Charmed Circle

By *James R. Mellow*

Charmed Circle:
Gertrude Stein & Company

Nathaniel Hawthorne
in His Times

Invented Lives:
F. Scott and Zelda Fitzgerald

CHARMED CIRCLE

Gertrude Stein & Company

JAMES R. MELLOW

Volume I
of the Lost Generation Trilogy

Houghton Mifflin Company
Boston

For information to reproduce selections from this book, write to Henry Holt
Company, Inc., 115 West 18th Street, New York, New York 10011.

Library of Congress Cataloging-in-Publication Data

Mellow, James R.
    Charmed circle : Gertrude Stein & company / James R. Mellow.
      p.   cm.
    Reprint. Originally published: New York : Praeger, 1974.
    Includes index.
    ISBN 0-395-47982-7
    1. Stein, Gertrude, 1874–1946 — Biography.   2. Stein, Gertrude,
1874–1946 — Friends and associates.   3. Authors, American — 20th
century — Biography.   4. Paris (France) — Intellectual life — 20th
century.   I. Title.
    [PS3537.T323Z72   1991]
    818'.5209 — dc20   91-19140
    [B]   CIP

Printed in the United States of America

AGM 10 9 8 7 6 5 4 3 2 1

Excerpts from hitherto unpublished letters of Alice B. Toklas appearing on pages
383, 472–75, and 477 © 1974 Lt. Col. Redvers Taylor and Louise Taylor.

Permission to reprint or quote has kindly been granted as follows:

Quotations from the unpublished correspondence of Gertrude Stein. Copyright © 1974 by Daniel Stein, Gabrielle Stein Tyler, and Michael Stein.
Grateful acknowledgment is extended to the Estate and/or Heirs of Gertrude
Stein for permission to quote from previously published letters of Gertrude Stein and from the texts of *Geography and Plays* and *The Making
of Americans*.
Quotations from the unpublished letters of Alice B. Toklas. Copyright ©
1974 The Estate of Alice B. Toklas.
Grateful acknowledgment is extended to the Estate of Alice B. Toklas for
permission to quote from the published letters of Alice B. Toklas.
Grateful acknowledgment is extended to the Collection of American Litera-
ture, The Beinecke Rare Book and Manuscript Library, Yale University,
for excerpts from published and unpublished letters to Gertrude Stein and
from the Radcliffe manuscripts of Gertrude Stein.
Grateful acknowledgment is extended to Random House, Inc., for use of the
copyrighted material from the works of Gertrude Stein.
From VIRGIL THOMSON by Virgil Thomson. Copyright © 1966 by Virgil
Thomson. Reprinted by permission of Alfred A. Knopf, Inc.
From THE FLOWERS OF FRIENDSHIP: LETTERS WRITTEN TO
GERTRUDE STEIN, edited by Donald Gallup. Copyright © 1953 by
Donald Gallup. Reprinted by permission of Alfred A. Knopf, Inc.
From TWO: GERTRUDE STEIN AND HER BROTHER. Copyright ©
1951 by Alice B. Toklas. Reprinted by permission of Yale University Press.
Grateful acknowledgment is extended to I.H.T. Corporation for permission
to quote from various articles from *The New York Herald Tribune*, dated
1934–35.

For my mother and father,
who taught me the quirky realities of life—
what was gently funny, what was interesting,
what might be beautiful,
what was worthwhile

. . . relations stop nowhere,
and the exquisite problem of the artist
is eternally but to draw, by a geometry of his own,
the circle within which
they shall happily *appear* to do so.

—Henry James

Contents

Sections of illustrations follow pages 84, 180, 340, *and* 436.

BOOK I

27, rue de Fleurus

"You must understand
that we lived in an atmosphere of euphoria, youth and enthusiasm
that can hardly be imagined today."
—D.-H. KAHNWEILER, *My Galleries and Painters*

CHAPTER ONE

The Atmosphere of Propaganda

I

A visitor to the studio at 27, rue de Fleurus in the early years of the twentieth century might well have believed he had been admitted to an entirely new form of institution—a ministry of propaganda for modern art. His knock upon the large double door that was secured by the only Yale lock in Paris's sixth *arrondissement* would have brought his hostess, a stout, impressive woman in her thirties, a woman with an imperturbable expression, a pair of frankly curious brown eyes, and a remarkable air of self-possession. Her customary response, if the visitor was not a familiar member of her circle of friends and acquaintances, would be a lax *"De la part de qui venez-vous?"* delivered in a contralto voice, the French tinged with a refined American accent.

Because anyone was admitted to the weekly at homes at the rue de Fleurus, the question was a mere formality. As likely as not, however, the guest might be forced to stammer, "But by yours, Madame." For Gertrude Stein, the hostess of these Saturday evenings, which combined excited talk with an extraordinary glimpse of the most outrageous modern paintings, was frequently in the habit of meeting interesting people, inviting them to her home—and promptly forgetting that she had.

The Yale lock was not for security. Although the whitewashed walls of the studio room were lined with paintings from eye level to the high ceiling—lined, tier upon tier, with stunning Cézanne oils and watercolors, with the brilliant smears of Matisse's Fauve landscapes, with the somber, brooding nudes and acrobats of Picasso's Blue and Rose Period paintings—the pictures had not acquired the astronomical values they were to have in later years. The Yale lock was a concession to Gertrude Stein's ingrained American sense of convenience. She found French keys a nuisance—too large and bothersome. The small key to her Yale lock could be dropped conveniently into her purse when she left the atelier for her usual afternoon walks. Or, it could be slipped into her pocket when she stepped out of the *pavillon*—the adjacent two-story apartment where she lived with her brother Leo—to open the studio doors for their arriving Saturday-evening guests.

The paintings were the principal attraction of the Steins' at homes. In the decade before World War I, few places in Paris could provide a similar glimpse of such modern audacities. For their services in exposing modern art to a continuous stream of international visitors— eager young German students, visiting Swedes and Hungarians, wealthy American tourists—the Steins could easily have claimed the distinction of having instituted the first museum of modern art. Within a few years of their arrival in the French capital, they had put together an astounding collection of everything the tradition-bound Parisian art world considered outrageous and revolutionary—and, more often than not, hoaxes of the most deliberate kind. Among the French it was considered sport to visit the Steins at least once, just to see the incredible trash the two gullible Americans had hung on their walls.

Moreover, the Steins themselves were an attraction. Open-minded, hospitable, they were both inveterate and enthusiastic talkers. Leo Stein discoursed on any subject from Picasso's painting style to the latest theories on diet, bringing to his discussion an amazing fund of odd information and queer observations. Gertrude, in those early years beginning to take herself seriously as a writer, was content to leave the aesthetic discussions to her brother Leo. She nonetheless admitted that argument was the very air she breathed. Among the assembled guests and, usually, at the center of a heated discussion, Leo cut an odd figure. He was taller and thinner than Gertrude, and his sharp profile, his straggly reddish beard and slightly balding head gave him a rabbinical appearance. He was a man of intense and antic gestures; in the middle of a conversation he would suddenly sit down and rest his feet on a bookcase, several inches above the level of his head, explaining that this was necessary for his cranky digestion.

Gertrude was formidable in appearance. On Saturday evenings her ample body was usually encased in a loose-fitting hostess gown. She looked monumental; the rounded, firm volumes of her head, her massive body seemed as if carved from stone. Even those who disliked her were struck by Gertrude's impressive bearing. Seated in one of the high-backed Renaissance chairs in the studio, her legs tucked under her Buddha-like, she gave the impression of an irresistible force disguised as an immovable object.

Dressed in brother-and-sister outfits of practical brown corduroy and wearing comfortable but unconventional sandals, the Steins were familiar figures on the streets of Paris and in the city's art galleries. On many occasions, they could be found in the tiny bric-a-brac shop where Mademoiselle Berthe Weill showed young and undiscovered artists, or in the little gallery on the rue Lafitte run by the ex-clown Clovis Sagot. More often they could be seen in another rue Lafitte establishment, picking their way through the disorderly stacks of canvases in the gallery run by the wily and unctuous Ambroise Vollard. Vollard, it was rumored, kept his better things hidden away in back rooms, waiting for prices to rise—among them a superb cache of Cézanne paintings he had been shrewd enough to acquire before the artist died. If one found a painting and took it to him to ask the price, the dealer was apt to put on a look of surprise, then baldly state that he had sold that picture just last month but had been unable to find it—meanwhile hurrying the canvas out of sight.

But Vollard sold regularly to the Steins, whom he professed to like. The Steins, he maintained, were less disposed to haggle over the price of a picture than were his richer clients. And the Steins paid promptly. As Vollard once confided to Leo, the rich paid only when they happened to think about it; their thoughts mostly ran to other matters. Among the patrons of the Parisian cafés, the Steins were considered to be wealthy American eccentrics. Leo, in fact, was referred to as an American Maecenas. But boulevard appraisals carried little weight with Vollard. He made it his business to know the precise financial situations of his customers. He had learned that the Steins' modest but comfortable income from San Francisco properties did not place them in the same category as his millionaire clients, such as the H. O. Havemeyers and Charles Loeser, who also bought Cézannes. But Vollard maintained that he liked dealing with Leo and his sister. They were the only clients, he said, who bought pictures "not because they were rich, but despite the fact that they weren't."

Gertrude and Leo Stein were not the only members of the family addicted to modern art. Their elder brother Michael and his wife, Sarah, were avid collectors, too. The Michael Steins maintained an apartment on the nearby rue Madame, having moved there from San Francisco with their young son Allan shortly after Leo and Gertrude had settled in Paris in 1903. Its walls were also studded with modern paintings, most of them handsome early works by Matisse. Michael Stein—a paunchy, dapper man with fastidiously trimmed mustache and beard—was the conservative, business-minded member of the family. With hard work and the shrewd sale of his father's railroad interests, Michael had turned the family holdings to sufficient account to endow each member with a comfortable income. It was Michael who kept a watchful eye on Gertrude and Leo's joint finances, cautioning them about their overdrawn accounts, advising fiscal responsibility. But it was Michael who advanced the necessary sums when Leo and Gertrude found themselves lacking the funds to buy a particularly tempting pair of Gauguins. His wife, Sarah—Sally to her friends—was a sweet, motherly-looking woman. An aspiring artist, she was one of the first and most dedicated students in the painting classes that Matisse conducted early in his career.

Disgruntled conservative artists whose works never entered the Stein collections referred to the family as the "Stein Corporation," as if it were an aesthetic cartel. Among such artists there was speculation as to whether the Steins bought their peculiar paintings because they liked them or whether they liked them because they had bought them. So familiar was the association of the Steins with everything radical in Parisian art that French art critics—horrified by the so-called infantile smears of Matisse's paintings and casting about for explanations— claimed that such work was clearly intended only for gullible and benighted Americans. The French, quite obviously, were not to be taken in by the crude hoaxes hanging on the walls of an upstart American salon.

The marvel was that the studio room at 27, rue de Fleurus—large by ordinary domestic standards but small for such a public function— should have held so many paintings, so many people. The Steins had set about collecting so industriously that the three available walls of the studio—the fourth was cut by the double door and oddly shaped windows that let in the northern light—were crammed with pictures hung row above row. In the dim and fluttering gaslight, only the lower ranges of art were clearly visible. Visitors had to shade their eyes from the glare of the low-hanging fixtures in order to pierce the gloom in which many of the pictures hung tantalizingly above.

But, even at the lower levels, there was enough to take in. Closely packed along one wall were a row of Cézanne watercolors, their exacting brushstrokes sketching out woodland glades and the rising fronts of austere mountains. Above them the brilliant fireworks of Matisse's Fauve pictures jostled Picasso's sober green-and-tan Spanish landscapes —pictures that carried in them the first hints of Cubist rectitude. A huge Picasso of a nude youth leading a horse, a painting from the artist's Rose Period, crowned the space above a cumbersome Henri IV buffet. Across the room the Picasso's scale was more than matched by Matisse's pastorale *Joy of Life*, a landscape idyll of frenziedly dancing figures and entwined nudes. On another wall a nude by Felix Vallotton —an attempt by a lesser man to recapture the shock of Manet's famous *Olympia*—sprawled out clinically on a crisp white sheet. Her quixotic expression and relaxed arm seemed to call attention to the small, precious Maurice Denis of a nursing mother and child hanging directly below it.

The pictures seemed like a seraglio—viewed in the modern manner. Nudes proliferated everywhere: in the awkward nakedness of Cézanne's *Bathers*, in the amiable roughhousing of Renoir's plump and gamboling females, in a Bonnard girl lying in suggestive exhaustion on a rumpled bed. There was Picasso's nude nymphet, wise beyond her years, holding a basket of flowers. It was this frankness of subject matter, this unembarrassed display of the Steins' sensual tastes, as much as the audacity of the painting styles that produced the expected shock for visitors who had come to be astounded.

The room was a jumble of furniture as well, crowding guests into a sense of intimacy. A long, sturdy Florentine table surrounded by Renaissance chairs was drawn close to the cast-iron stove at the back of the room. There were sideboards and buffets and bulky chests and little tables settled along walls and in corners. Each supported its full weight of accumulated objects: bronze Buddhas and fragments of bas-reliefs, a plaster head by Picasso, a coy modern Venus by Elie Nadelman, Matisse's early bronze *The Slave*. There were cheap porcelain figurines, costly Renaissance plates, tiny alabaster urns with alabaster doves balancing at the rims—objects Gertrude bought when she visited curio shops. Leaning against the walls were large portfolios of Japanese prints and Picasso drawings.

In time, the art burst out of the confines of this public room and was given refuge in the adjacent pavilion. There, Picasso and Matisse drawings were tacked to the double doors that led to the cramped dining room. In the dining room itself there were no pictures. The walls were lined with Gertrude and Leo's collection of books: college texts, books on psychology, philosophy, and history (Leo's amorphous territory); assorted volumes of English and American writers—cheap and expensive editions alike of Shakespeare, Trollope, and the English poets (Gertrude's special interest). But there were other spaces in the pavilion that could accommodate the overflow of their expanding art collection. Paintings that could not sustain their impact amid the exacting standards of the studio were transferred to Leo's small ground-floor study, which came to be known as the *salon des refusés*. Or they were lodged in the second-floor bedrooms. In one of these, Gertrude hung on the ceiling above her bed the testimonial of her enduring friendship with Picasso, the painter's little *Homage to Gertrude*—a picture at once intimate and extravagant in its pleasures, the canvas crowded with big-breasted angels accompanying a woman modestly bearing a plate of fruit.

II

If there had been such a thing as an international conspiracy to promote modern art in the early years of this century, 27, rue de Fleurus would have been close to the heart of it. "The place was charged with the atmosphere of propaganda," Leo remembered. The Steins, however, did not have sole custody of the modern movement. Many of the guests who crowded their Saturday evenings had come to the new art on their own. But the Steins had so placed themselves at the center of the network of journalists, publicists, advocates, and collectors who were spreading the gospel of modernism that, sooner or later, anyone interested in modern art would find his way to the rue de Fleurus. There he could assure himself of the continuing vitality of Matisse's and Picasso's stylistic ventures, and catch up with the latest cultural gossip.

Among the guests at 27, rue de Fleurus, there was an improbable mixture of types and nationalities: impoverished art students and wealthy collectors, ardent Swedish followers of the moderne, gregarious Americans looking for fun, irritating Germans who wanted to be shown things that had been placed out of reach. It did not escape Gertrude's attention that there was an unusually constant flow of Hungarians. She accounted for it as best she could. "It happened," she said, "that some hungarian had once been brought and the word had spread from him throughout all Hungary, any village where there was a young man who had ambitions heard of 27 rue de Fleurus and then he lived but to get there and a great many did get there . . . , all sizes and shapes, all degrees of wealth and poverty, some very charming, some simply rough and every now and then a very beautiful young peasant."

Inevitably, the tourists came because it was the thing to do when one was in Paris. A few went away converted, spreading the gospel of modernism among the heathen, sending fresh troops for later visits. Others came to scoff at the pictures, barely able to conceal their laughter before the doors closed behind them. Some came purposely to bait the artists. For on Saturday evenings, the perpetrators of these crimes against the traditions of art were on display themselves.

As special friends of the Steins, artists such as Matisse and Picasso were invited to supper beforehand on Saturday evenings. The meals were substantial if not lavish, consisting of roasts and simple fare prepared by the Steins' Norman *bonne à toute faire*, the stolid Hélène, who took pride in running the household on eight francs a day. Following the meal, the guests adjourned to the studio for the long evening, which began at nine and lasted into the small hours of the morning. There, Leo would hold forth inexhaustibly, surrounded by the curious and the incredulous, haranguing his guests in defense of modern art. Installed in one of the uncomfortable Renaissance chairs, Gertrude would occasionally press her hands down firmly on the arms, lifting her enormous bulk to greet a new visitor. Sometimes she could be heard replying with a firm, "Not just now. Perhaps later," when some guest asked to see a portfolio of Picasso drawings that had just been put away.

On a typical Saturday night, one might meet Matisse and find him eminently respectable-looking. With his gold-rimmed spectacles and carefully groomed reddish beard, dressed in a proper business suit, he was the very image of a staid academic, belying the impression created by his savage paintings. This tame appearance sometimes disturbed the painter himself. "I am always being taken for a solemn professor," he once complained, "but at heart, I am really quite gay." Beside him would be his wife, Amélie—another mark of his apparent conservatism; for amongst Matisse's bohemian colleagues, wives were the exception and mistresses frequently subject to change.

Madame Matisse provided her husband with a very creditable air. She was the personification of the bourgeois wife; a diligent and dutiful companion, a resourceful cook and housekeeper. She was, in other words, the admirable but somewhat plain wife of a man who had an appreciative eye for exotic-looking women. In order to supplement the meager family finances, Amélie Matisse had opened a small millinery shop—the inspiration, perhaps, for her husband's penchant for dressing his voluptuous and frequently nude young models in extravagant hats. Furthermore, she had elected to raise Matisse's daughter, his child by a previous, unsanctified liaison. During the years of hardship, when they were obliged to send their sons, Jean and Pierre, to live with grandparents, Madame Matisse had kept the older Marguerite—or Margot, as she was called—by her side, as solicitous of her welfare as if she had been her own child. There was about Madame Matisse something that Gertrude definitely liked, a way she had of pinning on her hat—inserting the long, lethal hatpin with deft authority—that Gertrude found fascinating. Matisse, as a gesture of friendship, made a drawing of his wife in this typical act and presented it to Gertrude.

At Matisse's side, on these Saturday evenings, there were sure to be one or two of his Fauve colleagues—Henri Manguin, perhaps, or the sullen André Derain, whose first meeting with Gertrude had resulted in a mutual though civil dislike. In the early years, the Fauve years, Georges Braque would also be in Matisse's company. Braque, puffing on his pipe, was distinctly noticeable in the crowd, for he loomed head and shoulders above his shorter colleagues. In the frequent rearrangements to which the Steins subjected their art collection, Braque good-naturedly held up the pictures while Gertrude and Leo stood back to assess the general effect.

Often Matisse would bring his great Russian patron, the millionaire textile importer Sergei Shchukine, to the Steins'. Shchukine was a small, impulsive man with a slight oriental cast to his eyes, a feature that Matisse pointedly emphasized when he sketched his benefactor. He was an avid collector of modern French painting and on a liberal scale that the Steins could seldom afford. Tiers of Gauguins and Cézannes hung in the dining room of his palatial home in Moscow. An entire room was set aside for the paintings of Matisse. Splendid Fauve landscapes and exotic studies like the *Spanish Dancer* and *Interior with Spanish Shawls* competed with ornate wall coverings and the rococo embellishments of his high-ceilinged salon. Shchukine's home might well have been another ministry for the modern movement had it been as accessible as the Stein's Parisian atelier. Even so, it was a principal source of information about the School of Paris for the rising generation of Russia's vanguard artists.

Matisse not only brought his patron to see the Steins but also, with commendable generosity, had introduced him to his then less successful rival, Picasso. It was the beginning of a number of significant purchases of the younger artist's work, including the large Picasso Rose Period picture of a lithe young acrobat balancing on a ball that had first belonged to the Steins. After the Russian Revolution this treasure horde of art was confiscated by the state, and Shchukine was appointed guide to his own collection in his former home.

At the Steins' the *cuadrilla* habitually surrounding Picasso was another matter. Black-eyed and frowning, Picasso stood in the midst of his friends like a small bullfighter, protected by his taller "seconds." Picasso's entourage, unlike Matisse's, did not consist of patrons and artist friends. It was more often made up of poets and women. One of these was the statuesque Fernande Olivier, the almond-eyed mistress of his early Parisian years. A superbly decorative female, somewhat indolent by nature but a shrewd observer, Fernande complained that Picasso kept her a near-prisoner in his Montmartre studio. Fernande had initially intended to become a schoolteacher. As a result of a chance encounter, she emerged as the first of the famous mistresses of a famous man. It had come about one sultry afternoon in the battered hulk of a building—dubbed the Bateau Lavoir because of its resemblance to a Seine laundry boat—in which Picasso maintained his studio. Fernande had been standing in one of its several doorways, waiting for an unusually severe cloudburst to stop, when the painter paused to pass the time of day. Before she knew what was happening, Picasso—a persuasive but agreeable spider—had whisked her off to the depths of his studio and the pleasures of his generally unmade bed.

In her memoir of her early years with the artist, *Picasso and His Friends,* Fernande noted that Picasso was invariably ill at ease at social gatherings like the Steins' Saturday evenings. His French at the time was hesitant and awkward; he knew no English. Unlike Matisse, he disliked talking shop with the transients of the salon. Most of the time he retreated, silent and glum, behind the security provided by friends such as the poets Max Jacob and Guillaume Apollinaire, who customarily went with him to the rue de Fleurus.

Jacob was a short, vivacious little man with a habitually droll expression. It was a quality that did not change significantly after he had a vision of Christ one day—October 7, 1909, to be exact—as he was entering his shabby quarters on the rue Ravignan. Following a second vision—this time while walking down the aisle of a movie house—he was converted from his unpracticed Jewish faith to Catholicism, a convert for whom Picasso served as godfather. Chronically poor, his usual luxury consisted of bouquets of flowers for his room. On one wall he had tacked an enigmatic message, *Ne jamais aller à Montparnasse.* Whether the injunction was strictly poetic or geographical is not quite clear. Certainly he went often to the Parisian Montparnasse—though not to court the muses. At the Steins', Jacob was invariably lively and witty, breaking out into extemporaneous performances of operas and plays, performing the female roles in a coy falsetto. With Fernande he loved to play the *vieux marquis,* kissing her hand with studied abandon, an act accompanied by a full repertory of lascivious smirks and leers. It may well have been the success of Max's little farces that goaded Leo Stein into an impromptu, fluttering rendition of the Dance of the Dying Swan that sent his audience into gales of laughter.

The most formidable member of Picasso's entourage was the poet, journalist, and man-about-town, Guillaume Apollinaire. Of uncertain parentage—among his friends it was rumored that the poet was the illegitimate son of at least a cardinal and perhaps a pope—he had led an extraordinary career. He edited everything from financial journals to physical-culture magazines. For several years he worked as the general editor of a series of pornographic books, the *Editions Briffaut,* providing appreciative introductions to the scatalogical masterpieces of the past. It was Apollinaire, in fact, who resurrected the Marquis de Sade from the bowels of the Bibliothèque Nationale, producing the first anthology of the author's works in 1909 and prophesying a new future for the old pornographer. When he was in need of money, Apollinaire contributed several original and racy novels of his own to the genre.

Florid in complexion, jut-jawed and with a regal profile, Apollinaire
cut an extraordinary figure in the Parisian art world. Picasso made innumerable sketches and caricatures of him wearing everything from a
papal crown and wristwatch (an allusion to his supposed parentage and
his role as critic among the Montmartre artists) to nothing at all as an
exemplar of the heroic physique. Expansive and convivial as a personality, Apollinaire was, however, notoriously close with a penny. "He
could often be tender and sympathetic to the point of tears," Fernande
observed. "I don't remember that he ever responded favorably to a request for a loan. I can hardly think of any friends he helped, whilst
nobody ever asked Max for help in vain; he always gave what he had."
Apollinaire's little apartment on the rue Henner was a model of neat-
ness. He had a particular fetish about the bed. No one was allowed to
put a coat on it, much less sit there. The slightest crease or hollow
caused Apollinaire to frown. One of his mistresses, a friend of Fernande's, told her that they never made love anywhere but in an armchair; the poet's bed "was sacred."

At the time that he frequented the Steins', Apollinaire's mistress was
the painter Marie Laurencin, a woman with seemingly chaste Clouet-
like features and poor eyesight—a disability that gave her an expression
of aloofness. At the Steins' they made a striking pair: Apollinaire, robust
and voluble, delivering intricate and racy stories about his experiences of
the day, Marie, slender and silent, peering nearsightedly at the pictures
through her lorgnette. So unusual was their appearance together, the
gentle painter Le Douanier Rousseau—one of Apollinaire's critical enthusiasms and a sometime guest at the Steins'—twice painted them in
stiff and straightforward poses as "The Muse Inspiring the Poet." In
both versions Marie Laurencin looks like a large, indisputable mother
who has just finished reprimanding her child.

Probably in emulation of the Rousseau portraits, begun in 1908,
Marie Laurencin painted her lover as well. Her group portrait, in a
sweetly primitive vein, included Apollinaire and herself, Picasso and
Fernande and Picasso's large, white, lamblike dog, a lazy creature that
cluttered up the artist's studio and which he was obliged to pick up and
move out of the way like a piece of furniture. Gertrude was so impressed with Marie's painting that she bought it. It was the first picture
Marie had sold, and she remained grateful for Gertrude's gesture even
when they were no longer on friendly terms.

For Apollinaire, Marie painted a larger and more elaborate picture in
the same vein, *Reunion in the Country*, adding to the original quartet
portraits of Gertrude, the poet Maurice Cremnitz and a now-unidenti-
fiable woman. A blonde angel, garlanded with fruits, presided over this
unusual gathering. The painting remained in Apollinaire's collection
until his death. By then, the idyllic pastorale had become a tender

souvenir of a love affair that was over and a commemoration of the bohemian way of life that ended with World War I.

In the decade before the war, the Stein salon was not limited to the celebrities of Parisian bohemia. It was at once democratic and congenial, an international meeting ground buzzing with transcontinental gossip. For Americans it was a kind of cultural halfway house between the European vanguard and the merest beginnings of the *avant-garde* in the United States. There was always a contingent of Americans, including Alfred Maurer, Max Weber, Patrick Henry Bruce, Morgan Russell, and Marsden Hartley, who were in regular attendance at the Steins' Saturday evenings. Gertrude entertained them, befriended them, and watched over their careers with absorbed interest. She was, for example, extremely fond of Maurer, a small, dapper man with an eye for the ladies. But she felt that as an artist Maurer was doomed to be a "follower" throughout his life—a judgment that was not altogether incorrect. It was "Alfy," Gertrude recalled, who, in the early years of her salon, held up a lighted match to the edge of a Cézanne portrait to assure his bewildered countrymen that the picture was, indeed, "finished," because it was framed. It was also Alfy, who, one summer in Fiesole, standing on a terrace overlooking the Arno valley, exclaimed, "There should be ten thousand houris there." Gertrude laughed. "But surely, Alfy, ten thousand are a great many." "Not for me," Maurer said.

Occasionally at the rue de Fleurus there were visits from royalty and the *haut-monde*. The Infanta Eulalia of Spain was brought by an American journalist and writer, Alice Woods Ullman. Her highness, more accustomed to Bouchers and Fragonards, had wanted to see the Steins' much-talked-of Matisses. Confronted by the dark passageway and the darker courtyard, however, she had turned back in fright. The Spanish-American War had not faded from her mind, and she had to be convinced that it was not, after all, an American ambush in which some outrage would be committed on her person. Once inside the studio, she was reassured by the people but unenlightened by the art. As Mrs. Ullman wrote Gertrude the following day: "HRH finds you are *delightful*, all of you, but your pictures 'horrors!' "

That aristocratic American painter, Mary Cassatt, friend of the Impressionists, was more uncompromising. In 1908 Miss Cassatt, who, like Gertrude, had been born in Allegheny, Pennsylvania, and lived in France, had been taken to a Saturday evening at the rue de Fleurus by an American hostess, Mrs. Montgomery Sears. Circling about the room with regal stiffness, inspecting the people, inspecting the pictures, she promptly returned to her friend and said sharply, "I have never in my life seen so many dreadful paintings in one place; I have never seen so many dreadful people gathered together and I want to be taken home at once." Fortunately Mrs. Sears had told her chauffeur to wait.

There was also the Marquise de S——.

At a tea party at the Ritz, people had talked of nothing but the Steins' Picassos and Matisses, and since the Marquise had not yet seen them, she had missed one of the events of the season. She had been told that Vollard was friendly with the Steins and asked if he could arrange an introduction. Vollard informed her that no introduction was needed. The Steins were very hospitable, and they received every Saturday evening.

Alas, the Marquise was leaving for Rome before Saturday. She was, however, a great friend of the Italian ambassador to France. Might not the Italian ambassador speak to his friend, the American ambassador, who in turn might speak to the Steins?

Vollard, playing the game to the hilt, informed the Marquise that it would be of little use: "I know that people have tried these arrangements between ambassadors before, but without success."

Nothing would do, then, but that the Marquise delay her trip to Rome. On the following Saturday evening, she was accompanied to the rue de Fleurus by Vollard himself. But as the dealer shrewdly observed: "People who came there out of snobbery soon felt a sort of discomfort at being allowed so much liberty in another man's house, and did not come again."

III

People who met Gertrude Stein for the first time were usually impressed with her remarkable head; the broad, smoothly modeled brow, the full, straight nose, the deep-set, candid, and sometimes mischievous eyes, a mouth that was generous but uncompromisingly straight. Some likened it to the head of a Roman emperor—but carved from American granite. Others were charmed by the lightness and suavity of her voice, by the irresistible fullness of her laughter. It was a laugh, one of her friends remarked, "like a beefsteak"—juicy and solid. Another thought it was like the fire kept banked in the studio's cast-iron stove. A sudden burst of inspiration could fan it into a roaring blaze, spreading a genial warmth.

She had a passion for acquaintanceship—"Give me new faces new faces," one of her lines intoned—but a limited capacity for untroubled friendship. Except for several durable relationships, her friendships were like her collection of bric-a-brac: delicate objects, curiosities that took her fancy, souvenirs from her travels or the gifts of her fame. They were seldom priceless; they were not intended to display a cultivated taste; they were replaceable. She had no patience for protecting them, for putting them out of danger. They had to withstand the lively traffic of her salon. The care and dusting of them—and the dusting off, one might add—were left to others. Frequently, through carelessness or inadvertence, the more fragile were broken and had to be discarded. She would be sorry or annoyed—but usually discovered that the pleasure of a new friendship could console her for the loss of the old.

Her reactions to most things—a new painting, a new face—were intense. Meeting someone for the first time, she had a disconcerting habit of fixing her eyes sharply on the visitor and asking a barrage of questions: Where was he from? How old was he? What did he do? What was his parentage? In later years, to the dismay of friends, she had refined the technique to the simple, "What is your blood?" For those who recalled that a "science" of the blood had led directly to the gas ovens at Auschwitz, the effect was sometimes chilling. The spectacle of human nature amazed and absorbed her. As the hostess of an international salon for the better part of her life, she watched those variable and interesting dramas—liaisons, marriages, ruptures, divorces, reconciliations—enacted many times. As a writer she was fortunate in having the human comedy played out in her living room.

One of the remarkable features of her career was its resiliency. Out of curiosity, plain affection, and an extremely shrewd understanding of how to conduct a career in the modern world, Gertrude cultivated the young in every generation. At the beginning of the century, she promoted the vanguard artists of Paris; in the twenties, she took on young writers, journalists, publicists, and the editors of the little magazines that had, as she was fond of quoting, "died to make verse free"; in the thirties, she sought out a new crop of admirers by lecturing college and prep-school students during a much-publicized American tour; in the forties, she adopted, wholesale, the American GIs of World War II—thus providing herself with a perennial audience. It was a splendid strategy.

Ridiculed, lampooned, and seldom published during much of her lifetime—and then often at her own expense—she nevertheless made a place for herself in American literature; if not at the head of the line, where she felt she properly belonged, at least in the front rank of her generation.

There were, to be sure, those who took an immediate dislike to her, who remembered only a monumental ego. Agnes Ernst, an ambitious young reporter for the *New York Sun* when she first met Gertrude, later the wife of Eugene Meyer, owner of the *Washington Post,* had an especially hostile reaction. In her memoir, *Out of These Roots,* Mrs. Meyer maintained that Gertrude "was and remained, in my opinion, a humbug who lived when I first knew her in 1909, on what she could assimilate from Leo, and later, on what like a busy magpie she could glean from other artists and intellectuals among the avant-garde thinkers in Paris." Mrs. Meyer admitted, however, that Gertrude had aroused immediate "antipathy" in her: "It is no doubt one of my limitations that I have always distrusted masculine women, and found their self-assertion distasteful. Gertrude Stein also offended my aesthetic sense, for in her middle thirties, she was a heavy woman who seemed to squat rather than sit, her solid mass enveloped in a monklike habit of brown corduroy."

Mrs. Meyer was much more appreciative of Leo, who, when he chose, could be distinctly charming and even flirtatious. "Most of the visitors to the Stein apartment in 1909," she recalled, "paid little attention to Gertrude. The center of attraction was Leo's brilliant conversation on modern French art." Leo, she contended, "was the only one of the many contemporary art critics I have known, not excepting Berenson, Roger Fry and Meier-Graefe, who achieved complete integrity in his relationship to aesthetic values."

There were those, too, who took both Steins with a grain of salt. The American painter Maurice Sterne, who knew Gertrude and Leo from summers in Italy and their years in Paris, was a frequent guest at the rue de Fleurus. A handsome young man, conservative in his artistic tastes, Sterne was distinctly liberal, even somewhat callous, about matters of the heart. Among his early conquests, he could count the exotic Russian actress Alla Nazimova. A note of condescension creeps into his description of Leo Stein. Although Leo, Sterne noted, "was very attractive both to women and to men, his female friends were never of the pretty, feminine type. They were intellectuals with fine minds and dull bodies and they were awed by Leo's keen intellect." But Leo was, he felt, "the undisputed ruler of the Stein clan. Gertrude had no taste or judgment in the visual arts; at best she was a reflection of her brother." Sterne's judgment may be accurate enough about Gertrude's role during the initial stages of their collection, but it hardly accounts for her acceptance and promotion of Picasso, whom Sterne tended to regard as a charlatan. He was prepared to admit, however, that Gertrude had an understanding of literature. He recalled, in particular, a walk they had taken together in Italy. He had asked her why she had never thought of becoming a critic, since she "spoke so intelligently about writing."

"It's funny that you should say that," Gertrude told him. "As a matter of fact, I did, long ago, but I found that analysis is not in my line.

I'll leave that to Leo—he loves to chew the cud. I want to do something more vital than write about the writings of others."

About Leo's aesthetic judgments, Sterne was suspicious as well. He had accompanied Leo to the spring Salon des Indépendants in 1906, the year that Matisse had entered the *Joy of Life*. Sterne disliked the picture on sight. He thought the color crude, the drawing poor. He was inclined to agree with the visitors who stood laughing in front of the picture. Leo was hesitant about evaluating Matisse's important painting. He said he would have to study it further. Such caution irritated Sterne; with pictures, as with love affairs, he made up his mind right away. When, two weeks later, Leo announced that he thought Matisse's painting was "superb" and that he intended to buy it, Sterne exploded: "It took you a hell of a long time to make such an astounding discovery!"

Leo reminded him tartly. "It took *you* much longer to see Cézanne."

If Sterne's views of Gertrude and Leo reflected his artistic prejudices and his own formidable ego, they nonetheless suggest the frankness, the give-and-take, that existed among the regulars of the Stein circle. Moreover, Sterne was not one of those intimates of the Steins who later felt obliged to take sides for or against either Gertrude or Leo. In his memoir, *Shadow and Light*, he dealt with them both even-handedly and with impartial malice. One of his remarks carried a beautifully honed cutting edge. At the time he first knew them, Sterne observed, Gertrude and Leo Stein gave the impression of being "the happiest couple on the Left Bank."

CHAPTER TWO

Rich, Right American Living

I

Since childhood, Gertrude and Leo Stein had been inseparable companions. The youngest and most bookish of the Stein children—Leo was born in 1872; Gertrude, two years later—they were separated from their brothers and sister. Before Gertrude and Leo were born, however, five children had been born to Daniel and Amelia (Keyser) Stein. Two had died in infancy. During spells of adolescent despondency, when Gertrude experienced a fear of death or "not so much of death as of dissolution," she reflected that, if the two infants had not died, she and Leo might never have been born. It was quite likely that they might not have. Their father, a man of earnest, if somewhat erratic, decisions, had determined upon having no more than five children. When she and Leo learned of this, Gertrude remembered, they never talked about it; it made them "feel funny."

About family loyalties, Gertrude was remarkably unsentimental, dispensing with them as readily as she did certain friendships in later life. For Michael Stein, born in 1865, both Gertrude and Leo maintained a certain devotion; Michael was the respected eldest brother. But, for Simon, the next in line, and Bertha—four years older than Gertrude—Gertrude had little concern. Early in her life, she seems to have dismissed them both as unimportant. They were both, she felt, "a little simple minded," which angered their father but which seemed to Gertrude "natural enough if no one had worried about it." Simon had a prodigious appetite and was overweight much of his life. Unable to learn, he was considered clownish by the rest of the family. He led an aimless life; for a time he was a gripman on one of the street railroads in San Francisco, going off to work with his pockets bulging with candy to give to children. After Simon died in middle age, Gertrude merely recorded that he had died "still fat and fishing." Her sister Bertha, she recalled in *Everybody's Autobiography*, "was not a pleasant person, she naturally did not like anything." Gertrude particularly remembered her sleepless nights. She shared a bedroom with Bertha, who had an irritating habit of grinding her teeth in her sleep. "Simon I liked," Gertrude concluded, "but I did not like Bertha."

Neither Gertrude nor Leo had any great love for their father. Leo, who suffered from digestive disorders for much of his life, attributed them partly to his father's bullying dietary regulations. He recalled, particularly, a day in childhood when he had been forced to eat boiled turnips and carrots, from which he was ordinarily exempted because those vegetables made him ill. His father, however, had instituted a new regimen—the children must now eat everything that was put before them—and one Sunday, in front of company, he chose to exert his parental authority: Leo was sick for the rest of the day. But Daniel Stein's authority was unpredictable: Laws that were laid down one day were allowed to lapse a few days later. He was especially erratic on the question of his children's education, insisting, at times, that they learn foreign languages and be tutored at home; then maintaining that they should, in democratic fashion, attend public schools as the neighboring children did. Gertrude remembered the succession of governesses and tutors hired and fired according to her father's educational whims of the moment. Leo's memories of his father were grim and unflattering: a "stocky, positive, dominant, aggressive person, with no book learning whatever (I never knew him to read a book)" and an "exceedingly disputatious" man.

Gertrude, in her autobiographical writings, pronounced Daniel Stein "depressing"—a characterization she applied to fathers in general. But, with the charity of fiction, she depicted him as a more complex figure, David Hersland, in her long novel of family life, *The Making of Americans*. There, she observed that the parental figure was, in some ways, a "splendid kind of person. . . . He was big in the size of him and in his way of thinking. His eyes were brown and little and sharp and piercing and sometimes dancing with laughing and often angry with irritation." David Hersland was a man of emphatic moods, of large ideas and big beginnings that were all too likely to dissolve in his own impatience. The Hersland household, like the Steins', was one

"where there was much fierce talking and much frowning, and then
the father would end with pounding on the table and threatening and
saying that he was the father they were the children, he was the master,
they must obey." Gertrude felt that this irascible man had encouraged
his children to be independent, had instilled in them a passion "to be
free inside them." Leo, unfortunately, seemed to inherit from his father
a fatal inability to complete any course of action he had begun.

Daniel Stein was one of five brothers—German Jews who had emigrated
to America before the Civil War. In 1841, the eldest brother, Meyer—
he was eighteen at the time—had arrived in Baltimore, then one of the
chief ports of entry for the North German Lloyd Line. Within months,
Meyer had established himself in the city and sent for the remainder
of the family. Immigration records indicate that Michael and Hanne
Stein (Gertrude's grandparents) had landed in Baltimore on September 2, 1841. With them were their four sons, Samuel (age ten), Daniel
(age eight), Solomon (age five), and Levi (age two). Their ship was
the *Pioneer*, and their last place of residence was given as Weigergruben,
Germany. Although Gertrude tended not to idealize her immediate
family circle, she held a romantic view of the pioneering spirit of her
forebears, particularly of her grandmother. In *The Making of Americans*, she included a vivid account—evidently based on family stories—
of the hardships and uncertainties of the Stein family's removal to the
new continent from their small Bavarian village. Gertrude's grandfather, it appears, was uncertain and hesitant about the move. It was
Hanne Stein who was the pillar of strength in the family—a "good
foreign woman who was strong to bear many children and always after
was very strong to lead them. The old woman was a great mountain."

In Baltimore, Meyer Stein opened a clothing store, specializing in
imported textiles, which prospered well enough over the years to allow
him to engage his four brothers in the firm. But the Steins were an
argumentative and independent clan, and, in 1862, Daniel persuaded
his younger brother Solomon to move to Pittsburgh, where they opened
a second Stein Brothers at the corner of Wood and Fourth streets. Although the new firm remained in business twelve years, it was not always a successful partnership. Leo remembered his Uncle Solomon, a
"very competent but gentle person," telling him that most of his time
had been spent getting back the customers that Daniel's abrasive
temper had driven away.

Nor was the family situation always harmonious. Daniel had married
Amelia Keyser, a member of a large family of German Jews who had
settled in Baltimore before the Steins. The two brothers had bought
twin houses in Allegheny, then a suburb of Pittsburgh and later ab-

sorbed into the city itself. Amelia Stein—Milly, as she was known to the family—was ordinarily a gentle-mannered, somewhat vague woman who was devoted to her family. Born in 1842, she was ten years younger than her husband. She had, as Gertrude recalled, a "quick temper" and could be steely and unforgiving. For several years she and Solomon's wife, Pauline, had been quarreling and had reached the point, shortly before Gertrude's birth, at which they were no longer on speaking terms.

It was on Western Avenue in Allegheny, around 8:00 in the morning of February 3, 1874, that Gertrude was born—a "perfect baby," so her father later informed her, a condition he sometimes reproached her with whenever she was ill. Despite the fact that her memories of Allegheny were nonexistent, Gertrude took a perverse pleasure in her place of birth. Throughout her later life in Europe, whenever she was officially required to establish her identity and birthplace, Gertrude would assert, in a firm and amused voice, that she had been born in Allegheny, Pennsylvania, to the consternation of the French clerks who tried to spell it. But she lived in Allegheny only until it was safe for an infant to travel, for Daniel and Solomon Stein had agreed to dissolve their partnership. Solomon moved his family to New York, where he went into banking, and late in 1874, Daniel Stein took his family to Austria, where he had business prospects. Until she was five, Gertrude lived abroad.

Her recollections of those years were sparse but vivid. Her father was frequently away from Vienna on business, but the family life was active. There was her mother and her aunt Rachel Keyser who served as a companion for her mother. There was a governess for herself and Bertha and for the boys a Hungarian tutor, Herr Krajoletz, who was so ardent a naturalist that the children began to collect plants, beetles, and snakes. Leo learned in German all the names of the common butterflies and beetles. Gertrude remembered with pleasure the formal public gardens. "And there was music and there was the old emperor who was a natural figure to have in a formal garden." She remembered her first books, "picture books but books all the same since pictures in picture books are narrative." And, on her third birthday, she had "a taste of Vienna beer." In 1878 Milly Stein grew restless in Vienna— her husband was back in the States on business, and her sister Rachel had also returned there. She moved to Passy, in the 16th *arrondissement* in Paris. Gertrude's recollections of Paris, where the family remained for more than a year, were mostly of food: the bowl of soup and the bread she was given at breakfast in the school to which she and Bertha had been consigned; at lunchtime, trading the mutton chops, which she did not like, for spinach, which she did. She recalled a day, too, when her three brothers—all of whom were learning to ride—came to visit her on horseback. When Gertrude was five, Amelia Stein, tired of living abroad and homesick, decided to return to America. There was a final, frantic shopping spree for sealskin coats and muffs and for "gloves dozens of gloves, wonderful hats, riding costumes, and finally ending up with a microscope and a whole set of the famous french history of zoology." Although she did not remember the event, Gertrude pestered her brother Michael to recount the story of their mother's great shopping excursion—it delighted her. There was, finally, a brief stop in London, where the family was taken to a performance of *H.M.S. Pinafore*. Gertrude did not remember the performance, only the "glitter" of the huge theater. Of the ocean crossing, she remembered nothing at all, nor did she remember "that any one ever said there was anything to remember."

II

When the family arrived in New York, relatives attempted a reconciliation between Amelia and Pauline Stein, but Amelia would not be reconciled. In later years, after Gertrude had gotten to know and rather admire her aunt Pauline, she was still grateful for her mother's intransigency. Had her father gone into partnership with her uncle Solomon once more, Gertrude thought, her branch of the family might have been considerably richer, but she would have grown up in New York—a dismal prospect—rather than California.

In 1880, after a stay in Baltimore, Daniel Stein, once more full of big prospects, moved his family to the West Coast. He had scouted the territory beforehand and decided that the business opportunities were best in the San Francisco area. There he invested in street railroads, real estate, the San Francisco Stock Exchange. At first, the family lived in a hotel in Oakland, across the bay from San Francisco; then it moved into a large house in East Oakland that Gertrude referred to as the "old Stratton house" and that she remembered fondly. It was situated on ten acres of property at Thirteenth Avenue and Twenty-fifth Street. A winding avenue of eucalyptus trees led up to the house, which stood on a rise. The gardens, a small orchard of apple and cherry trees, and the wide, unkempt lawns were surrounded by rail fences and thick hedges of roses. Recalling the pleasures of her California days in *The Making of Americans*, she described the joys of the Hersland children—the Stein children significantly reduced to three in number, with herself the eldest—with a lyricism that was full-blown:

The sun was always shining for them, for years after to all three of the children, Sunday meant sunshine and pleasant lying on the grass with a gentle wind blowing and the grass and flowers smelling, it meant good eating, and pleasant walking, it meant freedom and the joy of mere existing, it meant the pungent smell of cooking, it meant the fun ʟ ʰisfied sense of being stuffed up with eating, it meant sunshine and joking, it meant laughing and fooling, it meant warm evenings and running, and in the winter that had its joys too of indoor living and outside the wind would be blowing and the owls in the walls scaring you with their tumbling.

She was proud of the fact that in her early years she had escaped the "rich right american living" of the upper-middle class. She grew up among poorer, working-class families: "Mostly they were honest enough working men and women and their children went to school and went on to be decent enough men and women," though there was sometimes a "queer" side to some of the families with whose children she and Leo played. There were

some who were not good to earn a living, there were families where it was a little hard to understand how they were living, nobody did any working, nobody had money that belonged to them. In some of the families around them there was a father who was really not very existing, no one was certain that he was a husband of the woman and the father of the children.

Nevertheless, she was herself privileged. The Stein household, staffed with servants and a governess, had status among the poorer neighboring families. And, in the midst of her own family, Gertrude was the petted youngest child. "If that does happen it is not lost all the rest of one's life," she commented in *Wars I Have Seen*, "there you are you are privileged, nobody can do anything but take care of you, that is the way I was and that is the way I still am." Having a brother two years older only added to her sense of security: "you go everywhere and do everything while he does it all for and with you which is a pleasant way to have everything happen to you."

The Stein children attended public schools—primary schools in East Oakland, the Oakwood High School—though that educational program was altered on occasion when Daniel Stein revised his democratic principles and he decided his children should be proficient in European languages and hired tutors to teach them at home. Gertrude's memories of school years were relatively innocent—a prize essay, for example, written at about the age of eight, describing a sunset she had seen and which was selected to be written on parchment paper. Her handwriting was so bad that another student had been asked to transcribe it. Her teacher considered this a disgrace. She also recalled the Lend a Hand Society, in which the students were required to tell their good deeds for the day. Since she and Leo were bookish and had no chores to do at home, they were always hard pressed to find a good deed.

Leo's recollections of his school years were markedly different. In later years he was convinced that he had been the victim of an un-

happy childhood, a view that Gertrude felt did not fit the circumstances
and that she found meaningless, since it had developed long after the
fact. "What is the use of having an unhappy anything," she remarked.
"My brother and I had had everything."

Leo, however, remembered facts enough "to make a dozen neuroses."
High on the list were instances of his father's insensitivity, like the
episode of the boiled turnips. Abnormally sensitive himself, he was attracted to girls but habitually ran away from those that interested him.
With others he was "simply comradely." Once at a party at which the
inevitable kissing games were played, he jumped out a window rather
than pay the forfeit. During his school days, Leo maintained, he had
suffered from sexual repression, "never indulged in the private practices
common to boys" and never read bawdy dime novels. A minor episode
—it was the only incident of its kind, Leo admitted, that had occurred
—had instilled in him what he called the "Jew complex." There were
scarcely any Jewish families in East Oakland, and for much of the time
Leo was the only Jewish boy in his school. One day, a classmate produced a kazoo—the musical instrument was then in vogue—that he
had whittled down in order to have it fit conveniently in his pocket.
Since Leo had already had that idea, he promptly brought out his own
shortened kazoo, whereupon the boy made the slurring remark, "Oh,
those damned Jews always get ahead of us." Leo was mortified, felt he
should have started a fight then and there, but did not. This somewhat Freudian incident made him even more morbidly self-conscious.
Whenever anyone paid the slightest attention to him, he reported, he
blushed "so hard as sometimes to give me a headache." The childhood
dependency that developed between Leo and Gertrude seems to have
been marked by a certain element of desperation.

For both of them it was a bookish and argumentative period. In those
days, Leo "led in everything," Gertrude acknowledged. "He found a
good many books that I would not have found and I read a great many
books that did not interest him. . . . We both liked talking that is we
always had argued about anything." Her early reading consisted of Jules
Verne's adventures, "a few stray novels, a few travel books," and her
mother's gift volumes of Wordsworth and other English poets. She
"absorbed" Shakespeare in an annotated edition. In time she was given
reading privileges in the San Francisco Mercantile and Mechanics'
libraries "with their excellent sets of eighteenth century and nineteenth
century authors." She read the English novelists—Fielding, Smollett—
was particularly fond of Richardson's *Clarissa Harlowe*; she read nineteenth-century histories and biographies—Lecky's *Constitutional History of England*, Carlyle's *Frederick the Great*—and worried about the
time when there might not be anything further to read.

She and Leo attended the local theater—touring companies of *Uncle
Tom's Cabin* and melodramas such as *Secret Service*—and the "twenty-

five cent opera of San Francisco," where they first saw *Faust* and *Lohengrin*. Edwin Booth brought his production of *Hamlet* to the city, and Sarah Bernhardt, on a world tour, settled in San Francisco for a lengthy engagement. In the late 1880's, Gertrude and Leo had had their first glimpse of a "masterpiece" of French painting, Millet's *Man with the Hoe*, acquired by William H. Crocker, a San Francisco art collector. Leo had bought a reproduction of the picture, and they studied it carefully at home. They showed it to their brother Mike, who dryly commented that it was "a hell of a hoe." Their leisure hours were spent trekking up into the hills, munching on dry crusts of bread, and talking, so Leo recalled, "endlessly about books and people and things." Gertrude liked to remember the hot, sunny journeys into the countryside and the pleasure of dropping to the ground, exhausted after a long walk, lying on her back in a flowering meadow. But of those childhood jaunts with Gertrude, Leo was to remember, somewhat accusingly, that while they had discussed practically every subject then available to young people under the bright California sun, they had never, never disclosed to each other their most intimate thoughts and feelings.

Their idyllic life was clouded in 1885, when the family moved from the Stratton house to a smaller one on Tenth Avenue. Amelia Stein had been ill for some time—the illness was eventually diagnosed as cancer—and was forced to take a series of treatments. Amelia Stein's condition became progressively weaker. Bertha was obliged to accompany her mother on her visits to the nearby doctor. In the following year, when her mother was completely invalided, Bertha tended the household. In 1888, after a prolonged illness, Amelia Stein died. Gertrude was fourteen.

Her response to her mother's death was curiously unfeeling. Her fictional portrait of Amelia Stein in *The Making of Americans* had elements of sympathy and tenderness: "she had a gentle little bounty in her, she had a sense in her of superior strength in her from the way of living that was the natural way of being to her, she had a larger being from the children who were always to her a part of her." But in her memoirs she recorded pragmatically that because of her mother's long illness, "we had already had the habit of doing without her." Her father, however, became a figure to contend with: "After my mother died we went on doing what we had done but naturally our father was more a bother than he had been, that is natural enough. Hitherto we had naturally not had to remember him most of the time and now remembering him had begun."

Her brother Mike had returned from Johns Hopkins to manage the Omnibus Cable Company, the street railroad of which her father was vice-president. Bertha kept house, but each member of the family arranged his own hours, and meals were irregular. Leo, who was planning to attend the University of California at Berkeley, was "hastily, doing

three years' high school work in seven months." Gertrude, who had
dropped out of high school, was pursuing her own independent course.
Mike thought she should become a musician—Leo was practicing dili-
gently on the violin—but the idea did not excite her. "Naturally," she
noted, "my father was not satisfied with anything, that was natural
enough."

She and Leo would meet Mike at his office in San Francisco, having
stopped in the meantime in the bookstores along the way. They had a
regular allowance, which they regularly squandered on books—Shelley
in a green and morocco binding, an illustrated set of Thackeray—and
usually arrived at Mike's penniless. Glad to have their company, he
would take them out to dinner in the city.

"Then one morning," Gertrude noted in *Everybody's Autobiography*
—unable to recall whether that morning in 1891 had occurred in the
spring or the summer—"we could not wake up our father. Leo climbed
in by the window and called out to us that he was dead in his bed and
he was." Michael wrote to his uncle Meyer Stein in Baltimore that the
funeral "attended by many prominent men in San Francisco" had been
"conducted according to the Jewish rites by Rev. M. S. Levy," an old
friend of his father's. He had been appointed an executor of the estate.
The children, he noted, were all of age "except Leo and Gertrude to
whom I will act as guardian." There were the difficulties of probating
the will and settling the debts. Michael brought his father's books
home and went over the accounts while Leo and Gertrude looked on.
"There were so many debts it was frightening," Gertrude observed,
"and then I found out that profit and loss is always loss." But Daniel
Stein had left property in Baltimore and in Shasta County, California.
Michael Stein disliked business, but he managed to sell his father's
franchise for the street railroad—as well as Daniel Stein's never-realized
project for consolidating the various competitive street railroad systems
—to Collis P. Huntington, the railroad magnate. Mike's handling of
the deal, according to Gertrude, so impressed the tycoon that he hired
him. He stayed with the company for several years, becoming the division superintendent of the combined Market Street Railway Company
in 1895. In 1903, after the union had struck the line in the preceding
year, Michael retired, permanently. His sympathies, apparently, had
been with the workers.

Mike's perseverance had provided his charges with an independent
income if they chose to live quietly. For years he acted as a second father
for Leo and Gertrude, regularly sending them their remittances, advising them on their spending habits, advancing them money when necessary. Leo reckoned, years later, that his income during the pre–World
War I era was "perhaps a hundred and fifty dollars a month on the
average." When he and Gertrude were sharing expenses in Paris during
those years, they lived comfortably, bought pictures, traveled. It was

enough, Gertrude maintained, to keep them "reasonably poor." It was typical of Gertrude's taciturn relationship to her parents—even though she devoted reams of paper to explicating the minor twists and turns of family living—that she could conclude about her California years: "Then our life without a father began, a very pleasant one." The conventional pieties were never important to her.

III

In 1892—before Michael's coup with the sale of the Omnibus Cable Company franchise—Bertha and Gertrude were sent east to Baltimore to live with their mother's sister Fanny Bachrach. Leo, who was about to enter Harvard, accompanied them. At first, Gertrude had delighted in the presence of her several lively aunts, with their gossip, their curiosity, their daily affairs. And she was happy to be in the company of cousins her age or younger. Aside from the companionship of Leo, her adolescent years in California had been interior and introspective. "So many things begin around fifteen," she noted—"money, possessions, eternity, enemies, the fear of death." The logical conclusion would be that her fear of death had been precipitated by the death of her mother and father, but she seemed to relate it to larger issues, to an awareness— derived from history—that whole civilizations, like large family units, had disappeared from the face of the earth. In Baltimore, confronted with the large and busy Stein and Keyser clans, she began "to lose her lonesomeness." But she felt a certain strangeness, after the "rather desperate inner life" she had been leading in California, on moving into the "cheerful life" of her numerous uncles and aunts. There were gratifying trips to New York City, as well, where she took in the opera and the museums, met her uncle Solomon and his wife, Pauline, whose son, Fred, was a companion of Leo's at Harvard.

One of the consequences of the death of her parents, however, was that it increased her dependence on Leo. She seems to have trailed after him, like a satellite after a superior planet. Without him she grew restive and unhappy. As a result, she made a move that would bring them together again. She applied to Radcliffe—it was then called the Harvard Annex—to be enrolled as a special student. There were difficulties. She had not completed high school, and her education was spotty and informal. At first, it appears, she had no intention of working toward a degree, enrolling only as a special student.

The courses that she took at Radcliffe—philosophy and metaphysics under George Santayana and Josiah Royce, psychology (then considered a branch of philosophy) under William James, zoology, botany—indicate the variety of her interests and, probably, the unsettled nature of her ambitions. Her best marks—A's and B's—were achieved in those subjects. She did less well in required courses such as mathematics (B and C) and in the physical sciences (physics, C; chemistry, C minus). Her only course in literature was a survey course in French literature, taken in her sophomore year, and for which she received a C plus, testifying to her claim that "English" was her language and that French literature—though she lived in France more than forty years and knew many of the most important French writers of her time—was a matter of indifference to her.

Gertrude found life at Radcliffe agreeable. She lived in a boardinghouse in Cambridge for four years and found the occupants, mostly "New England" types, interesting. With her usual eye for the amenities and her own comfort, she graded the landlady "a very good boardinghouse keeper." Judging from one of her English composition essays, preserved at Yale, she accommodated herself easily to boardinghouse life and soon became a member of the group. The composition in question deals with an unidentified newcomer to the house, a girl with superior airs, whom the other boarders resent as an intruder: "She seems to have known all the great people since the time of Adam and they have all given her their private views on all subjects. Our landlady looks at her, drinking her in with open mouth, eyes and ears. She gives her a finger-bowl at dinner too and we poor plebes look on in envy and can only hope that some day we too will know some great man." Gregarious by nature, she served as the secretary for the Philosophy Club, inviting campus figures such as Royce and Santayana to read papers at their meetings. Royce offered her two choices—a paper on "Browning's Theism" and a more technical one on "The Principle of Individuation." The latter problem, he noted, "is a pretty one, and is of practical interest to people who desire to call their souls their own." Santayana answered that, if she didn't think the subject "too vast," he would like to talk about "Faith and Criticism." Gertrude also joined a dramatics group, the Idler's Club, which met to produce and discuss plays. A series of photographs at Yale apparently represent one of their productions. Gertrude, already impressive in size, was given a matronly role, set apart from the more slender couples, who evidently provided the love interest of the play.

She was socially active—took part in picnics and outings, often in the company of Leo, such as the cruise the pair took with friends in July 1897 on the *Vigilant*, sailing from Falmouth to Quisset on the south shore of Massachusetts. Her classmates remembered her as jovial and talkative, rather complacent about her size and indifferent to dress. On Saturday night she and her friends would often take a streetcar to the end of the line, for a walk in the country. They were not afraid, one of them remembered: "We said if we have any trouble with a

man, Gertrude will climb out on the furthest limb of a tree and drop
on him."

In her sophomore year at Radcliffe, Gertrude enrolled in English 22,
an English composition course, taught by the poet William Vaughn
Moody. Her Radcliffe themes represent her first serious efforts at writing, but they are instructive less for their hints of her later writing style
than for their indications of certain psychological attitudes when writing about family situations or disguised or fictionalized accounts of her
own state of mind. The writing is generally careless and often rambling,
with alternative words and phrases thrown down pell-mell and no final
choice indicated. "Your vehemence runs away with your syntax," one
of her instructors commented. The themes were frequently rewritten—
a task that she found uncongenial and that in her later career she dismissed as unnecessary, along with conventional forms of punctuation.
Her final grade in the course was a C.

In the Radcliffe themes the character of Hortense Sanger is generally
her own fictionalized persona. In one of the themes, "In the Library"—
marked "First chapter of a connected work"—Hortense is described as
a "dark-skinned girl in the full sensuous development of budding
woman-hood." She is sitting in "the library where most of her young
life had been passed," struggling with feelings of "wild impatience."
As she sits reading, she hears the strains of Chopin's "Funeral March,"
played by a military band, issuing from the street outside. " 'Books,
books,' she muttered, 'is there no end to it. Nothing but myself to
feed my own eager nature. Nothing given me but musty books.' " Suffering from a sense of oppression, the girl leaves the library, climbing
a steep hill overlooking the ocean, breathing in the cool air.

The piece continues with a passionate self-assessment that ends with
a very abrupt bit of Gertrude's own personal history:

Now the time had come when her old and well-beloved companions had begun to pall. One could not live on books, she felt that she must have some
human sympathy. Her passionate yearnings made her fear for the endurance
of her own reason. Vague fears began to crowd on her. Her longings and desires had become morbid. She felt that she must have an outlet. Some change
must come into her life, or she would no longer be able to struggle with
the wild moods that now so often possessed her.

Just at this critical time her father died and thus the only tie that bound
her to her old home was snapped. Not long after she accepted the invitation
of some relatives and left her old haunts and, she hoped her old fears, to
lead an entirely new life in a large family circle.

A pair of interwoven later themes—the first untitled, the second, rewritten and titled "The Temptation"—appears to be a continuation of
the Hortense story. They describe a minor sexual encounter with an

unknown man during a crowded church service in Baltimore. The incident leaves Hortense with a feeling of shame and guilt that she attempts to rationalize to herself and to explain away to her relatives who have observed it:

She had not noticed this man before, she did not look at him now, but he, taking advantage of the position, leaned toward her rather heavily. She felt his touch. At first she was (oblivious to) only half-aware of it, but soon she became conscious of his presence. The sensuous impressions (had done their work only too well. The magic charm of a human touch was on her) was in her and she (could) did not stir. She loathed herself but still she did not move.

Now she became conscious that possibly her friends would notice her proximity to this fellow. Even that did not stir her. Her busy brain was active in weaving excuses. She remembered her well-known tendency to absent-mindedness. "I can tell them I was unconscious and grow indignant if they accuse me.". . .

At last she noticed her (aunt) friend motioning to her. "Not yet," she said to herself, "I won't see her." Then with a quick revulsion she continued fiercely, "Liar and coward, will you continue this, have you no sense of shame?" and all the while her eyes were fixed on the preacher and she looked the embodiment of intelligent interest.

Professor Moody, after commenting that her analysis of the girl's reaction, "though unpleasant in the extreme, is not without psychological interest," went on to note: "Your work has shown at times considerable emotional intensity and a somewhat unusual power of abstract thought. It has frequently been lacking in organization, in fertility of resource, and in artfulness of literary method."

It is clear, at least, that early in her writing career Gertrude had developed a certain objectivity about her own character and a willingness to discuss it frankly, even though in supposedly fictional terms. Her Radcliffe essays, faltering in style, ungrammatical, poorly punctuated, are characterized by a painful honesty and an intense seriousness. Possibly the most ardent of the essays she wrote for Moody's course was an eloquent, if somewhat embarrassing, homage to one of her professors, William James:

Is life worth living? Yes, a thousand times yes when the world still holds such spirits as Prof. James. He is truly a man among men; (A) a scientist of force and originality embodying all that is strongest and worthiest in the scientific spirit; (A) a metaphysician skilled in abstract thought, clear and vigorous and yet too great to worship logic as his God, and narrow himself to a belief merely in the reason of man.

Aside from the fact that the whole essay testifies to her poignant admiration for the man, it has an odd psychosexual curiosity. In singing James's praises, Gertrude unconsciously adopted the lines of a popular song about a maiden whose virtue is being villainously threatened. She turned the negative, "No, no, a thousand times, no. I'd rather die than say yes," into a hearty affirmative.

In 1893, when Gertrude entered Radcliffe, William James was already famous as a psychologist, teacher, and lecturer. Three years before, at the age of 48, James had published his monumental two-volume *The Principles of Psychology*, which, with its shrewd insights and fresh literary style, helped to raise the then-fledgling discipline—an offshoot of philosophy—into a full-blown science of its own. There were those who claimed that James was "an impressionist in psychology." His admirers maintained that his book was "too lively to make a good corpse." The book was an almost immediate success and was readily adopted as a text in American universities with the more practicable one-volume edition published in 1892. It was required reading in Philosophy 1, an introductory course, with lectures by George Herbert Palmer, Santayana, and James himself, which Gertrude took in her freshman year.

James's behavior in the classroom was energetic and unconventional. In his enthusiasm or his absorption in a problem, he would assume unorthodox positions, sometimes sprawling on the floor to scribble on a hand-held blackboard. In his brown tweeds, students thought he looked "more like a sportsman than a professor." Others felt that he acted like a "nervous thoroughbred," fidgeting, active, high-spirited. Even those who found James's philosophy and classroom techniques wanting were prepared to admit that he was always "throwing off sparks." In his private life he suffered from bouts of morbid sensitivity, but in class he displayed an inveterate sense of humor, so that students frequently addressed him with, "But, Doctor, to be serious for a moment."

James was responsive to the young. He liked original minds and original observations. He liked to draw his students out, prodding them to tell him not what they had learned but what they thought. "The only states of consciousness that we naturally deal with," he claimed in his *Principles*, "are found in personal consciousnesses, minds, selves, concrete particular I's and you's." For James, knowledge gained from direct experience was apt to prove more valuable than knowledge learned *about* a subject. It was a philosophy Gertrude echoed years later, when she began a lecture on English literature with the sentence: "One cannot come back too often to the question what is knowledge and to the answer knowledge is what one knows."

In her sophomore year Gertrude enrolled in a course of laboratory experimentation conducted by Hugo Münsterberg, a brilliant young German professor and James's protégé at the Harvard Psychological Laboratory. Her work in the course was more than satisfactory. At the end of the term Münsterberg wrote her to thank her "above all for that model-work you have done in the laboratory and the other courses wherever I met you." "My contact with Radcliffe," he went on, "was in every way a most charming part of my Cambridge experiences. But while I met there all types and kinds of students, you were to me the ideal student, just as a female student ought to be, and if in later years you look into printed discussions which I have in mind to publish about students in America, I hope you will then pardon me if you recognize some features of my ideal student picture as your own." As a result of her work, James invited her to attend his seminar in her junior year and encouraged her to undertake several psychological experiments.

James was particularly interested in learning more about the distinction between the conscious and subconscious mind. He had, as well, an interest in spiritualism—much to the dismay of his more rationalistic colleagues—and in the ability of certain mediums to write out automatic messages while supposedly in a state of trance. He was, himself, somewhat ambivalent about whether such messages derived from the subconscious or issued from what he termed the "summer-land." But he wanted to investigate such phenomena under more normal conditions in the laboratory. What he proposed was a series of experiments in automatic writing in which the subject was tested under varying conditions of fatigue and distraction.

From the beginning, Gertrude had certain misgivings about the experiments. Moreover, she seems to have had a certain maidenly distrust of the unconscious or subconscious mind. In one of her Radcliffe themes, she described her experiences as a subject:

Next she finds herself with a complicated apparatus strapped across her breast to register her breathing, her finger imprisoned in a steel machine and her arm thrust immovably into a big glass tube. . . . Strange fancies begin to crowd upon her, she feels that the silent pen is writing on and on forever. Her record is there she cannot escape it and the group about her begin to assume the shape of mocking friends gloating over her imprisoned misery.

The series of experiments that she conducted with a graduate student and friend, Leon M. Solomons, was published in the Harvard *Psychological Review* in September, 1896, under the title "Normal Motor Automatism." Though largely written by Solomons, to whose

conclusions, she later claimed, she had deferred, it was her first published piece of writing. She and Solomons had been the only subjects
involved in the experiments. In one—an attempt at "spontaneous"
automatic writing rather than writing from dictation—Gertrude had
been the subject, and the exercise had produced a few lines that seem
characteristic of her later style: "When he could not be the longest
and thus to be, and thus to be, the strongest." Solomons had also
noted a "marked tendency to repetition," a tendency that Gertrude
developed into a stylistic feature of her later work.

A further series of experiments was conducted by Gertrude alone and
published after she had left Radcliffe in the *Psychological Review* of
May, 1898, under the title "Cultivated Motor Automatism: A Study of
Character in its Relation to Attention." It was an attempt to produce
automatic writing in a larger sample of normal subjects, fifty female and
forty-one male students from Radcliffe and Harvard. But, interestingly, Gertrude's principal concern was with the character of her
subjects, which she broke down into two types. Type 1, she noted, "consists mostly of girls who are found naturally in literature courses and
men who are going in for law," and which she defined as "nervous,
high-strung, very imaginative, has the capacity to be easily roused and
intensely interested." Type II was of a different order: "more varied,
and gives more interesting results. In general, the individuals, often
blonde and pale, are distinctly phlegmatic. If emotional, decidedly of a
weakish sentimental order." She also complained: "A large number of
my subjects were New Englanders, and the habit of self-repression, the
intense self-consciousness, the morbid fear of 'letting one's self go,'
that is so prominent an element in the New England character, was a
constant stumbling-block." If her character analyses were oversimplified,
they nonetheless attested to her need to group people in manageable
units—preferably two units—a habit of mind that she developed into a
program in the writing of her novel *The Making of Americans*. This,
rather than the actual literary style, may be what she had in mind when
she later claimed that "Cultivated Motor Automatism" was "interesting
to read because the method of writing to be afterwards developed in
Three Lives and Making of Americans already shows itself." But when
later critics attempted to attribute her mature writing style to her experiments in automatic writing, she was quick to scotch the argument.
She did not think that either she or Solomons had "been doing automatic writing, we always knew what we were doing." Furthermore, she
maintained that she "never had subconscious reactions," a rather large
generalization. As proof, she recalled an experiment conducted by one
of James's students who, in reading his report to the class, complained
that one of the subjects tested had had no responses at all. This had low-
ered the average and falsified his conclusions, and he asked if he might

eliminate that subject from his report. "Whose record is it," James had asked. "Miss Stein's," the student answered. "Ah," James said, "if Miss Stein gave no response I should say that it was as normal not to give a response as to give one and decidedly the result must not be cut out."

James kept up an interest in Gertrude's subsequent career and later visited her in Paris. He remained a hero for her until the end of her life. A few months before her death, she recalled the influence of her old professor. "Everything must come into your scheme," she said of the creative life, "otherwise you cannot achieve real simplicity. A great deal of this I owe to a great teacher, William James. He said, 'Never reject anything. Nothing has been proved. If you reject anything, that is the beginning of the end as an intellectual.' He was my big influence when I was at college. He was a man who always said, 'complicate your life as much as you please, it has got to simplify.' "

IV

In the late fall of 1895, Leo, invited to accompany his cousin Fred Stein, embarked on a world tour. They sailed from the West Coast to Japan on the first leg of their voyage. Leo recalled the early months of his trip with some fondness: "the first view of Fujiyama after nine days of storm at sea with all hatches closed; the wonder ride on the first evening ashore through the paper-lantern-lighted streets of Yokohama." Japan, at the time, was still shaking loose from its centuries' old isolation, and Leo was particularly proud of the fact that he had spent two months at Kyoto, out of bounds to most tourists, where there were very few foreigners. His glimpse of life untouched by the modern world he pronounced "fascinating."

The stormy crossing to Japan had also had its benefits. On board ship, he had met Hutchins Hapgood, a former Harvard student, later to become a celebrated writer and social critic. Hapgood's *The Spirit of the Ghetto*, published in 1902, was a pioneering work in sociology. A man of catholic tastes and old-fashioned liberal sentiments, Hapgood found Leo highly argumentative. In his autobiography, *A Victorian in the Modern World*, he recalled that on their initial meeting, Leo "couldn't leave the slightest subject without critical analysis. He and I argued the livelong day." One day, he remembered, they had argued whether a snowstorm falling over the ocean looked "natural" or whether it "represented a theatrical stunt."

He [Leo] was almost always mentally irritated. The slightest flaw, real or imaginary, in his companion's statements, caused in him intellectual indignation of the most intense kind. And there seemed to be something in him

which took it for granted that anything said by anybody except himself
needed immediate denial or at least substantial modification.

At twenty-three, Leo was still casting about for a suitable profession.
In his arguments with Hapgood, he had proceeded to drop one of his
options. With that erratic presence of mind that he claimed enabled
him to recall any and every detail of significance in his personal life
but that left him unable to "place" the woman who had sat next to him
at lunch and engaged him in a long conversation only three days before,
Leo remembered that it was exactly in mid-Pacific that he had announced to Hapgood that he had decided history was not a tenable
profession. From his boyhood, he had been intensely interested in history and had expected to make a profession of it. He had compiled lists
of the dynasties of Egypt and Assyria, had memorized the names of the
kings of England and France, the emperors of Germany. Gibbon was
his ideal. But even before he began his world tour, he had come to
the conclusion that history was "a mare's nest of illusory knowledge,"
subject to the unconscious and deliberate distortions of historians and
those who participated in historic events. He told Hapgood that until
some new "method of analysis was found which could get behind the
spoken word to the real intention, history was no better than fiction."

It was not until 1909, when he first read Freud, that Leo discovered
the method he had prophetically called for. He thought it a remarkable
coincidence that his insight into the fallaciousness of history—reached
in midocean in late 1895—was "exactly contemporary with Freud's first
publications." Freud's sexual theories did not, at first, interest him. It
was only later in life, when his neurotic inability to complete any project propelled him into a course of psychoanalysis, that Leo concerned
himself with such things as the Oedipus Complex. "There is the man
I long ago called for," he exclaimed to himself when he first heard of
the Viennese psychologist. What interested him about Freud was
Freud's discovery of the unconscious motives that distorted not only the
facts of one's personal life but the facts of history.

Leo's sojourn in Japan, however, was to provide him with at least one
consoling preoccupation. He had developed a serious interest in art and
in Japan began a study of Japanese prints, especially the works of
Kuninaga and Harunobu. This reawakening of his interest in art—as a
boy in California he had clipped out and mounted woodcuts from
Century magazine—had been prompted by his visit to Europe the
previous summer. He had devoted a lengthy stay in Paris to spending
his mornings in the Louvre. In the Salon Carré he had been particularly
impressed with Veronese's huge *Marriage in Cana* and Mantegna's
Crucifixion. He had even "discovered" Rubens' Marie de Medici deco-
rations, hung one after the other in the long gallery, where the public
and the critics considered them with condescension.

Aside from his experiences in Japan, Leo's world tour was to prove somewhat dispiriting. He was impressed with Canton, "with its mysterious, keenly, almost ferociously intelligent-looking crowds"; in Ceylon he had sat under a upas tree and found the streets of Colombo "Kiplingesque." But from Egypt to Italy to Carlsbad, where Fred Stein was to join his parents, the pleasures of the journey had begun to wane for Leo.

For Gertrude, Leo's journey represented her first prolonged separation from her brother, and she viewed it with a certain anxiety. She was scheduled to meet him in Europe at the end of his tour. In March, 1896, Leo wrote her from the Mena House Hotel in Cairo, in a tone of world-weariness with his role as companion: "I've reached a stage of momentary mental collapse. Never in my life I believe have I felt so completely dulled so intolerably stupid so inanely played out. I'm glad this thing will soon be over and may the weight of Cheops rest on my recumbent person if I ever undertake such a job again. I rather thought I was more completely bore-proof than I have proved to be." Nevertheless, in the next breath he was outlining a detailed itinerary for their summer together, including a tour of the Low Countries and Germany and a lengthy stay in Paris. He gave her some brotherly advice: "One thing that you want to attend to in time though is a letter of credit for 200 pounds which you want to write to Mike about so that you can attend to the signature business." He cautioned her that she should advise him of her plans early so that he could convey "certain other advices & directions concerning the passage Perilous."

With the end of the school term, Gertrude prepared somewhat tardily for her trip to Antwerp, where she was to meet Leo. They had finally decided upon a summer in Italy—which Leo had just visited— rather than Belgium and Holland. It had been a busy spring for Gertrude: she had been engaged in her laboratory experiments with Leon Solomons and with the writing of their report, "Normal Motor Automatism." And, as secretary for the Radcliffe Philosophy Club, she had been given the task of inviting lecturers for the club's irregular meetings. She had also found time to attend the regular concerts of the Boston Symphony. Early in June, her brother Michael wrote to her from San Francisco, worried about the lateness of her travel arrangements. "It is now June 2nd," he wrote, "and you had better let me know just when you are going to start and where you are going *to*, so I can get your letter of credit for you. Also let me know at once what drafts you want for use before starting. Also see that all your & Leo's bills (room rent etc.) are settled before you go so as to have everything in ship-shape."

Just before departure, she received a letter from a young Harvard student, Leo Friedman, with whom she regularly attended the symphony concerts. (It is perhaps not without some significance that during the year of Leo's absence, two of the men with whom she was companionable were named Leon and Leo.) Friedman wrote her on June 29:

Dear Gertrude,

I write to tell you good-by for somehow I could not do it while you were here—and to wish that you may have a happy trip. Weeks ago I felt how lonesome it would be here without you and I hope you will return early in the fall with Leo, who ought to be persuaded to come to the symphonies with us next year. Good-by—God bless you.

For some reason, Gertrude had conceived the idea—it was a measure of her dependence upon her brother and her anxiety about the trip—that after a year's time she would no longer be able to recognize Leo. She did, of course, spot him immediately, as he waved to her from the crowd gathered at the pier in Antwerp as the *Red Star* docked. But her anxiety about that moment—with its hint of the buried, fretful hostility that underlies most frightening dependency situations—indicates how thoroughly important Leo had become to her.

In her last two years at Radcliffe, Gertrude had come to a decision about her career. The decision, she claimed, had largely been prompted by William James, who advised her that she should take up either philosophy or psychology. For philosophy, James maintained, she would have to have higher mathematics. Since he gathered that mathematics had never interested her, he suggested psychology instead. "Now for psychology," James said, "you must have a medical education, a medical education opens all doors, as Oliver Wendell Holmes told me and as I tell you." In her junior and senior years Gertrude took the necessary courses, including mathematics, for graduation. But she had never completed her entrance requirements—principally an examination in Latin—and for that purpose she hired a graduate student, Margaret Lewis, to tutor her. The incident is worth recalling because it illustrates her somewhat thoughtless acceptance of her own situation in life and her capacity for learning something basic from even a minor experience. She had agreed to pay the young woman at the end of each month for the tutoring. But one month Gertrude had spent all her money going to the opera and asked the tutor if she would mind waiting, since she hadn't the money to pay her:

She said no reflectively and then she said what do you mean when you say you have no money, Oh I said I mean I have spent my month's money and I haven't any. Well she said reflectively your father and mother are dead you have your own money haven't you. Yes I said. Well then she said you have the money to pay me now I do not need it but you have it so you must not say you haven't got it. Yes I said but you see I cannot use that because that is what I have not got I only have a month's money, yes she said but you see those who earn money . . . when they have not got it they have not got it. I was much surprised and I never forgot it.

Leo, too, back at Harvard after his year's tour, was attempting to make up his mind about his future. He was, however, bored. When Gertrude communicated that fact to her sister-in-law—Michael and Sarah had been married in 1893—Sarah had written back uncharitably: "Tell Leo that I shall encourage Simon to go East with all my might, for I want him [Leo] to know what it is to be *really* bored to death." Like Gertrude, Leo had been enormously impressed with William James, and for a time he had toyed with the idea of becoming a philosopher. But philosophy was another of the options he dropped. Metaphysics, he decided, was too speculative an occupation; he lacked the credulity for maintaining belief in some watertight absolute. James, Leo felt, had "wanted a metaphysic as badly as anyone, but was too honest to shut his eyes to the no-thoroughfare signs, and remained, a bit uncertainly, on the outskirts." Pragmatism, Leo eventually decided, was the only philosophy worthy of serious consideration. Although he might well have absorbed its spirit in James's classes, Leo maintained that, "as was right and proper," he had discovered it "independently" before James had clearly spelled it out in his book of lectures, *Pragmatism*, published in 1907. James remained, however, the exemplary philosopher in Leo's mind. Late in life, Leo claimed: "Me and Billy James were the only really concrete-minded people I knew."

Gertrude had decided to pursue her medical career at Johns Hopkins University School of Medicine, in Baltimore, which had recently opened its doors to women students. Its location would bring her once again into contact with her lively Baltimore relatives. Furthermore, Leo —perhaps stimulated by the example of Gertrude's published laboratory work—had decided to pursue some independent research projects in biology there. Gertrude's choice of a medical career, however, prompted a warning from one of her old friends, Margaret Sterling Snyder, who had graduated from Radcliffe in 1895. In April, 1896, she wrote to Gertrude about her "lack of enthusiasm concerning your J. Hopkins plan."

Will it do you one bit of good as a deterrent if I tell you . . . that I now see I was one of the most deluded and pitiable of all these many young women who are aspiring after what is beyond them in our own day. My dear Gertrude, I have no explanations and no theories; I do not know enough to have. But I will say in a word that a sheltered life, domestic tastes, maternity, and faith are all I could ask for myself or you or the great mass of womankind. I overworked and overreached—too much ambition, too little faith in traditional ideals. . . . Now this I say not to preach to you—you are head-

strong as I was and will probably have to work it out for yourself—but that
when you begin possibly to waver in "being a useful member of society" in
the way you have outlined you may recall my experience and my affectionate
advice.

Gertrude was to receive virtually the same advice from her sister-in-
law. She had written to Sally Stein, early in 1897, reporting that Leo
had not been feeling well since his return from Europe—he was suffering from stomach disorders, a complaint that plagued him for several
years—and only vaguely mentioned their joint plans for the future.
"What do you mean by 'going to keep house and nurse him according
to all the latest medical school theories?' " Sally had responded, "Are
you going to Johns Hopkins, or Harvard Medical School, or New York,
or where? Mike and I feel quite hurt that Leon Solomons [then in San
Francisco] seems to know all your plans but we are in pitchy darkness."
Later in the year, when she and Mike had been dutifully informed
of Gertrude and Leo's move to Baltimore, Sally wrote to Gertrude
—ostensibly to pass on her husband's advice: "He also wishes that
you could make up your minds to board with the Bachrachs or some
other congenial people, while in Baltimore as he can't quite see who
will run the house when you are at college and Leo reading, and he particularly wonders at your investing in house-furnishings before you are
sure that you will enjoy house-keeping. If you feel it necessary to go
house-keeping alone, can't you rent a furnished flat?"

"Your financial condition," Sally noted, "after the August allowance,
which you will need to pay for your course of study, will be about
$300.00 on hand with $150—on Sept. 1st from Mk't Str. 5%s. and
$300—on Oct. 1st from Omnibus 6%s; then nothing until Jan. 10th."

But the real purpose of her letter was to convey to Gertrude her own
continuing happiness as the mother of a two-year-old son and to offer
some womanly advice: "There certainly is nothing in the line of happiness to compare with that which a mother derives from the contempla-
tion of her first-born and even the agony which she endures from the
moment of its birth does not seem to mar it, therefore my dear and
beloved sister in law go and get married, for there is nothing in this
whole wide world like babies—Leo to the contrary, notwithstanding."

It was advice that Gertrude never heeded.

V

Despite the worrying of Michael and Sarah, the housekeeping arrangements in Baltimore proved to be eminently practical. Leo and Gertrude
had found a house at 215 East Biddle Street and hired a housekeeper,

a firm but gentle German soul, Lena Lebender. Lena kept the house meticulous and shining; she admired "Mr. Leo," but "Miss Gertrude" was her pride. She doted on Gertrude like a mother, scolding her for mismanaging her allowance. Lena had brought with her Jack and Rags, her two dogs, which enlivened the household. Like their mistress, the animals were to figure in Gertrude's, "The Good Anna," the opening story of her book *Three Lives*. Gertrude had a fondness for gossip from any quarter. Even the backstairs gossip of her housekeeper with her stories of her life and her relationships, her problems with finding a suitable hired girl, was to serve Gertrude well in her later picture of an immigrant workingwoman. But Lena was a hard taskmaster, and whenever quarrels broke out in the kitchen or Lena asked her to "speak" to one of the transient girls, Gertrude made herself scarce.

Gertrude's first two years at medical school began auspiciously. She had arrived with a reputation as one of William James's favored students, with independent work to her credit. Her paper "Cultivated Motor Automatism" had appeared in the Harvard *Psychological Review* in the spring of her freshman year at Johns Hopkins. Her grades during her freshman and sophomore years—mostly for laboratory courses—were promising, ranging from the highest grade in anatomy (1) through normal histology (1.5), physiology (2) to physiological chemistry (2.5) in her first year, and pathology and bacteriology (1.5) and pharmacology and toxicology (2) in her second term. Like many of the women students at Johns Hopkins, she made models of brain tracts for Dr. Franklyn Mall, her professor of anatomy. Her female colleagues, she told Leo, felt obliged to do the work to earn favor with the male professor, though she didn't mind it since it was "purely mechanical work and rather restful." But the men in her class, she noted, "wouldn't waste their time on it." She passed on to Leo the remark of a German anatomist who visited Dr. Mall. On being shown the models, he observed that it was an "excellent occupation for women and Chinamen."

At the turn of the century it took women of stamina to survive medical-school training. At Johns Hopkins they were not only regarded as a form of coolie labor in that predominantly male domain but also were subjected to practical jokes and crude stories in the classroom. A fellow student of Gertrude's, Dorothy Reed, recalled a lecture by a nose and throat specialist: "He dragged in the dirtiest stories I ever heard, read or imagined, and when he couldn't say it in English, he quoted Latin from sources not usually open to the public." Even fifty years later, she claimed, the lecturer's remarks still came up in her mind, "like a decomposing body from the bottom of a pool that is disturbed." Dorothy Reed's impressions of Gertrude were not flattering: "She could do nothing with her hands, was very untidy and careless in her technique and very irritating in her attitude of intellectual superiority, which was marked, even in her youth." Miss Reed, however, seems to have been more familiar with Gertrude during her final years at medical school. Her concluding evaluation—"At medicine, she worked only in a half-hearted way, and her grades were always poor."—seems more applicable to the final years Gertrude spent at John Hopkins, when her interest in a medical career had begun to wane.

For Gertrude and Leo, life in Baltimore had its agreeable aspects. Although Leo's career in biology had begun to falter—he found he had no liking and no aptitude for laboratory work—he was still pursuing his interest in art. He frequently visited the Walters Art Gallery to study its collection of Chinese porcelains and its "choice" selection of works by the Barbizon painters. He had also begun collecting Japanese prints, and the walls of the house on Biddle Street were hung with these, as well as the modest number of etchings he and Gertrude had purchased.

Among their closer friends in Baltimore were the Cone sisters—Dr. Claribel and Etta—whom Gertrude and Leo had met when they first came to Baltimore from California in 1892. They had been introduced to the two sisters in the normal course of social life among the close-knit circle of well-to-do Baltimore Jews. Now, back in Baltimore, Gertrude and Leo often attended the Saturday night "evenings" that the Cones had established in their home on Eutaw Place. Etta Cone was particularly receptive to Leo's discourses on art.

There was a similarity in the family backgrounds of the Cones and the Steins. Herman Cone, Claribel's and Etta's father, was a German Jew who had come to America to make his fortune. His prosperous wholesale grocery business was sold when he reached retirement age, and his two eldest sons, Moses and Ceasar, turned that move to account by starting a successful exporting company for Southern-made textiles. Through bankruptcy and defaulted payments, the brothers acquired one Southern mill after another, laying the foundations for the highly profitable Cone Mills. Herman Cone died in 1897, and Moses and Ceasar generously turned over their shares of their father's estate to their unmarried sisters—Claribel was then thirty-three; Etta, twenty-seven—thus providing them each with a yearly income of $2,400.

Dr. Claribel, ten years Gertrude's senior, was a woman of independent mind and settled opinions on most matters. She had already asserted her rights by insisting upon becoming a doctor, graduating from the Woman's Medical College of Baltimore in 1890. She had a distaste for close physical contact and, so she claimed, decided against general practice after treating her first patient in Philadelphia. Thereafter she decided to devote her attentions to laboratory work and teaching, holding a professorship at her alma mater. When Gertrude enrolled at Johns Hopkins in 1897, Claribel was engaged in research in the Pathology Department at Johns Hopkins, and the pair frequently met each other en route to the university.

Etta Cone was of a less adventurous and more retiring disposition, and kept to her housekeeping duties, caring for her parents while they lived. But she had already developed an interest in art—an interest that was to become a consuming passion for both sisters, partly due to the inspiration of Leo and Gertrude. Etta's collecting had begun modestly. In 1898 her brother Moses had given her $500 to dress up the family homestead. Etta, on a shopping trip to New York, bought four paintings by the American Impressionist Theodore Robinson. The four landscapes, bought from a "widow's sale" of the painter's effects, proudly graced the parlor of Eutaw Place. Gertrude developed a special affection for the shy Etta. She liked to trail after her on visits to the dressmakers, and she valued Etta's advice on the proper materials to be selected for shirtwaists. In the next decade they frequently met or traveled together on trips to Europe, and they corresponded regularly. But there was often something condescending about Gertrude's attitude toward Etta, whereas she was genuinely awestruck by Dr. Claribel.

Claribel was the supreme authority, the dominant and domineering member of the pair. Stout and imperious, she took the tireless services of her sister entirely for granted. If, in their travels, Claribel decided their hotel room was not comfortable—even though Etta might argue that it was for only one night after a long day of sightseeing and shopping (the two were compulsive shoppers)—Claribel would insist that they must move immediately to better accommodations. Claribel would tell her weary sister, "Etta, one night is as important as any other night in my life, and I must be comfortable." When Dr. Claribel attended the theater, she bought two front-row seats on the aisle—one for herself and one for her packages. Etta would take a single seat, farther back. And when Dr. Claribel traveled, it was never, even for expediency, second class. She took a stateroom for two—for herself alone—or, failing that, a stateroom for three. If that were not available, she waited for the next ship. There was only one class in life for Dr. Claribel—first class.

For years Gertrude remained fascinated by the odd relationship of the two sisters: the one, outgoing, authoritative, magnanimously self-involved; the other, timid, patient to a fault—a born server. It was a relationship she would, later, attempt to establish for herself.

VI

In Baltimore, Leo had another of his epiphanies: "I had soon realized that I could do nothing in a laboratory, and one day I got a great idea in aesthetics—something along the lines of what [Benedetto] Croce later published—and I dropped biology and decided to go to Florence for a few years." His plans were vague, but he had an interest in Mantegna and thought he might work out his "great idea" through a study of art history. In the summer of 1900 he and Gertrude and Gertrude's friend Mabel Weeks, a Radcliffe graduate, had traveled through Europe together. Gertrude had left the pair behind—Mabel was to spend the winter studying in England—when she returned to Baltimore. Leo wrote to her soon after he had established himself in Florence. He had stayed a bit longer in Paris than he had expected. Gertrude had apparently acquired one or two color prints there before leaving. Leo informed her: "I also foolishly bought a couple of those color things that you were looking at at Hessel's so as to have them round continually and see what happened. They simply won't wash. I suppose that you have found that to be the case with those that you got." If he ever got back to Paris, he told her, he planned to exchange them "for some humble things in black and white."

In Florence, Leo wrote her, he had recently had lunch with the art historian Bernard Berenson and his companion, Mrs. Mary Costelloe —the handsome sister of the American writer Logan Pearsall Smith, who had left her dull English husband and placed her children with her Quaker parents, in order to devote her life to the well-being of the suave Harvard scholar and expert on Renaissance art. Berenson was a brilliant conversationalist and a highly opinionated man—the latter quality somewhat dimmed Leo's otherwise-favorable first impressions. "He has sense there's no doubt about that. He's rather younger than I thought him—only thirty-five—but he's been in Florence since he was twenty. His house is filled with beautiful old Italian furniture and hangings and he has a really magnificent art library." Leo described Mrs. Costelloe as "a large ruddy blonde, rather washed out by time, as she must be between forty and forty-five at best. She hasn't any very obvious intelligence and at first blush would seem intellectually merely an echo of Berenson." She married him that same year.

Leo pushed his acquaintanceship with Berenson steadily. Two days later, on October 11, he wrote Gertrude about another meeting: "I saw Berenson again Wednesday evening. He's certainly very conversable and in the main I find him very sensible. There's simply that tremendous excess of the I." Florence, he found, lacked the charm of Venice. The city was "so eminently serious minded, so erect in carriage and severe in temper that I feel it to be almost distant. I suppose however that after I've been here awhile and go back to Venice I'll feel the latter to be like my stummick—distinctly atonic." Leo was to spend two winters in the city, studying the paintings of *quattrocento* artists—della Francesca, Uccello, Veneziano—meeting frequently with Berenson and availing himself of Berenson's library. Perhaps, under the challenge of

Berenson's reputation, Leo also decided to write a biography of Mantegna, there being "no recent book on him in English" at the time. But like his "great idea" in aesthetics, his monograph on the Renaissance Italian master never reached fruition.

Florence, too, had its dismal aspects. "It rains and the wind is never weary," Leo wrote Gertrude in February, complaining, "Florentine weather can't easily be improved on in the direction of undesirability." He was feeling somewhat forlorn: "I believe I'm the only American in Florence, at least so the people here tell me. I blow the American trumpet as though it was the whole of Sousa's band that I had to work with. Mrs. Berenson however tells me that they have decided that my Americanism is just a bluff."

Mary Berenson, in fact, had come to the conclusion that all Leo wanted in life "was an ear." Berenson's judgment of his persistent American caller was equally unflattering. Leo Stein, he decided, was a man "who was always inventing the umbrella."

There is little doubt that Leo's defection contributed to the failure of Gertrude's medical career. She lost interest in her studies, failed to do her classwork, and, when asked questions in class, responded by saying she did not know the answer. She was bored; she "could not remember the things that of course the dullest medical student could not forget." But her grades had begun falling off in her junior year, before Leo's departure. She received a 3 in neurology, clinical microscopy, and obstetrics. The last subject she particulary disliked, largely because of her professor, Dr. John Whitridge Williams. She did, however, find valuable the casework in Baltimore's Negro quarter, when she had "to take her turn in the delivering of babies." Her glimpse of the hard life in the Negro community proved useful when she came to write the story of the young mulatto girl, Melanctha, in *Three Lives*. But there was some truth to her later contention, in *The Autobiography of Alice B. Toklas*, that while she found her early laboratory courses enjoyable, her last two years of medical studies, devoted to "the practice and theory of medicine," held no interest for her at all.

Moreover, she seems to have had some worries about her health. After Leo's departure, Gertrude moved to another house, on East Eager Street in Baltimore. Emma Lootz, a classmate at Johns Hopkins and a mutual friend of Mabel Weeks, had a room directly below Gertrude's large living room. She recalled that Gertrude "got alarmed" about the state of her own health, feeling that there was something wrong with her blood. Gertrude prescribed an unusual treatment for herself; she hired a welterweight to box with her. "The chandelier in my room used to swing," Emma Lootz remembered, "and the house echoed with shouts of 'Now give me one on the jaw! Now give me one in the kidney!' "

Leo, apprised of the situation, wrote Gertrude on her birthday, February 3, 1901, asking, "What is all this nonmedicated rumble that issues from your quarter? Is it representative of a phase or a general condition?" He offered her some mild advice: "It would be too bad if the first person in the family who had gone so far as to get the adequate preparation for anything should go back on it. Well I suppose you won't, especially as there's nothing else to be done. If you had my very superior talents for loafing it might do but you haven't so it won't." Despite Leo's lukewarm encouragement, Gertrude allowed herself to fail. Even the sharp remonstrances of close friends and colleagues did not move her. When Marian Walker, an ardent feminist, pleaded, "Gertrude, Gertrude, remember the cause of women," Gertrude shot back, "You don't know what it is to be bored."

Gertrude's account of her failure in *The Autobiography of Alice B. Toklas* is somewhat streamlined. One of her professors, Williams, the chief of obstetrics, had decided not to pass her. (According to Dorothy Reed, Williams, "an aristocrat and a snob, couldn't stand her marked Hebrew looks, her sloppy work and her intolerance.") After the term finals, Williams had called Gertrude in to tell her that she could, of course, take a summer course and in the fall get her degree. Gertrude had been planning to meet Leo that summer and travel in Spain. She surprised her professor by thanking him: "You have no idea how grateful I am to you. I have so much inertia and so little initiative that very possibly if you had not kept me from taking my degree I would have, well, not taken to the practice of medicine, but at any rate to pathological psychology and you don't know how little I like pathological psychology, and how all medicine bores me."

Actually, she had failed in four of her senior-year courses: obstetrics (5), laryngology and rhinology (5), ophthamology and otology (4), and dermatology (4). Nor did she give up her chances for her degree quite so readily. Dr. Mall, perhaps encouraged by Dr. Florence Sabin, who had gotten her degree earlier, had persuaded Gertrude to take on an independent project, promising to urge the faculty to give her another chance. Dorothy Reed, a friend of Florence Sabin's recalled: "Dr. Mall set her a problem similar to one Dr. Sabin had completed successfully in her fourth year. This was the sectioning of an embryo human brain and its reconstruction, and a study of the development of the centers of the brain and the tracts leading to them." Gertrude worked on the project for weeks and turned in her reconstruction to Dr. Mall. A few days later, Dr. Mall brought the model to Florence Sabin, saying, "Either I am crazy or Miss Stein is. Will you see what you can make out of her work?" "Florence," according to Dorothy Reed, "worked over it for several nights and came back to Dr. Mall with the answer that Miss Stein must have embedded the cord turned back under the embryo brain, instead of extended from it, and the centers of the outborne cells of the cord she had located in the brain, and other mysterious features of the reconstruction, could be explained only in this way." When Florence Sabin asked what she should do with the model, Dr. Mall had "shied the entire model and explanatory test into a waste basket."

It was a curious failure for Gertrude to make, for she was experienced in studying the anatomy of the brain. Earlier in her career, at Johns Hopkins, Dr. Llewellys Barker, a neurological specialist, had assigned her the task of studying the "nucleus of Darkschewitsch" of an infant a few weeks old. He had included Gertrude's report of her dissection of that section of the brain in his lengthy volume, *The Nervous System and Its Constituent Neurones,*" published in 1899. Even more curiously —although she no longer intended to take her degree—Gertrude returned to Baltimore, after the summer in Europe with Leo, to continue her research on brain tracts. Presumably, she was carrying on the project under the auspices of Dr. Barker—then at the Chicago Neurological Society. Dr. Barker wrote her on January 30, 1902, commenting on the work she had sent:

I have just gone through your second part with which I was more familiar because I studied these sections more thoroughly than the other set. I do not think that you have included too many drawings from sections. It seems to me that these are necessary in order to give a clear idea to the reader. Do you think that one drawing of the model will suffice? Dr. Mall's advice on that point will be valuable. I think that the photographs of the brains showing the planes of sections should be included, for they will be of special value to any research worker who wishes to identify convolutions.

He also asked her to go over her writing "with special reference to literary form." He was glad to hear that she planned to go to Europe, but he wondered what she would do there. "Are you to continue work on the nervous system?" he asked. "It would seem a pity not to, now that you have gone so far in this line of work and have so good a background."

VII

If it had not been for the prospect of a dreary English winter—the winter of 1902–3—Gertrude and Leo might have settled in London for a considerable stay. They were both now at loose ends, uncommitted as to the future. They had first taken rooms in London, at 20 Bloomsbury

Square, and were planning to spend five to six months in the English capital. But early in September, they had journeyed to Surrey to spend a few days with Berenson and his wife.

Berenson's impression of Gertrude, whom he had met during a previous summer in Italy, was more flattering than his impression of Leo. Years later, when he described her to an American interviewer, Aline Saarinen, he drew upon ancient and monumental associations. "Her apparently seamless garment," he said, "make her look like the proto-Semite, a statue from Ur of the Chaldees." He was always a little fearful, he noted, that her monolithic bulk might topple over. But Berenson was dismayed by the laxity with which the two Steins treated the books in his library. Moreover, Gertrude, in those years, gloried in the Italian sun and, with an entirely unladylike lack of concern, sweated profusely. She would hardly have appealed to a couple as fastidious as the Berensons.

Nevertheless, in 1902, the Steins were still on the best of terms with the art historian. Staying at Friday's Hill, the Berensons' country house, both Gertrude and Leo had been charmed by their glimpse of the English countryside in the warmth of a lingering summer. It proved so enjoyable, in fact, they took a cottage at nearby Greenhill-Fernhurst, prolonging their stay for another two weeks.

Their cottage, Leo wrote Mabel Weeks, was decidedly picturesque. It was set "among some fine oaks on a little hill soft with the springy English turf on which some nice red cows, lamby sheep, white ducks, lordly roosters and clucky hens wander in pastoral freedom." They continued to see the Berensons almost daily. They had also met Mrs. Berenson's sister, Alys, and her husband, Bertrand Russell—"a young mathematician of genius," so Leo informed Mabel. Berenson himself was rather frail, but Gertrude had put him on a diet of eggs and milk, under which, Leo was happy to report, the art historian was "flourishing like a Green Bay tree."

Friday's Hill, during that late summer, was the scene of a succession of lively debates. "Gertrude," Leo wrote Mabel, "was the other day trying to hold up the American end of a general discussion against Russell, Berenson and a young journalist, Dill." Leo wished that he had been there to mount a really proper defense of America. Although Gertrude was competent in the department of forensics, Leo, apparently, felt that she was no proper match for Russell. Unfortunately, he had been rather clumsily indisposed. Coming back from Friday's Hill one afternoon, he had been seized by an urge to do handsprings. Performing this stunt, badly, on a hillside, he had lost his footing and sprained an ankle. He had been laid up for several days.

He was confident, however, that he would have other opportunities to rout the Redcoats. "We have America versus England disputes all the time," he told Mabel. "The general theme is why in the name of all that's reasonable do you think of going back to America. It's quite impossible to persuade them that my Americanism is not a pose, and that I really think seriously of returning there—sooner or later. And truly at times it does seem quite impossible. On the whole, however, I remain constant, for after all there is something tonic—even over-tonic—about America, that I miss here and would not like to miss permanently."

"If America only were not so far away," Leo pontificated, "and if the climate in the possible parts were not so chilly. Those I think are my chief grievances against the land of my birth, though I suppose that they are not very profound ones. Someday I'll make up my mind that I can stand them and then Gertrude and I will retire to Connecticut or Duxbury or somewhere and live happily ever after." Leo's transatlantic sentiments were poignantly chauvinistic. Equally interesting was the fact that he had annexed Gertrude's life and was convinced that, having made up his mind about a course of action, Gertrude would inevitably follow.

For Gertrude, the arguments with Berenson and Russell meant more than a display of intellectual prowess. They started her meditating about her country and what she valued most about it. The seed of those meditations, planted at Friday's Hill, was to result in her mammoth homage to America and its middle class, her book *The Making of Americans*.

In the meantime, however, her loyalty to Leo was not proof against the rigors of a London winter. Installed in Bloomsbury Square, she found the progressive dampness, the cold, the lead-gray fogs unredeemably dreary and depressing. Even the long days spent in the reading room at the British Museum or the hours spent browsing in the London bookstalls offered no comfort. London had assumed a Dickensian aspect; but she did not care for the Dickensian squalor in real life. One day, as if in vindication of her arguments with Berenson and Russell, she announced to Leo that she was returning to America and promptly booked passage for New York. There she settled for the winter, taking up residence with Mabel Weeks and two girl friends, Harriet Clark and Estelle Rumbold, in a comfortable house, referred to as the White House, located at 100th Street and Riverside Drive.

When Gertrude set down her feeling about that dreary London winter a year later—she was then living in Paris and completing her first decisive effort as a writer—her impressions were still remarkably vivid. Describing the state of mind of her young American heroine, Adele, in the novelette *Quod Erat Demonstrandum*, she wrote with intensity and blunt awkwardness:

The time comes when nothing in the world is so important as a breath of one's own particular climate. If it were one's last penny it would be used for that return passage.

An American in the winter fogs of London can realise this passionate need, this desperate longing in all its completeness. The dead weight of that fog and smoke laden air, the sky that never suggests for a moment the clean blue distance that has been the accustomed daily comrade, the dreary sun, moon and stars that look like painted imitations on the ceiling of a smoke-filled room, the soggy, damp, miserable streets, and the women with be-draggled, frayed-out skirts, their faces swollen and pimply with sordid dirt ground into them until it has become a natural part of their ugly surface all become day after day a more dreary weight of hopeless oppression.

But it was more than the "hopeless oppression" of London that Adele—and her author—was fleeing from.

Left to himself in such a setting, Leo, too, became restless and dis-satisfied. An English acquaintance asked him about his plans for the coming Christmas holidays. Leo answered that since he had "no inti-mate acquaintances" in London, he would do the same as he did on any other day. The Englishman kindly invited him to spend Christmas Eve with his family; it was unthinkable that Leo should be "alone on Christmas Eve." The prospect of the impending festivities so dismayed Leo that he crossed the Channel to France on the afternoon of Decem-ber 24. He planned to return to America, by way of Paris and a brief stay in Florence.

CHAPTER THREE

The Vulgarity of Virtue

I

It was, apparently, an intolerable condition of rootlessness—both mental and physical—that led Leo Stein to settle in Paris instead of proceeding to America. There, early in 1903, he had come to the end of his professional options. History, philosophy, biology had all been tried and found wanting. His latest venture, art history, had also been abandoned. Art history, he reasoned, was no more reliable than history proper. Moreover, his projected study of Mantegna had faltered when he learned that the English art historian Maud Cruttwell was already at work on such a study. With the exception of Berenson, Leo found that the profession, as practiced in Florence, consisted of amiable, "frowsy-headed" English ladies. They seemed to cluster around Berenson like hens around an elegant bantam rooster.

No sooner had Leo stopped off in Paris than he launched himself in another career—that of artist. Dining, one night, in a restaurant with Pablo Casals—the cellist was then touring the European capitals as an accompanist for the singer Madame Emma Nevada—Leo confessed to Casals that he felt himself "growing into an artist." Pouring out this declaration into the ear of a listening friend had a salutary effect. Returning to his hotel room that evening, Leo made a roaring fire, stripped completely naked, and began to draw himself in the nude. His satisfaction altogether confirmed his new choice of vocation. It was typical that this moment of awakening in his career—which was a life of perennial self-analysis in the pursuit of self-esteem—should have come to him when he was staring at himself naked in a mirror.

From his own nude body, Leo progressed to sketching statues in the Louvre. Thereafter, he enrolled at the Académie Julian, the Parisian mecca for serious American students. It was clear, however, that in order to pursue his new career, he would need a proper studio and apartment. The difficulty was that Leo abhorred apartment-hunting.

Fortunately, a maternal uncle, the sculptor Ephraim Keyser, came to his rescue. Keyser was a portly, balding, and mustachioed older man with a glint in his eye that suggested he liked a good meal, followed by a good cigar and a good off-color story. His flair was for classically robed figures in artistic poses of the kind that graced Victorian parlors. His chief claim to fame was that he sculpted the tomb for President Chester A. Arthur. Keyser had just concluded a successful search for a studio when Leo confronted him with his own problem. Leo noted that his uncle must have taken the best studio he could find, but, in that case, what had been the next best? Ephraim told him the next best was 27, rue de Fleurus.

Leo inspected the premises on the rue de Fleurus, located on the Left Bank in a then less fashionable section of Paris. The street is short and angled, cutting off from the Boulevard Raspail and veering toward the nearby Luxembourg Gardens. The building was less than a decade old; the name of the architect, G. Pasquier, and the date, 1894, were chiseled on the stone façade. A central archway cut through the street front of the building through a dim corridor, past the concierge's tiny office on the left, to a pleasant, small, paved courtyard. To the right, jutting out from the main building, stood a compact two-story pavilion. Adjacent to it, slightly angled to catch the northern light, there was a studio. Leo found it exactly suited to his purposes.

By spring, he had installed himself in his new quarters. "What are your plans for the summer?" he wrote to Mabel Weeks, early in April. "I am fortunate in not needing to make a choice. I've got my house, my atelier, and my fencing school all engaged for the summer, as likewise a cook lady who didn't want to give me any eggs for breakfast this morning because it was Good Friday. However, when she saw that I had no scruples she relented—but nonetheless gave me fish both for lunch and dinner."

With only meager furnishings—the heavy Florentine pieces were bought later—Leo set about making an artistic environment. He hung his Japanese prints and the paintings he had begun to collect. In London he had bought his first "modern" painting by the English post-Impressionist Wilson Steer. The purchase had made him feel daring.

He discovered that "one could actually own paintings even if one were not a millionaire." In Paris he added a painting by another minor artist, Du Gardier—a small, late Impressionist painting of a woman in a white dress with a white dog posed against the sumptuous green of a summer lawn. The picture was to become an item of contention when both Gertrude and Leo set down their reminiscences of the early years at the rue de Fleurus. Gertrude mistakenly thought Leo had acquired it when they purchased their first Matisse. Leo set the record straight.

True to form, he had begun visiting galleries and attending the official salons with a certain enthusiasm. The newer salons, beginning around 1903, were brighter and livelier than the previous salons, which had been "full of pictures big enough to cover a wall, sprawling with pink nudes and landscapes painted with a kind of leaden color." Still, he found the new salons lacking: "There was a certain freshness and vivacity in many of the pictures, and yet they were somehow not art with a big A; they were essentially not complete things." Leo began to suspect he was devoting himself to art when it was becoming moribund.

Ironically, it was Berenson who introduced Leo to the work of the moderns and who, indirectly, started him off on what was to become, for however brief a period, his most satisfactory and influential vocation— that of critic and connoisseur of the modernist movement. Encountering Berenson on the street one day in Paris, Leo had complained about his boredom with painting at the moment. Berenson asked if he knew the work of Cézanne. If not, Leo should go and take a look at it in Ambroise Vollard's gallery. Leo knew the shop on the rue Lafitte; he had passed it often but never ventured in: It looked more like a junk shop than a plausible gallery. This time he stalked in and inquired about the Cézannes. Vollard brought out a few paintings for his inspection. Leo was so struck by the clarity and decisiveness of the pictures by the eccentric master from Provence that after only a few visits he bought his first Cézanne, an early landscape, *The Spring House*.

The following summer, in Florence—again through Berenson's good offices—he made a thorough study of the Cézannes in the collection of Charles Loeser, the heir of a Brooklyn department-store fortune. Loeser's Cézannes, bought from Vollard, were hidden in his bedroom and in the private rooms upstairs, out of the sight of his conservative visitors accustomed to the expectable Florentine madonnas that crowded the walls of his villa. That summer Leo indulged in what he referred to as a "Cézanne debauch." It was an important step in his career, for his study of Cézanne's method—the painstakingly analytical touches of paint that structured each object in its pictorial depth— prepared him for his early acceptance of the moderns.

Leo's career as a practicing artist, in the meantime, began to exhibit the inevitable course of slow decline. Though he continued painting for several years—and intermittently took it up again throughout his lifetime—he was never to make a success of it. But he did recall, years later, that even during this early period, before Cubism had been invented, he had created his first abstract drawings of planes and intersecting lines. The results he considered interesting as experiments; pictorially, the forms were confusing and unjustified, so he did not pursue it any further. Gertrude, who made a distinction between talking and doing, put the matter pointedly in *Everybody's Autobiography:* "My brother needed to be talking and he was painting but he needed to talk about painting in order to be painting, he needed to understand painting in order to be painting."

Her terse account of her arrival at the rue de Fleurus in the fall of 1903—also from the same source—suggests a certain displacement of Leo's artistic activities: "Well anyway he was painting, he had taken the pavillion and atelier on the rue de Fleurus although he was not painting there, he was painting at the school and drawing from the model at the afternoon drawing class as a matter of fact he never did paint at the rue de Fleurus atelier. I joined him and I sat down in there and pretty soon I was writing, and then he took a studio elsewhere and we lived together there until nineteen fourteen."

Gertrude, however, seems to have had some reluctance about committing herself to a life in Europe. Leo remembered that, when she first joined him in Paris, "she said she could stay there only on condition of a visit every year to America. I said she'd probably get used to it, but Gertrude is naturally dogmatic and said no, she was like that, and that was like her, and so it must be. That year she went to America for a visit and thirty-one years later she went again. No one really knows what is essential."

II

The novella of which Gertrude delivered herself shortly after her arrival at 27, rue de Fleurus, in 1903, was a subject of some embarrassment to her. It was her first-completed effort at serious writing and it was pointedly autobiographical in many of its details. The heroine of the book, Adele, is an unconventional woman who has suffered a series of unspecified disappointments while living in Baltimore. Adele spends the three summers encompassed in the time span of the story much as Gertrude had. The book opens with an ocean voyage to Europe, where Adele plans to spend the summer traveling in Spain—as Gertrude had, with Leo, in the summer of 1901, after she had given up on her medical career. The next year, Adele travels to Italy and then proposes to spend the winter in London, having first spent several weeks enjoying the English countryside. But like Gertrude, Adele finds the prospects of a London winter impossibly dreary and hurries back to New York, to the "clean-cut cold" of America. "I simply rejoiced in the New York streets," Adele confides to one of the principal characters in the story, "in the long spindling legs of the elevated, in the straight high undecorated houses, in the empty upper air and in the white surface of the snow. It was such a joy to realise that the whole thing was without mystery and without complexity, that it was clean and straight and meagre and hard and white and high." The final, climactic summer of the story is spent in Italy—first in Rome and then in Siena.

Adele is a creature of unconventional views, a champion of the middle-class way of life, from which her two shipboard companions in the initial voyage of the book, Mabel Neathe and Helen Thomas, are trying to escape. The two women are described as "college bred American women of the wealthier class," as is Adele herself. But they see themselves as emancipated women, and they find Adele's views rather contradictory.

"The contradiction isn't in me," Adele explains, "it is in your perverted ideas. You have a foolish notion that to be middle-class is to be vulgar, that to cherish the ideals of respectability and decency is to be commonplace and that to be the mother of children is to be low. You tell me that I am not middle-class and that I can believe in none of these things because I am not vulgar, commonplace and low, but it is just there where you make your mistake."

She then proceeds to outline what becomes the moral theme of the story: "You don't realise the important fact that virtue and vice have it in common that they are vulgar when not passionately given. You think that they carry within them a different power. Yes they do because they have different world-values, but as for their relation to vulgarity, it is as true of vice as of virtue that you can't sell what should be passionately given without forcing yourself into many acts of vulgarity and the chances are that in endeavoring to escape the vulgarity of virtue, you will find yourself engulfed in the vulgarity of vice."

The radical feature of Gertrude's short novel is its forthright discussion—without, however, labeling it as such—of the Lesbian relationship into which her heroine is initiated. Adele is drawn, by slow and perceptible stages, into a passionate affair with Helen, the tall, "American version of the English handsome girl." It begins as a mild flirtation, conducted—with pre-Freudian appropriateness—during their meetings on the afterdeck, above the "ploughing screw," the propellor of the ship. At first it involves minor petting and fondling and a good deal of talk about middle-class morality. At one point Helen taunts Adele:

"I am afraid . . . that after all you haven't a nature much above passion-ettes. You are so afraid of losing your moral sense that you are not willing to take it through anything more dangerous than a mud-puddle." But on their final night together, Adele suddenly feels herself "intensely kissed on the eyes and on the lips. She felt vaguely that she was ap-athetically unresponsive. There was another silence. Helen looked steadily down at her. 'Well!' she brought out at last. 'Oh' began Adele slowly 'I was just thinking.' 'Haven't you ever stopped thinking long enough to feel?' Helen questioned gravely." The affair is left at that inconclusive stage while Adele goes off to Tangiers and Spain, still puzzled about the nature of her relationship to Helen. In Tangiers she adopts an almost clinical attitude toward the possibilities of the affair: "It is something one ought to know. It seems almost a duty."

The relationship is renewed, after the summer, when Adele returns to Baltimore. She makes frequent trips to New York, where Helen is staying with her parents. For reasons that Adele cannot fathom, their meetings are conducted in an atmosphere of secrecy imposed by Helen. There is a certain poignancy to these encounters—the modern note of the lack of privacy in the large and impersonal city is struck quite clearly. They are conducted in public places, restaurants, museums, in long walks through the city streets. Only once, when they stop by the apartment of a friend who happens to be out, do they find the privacy for a passionate embrace—about as far, it seems, as their intimacies have developed at that point in the story. When Helen visits Baltimore, it is to stay with Mabel Neathe.

From the beginning, Adele has been aware that her intimacies with Helen have had to be managed out of the sight of Mabel Neathe's watchful eyes. But it is only during the course of the winter that she learns the nature of Helen's relationship with Mabel. Mabel, who has sensed an affair burgeoning between them, begins dropping vague hints about her own relations with Helen. Taunted sufficiently, Adele calls for a showdown:

At last the tension snapped. "Tell me then" Adele said to Mabel abruptly one evening. Mabel made no attempt to misunderstand but she did attempt to delay. "Oh well if you want to go through the farce of a refusal and an insistence, why help yourself," Adele broke out harshly, "but supposing all that done, I say again tell me." Mabel was dismayed by Adele's hot direct-ness and she vaguely fluttered about as if to escape. "Drop your intricate delicacy" Adele said sternly "you wanted to tell, now tell." Mabel was cowed. She sat down and explained.

The room grew large and portentous and to Mabel's eyes Adele's figure grew almost dreadful in its concentrated repulsion. There was a long silence that seemed to roar and menace and Mabel grew afraid. "Good-night" said Adele and left her.

The reader is never told explicitly what the relationship is, though the implication is that it is both physical and financial, for Helen's parents are miserly with her. Mabel's disclosures cause Adele to feel revulsion, though she seems incapable of giving up on the affair. There is a reconciliation just before Adele leaves for Europe, where she plans to spend the winter in London. The two correspond regularly, but, when there is a lapse of three weeks in which Adele does not hear from Helen, Adele guesses—correctly—that Mabel, who is staying with Helen, may have intercepted one of their letters. Adele waits until Helen will be alone at home and writes, suggesting that they end the affair: "I know therefore that you will not misunderstand when I beg you to consider carefully whether on the whole you had not better give me up. I can really amount to so little for you and yet will inevitably cause you so much trouble." Helen responds in endearing terms: "Hush little one . . . oh you stupid child, don't you realise that you are the only thing in the world that makes anything seem real or worth while to me." She has had a "dreadful time," she writes Adele. Mabel had read one of her letters. "The thing upset her completely and she was jealous of my every thought and I could not find a moment even to feel alone with you. But don't please don't say any more about giving you up. You are not any trouble to me if you will only not leave me."

Nevertheless, when Adele returns to spend the winter in New York, she avoids seeing Helen and goes to New England to spend a month with friends. She seems unwilling to accept the "turgid and complex world" of her emotions regarding Helen, and instead longs "only for obvious, superficial, clean simplicity." When she does return to New York and Helen, however, their affair reaches—in the vague terminology of the story—a consummation of sorts. They spend long sessions together in Helen's room, cultivating "the habit of silent intimacy." In one of these sessions, Adele is roused from her reveries by a kiss "that seemed to scale the very walls of chastity." She experiences a moment of revulsion and buries her face in her hands. Helen is in tears. Adele tries to rationalize her reaction. She is a talky lover: "You know I have always had a conviction that no amount of reasoning will help in deciding what is right and possible for one to do. If you don't begin with some theory of obligation, anything is possible and no rule of right and wrong holds. One must either accept some theory or else believe one's instinct or follow the world's opinion." Now, she explains, she has no theory, does not trust her instincts, and has really never regarded "the world's opinion." Adele is at a loss.

The affair now takes a different turn. In a curious passage, Gertrude analyzes the new relationship. Although the discussion is cast in terms of a psychological analysis, it reads, oddly, like a failing attempt to reach sexual climax:

This completeness of revulsion never occurred again, but a new opposition gradually arose between them. Adele realised that Helen demanded of her a response and always before that response was ready. Their pulses were differently timed. She could not go so fast and Helen's exhausted nerves could no longer wait. Adele found herself constantly forced on by Helen's pain. She went farther than she could in honesty because she was unable to refuse anything to one who had given all. It was a false position.

In the new relationship, Helen assumes the commanding role. Adele tries to puzzle out the "new dispensation," chafing under it: "Just how it came about she never quite realised but inevitably now it was always Adele that had to begin and had to ask for the next meeting. Helen's attitude became that of one anxious to give all but unfortunately prevented by time and circumstance." Their affair follows a path of quarrels and momentary reconciliations. Helen announces that she will be going to Italy with Mabel in the summer. Adele is not courageous enough to ask but the question "At whose expense?" is in her mind.

The two conspire to meet in Rome, but there the situation worsens; Mabel is glum and, at times, insolent, and Adele, for the sake of Helen, finds herself "toadying" to Mabel. In Florence the trio meet again. After an evening spent visiting with Helen and Mabel in their rooms, Adele leaves and Helen accompanies her downstairs. They kiss, indiscreetly, under a streetlight, and Adele has the feeling that Mabel has been watching them. Her suspicion turns out to be correct, and she learns from Helen that Mabel had made a scene. But Helen also shows her "an elaborate piece of antique jewelry" that Mabel has just given her. "Oh it's simply prostitution," Adele says to herself with bitterness. "How a proud woman and Helen is a proud woman can yield such degrading submission and tell such abject lies for the sake of luxuries beats me."

The final meeting takes place in Siena, some time later. Adele realizes that Helen has denied loving her, that Mabel has obliged Helen not to show her any affection. An uncomfortable and bitter silence develops between the two when they meet, while Mabel becomes more relaxed and civil. On their last night together, Adele and Helen still profess their love, but the occasion is joyless. Adele stays on in Europe; Mabel and Helen return home.

Adele writes Helen a final, abject letter: "Oh you know well enough what I want. I don't want you ever again to deny that you care for me. The thought of your doing it again takes all the sunshine out of the sky for me. Dear I almost wish sometimes that you did not trust me so completely because then I might have some influence with you for now as you know you have my faith quite absolutely and as that is to you abundantly satisfying I lose all power of coming near you." Helen's answer is to beg her "not to destroy the effect of her patient endurance all the summer." The same conditions, she assures her, could not happen again.

Adele's response is bitter: "Hasn't she yet learned that things do happen and she isn't big enough to stave them off. . . . Can't she see things as they are and not as she would make them if she were strong enough as she plainly isn't."

Dropping her head on her arms, she moans: "I am afraid it comes very near being a dead-lock."

That Gertrude viewed her novel about a Lesbian relationship as an unpublishable effort is, perhaps, indicated by the fate of the book. When she had written "Finis" at the end of the tale and inscribed the date—October 24, 1903—she put the manuscript aside in the large cupboard in the studio room at the rue de Fleurus. It was not until 1930 or 1931, when she was rummaging through piles of unpublished manuscripts, that she came across it again. Then, in some embarrassment, she turned it over to her visitors, Bernard Faÿ and Louis Bromfield, to read. The book was never published during her lifetime. When it appeared in a limited edition in 1950, four years after her death, it was slightly emended. Gertrude's original title for the book, *Q.E.D.* (Quod Erat Demonstrandum), was intended to point up the scientific nature of the enterprise. At one point in the story, Adele, puzzling out the nature of her emotional relationship with Helen, has a feeling of insight and exclaims, "Why it's like a bit of mathematics. Suddenly it does itself and you begin to see." When it was first published, the book was given an equally appropriate, if less decisive title, taken from one of the concluding phrases of the story *Things as They Are.*

Gertrude's embarrassment over *Q.E.D.* seems, in part, to have arisen from the fact that the writing of it was a therapeutic exercise. She had herself been involved in an affair much like the one she describes in the book. And the book was completed after she had settled into the rue de Fleurus, following a summer—the summer of 1903—whose adventures and itinerary prefigured those of her heroine, Adele.

In her last years at Johns Hopkins, after Leo had left for Florence, Gertrude had taken up with a circle of emancipated women, mostly graduates of Smith and Bryn Mawr colleges, who regularly met in the Baltimore apartment shared by Mabel Haynes and Grace Lounsbery, two Bryn Mawr graduates. The sessions were devoted to tea and spirited talk, in which Gertrude, evidently, was one of the principal debaters. One gets some impression of these meetings of ardent, college-bred women, from a letter to Gertrude written by Mabel Weeks, another regular of the Haynes-Lounsbery group. Following their summer together in Europe in 1900, Mabel wrote to Gertrude on December 21 from England, where she had remained to continue her studies. "Have you seen Miss Lounsbery and is she counting on me?" Mabel asked. "You and she will have to paddle on together and be as esoteric as possible with no alien New Englander to take short and fervid views of moral questions." Moral issues, much like the moral issues that figure in the discussions in *Q.E.D.*, were very much in the air in the Haynes-Lounsbery circle.

It was in this circle of young women that Gertrude met May Bookstaver, a protégée of Mabel Haynes's, with whom she had the affair described in *Q.E.D.* In the book May became Helen Thomas, and Mabel Haynes was transposed into the character of Mabel Neathe, the unsympathetic New England "spinster" possessed by "a nature of the tropics." The discovery of this affair and its relationship to Gertrude's early novel is the work of Leon Katz, who uncovered it while doing research for his doctoral dissertation at Columbia University on the subject of Gertrude's *The Making of Americans* and her related earlier writings. How closely the scenario of *Q.E.D.* follows the actual love affair between Gertrude and May Bookstaver is problematic. Much of the crucial documentary evidence is missing: Gertrude's letters to May have apparently not survived; May's letters, so Dr. Katz learned in the course of extended interviews with Alice B. Toklas, were destroyed by Miss Toklas "in a passion" in 1932—that is, after the manuscript had been resurrected. Dr. Katz also conducted interviews with friends of Gertrude's, such as Emma Lootz Erving and Mabel Weeks, who were aware of Gertrude's involvement with May Bookstaver and Mabel Haynes. From Miss Toklas he learned that in the writing of the book, Gertrude had literally transcribed passages from the correspondence between herself and May to create portions of the book's dialogue. On the strength of this research, he has reconstructed an account of Gertrude's affair with May in his introduction to the original version of *Q.E.D.*, published in *Fernhurst, Q.E.D. and Other Early Writings by Gertrude Stein.* His account largely follows the version in *Q.E.D.*, interpolating significant passages from the book to underscore the nature of the relationship among the three women.

To this reconstructed account, it is also possible to add a few tantalizing hints as to the state of Gertrude's emotions during this period. *Q.E.D.*, curiously, is a novel without men—except the unnamed man who accosts Helen in a restaurant one night, while she is waiting, alone, for Adele, who is late in arriving. (The incident precipitates one of their frequent quarrels.) Even Leo Stein, with whom Gertrude spent the summer of 1901—the troubled opening summer of the book in which Adele feels that she has had a "glimpse" of what her relationship to Helen means—is rendered as the nameless and genderless cousin with whom Adele is traveling in Spain and Tangiers. Whether Gertrude discussed the nature of her feelings for May with Leo during this summer it is impossible to say. But a letter that Leo wrote to her just after she left him in France suggests that they had established, between them, a certain frankness about sexual matters. "I had a perfect devil of a time the night that you left," Leo wrote her on October 25. "It cost me a hundred and fifty francs for champagne, eats and the lady between midnight and six o'clock but it was more than worth the price of admission."

In the Stein archives at Yale, there are, as well, certain letters that bear upon this period in Gertrude's life and her relationship with May Bookstaver. Gertrude was in active correspondence with Emma Lootz during the summer of 1903—the final summer of the book. Gertrude's letters to Emma Lootz were not preserved, but one can interpolate her point of view from the letters of her Baltimore friend, who took a lively but disapproving interest in Gertrude's relations with May and Mabel. (From her letters, however, it seems Mrs. Erving was not precisely aware of the nature of the involvement.) On August 10, after Gertrude had met May and Mabel in Rome, Emma wrote to her: "I did look disapproving when you said you had been marauding with your friends, but I may as well believe you when you say you were good tho I'm afraid our conceptions of virtue differ." She seemed equally concerned, however, about Mabel Weeks, with whom Gertrude was to take a walking tour near Siena: "I wish you would tell me about Mabel. Use your feminine intuition and your masculine reasoning and give me the result in writing. I think she is at a critical point—the boat of her soul is rocking in the waters of illusion and her sanity is a bit jarred." On September 3 she queried Gertrude: "How were your friends Miss H & B when you left them in Siena."

In October Emma wrote to Gertrude from Boston—she had recently married William Erving, a doctor, and they had moved to Massachusetts. Mabel Haynes, who planned to move to Boston after the summer, was expected shortly. "She is probably in N.Y." Emma commented. Emma and Mabel were to develop a friendship of sorts. On November 3 Emma reported to Gertrude: "I was called off to read Italian with Mabel Haynes. She and I are even more intimate than ever. She took me driving one day and she gave me a lufly Spanish drawn-work thing for a present and we drunk tea and discuss[ed] Henry James with extreme enthusiasm. She is looking forward to a lonesome winter."

Gertrude was still following the relationship between May and Mabel from afar. In response, apparently, to something Gertrude had written her, Emma wrote on February 15: "Mabel Haynes is at present in N.Y. with May. Are you a trifle fierce with her, Gertie?" Gertrude was sailing to New York herself, not long after. Emma had asked her to spend the week of April 11 in Boston, visiting with her and her new husband.

Whether the return to the United States, early in 1904, represented a final attempt at reconciliation with May or whether she was acting on her decision, as she had told Leo, not to settle permanently in Europe but to return home each year is not known. When she returned to Europe that summer, sailing with Etta Cone, it represented her last trip to America in thirty years.

Although the affair was over, the repercussions lingered on for some time. Emma, unfortunately, found herself caught up in the aftermath. In 1906 she was living in Washington, D.C., where her husband then had his practice. On March 20 she wrote Gertrude, telling her of a recent visit of Mabel Haynes and a friend. Her letter took on an ominous tone: "I'd like to see you and talk a few things over with you. It's useless to write, cause you would just get me hung up on some hook where I didn't intend to arrive and not let me get off again. Only I would remark that May Bookstaver would do as well not to show *all* the letters she receives from *everybody* to all chance acquaintances. However, my point of view just now is tainted with nausea."

Her next letter was more explicit:

In plain English I think that May Bookstaver has been and still is running amuck with her interest in melodrama. Whatever else Mabel Haynes may have been she has been honest in her feeling for May and May has treated her like dirt. When Mabel was on here I freely told her that I considered that she had been the victim of a plot all the time and that if she had any sagacity she would climb out. When she discovered that May had been showing her letters to most of her casual friends and acquaintances and finally to her family, it helped considerably. I say nothing about the nature of Mabel's affection for May and I see the provocation in it but all the same May hasn't been very decent. In the same way she might refrain from dissecting you at New York dinner parties and from showing your letters to her acquaintances. Her passion for conversation and her remarks become less and less sane. As for her elaborate explanation of my motives for cheating in examinations as she lays them before promiscuous assemblies, they are pictorial to a degree. She is welcome to deck me out in any fantastic dress that she pleases for the benefit of any one she chooses, for she owes me nothing. She is not justified in treating you in the same way, whatever her motives, and she has been rotten to Mabel. She is becoming more and more of an adventuress. . . .

Meanwhile her campaign between you and Mabel was fair to neither of you. Now tell me anything you like of my ugly disposition, my perverted intelligence and my general worthlessness. It may be all true what you think, there are six times as many sides to everything as there are people concerned —and here my contention is simply that May is exaggerating things.

Gertrude's response was, apparently, an unexpected and vehement defense of May Bookstaver. She seems, perhaps, to have pointed out that Emma's friendship with Mabel Haynes was on shaky grounds, that

Mabel had "knifed" her in the past. Emma answered her tartly on June 21:

Now, Gertie, you wrote me a lot of foolishness. Don't you mix me up with any situation that you and those two other misguided females created out of your emotions and sensations. If you have no objections to being served up by May for the pleasure of promiscuous publics, all right. Being fond of you I reserve the privilege to resent it. . . .

Mabel is now making a first class fight for her sanity and I respect decent fights. She's doing this for herself and as far as I can see isn't sticking her claws in any one else. When you say that I sacrificed hospitality and loyalty to vanity, I frankly don't see it and I'm sorry that you do. My surface relations with Mabel have never varied by a shade of politeness whether she was knifing me with my knowledge & realization or whether she was fighting you without, if you please (and dense I probably was) my realization of what was actually the state of things or of your feelings. . . .

The thing that I do resent in the whole business is that it has by some occult means raised any question between you and me.

Emma, it seems, feared for the sanity of her distraught friends and former classmates. Gertrude, it appears, was stuck fast in a loyalty to an old, misguided passion that had, nonetheless, awakened her to life. Ironically, the dust of this latest eruption settled quickly. On August 16 Emma scribbled a hurried card to Gertrude, informing her that May Bookstaver "was married yesterday in Newport to [Charles] Knoblauch." Within a year, Mabel Haynes had become Mabel Haynes Heissig, having married an Austrian Army captain. And very shortly after that, Gertrude had entered into a relationship that was to last a lifetime.

III

One day, late in 1904, Michael Stein announced to Gertrude and Leo that there was an unexpended balance of eight thousand francs in their account. They were overjoyed. It was an unexpected windfall, proving the wisdom of their having set up housekeeping together. Leo thought it a "criminal waste" to have the money lying idle when there were pictures to be bought. Gertrude approved, and the pair set off for Vollard's on the rue Lafitte. At Leo's instigation they bought two Gauguins—the bright yellow *Sunflowers* and *Three Tahitians*, a painting that eventually entered the collection of their Russian rival, Shchukine. Their growing assemblage of Cézannes was increased by a pair of small compositions of *Bathers*. Leo insisted on two more Renoirs, a painter for whom he had developed a special affection. Vollard, pleased with his sales, gave them a small Maurice Denis, a mother and child, for good measure. Leo was impressed with the Denis; he found in it "a distribution of blacks such as I have never seen in European art."

The second *Salon d'Automne*, which had opened at the Grand Palais in October that year, made a marked impression on Leo. There he first encountered the work of Toulouse-Lautrec, the subject of a special memorial exhibition. Impressed with Lautrec's skill as a draughtsman and designer and recognizing immediately the influence of Japanese prints on Lautrec's art, Leo was shortly to acquire the painter's *Le Divan*. But more importantly, the salon provided Leo with visual evidence for what was a prophetic analysis of the aesthetic foundations of the modern movement.

Writing to Mabel Weeks about the event, he warned her at the outset: "If this proves to be a treatise, not a letter, the responsibility will lie with the obligation that I have been under ever since the Autumn Salon, of expounding L'Art Moderne (you will observe that this is not the same thing as L'Art Nouveau). The men whose pictures we have bought—Renoir, Cézanne, Gauguin, Maurice Denis—and others whose pictures we have not bought but would like to—Manet, Degas, Vuillard, Bonnard, Van Gogh for example—all belong. To make the subject clear requires a discussion of the qualities of the men of '70 of whom the Big Four and Puvis de Chavannes are the great men and the inspirers in the main of the vital art of today." The Big Four, he maintained, were Manet, Renoir, Degas, and Cézanne.

Not only was Leo's choice of the precursors astoundingly prescient but also his detailed analyses of the qualities of each of them anticipated, by at least a decade, the canons of the modernist movement set forth by later critics. "Manet is the painter par excellence," he explained for Mabel's benefit. "He is not the great colorist that is Renoir but in sheer power of handling he has perhaps not had his equal in modern times. He had a great conception of art but few great conceptions." Of Renoir, he noted, seemingly unaware that the painter was still alive: "Renoir was the colorist of the group. He again was a man of limited intellectuality but he had the gift of color as no one perhaps since Rubens except perhaps Fragonard has had it—what you might call the feeling for absolute color, color handled not as the medium but as the stuff of art." Degas, he maintained, was the most "distinctively intellectual" painter of the group: "All his qualities are held together and brought to a focus by a perfection of control that only the finest mentality could give."

Fourth comes Cézanne and here again is a great mind, a perfect concentration, and great control. Cézanne's essential problem is mass and he has succeeded in rendering mass with a vital intensity that is unparalleled in the whole history of painting. No matter what his subject is—the figure, the landscape, still life—there is always this remorseless intensity, this endless unending gripping of the form, the unceasing effort to force it to reveal its absolute self-existing quality of mass. There can scarcely be such a thing as a completed Cézanne. Every canvas is a battlefield and victory an unattainable ideal. Cézanne rarely does more than one thing at a time and when he turns to composition he brings to bear the same intensity, keying his composition up till it sings like a harp string. His color, also, though as harsh as his forms, is almost as vibrant. In brief, he is the most robust, the most intense, and in a fine sense the most ideal of the four.

No one—in France or elsewhere—had arrived at so brilliant and concise an evaluation of Cézanne's method and of his monumental gifts. Cézanne, who had two more years to live, had by sheer perseverance acquired a few supporters in the last years of his life, but none of them had been able to explain the painter's achievements with the same incisiveness as his American collector, who was content to deliver the message in a letter or in a series of impromptu Saturday-night talks.

Leo's recognition of Cézanne's importance seems to have resulted in a further important purchase. Having studied the paintings in the Autumn Salon carefully, he was at first prepared to buy a Bonnard and a Vuillard from the show. Finding the sales office closed, he decided to have lunch and return. "But while eating," he noted in *Appreciation*, "I got an idea that was thrilling: to buy a big Cézanne figure, instead of a lot of little pictures." Gertrude agreed; Vollard was enthusiastic. Both Gertrude and Leo found it difficult to come to a meeting of the minds. Each of the pictures had its good and bad points, but many of them seemed "fragmentary and unfinished." Vollard, anxious that they should have the best possible range of choices, would suddenly declare, "Wait, I can get some other ones to show you," and the decision was postponed from one week to the next.

Then, one day, the dealer brought out an impressive picture of a woman—it was a portrait of Cézanne's wife, Hortense, seated in a red armchair, holding a fan. Vollard informed them, with strange logic, that ordinarily the portrait of a woman was more costly than that of a man, but with Cézanne, he supposed, it did not make much difference. The picture was imposing, and after repeated viewings and discussions, carried on at nearby Fouquet's, where they indulged themselves with honey cakes, Leo and Gertrude decided to buy the portrait. They carried it home triumphantly in a cab.

Judging from an undated letter that Gertrude wrote to Mabel Weeks, part of their problem may have been financial. They seem to have depleted their unexpected windfall. "We is doin business too," Gertrude wrote in the folksy style of her letters of the time. "We are selling Jap prints to buy a Cézanne at least we are that is Leo is trying. He don't like it a bit and makes a awful fuss about asking enough money but I guess we'll get the Cézanne."

Evidently Gertrude was planning another trip to America. "Goodby Mamie," she wrote to Mabel, "let me know whether there is a possibility of that walking trip materializing and look out for me on the 11th of March at North German Lloyd docks. Perhaps Leo will come along too, he seems to hanker after St. Louis." Neither Gertrude nor Leo made the proposed trip. At the conclusion of her letter, Gertrude had promised, "I will be writing a lovely story which you can jump on at your leisure."

The "lovely story" Gertrude had in mind seems to have been *Fernhurst*, a fictional account of another unhappy love affair, drawn not from her personal history, as *Q.E.D.* had been, but largely from the lively gossip encountered in Mabel Haynes's circle of Bryn Mawr graduates. The gossip concerned a triangular relationship involving the energetic and domineering dean of Bryn Mawr, Carey Thomas, an early champion of women's rights, and Mary Gwinn, her protégée, a brilliant, somewhat shy woman who was considered one of the intellectual lights of the Bryn Mawr faculty. Miss Thomas and Miss Gwinn lived together; they had been childhood friends and had studied together in Germany. The third member of the triangle was Alfred Hodder, a young Harvard graduate, whom Miss Thomas had hired as a teacher. Both Gertrude and Leo had known of Hodder from Harvard, where he had a reputation as a brilliant and promising student with an overly romantic disposition and a marked tendency for the ladies. Hodder was married when he arrived at Bryn Mawr, but he and Mary Gwinn fell in love and conducted a lengthy affair that was followed closely and with considerable interest by the young women at the college. Hodder eventually divorced his wife and married Miss Gwinn. He died not long after—"worn out with riotous living," according to Bertrand Russell.

Russell had lectured at Bryn Mawr in 1896 when the Hodder-Gwinn affair had been in progress. His wife, Alys, and Mary Berenson, his sister-in-law, were cousins of Carey Thomas's. Russell and his wife stayed with Carey Thomas during their visit to Bryn Mawr. In his *Autobiography*, he has left a vivid picture of the troubled life at the deanery. Miss Gwinn, he noted, "used to go home to her family for three days in every fortnight, and at the exact moment of her departure each fortnight, another lady, named Miss Garrett, used to arrive, to depart again at the exact moment of Miss Gwinn's return." Miss

Gwinn's romance with Hodder, Russell claimed: "roused Carey to fury, and every night, as we were going to bed, we used to hear her angry voice scolding Miss Gwinn in the next room for hours together."

This was the situation Gertrude chose to write about in *Fernhurst*, begun, probably, late in 1904. The dean of her story is Helen Thornton, who presides over the college of Fernhurst, which Gertrude locates in New Jersey. Interestingly, in view of the Berenson-Russell connection with Carey Thomas, Gertrude took the name of the college from the English village Greenhill-Fernhurst, where she and Leo had stayed while visiting the Berensons in 1902. Her Miss Gwinn is named Janet Bruce, while the Hodder role is given to Philip Redfern, described as a southerner, "trained in elaborate chivalry," a quality that evidently makes him attractive to women. He also is described as a "man of letters" who has failed everywhere: "In this life as in all his human relations his instincts gave the lie to his ideals and his ideals to his instincts." The author feels a strange sympathy for Redfern's plight: "He did not know how to win, how to avoid battle or how to yield— he only learned to dread the fire, he never learned to keep his fingers from it."

The Hodder-Gwinn-Carey Thomas triangle is, in fact, viewed as a restatement of her affair with May Bookstaver, with Mabel Haynes cast in the authoritarian role of the college dean, while Gertrude herself is Hodder. That she viewed it in that light is apparent from the ending she gave her fictional version. Whereas in actual life Hodder married Miss Gwinn, in *Fernhurst* Redfern does not succeed in weaning the ambivalent Janet Bruce from Dean Thornton's influence. The story ends in the same condition of stalemate with which Gertrude ended *Q.E.D.* Redfern is obliged to quit his job at the college. But, the author adds—a bit hopefully, it seems—"strange stories still floated about Fernhurst college. Redfern and Miss Bruce had been seen so it was said coming out of a hotel each with their own dress-suit case— other strange rumors about them were current but the energy and discretion of Miss Thornton kept them from ever becoming more than rumor and gradually they died away. Patiently and quietly the dean worked it out and before many years she had regained all property rights in this shy learned creature."

Gertrude also introduces the figure of Redfern's wife, Nancy, into the narrative, thus making a triangle a square. One of the failures of the story, in fact, is its lack of focus, for Gertrude has invested her sympathies in both the philandering husband and the wronged wife. Nancy Redfern is "full of moral purpose and educational desires." She has grown up with the easy, trusting manners of Western society. She is, in other words, another version of Gertrude herself—an idealized feminine version in contrast to the masculine version in Redfern. In the chapter dealing with Redfern's courtship of Nancy, which takes place in the midwestern college they are both attending, there is a good deal of amateurishly idealistic dialogue, much talk of "new worlds." One day, while they are trudging through the winter landscape, Redfern suddenly exclaims to her: "You are a comrade and a woman. It is the new world." When Nancy Redfern explains to him: "I am a Western woman and believe in men's honesty and in my own, while you—you seem always to doubt both," Redfern is silent for a moment and then bursts out: "You wonderful Western woman. . . . Surely you have made a new world." The dialogue sounds often as if it had been lifted from the novels of Gene Stratton Porter, for whose manly, clean-speaking heroes Gertrude once professed an early admiration.

Fernhurst is a decidedly minor and awkward piece of writing. Its chief interest lies in Gertrude's attempt to deal, once more, with her love affair with May Bookstaver. Curiously, she has split the affair into two functioning parts. Redfern's love for Janet Bruce is treated with all the idealized passion that Gertrude had felt for May Bookstaver. In a passage dealing with her hero's first meeting with Janet Bruce, one can sense the force of Gertrude's feeling even after her affair with May was over: "How these trivial incidents and words, the elm trees and the purple hills beyond and the group of people quietly talking remain fixed in the memory. There is a solemnity about a first meeting with those whose lives deeply affect our own that gives a sacredness to the most trivial phrase." On the other hand, the character of Nancy Redfern is burdened with all the misery of Gertrude's recognition of May's faithlessness and lack of will power.

No less curious a development is the fact that, five years later, she embedded the *Fernhurst* story, with only minor tailoring, into the ongoing narrative of her book *The Making of Americans*. At that point she changed the names of the headmistress and of Janet Bruce to Hannah Charles and Cora Dounor, and she assigned the thankless role of Redfern's wife, Nancy, to Martha Hersland, the character who represents Gertrude herself in the later narrative.

There is a good deal of editorializing in *Fernhurst*, though some of it has autobiographical interest. At one point Gertrude is discussing Redfern's "fateful twenty-ninth year," the year in which he meets Janet Bruce. In a lengthy editorial aside she goes on to note the importance of that year, when "all the forces that have been engaged through the years of childhood, adolescence and youth in confused and ferocious combat range themselves in ordered ranks." In the twenty-ninth year, she maintains, we reach "the straight and narrow gateway of maturity, and life which was all uproar and confusion narrows down to form and purpose and we exchange a great dim possibility for a small hard reality."

Significantly, she adds: "Also in our American life where there is no

coercion in custom and it is our right to change our vocation so often
as we have desire and opportunity, it is a common experience that our
youth extends through the whole first twenty-nine years of our life and
it is not till we reach thirty that we find at last that vocation for which
we feel ourselves fit and to which we willingly devote continued labor."

In 1904 Gertrude had reached that vantage point of thirty. She had
evidently determined that the "small hard reality" of her life would be
writing.

IV

For two winters in succession, in 1904 and again in 1905, both Dr.
Claribel and Etta Cone had remained in Europe. Claribel Cone was
furthering her medical studies, during those years, at the Senckenberg
Institute in Frankfurt am Main. Etta had spent the winter of 1904 in
Munich, visiting relatives and friends. Unlike her sister, Etta did not
develop a special affection for Germany and the Germans—even for her
Munich relatives, the Rosengarts. She had found life in Germany dull
and complained that Gertrude had not sent her any interesting tidbits
of news from Paris.

"You are an ungrateful brute," Gertrude replied in a jocular vein,
"so you are and I won't never have anything more to do with you, telling everybody that I don't tell you any news." She had then proceeded
to dispense news with a heavy hand: "Miss [Constance] Fletcher has
begun to work with Sally. . . . I am having corset-covers made by the
concierge's sister-in-law. . . . Mrs. Wellman almost had a miscarriage.
. . . Miss [Mildred] Aldrich writes plays, smokes cigarettes. . . . She
is a very interesting woman—she was here for dinner. . . . There's
going to be a Whistler show in London in February." Etta, she maintained, was not "so much on news" herself: "You haven't never told
me about how the girls spend their time or anything, you are very
neglectful and not me."

Among the assorted news and gossip, there was one item of personal
importance: Gertrude's meeting with Mildred Aldrich, who was to
become one of her most enduring friends and staunchest supporters.
At the time that Gertrude met her, she was fifty-one, a stern-looking
New Englander, doughty in figure, with a long face crowned with
white hair. Gertrude saw her as a female version of George Washington. Mildred Aldrich had had a lengthy career as an editor and critic,
writing on theatrical and cultural events for a variety of publications,
among them the *Boston Evening Transcript*. She had chosen to live
out her last years in France. When friends admonished her that she

should have retired in America, she told them that although she loved her native land, she considered it "the land of the young, the energetic, and the ambitious, the ideal home of the very rich and the laboring classes." Mildred maintained she was none of those: "I did forty-five years of hard labor there and I consider that I earned the freedom to die where I please." She had a wide circle of literary and cultural acquaintances—among them the Irish poet James Stephens and the American art critic Henry McBride—most of whom she introduced to Gertrude. Until her death in France, in 1928, she and Gertrude were fast friends.

Throughout the winter of 1904–5, Gertrude, and Leo, had kept Etta informed of events in Paris. Gertrude had also suggested a visit to London, but Etta declined. "It seems a little foolish to spend the whole winter in Deutschland," Gertrude had responded. "It isn't any more of a trip to London than going to Blowing Rock [the summer resort in North Carolina where Etta frequently visited her brothers] and you do that for a few weeks." "I got a cold in my nose," Gertrude went on, "in my left nose, everybody has a cold in their noses. Goodbye be a good girl and do everything the way you are told. Yours, Gertrude." Not to be outdone in epistolary humor, Leo had added a postscript: "Dear Etta, If I should ever get lost and you should ever hear of it just tip the police and tell them that if they look *inside* my shoes they'll probably find me."

When Etta sent Gertrude and Leo a Christmas gift of a box of cakes, Gertrude had thanked her heartily and went on to outline her newest plight: "My dear Etta: The cakes did arrive and dey was damn good, so says us and the Matthewses and little Roger who got a piece. Have just bought myself material for three pongee waists. Shall I have them made or shall I wait for your overseeing eye what I axed about in my postal." Gertrude, clearly, was willing to hand over such decisions to others. But when it came to some unconventional manner of dress, it was also clear she would do as she pleased. As she informed Etta in the same letter, "I have had my sandals blackened and wears them joyous in the streets of Paris."

After her first sojourn in Munich, Etta had resolved not to spend another winter in Germany. Accordingly, in the fall of 1905, she rented a flat in Paris at 58, rue Madame, the building in which the Michael Steins were living. The year before, on a visit to Paris, both Etta and Claribel had met Michael and Sarah and their young son, Allan. They had taken an immediate liking to Gertrude's eldest brother and sister-in-law, and the friendship of the four was to continue for years. Etta, fonder of children than the somewhat aloof Claribel, had warmed to the curly-headed Allan, then nine years old. Now that she had installed herself in Paris, she frequently took him to the Luxembourg Gardens and spoiled him with treats. Otherwise, she occupied her time with reading and visits to galleries and with piano lessons, taken from her landlady, Madame Vernot.

That winter, Etta was a frequent visitor at Gertrude and Leo's establishment. Their studio room was now filling up with new acquisitions, and Etta especially noticed the Cézanne portrait. Although Gertrude and Leo often had guests, the press of visitors had not yet reached the stage at which they would have to institute their regular Saturday evenings. During the day, Leo was busy with his art classes. Gertrude, who was now taking herself seriously as a writer—though she seldom discussed it openly—had begun her habit of writing at night. In the long quiet nights, when she could be sure there would be no further interruptions, she would sit at the long Florentine table in the studio room. Under the watchful eyes of Cézanne's magisterial portrait, in the dim light, she was writing out the slow, repetitive sentences of a new story about a tormented love affair. She would sit for hours, filling up the pages of a child's copy book with her exuberant scrawl, long after the lights in the ground-floor study of the pavilion—where Leo had retired to read, to ponder the imponderables, to write interminable letters to friends—had been extinguished. Finally the dawn light would seep into the studio. Outside, the concierge, bustling with the activities of a new day, would rouse Gertrude to the fact of morning. She would lock the atelier door and go to bed.

Gertrude's writing habits meant that she was not available in the mornings. She generally rose at noon, when Hélène served her breakfast, and then walked around Paris in the afternoon. Since both she and Etta were passionate shoppers and window shoppers, Etta would frequently join her on these excursions. Etta kept a combination diary and account book of her European journeys, setting down the principal events of the day, the cost of horse-drawn carriage rides, the price of shirtwaists. Gertrude's appearances in those pages are frequently wreathed with flattering remarks. In the late summer of 1901, for example, Etta noted down typical afternoon visits with Gertrude to the Louvre, to a gallery where Gertrude bought Japanese prints, even a session at the dressmaker's to which Gertrude had accompanied her: "She was quite amused and interested in the funny conglomeration of French people there. We then wandered along the Rue de la Paix to look in the jewelry shops . . . talked with Gertrude on her pet subject of human intercourse of the sexes. She is truly interesting."

Gertrude's remarks on the "human intercourse of the sexes," that afternoon, were, probably, more personal than Etta had guessed. She was then in the opening phase of her troubled love affair with May Bookstaver, a period of emotional turmoil for her, but a time when she felt she had gained some insight into her feelings for May. One catches a glimpse of the curious and fleeting mood of exaltation that sometimes comes at the beginning of an affair, in one of Etta's entries about Gertrude later that summer. Gertrude had arranged to sail back to America with Etta. The voyage had begun in thick fog as they left Southampton; then the ship sailed into clear weather. Etta's concluding remarks in her diary for that earlier summer trailed off in an incompleted sentence that was both suggestive and uninformative: "Clear beautiful day which I spent mostly below in a beautiful state of mind, but one which brought out the most exquisite qualities of Gertrude. My vanity . . ."

But now, four years later—in Paris, where she and Etta were continuing their walks—Gertrude was engaged in writing a story out of the painful wisdom gained from the end of her affair. It represented her third and most successful attempt to deal, fictionally, with her troubled emotions.

Three Lives, Gertrude's most important and influential early work, consists of three short stories, psychological portraits of impassive women—two German servants and a young black woman, Melanctha Herbert—women who were acted upon in life and who seemed incapable of understanding, much less mastering, their personal fates. The characters are drawn from types that Gertrude was familiar with, the servant girls she knew from childhood and the plodding, resigned women of the neighboring families in Oakland—and, in the case of Melanctha, from the Negro women whose lives she had witnessed during her outpatient work in obstetrics at Johns Hopkins.

Gertrude claimed that the stylistic method of the book had been influenced by the Cézanne portrait under which she sat writing. The portrait of Madame Cézanne is one of the monumental examples of the artist's method, each exacting, carefully negotiated plane—from the suave reds of the armchair and the gray blues of the sitter's jacket to the vaguely figured wallpaper of the background—having been structured into existence, seeming to fix the subject for all eternity. So it was with Gertrude's repetitive sentences, each one building up, phrase by phrase, the substance of her characters.

But the tone of dispassionate analysis that dominates *Three Lives* seems to have been drawn from other sources as well. The point of view of the book reflects the epigraph Gertrude affixed to the beginning of the stories, a sentence by the French writer Jules Laforgue, *"Donc je suis un malheureux et ce n'est ni ma faute ni celle de la vie."* (So, then, I am an unhappy one and it is neither my fault nor that of life.) The book also reflects the tone and general stylistic ambience of another French master, Gustave Flaubert, whose *Three Tales*—a late work by the master of the *mot juste*—Leo had urged Gertrude to read. On first settling in Paris, Leo had conceived an admiration for Flaubert—he especially appreciated *Bouvard et Pécuchet*, which he considered the "most admirable fooling." He directed his sister's budding career as a writer in constructive paths by urging her to translate Flaubert's *Three Tales*. It was while engaged in that work that Gertrude evidently conceived the idea of writing a trio of stories—equally analytical and dispassionate in tone—drawn from her own observations of character.

The first of her stories, "The Good Anna," is the most directly related to Flaubert, in particular to Flaubert's story of Félicité, a lonely, bovine servant girl who ends up her life believing that her only companion, a parrot, is the Holy Ghost. Gertrude's heroine, Anna, the domineering German housekeeper who looks after the large and complacent Miss Mathilda of the story, is patterned directly after Lena Lebender, who, with her two dogs, Jack and Rags, took care of Gertrude and Leo during their years at Johns Hopkins. In the story, Baltimore has been renamed Bridgepoint, Leo has been erased from the situation, and Lena's two dogs, now named Peter and Rags, have acquired a third companion, blind old Baby, a feeble creature that has to be saved continually from Peter's intemperate assaults.

The Miss Mathilda of the story is a caricature, though not a sardonic one, of Gertrude herself. She is a large, easygoing woman who avoids trouble whenever possible, who cannot bring herself to take sides in Anna's disputes with the hired girls, who spends too much on the theater and fine prints while the rigorously protective and frugal Anna complains and scolds. When Miss Mathilda comes home with an etching, Anna erupts: "And I slave and slave to save the money and you go out and spend it all on foolishness." When Miss Mathilda prepares to go out to dinner, wearing an old dress, Anna bars the way. "You can't go out to dinner in that dress, Miss Mathilda," Anna tells her. "You got to go and put on your new dress you always look so nice in." Secretly, Anna has "great pride in the knowledge and possession of her cherished Miss Mathilda," and boasts of Miss Mathilda's acquisitions to her friends.

In the end, however, Miss Mathilda goes abroad, where she plans to live permanently. It is the denouement of the Good Anna's life: She never again finds a mistress she can bully and fuss over as she had Miss Mathilda. She spends the remainder of her life managing a boardinghouse, wearing herself out in service to her transient boarders, unable to make ends meet. She becomes ill—the implication is that she has cancer—and submits to an operation from which she does not recover. The prose description of Anna's end is succinct: "Then they did the operation, and then the good Anna with her strong, strained, worn-out body died." With a clinical eye for the strange nature of dependency relationships, Gertrude made Anna's service to Miss Mathilda not the "romance" of her life, but the focal point of her energies—a focal point that was irreplaceable.

The second of the stories, "Melanctha," was, perhaps, the most remarkable attempt any white American writer had yet made in dealing with black experience. It was the story of a young and attractive mulatto, Melanctha Herbert, and her love affair with a Negro doctor, Jefferson Campbell. The social position of the Negro in American life—like the socially ostracized condition of homosexuality treated in *Q.E.D.*—provides no motivational impulse in the story; it is accepted simply as a given fact. The conditions of Negro life sketched in to provide the background of her story are not treated with condescending tolerance or sentimentalism. Gertrude's interest in her two Negro characters is in the passionate nature of their involvement—their love affair, which re-enacts, in heterosexual terms, the Lesbian affair between Adele and Helen in *Q.E.D.*

Significantly, the focus of the later story shifts from Adele to Helen. For Melanctha, the protagonist of the new inquiry into the nature of love, is a more complex and carefully realized version of Helen, while Jefferson Campbell, slow and circumspect, caught up in a passionate affair with the headstrong girl, is a masculine version of Adele. It is, probably, a relevant index of Gertrude's own emotional state at the time that she should have put so much of herself, of her own cautious approach to sex and love, into the role of Jefferson Campbell. With marvelous economy, too, she sublimated her own disappointed medical career in the character of a practicing doctor.

What is remarkable about "Melanctha" is the slow, patient, clinical manner in which the power and perversity of human character, the waywardness of passion, are analyzed and laid bare. The story is an anatomy of a love affair, of the progressive stages of dependency and the gradually changing roles by which Jefferson Campbell is brought to a state of resignation and dumb suffering. It begins with a psychologically acute analysis of Melanctha's character, of her uneasy relationships with her parents. Her father is an angry black man, hard on his daughter, given to bouts of drunkenness, who deserts his family; her mother, a pale, sweet, vague woman, incapable of dealing with either her husband or her unruly daughter. If Melanctha, as Gertrude characterizes her, is "always full with mystery and subtle movements and denials and vague distrusts and complicated disillusions" that relate her to her mother, she also draws force from her virile father:

Melanctha Herbert almost always hated her black father, but she loved very well the power in herself that came through him. And so her feeling was really closer to her black coarse father, than her feeling had ever been toward her pale yellow, sweet-appearing mother. The things she had in her of her mother never made her feel respect.

The theme of Melanctha's sexual initiation is treated frankly, but the language is curiously euphemistic. Melanctha's progress is described as a seeking after "wisdom," an almost biblical term, reminiscent of the definition of sex as carnal "knowledge." Her sexual searching, hesitant and timorous, at first—although the men think she is more practiced than she in fact is—is spoken of as learning the "many ways that lead to wisdom." In the beginning, she hovers around construction sites and railroad yards watching the brawny workers and mildly flirting with them. The men are responsive to her attractions, calling out to her:

"Heh, Sis, look out or that rock will fall on you and smash you all up into little pieces. Do you think you would make a nice jelly?" And then they would all laugh and feel that their jokes were very funny. And "Say, you pretty yaller girl, would it scare you bad to stand up here on top where I be? See if you've got grit and come up here where I can hold you."

In the course of one of these adventures, Melanctha falls and breaks her arm. Like Helen in *Q.E.D.*, who has a similar accident, she does not flinch under the pain. The men are impressed with her spunkiness. But with a nice sense of irony, Gertrude observes that it is not with the rough construction workers or yard men that Melanctha acquires "wisdom": "When the darkness covered everything all over, Melanctha would meet, and stand, and talk with a clerk or a young shipping agent who had seen her watching, and so it was that she would try to learn to understand."

There are in "Melanctha" echoes of the Lesbian relationship that figured in *Q.E.D.* Before she meets Jefferson Campbell, Melanctha takes up with Jane Harden, a sickly and, as her name implies, hardened Negro woman, one of Jefferson Campbell's patients. Jane Harden is described as having "many ways" in which to teach Melanctha: "She told Melanctha many things. She loved Melanctha hard and made Melanctha feel it very deeply. She would be with other people and with men and with Melanctha and she would make Melanctha understand what everybody wanted, and what one did with power when one had it." At first the pair would go out together on the streets, flirting with men. Then the relationship became so intense that they were content to remain with each other: "There was nothing good or bad in doing, feeling, thinking or in talking, that Jane spared her. Sometimes the lesson came almost too strong for Melanctha, but somehow she always managed to endure it and so slowly, but always with increasing strength and feeling, Melanctha began to really understand."

Melanctha's love affair with Jefferson Campbell is unpropitious from the beginning, for Campbell subscribes to views of life, to moral assumptions that are similar to Gertrude Stein's. He maintains that work is sufficient, that searching after novel forms of experience—"excitements," as he calls them—is self-defeating. He is a man given to slow and ruminative thoughts, who puzzles over his experiences, trying to explain them to himself, and the character of his thought virtually parallels the writing style of the book. This quality of mind places him at a disadvantage with the quick and unreflective Melanctha.

In their early meetings, sitting on a stairway outside the bedroom where Melanctha's mother is lying ill, Jefferson Campbell tries again and again to unravel his thoughts:

You see Miss Melanctha I mean the way so many of the colored people do it. Instead of just working hard and caring about their working and living regular with their families and saving up all their money, so they will have some to bring up their children better, instead of living regular and doing like that and getting all their new ways from just decent living, the colored people just keep running around and perhaps drinking and doing everything bad they can ever think of, and not just because they like all those bad things that they are always doing, but only just because they want to get excited.

Campbell, like the author, is the proponent of white, middle-class respectability.

But one of the striking features of "Melanctha" is that while Jefferson Campbell's comfortable moral assumptions are similar to the author's, as a writer, Gertrude Stein also underscores the hypocrisy of her own position. Melanctha, whose obsessive experiments with men in the search of "wisdom" have been unsuccessful, nevertheless exposes the shallowness of the bourgeois life view Jefferson Campbell is expounding: "Oh I know all about that way of doing Dr. Campbell, but that certainly ain't the kind of love I mean when I am talking. I mean real, strong, hot love Dr. Campbell, that makes you do anything for somebody that loves you." She puts it even more bluntly: "You certainly are just too scared Dr. Campbell to really feel things way down in you. All you are always wanting Dr. Campbell, is just to talk about being good, and to play with people just to have a good time, and yet always to certainly keep yourself out of trouble."

One of the finer aspects of the story is the manner in which these two antagonistic positions become enmeshed, instructive to each other. While "Melanctha" is written, in most respects, in a traditional vein, there is no plot in the conventional sense, only the disclosure of states of mind. The story moves forward not by means of novelistic incident, but through the slow, meditative process of the interior and spoken monologues. Awareness, the saddening "wisdom" that the characters arrive at, becomes a function of the language itself, drummed out by the insistent rhythms of speech, the simple, blunt, declarative sentences of the style. Gertrude Stein was never a writer for whom love was blind, but rather—like writing itself—a source of sharp, sometimes humiliating, consciousness.

In "Melanctha" the burden of this awareness falls to Jefferson Campbell. At one point he allows Jane Harden to tell him, at length, about
Melanctha's life before she met him. Like Mabel Neathe's disclosure of
her relationship with Helen, made to Adele, in *Q.E.D.*, Jane Harden's
revelations cause a strong feeling of revulsion in Jefferson Campbell. He
avoids seeing Melanctha for several days, and the affair is almost broken
off. When it does resume, his disloyalty hangs over their relationship.
His ruminative tendencies, his hesitations and doubts, become a source
of anguish for Melanctha. She, in turn, uses her pain and her weakness
as a source of new power over him, stifling his natural inclinations, forcing him into a subservient role. Finally, he bursts out: "You ain't got
no right Melanctha Herbert. . . . you certainly ain't got no right always to be using your being hurt and being sick, and having pain, like a
weapon, so as to make me do things it ain't never right for me to be
doing for you. You certainly ain't got no right to be always holding
your pain out to show me." Melanctha, however, has become the master
of the relationship, enforcing silence and resignation on Jefferson
Campbell, putting him off with vague professions of love. In the meantime, driven by her own urgencies, Melanctha has taken up with other
men. "Jeff knew now always, way inside him," the narrative continues,
"what it is to really suffer, and now every day with it, he knew how to
understand Melanctha better. Jeff Campbell still loved Melanctha Herbert and he still had a real trust in her and he still had a little hope that
some day they would once more get together, but slowly, every day, this
hope in him would keep growing always weaker." That is the manner
in which the relationship ends, dissipating away, leaving a residue of
painful awareness.

If the love affair between Melanctha and Jeff Campbell is disturbing and passionate, the situation in the third of Gertrude's stories, "The
Gentle Lena," is far different. It concerns a loveless arranged marriage
between two automatons, a trancelike coming together of a placid young
German servant girl brought to America by her aunt, and a young
tailor, Herman Kreder, who first runs away from the marriage and then
dutifully—at the insistent badgering of his parents—returns to go
through with it. It is a stolid affair that brings with it no poignant self-
awareness, simply a slow attrition of feeling until Lena dies of childbirth in a hospital. Only Herman seems to emerge from this brief but
sharp vignette of the German immigrant with some measure of independence and a prize—the three children who have brought some meaning into his routine existence and whom he raises by himself, freed
from his slavery to his unimaginative parents.

The power—and servitude—of love; that was the underlying theme
of Gertrude's three stories. For later readers it may seem. a failing in
the author's method, of the probity of her observations, that in dealing
with the lives of Negroes and German immigrants as she had witnessed

them in Baltimore at the turn of the century, there should be so little attempt to analyze, or take a stand against, the abuses of the period. One recognizes that there is, operative in the book, a feeling of determinism with respect to social problems. "Melanctha," however, remains a landmark performance by a white American author dealing with the Negro as a person of complexity and bewildering passions, not as a pawn in a propaganda treatise for social reform. Gertrude's treatment of the love affair between Jeff Campbell and Melanctha Herbert was written in terms of the democracy of human feelings.

Three Lives was a remarkable book for its time. Gertrude had begun it in the spring of 1905 and did not complete it until the spring of the following year. Publishing the book was to prove more problematic than the writing of it. Reaction in the family circle was mixed. Sally Stein was immediately enthusiastic; she recommended that Gertrude send it to a publisher. Leo, however, was perversely noncommittal about Gertrude's three stories. His silence was painful, and Gertrude complained about it in a letter to Mabel Weeks:

I am afraid that I can never write the great American novel. I don't know how to sell on a margin or do anything with shorts or longs, so I have to content myself with niggers and servant girls and the foreign population generally. Leo he said there wasn't no art in Lovett's book and then he was bad and wouldn't tell me that there was in mine so I went to bed very missable but I don't care there ain't any Tschaikowsky Pathetique or Omar Kayam or Wagner or Whistler or White Man's Burden or green burlap in mine at least not in the present ones. Dey is very simple and very vulgar and I don't think they will interest the great American public. I am very sad Mamie.

Nonetheless, Gertrude had decided to send the manuscript to a few friends for advice. The principal problem was to have the book typed. Gertrude was a thoroughly incompetent typist, and could barely manage the simplest sentence on the balky old Blickensdoerfer that was kept in the studio room. Etta Cone was therefore enlisted to make a typescript from Gertrude's barely decipherable manuscript. It was only after she had turned over the manuscript to her Baltimore friend, however, that Gertrude realized that she had not told Etta to read it first. "Baltimore," Gertrude observed in *The Autobiography*, "is famous for the delicate sensibilities and conscientiousness of its inhabitants." When she went to visit Etta at her rue Madame apartment shortly thereafter, Gertrude found her "faithfully copying the manuscript letter by letter so that she might not by any indiscretion become conscious of the meaning. Permission to read the text having been given the typewriting went on."

CHAPTER FOUR

A Good-looking Bootblack

I

The Autumn Salon, in the year 1905, was to become a historic event. When the exhibition opened at the Grand Palais on October 18, it created an immediate *succès de scandale*. Then in its third year, the salon had been established to encourage the work of young and untried artists in contrast to the more conventional and academic spring salons. In 1905 it included a roomful of canvases by relatively unknown painters whose work was characterized by slashing brushwork and savage color. The term "the Wild Beasts"—*Les Fauves*—had been promptly applied to the artists by Louis Vauxcelles, the conservative art critic for the journal *Gil Blas*. Catching sight of a Renaissance-type bronze statue in the midst of the brilliant and explosive canvases, Vauxcelles had exclaimed, *"Tiens . . . Donatello au milieu des fauves!"* His epithet, circulating quickly through the highly vocal Parisian art world, clung to the group. Vauxcelles had baptized the first of the twentieth century's radical art movements.

Claribel and Etta Cone, both in Paris at the time, had received invitations to the *vernissage*, and both attended. Making their way through the long halls crowded with conventional paintings, they suddenly found themselves in what appeared to be a jungle of people and brash color. "The walls were covered with canvases," Claribel recalled in an account left among her private papers, "—presenting what seemed to me then a riot of color—sharp and startling, drawing crude and un-even, distortions and exaggerations—composition primitive and simple as though done by a child. We stood in front of a portrait—it was that of a man bearded, brooding, tense, fiercely elemental in color with green eyes (if I remember correctly), blue beard, pink and yellow com-plexion. It seemed to me grotesque. We asked ourselves, are these things to be taken seriously." As they glanced around the room, they discovered their friends, the Steins, "all earnestly contemplating a can-vas—the canvas of a woman with a hat tilted jauntily at an angle on the top of her head—the drawing crude, the color bizarre." It was a painting they were soon to know a great deal about by an artist whose works they were to acquire with remarkable dedication.

Henri Matisse was thirty-five when notoriety propelled him into local fame as "The King of the Wild Beasts." Matisse, older than his col-leagues—men like Derain, Rouault, Marquet, Manguin, Jean Puy, Louis Valtat, all of whom participated in the 1905 Autumn Salon—was the least likely candidate for the title. Conservative in dress, serious—even grave—in manner, he had already achieved a certain renown as a promising traditionalist. In 1896 his painting *Woman Reading*, a con-ventional picture of a woman in an interior, exhibited in the spring *Salon de la Nationale*, had been acquired by the state. Matisse had also been elected an associate member of the generally conservative *Société Nationale*, a singular honor for a painter just beginning his professional career.

The Fauve exhibition, however, marked a definite break between Matisse and his early public. Sympathetic critics, like Vauxcelles, be-lieved that Matisse had pushed things too far or had been led astray by the enthusiasms of younger men. The general opinion among Parisian critics was that the entire exhibition was nothing more than the work of "practical jokers" and "maniacs." They could only view such paint-ings, at best, as the work of children turned loose with their paintboxes. The painting that they signaled out for special abuse was precisely the one in front of which the Steins had stationed themselves at the *vernissage*: Matisse's *Femme au Chapeau*—a portrait of the artist's wife in a superabundant hat, its somber blacks shot through with vivid slashes of orange and green. Although not by any means the greatest of Matisse's paintings, *Woman with the Hat*, by virtue of its celebrity, became a monument of the modern movement.

Matisse's artistic vocation might be said to have begun at the age of twenty while he was recuperating from an attack of appendicitis. He

had, in fact, been given a box of colors then and he began copying
chromoliths of Swiss landscapes. From these he proceeded to tightly
painted original still lifes. His father, a modestly successful grain mer-
chant in Bohain-en-Vermandois, in Picardy, had ambitions for his son,
and Matisse had begun his career as a dissatisfied law student and then
a bored clerk in a law office. It was only with the utmost persistence
that Matisse's father was finally persuaded to allow him to go to Paris
to study art—and then only with the provision that Matisse would enroll in the atelier of Adolphe Bouguereau, the reigning star of the
Parisian salons. Bouguereau, a painter of succulent nudes and contrived
genre scenes, had achieved success in the terms that mattered most to
middle-class sensibilities like those of Matisse's father. He had become
both rich and famous through his art.

Matisse's studies under the aging, industrious painter of seductive
nymphs and lecherous satyrs did not prove successful. The painter
found Bouguereau's method, which consisted of meticulously copying
the details of plaster casts, both mechanical and uninspiring. Bouguereau, after inspecting the young artist's efforts, announced with a
certain wrong-headed prescience: "You'll never learn to draw." In a
way, the remark was prophetic: Matisse was never to be satisfied with
mere proficiency. His lifelong ambition became the attempt to tran-
scend drawing, to construct an art of pure color. In the process, refining
his skills, exploring, inventing new techniques, he became the twentieth
century's most supple and, perhaps, its greatest draughtsman.

With Gustave Moreau, under whom he studied next, Matisse found
a more agreeable teacher. Moreau, a dedicated and retiring man, was a
painter of romantic tastes whose works displayed a distinct bias for the
evil heroines of history and mythology—Helen, Delilah, Salomé. It was
in Moreau's atelier, probably, that Matisse began developing that taste
for sensuous exoticism that marked a good deal of his later work. It was
there, too, that he encountered the artists—Manguin, Marquet, Rouault
—who formed the core of the Fauve group. But while Matisse had been
promoted to the leadership of the Fauves, he remained, throughout his
career, wary of aesthetic dogmas and radical styles. Years later he remarked: "My master, Gustave Moreau, used to say that the manner-
isms of a style turn against it after a while, and then the picture's
qualities must be strong enough to prevent failure. This alerted me
against all apparently extraordinary techniques."

Matisse's success at the *Salon de la Nationale*, at the age of 26, provided a happy augury for his future and a consolation to his skeptical
parents. It became clear, however, that his restless talent would not remain satisfied with official recognition. The large painting that he submitted to the salon in the following year, 1897, was *The Dinner Table*,
a heavy-handed feast of Impressionism, in which a servant girl is shown
preparing an elaborate banquet table. The Impressionists were still

considered anathema in conservative quarters, and Matisse's picture
was allowed in the exhibition only because he had been so recently
elected to the *Société*. He next began exploring a more radical technique, the divisionist method of Seurat and his followers, which broke
down the imagery of the painting into semaphoric dots of color. In
time, however, Matisse abandoned this technique. "All the paintings of
this school," he explained, "had the same effect: a little pink, a little
blue, a little green; a very limited palette with which I didn't feel very
comfortable." The results of this consistent probing of styles brought
him into disfavor. His paintings were no longer accepted by the *Société
Nationale*; his father, disgruntled by his lack of success, cut off his small
allowance. Matisse, now married—he and Amélie Payrayre had been
married in 1898—found himself in straitened circumstances with children to support. It was then that Madame Matisse opened her millinery shop on the rue de Chateaudun. The two sons, Jean and Pierre,
were sent to live with their grandparents. It was a gloomy period: Matisse had sold little or nothing for several years. When the storm of
critical abuse broke over his entries to the 1905 *Salon d'Automne*, his
prospects for the future looked exceedingly grim.

Neither Gertrude nor Leo was blessed with memories that were above
reproach. Years later, when they each wrote about the purchase of
Matisse's *Woman with the Hat*, they gave different versions. Gertrude,
delivering her third-person account in *The Autobiography of Alice B.
Toklas*, written thirty years later, remembered that she could not understand why people were roaring with laughter in front of the picture and
even scratching at the paint. "The Cézanne portrait had not seemed
natural," she related, "it had taken her some time to feel that it was
natural but this picture by Matisse seemed perfectly natural and she
could not understand why it infuriated everybody." She announced
that she wanted to buy it. Leo, she claimed, was "less attracted," but
agreed to buy it with her. He had found, she noted mistakenly, a picture of "a white-clothed woman on a green lawn and he wanted to buy
it." This was the Du Gardier that Leo had bought before her arrival in
Paris.
    Leo wrote about it more than forty years after the event, still smart-
ing under the celebrity that Gertrude had gained with her best-selling
autobiography. His account of his art adventures in Paris in the early
years of the century, he maintained in *Appreciation*, would be more
"veridical" than the "romance" Gertrude had concocted. In certain respects, it was, although it was also flawed by a telescoping of events and
a faulty recollection of the sequence of dates and happenings. Leo recalled that Matisse's painting had impressed him decisively: "It was a

tremendous effort on his part, a thing **brilliant and** powerful, but the nastiest smear of paint I had ever seen. It was what I was unknowingly waiting for." Still, he had wanted one or two days to think it over before making an offer for the picture. As for Sally Stein—Michael left no published recollections—she remembered that she had wanted to buy Matisse's picture because it bore a marked familial resemblance to her mother.

Matisse had set a price of 500 francs ($100) for the painting—on this, at least, both Gertrude and Leo agreed. At this point, in both their accounts, some unnecessary quibbling had intervened. The secretary at the salon had informed them that it was not customary to offer a painter his asking price. The Steins therefore made an offer of 400 francs, and the offer was forwarded to Matisse. Matisse's reply—in Gertrude's version—was that he wished to maintain his original price, so consequently the Steins paid it. Leo, however, maintained that Matisse told him he did not think his original price was excessive and "that he could not let it go for less than four-fifty." Leo responded, "I did not consider the price excessive either, that I had simply conformed to custom, and that if Matisse wished to innovate, I was quite content to follow him. So I did, and I had bought my first Matisse."

Gertrude's curiosity about people extended a good deal further than Leo's, so that when they met Matisse and his wife, she was pleased to learn from Madame Matisse about the family drama that had preceded the sale. Following her own recital of the buying of the picture from the Stein side, she set down the events of the transaction from the Matisses' point of view. According to Madame Matisse, her husband had been only too willing to accept the original offer. She, however, had urged her husband to hold out for the full price. The difference, she said, would mean winter clothes for Margot. There followed two anxious days of waiting during which Matisse became extremely anxious and Madame Matisse even more so. She was posing for her husband with a much-mended guitar, an old prop, when finally the Steins' *petit bleu* arrived. Matisse, opening it, made an extraordinary grimace. Madame Matisse let the guitar fall with a resounding thrum. "What is it?" she asked. "I was winking at you," Matisse explained, "because I was so moved I could not speak."

There was much about Matisse and his wife that Gertrude came to admire. The Matisse household—the family was living then in a three-room apartment on the Quai St. Michel, with a beautiful view of Notre Dame and the Seine, which Matisse often painted—was run as a resolutely bourgeois establishment. Madame Matisse, Gertrude observed, was an "admirable housekeeper" and a good cook. She remembered Madame Matisse's jugged hare in the style of Perpignan and the regional wines served at the Matisse table, particularly a good Madeira-type wine called Roncio. Matisse, she felt, was a man who had "an astonishing virility that always gave one an extraordinary pleasure when one had not seen him for some time. Less the first time of seeing him than later. And one did not lose the pleasure of this virility all the time he was with one." That curious judgment was further tempered with the observation that "there was not much feeling of life in this virility." Madame Matisse, on the other hand, "was very different, there was a very profound feeling of life in her for any one who knew her."

Gertrude recognized—and appreciated—in Matisse the selfishness that characterizes the creative life. During these years of hardship, he owned a small Gauguin and a small Cézanne, the latter a painting of three bathers, which he refused to sell, even though the advantageous price he might have gotten for either of the pictures would have helped the sagging family finances. Matisse claimed that he needed both works as inspiration, but more particularly, the Cézanne. Furthermore, at the time the Steins first met him, he had engaged a separate studio on the rue de Sèvres. The little top-floor apartment on the Quai St. Michel was too confining, particularly for the ambitious canvas he was working on, the *Bonheur de Vivre*, which Leo subsequently bought, much to the chagrin of Maurice Sterne.

What Gertrude admired in Matisse was his dogged persistence. He worked, she noted, "every day and every day and every day and he worked terribly hard." It was a quality Leo admired as well, one that sharply contrasted with his own hesitations and his inability to bring any project to a satisfying completion. Leo took note, too, of another virtue of the French painter: "Matisse has great maturity, and the temper of the eternal pupil: he is always willing to learn anyhow, anywhere, and from anyone." While Leo's remark does justice to Matisse's patience and receptivity, it also indicates, perhaps, Matisse's circumspection with regard to his new American patron. Leo, when visiting artists' studios, was in the habit of freely offering his advice on pictorial problems. He seldom understood it when a painter seemed less than happy when he pointed out some flaw in a composition.

The patronage of the Steins came at a crucial moment in Matisse's career. Matisse's biographer, Alfred H. Barr, Jr., has referred to the purchase of the *Woman with the Hat* as "an act of considerable courage and extraordinary discernment." In the next few years, Leo was to pick out important works from Matisse's production, like the *Bonheur de Vivre* of 1906 and the *Blue Nude* of 1907. Within a short time, the walls at 27, rue de Fleurus began to crowd up with brilliant Fauve landscapes, figure studies, and still lifes—*Landscape, Collioure* (1904–5), a portrait of *Margot* (1907), *Music* (1907), among them—to which was added a cast of Matisse's important early sculpture, the *Slave* (1900–3).

It was the Michael Steins, however, who were to become the most consistent and loyal patrons of Matisse. Their purchases were, at first, modestly scaled works such as the little portrait of Madame Matisse,

The Green Line (1905), and a charming, small still life, Pink Onions (1906), as well as Matisse's Self-Portrait of the same year. In time they added large and important pictures, such as the Young Sailor I (1906) and the impressive Blue Still Life (1907). Their large and airy° apartment on the rue Madame became, virtually, a shrine to the painter, hung with large and small works, ranging from intimate sketches to major statements like The Red Madras Headdress. They continued to buy the artist's work long after Gertrude and Leo's interest had waned.

Leo's appreciation of Matisse began to fade within three years of having discovered him. In Appreciation, he noted—somewhat incredibly—that he had reached the conclusion that Matisse's work was lacking in "rhythm," a quality he deemed essential in a work of art. His last purchase, he claimed, was Matisse's Blue Nude, painted in 1907. Thereafter he brought pictures home for consideration, but did not keep them. "For the moment," he wrote, "they no longer served me." It is worth noting, perhaps—since money considerations have a way of hastening such critical evaluations—that Matisse, by this time, had begun to acquire other patrons and collectors, notably the Russian collector Shchukine. And in 1909 Matisse entered into a series of contracts with the respectable firm of Bernheim-Jeune; thereafter the prices of his paintings climbed steadily.

Gertrude's relationship with the Matisses remained cordial until World War I. From the beginning, the painter was a welcome guest at the rue de Fleurus, often dropping by after his work at his studio and remaining sometimes for dinner. Gertrude even attributed the establishment of her Saturday evenings as due in part to the French painter. More and more frequently, people began dropping by to see the Matisse paintings—and the Cézannes: "Matisse brought people, everybody brought somebody, and they came at any time and it began to be a nuisance, and it was in this way that Saturday evenings began." Her enthusiasm for Matisse's painting faded about the same time that Leo's had, although she maintained a lively personal interest in the painter and his fortunes for a considerable time after that. What she discerned and appreciated in Matisse's work was the formidable sense of struggle that informed the early works, such as Woman with the Hat, the last Matisse she kept in her collection and which she sold to Michael and Sarah in 1915. With a lack of insight that corresponded to Leo's, she felt that the "struggle" had gone out of Matisse's later work. It was this, evidently, that she had in mind when she told him rather bluntly—in response to his discreet questioning—"there is nothing within you that fights itself and hitherto you have had the instinct to produce antagonism in others which stimulated you to attack. But now they follow." Gertrude did not record Matisse's response to their conversation, but he seems to have referred to it when he sent her a post-

Gertrude before the atelier door, *circa* 1907. (Courtesy Yale Collection of American Literature.)

Gertrude, age four, in Passy, France. (Courtesy Yale Collection of American Literature.)

Amelia and Daniel Stein. (Courtesy Yale Collection of American Literature.)

The Stein children in Vienna, *circa* 1876, with governess and tutor. (Courtesy Yale Collection of American Literature.)

Gertrude and Leo in Cambridge, Massachusetts, *circa* 1897. (Courtesy Yale Collection of American Literature.)

Sarah and Allan Stein with Gertrude in San Francisco, summer, 1899. (Courtesy Cone Archives, The Baltimore Museum of Art.)

Leo in the studio-room, *circa* 1904–5. (Courtesy Cone Archives, The Baltimore Museum of Art.)

Picasso, *Portrait of Leo Stein*, gouache, 1906. (Cone Collection, The Baltimore Museum of Art.)

The "Stein Corporation": Leo, Gertrude, and Michael, *circa* 1907. (Courtesy Yale Collection of American Literature.)

Michael and Sarah Stein with Matisse, Allan Stein, and Hans Purrmann, at 58, rue Madame, late 1907. (Courtesy Cone Archives, The Baltimore Museum of Art.)

Matisse, *Portrait of Michael Stein*, oil on canvas, 1916. (San Francisco Museum of Art. Gift of Mr. Nathan Cummings.)

Matisse, *Portrait of Sarah Stein*, oil on canvas, 1916. (San Francisco Museum of Art. Gift of Mr. and Mrs. Walter A. Haas.)

Picasso's mistress Fernande Olivier and an unidentified child. (Courtesy Yale Collection of American Literature.)

Picasso in his studio. The painting in the background is the portrait by Rousseau that initiated the famous Rousseau banquet. (Courtesy the Bettmann Archive, Inc.)

Vallotton, *Gertrude Stein*, oil on canvas, 1907. (Cone Collection, The Baltimore Museum of Art.)

Picasso, *Portrait of Gertrude Stein*, oil on canvas, 1905–6. (The Metropolitan Museum of Art, New York. Bequest of Gertrude Stein.)

card, some years later, in the spring of 1912, while visiting Tangiers. "The weather has been fine for three weeks and I have taken advantage of it to work," Matisse wrote her, "painting is always a very difficult thing for me—it's always a struggle—is that natural? Yes, but why so much trouble. It is so fine when it comes easily." It was a gentle reminder that not every painter's "struggles" were readily apparent.

It is clear, however, that Gertrude's evaluation of Matisse was distinctly colored by the personality and the work of the artist she met quite soon after she had been introduced to the "King of the Fauves."

II

Like a good many events in the life of Gertrude Stein, the circumstances of her first encounter with Picasso are buried under the slag of conflicting accounts and faulty recollections. Gertrude's version of their initial meeting is judicious enough. It was Leo, she acknowledged, who first saw and was struck by the work of the unknown Spanish painter in the shop of Clovis Sagot on the rue Lafitte. The painting was the *Jeune Fille aux Fleurs*, one of several canvases that Picasso, then twenty-four and hard up in Paris, had been forced to sell to the ex-clown-turned-picture-dealer for degradingly low sums.

Gertrude remembered that she did not like the painting at all when she first saw it; there was something "rather appalling" about the drawing of the legs and feet of the nude little nymphet, standing in an Egyptian profile, her head turned, holding a basket of red flowers. Sagot, catching the drift of the conversation between Gertrude and Leo as they stood examining the picture, had enterprisingly suggested that the girl could be guillotined. They could take only the head—a solution that did not recommend itself to either of them. Gertrude recalled, too, that she and Leo had quarreled angrily over the picture: "He wanted it and she did not want it in the house."

The gospel according to Leo presented a somewhat different story. The *Jeune Fille*, Leo maintained, was not his first Picasso at all. Earlier, at Sagot's, he had seen and bought a Picasso painting of an acrobat's family with an ape, a picture now in the Gotheburg Gallery in Sweden. Leo had every reason to remember this Rose Period picture, with its tenderly delineated mother and child and its vividly defined crouching ape. It demonstrated the superiority of his zoological knowledge over that, even, of an ex-circus performer such as Sagot. "The ape looked at the child so lovingly that Sagot was sure this scene was derived from life; but I knew more about apes than Sagot did, and was sure that no baboon-like creature belonged in such a scene. Picasso told me later that the ape was his invention, and it was proof that he was more talented as a painter than as a naturalist."

Leo also noted that he had met Picasso shortly after this purchase through one of his Parisian acquaintances, H. P. Roché—"a born liaison officer," as Leo referred to him. Roché, who knew everybody worth knowing in Paris and who made a profession of introducing people all around, was later to exploit his contacts by becoming the advance agent for a number of wealthy American collectors, the most notable of whom was the sharp-eyed New York lawyer and art patron, John Quinn. Leo liked Roché immensely because he was a good listener—"more ear than anything else." Once a month Roché would drop by 27, rue de Fleurus to spend an entire evening with Leo, listening patiently to his fund of observations on art and science and psychology. A man with distinct literary affiliations and, at the time, literary ambitions of his own, Roché introduced Leo to the stars of the Closerie des Lilas—Jarry, Moréas, Paul Fort—and even proposed to write a book to be called "Conversations with Leo Stein," a project that suitably flattered Leo but that, unfortunately, never materialized.

Gertrude, too, was impressed with the tall, red-headed Roché. He crops up often in her writings under the name of Vrais, a character whose response to most situations was "Good, good, excellent." She was also to devote one of her early and more comprehensible word portraits to him. Roché's wide circle of international acquaintances—Englishmen, Germans, Austrians, Hungarians, Russians—whom he brought round to the rue de Fleurus, would have made him attractive to Gertrude in itself. But he was also one of the earliest and most enthusiastic admirers of her *Three Lives*, and once, when she had told him something about herself, Roché had answered, "Good, good, excellent, that is very important for your biography." That remark permanently installed Roché in her memory, even after he had written her a frank, earthy, and disapproving letter about her later literary efforts. Annoyed by the rhythmic repetitions of her word portraits, he had commented: "More and more your style gets solitary—the vision remains great, and the glory of some occasional pages. Rhythm? oh yes. But that sort of rhythm is intoxicating for you—it is something like————." He advised her to shape her material more carefully and condense it by at least sixty to ninety per cent. "Are not you after all very lazy?" he concluded.

Despite what would have been a blow to any author's sensitive ego, Gertrude remembered Roché quite fondly in her autobiography as "a very earnest, very noble, devoted, very faithful and very enthusiastic man." She could not help repeating, however, Picasso's quip that Roché was very nice, "but he is only a translation."

It was Gertrude's recollection that she had met Roché first at the studio of a friend, Kathleen Bruce, a minor English sculptor who later married the celebrated explorer of the South Pole, Robert Scott. Gertrude had taken her nephew Allan Stein to the studio, where he was posing for a small statue by Miss Bruce. Discussing Leo's new acquisition of the Picasso painting, she discovered that Roché knew the painter, and she arranged, then and there, for Roché to take Leo to Picasso's studio. She had, it appears, so disliked the *Jeune Fille* that she had no interest in meeting the painter herself.

As is often the case in Gertrude's and, sometimes, in Leo's accounts of their early years at the rue de Fleurus, the dating of events is off by a year. As one of the newsy items in her letters to Etta Cone in the winter of 1904–5, Gertrude informed Etta that Kathleen Bruce was in the process of doing a sculpture of Allan. "It ain't much," she commented tersely. It seems unlikely—though not impossible—that Allan's sittings would have occupied a full year until the fall of 1905, when Leo acquired the Picasso. Leo's version was that he had already met Picasso when he and Gertrude looked at the *Jeune Fille* in Sagot's shop. Feeling that Gertrude had hogged all the glory—although she had acknowledged his discovery of Picasso and her immediate dislike of the painting—Leo went on to record the vivid details of their argument. On the day that he bought the *Jeune Fille*, he had come home late for dinner and found Gertrude already at the table. When he told her he had bought the picture, she threw down her knife and fork. "Now you've spoiled my appetite," Gertrude said. "I hated that picture with

Picasso, letter to Leo Stein, *circa* 1905. (Collection Mr. and Mrs. Perry Townsend Rathbone.)

the feet like a monkey's." But since he was an honorable man, Leo acknowledged that some years later, when he had been offered "an absurd sum" for the painting, Gertrude had refused to sell.

If Gertrude took an immediate dislike to Picasso's painting, her response to the painter was far different. Picasso impressed her as "a good-looking bootblack. He was thin dark, alive with big pools of eyes and a violent but not rough way." Her account of Picasso and Fernande's first dinner at the rue de Fleurus had its moments of marvelous hilarity. The painter was seated next to her at the table. When she absent-mindedly reached for a piece of bread, Picasso suddenly snatched it back with the fury of a hungry man. "This piece of bread is mine," he said loudly. Picasso's display of possessiveness, the sheepish look that came over his face when she burst out laughing, seemed to establish a bond of intimacy between them. It was all the more cemented when, after dinner, Leo began to bring out one portfolio after another of Japanese prints. Picasso looked through each of them with admirable constraint. Finally, under his breath, he muttered to Gertrude, "He is very nice, your brother, but like all americans, like Haviland, he shows you japanese prints. *Moi, j'aime pas ça,* no I don't care for it." As Gertrude noted, she and Picasso understood each other immediately.

For the next forty-one years, interrupted only by the quarrels that would inevitably result between two sensitive egos eager for acceptance and praise, they were to engage in friendly and familiar conversation. In Picasso's studio or at the rue de Fleurus, they would sit, knee to knee —Gertrude, large and formidable, in her chair; Picasso, small and intense, in his—discussing the personal fortunes and habits of friends, the difficulties of their own work, their struggles, the state of the Parisian art world. Picasso had a fund of malicious observations about mutual acquaintances that Gertrude appreciated and remembered. He had, too, a way of summing up, in razor-sharp and emphatic statements, his ideas about art and the creative life that complemented and influenced her own way of thinking. When he told her, for example, that the artist who first creates a thing is "forced to make it ugly," that "those who follow can make of this thing a beautiful thing because they know what they are doing, the thing having already been invented, but the inventor because he does not know what he is going to invent inevitably the thing he makes must have its ugliness," she set it down as one of the larger truths to be gained from listening to a genius. It was to become a consoling dogma for her own creative efforts and her struggle to achieve the recognition she felt was properly due her own literary genius.

In trade for such insights, she might offer her own breathtaking generalizations, such as her belief that the reason she and Picasso were so responsive to each other was that they represented the most advanced and most backward of modern nations, America and Spain. They had, therefore, the affinity of opposites.

For his part, Picasso was indebted to Gertrude—and to the Steins in general—for their support at a difficult period in his career. The brother and sister began to buy heavily—scores of drawings, paintings from his earlier Blue Period, stunning large canvases from the Rose Period in which he was working when he met them, paintings such as the *Boy Leading a Horse*, and the large, stolid, columnar nude posed against a sumptuous pink ground that was to become one of Gertrude's favorite paintings. Each year Gertrude and Leo selected and bought both the most lovely and most difficult of his works, displaying an extraordinary catholicity and discrimination as patrons. Not only did they offer him the hospitality of their home and their table, they displayed his works proudly, argued in his defense, and encouraged others to buy.

As for Gertrude's flights of inspiration, Picasso was disposed to listen to them politely and, sometimes, diffidently, nodding in apparent approval, interjecting, "*Expliquez-moi cela!*" when the logic of her remarks, as it sometimes did, escaped him. Despite the boundless enthusiasm of her conversation, Picasso was inclined to feel that she was as unhappy as he was—and told her so. It was only, he said, that she had more courage and did not show it. She would then give vent to one of her fine, boisterous laughs and disagree. Gertrude took stock of Picasso's character. In his personal life, she observed, "Picasso never had the pleasure of initiative. As he used to say of himself, he has a weak character and he allowed others to make decisions, that is the way it is, it was enough that he should do his work, decisions are never important, why make them." It was an attitude toward life, toward one's personal circumstances, that she knew very well.

Their estrangements, over the years, were never serious or sustained. Sometimes, early in their friendship, the two ardent patriots fell to arguing about the Spanish-American war—still recent in both their memories—and, as Gertrude noted, "Spain and America in their persons could say very bitter things about each other's country." Once, on a Saturday evening at the rue de Fleurus, Picasso discovered that the Steins had had two of his pictures varnished without consulting him. He felt that they had ruined them and fumed for the rest of the evening, even as they sent him reassuring glances over the heads of other guests. He stayed away for days, until Gertrude and Leo sought him out in his studio and restored amity. Occasionally the estrangement resulted from Gertrude's dissatisfaction with one of Picasso's successive love affairs. While she was ordinarily tactful about such matters and greeted each of the several women who entered and left Picasso's life as cordially as possible, she could be jealous of anyone who threatened her friendship. In consequence, the temperature of the friendship might cool and the invitations to dinner or to tea would not be offered so warmly or so handsomely. As a hostess, Gertrude found Fernande, the first of Picasso's women, rather "heavy in hand," but she got along well with Fernande and tried to steer an apolitical course between Picasso and his mistress when the pair quarreled and separated during the course of their stormy affair.

There were friends among the Stein circle who thought that Gertrude was overindulgent where Picasso was concerned. Maurice Sterne recalled a visit to Picasso's studio in the early years. Picasso was not there when they arrived. But they found a drawing tacked to the door, showing a man—with a marked resemblance to the painter—sitting on the toilet. Sterne recalled that Gertrude, without the least sign of embarrassment, had chortled, "Isn't he cute." Sterne thought it highly improper.

Matisse, apparently, regretted the friendship that was developing between Gertrude and Picasso. It was at the Steins' atelier, apparently as late as the fall of 1906, that the rival painters first met and took stock of each other. "North Pole, South Pole," was Matisse's private comment on the meeting. The two artists exchanged pictures, and Gertrude maliciously reported that each had picked the weakest example of the other. It got back to Gertrude that Matisse had told someone: "Mademoiselle Gertrude likes local color and theatrical values. It would be impossible for any one of her quality to have a serious friendship with any one like Picasso." It was around this time that she began referring to Matisse as *Cher Maître*, with a slight edge in her voice.

III

Neither Gertrude nor Picasso could remember precisely how it had come about that Picasso decided to paint her portrait. She thought it had been arranged at Sagot's, a very short time after Leo had bought the *Jeune Fille*. It was an unusual request on the painter's part, for Picasso had not been in the habit of working from a model. It seems to have prompted a renewed interest in portraiture, for he followed it with a portrait sketch of Leo and a little gouache portrait of Gertrude's nephew Allan, both completed in the following spring.

Gertrude remembered that her portrait had required eighty to ninety sittings during the winter and spring of 1905–6. Some afternoons she would take the horse-drawn omnibus at the Odéon, crossing Paris to the Place Blanche and then making her way up the steep ascent to his studio on the rue Ravignan. More often, as a confirmed advocate of walking, she would journey there on foot. On Saturdays or evenings when Picasso and Fernande had been invited to dinner, the trio would stroll back to the rue de Fleurus. Generally, however, her walks home after the long sessions of posing were solitary. She was fond of recalling those evening walks, when the sky turned an ever-deepening violet and the lights along the Seine began to sparkle. They were to become part of her personal history of her portrait, part of that "legend," by which, as Picasso once informed her, every picture was obliged to live after it had left the painter's hands.

Gertrude liked, too, the long quiet hours of posing, even in the midst of the chaotic drabness of Picasso's studio. Picasso's establishment in the ramshackle Bateau Lavoir was far different from the Matisses' tidy little apartment on the Quai St. Michel. It was a jumble of castoff furnishings. There was a large rumpled couch that served as bed and chairs; there were assorted tables; a small pot-bellied stove held together with lengths of wire. There were stacks of canvases everywhere; drawings littered the floor.

Picasso had posed her at an angle midway between profile and full face, sitting in a decrepit armchair with one of its arms missing. The chair, in fact, disappeared from view behind the generous bulk of her figure, clothed in her costume of brown corduroy, with a loosely draped white collar pinned with a favorite coral brooch. In some respects the pose was rather like that of Cézanne's portrait of his wife, which Picasso had studied in Gertrude's studio, the figure rising bluntly from the base of the picture, the left arm—hand resting on her lap—thrown out into an awkward contortion. In both cases the pose is that of a sedentary, monumental figure; but Gertrude is more accessible, leaning heavily toward the viewer, where her Cézannean counterpart sits ramrod stiff, the posture to which Cézanne had subjected his patient wife.

In the initial session, Picasso, dressed in his blue *singe*, or "monkey-suit," sat, so Gertrude recalled, "very tight on his chair" close to his easel, mixing brown and gray paint on a tiny palette. For Gertrude's amusement, Fernande read aloud from *The Fables* of La Fontaine. The readings were to prove unnecessary at later sittings because Gertrude was in the process of formulating a "portrait" of her own, the portrait of Melanctha in *Three Lives*. In the moments of sustained quiet, she pondered over the character of her sexually attractive, indolent, and yet strangely willful young Negro heroine who seemed to share a few of the traits that Gertrude had already observed in Picasso's mistress.

Late in the afternoon of the first session, Leo, Michael, and Sarah arrived to take a look at what had been accomplished. They brought with them an American friend, Andrew Green, one of the walk-on characters who populated the Stein circle. The Steins were impressed with Picasso's initial sketch. Green began to plead—rather too forcibly—that the artist should leave it exactly as it was. Gertrude watched Green's performance with a quizzical eye: She knew that he had no great liking

for modern art. Once, while staying at the rue de Fleurus while Leo
and Gertrude were away, Green had had all their pictures covered with
sheets. Picasso listened to the tall, young American's pleading, then
shook his head emphatically, *non*. As they left the studio, Green commented on Fernande's beauty. "He was indeed quite overcome," Gertrude noted. Green confided to her that if he could only speak French,
he would make love to Fernande and "take her away from that little
Picasso." Gertrude laughed. "Do you make love with words?" she asked.

The posing sessions continued through the late fall. Picasso's studio
was abysmally cold—in the winter months he and Fernande would
wake up in the morning to find the dregs of the previous night's tea
frozen in the cups. For Gertrude's visits the fire was stoked up until
the stove glowed red. In November, Gertrude brought Etta Cone for
her first visit to Picasso's studio. She had two reasons: She wanted Etta
to see the portrait and she wanted her to buy something to help out
the Picasso finances. Etta was compliant; she picked out a watercolor
and an etching for which she paid twenty dollars, dutifully noting it in
her account book. She did not like the portrait, however; she thought
it hardly a flattering likeness of Gertrude. The visit, nevertheless,
marked the beginning of more purchases of Picassos by the Cone
sisters. In the following March, when sister Claribel was visiting Paris
and Etta was completing the laborious typing of Gertrude's manuscript, both Cone sisters were taken to visit Picasso and selected eleven
more drawings and seven etchings. Earlier, in January, Michael and
Sarah had introduced them to Matisse, and they had bought a drawing
and a watercolor, the first of many subsequent purchases. The Cones
were to develop a solid and enduring friendship with the Matisse
family. And they bought regularly from the artist all during their years
of collecting art. With Picasso, however, they seem to have lost interest when he entered his Cubist phase. With only a few exceptions, they
chose works from Picasso's Blue and Rose periods.

Still, Etta Cone conceived a certain affection for Picasso and for the
glimpse of bohemian life she had caught in Picasso's studio. After she
had left Paris in the spring to consult a specialist in Germany—she was
suffering from what Gertrude in her medical-school slang referred to as
a "bum gut," a complaint she shared with Leo—Etta was glad to receive news of the Picassos. Gertrude, perhaps as a helpful hint, wrote
to her about the financial difficulties of the pair. Etta had responded:
"Poor little Picasso! But then I'd swap all around with his health and
genius, were it possible." But she made no offer of assistance. She was
soon to embark on a costly around-the-world tour with sister Claribel
and her brother Moses and his wife Bertha. Besides, she had, earlier
in the spring, made a loan of 500 francs to Gertrude, who was apparently overdrawn. She had reminded Gertrude again, in mid-May: "By
the way, don't you need some cash, don't hesitate and you needn't

luxuriate in the feeling of poverty, for it's no use to." Etta's charities, apparently, were more often confined to friends rather than needy artists. It seems to be the case, however, that Gertrude regarded Etta as something of a soft touch and felt few qualms about asking for assistance for herself or others.

In the spring of 1906, before Etta had left for Germany, Picasso's portrait of Gertrude came to a standstill. One day, in a fit of irritability, Picasso had painted out the head. "I can't see you any longer when I look," he told Gertrude. The painting remained unfinished all summer while Picasso and Fernande went off to Gosol in Spain, a trip that required new clothes for Fernande and a French cooking stove—expenses that no doubt made their financial situation even more difficult. When Picasso returned to Paris in the late summer—Gertrude and Leo were still away, summering at Fiesole—he completed the portrait without Gertrude. He gave her a strange, masklike face, with prominent eyes, a sharply angled nose, a straight, uncompromising mouth. The portrait became a stunning transitional work, lingering at the end of his Rose Period of harlequins and circus subjects. With its brown and somber coloring, its tawny hints of rose in the flesh colors and in the background, the painting represented the autumn of that style. But its sharp and angular characterization of the sitter looked ahead to the approach of Cubism.

When Gertrude returned to the rue de Fleurus, Picasso made her a present of the picture. She was thrilled with it. "I was and I still am satisfied with my portrait," she wrote later in her book on Picasso, "for me, it is I, and it is the only reproduction of me which is always I, for me." Leo was less convinced. He thought that Picasso's failure to reshape the picture around the newly introduced face had left the painting stylistically incoherent. The *Portrait of Gertrude Stein* was nevertheless given a prominent place in the atelier. When friends complained that Gertrude did not look at all like his painting, Picasso was in the habit of shrugging his shoulders and saying, "She will."

IV

Picasso, Gertrude maintained, had no need of collaboration with other artists. "He needed ideas," she claimed, "anybody does, but not ideas for painting, no, he had to know those who were interested in ideas, but as to knowing how to paint he was born knowing all of that." In her loyalty she overlooked the fact that one of the most important developments in Picasso's art, the invention of Cubism, had been the result of a close collaborative effort with Georges Braque. There is a plausible explanation for this oversight: Gertrude thought Braque a competent, uninspiring painter, and hardly the inventive type. In the early years neither she nor Leo appears to have bought a single painting by Braque. (In the twenties, Gertrude did acquire two small works, both still-life subjects, which she kept for several years.) It is possible, of course, that she and Leo might have made a token purchase or two in the early years, but in the sequence of photographs taken of the studio before World War I, there is no clearly identifiable work by Braque shown amid the pictures crowding the walls. Under the circumstances, it seems to have been a case of heroic forbearance on the part of the French painter, for Braque was a frequent guest at the rue de Fleurus.

Gertrude's remark, nonetheless, had its truth. It acknowledged the extraordinary precocity of Picasso's talent and the artist's lifelong habit of associating with poets and writers. Almost from his birth—on October 25, 1881, in Málaga—Picasso displayed a genius for drawing. He was encouraged by his father, José Ruiz Blasco, a competent painter and teacher of art. In 1896, after several years in Corunna, Picasso and his family moved to Barcelona, where his father had been appointed a professor at the Academy of Fine Arts. There, at the age of fifteen, he completed in one day the entrance examination for the academy, for which most students were allotted a month. At sixteen he had his first exhibition in a Barcelona gallery, and soon after, though hardly out of his adolescence, he was drawn into the bohemian life of the city, frequenting the popular artists' café Quatre Gats (Four Cats) and contributing illustrations to Art Nouveau periodicals such as *Pèl & Ploma* and *Joventut*. In 1900 he made his first visit to Paris, and in the following year, in June, had an unsuccessful exhibition at Vollard's gallery. For the next few years he traveled back and forth between Paris and Spain, picking up various stylistic influences like those of Toulouse-Lautrec and Gauguin, and applying them to Spanish subjects, such as the pair of Barcelona prostitutes in his morbid Blue Period painting *Two Women at a Bar*, a picture that Gertrude and Leo acquired shortly after they met him.

In 1904 Picasso settled permanently in Paris. When Gertrude met him, late in 1905, he was becoming one of the central figures in a widening circle of vanguard writers, artists, dilettantes, and café characters who thronged to the Montmartre bistros and cafés and regularly visited the Cirque-Medrano. In those early years, it seemed as if the various personalities had been drawn together by some irresistible magnetism. It was the Baron Mollet, an extravagant Parisian character—his title had been conferred upon him by Guillaume Apollinaire, who claimed that Mollet was his "secretary"—who introduced Apollinaire to Picasso and Max Jacob. It was Picasso who introduced Marie Laurencin, an art student he had met, to Apollinaire, telling the poet, prophetically, "I have a fiancée for you." Marie Laurencin, in turn, introduced Apollinaire to Braque, a former classmate in art school, and Apollinaire brought Braque, as well as his friend André Derain, to Picasso's studio. The poets André Salmon and Maurice Cremnitz, and the art writer Maurice Raynal, had by this time gravitated into the group as well. And it was this crowd of personalities that Picasso drew along in his orbit to the rue de Fleurus. His appearances there, flanked by such prepossessing figures as Apollinaire and later, Braque and Derain, were Napoleonic, Gertrude thought. Picasso was, she said, "every inch a chief."

The most vivid of the personalities surrounding Picasso, Gertrude felt, was Apollinaire. She was dazzled by his talk; he was "extraordinarily brilliant and no matter what subject was started, if he knew anything about it or not, he quickly saw the whole meaning of the thing and elaborated it by his wit and fancy carrying it further than anybody knowing anything about it could have done, and oddly enough generally correctly." At the time Gertrude met him, probably in 1906, Apollinaire had begun to take an abiding interest in the Montmartre painters. As a practicing art critic, he had already published an appreciative essay on Picasso's Rose Period harlequins and children in *La Plume,* and a bit later, in 1907, was to devote an equally flattering essay to Matisse in the pages of *La Phalange.* In the ensuing years he took up and championed each new development—Cubism as exemplified by Picasso and Braque, the Italian Futurists, the Orphism of Robert Delaunay. His tributes and laudatory essays were gathered into a volume, which became a landmark in the new art criticism, *Les Peintres Cubistes,* published in 1913. Apollinaire's artist friends took a condescending view of his art criticism without, however, disavowing its usefulness as publicity. In later years the artists he promoted claimed that he had understood little of what he was writing about, that he had simply passed on observations they had made to him. "He never wrote penetratingly about our art," Braque maintained. "I'm afraid we kept encouraging Apollinaire to write about us as he did so our names would be kept before at least part of the public." Picasso, rereading his old friend's collected art criticism later in life and remembering the importance it had when it was first published, was sad to find "how shallow" it was.

Apollinaire's published opinions on the artists of his circle were somewhat different from his private evaluations. He felt it his duty to praise a good deal of mediocre work in order to promote the newer developments in art. "It is for that reason, and for the sake of great artists like Picasso, that I champion Braque and the Cubists in my writings," he once confided to a friend. Standards of loyalty and frankness among the Picasso group were loosely defined. Fernande Olivier observed that while there was a certain community of spirit among the artists, there was little sincerity in their relationships. "Few of the friends in the group stood up for any who were not present," she said. "On the contrary, I often noticed that despite their seeming ties of affection, no sooner did one of them leave the house than the others would begin to speak ill of him.

It was Apollinaire's extravagant personality that Gertrude admired. In her recollections of the poet she scarcely ever commented on his writing. Apollinaire was, indeed, a marvelous figure. As a child he and his younger (illegitimate) brother Albert had led a helter-skelter existence under the charge of their mother, a handsome woman who claimed descent from Polish nobility and who for a time had served as a *femme galante* at the casino in Monte Carlo. The poet had grown up in an atmosphere of illustrious claims and great expectations all brought down to the shabbiest of realities—fleeing from creditors, skipping out of hotel rooms, evading the law. It was in Monte Carlo that Olga de Kostrowitzky—Apollinaire's *nom de plume* had been manufactured from two of his given names—took on the most permanent of her children's adopted "uncles," an Alsatian gambler, Jules Weil.

Apollinaire was living in a tiny bachelor apartment near Picasso in Montmartre when Gertrude first met him. Madame de Kostrowitzky and Weil had installed themselves in an apparently continuous state of domestic strife in a rented villa at Le Vésinet, on the outskirts of Paris. Apollinaire visited them regularly; the poet never relinquished his affection and dependence upon his difficult mother. He did, however, fortify himself with a few drinks before journeying out to Le Vésinet on a visit. He sometimes brought along a few of his new bohemian friends. Madame de Kostrowitzky found them so much riffraff, unworthy of her son. She did, nevertheless, develop a certain affection for the raffiné charms of Max Jacob. "Who *are* all these dumplings my son brings to the house?" she would ask the poet.

In Paris, Apollinaire was a restless gad-about. He seemed to know every quarter of the city. It became for him a perpetual mistress and a constant love object in his poems. He would arrive at Gertrude's and at friends, laden down with books and engravings he had picked up along the quays. His talk was full of pungent anecdotes—some of them true, some of them characteristically embroidered—about the odd corners he had discovered, the characters he had met. For several years he wrote a column, *"La Vie anecdotique,"* full of local gossip and local color, for *Le Mercure de France.* He was, as well, respected as a gourmet, ferreting out unheard-of Parisian restaurants and seducing his friends into dining with him, usually evading the bill. Invited to dinner, he proved a demanding but inexplicably charming guest. "Nobody but Guillaume," Gertrude remembered, "it was the Italian in Guillaume . . . could make fun of his hosts, make fun of their guests, make fun of their food and spur them on to always greater and greater effort."

There was something adventitious about Apollinaire's talents as a poet. Poems sprouted up for him like improbable flowers in the cracks of city pavements. He, like Gertrude, was impressed with the efforts of the Cubists and emulated their style, creating poems—collage-like—out of snippets of conversation overheard in a bistro on the rue Christine. He made poetry out of old legends, new encounters, found objects: He had a gift for the unlikely that caused critics and reviewers of his 1913 volume, *Alcools*, to compare him to an old junk-dealer. They complained, as well, about his lack of punctuation. "As for punctuation," Apollinaire answered, in terms that were very similar to Gertrude's explanations for her dismissal of the comma, the question mark, and other unnecessary accretions of grammar, "I have eliminated it only because it seemed to me useless, and it actually is useless; the rhythm itself and the division into lines provide the real punctuation and no other is needed." Whether the two had ever conferred on the subject is problematic: The similarities may be due to the coincidental fact that each had a highly developed aural sense of language, and in certain of their poems, at least, the structure of the lines was carried by repetitions, percussive phrases, natural pauses, the sense of sound. Punctuation in such cases was visual—superfluous. Apollinaire was in the habit of declaiming his poetry aloud in the cafés; Gertrude read her highly syncopated word portraits and poems aloud to friends in her studio.

Despite the parallel technical experiments one finds in both their writings at a similar period, neither Gertrude nor Apollinaire mentioned any discussion they might have had about their creative efforts. Apollinaire did devote a flattering paragraph to Gertrude and her family in his review of the 1907 Autumn Salon in the ephemeral *Je Dis Tout*, a publication that one of his enemies described as a "vague scandal sheet" put out for the amusement of seventeen readers. The occasion was Apollinaire's discussion of the paintings of the Swiss artist Felix Vallotton, one of which was a recent portrait of Gertrude:

He is exhibiting six paintings, among which is a portrait of Mlle. Stein, that American lady who with her brother and a group of her relatives constitute the most unexpected patronage of the arts in our time.
> *Their bare feet shod in sandals Delphic,*
> *They raise toward heaven their brows scientific.*
Those sandals have sometimes done them harm. Caterers and soft-drink vendors are especially averse to them.

Often when these millionaires want to relax on the terrace of a café on one of the boulevards, the waiters refuse to serve them and politely inform them that the drinks at that café are too expensive for people in sandals.

But they could not care less about the ways of waiters and calmly pursue their aesthetic experiments.

Aside from the amusing situation described, the piece is a gracious bread-and-butter compliment of the kind Apollinaire excelled at. In order to point up the story, he seems to have elevated Gertrude and Leo to "millionaires."

Gertrude's principal acknowledgment of Apollinaire as a writer dealt with his art criticism. Writing to a friend about the latest art-world gossip, in 1912, she described one of the little intrigues she enjoyed. It involved herself, Apollinaire, and the painter Delaunay, whom she found amusing as a person but negligible and overambitious as a painter. After his initial success, Gertrude felt, Delaunay's paintings "grew big and empty or small and empty." When the artist presented her with a small picture, claiming it was a "jewel," she mused: "It is small, but is it a jewel." Her letter on the subject of Delaunay and Apollinaire was chatty:

We have not seen much of the Delaunays lately. There is a feud on. He wanted to wean Apollinaire and me from liking Picasso and there was a great deal of amusing intrigue. Guillaume Apollinaire was wonderful. He was moving just then and it was convenient to stay with the Delaunays and he did and he paid just enough to cover his board. He did an article on Cubism and he spoke beautifully of Delaunay as having "dans le silence creet [sic] something or other of the couleur pur."

Now Delaunay does conceive himself as a great solitaire and as a matter of fact he is an incessant talker and will tell all about himself and his value at any hour of the day or night to anybody, and so he was delighted and so were his friends. Apollinaire does that sort of thing wonderfully. He is so suave you can never tell what he is doing.

Gertrude considered Apollinaire a remarkable personality and an influential propagandist for the new men of Paris but paid little attention to his career as a writer. Her old friend, Daniel-Henry Kahnweiler, who championed the Cubist painters in his gallery on the rue Vignon, felt that Gertrude, whose knowledge of English literature he considered amazing and profound, was shockingly ignorant of her French contemporaries. Kahnweiler, in his limited editions, was the first to publish the writings of Apollinaire and Gertrude Stein in France. He regarded her lack of understanding and interest in Apollinaire as a poet—though not as a critic—and in Max Jacob, as well, as something of a scandal in a writer as perceptive as he felt her to be. There was, perhaps, a certain disingenuousness about Gertrude's claim to needing no other language but English. She may have been overcautious about safeguarding the originality of her own radical literary efforts. But of the possibility that she and Apollinaire might have influenced each other in mutual discussions at the rue de Fleurus, the record remains intriguingly silent.

V

As their ties with the new artists developed, Gertrude and Leo found the character of their collection changing rapidly. The Japanese prints were taken down and replaced in rapid succession with ambitious works by Picasso and Matisse. From 1905, when they had acquired both Matisse's *Woman with the Hat* and Picasso's *Jeune Fille aux Fleurs*, the pictures that had hung in single file began to be tiered one above the other on the walls. From Matisse they bought the commanding *Joy of Life* and at least one of the related studies for the picture, the sumptuous *Still Life with Melon*, as well as several landscapes from Matisse's Fauve and earlier periods. Early in 1907, apparently, they bought the artist's *Blue Nude*, a startlingly contorted figure reclining among palm trees, a souvenir of Matisse's journey to Biskra, in Algiers, the year before. Gertrude's friend, the doughty Mildred Aldrich, inspecting the picture in the presence of the artist had found herself at a loss to say something about it. Finally she blurted out that she did not think she could assume that particular pose. Matisse had cocked his eye and laughed. *"Et moi non plus"*—nor me, either.

Within that period of a year and a half, the Steins' purchases of Picasso were even more pronounced. Fernande Olivier remembered that on their first visit to Picasso's studio, the pair bought 800 francs' worth of paintings and drawings (approximately $150), a purchase that the impoverished artist and his mistress considered an extraordinary bounty at the time. In the flush of discovery, they had bought heavily from both Picasso's earlier Blue Period works and the Rose Period, in which he was then engaged. From the former, they acquired the *Two Women at a Bar*, a *Seated Woman with Hood*, the *Dozing Absinthe Drinker*, as well as a haunting, somewhat coarse study *Woman with Bangs*, a painting the Cone sisters later acquired. Their Rose Period purchases were equally notable: the large and handsome *Boy Leading a Horse*, as well as several drawings relating to the painting, and the *Young Acrobat on a Ball*, whose superbly balanced, lithe figure of the acrobat may have inspired the same image in one of Apollinaire's loveliest poems, "Phantom of the Clouds":

And when he balanced on a ball
His slim body became so delicate a music that none of the
        spectators could resist it

During this period, as well, they bought Picasso's *Seated Nude*, now in the collection of the Musée d'Art Moderne, and the imposing *Grand Rose Nude*, one of the Picassos Gertrude kept for the remainder of her life. And they bought scores of drawings and watercolors that were kept in portfolios in the studio room. This earliest phase of their collection was capped off with Picasso's portrait of Gertrude.

As the paintings accumulated on the walls, Gertrude and Leo decided to give a luncheon party for the artists. Beyond the bare description of the event that Gertrude gives in *The Autobiography of Alice B. Toklas*, there is apparently no record of when the luncheon took place or of the guests who attended. One can only reconstruct the event from early photographs of the studio and Gertrude and Leo's discursive recollections of those years. Gertrude mentions it as having taken place the year before Alice B. Toklas had arrived in Paris, so that the fall of 1906, after Matisse and Picasso had met, might be a plausible date. Or even, given her vagueness with dates, the early winter of 1907. That it was a sizable luncheon one can determine from the fact that it was held in the atelier itself, rather than in the cramped dining room of the pavilion. It was the occasion for one of Gertrude's happiest displays of tact. "We had just hung all the pictures and we asked all the painters," she says in the *Autobiography*. "You know how painters are, I wanted to make them happy so I placed each one opposite his own picture, and they were happy so happy that we had to send out twice for more bread."

There is no record of the menu either—surprisingly, for a writer who had a taste for *gourmandise* and who, in later life, complained about authors who described families settling down to meals without telling what they had had to eat. The Steins' cook and housekeeper at the time was the staunch Hélène. Hélène had her standards for maintaining the honor of the household, and her views on propriety. She thought it improper, for instance, for a French guest—as Matisse had once done—to inquire of the cook beforehand what the hostess was serving for dinner. On that occasion, she had served up the eggs fried, rather than in a conventional omelet. On special occasions—and, no doubt, the Steins' luncheon for the artists would have been considered that—the meat course would begin with a fillet of beef with Madeira sauce, followed by a leg or saddle of mutton, and end with a chicken roasted to succulent perfection, one of Hélène's specialties. Hélène, however, deemed herself a plain cook and, as such, considered elaborate desserts beyond her capacities. Anything more than a soufflé was thought to be elaborate. For the honor of her employers, it is clear, the luncheon would have been substantial—a fact that was not lost upon the artists.

What artists might have attended? Matisse, we know from what later transpired, was definitely there. Picasso, the most favored of their discoveries, would have been invited together with Fernande. From the 1905 spring *Salon des Indépendants*, Leo had bought works by two minor artists, Henri Manguin and Felix Vallotton. Manguin was a follower of Matisse, a small, dark man, a fluent talker, who was often invited to the rue de Fleurus. Vallotton, whose stark nude sprawled across the back wall of the atelier, was a painter who had achieved a certain official success as a portrait painter. Leo found him a witty and cynical companion, but thought that Vallotton had "ruined his promise by marrying a rich wife—which a painter can rarely afford to do." Gertrude thought of him as a "Manet for the impecunious." Vallotton's portrait of her pictured her as an august and sleek personage in the loose, brown corduroy robe with a lapis-lazuli mandarin chain—a gift from Mabel Weeks—which she wore as a sort of official costume at her "at homes" on Saturday evenings. Sitting for Vallotton was something of an experience. "When he painted a portrait," she noted afterwards, "he made a crayon sketch and then began painting at the top of the canvas straight across." It was rather "like pulling down a curtain as slowly moving as one of his Swiss glaciers. Slowly he pulled the curtain down and by the time he was at the bottom of the canvas, there you were." Her feelings about the picture are no doubt reflected in the fact that it never appears in photographs of the studio in the early years, and later she unloaded the picture on the Cone sisters. Whether Maurice Denis, whose *Mother and Child* impressed Leo, or Bonnard, whose almost lascivious nude, *The Siesta*, was also displayed prominently in the atelier, were present at the Steins' luncheon is not known.

If the guest list was not limited to those painters whose works Gertrude and Leo had acquired, perhaps Braque attended. And there were several American artists who might have filled out the roster of guests. Alfy Maurer was one of the regulars at the rue de Fleurus at the time. Gertrude never mentioned owning a picture by the artist. But Maurer's style then was heavily influenced by Matisse's Fauve landscapes. It is at least possible that among the unidentifiable paintings of that type in the studio photographs, there was a painting by Maurer. Mahonri Young, the sculptor, was also a favored visitor. Etta Cone had met him at the rue de Fleurus, before she had embarked on her world tour, and she found him particularly agreeable. When Gertrude wrote her later that Young had recently married, Etta replied with a baleful: "Gee, don't tell me Young is married. My last hope." Gertrude and Leo owned a small plaster sculpture by Young, a portrait of Alfred Maurer in a flowing cape and peculiar cap. And it was at some point in the late fall of 1906 or early winter of 1907 that Leo had brought home a newly arrived young American painter, H. Lyman Sayen, whom he had met playing billiards at the Café du Dome. Sayen was an engineer-turned-artist, and while Gertrude seemed impressed with his work, she makes no mention of owning one. She was equally impressed with his resourcefulness as a handyman. Shortly after meeting the Steins, Sayen was called upon to devise a more convenient method for lighting the recently installed gas fixtures. The new fixtures that he installed for them might well have brought about the rehanging of the pictures that had precipitated the luncheon.

One can only picture the scene, then, and imagine the event: the artists, their wives and mistresses, seated around the long Florentine table, the room heavy with cigarette smoke, the voices, animated and sharp, as one course followed upon another. There would be Picasso's high, whinnying laugh, Matisse's solemn and considered phrases, Gertrude's sudden bursts of laughter as they discussed common gossip and rumors. And there would be the satisfaction of the guests as they looked up from their plates to gaze on some specially honored work of their own.

It was only after the luncheon, as the guests were leaving through the double doors, stepping out into the brisk air of the courtyard, that Matisse, turning back into the room and surveying the scene, noticed Gertrude's little trick. When he confronted her with it, some time later, he told her that it was proof that she was "very wicked." "Yes I know Mademoiselle Gertrude," he said, shaking his head, "the world is a theater for you, but there are theaters and theaters."

Among the theaters Matisse had in mind, undoubtedly, was the spectacular theater provided by his young Spanish rival. But by then Gertrude's loyalty to Picasso had been solidly established; her interest in Matisse was waning. Gertrude's so tactfully arranged little luncheon for the artists may well have celebrated the end, rather than the beginning, of a friendship.

CHAPTER FIVE

The Necessary Luxury Company

I

The earthquake that shook San Francisco at 5:30 in the morning of April 18, 1906, had caught William James in bed. Since January, James had been living in nearby Stanford, where he was giving a series of lectures at Leland Stanford University. Just before he had left Cambridge, a friend had said to him half-jokingly: "I hope they'll treat you to a little bit of an earthquake while you're there. It's a pity you shouldn't have that local experience." Now, as he lay, startled, in a quaking bed, the pictures dropping from the walls, the bureaus crashing to the floor, James said to himself: "Here's Bakewell's earthquake after all."

In his bedroom, that relatively small compartment of the larger experience, James had gathered no notion of the extent of the damage, but he had felt the force of the quake. Describing it in a letter, days later, he said: "The room was shaken like a rat by a terrier, with the most vicious expression you can possibly imagine, it was to my mind absolutely an *entity*." Still, in the midst of the upheaval, with his inveterate habit of drawing some object lesson from every new experience, James conceived, he said, "only admiration for the way a wooden house could prove its elasticity."

When he stepped outside, he noted that most wooden houses had re-mained standing, though brick chimneys were down everywhere. Sev-eral of the large brick university buildings had been reduced to heaps of rubble. People, hurriedly dressed and disbelieving, were milling about in the streets. There was, James noticed, a good deal of "Gabble and babble, till at last automobiles brought the dreadful news from San Francisco."

San Francisco had, indeed, fared badly. Water mains and gas mains had broken immediately under the force of the shocks, and the city was soon rocked by explosions. The waterfront had been demolished; fires began crackling up throughout the city, sending clouds of acrid black smoke into the strangely becalmed spring sky. Alice Toklas surveyed the scene from the large house, near the Presidio, where she lived with her widowed father and younger brother. Except for its completely demolished chimney, the house had escaped serious damage. Alice pro-ceeded upstairs to her father's bedroom. Ferdinand Toklas, incredibly, appeared to be asleep. Drawing the curtains aside and pushing up a window, Alice called to him: "Do get up. The city is on fire." Her father barely roused himself: "That will give us a black eye in the East," he said.

Ferdinand Toklas's spartan imperturbability was a quality his daughter admired and imitated. Alice was fond of relating another story about her father, a well-to-do Polish Jew who held property interests in the San Francisco area. The occasion was a vacation trip she and her brother had taken with him. One morning, her brother had gone out horseback riding with a young friend he had met at the hotel. When one of the horses returned riderless, the boy's mother had gone into hys-terics. "Be calm madam," Alice's father had told the woman, "Perhaps it is my son who has been killed."

From her mother, a quiet, determined woman who died when Alice reached college age, Alice had acquired a taste for the gentle arts: cooking, gardening, needlework—the accomplishments of a lady. From her grandmother, who had been a pupil of Clara Schumann, she learned to play the piano sufficiently well to think about a career as a concert pianist. She had a devotion to literature as well. Her mother had given her a membership card to the Mercantile and Mechanics Library, the same library where Gertrude had spent much of her San Francisco adolescence, though the two had not met. Alice's taste in reading had begun with a fondness for English and American novels and then proceeded to an interest in biographies and memoirs. At the age of nineteen she was a confirmed admirer of Henry James. She had once written to the novelist, suggesting that *The Awkward Age* would make a striking play. She had even offered to dramatize it. To her surprise, she received a "delightful letter" from James, which, to her regret, she did not keep, having become embarrassed at the thought of her boldness. Her affection for James as a writer lasted through her lifetime.

At the time of the earthquake, Alice was on the verge of her "fateful" twenty-ninth year and still unmarried. Small, sharp-featured, she was not attractive in any usual sense. There was a light down on her upper lip that in later years darkened so perceptibly it gave the appearance of a mustache, a feature that acquaintances found almost impossible to overlook. Yet there was something oriental and a bit sultry about her appearance in her younger years, qualities that seemed to be enhanced by her taste for elaborate earrings and exotically flowered print dresses. Her eyes were one of her most notable features. Gray-green and piercing, according to one observer, they gave an impression of "unblinking steadiness," as if Alice never relaxed her vigilance.

Her life in San Francisco consisted of what she termed the "gently bred existence of my class and kind." There were the inevitable social gatherings of her young women friends and the entertainments that the cosmopolitan city of San Francisco could offer: theatrical performances given by touring acting companies, evenings at the opera. The Tivoli Opera House had a year-round stock company, and Alice had heard Tetrazzini sing Violetta there. As a young girl, she, too, had been taken to view Millet's famous *Man with the Hoe.*

The earthquake had brought a severe break in the gently ordered continuity of Alice's life. But with that presence of mind that was to remain one of her admirable qualities, Alice soon began setting things to rights. The family silver was stored in a Chinese chest and buried in the back yard—in the event that the fire might spread to her house and as a safeguard against the looting that had broken out in parts of the city. She sent a servant out to buy whatever provisions could be found. A picnic lunch was prepared, and she and her friends dined out on the sidewalk in front of the house. In the meantime, her father, who had traveled down to the city to see that the vaults in his bank were holding firm, returned with four hundred cigarettes, all that he could find, for Alice and her girl friends. She was a chain smoker all her life.

In the days and months that followed, Alice managed with remarkable self-possession. She paid calls on friends, bringing with her large bouquets of carnations from a neighbor's garden. The unnatural heat from the fires in the city had brought them into bloom ahead of time. She even attended a performance by Sarah Bernhardt, who was appearing in Racine's *Phèdre*, in the Greek amphitheater in nearby Oakland. She managed to take a welcome bath, there, in the home of a friend.

The resourcefulness with which Alice and her friends restored the order of their pleasures, led one of their gentlemen friends, Frank Jacot,
to name them The Necessary Luxury Company.

One of the consequences of the earthquake was that it brought the
Michael Steins and their son, Allan, back to San Francisco to inspect
the damage that had been done to their income-bearing properties.
Stopping off in Baltimore in May, Mike dashed off a letter to Gertrude
and Leo: "We had a good deal of mail, the most interesting being
from Theresa who sees Mathews every day. Our houses she says are
practically all right; but the chimneys are gone and will have to be
rebuilt perhaps all the way down necessitating tearing open the walls to
reach them. . . . We telegraphed at once for answers to the questions
I asked in my Paris letter, and we will wait here for the replies. I am
more and more convinced that we will have to go out there *very* soon."
Sally reported that as soon as they had arrived, Lena Lebender had
hurried over to visit them. Lena, she noted, was "all reconciled to your
staying over there & now & instead of wishing Leo a bad tummy is
going to save up to take trip over to see you."

In October, from San Francisco, Sally wrote Gertrude about the
success their Matisses were having. They had brought three small paintings—the first Matisses to cross the Atlantic—including the startling
portrait of Madame Matisse with a green stripe running down through
the face. "I have had a pretty hot time with some of the artists," Sally
wrote Gertrude, "You see, Mikey sprang the Matisses on one just for
fun & since the startling news that there was such stuff in town has
been communicated, I have been a very popular lady. . . .

"Have been called to the telephone six times during this effort—six
more invitations, accepted 'em all—going morning, noon, afternoon,
evening, night—it's rather amusing—and I do love to show my clothes;
they always create such a sensation!

"And, oh, the slang. Gertrude, it's great.—I don't understand most of
it;—but when I do, I wonder—as I do at most everything."

Alice, introduced to the Steins—probably by her friend Harriet Levy,
who had met both Gertrude and Leo in Italy—was immediately struck
by the strangeness of Matisse's portrait of his wife and intrigued by the
stories Sally told her about the family's life in Paris. She saw them
often. Once, while they were out walking together, they met Alice's
father. When she returned home that evening, her father, with what
Alice referred to as his "Pole's prejudice," had promptly asked: "Who
did you say was the German memorial monument you were with today?"

Harriet Levy had been prodding Alice to take a trip to Europe with
her and Alice began to consider it seriously, though she was reluctant to
mention it to her father. When Sally Stein learned of their plans, she

offered to take Alice with them when they returned to Paris in November. Alice's reaction to the suggestion was one of those mystifications that crop up in her life. Recalling the incident in her memoir *What Is Remembered*, she said simply: "I was cool about accepting this invitation, so they compromised with a more accommodating and charming young girl." She was a woman with nice, though frequently undisclosed, reasons for many of her decisions.

Alice and Harriet Levy did not make the trip until the following year. Mr. Toklas's response had at first been a "noncommittal sigh," then in time he stated that he would close the house and move to his club. Alice's brother planned to live at Berkeley for his last two years at the university. In September, 1907, Alice recalled, she and Harriet began the long hot journey across the continent by train, stopping in New York for a day or two, where they caught a glimpse of the reigning beauty, Lillian Russell, dining in the roof garden of their hotel. Alice's friend, Nellie Jacot, formerly Eleanor Joseph of The Necessary Luxury Company, had married Frank Jacot; the couple were living in New York. Nellie took Alice to a matinee performance of Alla Nazimova in Ibsen's *A Doll's House*, a performance Alice considered memorable because she liked neither the play nor the acting. Nazimova's Slavic temperament, she felt, did not suit the role of Nora. On the day of departure, Nellie had thoughtfully supplied their stateroom with bouquets of flowers, baskets of fruit, and, for Alice, a copy of Flaubert's letters. Alice spent the ocean crossing reading Flaubert on deck and conducting, with disapproving glances from her traveling companion, what turned out to be a mild flirtation with a distinguished-looking elderly gentleman, a commodore. Shortly after their arrival in Paris, the commodore sent Alice what she considered "a most compromising letter." She tore it into shreds, dropping them into the artificial lake in the Tuileries Gardens.

The first order of business in Paris, however, once the pair had settled into their rooms at the Hotel Magellan, near the Étoile, was a call on the Michael Steins in their spacious flat on the rue Madame. The walls were hung with even more vivid examples of Matisse than those Alice had seen in San Francisco. But amid the clatter of tea things, the flow of talk about their trip, it was not the paintings that held Alice's attention: It was the figure of Gertrude Stein, just returned from a summer in Italy. "She was a golden brown presence," Alice remembered, "burned by the Tuscan sun and with a golden glint in her warm brown hair. She was dressed in a warm brown corduroy suit. She wore a large round coral brooch and when she talked, very little, or laughed, a good deal, I thought her voice came from this brooch. It was unlike anyone else's voice—deep, full, velvety, like a great contralto's, like two voices."

On that first encounter, according to the legend Gertrude later propagated, Alice had heard bells, the bells that signaled her encounter with the first of the three then-unheralded geniuses she was to meet—the others being Picasso and the philosopher Alfred North Whitehead. As Alice was preparing to leave on that interesting afternoon, Gertrude took her aside and asked, rather pointedly, it seemed, that Alice meet her at the rue de Fleurus on the following afternoon: They would take a walk together in the Luxembourg Gardens.

On the following day it was clear that Alice might be late for her appointment with Gertrude. Harriet had insisted that they must lunch together in one of the open-air restaurants in the Bois de Boulogne, so Alice sent Gertrude a *petit bleu*, the convenient Parisian telegram, making her excuses in advance. She arrived at the rue de Fleurus a half-hour late. If Gertrude remembered that Alice, on their first meeting, had heard bells, Alice, in her reminiscences, suggested that Gertrude had been struck by *un coup de foudre*, that flattering device perennial to all romantic novels—love at first sight.

"When I got to the rue de Fleurus and knocked on the very large studio door in the court," Alice related, "it was Gertrude Stein who opened it. She was very different from the day before. She had my petit bleu in her hand. She had not her smiling countenance of the day before. She was now a vengeful goddess and I was afraid. I did not know what had happened or what was going to happen."

"Nor," Alice added mysteriously, "is it possible for me to tell about it now. After she had paced for some time about the long Florentine table made longer by being flanked on either side by two smaller ones, she stood in front of me and said, Now you understand. It is over. It is not too late to go for a walk. You can look at the pictures while I change my clothes."

When Gertrude returned, she was in a more accommodating frame of mind and asked familiarly about Harriet. She and Alice proceeded on the first of many walks, along the few short blocks of the rue de Fleurus and into the Luxembourg Gardens, through the tree-lined avenues, past the little parks with their statues of forgotten poets and famous composers, past the nursemaids in their starched white caps and the children rolling hoops. Gertrude called to her, "Alice, look at the autumn herbaceous border." But Alice, musing over Gertrude's frightening performance, was not disposed to return the familiarity. The opening day of their long lives together, after that first and premonitory upheaval, ended in a patisserie off the Boulevard Saint-Michel, where they sat together calmly eating praline ices and the most delicious cakes in the quarter.

II

Alice's first visit to the studio of her second genius, Picasso, took place after she had settled down to the pleasures of Parisian life. She had met Picasso and Fernande earlier at a Saturday-evening dinner at the rue de Fleurus. She found Fernande strangely attractive, an "oriental odalisque," but a bit ponderous. Picasso made the most forceful impression; Alice was struck by his "marvelous, all-seeing brilliant black eyes." Her visit to his studio in the Bateau Lavoir was hedged around with difficulties. Picasso and Fernande had temporarily separated. Although Fernande was somewhat indolent by nature, she nevertheless found life in the studio dull. There was little for her to do in the way of housekeeping because the painter seemed to resent any attempts to tidy up the apparently fruitful disorder in which he lived. Picasso, absorbed in his work, was frequently noncommunicative; Fernande found his silent moods difficult. At times, it seemed, she was relegated to the status of a household pet—like the white mouse, the stray cats, the dogs of uncertain lineage, even the monkey that made up Picasso's menagerie over the years. Picasso confided to Alice that his mistress was, quite frankly, bored—a disease that he warned Alice might be contagious among women. When the couple did finally separate five years later, Picasso explained that although Fernande's beauty had always held him, he could never stand "any of her little ways." For the moment their life together had become constraining and tiresome: Fernande had taken a little apartment of her own, a short distance from Picasso's studio.

Gertrude had pressed Alice into taking French lessons from Fernande, and it was for the purpose of making the arrangements that she and Alice had boarded the horse-drawn omnibus that took them across Paris from the Place de l'Odéon to Montmartre. First they stopped to visit Picasso. The painter greeted them at the door, wearing his monkey suit, with the belt dangling behind like a tail. Alice, overpowered by the smell of turpentine and dog, looked around for a chair in response to Picasso's offer that the ladies be seated. But as Alice was to observe, in artists' studios one mostly stood; there were few items of furniture and most of these were paint-splattered. While Gertrude and Picasso stood talking, her eyes were drawn to a huge, barbarous canvas leaning against the wall, a painting of a group of women in menacing postures. The forms were brash and angular. Her impression of the painting, as Gertrude was to report it in the *Autobiography*, was that "there was something painful and beautiful there and oppressive but imprisoned."

Finally, Gertrude announced: "Well, we have to go. We are going to have tea with Fernande."

Picasso looked sheepish. "Yes I know," he said.

"How often do you see her?" Gertrude asked with that touch of malice she liked to exercise on occasion, making an awkward situation slightly more uncomfortable.

"I have never been there," Picasso said resentfully.

Gertrude laughed. "Well, anyway, we are going there and Miss Toklas is going to have lessons in French."

"Ah, the Miss Toklas," Picasso countered, "with small feet like a Spanish woman and earrings like a gypsy and a father who is king of Poland like the Poniatowski's, of course she will take lessons."

As they started out the door, Gertrude handed Picasso a bundle of newspapers. It was the comics section from one of the American Sunday papers: The painter was an avid follower of the Katzenjammer Kids and of Little Jimmy. Picasso beamed and thanked her.

The scene at Fernande's little flat, farther up the steep hill, was quite different. Alice, with her eye for domestic appointments, thought it had been done up in wretched taste. There was a large upright piano, a bed and a table covered with Turkish throws, and an unaccountably large number of opaque glass bowls and ashtrays. Two of Fernande's friends, Alice Derain and Germaine Pichot, had already arrived to take tea in the English fashion—a new fad in Paris. Alice Derain was a woman of charm, virgin-like in appearance, with a gift for racy language that Fernande eventually decided was too crude for Harriet Levy's ears but not for Alice's. Germaine Pichot, on the other hand, was quiet and serious, but the heroine of a number of libidinous adventures, a few of which Fernande related to Alice as part of her course in conversational French. Germaine, at the time, was married to the painter Pichot, one of Picasso's colleagues.

The tea-time conversation dragged on pleasantly, but in no important direction. It was a relaxed and an amiable affair. The ladies looked pleased and smiled a good deal, venturing some new topic of conversation that Alice negotiated successfully, but that soon caused Gertrude to fidget in her chair. The only rousing business of the afternoon occurred when Fernande, who was also addicted to the Katzenjammer Kids, asked Gertrude if she had any more comics supplements.

Gertrude—quietly—answered that she had just left them with Picasso.

Fernande lashed out in a rage. "That is a brutality that I will never forgive him," she cried. "I met him on the street, he had a comic supplement in his hand, I asked him to give it to me to help me to distract myself and he brutally refused. It was a piece of cruelty that I will never forgive.

"I ask you Gertrude," she implored, "to give to me myself the next copies you have of the comic supplement."

Gertrude was nonplussed. "Why certainly," she said, "with pleasure."

After she and Alice had left Gertrude remarked that it was to be hoped that Fernande and Picasso would be together again before the next installments of the Katzenjammer Kids arrived. Otherwise, she concluded, "I will have to lose them or have my brother give them to Pablo by mistake."

The strange, barbaric picture that had troubled Alice on her first visit to Picasso's studio was to have formidable consequences in the development of modern art. It marked, with all the ugliness of the process exposed to view, the painful transition of Picasso's style from the early representational manner of the Blue and Rose periods to the first radical phases of Cubism. Dubbed *Les Demoiselles d'Avignon*, a sardonic commemoration of the ladies of a well-known house on Avignon Street in Barcelona, it became a monument in the history of modern art, a painting that changed the conventions of pictorial structure for several decades thereafter. Painted in the spring of 1907, it was preceded and followed by a number of sketches and watercolors, studies of savagely distorted heads and posturing women, several of which the Steins acquired and which were hung in the studio at 27, rue de Fleurus.

According to Gertrude, it was Matisse who introduced Picasso to one of the important stylistic influences for the *Demoiselles*. Matisse, she claimed, drew Picasso's attention to Negro sculpture not long after Picasso had completed her portrait. The older painter, she noted, was in the habit of browsing in the local shops, and on the rue de Rennes there was a curio dealer who always had a great many African wood carvings in his window. Matisse's testimony in a 1945 interview confirms her recollection. While on his way to visit Gertrude one day, he had bought a Negro statuette in the shop of Père Sauvage on the rue de Rennes. He took it along to show Gertrude. Picasso arrived unexpectedly. When he saw Matisse's new purchase, he was immediately enthusiastic. The graphic and expressive distortions of African sculpture do, indeed, figure in Picasso's painting, but Gertrude was to contend that Picasso's use of them was quite natural. African sculpture, she observed, was not naïve at all, but "very ancient, very narrow, very sophisticated." She liked it "well enough" but thought that it had "nothing to do with europeans." Yet she acknowledged that it had served Picasso's vision at the time. "African art which was naïve and exotic for Matisse," she claimed, "was for Picasso, a Spaniard, a thing that was natural, direct and civilised."

Another source for Picasso's strange picture may have been the awkward posturing nude figures of Cézanne's *Bathers*, which the artist could study regularly at the rue de Fleurus. But there was a more direct form of inspiration in Gertrude's studio room. Matisse's biographer,

Alfred H. Barr, Jr., has suggested that Picasso's decision to attempt so ambitious a picture was triggered by his rivalry with Matisse, whose large *Bonheur de Vivre*, completed the year before, was hanging at the rue de Fleurus. Confronted by Matisse's huge idyll on the joys of life each time he visited the Steins, it is significant that Picasso should set the scene for his own equally large but mordant celebrations of pleasure in a bordello. The bourgeois idyll has been brought down to venal realities. An early study for the picture shows a fully clothed sailor seated amid strutting nude women; another has a man entering through the curtains at the left, carrying a skull—an ironic reference to the Spanish conventions of the *memento mori*, a recollection of death in the midst of worldly pleasures.

In the completed picture, the men have disappeared; there are only five savage women. The three *"demoiselles"* on the left of the canvas were painted in Picasso's then current manner, their tawny bodies, however, only slightly modeled. The faces are done in the masklike style adapted from Iberian sculpture, which Picasso had used in his portrait of Gertrude. But as Picasso worked on the contorted figures on the right and the extraordinary still life of a melon slice and oddly phallic fruits at the lower center of the picture, the forms were subjected to even more bizarre distortions. The faces, in particular, closely approximate the conventions of African sculpture, with flat and twisted noses and slanted eyes. Throughout the picture, the safe conventions of nineteenth-century art have been radically dismissed; even the space in which the figures are situated has been treated as if it were nothing more than a sheet of crumpled blue paper.

Les Demoiselles was never exhibited publicly in those early years; nevertheless it achieved a formidable underground reputation and created noticeable divisions in the Parisian vanguard. It was the opening gun in the battle for Cubism, and artists took sides for and against the picture. In the course of its subterranean history and the later stylistic developments that issued from it, artists as diversely talented as Marcoussis, Gleizes, Metzinger, and Léger were to be drawn into Picasso's orbit. Matisse was notably cool to Picasso's innovations at the beginning; it was even rumored that he had vowed to "get" Picasso when former recruits in the Fauve movement, such as Braque and Derain, were among those to be won over by his rival.

Gertrude recognized the immense struggle that the painting entailed. It constituted, in fact, the real subject of Picasso's painting, the effort to create a new method, a new manner of seeing, a new composition, "a composition that had neither a beginning nor an end, a composition of which one corner was as important as another corner, in fact the composition of cubism." And she acknowledged in it a certain indebtedness to Cézanne. "It is true certainly in the water colors of Cézanne," she remarked about the development of Cubism, "that there was a tendency to cut the sky not into cubes but into arbitrary divisions, there too had been the pointilism of Seurat and his followers, but that had nothing to do with cubism, because all these other painters were preoccupied with their technique which was to express more and more what they were seeing, the seduction of things seen."

"Matisse and all the others," she concluded, "saw the twentieth century with their eyes but they saw the reality of the nineteenth century, Picasso was the only one in painting who saw the twentieth century with his eyes and saw its reality and consequently his struggle was terrifying, terrifying for himself and for the others, because he had nothing to help him, the past did not help him, nor the present, he had to do it all alone."

Gertrude was also aware of the consternation Picasso's radical new style was causing among his former admirers. Picasso's Russian patron, Shchukine, after viewing the *Demoiselles*, had turned up at her studio, wailing, "What a loss to French painting." For a time Shchukine was wary of acquiring further Picassos. Picasso told her, in a mixture of heroic pride and bitterness: "They say I can draw better than Raphael and probably they are right, perhaps I do draw better but if I can draw as well as Raphael I have at least the right to choose my way and they should recognize it, that right, but no, they say no."

There was dissension even within her own walls. Leo thought the *Demoiselles* a "horrible mess"—one reason, no doubt, why the Steins made no move to acquire the picture. Leo conceded that he had been willing to buy some of the sketches and paintings related to the picture —what he termed Picasso's "Negroid things"—"in hopes of something better." His opinion was that the Negro influence had been necessary because "Picasso's interior resources were too small for his then needs, and he had to have support from the outside." His opinion, he felt, was confirmed by Matisse, who, one day, looking over the Picasso sketches at the rue de Fleurus, said: "Ye-es, it's very ni-ice, very ni-ice, but— isn't it just the same thing?" Leo explained Matisse's remark: "Of course what Matisse meant was that though the forms were larger and the curves more sweeping, the forms were not really any bigger than they had been. In spite of the pretense, the difference was only a matter of illustration."

The *Demoiselles* marked the beginning of the end of Leo's support for Picasso. He still followed Picasso's progress conscientiously and continued to buy his works, but Leo's acquisitions, from then on, were apt to be made in return for sums of money he had advanced the painter from time to time. Eventually Picasso found the defection of his former patron hard to take. For once, Leo, who ordinarily assumed that painters welcomed his informed criticisms, had tactfully decided to remain silent. But Picasso, according to Leo, was unable to leave the subject alone. "Why don't you like my painting?" he would ask Leo repeatedly. Leo's account of their arguments at the rue de Fleurus have a special poignancy: "He [Picasso] would stand before a Cézanne or a Renoir picture and say contemptuously, 'Is that a nose? No, this is a nose,' and then he would draw a pyramidal diagram. 'Is this a glass?' he would say, drawing a perspective view of a glass. 'No, this is a glass,' and he would draw a diagram with two circles connected by crossed lines. I would explain to him that what Plato and other philosophers meant by 'real thing' were not diagrams, that diagrams were abstract simplifications and not a whit more real than things with all their complexities." Once, Picasso blurted out angrily: "You have no right to judge. I'm an artist, and you are not." One evening the argument became so heated that Leo stormed into his study, slamming the door behind him. When he emerged a few minutes later, armed with fresh arguments, Gertrude, who was standing in the dining room with an armful of books, deliberately threw the books down on the floor, thus putting an end to the discussion.

There was some justice, then, to Gertrude's remark: "I was alone at this time in understanding him, perhaps because I was expressing the same thing in literature, perhaps because I was an American and, as I say, Spaniards and Americans have a kind of understanding of things which is the same."

III

In the summer of 1906 Gertrude had begun work on a long, plodding book that she intended to be a history of a "decent family's progress." In the course of the five years required to complete her novel, it became something more than a narrative of a family's progress. It became a queer psychological experiment in which the author, with more ambition than insight, attempted to write a "history of every one who ever can or is or was or will be living." Gertrude, in time, was to regard the book as her masterpiece—and even more than that, as a landmark in the history of modern literature. Few readers were to agree with her. In the beginning, few readers were to have the opportunity of doing so. The book remained unpublished for more than a decade. When it was published in Paris, in 1925, it ran to 925 pages and bore the title *The Makings of Americans*, and the subtitle "Being a History of a Family's Progress." Gertrude affixed the dates 1906–8 as the period of its composition. Actually, while those dates may represent the period of her most concentrated effort on the book, the period of its composition extends both before and after. An early sketch for the opening segment of the book, dealing with the Dehning family, which was, originally, the family whose progress she was to describe, has been found in the Stein archives at Yale. Textual evidence suggests that it had been written while she was living in the White House in New York, either during the winter of 1902–3, when she had returned from her dismal stay in London, or early in 1904, when she made her last visit to the United States before permanently settling at the rue de Fleurus. Nor did she complete it until the fall of 1911, when she began sending out segments of the book to the English publisher Grant Richards, as well as to friends in New York whom she had enlisted to place it with a publisher there. Publishers, however, awed by the formidable length of the manuscript and even more by its erratic literary style, scarcely considered it. One reader, Mrs. Westmore Willcox, on the staff of the *North American Review*, had warned, "I am sure no American publisher will be able to cope with your book. It is too expensive a venture for too uncertain returns."

The writing style of the book was slow and ponderous; the simplest ideas and observations are introduced and worried over endlessly. The pace of the novel is elephantine; the plot, such as it is, lumbers forward, foraging about in strange jungles of psychological observation. Gertrude was to make no concessions to the patience and endurance of her readers. Yet *The Making of Americans* was to serve as the laboratory of her later style, of her antic philosophy of human nature, and even of her habits as a creative writer. In the years she devoted to its writing, she kept long nightly vigils, watching over its progress, pondering over its directions, while the city of Paris was in darkness and the rest of her household was asleep. "I am writing for myself and strangers," she announced in the book. In later years she conceded that even the inclusion of "strangers" might have been an unnecessary compromise of her artistic principles.

The Making of Americans is a sprawling, jerry-built structure. The original theme of the novel, the succession of generations, is suggested by its opening anecdote:

Once an angry man dragged his father along the ground through his own orchard. "Stop!" cried the groaning old man at last, "Stop! I did not drag my father beyond this tree."

The next paragraph announces what is to become the motivational force of the novel, the attempt to deal with and analyze human character, an attempt that becomes grandiose in its ambitions and takes over the novel's original narrative intentions.

It is hard living down the tempers we are born with. We all begin well, for in our youth there is nothing we are more intolerant of than our own sins

writ large in others and we fight them fiercely in ourselves; but we grow old
and we see that these our sins are of all sins the really harmless ones to own,
nay that they give a charm to any character, and so our struggle with them
dies away.

Gertrude was thirty-two, approaching middle age, when she took up
her earlier version of *The Making of Americans* and proceeded to make
a new and more ambitious novel of it. The opening paragraph of that
earlier version suggests what might have been the initial stimulus for
the book—the spirited debates she had had with the Berenson circle at
Friday's Hill in September, 1902. One can hear, in its opening phrases,
the kind of ebullience that may have grated on the sensibilities of
Berenson and Bertrand Russell when she argued with them about the
merits of American democracy:

It has always seemed to me a rare privilege this of being an American, a real
American and yet one whose tradition it has taken scarcely sixty years to
create. We need only realise our parents, remember our grandparents and
know ourselves and our history is complete. The old people in a new world,
the new people made out of the old that is the story I mean to tell for that
is what really is and what I really know.

The pride of patriotism in being an American, however, though re-
stated early in the final version of the book, was one of the themes that
was soon discarded in the course of the novel.

In the original version, it appears, Gertrude had intended to deal
only with the Dehnings, a family based on the New York branch of
the Stein family, and in particular with Julia Dehning, the eldest
daughter in the family, and a character based on Gertrude's cousin Bird
Stein, later Bird Gans. In reshaping the material for her new book, she
moved the family to Bridgepoint, the fictional name she had chosen
for Baltimore in *Three Lives*, and she chose a second family, the Herslands, described as "a western family." The Herslands represent her
own family in Oakland. In the novel, David Hersland and his wife,
Fanny, whose fictional characters approximate those of Daniel and
Milly Stein, have three children: Martha, Alfred, and young David. As
Martha Hersland, Gertrude promoted herself from being the baby of
the family to the eldest of the Hersland children and dispensed with
two members of her own family, Simon and Bertha. Interestingly, too,
the name she chose to replace Oakland as the scene of her California
childhood was Gossols—an adaptation of the Spanish city of Gosol,
where Picasso and Fernande were spending the summer when she was
beginning her novel in Italy. It is, perhaps, an early, unconscious example of her affiliation of Spain with America.

At first, Gertrude operated under the conventional methods of the novel; she introduces her characters, provides some narrative account of the lives of the Dehning and Hersland families, and a few scant physical descriptions of her leading characters. As a matter of structural convenience, rather than structural necessity, the stories of the two families are interwoven when Julia Dehning marries Alfred Hersland. The most graphic portions of this early segment of the novel, however, are those that deal with the three Hersland children growing up in Gossols and their fight to establish their independence from their irascible father. In these sections, Gertrude even admits to a certain loving kindness for the character of her fictional father, David Hersland:

His hair was grey now, his eyebrows long and rough and they could give his eyes a very angry way of looking, and yet one could love him, in a way one was not afraid of him. He never would go so far as his irritation seemed to drive him, and somehow one always knew that of him. He had not so much terror for his children as fathers with more kindness and more steadfast ways of doing. One always had a kind of feeling that what one needed to protect one from him was to stand up strongly against him. . . . All one had to do was to say then to him "Alright but I've got a good right to my opinion. You started us in this way of doing, you have no right to change now and say that it's no way for us to be acting."

Midway through the novel, after interminable discussions of the servants, governesses, cooks, and seamstresses associated with the Hersland household, Gertrude resorted to an older piece of writing, the *Fernhurst* episode, in order to carry forward her history of Martha Hersland. The earlier novella was condensed, the more puerile passages were discarded, and the episode was patched into her new novel with Martha cast in the ineffectual role of Phillip Redfern's wife. It is a makeshift device, at best, and in one of the many author's asides that occur in *The Making of Americans*, Gertrude admits to a certain sense of dismay in rereading her earlier material:

This is very true then that to many of them having in them strongly a sense of realising the meaning of the words they are using that some words they once were using, later have not any meaning and some then have a little shame in them when they are copying an old piece of writing where they were using words that sometime had real meaning for them and now have not any real meaning in them.

Nonetheless, the *Fernhurst* episode was copied into the wayward stream of the new novel, along with the author's admission of shame.
But narrative episodes of this kind, as the novel progresses, become less important for the author, become like ice floes in the long, ruminative stream of the prose style. At times they become leitmotivs, attaching themselves to a character, and are repeated whenever the character

is reintroduced. A childhood episode in the life of Martha Hersland, for instance, describes a moment of "angry feeling" when she is just starting school. Returning home one day, her friends run off ahead of her:

She was in the street and it was a muddy one and she had an umbrella that she was dragging and she was crying. "I will throw the umbrella in the mud," she was saying, she was very little then, she was just beginning her schooling, "I will throw the umbrella in the mud" she said and no one was near her and she was dragging the umbrella and bitterness possessed her . . . ; "I have throwed the umbrella in the mud" burst from her, she had thrown the umbrella in the mud and that was the end of it all in her.

But it is not the "end of it" in the novel, for the incident cited on page 388 recurs on pages 389, 393, 407, and 426, as Gertrude, after one excursion after another, returns to the central character of her discussion. What takes over the novel, in fact, is a gradually evolving system of character analysis with which the author attempts to categorize her fictional characters and proceeds to make lengthy inventories of characterological types—usually anonymous but sometimes given fictional names—that are related to them.

The system that Gertrude evolved was a queer one. As she later explained it, it was her attempt to get at "the bottom nature in people."

I began to get enormously interested in hearing how everybody said the same thing over and over again with infinite variations but over and over again until finally if you listened with great intensity you could hear it rise and fall and tell all that that there was inside them, not so much by the actual words they said or the thoughts they had but the movement of their thoughts and words endlessly the same and endlessly different.

For the purpose of defining the "bottom nature" of individuals, she not only analyzed the fictional characters in her novel but also imported into the course of it her analyses of the friends she had known and the acquaintances she had made in her new life in Paris. She devised two categories, or types—the independent-dependent and the dependent-independent—into which she fitted everyone she knew as well as a few historical specimens such as Lord Byron and Oscar Wilde and the philosopher Herbert Spencer, in the vain hopes of writing a "history of every kind of men and women, every kind there is of men and women." When these two categories proved too broad for her study of character, she further refined them to include various types of "being" as subdivisions within each type—"resisting being," "attacking being," "loving being." She also resorted to making charts and diagrams as aids for determining the resemblances between her complicated subject types. Under the stress of this system the language of *The Making of Americans* seems to have turned eccentric:

There must now then be more description of the way each one is made of a substance common to their kind of them, thicker, thinner, harder, softer, all of one consistency, all of one lump, or little lumps stuck together to make a whole one cemented together sometimes by the same kind of being sometimes by other kind of being in them, some with a lump hard at the centre liquid at the surface, some with the lump vegetablish or wooden or metallic in them.

One odd type is described as having "a mushy mass of independent dependent being with a skin holding it together from flowing away." Another, we are told, has a substance that "just sort of bobbled up and down in her." The straining after analogies becomes inadvertently comical when one character is described as a "cannon-ball resting on a bag of cotton," and the author complains that the description had been invented by someone else and she was uncertain about using it. At times the author forgets the category to which she has assigned a character. Dean Hannah Charles is classified as an independent-dependent type and, within a very few sentences, is cast into the dependent-independent category. Another character begins with "dependent independent resisting being" and, at the end of a very lengthy paragraph, emerges as a "reasonably just and a little fearful and quite impersonal and somewhat loving quite very good resisting independent dependent one."

From time to time, odd case histories float up to the surface of the novel, such as the woman who believed that her menstrual periods had some connection with her religious affiliations:

She was a child of Plymouth Brethren and she thought that what happens to all women every month only happened to Plymouth Brethren women, women having that religion, she was twenty eight years old when she learned that it happened to every kind of women.

Although the terms are genteel, there is an attempt to deal with the sexual mores of various types:

Frank Hackart attributes his doing anything to the philanthropy in him, she was lonesome and threw herself on him, took possession and what did he do but take care of her. . . . Mary Helbing always puts it down to, that they wanted it and she gave it but she had no responsibility, it was because she was so game that she did it.

At one point Gertrude confesses: "Loving being, I am filled just now quite full of loving being in myself and in a number of men and women. . . . I have loving being in me more than I knew I could have in me. It was a surprising thing to find it so completely in me." She goes on to acknowledge: "I am realising just now with lightness and delight and conviction and acquiescing and curious feeling all the ways anybody can be having loving feeling. I have always all along been telling a little about ways of loving in different kinds in men and women."

Gertrude's odd characterological system seems to have been partly inspired by a book she had read, *Sex and Character*, by a young Viennese psychologist, Otto Weininger, who had ended a brilliant career by committing suicide in 1903. There were several aspects of Weininger's study that appealed to Gertrude at this stage of her own career, for Weininger had attempted to "apply characterology" to such problems as the nature of genius and talent, the relation of identity to genius, and, above all, the relationship of the sexes. Weininger, basing his theory on certain phases of fetal development, believed that all human beings had an underlying bisexual nature. Despite his stated aversion to a statistical approach to questions of human character and motivation, he nevertheless undertook to arrive at something new, a mathematical formula for "a law of sexual attraction," which, based on the proportions of male and female characteristics in individuals, would not only account for but also justify both normal and abnormal sexual tendencies. If Weininger's theory of a sexual calculus did not directly inspire Adele's eureka in *Q.E.D.* when she suddenly found that her tangled emotional relationship with Helen was "like a bit of mathematics" that did itself and provided new insights, it certainly echoed Gertrude's thoughts.

Although Weininger's book took an enlightened stand on homosexuality, advocating a "repeal of the ridiculous laws" directed against it, his psychological formula for dealing with it is simplistic: mating the male invert to "the most man-like woman, the Lesbian or Sapphist type." A psychologist who can claim that "in all cases of sexual inversion, there will be found indications of the anatomical characters of the other sex," and that "the men who are sexually attracted by men have outward marks of effeminacy, just as women of a similar disposition to those of their own sex exhibit male characters," seems to have had little basic experience in the field. Moreover, there is a good deal of rabid philosophizing in Weininger's book that is frankly antifeminist and anti-Semitic. Women are denied any possibility of genius simply by their nature, which is "devoted wholly to sexual matters, that is to say, to the spheres of begetting and of reproduction." "The most appallingly decisive proof of the emptiness and nullity of women," Weininger goes on to say, "is that they never once succeed in knowing the problem of their own lives, and death leaves them ignorant of it, because they are unable to realise the higher life of personality." The Jew, according to Weininger, is also incapable of genius and has the same social nullity as women: "As there is no real dignity in women, so what is meant by the word 'gentleman' does not exist amongst the Jews. The genuine Jew fails in this innate good breeding by which alone individuals honour their own individuality and respect that of others."

Whether Gertrude, as a woman and a Jew, overlooked or dismissed the more rabid philosophizing of Weininger is not altogether clear. But she had, clearly, read the book, or portions of it, and had subscribed to certain of its views. She had even recommended it to Marian Walker, her ardent feminist friend of Johns Hopkins days. Marian Walker Williams, married and "producing a fine baby every two years," for the express purpose, so she claimed, of Gertrude's returning to America to play with them, wrote to Gertrude on June 11, 1909:

By the way, in an idle moment I read the book on sex which you said exactly embodied your views—the one by the Viennese lunatic. It struck me that you made a mistake in your statement—it was evidently before not after he wrote the book that he went insane. We had a considerable amount of fun, however, in calculating the percentage of male and female in our various friends according to his classification. But he was really a very half-baked individual.

Gertrude's system of character analysis avoided the bisexual drama of Weininger's and concentrated, instead, on the more general conflicts of dependency relationships in which sex played an obvious, if symptomatic, part. But among the notes she made while *The Making of Americans* was in progress, there is one that suggests that she had taken Weininger's view of male superiority to heart: "Pablo & Matisse have a maleness that belongs to genius. Moi aussi perhaps."

There is a large element of crank philosophy, of behavioral theory gone awry, of the "half-baked" in *The Making of Americans*. Overlong, maddeningly repetitive, tedious in its rhythms, the method of the book was little more than the accumulation of each day's writing stint. It flows along aimlessly, catching up bits of psychological lore, sharp fictional portraits, too-generalized observations drawn from life, fragments of the author's personal emotions. The author exults as the task progresses: "Always I love it, sometimes I get a little tired of it, mostly I am always ready to do it, always I love it." The author confesses: "It is sometimes a very hard thing to win myself to having been wrong about something. I do a great deal of suffering." The author makes an odd admission: "I can never have really much feeling of what specifically they will be doing from moment to moment in their living. . . . I just felt like mentioning this thing and so I have just mentioned it here so that every one can be certain that I have not any dramatic constructive imagination." The personal joys and woes of the author float by like messages in bottles, bobbing on the stream of the prose.

Yet *The Making of Americans* is a queer and interesting work, a work fixed permanently—like Picasso's *Demoiselles*—in a state of awkward transition. It makes a virtue of amateurism, of amateurism raised to a principle of revolt against academic conventions, and in that sense *The Making of Americans* is strictly modern. Gertrude was later to claim for it that it was one of "the three novels written in this generation that are the important things written in this generation"—the others being Proust's *Remembrance of Things Past* and Joyce's *Ulysses*. Yet, her book lacks the carefully observed social history of Proust and the concise dramatic structure of Joyce. In an interview, in the last year of her life, she suggested that Joyce smelled of the museum, that he had "one hand in the past" and it was for that reason that Joyce was accepted and she was not. In her own work she said, "The newness and difference is fundamental."

But in a moment of reflection, in the same interview, she conceded: "Nobody enters into the mind of someone else, not even a husband and wife. You may touch, but you do not enter into each other's mind." That admission seems to relegate her odd characterological system, her attempt to divine the "bottom nature" of every conceivable human being, and the novel that housed it, to the status of a ruined enterprise. If *The Making of Americans* can make any claim to being a monument in the history of modern literature, it is as an architectural folly—something like the Güell Park of Antonio Gaudí or the Watts Towers of Simon Rodia.

IV

Ordinarily, each summer, Gertrude and Leo rented the Casa Ricci in Fiesole, near Florence. The villa was perched high on the hilltop overlooking the valley of the Arno with the domes and spires of Florence easily observable in the distance. But before the summer of 1908, Gertrude informed Alice that she and Leo would be taking a larger villa, the Villa Bardi, on the other side of Fiesole, with Michael and Sarah and young Allan. Therefore, Gertrude suggested, Alice and Harriet could rent the Casa Ricci. It was Gertrude's idea that she and Alice might spend the summer together, exploring the Tuscan countryside. She also wanted Alice to see Assisi, in nearby Umbria, one of her favorite spots in Italy. She was slowly initiating Alice into what was important in her own life.

Alice's long hot summer in Italy consisted largely of interminable walks in the company of Gertrude. Harriet was left to the Stein family and her own devices. Gertrude was an indefatigable hiker, striking off down country roads and up the hilly terrain with an easy, ponderous masculine stride. A late riser—she was still devoting nightly sessions to writing *The Making of Americans*—she had a habit of beginning her walks in the heat of the noonday sun. Her usual costume was a brown corduroy skirt and a pongee shirtwaist; in the stifling heat she sweated profusely, a fact that never deterred her. Alice, trying to keep up at a dignified pace, found the walks frequently intolerable. The heat was unbearable, and several times she was close to tears. Once she had no recourse but to step behind some bushes and discard her silk combination and stockings. When Gertrude grew weary, however, she simply flung herself down in the nearest field, bidding Alice to do the same. Lying on her back, Gertrude would stare up into the bright, cloudless glare of the sky.

They were, it seemed, in sainted territory. Nearly every village and hillside harbored its legends from that extraordinary flowering of sanctity among the Franciscan and Dominican orders during the thirteenth and fourteenth centuries. It was the country of Saint Dominic, Saint Bonaventure, Saint Clare, Saint Catherine of Siena. Gertrude had little interest in religion per se, but she had developed a lively interest in certain Catholic saints, notably Saint Teresa of Avila and Saint Francis of Assisi. She liked to make pilgrimage journeys to sites associated with them. Alice's devotions to the saints were less arduous and more practical. She had a distressing habit of losing articles of clothing or items of personal value. Whenever she visited churches, therefore, she made a point of putting money in the box before Saint Anthony of Padua, the patron saint for recovering lost articles. Michael Stein was to claim that if Alice were a general, she would never lose a battle, "only mislay it." At first Gertrude laughed at Alice's precautions, but later in life she recognized the need for them. When Alice was not with her, she would always make an offering to Saint Anthony on Alice's behalf.

As one of their pilgrimage jaunts, Alice recalled a long, steep climb up a mountain where, legend had it, Saint Francis and Saint Dominic had met for the first time. The road had been dry and dusty and the two women had arrived barefoot at the summit, sitting among the clouds, lunching on the sandwiches Alice had brought. The most grueling journey of the summer, however, and one that Gertrude had insisted upon, was a series of walks to Saint Francis's cathedral at Assisi. They journeyed, first, by train to Arezzo, then on to Gubbio and Perugia, where they put up overnight in a hotel in order to see the Fra

Angelicos in the local museum. At Perugia they sent one of their bags ahead to Assisi and another back to Fiesole and made their way on foot to the pilgrimage site. Along the way they encountered crowds of peasants from every region of Italy. Gertrude walked jauntily ahead, striking up conversations with one group of peasants after another. Alice thought the peasants "beautiful beyond words," but "malodorous if one caught nothing more than a whiff." She maintained her distance. The climb to the cathedral itself took several hours, and once there, Alice wearily went in to pray. Gertrude wandered off to inspect the Cimabue frescoes. Later, as planned, they joined Harriet at an inn in Assisi. Harriet had preferred to travel more conveniently by train and hired carriage.

At some point during their summer in Italy they seem to have journeyed north to Venice—perhaps accompanied by Harriet. Although neither Gertrude nor Alice recorded their impressions of the city of the doges, there is, in the Stein archives at Yale, a charming photograph of the pair, taken at the principal tourist spot, the piazza in front of Saint Mark's. Alice is standing, wistful and solemn, staring straight at the photographer, wearing the dark cotton batik dress that she wore on her jaunts with Gertrude. Gertrude stands massive and stalwart in her skirt and shirtwaist, wearing an impressive straw hat bedecked with large artificial pansies, one of her favorite flowers. They are ringed around by pigeons, Gertrude feeding two of them in her cupped hands. It is a striking vignette: two unusual tourists, posed in a happy moment in a celebrated spot.

In Florence that summer Gertrude had introduced Alice to Berenson and his wife, Mary, as well as Mary's brother Logan Pearsall Smith, then visiting the couple at Berenson's villa, I Tatti. She also took her to meet two women friends, Florence Blood and the Princess Ghyka, living in the Villa Gamberaia, at Settignano. The two women were in the process of restoring the villa's famous gardens with grottoes and water parterres. One day in June, Alice went to lunch to meet Dr. Claribel Cone and her sister Etta for the first time. Gertrude had not seen the sisters since they had embarked on their world tour in 1906. The luncheon had begun easily enough. The four women sat back, relaxed and casual in the bright summer light. Claribel and Etta were full of news about family affairs and mutual friends in Baltimore. Alice liked Dr. Claribel immediately, but found her sister less attractive as a person. Dr. Claribel, she decided, was "handsome and distinguished, Miss Etta not at all so." In the course of the meeting, Etta remarked that generally she could forgive but not forget an offense. Alice maintained that while she could forget, she could not forgive. She and Etta were to have a minor disagreement over which of them would do the honors in paying the bill. It was only a slight contretemps, but it remained in Alice's memory more than fifty years later, when she gave an account of it in *What Is Remembered*. In this case, it seems, Alice neither forgot nor forgave. She was to remain remarkably cool about Etta Cone. Perhaps she was jealous of Gertrude's earlier, intimate friendship with the younger Cone sister. In the end, Alice's response was to color Gertrude's attitude toward Etta as well.

Three Lives, which Etta Cone had so dutifully typed from Gertrude's longhand manuscript in the spring of 1906, had been a source of disappointment to Gertrude ever since. Leo's noncommittal response to the book had troubled her, and, as she had written to Mabel Weeks, at the time, she was uncertain whether it would interest "the great American public." Despite her misgivings about the reception of the book, she had sent the typescript to Hutchins Hapgood. In a later letter to Mabel Weeks, she had even been somewhat jaunty about *Three Lives:* "It will certainly make your hair curl with the complication and the tintinabulation of its style but I'm very fond of it, nothing will discourage me. I think it a noble combination of Swift and Matisse. I am now just starting a new one [*The Making of Americans*], now that the other has been once sent to Hutch, it does not seem to matter much to me whether it gets published or not." Her apparent indifference, however, does not fit the story of her persistent efforts to see *Three Lives* in print.

Hapgood, who was staying in Settignano when Gertrude sent him the manuscript, was an established writer and journalist, well connected in New York publishing circles. His wife, Neith Boyce, was also a successful writer. They were people whose opinions Gertrude valued. In April, 1906, Hapgood wrote her an enthusiastic letter about the book. "In the essentials," he said of the stories, "they seem to me extremely good—full of reality, truth, unconventionality. I am struck with their deep humanity, and with the really remarkable way you have of getting deep into human psychology. In this respect, the Negro story seemed to me wonderfully strong and true, a powerful picture of the relations between a man and a woman and the inevitable causes of their separation."

Hapgood voiced what was to become the accepted view of Gertrude's first published work, that the central and longest portion of the book, the love affair between Melanctha Herbert and Jeff Campbell, was a tour de force. But his enthusiasm was somewhat tempered because of Gertrude's unconventional writing style. He suggested she would have difficulties finding a publisher. "They lack all the minor qualities of art," Hapgood noted, "—construction, etc., etc. They often irritate me by the innumerable and often as it seems to me unnecessary repetitions; by your painstaking but often clumsy phraseology, by what seems sometimes almost an affectation of style." He feared she would have difficulties with publishers, partly for the "idiotic" but nonetheless real reason that the stories were "not the right length, and partly (and this the most important) because to get their real quality, patience and culture are demanded of the reader." Nevertheless, he offered to send her manuscript on to Pitts Duffield of Duffield & Co., a respectable New York publishing firm. Duffield was, in his opinion, "the most likely man to get into the quality of your work, that I know; and, if he likes it, he is less likely to allow strictly commercial reasons to interfere with his publishing it." Hapgood also offered to write Duffield "and call his attention to what I think the great excellence of your work."

Gertrude wrote Hapgood, asking him to send the manuscript on to the publisher. She then waited three months before hearing from him. In August, Duffield wrote, apologizing, first, for the lengthy delay in writing to her about the book:

But to report at last:—we hardly see our way clear to making you any offer of publication for "Three Histories" [Gertrude's original title]. The book is too unconventional, for one thing, and if I may say so, too literary. Where one person would be interested in your application of French methods to American low life, a hundred, ignorant of any sense of literary values, would see only another piece of realism; and realism nowadays doesn't go. This, at any rate, would be our unfavorable prognosis.

As a consolation, he offered to turn the manuscript over to a literary agent, Flora Holly, if Gertrude would cable him at the publisher's expense. Gertrude cabled the economical code word "Holly" that Duffield had suggested.

In January, 1907, in response to a query from Gertrude, Miss Holly finally wrote about her difficulties in getting around to Gertrude's manuscript. "I have been delayed in writing you," she informed Gertrude, "because I have been having trouble with my eyes and all reading was forbidden for a number of weeks." After complaining about the faintness of the typewriting, Miss Holly went on to say, "I doubt very much if I could find a publisher who would consider these three stories for book publication. They seem to me to be more character sketches than anything else, while the characters themselves would not appeal to a large audience." Miss Holly also took a dim view of possible magazine publication: "On the other hand, these stories, if taken separately would be too long for publication. Miss Roseboro is still with Mc-Clure's, and I will send the manuscript over there as you suggest, and if she is not interested I will notify you at once in order that you may advise me as to the further disposal of the material."

Gertrude had forwarded a note to Viola Roseboro, a reader at *Mc-Clure's* magazine whom she knew. Miss Roseboro, however, was unable to use the stories and sent the manuscript back to Miss Holly with a note for Gertrude. Miss Holly communicated the information to Gertrude, saying that Miss Roseboro had sent a "nice note," but failed to forward it. She also asked if Gertrude had any further suggestions. Gertrude answered, tartly, that she had "supposed it was the agent's business to do the suggesting." Miss Holly confessed that she could think of nothing further. Exasperated, Gertrude asked her to give the manuscript to Mabel Weeks. As she later told a friend, she had paid Miss Holly "five dollars for the privilege."

For more than a year, Mabel Weeks tried, but unsuccessfully, to place the book with a publisher. "Your manuscripts are in the hands of a reader for Macmillan," she wrote Gertrude in April, 1907—and when her resourcefulness failed, she turned the book over to May Bookstaver, then Mrs. Charles Knoblauch. It was a curious turn of events. In April, 1908, Mabel reported to Gertrude that May "doesn't in the least recognize herself in Melanctha, though she says that all those talks between Jeff and Melanctha are practically verbatim." For Gertrude's benefit, she also reported on May's husband. Mr. Knoblauch, she told Gertrude, "is what the American magazine story would call a 'man's man.'"

May Knoblauch finally placed the book with the Grafton Press, a New York publishing firm that specialized in limited editions published at the author's expense. In November, 1908, she wired Gertrude: "Grafton will publish six hundred sixty dollars shall I sign contract—Knoblauch." Discouraged, Gertrude agreed to the terms the house offered—1,000 printed copies, 500 bound copies, for the specified fee. Even then it was not the end of her problems. F. H. Hitchcock, the director of the Grafton Press, in sending her the galley proofs of the book in mid-January, 1909, noted, "My proof-readers report that there are some pretty bad slips in grammar, probably caused in the typewriting." He suggested that the author allow his firm to make the corrections—"We would make the charge, of course, as little as possible"—or that she use an editor in Paris whose work they had found entirely satisfactory, Alvin S. Sanborn, who lived at 61, rue Lepic. Gertrude ignored both offers, only to find Mr. Sanborn knocking at her door one day. Mr. Sanborn informed her that the publisher had thought she might be a foreigner, unfamiliar with the English language. Gertrude told him, in no uncertain terms, that she was an American, that she was thoroughly familiar with the English language, that the stories were written exactly as she had intended, and that they were to be printed exactly as written. She returned her corrected galleys to the Grafton Press.

Even there the matter did not end. Mr. Hitchcock wrote her again in April, saying that he had received her corrections and read through the proofs. At his request, Mrs. Knoblauch had kindly come to the office to explain Gertrude's position in the matter; the book would be printed as she wished. He did, however, make one suggestion that Gertrude adopted; he recommended that the title be changed from *Three Histories* to *Three Lives*. The former title seemed much too formal and the new title would avoid any confusion with the "real historical publications" on his list. He also suggested that an introduction by Mrs. Hapgood, already known to the reading public, would be a distinct advantage. When the book finally appeared, late in 1909, it carried no introduction, but blurbs by both Hutchins Hapgood and Neith Boyce were printed on the dust jacket.

"I want to say, frankly," Mr. Hitchcock had concluded his letter, "that I think you have written a very peculiar book and it will be a hard thing to make people take it seriously."

It was a refrain with which Gertrude was to become thoroughly familiar in her long career.

V

Alice had begun to make herself useful, even indispensable, at the rue de Fleurus. With the copybook volumes of *The Making of Americans* piling up, Gertrude was in need of a typist. She found a willing helper in her new friend from San Francisco. Alice agreed to take on the formidable task of transcribing Gertrude's bold and often illegible script, a task that was to develop into a lifetime occupation. She became so proficient at it, in fact, that there were times when she was the only person capable of reading Gertrude's handwriting—Gertrude, herself, being unable to decipher the words. To facilitate the work, Gertrude disposed of her ancient Blickensdoerfer and bought a new Smith-Premier, an object that, in its massive metal cover, figured prominently amid the clutter of the studio room. Ordinarily, Alice came in the morning, while Gertrude was still asleep after her night's work. She typed out the work of the previous day until Gertrude got up at noontime. Alice was to regard the years she devoted to transcribing *The Making of Americans* as a "very happy time" in her life. "It was like living history," she remembered. "I hoped it would go on forever."

Moreover, Gertrude had initiated Alice into the strange system of character analysis she was evolving while her novel was progressing. During their hours of companionship, sitting in the studio, walking in the Luxembourg Gardens, Gertrude and Alice would discuss the parade of characters who were beginning to figure in *The Making of Americans*. Gertrude would query Alice on her impressions of the friends, relatives, casual visitors to the studio who were to become frozen in the glacier-like progress of the novel. As part of her characterological analysis, Gertrude had teasingly designated Alice's type as that of an "old-maid mermaid," a characterization that Alice resented. The Freudian implications of the description suggest that Alice may have been suffering from sexual inhibitions, or inabilities, early in her relationship with Gertrude. But as Alice was to remark, somewhat archly, "By the time the buttercups were in bloom, the old-maid mermaid had gone into oblivion and I had been gathering wild violets." These flower-gathering sessions were literal. By springtime Gertrude and Alice had become constant companions, and the pair would venture out to the forest of Saint-Germain to pick hyacinths and forget-me-nots and lilies of the valley.

Even before she moved into the rue de Fleurus, Alice was to provide a good many services toward Gertrude's general comfort. Gertrude had developed a hankering for American cooking. Alice agreed that on Sunday, Hélène's day off, she would prepare the evening meals. Although she maintained that she was, in the beginning, a diffident cook, she began preparing chicken fricassee, corn bread, apple and lemon pies for Gertrude's approval. For their first Thanksgiving dinner together, Gertrude decided that they must have a roast turkey, but she was unable to make up her mind whether the stuffing should be made with mushrooms, chestnuts, or oysters. Alice concocted a version that included all three: It became standard fare for holiday feasts thereafter.

One evening, while Alice was preparing supper, Gertrude marched into the kitchen to tell her that she must stop whatever she was doing. Gertrude had just written something that she wanted Alice to read. It was a little prose vignette, a kind of happy inspiration that had detached itself from the torrential prose of *The Making of Americans*. Alice was reluctant, concerned that the supper would be spoiled. She liked her food served piping hot, while Gertrude did not. But they had arrived at an agreement—one measure of Gertrude's affection for her—that Alice could serve the meals as hot as she liked while Gertrude would wait for her plate to cool. On this occasion, however, Alice took the meal off the stove and dutifully followed Gertrude into the dining room, where she sat down to read.

The story began with a description of an indecisive young man, Barnes Colhard, who sounded much like Alice's brother, and of his father, who sounded even more like Ferdinand Toklas. It then went on to describe a dissatisfied young woman named Ada, who felt herself trapped in an unrewarding family situation. Ada's mother had died, and she was now keeping house for her father and her brother. Alice read the description of Ada: "She had been a very good daughter to her mother. She and her mother had always told very pretty stories to each other. Many old men loved to hear her tell these stories to her mother. Every one who ever knew her mother liked her mother. Many were sorry later that not every one liked the daughter. Many did like the daughter but not every one as every one had liked the mother. The daughter was charming inside in her, it did not show outside in her to every one, it certainly did to some." Alice began to feel hurt; she thought Gertrude was making fun of her.

The prose ran on in sonorous repetitions of words and phrases. There was an account of an inheritance from Ada's grandfather and of how Ada had decided to move away from her family, of how her father waited for her return and how Ada wrote "tender letters" to him but never went back. In the final paragraph the portrait of Ada turned into an idyll of sorts. Ada had met a genderless "some one," a storyteller, too, and ostensibly a writer, who loved Ada and listened patiently to her charming stories:

That one who was loving was almost always listening. That one who was loving was telling about being one then listening. That one being loving was then telling stories having a beginning and a middle and an ending.

The "portrait" ended on a note of affection and bliss: "Trembling was all living, living was all loving, some one was then the other one. Certainly this one was loving this Ada then. And certainly Ada all her living then was happier in living than any one else who ever could, who was, who is, who ever will be living."

It was, in effect, a love poem in which Gertrude declared both her love for Alice and her notion of the benevolent effect her love had had upon Alice's previously unsettled emotional life. In Gertrude's view, the happiness of Ada-Alice stretched far away into the future.

The reticence with which Gertrude's love affair with Alice Toklas has been treated in the past seems unnecessary now. Friends, even enemies, writing about the pair in memoirs and autobiographies, tended to treat it as a privileged subject. Earlier biographers, writing, it is true, while Alice Toklas was still alive and had contributed to their researches, were discreet. It was enough that Alice should be described as a dedicated friend, companion, and secretary for forty years, leaving the reader to infer the nature of the relationship. That it was in the nature of a marriage, an odd marriage that, in fact, proved more durable and productive than many of the more orthodox marriages among the members of their immediate circle, seems clear. Richard Bridgman, in his critical study, *Gertrude Stein in Pieces,* published in 1970, has discussed the nature of the relationship openly, on the basis of the abundance of the allusions in Gertrude's later writings in which she refers to herself and Alice in the conventional terms of husband and wife: "She was born in California and he was born in Allegheny Pennsylvania," for example. And Leon Katz, in revealing the Lesbian relationship that served as the basis for *Q.E.D.*, has shed light on some of the obscuring tendencies of her style.

Ernest Hemingway, who had a notably bitter falling-out with Gertrude, in later years, was among the first to hint at the subject—but only obliquely. Writing an appreciation on Joan Miró's painting *The Farm*, a picture that he had once owned, Hemingway noted that it had taken the artist nine months to paint his picture, the normal human period of gestation. He clearly had Gertrude in mind when he went on to state that "a woman who isn't a woman can usually write her autobiography in a third of that time." It was his reply, nursed in bitterness, to Gertrude's demeaning portrait of him in *The Autobiography of Alice B. Toklas*, in which she charged that Hemingway was, after all, a bit "yellow." In an ironic way, Hemingway's jibe had echoed a remark that Gertrude had voiced through Adele, the heroine of *Q.E.D.* Exasperated by a display of feminine insincerity between her shipboard companions Mabel Neathe and Helen Thomas, Adele blurts out, "I always did thank God I wasn't born a woman."

Like most loving couples, Gertrude and Alice fell into the habit of using pet names with each other: Gertrude was "Lovey" and Alice was "Pussy." In later years, long confirmed in the habit, they would address each other that way, even in the company of comparative strangers, such as the American GI's who crowded into their apartment after World War II.

VI

The portrait of Ada was to open up an important new vein in Gertrude's writing, one that occupied her for many years thereafter. With a burst of creative enthusiasm, she began writing word portraits of friends, relations, and the notables of her salon. She attempted pairs and groups of people: the Cone sisters in "Two Women," Ethel Mars and Maud Hunt Squire, two minor painters who frequented the rue de Fleurus, in "Miss Furr and Miss Skeene." She went on to attempt "portraits" of large groups of people and incidents she had witnessed in her shopping tours of the Parisian department stores—"Bon Marché Weather," "Flirting at the Bon Marché," "*Aux Galeries Lafayette.*" Though more succinct and individualized, her early portraits, such as "Ada," continued on with the slow-moving, repetitive sentence structure she had developed for *The Making of Americans*. When she attempted prolonged analyses of large groups of people, as she did in *Two: Gertrude Stein and Her Brother*, *Many Many Women*, and *A Long Gay Book*, the pieces went on interminably, freighted with monotonous repetitions, becoming book-length studies largely, it seems, through the inertia of the daily writing stint. Eventually she dispensed with any attempts at narrative action and description, qualities that

made "Ada" and her earlier portraits at least comprehensible to the
reader. Later she tried very short, abstract portraits of no more than
three or four lines, like her 1912 portrait of "Guillaume Apollinaire":

Give known or pin ware.
Fancy teeth, gas strips.
Elbow elect, sour stout pore, pore caesar, pour state at.
Leave eye lessons I. Leave I. Lessons. I. Leave I lessons, I

By then, the language had been purged of most of its associational
values, had become like a Cubist painting, with only hints and guesses
of the subject that lay behind her disjunctive style. She moved into new
and radical experiments with syntax and punctuation, attempted novel
forms of drama, as well. The possibilities of the genre lay all before her,
and with dogged persistence, she was to explore them all, well into the
twenties and thirties.

"Two Women," her portrait of Claribel and Etta Cone, is typical
of her early method. It appears to have been written some time after
her portrait of Alice. There is very little narrative incident in the
piece and only the barest physical description of the subjects. The names
that Gertrude eventually chose for Claribel and Etta are significant.
After having considered Bertha for Claribel, she finally chose the name
Martha—the name she had enlisted for herself in *The Making of
Americans*. And for Etta she chose Ada—the name she had already assigned to Alice. The choices represented a possibly conscious recognition that there was a similarity between the authoritative Claribel's relationship with her subservient sister and Gertrude's relationship to
Alice. The portrait, however, describes the two sisters in only general
terms: Martha as the dominant and aggressive one; Ada, characterized
by passive receptivity.

She did some things. She did go on being living. She was more something
than any other one. She did some things. She went on being living. She
did this thing, she went on being living.
   The younger one did some things. She was receiving some things more
than any other one. She went on receiving them. She went on being living.
She received this thing, she went on being living. She did some things.
She did go on being living.

The portrait rambles on in this fashion for several pages—it is one of
Gertrude's longer exercises in the genre—but it gives few particulars.
The sisters are described as "rich ones"; Martha-Claribel is "a person
of some distinction"; Ada, we are told, had been "suffering and she was
suffering in there being a connection between tender feeling and listening, and between liking and listening," a malady that seems to imply

that Etta experienced hurt feelings when others did not take her seriously and listen to her—an ailment that the self-centered Claribel did not suffer from at all. But it is difficult, even impossible, to recognize in the bland repetitions and the generalized talk any very sharp features of the subjects. These can be found more readily in the notes Gertrude made in the original autograph manuscript. In her longer portraits, apparently when she broke off in the course of writing, Gertrude left notes for herself on what to take up when she resumed. One of the notes about "Two Women" reads:

Tell about the others connected with them, their duties and how they did them, what effort they had when they were traveling, how they quarreled, how they spent money, how they each had what they wanted [Martha] when she wanted it, Ada when she was going to want it. Stinginess, buying scarves. Heaping things, patting hair, a little crazy, dress-making scenes, friends of each. Pleasing anybody. Etta and no father no mother. Sex in both.

"Sex in both"—the absence of such particulars in the finished portrait offers a revealing clue to what the portraits were intended to make plain while the odd, generalizing tendencies of the writing were martialed to disguise it.

This was not true of all the earlier portraits. Helen Furr and Georgine Skeene, "that touching pair of left-hand gloves," as the critic Edmund Wilson once referred to them, are depicted in less guarded terms in the double portrait "Miss Furr and Miss Skeene." The originals of the portrait were Miss Mars and Miss Squire, two midwesterners with cultural ambitions—they both dabbled in watercolors—who had arrived in Paris, early in the century, somewhat mousy, tailored, and prim. Within a year they were habitués of the local cafés. Miss Mars had dyed her hair flaming orange, and both appeared in public so heavily made up their faces had the appearances of masks. Alice had met Miss Mars at one of the Saturday evenings at the rue de Fleurus, and they had discussed make-up together—it was, then, a new fashion—classifying the women present according to types: Fernande was obviously *femme decorative*, while Madame Matisse, with more difficulty, was assigned *femme intérieure*.

In the portrait, Helen Furr is described as a "pleasant woman," who has left her husband and moved away to another city to live with Georgine Skeene. Both women are "cultivating their voices." While they are often seen sitting in the company of many "heavy and dark men," the portrait hints at other inclinations:

They were both gay there, they were regularly working there both of them cultivating their voices there, they were both gay there. Georgine Skeene was gay there and she was regular, regular in being gay, regular in not being gay, regular in being a gay one who was one not being gay longer than was needed to be one being quite a gay one.

It is difficult to know whether the term "gay" had, then, the connotation that it has recently acquired, but the persistent use of it in the portrait suggests a way of life rather than a transient emotion. It was on the basis of the portrait of "Miss Furr and Miss Skeene," as well as other examples of Gertrude Stein's writings, that Wilson, in 1951, came to the significant conclusion, about Gertrude's writings, "that the vagueness that began to blur it from about 1910 on and the masking by unexplained metaphors that later made it seem opaque, though partly the result of an effort to emulate modern painting, were partly also due to a need imposed by the problem of writing about relationships between women of a kind that the standards of the era would not have allowed her to describe more explicitly. It seemed obvious that her queer little portraits and her mischievously baffling prose-poems did often deal with subjects of this sort."

Wilson, however, later felt that he may have exaggerated "the Lesbian aspect of Gertrude Stein's obscurity." Reading *Two: Gertrude Stein and Her Brother*, the posthumously published volume of word portraits that Gertrude had written between 1908 and 1912, and which Yale issued in 1951, Wilson confessed that he had found little to substantiate his theory: "One feels rather that the ruminative dimness is the result of an increasing remoteness in her personal relationships." He apparently overlooked the portrait "Men," included in that volume, a portrait that clearly describes a homosexual situation involving three men.

"Men" begins explicitly:

Sometimes men are kissing. Men are sometimes kissing and sometimes drinking. Men are sometimes kissing one another and sometimes then there are three of them and one of them is talking and two of them are kissing and both of them, both of the two of them who are kissing, are having their eyes large then with their being tears in them.

But, thereafter, it becomes difficult to thread one's way through the boozy episode. Gertrude's habit of describing each of the subjects with the generalized "one" makes it problematic in keeping each of the subjects straight. Moreover, the portrait skips ahead in time to describe later encounters among the three men. Nevertheless, a careful reading of the portrait does yield some elements of a story line. During the kissing episode, for example, a fight develops between the two men who have been kissing. One man knocks the other down. This display of aggression has a curious psychological effect; the two become lovers. The man who was the aggressor is described:

One of them is then large with this thing quite large with having tears on him. This one is quite large then and has been winning in having another one knocked down by him. He is large then and kissing the other one then and is certain then that the other one is one to hear everything.

The man who has been knocked down, it is suggested, has been initiated into homosexuality as a result of the fight:

The one who had been knocked down in being one coming to be loving and kissing and drinking might have knocked down the one who had knocked him down then. He might have knocked down the one who knocked him down, and then he loved him and he kissed him, and they told then that they both then knew everything. He might have knocked down the one who knocked him down and he would then not have been loving and kissing and knowing then everything.

There has been, it appears, a break between the winner of the fight and the third member of the trio. The "third one," we are told, is someone the man who won the fight "would not then have near him." The third man is described, cryptically, as someone who "is filling something." The assailant of the story appears to have gained some psychological advantage from the break; he becomes "a large one from not wanting a meeting with the one who was then filling something." Still, at some point in time, all three men have been intimately involved:

Each one of the three of them was such a one, one drinking and talking and loving. Each one of them, each one of the three of them had been one drinking with the other one loving one of the three of them, loving two of the three of them, loving all of the three of them, kissing one of them, crying some then. Each one of the three of them were such ones.

Their later meetings are inconclusive. The first man, the winner of the fight, seems to have a change of heart, is "just then a large one in being one not needing to be loving any one he had been knowing; who did want to be one not liking kissing, not liking any one who had been one." The man who was knocked down "lost that thing, he had lost being one liking that one being a large one from kissing and crying." The portrait ends with Gertrude's attempt to describe, in none-too-explicit terms, what it meant to each of them "in being such a one."

The sexual ambiguities of the Stein circle were apparent. Picasso once commented on the "virginal" quality of the Americans who visited the rue de Fleurus. "They are not men, they are not women, they are americans," he would say of them. There was, Gertrude acknowledged, "a type of american art student, male, that used very much to afflict" Picasso. His usual comment would be "No it is not he who will make the future glory of America." Both Gertrude and Leo, it appears, were tolerant about the unorthodox sexual habits of the expatriates who visited their studio. One gets some notion of the sexual versatility of their friends from the fact that the original title of "Men," which she had scrawled across the cover of the copybook manuscript, was "Hutch and David and Sterne." Hutchins Hapgood was, of course, married to Neith Boyce at the time, and Sterne had had a recent and passionate affair with Alla Nazimova, the actress. The David of the portrait was David Edstrom, a tall, good-looking Swedish sculptor who was married to the daughter of a Swedish magistrate. Edstrom and his wife did not live together. Gertrude, who had met Mrs. Edstrom in Florence, found her an odd intellectual type who wore men's hats and boots. Alice met Edstrom in Paris not long after she had arrived. The sculptor seems to have carried on a mild flirtation with her traveling companion, Harriet Levy. Alice thought him a bit "silly," but admitted to a certain affection for him. Gertrude's notes in the original manuscript version of "Men" reveal that it had been Edstrom who had knocked down Sterne.

That Gertrude and Leo served as mother- and father-confessor in the affairs of their friends seems indicated by one of Leo's recollections in *Journey into Self*. He recalled a quarrel that Hapgood and Edstrom had had in Florence. Leo was in Paris at the time, but Edstrom had come to Paris and had told him about it. Leo wrote to Hapgood, saying that it would be better if they did not discuss Edstrom, since he tended to agree with Edstrom's point of view. Hapgood replied by saying that in that event, he wouldn't bother to see Leo when he came to Paris. Leo relented and agreed to discuss the matter. When Hapgood arrived in Paris, Leo visited him in his hotel and heard Hapgood's side of the story. Leo concluded that although the facts in both cases were identical, he still tended to believe in "Edstrom's interpretations" and told Hapgood so. As a consolation, Leo then said, "Come home to lunch and Gertrude and you can begin to talk over the matter for the next month or two," which, he reported, is exactly what Hapgood and Gertrude did. Leo's point was that Gertrude had a large appetite for gossip, while he liked very little of it unless it was "intrinsically entertaining." But it was clearly more than gossip for Gertrude; it was the stuff of which her word portraits were made.

Long after Gertrude's invention of the genre, in a lecture, "Portraits and Repetition," which she delivered to American audiences in the mid-thirties, Gertrude explained the motivating force behind her word portraits:

I had to find out what it was inside any one, and by any one I mean every one I had to find out inside every one what was in them that was intrinsically exciting and I had to find out not by what they said not by what they did not by how much or how little they resembled any other one but I had to find it out by the intensity of movement that there was inside in any one of them.

It was a strange, crabbed, obstinate experiment for a writer to attempt, and it effectively consigned much of her writing to the status of closet literature. The phrase is applicable quite literally, for the repository for the piles of copybook manuscripts of her puzzling word portraits and prose poems was the large, dark Henri IV cabinet that stood in the studio room. For years the mounting pile of manuscripts served as a nagging reminder of her failure to find either willing publishers or a responsive audience for her work.

CHAPTER SIX

Couples

I

No event during the first years of Gertrude and Alice's friendship was to assume such symbolic importance as the Rousseau banquet. It became the legendary fete of that era of high spirits and radical ventures, a kind of serio-comic celebration of the new and the absurd. And no event was better calculated to confirm Leo Stein's theory that history was a barely creditable discipline dealing in psychologically motivated falsehoods and misstatements of fact. That the banquet did take place —on some still-undetermined day in the late summer or fall of 1908—in Picasso's Bateau Lavoir studio are the two incontrovertible facts. Beyond that the accounts of those who witnessed the affair differ in most respects. Even the occasion for the banquet is not beyond contention. Supposedly it had been prompted by Picasso's purchase of a Rousseau painting. He had come across the picture, a portrait of a woman, in a shop on the rue des Martyrs. The dealer offered it to him for five francs, saying that the canvas could be painted over. Picasso bought it immediately; he called it "one of the most truthful of all French psychological portraits." According to Fernande Olivier, the banquet was entirely Picasso's idea; he had mounted it at his own expense in honor of the aged and gentle Rousseau.

But Leo Stein, an ardent investigator of first causes and first principles, maintained that it was he who had been the prime mover of the event:

One day I had gone to see Picasso, who was not at home. While I was talking with Fernande, Rousseau came in to rest for a moment, for he had been giving a violin lesson in the neighboring Rue Lepic. As I had never heard him, I asked him to play, but he excused himself: he was tired, and the day was hot. Then Fernande said, "Monsieur Rousseau, you must come to dinner soon and play for us and a few friends." Rousseau said he would be delighted, whereon Fernande added, "Let's not leave it at some time; make it a week from Saturday, and I'll ask the Steins, and Braque and Apollinaire and Marie Laurencin." That was agreed to, but when the news got around, so many others wanted to come that the dinner was changed to a picnic supper, famous through all the world as the Banquet Rousseau. Great oaks from little acorns grow. If I had not that drowsy summer afternoon asked Rousseau to play, there would have been no banquet and no post-fabricated explanations to account for it.

Gertrude's "post-fabricated" account, for it was her version, included in *The Autobiography*, which had aroused Leo's antagonism, had been published twenty-five years after the event. Vividly written, it was the first account of the affair in English: Maurice Raynal, another of the guests, had written a commemorative essay on the banquet for a special Rousseau issue of Apollinaire's short-lived publication, *Les Soirées de Paris*, in January, 1914; and Fernande Olivier's account of it, in *Picasso et ses Amis*, appeared in the same year as Gertrude's, that is, in 1933. Some measure of Gertrude's skill as a publicist is indicated by the fact that nearly every reviewer of her best-selling memoir mentioned her description of the banquet. She had taken an improvised party and propelled it into legendary status as a symbol of the freewheeling bohemian life of Paris in the decade before World War I. Moreover, her book, and her recollections of the banquet, sparked a lively controversy, one of the indispensable conditions for making an event famous. For a special supplement of *transition*, in 1935, Matisse, Tristan Tzara, Eugene and Maria Jolas, Braque, and the poet André Salmon—the last two having been guests at the banquet—produced a "Testimony Against Gertrude Stein," complaining against her falsifications and her general lack of comprehension.

According to Gertrude's version, as witnessed through the eyes of Alice Toklas, Apollinaire had also played an important role in the event: "It was Guillaume Apollinaire, as I remember, who knowing Rousseau very well had induced him to promise to come and was to bring him and everybody was to write poetry and songs and it was to be very rigolo, a favorite Montmartre word meaning a jokeful amusement." She also recalled that the banquet had taken place in the late fall, because Alice had bought her first winter Paris hat, a large black velvet hat trimmed with brilliant yellow feathers. The hat was to figure notably in the proceedings.

Gertrude's account continued: She, Alice, Leo, and Harriet Levy had gathered earlier in the evening at a café at the bottom of the hill below Picasso's studio. A number of the guests had already assembled there, several of them having progressed through many rounds of *apéritifs*. In the absense of Apollinaire, who had gone to fetch Rousseau, Marie Laurencin, unused to drinking, had become very drunk. She was revolving around in an aimless, exotic dance, her arms flailing about in the air. These preliminary festivities were suddenly interrupted when Fernande broke in, angrily, saying that Félix Potin, the caterer, had not delivered the food for the meal. Alice, in her element, taking charge of an emergency, rushed off with Fernande to see if it were possible to telephone Potin's—but to no avail, the store was closing and they would not deliver. The two proceeded through the neighborhood, buying whatever was necessary to supplement the huge amount of *riz à la Valenciennes* Fernande had begun to prepare. As they trudged up the hill to the studio, they passed the other guests making a slow ascent. Gertrude and Leo were alternately pushing and pulling the drunken Marie.

At the Bateau Lavoir, the studio of Jacques Vaillant, a young artist resident, had been commandeered for a ladies' coatroom, while the studio of Max Jacob—who, according to Gertrude, had had a recent spat with Picasso and did not attend the banquet—was to serve as the men's coatroom. Alice deposited her coat and her new hat in Vaillant's studio and proceeded to help Fernande. In Picasso's studio an improvised table made from planks of wood laid on carpenters' trestles occupied much of the room. Benches had been clustered around it, and at the place of honor the newly acquired Rousseau painting was hanging, draped in flags and wreaths.

The guests began to arrive. Fernande, however, barred the way: Marie Laurencin, she declared, was too drunk and would spoil the seriousness of the occasion. Gertrude, arguing both in French and English, said that she would be "hanged" if after all the work of pushing Marie up the hill she was going to allow her efforts to be wasted. Picasso, who had been hovering behind Fernande, finally asserted himself. Marie was allowed to take her place at the banquet table.

No sooner had the guests settled down—the Steins, Braque, the Pichots, Salmon, Raynal, the poet Maurice Cremnitz, and the momentarily becalmed Marie Laurencin—than Apollinaire arrived with the guest of honor. There was a wild burst of applause: Rousseau, shy, "a little small colourless frenchman with a little beard, like any number of frenchmen one saw everywhere," was dwarfed by Apollinaire. The guests were served up liberal quantities of Fernande's rice and liberal quantities of wine. But as the dinner started, the previously dormant Marie Laurencin suddenly erupted into wild cries. Apollinaire took her downstairs for a talking to. After a few moments she returned sober and slightly bruised.

It was now time for the testimonials. Apollinaire began with a gracefully rhymed homage, citing Rousseau's altogether fictional service with the army in Mexico as the inspiration for his exotic landscapes. He went on to link the names of the painter-host and painter-guest in rhyme:

Nous sommes réunis pour célébrer ta gloire,
Ces vins qu'en ton honneur nous verse Picasso,
Buvons–les donc, puisque c'est l'heure de les boire
En criant tous en choeur: "Vive! Vive Rousseau!"

We are gathered to celebrate your fame,
And so let us drink the wine Picasso is pouring
To honor you, for it is time to drink it
Crying all in chorus, "Long live! Long live Rousseau!"

The guests shouted out the rousing refrain *"Vive! Vive Rousseau!"* The poems and speeches, the elaborate testimonials flowed on as steadily as the wine. Then André Salmon leaped up on the shaky table to declaim his homage. He promptly followed this by grabbing up a full glass of wine and drinking it down, then went suddenly "off his head" and began to fight. Leo moved to protect the fragile Rousseau and his violin, while the others dragged Salmon to the front studio. Dead drunk, he went to sleep peaceably among the ladies' hats and coats.

The party restored to calm, it took on the aspects of a pleasant musicale. Marie Laurencin, now sober, sang old Norman songs. Pichot danced some Spanish dances. Rousseau, "blissful and gentle," played several works of his own composition. Apollinaire approached Alice and Harriet Levy, asking them to sing a few songs of the red Indians— a request with which, unfortunately, they could not comply.

At three in the morning the banquet finally broke up. When the ladies went to the cloakroom, they found Salmon still asleep. Next to him were the chewed-up remains of a box of matches, a telegram, and the yellow *fantaisie* from Alice's hat. Awakened, the poet was apparently sober and perfectly charming. But, while Leo and Gertrude were helping Le Douanier into a cab—they took him home together with Harriet and Alice—Salmon rushed past them and disappeared down the hill with a blood-curdling scream.

In Fernande's version the banquet had progressed along no less eventful, but somewhat different lines. She recalled that there were about thirty guests, Max Jacob among them, and that the diners were already assembled in the studio when she realized that the caterer was not going to deliver the meal. (It arrived, in fact, at noon on the following day, when the studio was in complete disorder.) While Fernande set out in search of additional food in the local bakeries and restaurants, several of the guests returned to the bar for more *apéritifs* and proceeded to get even drunker. When they returned, the festivities began. Marie Laurencin was very drunk indeed and promptly demonstrated her condition by falling into a tray of jam tarts that had been placed on the sofa. Her hands and dress covered with the sticky jam, she started around the room, embracing everyone in sight until Apollinaire, in the course of a highly vocal argument with her, packed her off to her mother's.

Throughout the seemingly interminable homages and drunken tributes, the gentle Rousseau—according to Fernande's account—listened dreamily while wax, dripping from one of the Chinese paper lanterns strung around the studio, formed a little conical cap on his head. He was aroused from this trancelike state only when one of the lanterns caught fire and there was a flurry of excitement.

It seemed to Fernande that everyone in the neighborhood, drawn by the boisterous sounds of festivity, descended upon the party. Groups of hungry neighbors circulated around the room, stuffing their pockets with *petits fours* even under the hostess's glaring eyes. Fernande did not mention—though Gertrude had—the arrival of Frédé, the proprietor of the neighboring Lapin Agile, who wandered in, accompanied by his constant companion, a donkey named Lolo. If Alice and Gertrude remained convinced that it was Salmon who had eaten Alice's hat, there was, in all probability, a more likely culprit. Fernande, in her memoir, had previously noted the donkey's voracious appetite and queer tastes. On one of its visits to the studio, the animal had eaten a package of tobacco and two scarves. The meal of a telegram, a box of matches, and part of a hat sounds suspiciously like Lolo's.

Fernande also mentioned two or three American couples, apparently in evening clothes, who stood out in the crowd of less showily dressed Montmartre bohemians. They appeared to be having difficulty keeping straight faces as the evening progressed. Fernande felt that it was their presence that goaded Salmon and Cremnitz, late in the evening, into chewing up a bar of soap and frothing at the mouth in a mad display of delirium tremens.

To Fernande, it seemed that most of the guests on that legendary evening had taken the whole affair as a lively joke on the gullible Rousseau. But she and Picasso had intended it as a sincere tribute. She was quite touched, therefore, when the old man, taking it all on faith as a recognition of his genius, sent Picasso a sweet and affectionate letter of thanks.

André Salmon's version of the Rousseau banquet, given in his 1956 memoir, *Souvenirs sans fin*, is chiefly a rebuttal of Raynal's "Ubuesque" account in Apollinaire's magazine. Apollinaire, Salmon thought, must have passed over Raynal's farcical account, with its glaring errors, without regard for its dangers for future historians. Salmon thought it a "gross" mistake, a slur upon Picasso's honor and Fernande's resourcefulness, to suggest, as Raynal had, that the catered meal had never arrived. To begin with, there was no caterer at all. The slender means and the contributions of the assembled guests would not, it seems, have allowed such an extravagance. The food had been bought from the local victualers along the rue Ravignan and rue Lepic. Salmon seems to have overlooked or forgotten about Fernande's earlier crisis with the caterer. The poet was also disturbed by Raynal's lively sketch of Apollinaire sitting calmly at a corner of the table, in the midst of all the hubbub, catching up on his two-month-old correspondence and incidentally writing out his "tribute" to Rousseau. Salmon pointed out that Apollinaire had written his homage earlier in the afternoon in his own apartment.

In his lengthy chapter *"Le Douanier Rousseau Dine Chez Picasso,"* Salmon also takes Gertrude to task for the inaccuracies of her account. Rousseau, he maintained, went home around midnight, put into a cab by Picasso. The events, he claimed, that Gertrude related as happening during the banquet had really taken place during the frolics after Rousseau's departure. He expressed surprise that Gertrude, admirably sober throughout the affair, should have "coldly" described "the terrifying spectacle of an attack of *delirium tremens*" that he and Jacques Vaillant had so carefully staged. In his haste to correct the mistakes of others, Salmon added a few of his own. Coldly or otherwise, Gertrude hadn't mentioned delirium tremens at all—only that Salmon (with no mention of Vaillant) had gotten extremely drunk, "went off his head," and started a fight. It was Fernande Olivier who supplied the details of the delirium tremens, down to the fake frothing at the mouth.

In his *transition* rebuttal, Salmon admitted that he had only once visited the Steins at the rue de Fleurus. On the strength of that one visit, apparently, he created, in his later memoir, a picture of the Steins during a typical Saturday-evening at home. It is an odd picture: Leo holds forth in the large studio room surrounded by the pictures of the artists he has discovered. Gertrude holds herself aloof from this gathering, awaiting the "respectful homages" of her guests in a "little boudoir" decorated with the works of "her choice"—the Renoirs that were, actually, Leo's treasures. Salmon cites the Renoirs, however, as evidence of Gertrude's conservative tastes. It took no audacity, he maintained, to "discover" Renoir in the years between 1905 and 1908.

"It is evident," Salmon noted in his earlier *transition* attack, "that Miss Stein understood little of the tendency we all had, Apollinaire, Max Jacob, myself and the others, to frequently play a rather burlesque role. We made continual fun of everything." Of Gertrude's comic account of the Rousseau banquet, he concluded, "And what confusion. What incomprehension of an epoch! Fortunately there are others who have described it better."

Such was the Rousseau banquet in all its lovely contradictions. It seems almost a superb fiction, one of the marvelous inventions of that extraordinary decade.

II

Now that Alice was spending much of her time at the rue de Fleurus, her living arrangements with Harriet were becoming complicated and bothersome. She and Harriet, after their first summer in Italy, had taken a small apartment at 75, rue Notre Dame des Champs. It consisted of four sunny rooms and a kitchen, and they furnished it in the Stein manner with items of Renaissance furniture picked up in Florence. They also engaged a servant—or a series of servants. The first, Célestine, proved to be no cook at all; the second, Maria Lasgourges, a Basque woman, was "a treasure, an excellent cook, resourceful and experienced." But the services of Maria and her "unfailingly delicious food" lasted only until the spring, when she decided to retire. She was replaced by another Maria—Maria Entz—who had, according to Alice, "all the Swiss virtues and limitations." She was "clean, hard-working and honest," but her cooking was indifferent. She liked to prepare dishes in which cheese and chocolate were the main ingredients. Alice, who was to measure out her life in servants, was developing that discerning eye for the peculiarities of household help that was to keep 27, rue de Fleurus running smoothly for years.

When Alice began to spend not only most of her days with Gertrude but also many of her evenings as well, Harriet became plainly disapproving. She thought it dangerous and improper for Alice to be returning late at night without an escort. On most occasions, Alice's nightly travels were unadventurous, but one evening, not long after the

Rousseau banquet, she was disturbed by the sound of footsteps following behind her. As she hurried along the deserted street, the footsteps
seemed to be overtaking her. She heard a voice calling, "Mademoiselle,
Mademoiselle." Outraged, Alice turned—only to discover old Rousseau
hurrying after her. The painter lectured her on the inadvisability of a
woman's traveling about alone on the streets after dark. He insisted on
taking her to her door. It may have been more than gallantry on Rousseau's part. One Saturday evening at the rue de Fleurus, he confided
to Alice that she bore a striking resemblance to his long-dead wife,
Clémence.

Throughout that winter, Alice was drawn into the management of
two households—the apartment on the rue Notre Dame des Champs
and the pavilion on the rue de Fleurus. At Gertrude's, she welcomed
guests at the door and helped to entertain them. She paid attention,
too, to the daily menus, but tactfully avoided intruding too far into
Hélène's domain. Hélène, an old-fashioned servant, thought it out of
place for a lady to concern herself too much with the kitchen. Alice's
morning activity consisted of typing up the preceding day's sheaf of
Gertrude's manuscript. In the afternoons she and Gertrude went walking or window-shopping or visited friends. Their evenings together were
often devoted to long conversations on the progress of Gertrude's writing. On occasion, Leo availed himself of Alice's secretarial skills, asking
her to type up various projects, such as a series of notes on education
he wanted to send Mabel Weeks.

Three Lives was published in the summer of 1909. Gertrude seems to
have forgotten about the publication date—July 30. She and Alice were
staying then at the Villa Bardi in Fiesole. But she was reminded of it
when an old Boston friend, Thomas Whittemore, the later discoverer
of the mosaics in the Hagia Sophia, presented her with a handsome
bouquet in honor of the occasion. From Le Trayas, on the French
Riviera, where the Michael Steins were spending the summer, Sally
offered some mild encouragement. On August 7 she wrote Gertrude
that she had "put in the afternoon reading Anna and Melanctha," and
found that "they read along very well."

In the fall, when they had returned to Paris, Alice began to busy
herself with the promotion of the book as earnestly as if it had been
her own. Gertrude was anxious to have the book reach a few notable
writers. The pair enlisted the services of Emily Dawson, a Quaker relative of the Berensons who lived in London, asking her to forward
copies to H. G. Wells, Shaw, Galsworthy, and Arnold Bennett. Miss
Dawson, whom they had met in Florence, was evidently flustered by
the commission. She wrote that she had been unsuccessful in persuad-

ing some "discriminating & clever" English friends to write special covering letters to Gertrude's "4 Olympians." After Christmas, she promised, she could write the letters herself.

There were certain comic aspects to Gertrude and Alice's early efforts at promotion, but they were to become a good deal more expert as the years passed. Only Wells acknowledged receiving the book—and then, more than three years after publication: They seem to have had difficulty in locating the English novelist. Wells admitted that, at first, he had been "repelled" by Gertrude's "extraordinary style," and that he had put the book aside. "It is only in the last week I have read it," he wrote her in January, 1913. "I read it with a deepening pleasure & admiration. I'm very grateful indeed to you for sending it to me & I shall watch for your name again very curiously & eagerly." Gertrude treasured Wells's letter and developed a habit of referring to his endorsement whenever she wanted to convince others of the seriousness of her writing. She may also, during this time, have tried to get a copy of *Three Lives* to Henry James. Among the Stein papers at Yale, there is an undated draft of a letter in her hand (probably intended for Alice to type) addressed to the New York publishers Harper & Company. It is a mere two lines: "Sirs, Will you have the great kindness to send this package to Mr. Henry James. I am very anxious to have him receive it promptly." There is, however, no record of the novelist's having received *Three Lives* or any of Gertrude's later writings. But it is clear that she was aiming for the top of her new-found profession.

Gertrude had less difficulty in reaching the novelist's brother, William James. She had last seen her former professor in 1908, when James was touring the Continent after delivering a series of lectures at Oxford. Gertrude had gone to meet him at his hotel in Paris. To her delight, James was enormously interested to hear about her new career as a writer, and equally interested in her newly begun collection of paintings. With that brisk acceptance of a new experience that characterized the man, James had returned to the rue de Fleurus with her. He had an interest in art: As a young man he had once considered it as a profession and now his son Billy was making a career for himself as a painter. But James was not quite prepared for the sight of the strange pictures in Gertrude's studio room. With a slight gasp, James stepped back and surveyed the riot of color and the strangely distorted figures. "I told you," he said, half in admiration and half in wonder, "I always told you that you should keep your mind open."

Now that her first book had been published, Gertrude forwarded a copy of *Three Lives* to her former professor. There was no immediate response, and she next sent him a volume of Péguy's writings, accompanied by a letter. Late in May, 1910, James wrote her from Bad-Nauheim in Germany. He had been ailing with a serious heart condition and was taking a rest cure at a sanatorium there. If the flesh was weak, James's mind and spirit were as alert and refreshing as ever. "I have had a bad conscience about *Three Lives*," he wrote Gertrude.

You know how hard it is for me to read novels. Well I read 30 or 40 pages, and said "this is a fine new kind of realism—Gertrude Stein is great! I will go at it carefully when just the right mood comes." But apparently the right mood never came. I thought I had put the book in my trunk, to finish over here, but I don't find it on unpacking. I promise you that it shall be read *some* time! You see what a swine I am to have pearls cast before him! . . .

How is the wonderful Matisse and his associates? Does he continue to *wear?* My wife and I will probably return to England through Paris by the middle of July, and if so we shall certainly look you up.

The meeting never occurred, nor did James have an opportunity to finish *Three Lives*. Dangerously ill, accompanied by his worried wife and equally worried brother, Henry, he had stayed only overnight in Paris and went on immediately to London. On August 26, after a troubled ocean crossing, James died in New Hampshire. His widow recorded the medical diagnosis and her own in her diary: "Acute enlargement of the heart. He had worn himself out."

Leo heard the news during a visit to London. He wrote Gertrude a few stunned sentences: "I got a really painful shock the other day. James is dead. He died in his summer home." Gertrude had probably already heard: In Paris both the *Temps* and *Figaro* had responded with generous obituary notices, the latter paper announcing: "One of the greatest philosophical minds of the age has died."

Three Lives had a disappointing sale. By February, 1910, the Grafton Press reported, only 73 of the 500 bound copies had been sold and 37 of these to bookstores at 75 cents per copy. Seventy-eight more copies had been distributed free to book reviewers and friends. Despite this, Gertrude received a letter from an editor at Grafton, dated February 28, suggesting that she appropriate $200 to $300 more for special advertising. The book, the editor noted, had aroused "more favorable comments" than had been expected and "certainly appeals very strongly to a class of readers." With special circularizing and advertising, he suggested, they "might succeed in selling a fair number of copies." Gertrude, apparently unwilling to invest more, seems to have declined the offer.

Nevertheless, the book had a surprisingly durable underground reputation for years. Several of the influential and useful people Gertrude met later in her career—the American critics Henry McBride and Carl Van Vechten, for example, and the English art critic Roger Fry—acknowledged that they had read the book when it first appeared, admired it, and had become curious about its author. In the meantime, Gertrude had the solace of her sparse but largely favorable reviews. An extremely perceptive notice in the Kansas City *Star* became Gertrude's favorite. The unsigned reviewer called the book "a very masterpiece of realism." He especially singled out the story of Melanctha:

As character study one can speak of it only in superlatives. The originality of its narrative form is notable. As these humble lives are groping in bewilderment, so does the story telling itself. Not written in the vernacular, it yet gives that impression.

"Here is a literary artist of such originality," the reviewer went on, "that it is not easy to conjecture what special influences have gone into the making of her. But the indwelling spirit of it all is a sweet, enlightened sympathy, an unsleeping sense of humor and an exquisite carefulness in detail." The writer hailed Gertrude as a "new and original artist come into the field of fiction."

Three Lives became a distinct critical success, as the reviewers echoed one another. In the Boston *Morning Herald* of January 8, it was called "an extraordinary book. With its strange unconventional English, its haltings, its endless repetitions, it furnishes hard reading and yet somehow its unfamiliar, almost uncanny, style grips the reader firmly." *The Nation*, on January 20, noted that the book had "the sense of urgent life one gets more commonly in Russian literature than elsewhere." The *Brooklyn Daily Eagle*, on March 2, termed it "an extraordinary piece of realism," and as late as August the reviewer for the Springfield, Massachusetts, *Union* was echoing the *Eagle*'s praise, saying that it was "not an over-extravagant claim." He noted, correctly, too, that "It is not a book that will command general or popular reading."

Gertrude had kept track of her American reviews by means of a press-clipping service, the Romeike Agency. As a budding author, she pasted them into a small notebook for safekeeping. The Romeike firm had been recommended to her by Alice Woods Ullman, the American journalist who had brought the Infanta Eulalia on a visit to the rue de Fleurus a few days before Christmas, 1909. Following that visit, Mrs. Ullman wrote Gertrude recommending the Romeike firm as the "most satisfactory establishment" she had dealt with. She recalled that the fee was five dollars for a hundred reviews. Mrs. Ullman went on to render her verdict on the Stein art collection. She had been impressed with the Vallotton nude and had seen "the color in the Matisse things," but she was not prepared for the Picassos: "The Spaniard's things, mmm—I'm sure I do not at all know what." Pictures aside, Mrs. Ullman told Gertrude, she had thoroughly enjoyed her visit and hoped that she would be invited again. In conclusion, she added a sentence that must have brought a flush of pleasure to Gertrude: "What a beautiful young woman you have stopping with you!"

In her subtle but insistent way, Alice was becoming a presence at the rue de Fleurus.

III

It appears to have been in the spring of 1909 that Gertrude first asked Alice to live with her and that Alice agreed. Leo had undoubtedly been consulted and gave his approval. For reasons of his own, he was to regard Alice's move to the rue de Fleurus as a "blessing." But although Gertrude and Alice had made up their minds, Alice did not move into her new quarters officially for another year. The problem was Harriet.

Neither Gertrude nor Alice wanted to tell Harriet of their decision. Instead, they tried to find out from her what her plans were for the coming winter—whether she would be staying on in Europe, living in the apartment on the rue Notre Dame des Champs for another year, or whether she would be returning to the States. They seem not to have asked Harriet very pointedly, merely questioned her about her plans. Whether deliberately or unintentionally, Harriet misunderstood the nature of the question and told them that she hadn't made up her mind about the coming summer. Gertrude and Alice's reticence suggests that they expected some unpleasantness and were careful to avoid it. Gertrude tended to be cowardly about difficult personal confrontations and did her best to avoid them. Even in her later years, when she had become a celebrated public personality, given to expressing her views frankly, she was inclined to let Alice dispose of sticky personal problems. Banishment of former friends was usually accomplished by means of a sharp note or a telephone call or, simply, a curt message that she was not at home to the person who was calling. On this occasion she and Alice were obliged to wait—impatiently—while Harriet delayed making any decision.

This awkward situation nonetheless provided Gertrude with the inspiration for one of her more amusing word portraits—a study of Harriet refusing to make up her mind. Written in her early style of baldly repeated simple sentences, the constant repetition heightens the effect of a maddening impasse. The portrait begins by dumbly stating the problem, then offering a too-general response. It then corrects itself to take into account all parties interested in Harriet's not having made any plans.

She said she did not have any plans for the summer. No one was interested in this thing in whether she had any plans for the summer. That is not the complete history of this thing, some were interested in this thing in her not having any plans for the summer. She was interested in this thing in her not having any plans for the summer. Some to whom she told about this thing were interested in this thing. Her family were interested in this thing in her having not yet made any plans for the summer. Others were interested in this thing, her dress-maker was interested in this thing and her milliner.

It then proceeds to outline the very special case of the author and Alice:

Some who were not interested in this thing in her not having made any plans for the summer would have been interested in this thing in her not having made any plans for the summer if she had made plans for the winter.

The portrait travels through a circular route in time:

What would be her plan for the summer. She would not have any plan for the summer. She would not really come to have a plan for the summer and the summer would be a summer and then there would be the winter. She would not have any plan for the winter and some would ask her what was her plan for the winter. There would not be then any more summer. There would be then a winter.

Gertrude then moves on to express a certain sympathy with Harriet's plight and her dependence upon Alice: "It was not easy for her to come to have a plan for the winter, some whom she was needing to have with her would be leaving her." She also writes of Alice's inability to move to the rue de Fleurus with her belongings as long as Harriet has decided to remain. The portrait then concludes from the vantage point of the end of summer, with no successful outcome. Gertrude and Alice are facing a winter of discontent: Harriet is still undecided:

She could not tell any one in the beginning of winter that she had not a plan for the winter because she would be knowing then that it was winter and she would be knowing then that what she was doing then was her plan for that winter, every one could know that, any one could know that, she could know that that what she was doing in the winter was the plan she was carrying out for that winter. There was then coming to be the end of summer and she was then not answering anything when any one asked her what were her plans for the winter.

Interestingly, the situation described in "Harriet" ends, as did *Q.E.D.*, with three women at an impasse, one of them exercising control over the actions of the other two. The difference is that the author's attitude is humorous rather than despairing.

During that winter, Harriet had felt increasingly lonely, with Alice at the rue de Fleurus much of the time. She wrote to a friend in San Francisco, Caroline Helbing—a friend of Alice's as well—suggesting she visit them in Paris. Caroline obliged, and the situation was eased somewhat, now that Harriet had company. The four women—Gertrude, Alice, Harriet, and Caroline—frequently lunched and dined together. Caroline was taken to galleries and shopping and to meet Mildred Aldrich and Marie Laurencin. On one occasion they were invited to tea, to meet Marie's mother at their little flat near the rue Fontaine. They started out on the Métro, but at the very first stop, Gertrude, hating the claustral atmosphere, commanded: "Come on, we are getting off here, we will take a fiacre." "The Métro," Alice noted years later, "was not to be an experience for us."

When the time came for Caroline to leave, Alice accompanied her to the boat train. As they drove to the station, Alice said firmly and sweetly, "Caroline dear, you must see that when Harriet goes back to America she does not return to Paris because it is already arranged that I should go to stay with Gertrude and Leo at the rue de Fleurus."

"That is what I suspected," Caroline said. "You can count on me."

Harriet, however, did not leave Paris until the summer of 1910, when she returned to America with the Michael Steins. Sarah Stein's father had been taken ill, and the family, including Allan, had returned to San Francisco for a lengthy stay that was further prolonged when Mr. Samuels died in November. From San Francisco, in mid-August, Michael Stein wrote that they had seen Alice's father. With Sally's help, Mr. Toklas was becoming reconciled to his daughter's extended stay in Europe. Mike's postcard reported: "Alice's father spent an afternoon with Sally and Sally made such an angel of Alice that her father is still walking on air."

That September, when Alice and Gertrude returned from their summer in Italy, Alice moved into the rue de Fleurus permanently. Not long after, Harriet wrote to Alice, suggesting she close up the flat, asking her to have the paintings she had bought, especially a recent Matisse, *La Femme aux Yeux bleus*, carefully packed and sent to her, since it was likely she would be remaining in California for some time. Gertrude and Alice's patience had been rewarded.

Leo Stein proved marvelously accommodating about Alice's move; he willingly gave up his small study for Alice's use as a bedroom. And when Alice ran into difficulties with the landlady of the rue Notre Dame des Champs apartment, he helped her in preparing the letters and necessary papers for the lawyer she was obliged to hire. Alice, as a precaution, perhaps, had told the landlady that she would pay rent for the apartment until the following spring. The pictures and furnishings,

however, were to be shipped to San Francisco. Madame Bouguereau
had objected. It was illegal, she said, to leave the apartment un-
furnished.

At the time of Alice's move, Leo was involved in a critical opening of
a long-protracted love affair. He had taken up with a young model, a
girl of the quarter, Nina Auzias, who had had innumerable affairs with
the artists for whom she posed. Nina had come to Paris at the age of
eighteen to study singing, had lost her voice through hard luck, and,
it seems, dissipation. When Leo met her, in 1909, she was twenty-six,
and involved in three separate love affairs, one of them with an English
artist who, according to Leo, had done nothing "but paint innumerable bad portraits of her" for seven years. One of Nina's lovers had
threatened to kill Leo and himself if Nina should leave him; a second,
more considerate in a peculiar way, threatened to do some killing if
Nina should leave lover No. 3 for anyone but himself. Leo found himself in "a perfect whirlpool of tragicomic romance."

Like everything else in Leo's life, his love affair was conducted in an
original fashion. His lengthy and erratic courtship with Nina did not
end in marriage until 1921. Nina appears to have pursued him. As he
explained to Gertrude, he liked Nina "for herself" and "loved her for
her love." Nor, it seems, was he immediately aroused by her physical
charms. (In the bloom of passion, however, he once described her as
"a feminine version of St. James the Less" in a Correggio painting, and
found her eyes "absolutely bottomless.") Although Nina had delicate,
doll-like features, crowned with a head of generally unmanageable hair,
she thought her body unattractive, and Leo was inclined to agree with
her. In a strangely touching memoir, printed together with Leo's
papers in *Journey into the Self*, Nina recalled a posing session in which
Leo, continually whistling through his teeth while he sketched, set her
nerves on edge. Finally, Leo remarked, "Yes, you are right, you are
badly built and not at all inspiring." Chagrined, Nina remained silent
until she could stand it no longer.

And suddenly I rushed toward him, seized his head and kissed him. Without a word he arose—and spat on the floor. That was too much. I said, "No,
I do not wish to pose any more. I am too ugly. I am going."

When they next encountered each other in a sketching class, several
months later, Leo asked her to resume her posing for him. Nina reminded him that she was "too uninteresting."

"Yes, that is right," Leo answered, "but you can come to visit me as
a psychological model. I am sincere. You have had many experiences
and have much to tell me. That interests me a great deal, and I shall
pay much more than for an ordinary model. Come tomorrow."

The relationship was resumed, and the "posing" sessions took a strange turn. "Very dignified and calm," Nina related, "I sat on the sofa. Not far from me he sat also. And looking only at the wall opposite, I began to relate to him my fantastic adventures, like a modern Scheherazade to her modernistic Sultan."

While Gertrude's romance with Alice was being conducted in person and on the premises—with only the sparsest hints of it in their recollections—much of Leo's courtship with Nina was conducted long distance and by letter. Perhaps because Alice was living at the rue de Fleurus, or because restlessness was a condition brought on by love, Leo traveled considerably during 1910 and 1911, journeying to Florence, Rome, Berlin, and London. From these distances, he counseled Nina on her subsequent love affairs while she supplied him with details in the fashion of a patient with an analyst. In an undated letter from Florence, Leo wrote her:

My Dearest, I have just received your second letter (the other has also arrived safely) and I am very happy that S. has once more made his entrance upon the scene. That would really have been disgusting if such a grand flame of love had been extinguished so soon. Why had he not written to you for a whole week? . . .

Thus, good luck, but try at the same time to conduct yourself and to use a little moderation. Love and kisses, Stein.

Interspersed with his counsels were confessions of his inadequacies: "I deeply hope that this summer it will be possible to be together for at least a month. I do not think I shall be capable of a passionate love like that of R., or B., etc., not because I am too much soul and not enough flesh, but rather becauses these elements are not sufficiently mixed." Other letters contained long-distance professions of tenderness ("Nina darling, each time that I think of that gift of your love I am filled with a profound emotion of gratitude and well-being") and advice about a problematic suitor ("I am really of the opinion that save in the case that M.R. leaves Paris, it would be most imprudent to rejoin me here [i.e., Florence]. It is hardly likely that his love will bloom again, but under the circumstances if he thinks that this tragicomedy is being played on purpose, his wounded pride would turn to hate and the results would be fearful"). Even Nina's lovers, it seemed, applied to Leo for counsel. As he wrote to Nina in July, 1910, "I received today another letter from M.R. It is on the same subject as the other, and I answered with a letter full of very wise reflections. I shall not repeat them because they are very profound and you, poor dear, you would not understand them."

Not only did Leo keep up his epistolary romance with Nina for several years, he regularly supplied his sister and his friend Mabel Weeks with progress reports. To Gertrude and Mabel he sent reports on

Nina's emotional state, verbatim snippets of her love letters to him, and paraphrases of the letters Nina received from her other lovers. From Berlin, in July, 1910, he wrote to Mabel Weeks: "Matters with Nina are going nicely. She seems to have gotten rid of my 'rivals'; in fact the last and fiercest of them is the profoundest admirer and most intelligent disciple that I have among the younger men. Nina and I have corresponded actively all summer, and her letters are invariably good." From London, later in the year, however, he wrote to Gertrude that Nina had gone off on another adventure, this time to Spain, and he supposed that the affair was finished: "She sends her postal cards in pairs. In the last pair it reads on one that she'd rather tell the story than write it, and the other is worded as follows: *Je languis de vous revoir et de vous raconter toute l'aventure. Je sais que j'ai un grand ami en toi et si tu ne m'aimes plus d'amour . . . ce sera un amitié, n'est ce pas?*" Leo's conclusion was admirably level-headed. "I think that on the whole, considering what I am and what Nina is, the course has been quite ideally run," he wrote Gertrude.

Yet the course was not run. When he returned to Paris, he and Nina resumed their affair. It was to continue on for years, fretted over, discussed, analyzed. In March he was writing to Nina: "In truth, if I were more egotistical, I should like to have you all to myself, but knowing how little I can offer you I always have a fear of making you miss a greater self by putting myself between you and your fate." By the end of the summer, when he returned to Paris early from Italy, where Gertrude and Alice had stayed longer, he was writing to Gertrude about Nina's reinvolvement with a composer, "I saw a couple of his letters—he writes to her every day—the regular better fifty years of Europe than a cycle of Cathay sort of thing. He can't live except in the light of her eyes. If she will only take him he will have a real inspiration and write the music of the future."

Leo was lover, counselor, analyst, friend; he had been blessed with such a dispassionate intelligence that he could never take love hard.

IV

Both Matisse and Picasso "sat" for early word portraits by Gertrude. Oddly, it was on Matisse that Gertrude, writing in 1909, conferred the title of greatness. The Matisse portrait begins with a slow, lengthy single sentence that encompasses both the painter's distrust of his own methods and his gradual feelings of self-assurance. It ends with the author's assertion that the painter's estimate is a true one:

One was quite certain that for a long part of his being one being living he had been trying to be certain that he was wrong in doing what he was doing and then when he could not come to be certain that he had been wrong in doing what he had been doing, when he had completely convinced himself that he would not come to be certain that he had been wrong in doing what he had been doing he was really certain then that he was a great one and he certainly was a great one. Certainly every one could be certain of this thing that this one is a great one.

From this pinnacle of certainty, however, the portrait quickly runs downhill to ambivalence. It takes into account both Matisse's followers and his critics, those who feel the artist is "greatly expressing something being struggling" and those who do not. The terminal sentence— "This one was one, some were quite certain, one not greatly expressing something being struggling"—may well represent the author's point of view, for the "wonderful Matisse," as William James had referred to him, did not continue "to wear" for Gertrude.

Part of the problem may have been the sense of assurance that Matisse had painfully earned. In the notebooks Gertrude kept while *The Making of Americans* was in progress, she jotted down a sharp observation about the painter: "Brutal egotism of Matisse shown in his not changing his prices." Matisse's contract with Bernheim-Jeune had afforded him a certain measure of financial security. Evidently he did not feel it necessary to make special concessions for old patrons. Matisse was coming up in the world. He had consolidated his position as a leader of the vanguard by means of the "Matisse Academy," the classes in painting and sculpture that Sarah Stein, who became one of his most ardent students, and the young German painter Hans Purrmann had urged him to conduct. During the four years the academy was in existence—from the winter of 1907–8, when it opened in a former convent on the rue de Sevres, until 1911, when Matisse abandoned teaching as an unnecessary chore—the school had attracted an international roster of aspiring art students. The original class had included ten students, among them Sally Stein and the American painters Patrick Henry Bruce and Max Weber, both of whom were frequent visitors at the rue de Fleurus. Other Americans, like Maurice Sterne and Walter Pach, made a habit of dropping in on the classes. By the spring of 1908, Matisse was obliged to find larger quarters, which he did in the eighteenth-century Hôtel Biron, on the rue de Varenne, not far distant from Gertrude. The class, by then, had become international. Purrmann, who served as class monitor, had encouraged a number of German friends to enroll. For some reason there was a large contingent of Scandinavians and a fair sprinkling of Hungarians.

From the beginning, there was some difficulty in determining whether the students were more radical than the master. Matisse chose to run his classes along conventional lines, stressing anatomy and drawing from the live model. It was his habit to meet with his classes on Saturdays to criticize the week's work. On the first of these visits he had been aghast to find the students' work full of slashing gestures and brash colors that "out-Fauved" the Fauves. He immediately brought out a cast of a Greek sculpture and admonished them to start drawing from the "antique," a practice that most of them, in their yearning to be modern, had felt they had put behind them. The ideology of the class was demonstrated by one young woman who, when asked by the master what she had in mind by the brash sketch she offered for approval, declared, "*Monsieur, je cherche le neuf.*" Sally Stein, regarded jealously by the other students as Matisse's favorite, took notes on Matisse's classroom pronouncements. They provide a valuable record of the artist's ideas and methods. "The antique above all," Matisse told his students, "will help you to realize the fullness of form. . . . In the antique, all the parts have been equally considered. The result is unity, and repose of the spirit." He cautioned them against modernistic effects: "In the moderns, we often find a passionate expression and realization of certain parts at the expense of others; hence a lack of unity, consequent weakness, and a troubling of the spirit." Since there were few "moderns" at the time, it sounds suspiciously as if Matisse had the savage modernism of Picasso's recently completed *Demoiselles* in mind.

The academy, split by jealous factionalism, was rife with minor, but amusing, scandals. Gertrude looked forward to the Saturday evenings when Matisse, fresh from his critical sessions with the students, stopped by the rue de Fleurus to recount the latest gossip about the poor Hungarian student who had been discovered eating the stale bread used for erasers or the other impoverished student who had posed nude for the class so that he could earn some extra money. After that exposure, several of the emancipated young women in the class would not allow the young man to set up his easel next to them. The most blatant transgressor, however, was the American who pleaded poverty and was allowed to take the classes free. It was discovered that he not only had bought a small Matisse painting but a small Picasso as well—and that was clearly regarded as treasonable.

In 1909, Matisse's Bernheim contract and a commission from his Russian patron, Shchukine, for two large murals, *Dance* and *Music*, enabled the artist to move to a country house in suburban Issy-les-Moulineaux on the Clamart Road. There he had a garden, a source of pleasure for himself and Madame Matisse. He also erected a prefabricated wooden studio large enough to accommodate his sizable mural projects. Country life and his spacious studio provided a spur to his creativity; his painting entered a new and ambitious phase with a series of large, colorful works that celebrated both art and life. Fragments of his *Dance* mural figured as a backdrop in his still-life paintings; the dramatic *Red Studio* of 1911, one of the superb decorative masterpieces of the period, pictures his paintings and sculptures stationed about the studio, rendered against a flat, earthy red ground. His new prosperity also allowed him to travel. Matisse visited Spain and Morocco for months at a time, bringing back exotic and colorful paintings and equally colorful shawls, rugs, and Arabian costumes that shortly appeared in paintings executed in the quiet of his studio.

It was on the decorative aspect of Matisse's work that Gertrude most misjudged the artist, comparing him unfavorably with Picasso. In her notebooks, she observed:

I am quite sure that it is true of Matisse that he cannot do pure decoration because he has to have the practical realism of his group as his point de depart always. He must paint after nature, his in between decorative period was and is a failure, it is only carried by his beautiful colors and his power in drawing but they have no real existence. He has always failed in such flat painting, he then of course not understanding his own failure cannot understand Pablo who succeeds in just this.

Matisse became the twentieth-century master who raised the decorative approach and flat painting, through the sheer tenacity of his efforts, to unsurpassed heights.

Gertrude was on surer ground with Picasso. In her attempts to understand the artist and his work, intimacy proved more useful than aesthetic judgments. Her raw notes, leading up to her word portrait of the painter, suggest a mingling of their personalities. Picasso's character, in a sense, defined her own:

Do one about Pablo his emotional leap and courage as opposed to lack of courage in Cézanne and me. His laziness and his lack of continuity and his facility too quick for the content which ought to be so complete to do what he wants to do. Too lazy to do sculpture. His work is not because it is too strong for him to resist but because his resistance is not great enough. Cézanne resistance great but dragged along. Pablo is never dragged, he walks in the light and a little ahead of himself like Raphael, therefore his things often lack a base. Do him.

The Picasso portrait, written in the same year as her "Matisse," offers no assurances of greatness or genius. It starts out with a recognition of the artist's personal qualities and of his "following" among the younger artists: "One whom some were certainly following was one who was completely charming." It goes on to acknowledge his erratic working habits, his struggles, the process by which he seemed to "empty" himself of successive influences. In a particularly effective passage, Gertrude spelled out the infinite variety of Picasso's production:

This one always had something being coming out of this one. This one was working. This one always had been working. This one was always having something that was coming out of this one that was a solid thing, a charming thing, a lovely thing, a perplexing thing, a disconcerting thing, a simple thing, a clear thing, a complicated thing, an interesting thing, a disturbing thing, a repellant thing, a very pretty thing.

Picasso's "following" did not constitute an academy; it was loosely comprised of that gang of Montmartre artists—Braque, Marcoussis, Gleizes, Delaunay, Derain, Léger—who met in one another's studios or saw one another in the Montmartre cafés and bistros in the evenings. Max Jacob referred to these years, the years between 1909 and 1913, as the "heroic age" of Cubism. Gertrude seconded the definition, but with a qualification. "All ages are heroic," she claimed, "that is to say there are heroes in all ages who do things because they cannot do otherwise and neither they nor the others understand how and why these things happen." It was a period of prodigious energy and far-reaching innovations for the painters who clustered around the dynamic figure of Picasso. The collaboration between Picasso and Braque, the co-inventors

Picasso, study for *Violin*, 1912. (Marlborough Gallery, Inc., New York.)

of the style, was particularly close. It was even rumored that they had maliciously signed each other's paintings in order to confound the enemy. Braque maintained that they had been "engaged in what we felt was a search for the anonymous personality. We were inclined to efface our personalities in order to find originality." If "amateurs" mistook their paintings, it was "a matter of indifference" to them both. Picasso, jealous of his reputation, seems to have put the collaboration on a different footing entirely. "Braque, he is my wife!" he is reported as saying, a few years later, when their friendship had cooled.

The most striking innovation of the Cubist confraternity was its complete overthrow of the conventional methods of pictorial structure. The Cubists pointedly dismantled the familiar objects of still life, landscape, and even figurative painting, breaking everything down into planes seen simultaneously from every direction. They dispersed these elemental forms across the entire surface of their pictures until the subject matter was barely recognizable. Their pictures became shimmering surfaces of silvery gray and brown planes with glints of light and dappled shadows, rather like looking down at pebbles seen through a clear, shallow stream. Then, around 1910, when Cubist painting seemed close to pure abstraction, the painters pulled back, introducing fragments of lettering —the JOU of a newspaper logo, the labels of a bottle of Marc or ale— establishing the brand names, as it were, of the objects they were abstracting.

In 1911, Picasso and Braque created another innovation, pasting into their pictures bits of newspaper, sections of patterned oil cloth and wallpaper, combining the found objects of daily life with *trompe-l'œil* segments of painting—a spirited playing off of one form of reality against another. Their innovations were to alter the course of painting for years. Looking back on the period, Gertrude once remarked to Picasso that it was incredible, the amount of work that had been accomplished in those years. "You forget," Picasso answered, "we were young then."

In a more modest way, Picasso, too, was moving up in the world. In 1909 he and Fernande had taken a new apartment, with a large studio and drawing room on the boulevard de Clichy. It was furnished with a large piano on which Fernande occasionally picked out a melody and with odd pieces of furniture, including a Louis Phillipe sofa upholstered in purple velvet, to which Picasso had taken a fancy during his walks in the neighborhood. They also hired a servant who, like Hélène, could make a decent soufflé. It was around this time that they were taken up by the legendary *couturier*, Paul Poiret, who invited them to one of his lavish parties, given on his houseboat in the Seine. Poiret presented Fernande with a rose-colored scarf and a spun-glass *fantaisie* for a hat. Fernande, perhaps to replace the one that had been demolished at the Rousseau banquet, gave the *fantaisie* to Alice, who wore it for years.

Picasso seems not to have found his new quarters conducive to working. He hired a studio on the lower floor of his old haunt, the Bateau Lavoir. One day, in the spring of 1912, Gertrude and Alice stopped by the studio to pay a visit. Finding that Picasso was not in, Gertrude, as a joke, had left her calling card. Some days later, when they returned to the rue Ravignan studio, they noticed a large and beautiful oval composition. It pictured a table with various objects in the high style of Analytical Cubism. At the bottom of the picture, Picasso had painted in a replica of Gertrude's calling card. To one side were the words "Ma Jolie," a reference to a popular song: "O Manon ma jolie, mon coeur te dit bonjour." Gertrude acquired the painting, officially titled The Architect's Table, not long after. The purchase was not without its difficulties. Gertrude thought the price of 1,200 francs was more than she could afford. When Picasso refused to come down on the price, Kahnweiler, who had recently become his dealer, arranged for her to buy it in two installments.

But on the day that she had first seen the picture, she had found it somewhat mysterious. As they left Picasso's studio, Gertrude turned to Alice. "Fernande is certainly not Ma Jolie," she said. "I wonder who it is."

She was not to learn the outcome of Picasso's newest amorous adventure until that summer, when she and Alice were traveling in Spain.

V

On May 1 Gertrude and Alice began an extensive journey through Spain in sweltering heat. They traveled southward by train, criss-crossing through central Spain, stopping first at Burgos and Valladolid, then moving on to Avila.

Alice was immediately struck with Avila. From the train station, they had ridden over the cobbled streets to their inn in a coach with four mules, the harnesses jingling with bells. Finding the inn pleasant and clean, Alice announced that she wanted to stay forever. Gertrude had a fondness for the natal city of Saint Teresa, who was to become the heroine of her later opera libretto, Four Saints in Three Acts. But she was not disposed to remain long in Avila when the rest of their long trip was still ahead of them. Their argument became nearly violent. Finally Gertrude conceded. "Well, I will stay two weeks instead of two · days," she informed Alice, "but I could not work here, you know that." On their first morning there, they visited Saint Teresa's church. They also toured the surrounding countryside. One day they attended a High Mass in the cathedral given in honor of a visiting bishop. The Mass was to be followed by a sumptuous lunch, and in a local pastry shop

Alice had inspected the food that was to be served: "Foods of all kinds fantastically decorated with vegetables, salads arranged to represent the cathedral, pieces mounted in caramel and meringue." She found the cooking in Avila better than in most of the towns they were to visit.

In Madrid, where they arrived early in June, they found a letter from Leo awaiting them. He reported that there were some strange goings on in the Picasso household. Picasso, according to one rumor, had run off with another woman. In any event, the painter was no longer in Paris. According to another rumor, Fernande had gone off with another man. Although Gertrude did not learn the details of the affair until later, both rumors proved to be true. The *Ma Jolie* of Picasso's painting was Marcelle Humbert, the frail and delicate mistress of his painter colleague Louis Marcoussis. Picasso's break with Fernande was final; he renamed Marcelle, calling her Eva, symbolizing that she was the first woman in his life. As he told his dealer friend, Kahnweiler, "I love her very much and I shall write her name on my pictures." With the same sentiments as a young lover carving his beloved's name on a tree trunk, Picasso inscribed his paintings with Eva, or the "*Je t'aime Eva*," for the next few years. More often, he resorted to the already familiar sobriquet *Ma Jolie.*

Fernande, too, had run off. She chose a charming young Italian painter, Ubaldo Oppi, in the apparent hope of making Picasso jealous. The stratagem had not worked. Picasso, freed of his former mistress, took off with his Eva for Céret, the city in the French Pyrenees where he and Fernande had spent a previous summer with Braque. The situation there might have been ideal had not the repentant Fernande turned up to stay with the Pichots. Among the small colony of Parisian artists stationed there—Picasso's compatriot, the sculptor Manolo, Juan Gris, Braque and his wife, Marcelle—the Picasso affair was watched with vital interest. In the local cafés it became the topic of the day. Picasso solved the situation by leaving quietly with Eva, taking a house at Sorgues, near Avignon.

In Madrid, Gertrude and Alice spent their mornings at the Prado studying the paintings of Goya and Greco and Velásquez. In the evenings they sampled the night life of the cafés and music halls. They both developed an infatuation for the famous Spanish dancer La Argentina and every night took in her performances. They attended the bullfights as well. Gertrude, having seen them years before with Leo, advised Alice to look away when the horses were gored. When they had been dragged out of the arena, she told Alice to open her eyes. For these occasions, Alice had taken to wearing what she termed her "Spanish disguise," a long black satin coat with a black feathered hat, black gloves, and a fan.

In Madrid, too, they heard the singer Preciosilla, appearing at one of the cafés. Alice thought her eyes as brilliant and flashing as the enormous diamond earrings the singer wore at her performances. Apparently

Gertrude thought so as well, for when she wrote a word portrait of the
singer, the word "diamonds" recurred frequently in the long, crescendo-
like sentence that climaxed her prose poem. Under the influence of the
flamenco rhythms of the Spanish songs, Gertrude explored a new mode
of syntax in which there were barely any associative meanings to the
words she chose, only an insistent rhythm that ended in an astonishing
burst of abstract language.

Not so dots large dressed dots, big sizes, less laced, less laced diamonds,
diamonds white, diamonds bright, diamonds in the in the light, diamonds
light diamonds door diamonds hanging to be four, two four, all before, this
bean, lessly, all most, a best, willow, vest, a green guest, guest, go go go go
go go, go. Go go. Not guessed. Go go.
   Toasted susie is my ice-cream.

From Madrid, Gertrude had sent a brief note to Mildred Aldrich on
their stay in the city. It had been written on a postcard with Goya's
portrait of Charles IV and his family. The picture delighted Mildred.
Writing back to the "girls," she recalled Théophile Gautier's description of the group portrait as looking "like a grocer's family that had won
the big lottery prize." Mildred also informed them that she had had a
long and chatty letter from Harriet Levy, Alice's friend, who had apparently resigned herself to living in California. Harriet had installed
herself at Mount Carmel—"that resort of all geniuses," as Mildred
termed it.
   In Toledo, they witnessed a Corpus Christi procession; in Cuenca, a
tiny village that had been recommended by Gertrude's painter friend
Harry Phelan Gibb, they were considered with such curiosity by the
natives that two civil guards were assigned to accompany them in order
to spare them any annoyance. In Cordova and Seville the heat proved
unbearable, day after day. In Seville, Gertrude had a frightening attack
of colitis. The pair hurriedly took a train to Gibraltar, where she re-
covered in a few days. From Gibraltar, they crossed the Mediterranean
to Tangier.
   Matisse and his wife had been there earlier in the year. Matisse had
been particularly taken with the lush tropical gardens, which he could
see from his window in the Hôtel de France. He had made several
paintings of the subject, a series of green paradises. On Matisse's recom-
mendation, Gertrude and Alice decided to stay in the same hotel and
found it pleasant and amusing.
   There had been some recent difficulties between the sultan of Tangier and the French authorities, and there were areas of the city that
were considered unsafe for foreigners to visit. Accordingly, during their
stay, they hired a guide, a voluble young man named Mohammed.
Mohammed presented himself as an adopted son, one of several, of the

sultan of Tangier. He spoke fluent French and had a smattering of English. Alice thought him intriguing, particularly when he told them about the sultan's plans to abdicate. Mohammed not only told them the date—Alice remembered it because it was her brother's birthday—but the amount of money the sultan would demand from the French for doing so. They were surprised, some time later, to pick up a newspaper and read that Mohammed's prediction had come true in every detail. It was not, however, the end of the story. Three years later, when Gertrude and Alice were staying at Palma de Mallorca, they had occasion to relate the incident to Monsieur Marchand, the French consul on the island. "If you had only told us," Monsieur Marchand groaned. "Fancy your knowing what we wanted and needed to know." At the time, he had been the liaison officer between Marshal Lyautey, the resident general of Morocco, and the Arabs. Now he learned that two foreign ladies, idling in Tangier, had been given the information gratis by a talkative young man. It was precisely the kind of ironic denouement that Alice loved.

Returning to Spain, Gertrude and Alice made their way slowly northward. They spent a few uneventful days in Ronda, a village in Picasso's native province of Málaga. Alice thought the small houses there looked, somehow, Elizabethan. Mostly they took walks in the surrounding country. On one of these they came upon a stream. Gertrude, with the grace that large women sometimes have, stepped deftly across, moving from stone to stone. "Come on," she taunted Alice, "Why do you hesitate?" Alice picked her way cautiously across. Reaching the safety of the other side, she muttered that they were "not stepping stones but skipping stones."

From Ronda they moved on to Granada. Gertrude had visited it before with Leo in 1901, during that first troubled summer when she was trying to puzzle out her relationship with May Bookstaver. She had developed a special fondness for the city, connecting it, it seems, with special and sensuous insights. In *Q.E.D.*, she had described Adele as sitting in the court of the Alhambra with the swallows flying in and out of the crevices in the walls, the scent of oleander and myrtle heavy in the air. Adele had given herself up to the hot sun burning on her face, losing herself in a feeling of "sensuous delight." It was in Granada, too, that Adele is described as having had a sudden illumination, while reading the tale of Dante and Beatrice in the *Vita Nuova*. "At last," Gertrude's heroine exclaims, "I begin to see what Dante is talking about and so there is something in my glimpse and it's alright and worth while." But Gertrude also described a simpler, earthier experience that had happened to Adele:

One day she was sitting on a hill-side looking down at Granada desolate in the noon-day sun. A young Spanish girl carrying a heavy bag was climbing

up the dry, brown hill. As she came nearer they smiled at each other and
exchanged greetings. The child sat down beside her. She was one of those
motherly little women found so often in her class, full of gentle dignity and
womanly responsibility.

They sat there side by side with a feeling of complete companionship,
looking at each other with perfect comprehension, their intercourse saved
from the interchange of commonplaces by their ignorance of each other's
language. For some time they sat there, finally they arose and walked on together. They parted as quiet friends part, and as long as they remained in
sight of each other they turned again and again and signed a gentle farewell.

In Granada, this time with Alice, Gertrude had decided to remain for
several weeks. During their stay there, they met several people from
the sizable English community, including the English consul, who took
them on "long walks over the roofs of some houses." Gertrude found
that she could work well in Granada. She was impressed with the dancing of the Spanish gypsy women and their graceful, easy way of walking
in their wide skirts and she attempted to capture the rhythms in a
long prose poem, "A Sweet Tail (Gypsies)":

This is the sun in. This is the lamb of the lantern with chalk. With chalk a
shadow shall be a sneeze in a tooth in a tin tooth, a turned past, a turned
little corset, a little tuck in a pink look and with a pin in, a pin in.
　　Win lake, eat splashes dig salt change benches.
　　Win lake eat splashes dig salt change benches
　　　Can in.

In Spain, the birthplace of Picasso, she had arrived at a new phase of
her writing, a phase of radical disassociation, in which her language became increasingly abstract. Her intentions, as she described them to a
friend shortly after her Spanish trip, were blunt: "Well, Pablo is doing
abstract portraits in painting. I am trying to do abstract portraits in *my*
medium, *words*." In later years she was less explicit. She said of the
period her work was then entering, "I became more and more excited
about how words which were the words that made whatever I looked
at look like itself were not the words that had in them any quality of
description. This excited me very much at that time."

In Spain, it seems, she had arrived at a means of describing an experience without the usual "interchange of common-places"—and without the necessary communicative terms of language. She had in a sense
perfected a "foreign" language of her own.

CHAPTER SEVEN

Made in America

I

On their return from Spain, Gertrude and Alice were bombarded with telegrams and letters from Mabel Dodge, inviting them to visit her in Italy. Gertrude had met Mrs. Dodge, the woman who was to do much to promote her early reputation in America, nearly two years before when Mildred Aldrich brought her one day to the rue de Fleurus. An indefatigable hostess, a collector of celebrities, husbands, lovers, artists, and writers, Mrs. Dodge was a perfectly featured but plain, somewhat buxom woman. She nonetheless saw herself, and was regarded by friends, as a *femme fatale*. Gertrude sensed that behind Mabel Dodge's carefully emancipated front there lurked an equally cautious tease. She described her as having "very pretty eyes and a very old fashioned coquetry."

At the time of their first meeting, Mabel was married to Edwin Dodge, a taciturn Boston architect who had met her and wooed her on a transatlantic crossing to Europe. Mabel had been recently widowed. Her first husband, Karl Evans, whom she seems to have married hastily and for want of something better to do in Buffalo, New York, had died not long after their marriage, leaving her with a young son.

Having left the dull precincts of her native city behind, Mabel Dodge chose to live in style. She and her new husband had taken over an imposing villa in Arcetri, near Florence. The gardens of this establishment were lined with ancient cypresses, and the lawns were studded with strident white peacocks. The house itself, according to local legend, had once been lived in by Raphael. It was also supposedly haunted by ghosts and poltergeists who frequently frightened her guests. On one occasion, so Mabel had eagerly written Gertrude, the spirits had been particularly active and had so terrified three of her guests—the sculptor Jo Davidson and his wife, Yvonne, and the American actress Florence Bradley—that the trio had taken a midnight train to Rome rather than risk another sleepless night.

When Mrs. Dodge traveled in Europe, she did so with incomparable flair, accompanied by several young men whom the French society painter Jacques-Émile Blanche, another of her cultural conquests, referred to as Mabel's *"jeunes gens assortis."* Husbands seldom encumbered Mabel Dodge's mode of life for long. When Edwin Dodge's stodginess proved unbearable, she divorced him. She next pursued a mild flirtation with Hutchins Hapgood, to whom she had been introduced by Gertrude. This was followed by a serious and temperamental affair with the writer John Reed, whose later account of the Russian Revolution, *Ten Days That Shook the World*, made him a radical hero of the period. After the Reed affair, she married the painter Maurice Sterne. That marriage, tempestuous and moody from the beginning, ended in divorce as well. By 1933, when she began publishing her four-volume memoirs, significantly titled *Intimate Memories*, she was Mabel Dodge Luhan, having married Antonio Luhan, the virile Indian who worked for her on her Taos, New Mexico, estate. It was at Taos, too, where she established an artists' colony, that she provided refuge for D. H. Lawrence and his wife, Frieda, a stormy association that Mrs. Luhan commemorated in her book, *Lorenzo in Taos*. Gertrude, who had followed Mabel's brisk amatory and marital adventures for several years but had discontinued their friendship, queried a friend: "Is she completely mired in D. Lawrence who it seems does *not* want to put her in a book?"

Despite the cultivated disorder of her emotions and her breathless acceptance of new flirtations and new artistic causes, Mabel Dodge had an eye for the genuine article. After her first visit to the rue de Fleurus in the spring of 1911, Mabel cultivated Gertrude assiduously. She had taken away with her a portion of the manuscript of *The Making of Americans* and wrote back about it in perceptive and flattering terms. "There are things hammered out of consciousness into black & white that have never been expressed before—so far as I know. States of being put into words, the 'noumenon' captured—as few have done it. . . . It is as new & strange & big as the post-impressionists in their way &, I am perfectly convinced, it is the forerunner of a whole new epoch of

new form & expression." Her early friendship with Gertrude bristled
with such superlatives. In the summer of 1911, Gertrude and Alice had
visited Mrs. Dodge at the Villa Curonia, to have tea and meet Constance Fletcher, the once-beautiful but now aged and obese author of
Kismet. After the visit, Mabel had dispatched a breathless letter: "*Why*
are there not more real people like you in the world? Or are there & one
doesn't attract them. Miss Fletcher & I both felt as though we had
been drinking champagne all afternoon. . . . I am *longing* for your
book to get born!"

Such letters were balm to Gertrude, who was despondent over her
failure to find a publisher for her work. After another of Mabel's
salutory letters, written early in 1912, Gertrude had answered gratefully:

Your letter was a great comfort to me. I was kind of low in my mind about
that publication end and even Wagner's letters were ceasing to be a comfort
to me. I have been trying some English publishers with collections of the
shorter and longer things, those you saw and the ones I did this summer
when I first came back, there is nothing doing. . . .

I am still sending the volumes of the short and longer things about but
they come back quite promptly and with very polite and sometimes regret-
ful refusals. The long book is in America. I have not heard anything of it
for a long time. You can understand how much I appreciate your letter.

In a brightened mood, Gertrude went on to relay the gossip of the volatile Parisian art scene:

It has been wonderfully spring here for two weeks now. Also the futurists
are in town. You know Marinetti and his crowd. He brought a bunch of
painters who paint houses and people and streets and wagons and scaffold-
ing and bottles and fruits all moving and where they are not moving there
are cubes to fill in. They have a catalogue that has a fiery introduction
demolishing the old salons and they are exhibiting at Bernheims and everybody goes. Marinetti has given several conferences and at the last he attacked the art of the Greeks and Nadelman who was present called him a
bad name and Marinetti hit Nadelman·and they were separated.

Gertrude's association with Mabel Dodge was commemorated by a
word portrait, one that brought its author as well as its subject some
welcome notoriety. The "Portrait of Mabel Dodge at the Villa Curonia"
was written, as its title suggests, at Mrs. Dodge's luxurious establishment. Returning from Spain, reluctant to end their holiday, Gertrude
and Alice had journeyed to Florence, where they spent several weeks as
Mabel Dodge's guest. For her nightly writing sessions, Gertrude was
given Edwin Dodge's study, next to Mabel's white, linen-hung boudoir.
There, according to her hostess, Gertrude sat each night at Edwin's
table "writing automatically in a long weak handwriting—four or five

lines to a page—letting it ooze up from deep down inside her, down onto the paper with the least possible physical effort." In the morning Alice would gather up the pages and type them.

Gertrude's portrait of her hostess begins with a simple connective sentence expressing pleasure in the surroundings: "The days are wonderful and the nights are wonderful and the life is pleasant." But from there it proceeds through a series of leisurely sentences in which the highly abstracted, elusive meaning of the words is played off against the relatively conventional syntax:

Bargaining is something and there is not that success. The intention is what if application has that accident results are reappearing. They did not darken. That was not an adulteration.

So much breathing has not the same place when there is that much beginning. So much breathing has not the same place when the ending is lessening. So much breathing has the same place and there must not be so much suggestion.

When the completed portrait was read aloud to Mrs. Dodge, she was delighted. She insisted on having it published immediately and arranged to have a private edition of three hundred copies printed in Florence, bound with handsome wrappers of flowered wallpaper. These she began to distribute liberally among her friends. In a rash of underlining and fervid identification with her prose persona, she wrote to Gertrude—then back in Paris—about the portrait's reception:

What they see in *it* is what I consider they see in me. No more no less. . . . My English friend Mrs. Napier . . . writes "it is bold effrontery to do this sort of thing" (*If* she knew me! ! !). Others say (as they would of me! they know *so little* they *are* saying it of me!) "there is no beauty in it." . . .

When I say it seems to me "middleclass, confused & rather sound," Edwin laughs with contempt at my daring to mention the word "sound" in connection with myself not to mention *it!*

When she later wrote about the event in her memoirs, Mabel Dodge described an amusing episode, a comically prolonged seduction scene, that had taken place in her adjacent boudoir while her portrait was being written. While her husband was away in America, she had been conducting a little flirtation with her son's twenty-two-year-old football-playing tutor. One night, while Gertrude sat writing by candlelight in Edwin's room, Mabel's would-be suitor presented himself at her bedroom door. Fearful that Gertrude might hear him whispering her name in the corridor, Mabel let him in. The scene, described in Mabel Dodge's vivid prose, was equal to anything that might have been produced by her friend the theatrical designer Gordon Craig: The lovers, clasping each other in silence, edged toward the "wide, white-

hung bed—until we were lying, arms about each other—white moonlight—white linen—and the blond white boy I found sweet like fresh
hay and honey and milk." Despite this passionate embrace, Mrs. Dodge
assured her readers she had sustained her much-tempted virtue. She was
rewarded when, finally leading her suitor to the door, he whispered
hoarsely in her ear: "I love you so—and the wonderful thing about you
is that you're *good!*"

Mabel was relieved that Gertrude had remained in the study, unaware
of the encounter, sitting at the desk writing, "like a great Sibyl dim
against the red and gold damask that hung loosely on the walls." But
since an "adulteration" and a good deal of heavy "breathing" figure
ambiguously in Gertrude's text, it seems possible that, subliminally, at
least, Gertrude may have been aware of the footsteps passing down the
red-tiled corridor to Mabel Dodge's bedroom. One cryptic passage in
the portrait reads: "A walk that is not stepped where the floor is covered
is not in the place where the room is entered." The concluding sentence
is even more suggestive: "There is not all of any visit."

Late in 1912 Mabel Dodge returned to America. In New York she installed herself in a Fifth Avenue apartment and opened a "salon" that
brought together an odd mixture of types—capitalists, anarchists, artists,
writers, and actresses. Mabel's Wednesday "evenings" were likely to
draw such disparate types as the poet Edwin Arlington Robinson and
the fervent anarchist Emma Goldman. Max Eastman, Margaret Sanger,
and the young Walter Lippmann were among her regulars, along with
Hutchins Hapgood, Lincoln Steffens, Marsden Hartley, and Charles
Demuth.

In January, Mabel wrote to Gertrude about a new cause she was
helping to promote, an art exhibition that she was sure would be
"the most important public event that has ever come off since the
signing of the Declaration of Independence." Her letter was characteristically effervescent:

Arthur Davies is the President of a group of men here who felt the American people ought to be given a chance to see what the modern artists have
been doing in Europe, America & England of late years. So they have got
a collection of paintings from Ingres to the Italian futurists taking in all the
French, Spanish, English, German—in fact *all* one has heard of. This will
be a *scream!* 2000 exhibits in the great armory of the 69th Regiment! The
academy are frantic. Most of them are left out of it. . . . Somehow I got
right into all this. I am working like a dog for it. I am *all* for it. . . . There
will be a riot & a revolution & things will never be quite the same afterwards.

Gertrude and the entire Stein family, however, already knew of the

exhibition that was to become the historic Armory Show. In the preceding November, Davies and Walt Kuhn, another member of the organizing committee, had called at 27, rue de Fleurus and at the
Michael Steins' flat on the rue Madame. Leo had agreed to loan Matisse's *Blue Nude* to the exhibition, as well as two Picasso still lifes, one
of them the beautiful gray and green *Vase, Gourd and Fruit on a
Table*. From the Michael Steins, Davies had selected two Matisses, *Le
Madras rouge* and *La Coiffeuse*. Moreover, Walter Pach, one of Leo's
converts to the modernist faith and a frequent guest at the rue de
Fleurus, had served as an agent for the exhibition, securing loans from
the Parisian dealers Kahnweiler, Vollard, and Hessel—all of whom
were on friendly terms with the Steins. Undoubtedly the Steins' willingness to lend to the exhibition had given the affair status in the dealers'
eyes.

In her letter about the Armory Show, Mabel had an important piece
of news for Gertrude. She had been distributing copies of Gertrude's
"Portrait" to the journalists and editors she had begun to meet. As a
result, she had been asked to write an article about Gertrude Stein and
her writing by F. J. Gregg, a newspaperman hired to do the publicity
for the Armory Show. "Now, my poor darling Gertrude," Mabel wrote,
"I have written an article called 'Speculations' somehow drawing a comparison between you & Picasso & it is going to come out in some art
magazine in February & be on sale for a month at that show. . . . I
don't mind telling you that I am petrified at having done it & in my
dreadful *dead* language! At the same time, as you perceive, it *will*
make your name known by & large, as the writer of 'post impressionistic
literature.' . . . So there Gertrude is my confession. I am your faithful
& incomprehending Boswell. If I dare, I'll send you some copies."

"Speculations, or Post-Impressionism in Prose," actually appeared in
the March, 1913, issue of *Arts and Decoration*, an issue devoted entirely
to the Armory exhibition. Advance copies of the magazine, carrying
articles on the new art by Davies, the collector John Quinn, and
painters William Glackens and Guy Pène du Bois, went on sale shortly
after the exhibition opened on February 17. Mabel Dodge's article,
written in a deliberate and serious style that was far different from her
usually breathless letters, presented a picture of Gertrude soberly at
work in her Paris studio, surrounded by the revolutionary art of Matisse and Picasso. "She has taken the English language," the article announced, "and, according to many people has mis-used it, or has used it
roughly, uncouthly and brutally, or madly, stupidly and hideously, but
by her method she is finding the hidden and inner nature of nature."
Mrs. Dodge went on to link Gertrude Stein's intentions as a writer with
those of Picasso as a painter in a way that prefigured later critical approaches to her work:

In Gertrude Stein's writing every word lives and, apart from concept, it is so exquisitely rhythmical and cadenced that if we read it aloud and receive it as pure sound, it is like a kind of sensuous music. Just as one may stop, for once, in a way, before a canvas of Picasso, and, letting one's reason sleep for an instant, may exclaim: "It *is* a fine pattern!" so, listening to Gertrude Stein's words and forgetting to try to understand what they mean, one submits to their gradual charm.

The Armory Show was a publicist's dream. Thousands of people attended it during its month-long stay in New York. The exhibition and the artworks were hotly debated and ridiculed in the press. In New York it was Marcel Duchamp's *Nude Descending the Staircase* that received the lion's share of attention, one unfriendly critic labeling it an "explosion in a shingle factory." Another called the Cubist group, which included Picasso, Delaunay, and Braque, a "Chamber of Horrors." Editors, sensing good copy, kept up their attentions to the show in newspapers and magazines for months. When the exhibition traveled to Chicago and Boston, there were fresh outbreaks of satire and ridicule. Although the paintings that Leo and Gertrude had loaned were listed in Leo's name, it was Gertrude, largely because of Mabel Dodge's article, who was singled out for notice. Like the Armory Show itself, she had become good copy.

At the huge beefsteak dinner that the association gave for the "friends and enemies" of the press at Healy's Restaurant on the evening of March 8, a burlesque telegram, parodying Gertrude's style, was read out as part of the highjinks of the affair. When G. P. Putnam's published a parody version of a children's primer called *The Cubies' ABC*, Gertrude was commemorated:

G is for Gertrude Stein's limpid lucidity
   (Eloquent scribe of the Futurist Soul,)
Cubies devour each word with avidity:
"*Alone* words lack sense!" they affirm with placidity
"But *how* wise we'll be when we've swallowed the whole."
—G is for Gertrude Stein's lucid limpidity.

In Chicago it was the Steins' *Blue Nude* by Matisse that scandalized the conservative public. A group of irate art students made a replica of the painting and an effigy of the artist and burned both. Gertrude was remembered in a brisk quatrain that appeared in the *Chicago Tribune*:

I called the canvas *Cow with Cud*
And hung it on the line,
Altho' to me 'twas vague as mud,
'Twas clear to Gertrude Stein.

"You are just on the eve of *bursting!*" Mabel Dodge wrote Gertrude a few days before the exhibition opened in New York. "Everybody wherever I go—& others who go where I don't say the same thing—is talking of Gertrude Stein! There is an article coming out in the N.Y. Times this Sunday & the editor sent a young man around to see me & talk about you as he (the ed.) had got hold of a copy of yr portrait of me & he said he *must* get hold of it all *first* as it was new, etc. etc."

The young man from the *Times* was Carl Van Vechten, a music critic for the paper who, a few months later, met Gertrude in Paris and was to become a lifelong friend and one of the most dedicated of her publicists. The article in question was not printed, as expected, in the Sunday issue of the *Times*, but in the Monday-morning edition, February 17, the day the Armory Show opened. It appeared in the most unlikely of sections—on the financial page—and in only one edition. Still, it was more grist for the publicity mill.

Nothing indicates more clearly Gertrude's thirst for what she termed "*la gloire*" than the series of letters she addressed to Mabel Dodge during the period of the Armory exhibition. With the news that she was to be the subject of Mabel's article and one by Van Vechten in the *Times,* her letters displayed a mounting impatience. Writing to Mabel from the Knightsbridge Hotel in London, where she and Alice had gone late in January in an attempt to interest English publishers in her work, she congratulated her "faithful and incomprehending Boswell": "I am completely delighted with your performance and busting to see the article, send it as soon as it is printed. You must be having an awfully amusing time and there will be lots of stories to tell. It takes lots of showing to make them take me, but I guess you will do it." Mabel's portrait, Gertrude reported, was creating a stir in London. The "most unexpected interested person" was Logan Pearsall Smith:

Among other things he read it to [Israel] Zangwill and Zangwill was moved. He said, "And I always thought she was such a healthy minded young woman, what a terrible blow it must be for her poor dear brother." And it seems he meant it.

In one of her letters Gertrude noted, "It's a good time to see publishers but I am awfully cold-footed about it. Like Davidson, I haven't got much courage." In a later letter she reported that the publisher John Lane and the *English Review* were both "nibbling." The former was considering an English edition of *Three Lives;* the latter had a number of her shorter pieces, including the "Portrait of Mabel Dodge." The English art critic Roger Fry, a pioneering sponsor of the new art, who had visited her in Paris the year before, had agreed to help Lane "land" her. Fry, she wrote, was being "awfully good about my work. It seems that he read *Three Lives* long ago and was much impressed with it and so he is doing his best to get me published. His being a Quaker gives him more penetration in his sweetness than is usual with his type, it does not make him more interesting but it makes him purer."

In the meantime, she and Alice were enjoying their glimpse of English society. They attended the opening night of the Russian Ballet and a performance of Richard Strauss's *Elektra*. Although not an ardent music lover, Gertrude had found the Strauss opera illuminating: "It made a deeper impression on me than anything since Tristan in my youth. He has done what Wagner tried to do and couldn't, he has made real conversation and he does it by intervals and relations directly without machinery. After all we are all modern." They were given a "handsome" dinner by the singer Paul Draper and his wife, Muriel, friends of Mabel's, "the table a complete scheme in white only broken by the vivid color of food and wine." On February 13 they met both George Moore and Lytton Strachey at a dinner given by Miss Ethel Sands— "the incorrigible old Sapphist," as Strachey unkindly referred to his hostess. Strachey sat next to Alice, talking in "a faint high voice." They discussed Picasso and the Russian Ballet. The biographer of Queen Victoria admitted that he had "gleaned a certain amount of information about Picasso" that interested him, but, as he wrote a friend, he had found his conversation with Miss Stein's friend "vexing." He had wanted to listen to George Moore and couldn't manage it.

None of Gertrude's English prospects materialized, and she and Alice returned to Paris later in the month with only a handful of polite rejection letters and a few vague hopes. Lane was still considering *Three Lives*. The *English Review* had turned her down, but Logan Pearsall Smith was hopeful that the *Oxford Fortnightly* might take some of her word portraits. Her English campaign had put a dent in her finances. "Owing to the stress of poverty," she told Mabel, "we will be staying in Paris surely through June."

Understandably, Gertrude was even more impatient for the harvest of publicity she seemed about to reap in New York. Her letters to Mabel expressed her growing anticipation: "Nothing has come yet, not your article or clippings, but I guess they are on the way and if you have not sent a catalogue of the show will you send one." She wrote again: "Your letter via Jo Davidson has just come, but not your article. Please send that I want to see it, surely I will like it. Please send it quick."

Finally, the longed-for copies of *Arts and Decoration* arrived. Gertrude was thrilled:

I've just gotten hold of your article and I am delighted with it. Really it is awfully well done and I am as proud as punch. Do send me half a dozen copies of it. I want to show it to everybody. Hurrah for gloire.

Her first enthusiastic response was seconded immediately by another letter:

I have just read your article over again quietly and I am startled to see how completely and fully you have told your story. It is admirable in its measure and amplitude.
  Your sentences are full and simple. I am delighted and more than delighted.
  I expected to be pleased and I am really stirred.

When Mabel sent her a batch of clippings and letters, Gertrude experienced a new surge of excitement:

I have just gotten through the clippings, golly there were a lot of them. I was delighted with the letters to you from total strangers. Who did the typewritten parody about you and your entourage, it was thorough and intelligent and at times extremely good. . . . I get awfully excited about the gloire but this last batch has quite filled me up. . . . Bully for us, we are doing fine.

II

There were, however, a few clouds gathering over the recent and amiable partnership between Gertrude and Mabel Dodge. In an earlier letter, Gertrude mentioned having sent a manuscript, *Many Many Women*, to a New York publisher, Mitchell Kennerley. The book was a tediously long, repetitious group portrait written in her *Making of Americans* manner. Kennerley, Gertrude told Mabel, had had the book for about four months. "He said he wanted to see something of mine because Stieglitz had spoken of me to him and so I sent him that, but he has never written anything about it. I have not wired him because I supposed he was making up his mind." Her next mention was more pointed: "I wonder if Mitchell Kennerley is going to do anything with my ms. Will you ask him sometime. There is no use my writing to him as he does not answer. Perhaps you can find out." There seems to have been an element of bad faith in Gertrude's handling of the Kennerley business, for May Knoblauch, also acting as Gertrude's agent, had placed several shorter pieces with the publisher, as well as the manuscript of *The Making of Americans*. Gertrude apparently felt that Mabel Dodge would be a more forceful representative. Mabel, unable to make contact with Kennerley, who refused to see her or talk with her on the telephone, promptly started legal action to recover the manuscripts. Having learned from May Knoblauch that Kennerley also had the manuscript of *The Making of Americans*, she asked Gertrude for written authority, "*at once*," to get possession of the book. She proposed turning it over to Flora Holly, the literary agent. Writing to Gertrude on May 2, 1913, Mabel told Gertrude, "The lawyer expects today a reply from K. as he has now delivered an ultimatum. He must deliver up *all* the mms. & take or reject the *one* he wanted—& state terms." Mabel's pressure tactics at first seem to have been successful. Kennerley proposed publishing six of Gertrude's shorter pieces.

Gertrude was cool about the Holly proposal; she related the history of her unsatisfactory dealings with Miss Holly over *Three Lives*. But she was plainly grateful for Mabel's efficiency: "I am delighted about Mitchell Kennerley. I have not written to him about it because I knew you could do it for me so much better. I cannot tell you how happy I am about it all." She was, it seems, content to rely on Mabel's services. In a later letter, she asked: "And what book is Mitchell Kennerley doing and when is it coming out. He has an interesting handwriting and seems to have an extremely hopeful temperament. He sounds all right." Gertrude's optimism proved unfounded. The Kennerley deal did not materialize. The manuscript of *The Making of Americans* was returned to her by way of May Knoblauch.

In the meantime, Gertrude had been sending Mabel Dodge examples of her recent writing. Sensing that the publication of Mabel's article about her and the publicity surrounding the Armory Show might create an interest in her work, she evidently expected Mabel would be as dedicated to her career as she was herself. From London she had written Mabel: "I will send you a little bunch of short things so that you will have something if you get a chance to place it, but make them pay for them because I don't want to get known as giving them away." Moreover, she had begun experimenting with playwriting as a logical outgrowth of her portrait writing. Gertrude's "plays" were generally brief pieces, made up of what appeared to be conversational fragments but written in elusive language. Often they gave no indications as to which characters were speaking which lines. It was her playwriting activities that had led her to recognize in Strauss's *Elektra* the attempt to make "real conversation" without the usual stage "machinery." One of Mabel Dodge's friends, the actress Florence Bradley, had read several of Gertrude's plays during a visit to Paris in 1912. According to Gertrude, Miss Bradley had been excited and enthusiastic about them. Nourishing hopes that her latest literary innovations might be produced, Gertrude sent several of her short early theater pieces to Mabel, hoping Mabel and Florence Bradley would find a producer for them. She was, in fact, to wait twenty years before the first of her plays to be performed, *Four Saints in Three Acts*, was produced as an opera with a score by Virgil Thomson.

The first serious rift in the friendship occurred over the plays. When Mabel suggested publishing them without waiting for production, Gertrude's tone became peremptory: "No decidedly not," she wrote Mabel. "I do *not* want the plays published. They are to be kept to be played. Florence Bradley understands about that perfectly." On the subject of the other works languishing in Mabel's keeping, Gertrude was equally sharp—in fact, rude: "I want the short things you have to be published in magazines as I told you. I think that is the important step now. If you cannot arrange that send them back and I will do it from over here but it must be in good *monthlies*. I definitely do *not* want anything of mine published in newspapers or weeklies."

A critical episode in their dissolving friendship centered around the publication of *Tender Buttons*. A young poet, Donald Evans, a colleague of Van Vechten's at the *New York Times*, had embarked on a new publishing venture, the Claire Marie Press, intending to sponsor vanguard literature. He wrote to Gertrude in February, 1914, asking if he might bring out a volume of her plays. Anticipating Gertrude's objections, Evans had countered: "My bringing out the volume, my dear Miss Stein, would not in any way hurt the producing value; in fact, it would stimulate interest in their production in the theater." Evans made her a bona fide offer—"10% royalty on the first 500 copies sold and 15% on all after that." It was the first legitimate offer Gertrude had received—that is, one in which she would not have to pay for the privilege of being published. Furthermore, Evans was extravagantly optimistic about what he could do for the book: "I can give you a book of more distinguished appearance than any other publisher in America and I can also get you more publicity for it," he told Gertrude. "My public also is the most civilized in this country."

Her appetite for *la gloire* already whetted, Gertrude could scarcely resist such an opportunity. Still, she was reluctant to have the plays published. She sent Evans, instead, the manuscript of *Tender Buttons*, a collection of short pieces divided into three segments entitled "Objects," "Food," and "Rooms." The book was a much more revolutionary work than *Three Lives*.

Ostensibly, the poems or prose pieces (they are difficult to categorize) were verbal re-creations of the objects and foodstuffs Gertrude was considering— "A Long Dress," "A Red Hat," "Milk," "Eggs," a "Single Fish." But in *Tender Buttons* Gertrude had pushed the disjunctive language of her Spanish exercises to even greater hermetic lengths. Very few clues are offered to the reader. In the generally brief pieces that make up the first two sections of the book, the language is undeniably cryptic, while the syntax is conventional. "A Long Dress" is typical of the method she employed through much of the book:

What is the current that makes machinery, that makes it crackle, what is the current that presents a long line and a necessary waist. What is this current.

What is the wind, what is it.

Where is the serene length, is it there and a dark place is not a dark place, only a white and red are black, only a yellow and green are blue, a pink is scarlet, a bow is every color. A line distinguishes it. A line just distinguishes it.

Occasionally Gertrude pruned the prose poems to the limits of brevity. "Dining" in its entirety reads:

Dining is west.

Each of the pieces has its carefully contrived rhythm—abrupt or languid, the words frequently repeated for percussive effect. The most curious piece, "This is This Dress, Aider," which Richard Bridgman, in his critical study, translates as "This is Distress, Ada," seems to hint at some sexual connotation. It reads:

Aider, why aider why whow, whow stop touch, aider whow, aider stop the muncher, muncher munchers.

A jack in kill her, a jack in, makes a meadowed king, makes a to let.

The exclamatory "whow stop touch" seem nearly orgiastic. But only seldom do such hints of meaning and sense rise to the surface of the poems.

The final segment of the book, "Rooms," is a long, uninterrupted prose poem. Brief references to a large stove, a large table, and double doors—"what is the use of a covering to a door. There is a use, they are double"—suggest that Gertrude is describing, abstractly, her own studio room and, perhaps, the rooms of the adjacent pavilion, which opened onto the courtyard: "Harmony is so essential. Is there pleasure when there is a passage, there is when every room is open." There are occasional joking allusions that may be personal: "The sister was not a mister. Was this a surprise. It was." After a fleeting reference to a "description," there is the announcement: "The author of all that is in there behind the door."

Although Gertrude's recollections of the dates at which various of her works were written are not always accurate, she maintained in her autobiography that *Tender Buttons* was begun during her summer in Spain and completed when she returned to Paris. The style corroborates that dating, and in "Rooms" there is internal evidence to suggest that that section had been written in Paris. Midway through the piece, a three-sentence paragraph occurs:

Giving it away, not giving it away, is there any difference. Giving it away. Not giving it away.

The passage apparently relates to a visit the wealthy and irascible American collector Dr. Albert Barnes, a patent-medicine millionaire, made to the rue de Fleurus late in 1912. As Gertrude wrote Mabel Dodge, Barnes "did literally wave his cheque book in the air." It appears to have been Barnes who, standing before Picasso's portrait of her, bluntly asked Gertrude how much she had paid for it. "Nothing," Gertrude said. "Nothing?" the collector exclaimed. "Nothing," Gertrude repeated, "naturally he gave it to me." When she related the incident to Picasso a few days later, the painter smiled: "He doesn't understand that at that time the difference between a sale and a gift was negligible."

It was Gertrude's contention that in *Tender Buttons* she had struggled to rid herself of nouns in her writing: "I knew nouns must go in poetry as they had gone in prose if anything that is everything was to go on meaning something." What she wanted to do, she claimed, was what Shakespeare had done with the Forest of Arden: create a scene, a setting, an object without consciously describing it. "You feel it all but he does not name its names." *Tender Buttons* fairly bristles with nouns—the "perchings" rather than the "flights" of language and thought, as William James had put it—but it is true that they have been deprived of their focal meanings. They no longer stand as the comforting "names" of things in Gertrude's sentences. The language having become dissociative and abstract, the nouns were shorn of their meaningful associations. Still, she could admit to only a partial success. She could not dispense with them entirely. "I struggled I struggled desperately with the recreation and the avoidance of nouns as nouns and yet poetry being poetry nouns are nouns."

Gertrude's decision to publish the book with Donald Evans—*Tender Buttons* was eventually published in June, 1914, a slender volume with yellow covers and a circular green label—created a serious rift in her relations with Mabel Dodge. In March, Mabel had written to Gertrude in a perhaps fatal proprietary manner. "Dearest Gertrude," Mabel began, "This is going to be a letter."

Now in the first place. About your stuff. I cabled you *not* to publish with D. Evans after having a long talk with E. A. Robinson who is our "dark poet" here, & who knows more about things than most people. He knows Evans & believes in his ability but he thinks the Claire Marie Press which Evans runs is absolutely third rate, & in bad odor here, being called for the most part "decadent" & Broadwayish & that sort of thing. He wrote Evans to get out of it, to chuck it & stop getting linked up in the public "mind" with it. I think it would be a pity to publish with him *if* it will emphasize the idea in the opinion of the public, that there is something degenerate & effete & decadent about the whole of the cubist movement which they *all* connect you with, because, hang it all, as long as they don't understand a thing they think all sorts of things. My feeling in this is quite strong."

It was just the kind of letter, preceded by a peremptory telegram, that would put Gertrude off. She knew the value of publicity—good and bad. She had been through the campaigns when Matisse and Picasso were scorned and ridiculed. Now they both had dealers, and their canvases were bringing advantageous prices. But if Gertrude was rankled by the abrupt tone of Mabel Dodge's letter, their friendship did not terminate on the spot. It was allowed to cool in easy stages.

Mabel sensed that "for some obscure reason," Gertrude was angry. She noted in her memoirs that "we still wrote back and forth for I had business to do for her, though I was the last who should have tried that —being so muddle-headed, forgetful and self-centered." When, a few years later, she asked Leo Stein what had caused the coolness between herself and Gertrude, Leo intimated that Mabel had stepped out too far into Gertrude's limelight. There was some doubt in Gertrude's mind, Leo told Mabel, "as to which was the more important, the bear or the one leading the bear."

Mabel Dodge, however, ascribed the break to other causes. In her memoirs, she maintained that she had been especially puzzled by the character of Alice Toklas, whom she described in terms that were both sultry and bizarre: "like Leah, out of the Old Testament, in her half-Oriental get-up—her blues and browns and oyster whites—her black hair—her barbaric chains and jewels—and her melancholy nose. Artistic." It was Mabel's impression, during that autumn visit to the Villa Curonia, that Alice was forever manicuring—Mabel did not say sharpening—her nails: "Every morning, for an hour, Alice polished her nails—they had become a fetish with her. She loved her hands." But what perturbed Mrs. Dodge most was Alice's implacable calmness. One day she asked Alice outright: "What makes you contented? What keeps you going?"

Alice answered, "Why, I suppose it's my feeling for Gertrude."

Leo Stein had given Mabel a disturbing picture of life at the rue de Fleurus after Alice moved in. Alice "did everything to save Gertrude a movement—all the housekeeping, the typing, seeing people who called, and getting rid of the undesirables, answering letters—really providing all the motor force of the menage. . . . And Gertrude was growing helpless and foolish from it and less inclined to do anything herself." As Leo observed, he had "seen trees strangled by vines in this same way."

The basic cause of the break in her friendship with Gertrude, however, Mabel Dodge attributed to an incident that had occurred that autumn of 1912 when "The Portrait of Mabel Dodge" had been written. An incurable romantic, who saw herself at the center of many romances—whatever the gender of her admirers—Mabel had noticed that during the writing of the portrait, Gertrude seemed "to grow warmer to me." Mabel had, she confessed, responded in "a sort of flirtatious way," though her thoughts were taken up with the young blond tutor.

One day at lunch, "Gertrude, sitting opposite me in Edwin's chair, sent me such a strong look over the table that it seemed to cut across the air to me in a band of electrified steel—a smile traveling across on it—powerful—Heavens! I remember it *now* so keenly!" Alice, according to Mrs. Dodge, caught sight of this exchange. She got up from the table immediately and rushed out onto the terrace. When she didn't return, Gertrude followed after her. Several minutes elapsed. Gertrude came back without Alice. "She doesn't want to come to lunch," Gertrude explained. "She feels the heat today."

The process was slow and piecemeal, Mabel Dodge noted—"*poco-poco*" was her phrase—but the result was, inevitably, the same: the end of her friendship with Gertrude. The dissolving of their friendship, Mabel was sure, had been "Alice's final and successful effort in turning Gertrude from me—her influencing and her wish."

In this welter of motivating forces—Gertrude's heady personal ambitions, her responsiveness to admiration and flattery; Alice's possessiveness, her sense of insecurity despite her outward calm; the intrusion of a third person whom Gertrude flirtatiously encouraged—there lay all the classic elements for many of Gertrude's later estrangements.

III

Mabel Dodge's laudatory article in *Arts and Decoration* had done much to promote Gertrude's American reputation as a leader of the artistic vanguard, but it had not done everything. By 1913, Gertrude's contacts with the American chapter of the international vanguard had already been firmly established. She had become a fixture of the Parisian scene, a celebrated hostess whose collection of modern art was considered a must for visiting American artists. For many of them, 27, rue de Fleurus became a kind of American oasis on the banks of the Seine. One could always get there the most recent news from home and the latest word on the heated controversies of the Parisian art scene. Old friends brought new acquaintances; new arrivals came with letters of introduction from former visitors. Artists stationed in Paris for their indoctrination into the school of Paris regularly brought their friends and colleagues from the States.

The Steins' hospitality extended to most of the major and minor figures of America's first wave of modernists—that generation of artists who, like Alfred Maurer, Max Weber, Marsden Hartley, struggled against

Leo and Nina in Settignano, Italy. (Courtesy Yale Collection of American Literature.)

Alice and Gertrude in Venice, *circa* 1908. (Courtesy Yale Collection of American Literature.)

Laurencin, *Group of Artists* (Picasso, Laurencin, Apollinaire, and Fernande Olivier), oil on canvas, 1908. (Cone Collection, The Baltimore Museum of Art.)

Marie Laurencin. (Courtesy Yale Collection of American Literature.)

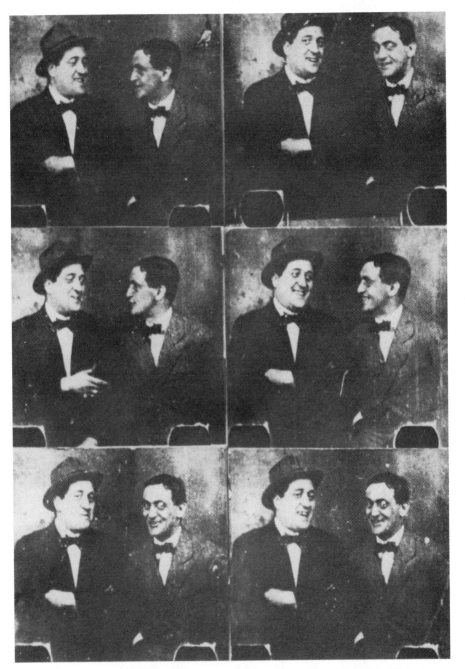

Guillaume Apollinaire and André Rouveyre, Paris, August 1, 1914. The photograph, taken on the eve of World War I, was presented to Gertrude in 1939, on the eve of World War II. (Courtesy Yale Collection of American Literature.)

Picasso, *Still Life with a Calling Card*, pasted paper and crayon, 1914. (Collection Mrs. Gilbert W. Chapman, New York.)

Picasso, *The Architect's Table*, oil on canvas, 1912. (Collection of The Museum of Modern Art, New York. Gift of William S. Paley.)

Picabia, object-portrait, *Here, This Is Stieglitz*, 1915. (Courtesy the Washburn Gallery, New York.)

Demuth, poster portrait, *Love, Love, Love* (Homage to Gertrude Stein), oil on board, *circa* 1928. (Courtesy Lee Ault and Co., Inc.)

Alvin Langdon Coburn, portrait photograph of Gertrude Stein, 1913. (Courtesy Yale Collection of American Literature.)

With Claribel and Etta Cone. (Courtesy Yale Collection of American Literature.)

"Alfy" Maurer. (Courtesy the Weyhe Gallery, New York.)

Janet Scudder. (Courtesy Macbeth Gallery Records, Archives of American Art, the Smithsonian Institution.)

Mildred Aldrich in her pony-cart. (Courtesy Yale Collection of American Literature.)

Henry McBride in Mildred Aldrich's garden. (Courtesy Yale Collection of American Literature.)

The studio at the rue de Fleurus after Leo's departure, winter, 1914–15. (Courtesy Yale Collection of American Literature.)

Gertrude and Alice with "Auntie," in service, *circa* 1917. (Courtesy Yale Collection of American Literature.)

the hard American grain, attempting to translate the lessons of Parisian modernism into the American idiom. Aside from providing a convenient study collection of what was currently happening in Parisian art, the Steins could be counted upon to arrange introductions to painters such as Matisse and Picasso and to accompany their guests on studio visits, serving as translators if needed.

In time a network of associations stretched across the Atlantic from the Left Bank of Paris to New York. Gertrude's early favorite, Alfy Maurer, brought William Glackens, one of the New York Eight, to see the Stein collection early in 1912. In turn, Glackens brought his patron, Dr. Barnes, later in the same year. It seems likely, too, that Maurer had introduced the young American painter Arthur Dove to the rue de Fleurus, around 1909, when Dove was in Europe. Max Weber, the small, doughty painter from New York, one of the first Americans to enroll in the Matisse Academy and a visitor to the rue de Fleurus until he returned to America in 1909, sent the American photographer Alvin Langdon Coburn—the friend and illustrator of Henry James. Coburn had sought the introduction as a means of photographing Matisse for his *Men of Mark*, published in 1913. Struck by Gertrude's appearance and her reputation—he seems to have been considering a companion volume on notable women—Coburn asked to photograph Gertrude as well. Gertrude was impressed: It was the first time she had been photographed by a celebrated professional photographer. Coburn, who was living in London at the time, was pressed into further useful services, helping to promote Gertrude's cause among the English publishers of his acquaintance.

Walter Pach, Leo's convert to modernism and a sometime student of the Matisse Academy, brought the Italian-born American painter Joseph Stella in 1911. Gertrude found the big and boisterous painter rather like Apollinaire; they both had a fund of sarcastic wit that was frequently turned on their hosts. Stella, whose literary style ran to *bel canto* flourishes and misspellings, left a sardonic account of a visit to the Steins among his fragmentary autobiographical notes:

Somehow in a little side street in Montparnasse there was a family that had acquired some early work of Matisse and Picasso. The lady of the house was an immense woman carcass austerely dressed in black. Enthroned on a sofa in the middle of the room where the pictures were hanging, with the forceful solemnity of a pitoness or a sibylla, she was examining pitiless all newcomers, assuming a high and distant pose.

Another account of a visit to the rue de Fleurus made in 1910 by a little-known but creditable modernist painter, Manierre Dawson, gives a vivid impression of the easy, democratic manner in which the Steins conducted their Saturday evenings. Dawson, an architect turned

painter, had arrived in Paris with an introduction from one of his colleagues in a Chicago architectural firm. Calling at the Steins'—it was a
Wednesday afternoon—he was met at the door by Alice, who informed
him that "Miss Gertrude" was busy that afternoon, but would be at
home on Saturday evening.

"Telling Whitley about it," Dawson wrote in his journal for November 2, "he suggested we call together and also suggested I take along a
wood panel to show. He said Saturdays brought a mixture of nationalities to Miss Stein's, but while there was much confusion and the
light was not good, one could see an extraordinary jumble of paintings,
a few of them remarkable and well worth examining."

On the following Saturday, the pair presented themselves at the
rue de Fleurus. Dawson was introduced to Gertrude and informed her
that he was "a fellow draughtsman of Lebenbaum's," that he was more
interested in painting than in architecture, but that he "could not stay
long in Paris because money was running out." His journal account
continued:

After some time she beckoned me to her chair. With some diffidence I
showed her my little painting which I had carried under my arm. Looking
at it for a while steadily, she passed it to a bearded Frenchman who said
a few words in comment, raised his eyebrows and with just a suggestion of
a bow, returned it to me. Then came the surprise. "Can I have this?" said
Miss Stein. "Do you mean to buy it?" I asked smiling and thinking I would
gladly give it to her. "Yes," she said, "Would 200 francs be right?" "Yes."
This is the first painting I ever sold.

Charles Demuth, the later Precisionist painter, visited the Steins
often during his 1912–14 sojourn in Paris when he was studying at
various Parisian academies. An elegant homosexual, something of a
dandy, witty and friendly, Demuth, at the time, was also pondering a
career as a writer. Gertrude knew little of his artwork; Demuth impressed her because he was among the first to express an interest in
her newly written plays. He and Florence Bradley, she claimed, "were
always talking them over together." Writing about Demuth in her
autobiography, Gertrude maintained—incorrectly—that she had never
seen Demuth since those early years but that they sent messages to each
other through mutual friends: "Demuth always sent word that some
day he would do a little picture that would thoroughly please him and
then he would send it." One day, in the early thirties, the painting
arrived, "A remarkable little landscape in which the roofs and windows are so subtle that they are as mysterious and as alive as the roofs
and windows of Hawthorne or Henry James." The comparison was apt,
for among Demuth's better works are his watercolor illustrations for
the stories of Henry James.

Another Precisionist painter, Charles Sheeler, had his first glimpse of modern art in the flesh not at the rue de Fleurus, but at one of Sarah Stein's "evenings." Traveling in Europe with his parents in 1909—Sheeler was then twenty-six—he had gone to the Steins' at home with an introduction from a mutual friend. The walls of their living room, he recalled years later, were "plastered" with Matisses and Picassos. "I went to a couple of galleries, but I didn't see as much there as I saw at the Steins on that one evening." Sheeler's brief exposure to the modernists, however, made a deep impression: "I didn't understand them in the least, but I did carry the conviction that the artists knew what they were doing."

Aside from visiting countrymen, there was a contingent of American artists living in Paris before World War I who regularly frequented the rue de Fleurus. Most of them—Patrick Henry Bruce, Arthur B. Frost, Jr., Morgan Russell, H. Lyman Sayen—were under the influence of Matisse during the early years when Gertrude and Leo knew them. Bruce, an aristocratic Virginian, was an ardent Matisseite. His friend Frost, another member of the Matisse Academy, was the son of the highly successful illustrator A. B. Frost. The elder Frost took a dim view of his son's dabbling in such exotic forms of art. Gertrude recorded a conversation in which the father complained to Bruce that "it was a pity that Arthur could not see his way to becoming a conventional artist and so earning fame and money." Bruce countered, "You can lead a horse to water but you cannot make him drink." "Most horses drink, Mr. Bruce," was the elder Frost's starchy answer.

Morgan Russell was a practicing sculptor when he first met Gertrude and Leo, around 1908. For two years he worked with Matisse as a sculptor and then reverted to painting. In later years, only modestly successful as a painter, he referred to himself as "a sculptor *manqué*." Russell was one of Nina's three tempestuous suitors when her affair with Leo had just begun. With incredible patience, Leo listened to Russell's woes, discussed art with him, and on occasion loaned Russell money. Although Leo regarded this three-sided affair as something of a "tragi-comedy," he seems to have been on guard against any sudden burst of passion on Russell's part, as when he advised Nina not to visit him in Italy. In the course of his discussions with Russell, Leo, too, had apparently opened up. He once told Russell that he wanted "above everything to be a painter, that he had sat in front of a plate of fruit for days, hoping to be able to express something in paint and had finally given it up."

Another American painter who met the Steins during this period was Stanton Macdonald-Wright, who, together with Russell, Bruce, and Frost, a few years later, formed the nucleus of the Synchromist group. Wright thought the Steins an "ill-assorted pair," yet he genuinely admired Leo's "retiring but authoritative presence." He found it far different from Gertrude's "exhibitionism and forwardness." Wright recalled a visit he and Russell had paid to the rue de Fleurus, one evening in 1909, just after Leo had bought some Cézanne watercolors. Gertrude "was standing in front of them dressed in a long brown corduroy kimono, swaying gently from right to left, pontificating as usual. Her summation of their artistic value was 'they seem to float.' Whereupon, suddenly, she levitated, cigarette and all, and alighted in the pose of Ingres' 'Odalisque' on a couch with a beatific smile. The whole episode struck Morgan and me as highly ludicrous as G was no sylph and as I had myself bought four of those watercolors in which we found something vastly more than their lighter than air qualities."

Several of these younger artists—Pach, Russell, Frost, among them—were to "sit" for Gertrude's verbal portraits. Written in the comprehensible, repetitious style of her Matisse and Picasso portraits, these verbal studies of the American artists in her circle are much less decisive in tone and rather maundering. Part of her difficulty, apparently, was the youth of her subjects and her indecision about whether they would be successful or not. With Pach, age appears to be a determining factor in the question of his uncertain future prospects: "If he is a young one now he will perhaps be succeeding very well in living. If he is not a young one now he will perhaps be succeeding well in living." With Russell, Gertrude had an abrupt change of mind before completing her portrait: "One was quite certain that he would be one succeeding in living and then that one was quite certain that he would not be one succeeding in living." "Frost" is the most flaccid and aimless of the studies. The artist, it appears, was a respectful listener—a quality Gertrude responded to: "He certainly did listen and listen again and again, he certainly quite steadily did this thing."

"I do miss 27—I shall sometime paint why I miss 27—It is a place of living issues and the dead ones that come there don't affect it." The writer was the American painter Marsden Hartley. He was writing to Gertrude from Germany in the summer of 1913, where he had become acquainted with the artists of the Blue Rider group and those associated with Herwarth Walden's vanguard publication *Der Sturm*. Not long after, Hartley was invited to exhibit in the first German Autumn Salon, held that year in Berlin—a singular honor for an American artist so recently acquainted with the European scene. Hartley was much impressed by the creative *élan* of his German colleagues; he was equally taken with the handsome, athletic appearance of the young men in Germany. In Hartley, it seemed, the soul of a voluptuary had been imprisoned in the frame of a proper, but not too proper, New Englander. Thirty-six, tall and lumbering, hawk-nosed, dour in expression, he was possessed of a pair of the lightest, most intense blue eyes imaginable. They gave the stern, craggy features of his face an almost incandescent look.

In the spring of 1912, Hartley had made 27, rue de Fleurus one of his first stops on his inaugural trip abroad. At the Steins' he had been much impressed by the Cézannes and the Picassos, but he had not had time to look through Gertrude's albums of Picasso drawings. That fall, after Gertrude and Alice returned from their vacation in Spain and Italy, he wrote, asking if he might visit the rue de Fleurus to study the Picassos. He also asked if he might bring a new friend, a German sculptor, Arnold Rönnebeck, who found Picasso "as impressive as I myself do."

Gertrude and Alice developed an interest in both men, and Hartley and Rönnebeck were often invited to the rue de Fleurus during the winter. Rönnebeck, who had an amiable and flattering manner, spoke English and French in addition to his native German. On reading Gertrude's "Portrait of Mabel Dodge," he claimed that Gertrude's style was "photographic,"—a description that pleased her. Although she stoutly maintained that she did not like Germans, Gertrude admitted that Rönnebeck was an exception. He was, plainly, "charming" and was always invited to dinner.

Gertrude also took an interest in Rönnebeck's work. In a brief memoir, published many years later, Rönnebeck recalled a visit that Gertrude and Alice had made to his studio. Gertrude took it upon herself to offer some critical advice. Studying his sculptures, Gertrude told him: "Get that real roundness into them. This way I just don't like them." "After all," she added, "a form is a form is a form." The phrase recalls her famous description of a rose in "Sacred Emily," a poem that she seems to have been working on at the time. As a favor, Rönnebeck had offered to translate her Mabel Dodge and Picasso portraits into French and German. The Picasso portrait was read aloud to its subject, one day, at the rue de Fleurus. After only the first half page, Picasso moaned, "*Assez, assez, oh mon Dieu!*" The group broke out in laughter at Picasso's consternation. Finally, he turned and said, "Gertrude, I just don't like abstractions."

Gertrude's friendship with Rönnebeck became a casualty of World War I. Her relationship with Hartley was more solidly based. It was a mark of their mutual respect for each other that Hartley left four pictures with Gertrude for safekeeping when he went to Germany in April, 1913. He offered Gertrude one of these as a gift. Gertrude refused, insisting that she would rather buy something from the artist, and eventually chose one of his drawings. Hartley agreed, but asked that she keep the money—twenty dollars—until such time as he needed it. The time came in October, while Hartley was living in Berlin. Gertrude telegraphed the money, sending an equal amount as a gift.

In response, Hartley wrote her a long, grateful letter in which he discussed his career. He had written to her several times throughout the summer, expressing his enjoyment of "Deutschland" and his relief at having escaped from the high-powered aestheticism of Paris: "I feel like a neophyte who has left the theologians to their arguments and has come out to sit in the sun and ponder on bright flowers and nice meaningless smiles." His October letter, however, written from 4 Nassauischestrasse, was one of the lengthiest and most detailed of their correspondence. He gave Gertrude a strikingly poetic account of his personal background ("I am without prescribed culture. I have grown up out of a strange thicket—") and noted his indebtedness to his New York dealer, Stieglitz ("I owe him everything for the success of the past"). He mentioned that it was the Cézanne watercolors he had seen at the rue de Fleurus as well as those he had recently viewed at Bernheims that had given him the "most inspiration as expressing the color & form of 'new places.'" His outpouring of aspirations and feelings to a sympathetic listener, however, seems to have occasioned some moments of anxiety. His letter is punctuated with deferential asides: "However you will be bored to death—by this time. If I were sitting with you in 27, it would all be but one of my conversations."

Gertrude, engrossed in studying the men in her circle—especially the men with creative abilities—considered Hartley a worthy case. She introduced him as one of the characters in a curious play titled "IIIIIIIIII." The title can be taken as a series of Roman numerals or else as ten instances of the first person singular. In her wayward fashion, however, there are more than a dozen characters in the play, each identified by an odd series of initials or segments of their names. Hartley, for instance is M——N H——, while his friend Rönnebeck appears as R——K. Other roles are assigned to Gertrude's Boston friend Thomas Whittemore (T——S WH——) and probably the painter Alfred Maurer (ALF——). Interspersed between the set "speeches," written in Gertrude's most hermetic vein, there are, as well, a series of queerly titled statements ("Incline," "Banking," "The Wedding," for example) that seem to indicate the persona of the author. "Points," for instance, reads:

The exchange which is fanciful and righteous and mingled is in the author mostly in the piece.

Hartley's monologues, as with other speeches in the play, occasionally hover at the edge of meaning:

A sound is in the best society. It hums and moves, it throws the hat in no way away and in no way particularly at paving. The meanness is a selection of parts and all of that is no more a handkerchief merely and large.

Gertrude sent a copy of the play to Hartley in Germany and received an enthusiastic response. "It seems to have another kind of dynamic power," Hartley wrote, "—a kind of shoot to it and I feel my own color very much in what I say—my own substance. 'Peaceable in the rest of the stretch' I say somewhere. It is so good for I feel that way." Not one to pass up an opportunity, Gertrude suggested to Hartley that Stieglitz—who had already printed her word portraits of Picasso, Matisse, and Mabel Dodge in his magazine *Camera Work*— might be willing to print her play accompanied by illustrations of Hartley's work. Hartley, who was scheduled for an exhibition at Stieglitz' "291" Gallery, was enthusiastic. A segment of the play, comprised of three of his "speeches," followed by "Points," which incorporated several more of his isolated lines and "The Wedding," was printed in the catalogue for Hartley's exhibition, which opened in January, 1914. That Gertrude was willing to dismember the play for publication indicates a certain sense of expediency on her part—all the more notable, since at the same time she was being so adamant with Mabel Dodge on the subject of not having her theater pieces published before they were performed. Mabel Dodge contributed an introduction to the same Hartley catalogue. If she was aware that the Hartley "portrait" had been extracted bodily from one of Gertrude's plays, she must have been aware, as well, that Gertrude had one set of rules for herself and quite another for her harried promoters.

Gertrude's more explicit judgments about Hartley's work are revealed in her letters. While she entertained hopes for Hartley's success, she thought the artist was a slow starter. "I am glad you are all interested in Hartley," she wrote to Mabel Dodge when the painter returned to the States. "He is an interesting person alright, he ought to have time given him, he will need plenty of it, he is not a quick developer." It was an accurate assessment of Hartley's subsequent career, which explored several stylistic avenues before settling into the primitivistic vein of his late paintings.

A 1913 letter that Gertrude wrote to Stieglitz on the subject of Hartley provides a long critical estimate of his art. Whether one agrees with Gertrude's high evaluation—she compares him favorably with Kandinsky, Picasso, and Matisse—the letter offers explicit evidence that despite the judgments of her contemporaries and some later critics, Gertrude had arrived at a firm understanding of some of the most important formal issues of modern painting.

"In his painting," she wrote Stieglitz, "he [Hartley] has done what in Kandinsky is only a direction. Hartley has really done it. He has used color to express a picture and he has done it so completely that while there is nothing mystic or strange about his production it is genuinely transcendent. Each canvas is a thing in itself and contained within itself, and the accomplishment of it is quite extraordinarily complete. . . . In some way he has managed to keep your attention freshened and as you look you keep on being freshened. There is not motion but there is an absence of the stillness that even in the big men often leads to non-existence.

"He seems to be entirely on the right track. He is the only one working in color, that is. considering the color as more dominant than line, who is really attempting to create an entity in a picture which is not a copy of light. He deals with color as actually as Picasso deals with his forms. In this respect, he is working in a very different way from the neo-impressionist Delaunay etc. who, following out Van Gogh and Matisse, are really producing a disguised but poverty-stricken realism; the realism of form having been taken away from them they have solaced themselves with the realism of light. Hartley has not done this, he deals with color as a medium for creation and he is doing it really."

A further reference to Matisse in this context reveals Gertrude's misgivings about the course of that painter's development. "Of course Matisse with his feeling for the vitality of the human form and his superb gift of color has achieved marvels but I have always felt that in the picture the *Femme au Chapeau* he was headed in the other direction and not knowing it beguiled himself with decoration which took him back to light which was not really what he was meant to do." In her way, Gertrude had become as theoretical—and perhaps as officious —as her brother Leo on the subject of modern art.

The years 1912 to 1914 proved to be crucial ones in the building of Gertrude's American reputation. Both Stieglitz and Mabel Dodge had done much to promote her name. The publication of the Matisse and Picasso portraits in the August, 1912, issue of *Camera Work* brought her notoriety as a difficult and eccentric writer. Mabel Dodge's timely article confirmed her affiliations with the artists of the Armory Show. Over the next two years both Gertrude's reputation as a queer literary personality and the fame of the Stein art collection brought a throng of new visitors to the rue de Fleurus, while her reputation in her native land continued to gain ground. During these years, Hutchins Hapgood, writing regularly for the New York *Globe*, discussed Gertrude and her work on several occasions, once equating her work with that of Anton Johannsen, a labor leader indicted in a dynamiting conspiracy. Of Gertrude, Hapgood had said: "She tries to express in objective words the deeper mood which is not susceptible of being expressed conventionally. She tries, through a new form, to suggest the total content of her consciousness at any one moment." After suggesting that Johannsen's "fragmentary, vital talk," was a form of post-Impressionism, Hapgood compared the radical intentions of his two subjects: "A temperament that can express with vitality the turbulent reaching out and reaching up for a new life of submerged masses of men has something esthetically and emotionally similar to an artist who is strenuously seeking to express feelings and words hitherto unexpressed in art forms, and to express which means the breaking of the academical habits." For Gertrude, confirmed in her middle-class social habits, it was, probably, one of the oddest comparisons in her critical literature.

From New York, at the end of 1913, Marsden Hartley wrote Gertrude: "You are much talked of—even in Philadelphia you are said to be a creator of style—isn't that interesting—you are a new value in the eyes of many—not in the eyes of some." From Baltimore, early in 1914, Claribel Cone reported that at the conclusion of a lecture on Whistler, the respectable academic painter William Merritt Chase had launched into a discussion of the modernist movement, saying: "There is a Gertrude Stein, a sister of a man of considerable means who is buying Matisse's works and making him known. Each one of these paintings is a gold brick to the owner." Chase then read aloud portions of her Matisse and Picasso word portraits. The following day, in connection with Chase's lecture, Gertrude was mentioned in the *Baltimore Sun*. "Do keep me posted as to what goes on," Claribel requested, "as I shall you—as I get information as to your fast-growing American fame."

One of the unexamined consequences of her "fast-growing American fame" is the fact that the publication of her literary invention, the abstract word portrait, seems to have provided the inspiration for an equally novel invention in the visual arts—the object portrait. This peculiar genre, which one critic has described as an attempt to repudiate the portrait "likeness" and substitute in its place "a new symbolic-associative language," has a peculiar history. It is virtually the product of the artists of the Stieglitz group and its interchangeable members in the Arensberg circle, the salon of artists and writers that the wealthy poet and collector Walter C. Arensberg and his wife, Louise, instituted in New York just prior to World War I. Among these artists, the abstract-portrait mode extended from around 1915 to the late 1920's. While its formal resources were drawn from Cubism, especially Cubist collage, and some of the machinist aesthetics of Dada, it is remarkable that it was confined to artists such as Hartley, Demuth, and Francis Picabia, who were familiar with Gertrude's writing.

The dim beginnings of this new mode can be traced back to the pages of Stieglitz's *Camera Work*, in which one of its editors, Marius de Zayas, a Mexican writer and artist, proclaimed the death of old forms and called for the birth of new ones. In the July, 1912, issue of the magazine, a month before Gertrude's Matisse and Picasso portraits appeared, de Zayas announced, "Art is dead." In the June, 1913,

issue this note of anarchy and freedom was seconded by a new voice—
that of the Cubist painter Francis Picabia, who was visiting New
York in connection with the Armory Show. Picabia became the celebrity of the hour. He was the subject of a full-page illustrated article in
the edition of the *New York Times* on the eve of the Armory opening.
His two large Cubist paintings in the exhibition, *Dances at the Spring*
and *Procession, Seville*, were as talked about as Duchamp's *Nude
Descending the Staircase*. In the same issue of *Camera Work* in which
Gertrude's "Portrait of Mabel Dodge" appeared, Picabia issued one of
the preliminary manifestoes of what was to become the New York
branch of Dada and Company, announcing the beginning of a school
of amorphist art, *L'Ecole Amorphiste,* and signing it with a pseudonym,
Popaul Picador. With the manifesto, he included diagrams of two
blank canvases, entitled *Femme au Bain* and *La Mer,* thus demolishing
a brace of time-honored academic themes.

That Picabia was familiar with Gertrude's writing at the time, we
know from Mabel Dodge. The Parisian-born Cuban painter had been
invited to her salon as soon as he arrived on the scene. He was promptly
handed a copy of Gertrude's portrait of his hostess. On February 13
Mabel wrote Gertrude that "Picabia the painter is here & very intelligent & understands it all [the portrait] perfectly. I asked him to write
down what he said & I will send it to you. I will give him a letter to
you as you & Leo will *both* (strangely enough) like him." Whether
Picabia did, in fact, write out his analysis of Gertrude's portrait and
whether Gertrude received it is uncertain. It has not turned up among
her papers at Yale. She did, however, meet the painter when he returned to Paris with an introduction from Mabel Dodge.

Picabia was another of those volatile, erratic personalities who
crowded the stage of the Parisian vanguard in the early years of the
century. Thirty-four when Gertrude met him, he was handsome, flashy,
and a womanizer. The son of a wealthy Cuban father with business
connections in Spain and a mother from a *nouveau riche* Parisian family, Picabia began his amorous career at the age of eighteen by running
off to Switzerland with the mistress of a Parisian journalist. He liked
night life, night clubs, luxurious living. During the course of his lifetime, he owned a hundred automobiles, including an emblematic Rolls-
Royce. Picabia took up new ideas, new ways, with a Nietzschean fervor.
"If you want to have clean ideas," he maintained, "change them as
often as you change your shirts." When, late in his career, he abandoned his radical artistic affiliations and was made a knight in the
French Legion of Honor and spent his time cruising the Mediterranean
in his 70-foot yacht, his critics accused him of deserting the modernist
cause. Picabia answered: "To make love is not modern, but that is still
what I like best."

Gertrude seems to have had a preference for Latin men with pronounced sexual drives. She found Picabia interesting and likable, though her close friendship with the artist did not develop until much later, in the thirties, when he was a much less radical figure. Of her early meeting with him, she wrote Mabel Dodge, "I like him. He has no genius but he has a genuinely constructive intelligence and solid harmony." She noted, with some prescience: "The things he did in New York are much more interesting than the things he did here just before."

Picabia's first visit to New York did represent a critical phase in his career. Before that his art had coursed through Impressionism and Fauvism to settle into a stage of Cubism. Impressed with the pace and activities of life in New York, he produced some highly abstracted watercolors and gouaches of dockyards and Negro performers in night clubs that Stieglitz promptly exhibited in his gallery, "291." On returning to Paris, he executed several large canvases, attempting to convey his impression of America. One of these, an abstracted portrait of a "young American girl," was entitled *Udnie*, a cryptic amalgam of *Undine* and *nudité*. These paintings, he told a reporter from *Le Matin*, were "memories of America, evocations from there which, subtly opposed to musical harmonies, become representative of an idea, of a nostalgia, of a fugitive impression."

His most consistent development of the object portrait, however, began in 1915, after his meeting with Gertrude, when he had returned to New York, escaping from the European war. There, he renewed his friendship with Stieglitz and in collaboration with de Zayas helped to create the short-lived magazine *291*, sponsored by the art dealer and titled after his gallery. It was in New York that he began producing his machinist portraits, images of Stieglitz and others in the forms of mechanical equipment. His portrait of Stieglitz, printed in *291*, was a malfunctioning camera with the word "Idea" inscribed above it in heavy Germanic type—possibly a reference to Stieglitz' inability to convince the American public of the value of modern art and photography. Picabia's wife, Gabrielle—who had remained behind in Paris but soon joined her husband—was portrayed as an automobile windshield, labeled with the sentence, "She corrects manners laughingly" (*Elle corrige les moeurs en riant*). It was mockingly signed, "The faithful Picabia." It was, apparently, some question about the accuracy of that phrase that had prompted Madame Picabia's New York trip.

Other artists in the Stieglitz and Arensberg circles took up the object-portrait mode. De Zayas, working in collaboration with Picabia, produced many caricatures of public personalities created from typographic elements. Morton Schamberg, another artist of the group, made a sculpture portrait, *God*, out of a plumber's joint. Dove and Demuth also experimented with the symbolic portrait. Dove produced collage portraits of Stieglitz and the archconservative art critic Royal Cortissoz.

His Stieglitz portrait employed an actual photographic plate, a bit of coiled metal, and a piece of steel wool. Demuth's portraits were pure painting, notably a handsome "poster-portrait," an homage to Gertrude, entitled *Love, Love, Love,* in which a mask floated in space amid the printed words and numbers. He made similar portraits of the painter Georgia O'Keeffe, Stieglitz's wife, and the American poet William Carlos Williams. Both these artists, it is true, adopted the mode later, in the twenties, when it had already gained currency among the New York Dadaists and the germ of the idea in Gertrude's Matisse and Picasso portraits had been well buried.

Marsden Hartley's adoption of the portrait mode, however, was early and had direct links with Gertrude's word portraits. "I have always liked very much all I have read of yours," Hartley had written Gertrude early in their relationship, "because it always had for me a new sense of depth and proportions in language—a going into new places of consciousness—which is what I want to do also—to express a fresh consciousness of what I see and feel around me—taken directly out of life & from no theories & formulas as prevails so much today." He had also written her from Berlin, in August, 1913, about new sources of visual inspiration he had come across in Germany: "There is an interesting source of material here—numbers & shapes & colors that make one wonder—and admire."

Hartley employed some of these elements—notably numbers and German military insignia—in a series of colorful abstractions he painted in Berlin during 1914 and 1915. He had remained in the German capital throughout the opening phases of World War I, apparently under the spell of his attraction to a young German officer who was killed in the early stages of the war. The officer's initials, K v F, occur like a leitmotiv in several of Hartley's pictures of this period, including his abstract *Portrait of an Officer,* dated 1914.

IV

In 1913, Gertrude met the two men who were to do most to further her American reputation. Both were persevering journalists and critics; both were old enough and settled enough in their convictions to offer that slight resistance to her personality that augured well for a successful friendship. Carl Van Vechten, the "young man" from the *New York Times* whom Mabel Dodge found "temperamental . . . but rather nice," was thirty-three, and the music critic for that paper. Henry McBride was the forty-six-year-old art critic of the New York *Sun.* Both men had achieved a certain status in their professions, a consideration that Gertrude was too shrewd to overlook in matters of friendship. Both were in positions that could prove helpful to her career. With Van Vechten, Gertrude formed one of the most durable friendships of her lifetime. A prolific journalist, book reviewer, novelist, critic of arts and letters, Van Vechten kept her name before the public, promoted her reputation, arranged for the publication of her books. He became, in effect, her lifetime American agent—without pay.

With McBride, after their initial meeting in Paris, Gertrude kept up a steady correspondence, particularly in the early years of their friendship. McBride, the most astute and entertaining art critic of his generation, mentioned her frequently and favorably in his columns for the *Sun*, often quoting her at length. His promotion of her work and her reputation during the years of World War I kept her name before the public. Gertrude had met McBride through Mildred Aldrich—"Mick," as the art critic called her—in the spring of 1913. He had, of course, an interest in the Stein art collection, which he referred to in later years, "in proportion to its size and quality," as "just about the most potent of any that I have ever heard of in history." What differentiated Gertrude from other collectors, McBride felt, was "the fact that she collected geniuses rather than masterpieces. She recognized them a long way off." But McBride was equally interested in her plays. In August, 1913, he wrote to Gertrude in Spain, where she and Alice were summering for the second time: "I am disgusted really, at not seeing you again. I wanted to read those plays over again and talk with you about them." He was, he told her, trying to convince Willis Polk, a commissioner for the forthcoming San Francisco Fair, to stage them. "In the meantime," he added, "I still think they should be done next winter in New York, and if they are done, I hope I shall be allowed to help." McBride's optimism had undoubtedly encouraged Gertrude to adopt a high-handed attitude in dealing with Mabel Dodge.

Gertrude had an unusually warm response to the man. "You do make fun charmingly. I like your things," she wrote McBride in December, 1913, apparently in response to some of his articles. Although they saw each other only infrequently, when McBride made irregular summer trips to Europe, Gertrude looked forward to their meetings. In later years she once addressed him, playfully, as "My only dear." There was, however, an area in which they were not in accord. McBride had a distaste for popular success and cautioned Gertrude against it. "So you don't want large editions for me," Gertrude answered. "Damn it all it isn't the size of the editions, it's getting anything at all printed that's my worry." McBride's distrust of success was more than rhetorical. Mildred Aldrich described it as "a congenital contempt for successful people."

McBride's position in the New York art world proved beneficial to Gertrude. When her catalogue text for Hartley's show was published,

McBride printed significant portions of it in his regular column for the *Sun*. And Gertrude availed herself of McBride's services in other ways. When Ambroise Vollard's book on Cézanne was published in Paris, she wrote McBride about the book and the author: "It's about Vollard. He has just finished a book about Cézanne and it's really extremely good. . . . He is delightful he comes in in great haste in a cab, you remember how big he is, with original paintings and drawings and reproductions and a page of texts and asks to be admired and you do and he says he esteems your advice and he litters the floor with papers and then cab and all goes off and he comes with a new supply. I have done rather a nice sketch of him." The latter point may well have been the object of Gertrude's letter. McBride not only reviewed Vollard's book but also had Gertrude's portrait sketch "M. Vollard and Cézanne" printed in the October 10, 1915, issue of the *Sun*. In March of that year, reviewing the first issue of a new literary magazine, *Rogue*, in which Gertrude's prose piece "Aux Galeries Lafayette" had appeared, McBride observed: "*Rogue* was certainly astute from a business point of view in engaging the interest of Miss Stein whose extraordinary and attractive art will tide a magazine, if anything can, over the first few anxious trial numbers." It may have been the origin for one of Gertrude's long-cherished assumptions, that her name and literary reputation were always an asset to little magazines.

The publication of her piece in *Rogue* occasioned a brief misunderstanding with her self-appointed and hard-working literary agent, Carl Van Vechten. It was Van Vechten who had placed the piece with Allen Norton, the publisher of the short-lived magazine. Gertrude, having heard poor reports about Norton's literary venture, cabled Van Vechten to withdraw it. Van Vechten wrote her apologetically:

Your cablegram arrived too late as *Rogue* is already published and it includes *Aux Galeries Lafayette*. I am sending it to you with your other three manuscripts by registered post—and in this letter I am enclosing a cheque for *Aux Galeries Lafayette*. I am sorry that I have given something to Norton—if you didn't want me to—but you wrote me to get you an agent, and an agent, of course, would sell to anyone he could sell to—even a newspaper. Naturally, I thought this would be all right."

It was not the first or the last occasion when Gertrude, on the verge of publication—always, it appears, a climactic moment for her—would display symptoms of indecision, irritability, impatience. Van Vechten offered a few softening words: "Everyone admires *Aux Galeries*. I read it aloud with great effect! and I am frequently asked to do so." His letter—and the check—had a mollifying effect.

Carl Van Vechten was a born promoter and publicist; he had a penchant for championing whatever was new and shocking. In the twenties, when his reputation hit its stride, he promoted Negro blues, American jazz, such out-of-the-way novelists as Ronald Firbank and Ouida. A kind of perverse Trollope of the twenties, he wrote about the smart set, its Manhattan parties, its Harlem jaunts, its boozy Long Island weekends, in crisp and polished novels like *Peter Whiffle* and *The Blind Bow Boy*, which earned him a considerable reputation. They described a world of decorous heroines, attractive and emancipated women like Campaspe Lorillard and Edith Dale—the latter patterned after Mabel Dodge—and men who were handsome, wooden, intelligent, and slightly effeminate. It was a world in which taste—*toile de Juoy* hangings, Directoire furnishings, paintings by Matisse, perfumes by Houbigant and Coty—served as the index of character. As much as any writer, Van Vechten invented the myth of the "splendid drunken Twenties." Caustic critics like Dorothy Parker claimed: "Carl Van Vechten writes with his tongue in someone else's cheek." Van Vechten retorted that Miss Parker's sally was "probably not without envy." Gertrude, more favorably disposed to the author, thought Van Vechten "the most modern the least sentimental and the most quietly persistent of the romantics."

Van Vechten's modernity had been earned the hard way, growing up in not-so-quiet desperation amid the meager cultural rewards of Cedar Rapids, Iowa. There, at most, he could look forward only to the one-night stands of traveling theatrical companies—performances of Otis Skinner in *Romeo and Juliet*, Richard Mansfield in *Beau Brummel*—at Greene's Opera House, and to playing Schubert *lieder* and Sousa marches on the parlor piano. His doting parents—Carl was a late child; his brother Ralph was eighteen years older; his sister Emma, sixteen—indulged him. As a youngster, he was given to tantrums and showing off. In his teens, his one adult friend in town was a wealthy matron, Mahala Dutton Benedict Douglas, a woman with advanced views who later inherited the Quaker Oats Company when her husband went down on the *Titanic*. Mrs. Douglas was not considered fit company for impressionable adolescents; Carl therefore cultivated her friendship. Once, sitting on her porch at the end of a tedious summer day, he grumbled, "I'm so damn bored with this town, I'd like to put on a bath towel and run through the streets naked." Mrs. Douglas hunted up a towel and handed it to him, saying, "Go ahead, Carl."

At the age of nineteen, Van Vechten escaped from the doldrums of Cedar Rapids. Enrolling at the University of Chicago, he threw himself into a frenzy of activities: studying under Gertrude's former Radcliffe teacher, William Vaughn Moody, writing prematurely cynical sketches for the school weekly, composing ballads and waltzes for piano and violin, attending regular performances of the symphony and opera.

The highlight of his senior year was a theatrical enterprise he produced for the benefit of his fraternity, Psi Upsilon. A spoof on the amorous affairs of Madame du Barry, Van Vechten enacted the title role on a queen-size bed—the production's only bit of scenery—while his fraternity brothers paraded through in blackface, providing the love interest of the randy drama.

On graduating in 1903, he went to work on William Randolph Hearst's *Chicago American*, where he reported on the breakfast fare of the visiting Sarah Bernhardt—poached eggs, porterhouse steak, Budweiser beer—covered the 1904 Presidential elections and the tragic Iroquois Theater fire, in which nearly six hundred people lost their lives. Under the name "Chaperone," he wrote the paper's society column, covering the social events of the season and such Chicago notables as Mrs. Potter Palmer.

With money borrowed from his parents, he transferred his activities to New York. There, alert and enterprising, he wrote a long and timely article for Theodore Dreiser's *Broadway* magazine on Richard Strauss's controversial *Salomé*—scheduled for its first American performance at the Metropolitan Opera. Labeling it "the most sensational opera of an age," Van Vechten wrote authoritatively about the difficulty of the music and the strenuous "Dance of the Seven Veils," which he claimed was beyond the abilities of any singer who had to cope with the "trying music" that followed it—even though, as his biographer, Bruce Kellner, notes, Van Vechten had never yet heard the score and was writing about the opera from reports of its first performance in Dresden sent to him by the hometown girl, Anna Snyder, whom he shortly thereafter married.

After his *Salomé* article, Van Vechten was hired as an assistant music critic for the *New York Times*. He covered the city's principal operatic events and interviewed the great prima donnas of the period— Olive Fremstad, Geraldine Farrar, Mary Garden. He ghosted Luisa Tetrazzini's memoirs of her operatic career for an issue of *Cosmopolitan* and then added to his critical faculties by becoming the *Times*'s, and the country's, first dance critic, reporting regularly on the performances of Pavlova, Loie Fuller, Isadora Duncan. Gertrude became one of the long list of women celebrities whom Van Vechten courted, promoted, flattered in print. In his critical interests, he was decidedly a ladies' man.

Van Vechten's first meeting with Gertrude in May, 1913, had its comic aspects. He had arrived in Paris in advance of Mabel Dodge, with whom he planned to travel to Italy, and wrote promptly to Gertrude, who invited him to dinner on the following Saturday. Gertrude, evidently believing that Van Vechten wanted to interview her for the *Times*, wrote to Mabel about the impending visit: "He wants me to tell him about myself. I hope I will be satisfactory." But Van Vechten had just resigned his position with the paper, having accepted the post of drama critic for the *New York Press*. He had come to Paris, in the interim, to take in the new season of Diaghilev's Ballet Russe, having missed its performances on an earlier jaunt to Europe. He was present at the riotous opening-night performance of Stravinsky's *Le Sacre du printemps*, in which the uproar was so loud that it drowned out the music, forcing the choreographer, Nijinsky, to stamp out the difficult rhythms of the dances in the wings. Van Vechten attended the equally raucous second performance as well.

Gertrude and Alice also attended the second performance. In the audience that night Gertrude had spied Apollinaire: "He was dressed in evening clothes and he was industriously kissing various important looking ladies' hands. He was the first one of his crowd to come out into the great world wearing evening clothes and kissing hands. We were very amused and very pleased to see him do it." Meanwhile, Gertrude's attention had gravitated to the man who was occupying a seat in their box. Unknown to her, it was Van Vechten, her dinner guest of a few evenings later. Tall, lanky, fair-haired, Van Vechten had a set of natural but obstreperous teeth that gave him a joke-store grin when he smiled and a pouting look when he didn't. It was not, however, this unfortunate feature that Gertrude noticed. What piqued her interest was the gorgeously ruffled evening shirt the man was wearing. After the performance, which had been "incredibly fierce"—there were catcalls and fights; the man in the box next to Gertrude's brought his cane down sharply on the opera hat of the man next to him—Gertrude went home and wrote a word portrait of the anonymous man in the "much pleated" evening shirt. She titled it "One." There is no suggestion of the violence of the evening in her portrait, but there is a sartorial note: "A touching white shining sash and a touching white green undercoat and a touching white colored orange and a touching piece of elastic suddenly." Otherwise, the portrait is written in her usual hermetic style of the period, ending with the shaggy line: "Four between and a saddle, a kind of dim judge and a great big so colored dog."

There was one more thread of coincidence in the story of Gertrude's meeting with the critic and novelist. Van Vechten's marriage to Anna Snyder—the couple had been married in 1907—had been a casualty of his frantically paced New York career. Carl was keeping irregular hours, attending opening nights and theater parties; he had developed a new circle of friends, of whom his wife disapproved. The pair discovered they were less compatible than they had supposed. In the spring of 1912, Carl had agreed to the customary divorce proceedings in New York; he was "discovered" by prearranged witnesses in a hotel room with another woman.

Van Vechten's visit to the rue de Fleurus had been preceded, two weeks before, by a visit by his former wife. Anna Van Vechten, a former Wellesley girl, had been brought to meet Gertrude by a Wellesley acquaintance, Mrs. Gordon Caine. In the course of the evening, Anna Van Vechten had discussed her unhappy marriage. In her autobiography, Gertrude claimed that she had been uninterested in Mrs. Van Vechten's complaints, but she appears to have remembered some of the significant details. When Van Vechten came to dinner—turning out to be both the man in the pleated evening shirt and the "hero or villain of Mrs. Van Vechten's tragic tale"—Gertrude made use of them. She was in a teasing mood and began dropping one hint after another that suggested she knew a good deal about the critic's marital history. Her remarks punctuated the interminable series of hors d'oeuvres that Hélène, in one of her rare failures, served up in advance of a culminating sweet omelet. Van Vechten—no coward at displays of temperament —sat through the meal mystified and uncomfortable. Alice, perplexed, watched over Gertrude's behavior and each of Hélène's appearances with suppressed astonishment. It was an uneasy evening; nevertheless, it was the beginning of a friendship that lasted until Gertrude's death.

Van Vechten's first article about Gertrude, headlined "Cubist of Letters Writes a New Book," in the *Times,* had been written before his meeting with the author. The subject of the piece was Gertrude's "Portrait of Mabel Dodge," and it is clear that many of the critical observations had been supplied by Mrs. Dodge, who is referred to in the article as "a friend." Van Vechten, however, hazarded some views of his own and did not miss the opportunity to display his own erudition with reference to both the French Symbolists and the Italian Futurists with whom Gertrude, actually, had little in common. Van Vechten quoted lengthy passages from both Gertrude's portraits of Mabel Dodge and Picasso and offered some uncertain conclusions: "Perhaps she [i.e., Gertrude] intends the reader to make his pictures with each word, instead of with each phrase, a rapid-fire sort of quick wittedness which could not be expected of a reader untrained as yet in such eccentricities of expression. Or perhaps she expects nothing of the sort; perhaps she demands no intelligence or perception at all. The reader should draw his own conclusions."

In 1914 Van Vechten wrote a more detailed exposition of the Stein prose method, "How to Read Gertrude Stein," for the August issue of *Trend* magazine, a transient publication for which he wrote a regular column on theatrical events and personalities and to which Mabel Dodge and Hutchins Hapgood contributed as well. After his meeting with Gertrude, Van Vechten had become more authoritative on the subject. In his *Trend* piece, he explained:

The English language is a language of hypocrisy and evasion. How not to say a thing has been the problem of our writers from the earliest times. . . . Miss Stein . . . has really turned language into music, really made its sound more important than its sense.

Gertrude, warm to Van Vechten's attentions, began sending him selections of her shorter pieces. Van Vechten reported that he had taken them to several literary agents but always had the same response, being told that they could do nothing with "work so advanced." *Trend*, he reported in January, 1915, had folded. But he offered to hold on to the manuscripts in case some other opportunity turned up. It was the kind of dedicated service that he offered Gertrude for a lifetime.

CHAPTER EIGHT

War Zones

I

By 1913 Leo no longer bothered to attend the Saturday evenings; they had become, it appears, Gertrude's affair. In February of that year, while Gertrude and Alice were in London attempting to win over English publishers, Leo simply dispensed with them altogether. Writing to Gertrude in a jocular vein—it was on her thirty-ninth birthday— he informed her: "A lot of Hungarians, Turks, Armenians & other Jews came here Saturday to celebrate your birthday but I told them it was the wrong day & that besides there was no one at home."

On the following day he sent off to his transatlantic confidante, Mabel Foote Weeks, a long letter he had been composing for some time. "You people in New York will soon be in the whirlpool of modern art," he told Mabel. "I, on the other hand, am out of it. The present enthusiasm is for cubism of one species or another and I think cubism whether in paint or ink is tommyrot." He claimed, clearly referring to Picasso and Gertrude, that it was "the intellectual product of the unintellectual and I prefer the unintellectual to manifest themselves on a merely intelligent plane."

To prove a point—that anyone could write such stuff as Gertrude was now writing—Leo had begun composing parodies of "The Portrait of

Mabel Dodge." One version, decidedly puerile, is included among the
Stein papers at Yale:

Mabel Dodge
Hodge Podge
What is up,
What is down,
What's a smile,
What's a frown,
What is passion,
What is pose.

Another attempt, included in his letter to Mabel Weeks, made a more
serious effort to imitate Gertrude's style:

Size is not circumference unless magnitude extends. Purpose defined in
limitation projected. It is the darkness whose center is light.

Gertrude, and even Alice, Leo told Mabel, had had "the cheek to pretend that they understood this." Then he added, somewhat ambiva-
lently, "which I can do in part sometimes." But since Gertrude
"thought it very nice and I had very sarcastical intentions we evidently
didn't understand it the same way."

"As for Picasso's late work," Leo continued, "it is for me utter
abomination. Somebody asked me whether I didn't think it mad. I said
sadly, 'No, it isn't as interesting as that; it's only stupid.' " Having
absented himself from the Saturday evenings, he was now "a rank outsider . . . no longer a prophet in Israel or at best only a Jeremiah." He
proposed to take his deposing "good-humoredly"; he found it a relief
"not to be obliged" to look at pictures. With respect to the attention
Cubism was receiving, he could only conclude that "either I have lost
all my cunning in aesthetic perception or else I am superannuated, or
else it is a silly blunder."

Still, it was difficult for Leo to step down entirely. Midway through
his letter he added a pathetic aside: "If there is anything in these
pages that is intelligible enough to be interesting, and you want to ask
any questions about it—do, for I don't mind at all writing in response
to the stimulus of an immediate question. What I can't do is just to
write." His condition was far different from that of Gertrude, who was
writing and doing it with an aggravating confidence.

Leo did not wait for a response from Mabel Weeks. Three days later
he wrote her again. His second letter was even longer, a true jeremiad
on the subject. On the face of it, it was a very optimistic letter. He had,
it seems, reached another of those plateaus in his life, a little over a
month before, when his "philosophical conceptions came to be rounded
out and in essentials completed." He had, he informed Mabel, "hit

upon the explanation of the function of consciousness and upon why science and aesthetics, which for me are the only essential intelligent activities—why science and aesthetics exist." Without going into details about the nature of his discovery, he maintained that it had given him a liberated feeling, a feeling of "being released from all obligation of a pressing kind, like a person who had just put the roof upon his house and so being sheltered could spend his time furnishing and decorating it." It left him in a "most pleasing state of tranquillity."

"One of the greatest changes that has become decisive in recent times," he wrote Mabel, "is the fairly definite 'disaggregation' of Gertrude and myself. The presence of Alice was a godsend, as it enabled the thing to happen without any explosion." There was, he said, "practically nothing under the heavens that we don't either disagree about, or at least regard with different sympathies." The most serious issue was their separate vocations:

The crucial thing of course is our work. In my case, this is of comparatively little importance because in the first place I never suspected Gertrude of having any interest in the criticism of ideas, and in the second place I have no desire for glory. I want to be right of course, but I'm fairly well satisfied if I'm convinced of that myself, and I want those ideas which I believe to be right to prevail, but I don't care in the least who makes them prevail and gets any reward that attaches thereto."

The remark is curiously disingenuous, considering the fact that Leo was constitutionally incapable of leaving another man's ideas intact, nagging at them until he had convinced himself of the superior rightness of his own judgments.

"Gertrude on the other hand," he continued, "hungers and thirsts for gloire, and it was of course a serious thing for her that I can't abide her stuff and think it abominable. This would not have been so bad if there had been any general recognition without; a prophet can support not being honored in his own country when other lands sufficiently acclaim him, but when the acclamation otherwhere is faint the absence of support at home is painful. To this has been added my utter refusal to accept the later phases of Picasso with whose tendency Gertrude has so closely allied herself."

Gertrude simply didn't have, Leo felt, the capabilities for the course she was pursuing. Her artistic capacity was extremely limited, and her mind was "about as little nimble as a mind can be." "The Portrait of Mabel Dodge" was a case in point—he harked back to that again. If a person like himself, who knew the subject and who was "a far from inexperienced reader with no prejudices in the matter," could not understand it, then there was something wrong. He thought it "damned nonsense." The same was true of Picasso's recent efforts. "Both he and

Gertrude," Leo concluded, "are using their intellects, which they ain't got, to do what would need the finest critical tact, which they ain't got neither, and they are in my belief turning out the most Godalmighty rubbish that is to be found."

His relationship with Gertrude, Leo decided, had been "the only thing that was in any way a check on my independence." The "domestic discord" at the rue de Fleurus and Alice's arrival had had a salutory effect. "In many ways," he maintained, "freedom has come to me." He had had another "liberation" as well. Although he nowhere mentions that Alice's arrival might have prompted it, Leo had conducted a series of investigations on the subject of food. The previous May, he informed Mabel, he had been inspired "to study the matter thoroughly." "For about two months," Leo noted, "I ate my meals in the crack joints of this town and got so I could build up a menu that was impeccable as a work of art and distinguish the nth part of a hair in the merits of a dish as prepared at Ciro's, the Ritz, the Café Anglais or Voisin's, and when I was through with this I was through, through, through, and not the most beautiful name of the most wonderful dish can further tempt me." He had overcome his *gourmandise* completely and now preferred "bread and milk and fruit to all the luxuries that the best cook can supply."

Strangely, his dismissal of *gourmandise* was connected to his dismissal of the regular Saturday evenings. "I have long since given up the Saturday evenings," he announced in the next sentence. "They still go on but I absent me from that felicity, and I would rather harbor three devils in my insides, than talk about art."

His affair with Nina, he could report, was "solving itself beautifully also." Nina's voice had returned, indirectly it appears, as a result of a tempestuous affair with an English musician. "It was a whirlwind of passion on both sides," with the result that Nina's health had broken down. Leo's patient management and dietary restrictions had not only restored her health but her voice as well. Their relations were now those of "absolute confidence, perfect candor, complete toleration and unlimited goodwill, affection and mutual esteem."

Yet, despite the buoyant account of his liberating experiences, Leo sounds like a man cautiously taking in sail. His letter to Mabel Weeks ends on a note of resignation: "I have no interest in intimate contact with the 'world' because I cannot do anything toward bringing about what seems to me at present the most desirable of reforms, the social and economic ones. (For conversation as an art I have no talent and of the other kind, outside of gossip of which I soon have enough, I find it consists mostly of having people tell you things you already know and of telling them things that bore them.)"

If his "latest liberation" had, so to speak, put a roof over his philosophical house, he was beginning to feel the need to change his physical residence. "It is likely," he told Mabel, "that before long I shall leave the city and settle somewhere in sunshine land."

Gertrude's response to the "disaggregation" was consigned to her writing. In February, 1912, she had written to Mabel Dodge about several works in progress: "Another is a study of two, a man and a woman having the same means of expression and the same emotional and spiritual experiences with different quality of intellect. That is going very well and slowly." *Two: Gertrude Stein and Her Brother* is one of Gertrude's lengthy and frequently boring word portraits; it sprawls through 142 pages of the posthumously published Yale volume that bears its title. The opening sentences establish the unaccommodating style of the piece, with its generalized distinctions and persistent repetitions:

The sound there is in them comes out from them. Each one of them has sound in them. Each one of them has sound coming out of them. There are two of them. One of them is a man and one of them is a woman. They are both living. They are both ones that quite enough are knowing.

"Sound" in the portrait seems to be an all-encompassing term that signifies talking, sociability, personal expression, the repetitions that reveal the "bottom-natures" of the two subjects. But the analysis of the "sound coming out of them" goes on for page after page, the author seemingly hypnotized by the rhythm of the words, the sound of her own voice. By page 85, the process of comparison has reached no climax:

The sound coming out of him and sound was coming out of him and did come out of him the sound coming out of him expressed his being one beginning all of saying everything. Sound coming out of him expressed his being one hearing what he was saying.

Two pages later, she returns to her own self-analysis in similarly boring terms.

In sound sounding and coming out of her she was reminding herself that she had been asking all of saying that which she was saying. In sound sounding coming out of her she was expressing all of feeling all she was feeling and asking all of saying what she was saying.

Still, it is worth noting that despite the vagueness of the language, the lack of particulars and of action, the tone of these ruminations is surprisingly benign. The abstractness of the language was not a veil for hostility. Leo's new-found sense of freedom had been sensed by Gertrude as well: "He had freedom when he was walking and thinking. He had freedom when he was talking and leaving. He had freedom." Each of a long series of paragraphs, in the portrait, ends with complimentary negatives: "He was not monstrous." "He was not ashamed." "He was not childish." "He was not derogatory." One might regard *Two* and the writing of it as a form of remedial therapy undertaken by the author during a difficult period in her life.

Gertrude, however, was more explicit in discussing her break with Leo in *Everybody's Autobiography*. Leo had always been the principal talker during their Saturday evenings, Gertrude noted, but there came a time when she no longer listened to him: "This had never happened to me before up to that time I had always been listening sometimes arguing very often just being interested and being interesting and very often it was just that we had always been together as we always were." The change had come about in an unexpected way, in a strange assertion of her own ego: "Slowly and in a way it was not astonishing but slowly I was knowing that I was a genius and it was happening and I did not say anything but I was almost ready to begin to say something." It was odd, she mused, "this thing of being a genius, there is no reason for it, there is no reason that it should be you and should not have been him, no reason at all that it should have been you, no no reason at all."

One precipitating factor may have been the celebrity that Gertrude was beginning to achieve. Leo began expounding his view that Gertrude's writing owed too much to her own personality, that her word portraits, like the "Portrait of Mabel Dodge," were meaningless to the outsider.

"He did not say it to me but he said it so that it would be true for me," Gertrude noted. But she found that Leo's remarks no longer bothered her: "It did not trouble me and as it did not trouble me I knew it was not true and a little as it did not trouble me he knew it was not true. But it destroyed him for me and it destroyed me for him."

The actual date on which Gertrude and Leo decided to break up their housekeeping arrangement is not certain. It appears to have happened in the fall of 1913. Gertrude and Alice had spent that summer in Spain. In September, Leo had written to them from Florence, asking when they expected to return. He proposed to return to Paris after October 1. By the end of October he had told them of his plans to move to Italy permanently. By that time, as well, Gertrude and Alice had decided to move. Their rue de Fleurus apartment was badly in need of repairs, but in the past their elderly landlady had been adamantly against efforts at modernization. On October 28 Mildred Aldrich had sent Gertrude a *petit bleu* suggesting they look at a pavilion at 75, avenue Denfert Rochereau, so they had already begun apartment-hunting. By mid-December Gertrude was able to announce definite plans of their move. She wrote Mabel Dodge: "We have after much hunting found an apartment in the Palais Royal with a balcony that promises to be very nice. We don't move until July." In late December she wrote to Henry McBride: "We have been very busy finding an apartment because my brother has decided to settle in Italy and I decided to stay in Paris."

By spring, however, Gertrude and Alice had learned that there would no longer be any objections to renovating the studio at the rue de Fleurus. The landlady's agent gave them permission to make whatever changes were necessary. "We have changed our minds about moving," she wrote Mabel Dodge. "We found we liked it best here after all and so we are making ourselves a bit more comfortable." The changes in the studio room were extensive, resulting in complete upheaval there. A fireplace was installed in place of the old cast-iron stove. And the studio and pavilion were wired for electricity by their friend Sayen, the engineer-turned-painter. Also they had a sheltering passageway constructed between the pavilion and the studio room. This necessitated the cutting of a new doorway and a closing off of the old double doors.

Leo's move from the rue de Fleurus was not altogether amicable. Considering the years they had been together, considering the ties of former affection and dependency, it was natural that some emotion accompanied their break. At one point Gertrude and Leo were not talking to each other. "Your brother-in-law is still mad," one of Gertrude's lines informed Alice in the poem "Possessive Case," written during this period of domestic strife. They seem to have resorted to notes as a means of necessary communication. Some of Leo's notes to Gertrude have survived among her papers at Yale, but Gertrude's have not turned up. One of Leo's involved a painting he had removed from Gertrude's room: "So far as I can make out, the situation boils down to this. You left out of consideration the effect on my mind of not only having asked my advice but of *having taken* it throughout, while I left out the effect on your mind of its being your room and that you arranged it to suit yourself. As though whose omission is the more flagrant depends upon the question of whether the act of removing that picture which produced the effect on your feelings was or was not justified by mine."

A folded note from Leo, with Gertrude's name scrawled hastily on the outside, seems also to date from this period. "I told you, one time since," Leo complained, "that I found it very disagreeable to come downstairs or into the house in the morning & find the light burning in the front hall. You said then that it was accidental, etc. Now if you leave it on on purpose because you don't like to go upstairs in the dark or what not I'll try and get used to it but if it's only carelessness, I wish you'd jog your memory a little."

Inevitably the separation involved questions of money. And this was tied to the problem of the division of their art collection. Although a satisfactory division was finally made, the process had occasioned some bursts of temper. At one point in the transaction, since Gertrude and Leo were not speaking to each other, Alice was obliged to carry paintings back and forth between Gertrude in the atelier and Leo in the pavilion.

An undated note, really a letter, written by Leo on rue de Fleurus stationery, goes into the matter with some thoroughness. Leo was in the process of selling the remaining Japanese prints in the collection and Gertrude had raised the issue of her share. "Dear Gertrude," Leo's letter began, "It's impossible simply to answer yes or no to your note because there are a number of mistaken beliefs affirmed to which a mere yes or no would not satisfactorily fit.

"In regard to the value of the prints which you had owned, with the exception of the few bought from Bing & Hoyashi & the triptych from N.Y., the value is inconsiderable. If I make something substantial out of the sale it will be with the Harunobus, Kuninagas, Chinchos etc. that I got afterwards."

Because the issue of money had been raised, Leo went into some detail about their prior financial arrangements: "It is true that I have the reproductions etc., but if one were to go into details it would appear that during the second year that Alice lived with us my allowance for living expense was based on what it actually cost me plus 50 fr. a month and that not at first, so that I was contributing a grossly disproportionate share to the household expenses, and the year before that your expenses kept up their proportion very fully." Furthermore, Leo noted that while Gertrude and Alice had been in London, the gas bill had arrived, and "Although I was experimenting in cooking a good deal then, I was astonished at the disproportion." Finally it came down to the dirty linen—among other things: "Of course, for coal, for washing service (postage which then—I believe I did all the mailing—was no small item) my share since Alice has been here has been small. I was perfectly satisfied, however, as it offered a simple method for our individual liberation and I considered it cheap at the price." Leo proposed that since the "natural surplusage" had gone to Gertrude on those occasions, the books and reproductions should go to him.

At the end of his letter, he made a generous offer on the subject of the paintings:

The Cézanne apples have a unique importance to me that nothing can replace. The Picasso landscape is not important in any such sense. We are, as it seems to me on the whole, both so well off now that we needn't repine. The Cézannes had to be divided. I am willing to leave you the Picasso oeuvre, as you left me the Renoir, and you can have everything except that. I want to keep the few drawings that I have. This leaves no string for me, it is financially equable either way for estimates are only rough & ready methods, & I'm afraid you'll have to look upon the loss of the apples as an act of God. I have been anxious above all things that each should have in reason all that he wanted, and just as I was glad that Renoir was sufficiently indifferent to you so that you were ready to give them up, so I am glad that Pablo is sufficiently indifferent to me that I am willing to let you have all you want of it.

Leo invited Gertrude to make a "clean sweep of the Picassos," with the exception of a few "presentation" drawings. "I very much prefer it that way," he ended, "and I hope that we will all live happily ever after and maintain our respective and due proportions while sucking gleefully our respective oranges."

It was the end of a long and complex personal involvement. Gertrude had loved Leo, followed after him, listened to his word as gospel. Caught up in her romance with Alice, with her career seeming to offer some promise, she had allowed Leo to go with few regrets but, perhaps, some bitterness. Her feelings, at the time, may well have been transferred to her anxieties about her professional career and her haughty dealings with Mabel Dodge.

That Leo's departure had caused some consternation in both Stein households—at the rue de Fleurus and the rue Madame—seems clear from a letter that Mabel Foote Weeks wrote to Gertrude. Mabel's letter was in response to one from Gertrude, in which Gertrude had spoken vaguely of her troubles but suggested that she was dealing with them in her writing. Whether the writing involved was *Two: Gertrude Stein and Her Brother* is not certain.

"You did not suppose, did you," Mabel complained, "that I could possibly be satisfied with its vague hints of something bothering you. Cannot you tell me more even if you do not tell it in the best and fullest way. Please do not make me wait until the book is done."

"I have always had a curious feeling about Sally," Mabel continued, "that she had a certain power over Leo, a certain skill in manipulating him and when you both broke with Leo, more or less, I think she was filled with a sort of blind rage. When she felt that Leo no longer noticed her as an artist she had to stop painting."

At the head of her letter, Mabel had written: "Please do not let anyone read this letter." Unfortunately—since Alice was in the habit of filing Gertrude's correspondence—Mabel reiterated her point once more: "Don't read this to Alice. Unless I feel that sometimes I can write just to you, it's no fun to write."

Leo's move to Settignano, near Florence, took place in April, 1914. Early in the month he wrote to Michael on the back of a letter from the shipping agency that had transported his household effects; the letter is dated April 8. A few days later he wrote to Gertrude thanking her for a gift of a set of kitchen knives that he especially appreciated. In the course of his move, it seems, he had lost a silver carving knife that he particularly prized. In June, learning that Gertrude and Alice were planning soon to go to London, Leo wrote Gertrude again, asking her to buy a copy of Boswell's *Life of Dr. Johnson* for him.

Hutchins Hapgood, who had first met Gertrude in Heidelberg, when she was traveling with Leo at the end of Leo's *wanderjahre*, had been struck by her absolute devotion to her brother. "At this time in Heidelberg," Hapgood noted, "and for some years afterwards, Gertrude was possessed by a singular devotion to Leo; she admired and loved him in a way a man is seldom admired and loved; it was part of her profound temperament."

Gertrude's life with Leo, during the long, eventful decade when they lived together in Paris, had been like the tying—and the cutting—of a complicated knot.

II

The spring and summer of 1914 were unusually busy for Gertrude and Alice. Leo's departure and the renovations at the rue de Fleurus had been upsetting. They decided to take a brief vacation. In late April or early May they spent several days in Brittany, where, so Gertrude wrote Henry McBride, she had had "lots of fun and did poems, quite funny ones." In Paris they had a succession of visitors from America. Marsden Hartley stopped on his way to Berlin; Dr. Claribel Cone spent several days in Paris before journeying on to Munich. Early in the summer, Henry McBride arrived in the French capital. They had, too, a surprise visit from John Lane, the English publisher. He was fairly well committed to bringing out an English edition of *Three Lives* and advised Gertrude to come to London in July. He intimated that a contract would be ready then.

Before leaving, Gertrude acquired three still lifes by a new painter, Juan Gris. She had seen the first two, *Glass and Bottle* and *Book and Glasses*, in Kahnweiler's gallery early in June. The third, one of the most beautiful of Gris's Cubist collage paintings, *Roses*, Gertrude seems to have bought just before her London trip. Although in later years she was to speak of her friendship with the Spanish artist as a long-standing one, she was not particularly taken with Gris when she first knew him as one of the Cubists in Picasso's entourage. Gris, who was twenty-seven when Gertrude acquired his paintings, lived in the

Bateau Lavoir with his wife, Josette. Gertrude found him "a tormented and not particularly sympathetic character. He was very melancholy and effusive and as always clear sighted and intellectual." He had a habit of addressing Picasso as *cher maître*, much to Picasso's annoyance. Although often moody, Gris had a volatile and explosive temper. He had a passion for dancing and often visited the dance halls. He was, as well, a womanizer. He loved his wife in his fashion, but their marriage was subject to sudden quarrels. (Once, in a fit of rage, he had poured a cup of *café au lait, croissant* and all, over Josette's head.) As a painter, Gris had come to Cubism late and adopted the style wholeheartedly. He brought to it an order and clarity that some observers felt was too cold and too calculating, but that Gertrude found wholly admirable. Their friendship traced an erratic pattern over the next several years.

Late in June, Gertrude wrote to Mabel Dodge: "We are still in Paris. We are going to London for a few weeks and then are coming back here and late in August will go to Spain." She told Mabel that she had heard from Leo; her brother seemed "very pleased with Florence." On the Fourth of July, she had a note from Carl Van Vechten, who was in Paris and wanted to pay them a visit. He was eager to tell Gertrude "the latest gossip about *Tender Buttons*, Mabel, Hutch and everybody." He also wanted to introduce "a little Russian called Fania." The "little Russian" was the actress Fania Marinoff, whom he had met in New York and whom he was planning to marry. Gertrude sent Van Vechten a hasty postcard, inviting him and his friend to lunch on the following day, Sunday. She and Alice, she advised him, were leaving town on Monday. Whether Van Vechten and his bride-to-be received Gertrude's note in time to keep the appointment is not clear.

It was not a propitious time for a journey. The papers were full of the assassination of the Archduke Ferdinand at Sarajevo. There were rumors of war. Neither Gertrude nor Alice expected it would come to that. On July 6 they left for London, financially ill-prepared for a lengthy stay. But the prospects were too seductive. Gertrude was looking forward to signing her contract with Lane, and they planned to visit with friends.

On their first Sunday in London, they went to tea at the home of John Lane. There were a good many people there, including Hugh Walpole and an editor for one of the London dailies, who got into a discussion of war, the editor complaining that he would not be able to eat figs in Provence, as was his custom. John Lane informed Gertrude that he would be away for several days but that she should come to his office at the end of July, when her contract would be ready. He had, it appears, considered publishing something more recent than *Three Lives*, but conditions being what they were, he maintained he "would rather begin with that than with something more entirely new." Lane said he had confidence in *Three Lives.* His wife, whose opinion he valued, was also enthusiastic.

Since they now had ample time, Gertrude and Alice accepted an invitation to spend several days at Cambridge. The offer had come from the mother of a young woman, Hope Mirlees, whom Gertrude and Alice had met in Paris. They spent ten days there; the weather was beautiful, the food excellent, and Gertrude thought the house extremely comfortable. She could work in the privacy of her room or sit quietly in the garden, blooming with roses, and far removed from the lively conversations of the other guests. One day they were invited to lunch at Newnham, to meet Jane Harrison, the classical scholar. But sitting on the dais next to Miss Harrison, Gertrude had not found the conversation "particularly amusing." She and Miss Harrison, she judged, "did not particularly interest each other."

At a dinner given in their honor by Mrs. Mirlees, they met Alfred North Whitehead and his wife, Evelyn. Gertrude was particularly impressed with the English philosopher and co-author, with Bertrand Russell, of *Principia Mathematica.* She was to conclude—apparently on no other basis than her intuition—that it was Whitehead who had contributed the really significant ideas in their famous book. In her autobiography, she described him as "the gentlest and most simply generous of human beings." She liked his easy way with people.

During the dinner, Alice had sat next to the poet A. E. Housman. They had struck up a lively conversation when Housman, on learning that Alice had come from California, wanted to know about the famous ichthyologist David Starr Jordan, who had been a friend of her grandfather. But she was more impressed with the quiet conversation she had with Professor Whitehead while taking coffee in the garden. It was then that she heard the imaginary bell that signaled her meeting with her third genius. Whitehead, she claimed, "had a most benign sweet smile and a simplicity that comes only in geniuses." For their part, the Whiteheads were favorably inclined toward Gertrude and Alice; they invited them to dinner at their house in London.

What was to have been their last week in London proved eventful. They had begun by ordering some new furniture—a large couch and comfortable chairs covered in chintz to replace the furniture Leo had taken with him to Florence. They dined one evening with the Whiteheads and found that they not only liked the Whiteheads more on their second meeting but also that the Whiteheads "liked us more than ever and were kind enough to say so." The Whiteheads invited them to spend the weekend at their country house, Lockeridge, near the Salisbury Plain. Gertrude and Alice accepted with pleasure.

Gertrude had also contacted the photographer Alvin Langdon Coburn. Gertrude thought Coburn a somewhat "queer American" and seemed to view his wife as a kind of "adopted mother." But she had

been genuinely impressed with the series of photographs that Coburn
had taken of her the year before in Paris. Coburn had also proved
helpful—if unsuccessful—in trying to interest the publisher Gerald
Duckworth in her work. On July 27 Gertrude and Alice had gone to
tea with Coburn and his wife at their house in Hammersmith. While
there, probably at Alice's instigation, Coburn had offered to try to
arrange a meeting with Henry James, who was then living at Rye. On
the following day Coburn wrote Gertrude that he had no word from
James yet. He hoped that James was not abroad. Later that afternoon
he wrote Gertrude again:

Alas, I have just received the enclosed telegraph from Henry James. Perhaps another year when you are over he will be in town and we can make
an arrangement for a meeting.

It looks as if the dear man were ill again. He is never well for long at a
time these days. Anyway I have done my best and we will hope that he will
be in town and well the next time you come this way.

James was not ill; he was not disposed to receive any visitors. Moreover his niece, Peggy, had come to spend the weekend at Lamb House.
His telegram had read simply: "Sorry to say unable to receive here at
present any visits from London. Have come down for complete retirement. Henry James." Gertrude saved the master's telegram; it survives
among the letters, notes, bills, scraps of paper in the Yale archives. The
hoped-for meeting with him never took place. James did not survive
the war—the "grand Niagara," as he called it—which swept away the
glittering era whose values he had discerned and shaped.

On the morning of July 31 Gertrude kept her appointment at the
Bodley Head offices of John Lane. For what seemed an interminable
length of time, Alice waited outside, inspecting one shop window after
another. Finally Gertrude emerged, beaming. The contract had been
signed: "It was a gratifying climax." Late that afternoon they took a
train from Paddington Station. At seven in the evening they arrived
at Marlborough in Wiltshire, where Professor Whitehead was waiting
to meet them at the station. They brought with them only a weekend
trunk, having left the rest of their baggage in their London hotel. Their
weekend in the country, however, was to last eleven weeks.

They were at Lockeridge when the Great War began—the hurried conferences, the ultimatums, the declarations of war. In a state of uncertainty, Gertrude and Alice planned to return to London, but Evelyn
Whitehead insisted that they remain at Lockeridge. There was no possibility of their returning to Paris at the moment; they must stay until
they could. Gertrude and Alice gratefully accepted. Accompanied by

Mrs. Whitehead and her daughter Jessie, they made a brief trip to London to get their luggage and to draw on their letters of credit. Fortunately Alice's letter of credit—for only a small amount—was drawn on a California bank. Gertrude's, however, was on a French bank, and funds were frozen. She cabled to her relatives in Baltimore.

The anxious days seemed to merge one into the other. Then came the news of the invasion of Belgium. Gertrude remembered Professor Whitehead, in a gentle voice, reading out the stories of the destruction of Louvain. "Where is Louvain," Gertrude asked Alice, in a state of dejection. "Don't you know," Alice asked. "No, nor do I care," Gertrude answered. "But where is it?"

The Whiteheads' son North had secured a commission; their younger son, Eric, was not of military age. North, who had been away when the war broke out, spent three days at Lockeridge learning how to drive, then had to report to duty. He was shipped over to France almost immediately. His mother worried that he had not taken enough warm clothing; he had gone off without an overcoat. Evelyn and Jessie Whitehead kept themselves busy with Belgian relief work. Alice helped them as best she could. Gertrude and Professor Whitehead took long walks in the countryside, discussing philosophy and history. They seemed to find some comfort in the quiet optimism of the local game-keeper, whom they met regularly on their walks.

During the gloomy early weeks of the war, when the German advance could not be stopped, Gertrude and Alice became worried about friends in France. Alice was concerned about the Jacots, who were living near Boulogne-sur-Seine. Gertrude was worried about Mildred Aldrich, who had permanently given up her Paris apartment in June and had taken a farmhouse in Huiry on the Marne, where she proposed to live out the rest of her life. Mildred was directly in the path of the German army as it advanced toward Paris. There were anxious days of waiting. One afternoon, as Gertrude and Whitehead were walking through a rough stretch of woods, he asked her, gently, if she had copies of her writing with her. Gertrude said that everything was in Paris. Whitehead paused. He didn't like to ask, he told her, but he was beginning to worry. The capture of Paris seemed imminent.

Gertrude was miserable. She was concerned about her work and her pictures, of course, but the thought that Paris, a city that she loved, might be destroyed, as Louvain had been, was unbearable. On the day the Germans were finally stopped at the Marne, Gertrude had taken to her room, disconsolate. When the news came, Alice went upstairs and called out to her, "Paris is saved, the Germans are in retreat." Gertrude turned away, disbelieving. "Don't tell me these things," she moaned. Alice finally convinced her. The two of them stood together and wept.

Alice cabled the Jacots. Nellie's reply, *"Tout va bien, nullement de danger,"* seemed encouraging to the Whiteheads, though Alice thought it overoptimistic. A few days later, they heard from Mildred. She had remained in her farmhouse throughout the battle. When the towns to the north were evacuated and the roads were crowded with refugees—women pushing hand carts and baby carriages, farmers herding their cattle, wagons loaded with household effects—Mildred hoisted the stars and stripes above her gate and stayed. She had her garden and her books; this was her home. She was sixty-one, too old for the road. She decided, she said, to keep her face "turned toward Fate rather than run away from it. To me it seemed the only way to escape a panic—a thing of which I have always had a horror."

Her house proved to be an ideal observation point. Perched on a hilltop, it looked down over the Marne, over the low-lying fields and woods, with the neighboring villages clearly observable in the distance. French and British troops, on their way to the front, were billeted on her property. She entertained the officers, brewed tea, and got out her emergency stores of tinned biscuits and jam for the men. Mildred had experienced some moments of fright. One night when she was alone, a detachment of Uhlans, German cavalry, had broken through the Allied lines and camped in the woods below her house. Their horses could be heard neighing in the night. Then there were the days when the sounds of the artillery grew shatteringly near. "For seven days—from Thursday noon September 3 to Wednesday noon September 11—how many days is that," she wrote Gertrude, "I was within sight and hearing of the smoke and the cannonading, and just before noon on Saturday September 5 the battle advanced into that plain before my garden and for eight hours right under my eyes they pounded their heavy artillery and ended just after dark by shelling the plain and retreated leaving all the towns and villages in sight . . . in flames, and four thousand unburied Germans on the field." The war had come to her backyard and then like an ominous wave had receded. "But I'll tell you all about it later," Mildred promised, "all the stories of the soldiers, and of the battles, and of me feeding and cleaning, and serving cigarettes to the boys, and in spite of my almost collapsed condition, swearing that I would *not* get *demoralized,* and proving it by putting on a white dress every day, and white shoes and stockings and black ribbons in my hair in honor of the boys that were dying within sight of my door. I feel now that I shall never be able to look out on that plain again with the joy it once gave me."

Mildred's letter was shown and read to all of the Whiteheads' neighbors. It was, in fact, from letters such as the one she sent Gertrude that Mildred wrote a book, *A Hilltop on the Marne,* which recounted her experiences during the battle. It became a best seller in America when it was published in 1915, and ran through seventeen printings. The public was eager for first-hand accounts of the war, and

Mildred's terse, journalistic account was one of the first to fill the need.

Gertrude took heart from Mildred's letter. She upbraided the English she met who talked mournfully about the superior organization of the Germans. Any two Americans, she claimed, any twenty Americans, could organize themselves to do something, but not the Germans—they needed to have a method imposed upon them. They were a backward nation, Gertrude claimed; they could not possibly win the war because they were not modern.

Her self-composure restored, Gertrude even managed to come to the assistance of the Whiteheads during a difficult visit by Bertrand Russell. With their son in France, the Whiteheads hoped to avoid óne of Russell's lectures on pacifism. Gertrude obligingly turned the discussion to education, a subject on which Russell was a willing antagonist. He launched into a brilliant diatribe on the weaknesses of the American education system, particularly its "neglect of the study of Greek." Gertrude took him off guard by pointing out that Greece—if not actually an island—had had an insular culture that was perfectly appropriate to another insular culture like that of England. But America was a continent and would naturally look to a continental culture—therefore Latin was the appropriate culture for American studies. It was precisely the kind of argument guaranteed to fuss a logical mind, and it fussed Russell to the point that he "became very eloquent" on the issue of education. Gertrude, pushing her argument further, discoursed on the "disembodied abstract quality of the american character" and began mixing "automobiles with Emerson" in a way that fussed her opponent even more until it was time for everyone to go to bed.

With the news that Paris was spared and that travel restrictions had finally been eased, Gertrude and Alice prepared to return to Paris. Alice's father and Gertrude's Baltimore cousin, Julian Stein, had sent them much-needed funds. Mrs. Whitehead, on friendly terms with Lord Kitchener, the Secretary for War, had secured a military pass to go to France with them; she wanted to bring North an overcoat. On October 17 the trio took a Channel boat to France. It was daylight when they boarded; the ship was full of Belgian soldiers and officers who had escaped from Antwerp and were now on their way to the battlefront in France. It was Gertrude's first experience of seeing "the tired but watchful eyes of soldiers." It was ten o'clock at night by the time the boat train reached Paris. They rode to the rue de Fleurus in a taxi. Gertrude looked out the window, grateful to see the city of Paris "beautiful and unviolated."

The Paris to which they returned seemed strangely becalmed. There were few vehicles to be seen, and the streets seemed depopulated. Yet, for Gertrude, it was somehow familiar; she decided that it reminded her of the Paris of her childhood. There were food and fuel shortages to contend with in wartime Paris; coal and wood were scarce; many foods were in short supply. Foreign-owned stores were closed and shuttered. Certain streets seemed almost deserted. Kahnweiler's gallery had been closed and his stock of paintings confiscated as the property of an enemy alien. Picasso had warned him that he should take out naturalization papers, but the dealer had not thought it necessary. He was in Italy when the war broke out and could not return.

They visited Mildred Aldrich in the war zone and found her as sturdy as a French peasant. She was, as usual, hard up, having spent her meager funds helping refugees and the schoolchildren of her little village and bringing cigarettes to hospitalized soldiers. Gertrude and Alice were to make the journey to Huiry several times during the first winter of the war. In Paris, Alfred Maurer called on them; the painter was returning to the States. His father had cut off his funds as a means of forcing him to return home. Maurer had been caught in a village on the Marne when the Germans advanced toward Paris; he told them of his desperate efforts to escape the German army. Mrs. Whitehead, with Gertrude at the time of Maurer's visit, was dismayed by the artist's lack of bravery. Gertrude explained that, of course, Alfy had had his girl with him and was "scared to death lest she should fall into the hands of the Germans." Gertrude worried about Marsden Hartley, who had not been heard from since he went to Germany. In her letters to Mabel Dodge and Carl Van Vechten, she asked repeatedly for news of the artist. Finally Van Vechten wrote that Hartley was still in Berlin "working away," apparently unaware that there was a war.

Gertrude's concern over the wartime fate of the artists she knew also got her into difficulties. Juan Gris and his wife, Josette, were trapped, penniless, in Collioure when the war began. Since his dealer, Kahnweiler, could no longer send him money, their situation was desperate. In September, Gertrude sent him a money order. Gris, thanking her for her generosity, wrote that he would remain in Collioure for the time being; her check would keep them for two months there whereas he would have to spend half of it for the return trip to Paris. Gertrude then became involved in a scheme with Matisse and the American art dealer Michael Brenner. The three of them planned to provide Gris with 125 francs a month—Gertrude's contribution being 50 francs—in return for paintings. Kahnweiler, however, interpreted the move as a breach of his contract and adamantly refused to give his permission, leaving Gris in an awkward position. The arrangement broke down by Christmas, with Gertrude and Brenner both angry at having paid for pictures that they did not receive. Gertrude later wrote Gris that her 200 francs had been a gift, but it caused a rift in their friendship that was not mended until after the war. Eventually, Kahnweiler, to everyone's relief, arranged to send Gris money by way of the painter's sister in Spain.

To escape the wartime rigors of Paris, Gertrude and Alice decided to take a trip to Spain in the spring. But Gertrude was short of money, and in February she decided to sell her remaining Matisse, the *Femme au Chapeau*. Michael and Sarah, who were staying at Agay, on the French Riviera, were eager to buy the painting. Their collection of Matisses had been a casualty of the war. In the summer of 1914 they had loaned nineteen of their Matisses for a large exhibition that was to be held in Berlin. When war was declared, they were unable to get them back. The price that was agreed upon for the *Femme au Chapeau* was $4,000, and on February 12 Michael wrote Gertrude enclosing a draft for $2,000, promising to send the balance in March. "For the present," he told Gertrude, "the picture had better remain at your place as it is covered by your policy. Should you want to leave earlier let me know and I'll send the second draft to you in Spain. Do you plan to leave your Cézannes in your studio when you leave? If not put the *Femme au Chapeau* with them."

That winter there were zeppelin alarms. The first had come, one night in March, after Alice had gone to bed. Gertrude was working late in the studio. She heard a commotion outside and the sounding of a siren. Quietly she went to the pavilion and woke up Alice, telling her she had best come downstairs. Gertrude warned her not to turn on the light, and the two slowly made their way down the dark stairway. Downstairs, Alice settled on a couch, but her knees were shaking uncontrollably. Gertrude broke out into laughter. "Wait a minute," she said, "I will get you a blanket." "No," Alice wailed, "don't leave me." The darkness was punctuated with a few loud booms, and then there was a long silence. Finally there was a sound of horns blowing in the streets; the alert was over. They went to bed.

In a few days they had Mildred's opinion on the matter:

Well I am glad you heard the damned thing since it got there, just as a matter of experience, but I'll be hanged if I understand how, with the big aerial fleet that the allies have, it crossed their lines, much less got back safely. That is a mystery. They are *fort* those g— d— bosches.

From her own front, Mildred reported that a *cantonnement de régiment*, "reinforcements going to the Reims section—in fine spirits and condition," had stopped at Huiry the day before. Her garden was beginning to show signs of life, though it looked "a little naked." "No cannon heard here for several days & I am that glad," she added.

Not long after this first of modern air raids, a second one interrupted a dinner party that Gertrude and Alice gave for Picasso and his new mistress. He and Eva were living in an apartment on the rue Schoelcher, in Montparnasse. Gertrude and Alice had visited them several times and were surprised at Picasso's happiness. Eva was a rather frail creature, with delicate features and pale skin, and she was frequently ill with colds and bronchitis.

On the night of the alert, the four of them were at the table when the alarms sounded. Gertrude and Alice had been told that the two-story pavilion and the studio would afford them little protection in the event of a bombing. They and their guests went to the concierge's room in the main building, together with Jeanne, the new Breton maid-servant. The alert was a long one, and everyone soon became restless and bored. Jeanne returned to the pavilion to finish washing the dishes. Gertrude and Alice, with their dinner guests, went to the studio room. They put a candle under the table to shade the light. Alice and Eva attempted to sleep on the couch. Gertrude and Picasso stayed up talking until two in the morning.

"It was a strange winter and nothing and everything happened," Gertrude recalled in her autobiography. The old crowd had been dispersed. Braque and Derain had enlisted. Apollinaire, although he was not a naturalized citizen, had volunteered, too, and was serving in the artillery. Marie Laurencin had broken off her affair with the poet. Now married to a German, she was living in Spain. The Picabias were in New York. Picasso joked grimly about the time when Braque and Derain would return from the war and, putting their wooden legs on the table, would talk about the fighting. But the Great War was to put an end to the charmed and lively society they had all known before. It put an end to the "heroic" years of Cubism as well. Years later, the painter described the effects of the war and the mobilization of his friends: "On August 2, 1914, I took Braque and Derain to the Gare d'Avignon. I never saw them again."

III

Gertrude and Alice's vacation in Spain lengthened into a year-long stay. In May they took a train to Barcelona, where they stayed for several days. Then they took a boat to Majorca. The crossing was somewhat uneasy; they were told a German submarine was following in their wake. At Palma they put up in a pension that had been recommended by friends, but decided it was unsuitable. They found rooms at the Hotel Mediterraneo with a view overlooking the harbor. From there, Gertrude studied the activities of the ships in the harbor, in particular a rusting German steamer, the *Fangturm*, interned at Palma since the outbreak of the war. Suspicious of all things German, Gertrude and

Alice thought the *Fangturm* might be one of the network of ships that were refueling the German submarines in the Mediterranean.

They had planned to spend only a few weeks in Majorca, but they found life there calming and idyllic after the air raids and wartime shortages of Paris. Through the postman, they learned of a house for rent on the Calle de Dos de Mayo, in Terreno, on the outskirts of Palma. It was a pleasant villa with a terrace, though it proved to be damp and chilly during the rainy season. Having made up their minds to spend the next winter in Majorca, they took the villa. They moved in that summer and sent for their maidservant in Paris.

There were several English families on the island with whom Gertrude and Alice became friendly, including a Mrs. Penfold, a descendant of one of Nelson's captains, who was to figure spasmodically in the poems and plays Gertrude wrote at Majorca. There was also the French consul, Monsieur Marchand, to whom they told their story of the abdication of Moulai Hafid, the sultan of Morocco. The only other American on the island was the painter William Cook, vacationing with Jeanne, his Breton wife. Gertrude and Alice saw the Cooks almost daily. They took long walks with them to the outlying towns and up into the hills terraced with olive groves. Gertrude regarded Cook as a dependable and useful friend. He had recently worked in an American hospital for the French wounded and was later to join the American expeditionary forces. When he and his wife returned to Paris, in 1916, Cook, hard up for money, went to work as a taxi driver. It was in Cook's Renault taxi that Gertrude learned to drive.

Gertrude and Alice would have nothing to do with the Germans on the island. "We have made a vow never to speak to a German," Gertrude announced resolutely in "All Sunday," one of her Majorcan poems. They did, however, engage in a battle of sorts with the German governess of one of their neighbors who hung out the German flag every time there was a German victory. But, as Gertrude acknowledged sadly, in her autobiography, "We responded as well as we could, but alas just then there were not many allied victories." They were consoled by the fact that the lower classes were all for the Allies. With the exception of King Alfonso, they learned from the American dentist in Barcelona who treated the king, the Spanish government and the upper classes were decidedly pro-German.

Their stay on the Mediterranean island was peaceable—a kind of prolonged Sunday of the mind and emotions, isolated from the world at war. The sunny days merged one into the other; each day's leisurely activities were woven into the fabric of domesticity. In the sultry afternoons Gertrude read aloud from the *Letters of Queen Victoria*. Alice, who had been taught to knit by Madame Matisse, made socks and sweaters for French soldiers. Gertrude, who subscribed to Mudie's Library in London, developed a passion for biographical literature—for autobiographies of missionaries and accounts of campaigns and military diaries by English officers. Lord Roberts's *Forty-One Years in India* became one of her favorite books. They went for long walks in the country, taking picnic lunches and bringing back bunches of wildflowers. On their trips to Barcelona to visit the dentist, they bought pots of tuberoses, Gertrude having discovered that she liked their heavy, sweet, summery fragrance. They also bought their first dog, a Majorcan hound, an animal with an antic disposition that took to eating the tuberoses. Polybe—he was named after the *Figaro* critic whom they both admired —became a nuisance. He had an "incurable passion for eating filth," as well as tuberoses, and had to be muzzled. Allowed to run loose, he bounded off into the fields, chasing sheep and goats. Cook warned them that the peasants had sworn to kill the animal if they caught him. Tied in the yard, Polybe howled so constantly that the neighbors complained. Finally, they were obliged to give the dog away. Polybe became a persistent and mournful subject in her writing of this period.

Occasionally Gertrude and Alice made short trips on the island. They went, once, with Cook to nearby Inca to watch the bullfights, at which it was rumored Belmonte might appear. The event triggered narrative prose poems: "What Does Cook Want to Do," a portrait study of her American friend, and "I Must Try to Write the History of Belmonte." In the latter poem the leitmotiv was the nonappearance of the famous bullfighter: "The story of Belmonte is that we know he is hurt in the leg. A Mexican is to take his place." Gertrude, however, delivered her judgment on the bullfighters who did appear: "The one who was advertised was a failure. The other one the one we had seen had learnt how to do some things very nearly and he did it using all his old vigor and carrying it successfully. A man of talent and plenty. He had blue eyes." In its clean, straightforward language, the prose poem of Belmonte is representative of the leaner, more explicable writing style that Gertrude developed in Majorca and continued for some time after. Returning the favor of Cook's invitation, Gertrude and Alice invited him to a week-long festival of bullfighting and dancing that was held in Valencia, on the mainland. On their return to Majorca, to Alice's dismay, they discovered that in their absence, their Breton maid and Cook's Breton wife had become very friendly. Alice felt it made for a difficult social situation. Considering the intimacy of her life with Gertrude, she may also have thought it an uncomfortable breach of privacy.

The Majorcan year was one of the most relaxed and happily sustained periods of Gertrude's writing career. Her daily life with Alice, an island of domesticity in a calm sea, became the focal point and sustaining theme for a series of long poems, short poems, and plays. Like the Cubist painters, Gertrude seems to have pulled back from the hermetic style of *Tender Buttons*. Her writing gave way to more "readable"

forms of exposition. Snatches of conversation, the ruminations of the
author, bits of dialogue between herself and Alice thread their way
through the still-elliptical situations of her writing. It is not always clear
who the speaker is—their two personalities, on occasion, become
merged in a kind of marital union. Nor is it always clear whether Alice's
remarks are actual or invented, in a form of interior dialogue in which
Alice became Gertrude's literary alter ego.

An overriding convention in this spate of writing is that of the domestic life of a husband and wife—in which Gertrude plays the role of
the husband. "Farragut or A Husband's Recompense," for example, is
not about the American admiral—although the idea may have been inspired by Gertrude's reading. In its more lucid passages it is about their
life together on the island and a boat trip they made to the mainland.
There are moments of doggerel sentiment:

Alright I will be natural.
B is for birthday baby and blessed,
S is for sweetie sweetie and sweetie.
Y is for you and u is for me and we are as happy as happy can be.

And there are simple assertions:

Dearest, supposing you tell me that you love me.

There are reprimands to Alice for having incorrectly transcribed some
earlier section of writing:

If you had read the word the other way I wouldn't have minded. I have
forgotten what was mentioned.

There are admissions of marital difficulties:

How well I remember the quarrel. I don't often mention such things, They
never can happen. But once it was very suddenly authentic.

And what appears to be a more detailed account of a quarrel:

I can't remember the detail. The first that I can remember is asking do
you mean to deny that you heard me. I asked that often. The next thing
that I remember is asking were you nervous again. The next thing that I
can undertake to be remembering is were you flattering. Were you flattering me by voicing an objection. If so don't bother.
I don't really mean to be a slave.

At times, in this and other pieces of the period, one has the distinct
impression that the form of the poetry had become such a vehicle of

personal expression that Gertrude used it as a means of having a final word in one of her spats with Alice, who was still transcribing her daily writing into legible form.

Despite the intermittent bickering of "Farragut," however, the tone is one of placid conversation. The title of the second part, "How Farragut Reformed Her and How She Reformed Him," suggests Gertrude's recognition that their marriage was a process of mutual reformation. At times Gertrude even owns up to certain faults:

When I was wishing and sitting I wished for a clock. I meant to pick out an expensive one. I did so and now dear one is economising.

This confession of self-indulgence is followed by a charming wish-fulfillment fantasy:

And some day we will be rich. You'll see. It won't be a legacy, it won't be selling anything, it won't be purchasing, it will just be irresistible and then we will spend money and buy everything a dog a Ford letter paper, furs, a hat, kinds of purses, and nearly something new that we have not yet been careful about.

Although such quotidian material might not seem promising, Gertrude's Majorcan poems and plays—and the works that followed them for several years—provide one of the most authentic and accessible regions of her "difficult" writing. In them she was able to use every incident of her daily life—her tender and mock-tender sentiments for Alice, the events of the day, her reflections on writing, her evaluations of her own work in progress—as the legitimate subject matter of her work. She produced, in a way, a kind of radical lyric form—cryptic and readable, by turns. In "He Said It," moments of comic reflection interrupt the on-going dialogue:

I said I was careful of climbing. Not into bed. Yes into bed. Why. Because you can never tell about the slats.

There are, as well, confessions of selfishness:

You mean that I make it too cold. Well to be sure I am selfish I sit before the fire. I really ought to give you the best place only I don't like to change. You dear you are so sweet to me.

Occasionally there are moments of idyllic good humor:

We are going to have a picnic. With chicken not today today we are going to have eggs and salad and vegetables and brown bread and what else.

False smuggled contraband tobacco. You mean by that that it isn't tobacco.
No it's only leaves. I laugh.

In other poems of the Majorcan period and later, there are frequent
references to Alice and their on-going love affair:

Pussy how pretty you are. ["Lifting Belly"]

Do you love me sweetest just as much as if I were English. ["One Sentence"]

For instance our loving. We are loving. We can say that honestly. ["I Have
No Title To Be Successful"]

There are lines that are overtly sexual:

Kiss my lips. She did
Kiss my lips again she did.
Kiss my lips over and over and over again she did. ["Lifting Belly"]

Others are vaguely tinged with eroticism:

Lift brown eggs.
To me. ["The King or Something"]

There are declarations of Gertrude's affection and gratitude:

Oh you blessed blessed blessed planner and dispenser
and joy. ["The King or Something"]

Gertrude's writing and her ideas about writing are a matter of constant
preoccupation in the poems of this period:

I have very bad headaches and I don't like to commit to paper that which
makes me very unhappy. ["One Sentence"]

At times she congratulates herself on a particularly successful stretch
of writing:

A splendid instance of good treatment. ["The King or Something"]

Or boasts out loud:

What did I say, that I was a great poet like the English
only sweeter. ["Lifting Belly"]

Or queries herself:

I don't understand why I like narrative so much to read.
I do like it. ["Advertisements"]

She announces a change in her habits as a writer:

I will write in the daytime. ["I Have No Title To Be Successful"]

And in the concluding and resolute "Oh shut up," of her poem "Marry
Nettie," there is the suggestion that the author has become exasperated
by the sound of her own interior voice.

During this period Gertrude also wrote a number of plays. In "Captain Walter Arnold" she explains one of her dramatic methods:

Can you recollect any example of easy repetition.
    I can and I can mention it. I can explain how by twice repeating you
change the meaning you actually change the meaning. This makes it more
interesting. If we attach it to a person we make for realization.

Although the play is cast in two acts, Act II, in its entirety, reads: "A
dazzling dress. We dazzle altogether." It is a "play" chiefly by reason
of its dialogue construction with two unidentified voices.

That she found playwriting a congenial activity seems evident from
a letter she wrote Henry McBride in September, 1915. "The play that
I am doing now," she told the critic, "is inspired by the Mallorcans a
very foolish lot of decayed pirates with an awful language. It has begun
well. I am ever so pleased." Most of the plays of the Majorcan period
—"Do Let Us Go Away," "Counting Her Dresses," "Turkey and Bones
and Eating," "For the Country Entirely"—were not printed until 1922,
in the volume *Geography and Plays*, which was published in America
at her expense. But in the Majorcan plays, through the sheer wish to
make theater out of pure dialogue rather than dramatic action, she
arrived at one of the most advanced concepts of theater in her time.
Well before the modern Theater of the Absurd, she had decided to
dispense with most of the established conventions of dramatic form.
The divisions into acts and scenes in these plays is entirely erratic
and arbitrary. There is no sense of plot, of character development,
no continuity of dramatic action. She dispensed, too, with scenery
and decor; there are only such hints as might be gathered from the
conversational elements of the play. Gone, too, is the concept of the
actor's role; there are often no indications of when his speeches begin and
end. After she had made this audacious housecleaning of the dramatic
form, only the simplest of necessities were left—the bare stage and the
actors, stripped of everything except the spoken word. Few playwrights
had ever gone so far.

The voice in these poems and plays is the authentic, private voice of
the author. In her isolation, Gertrude had tapped the resources of the

personal life, the ruminations of the private mind. Her work became the record of her observations, insights, her descriptions of the banal or idyllic events of the day, her acknowledgments of the sustaining eroticism, the sexual politics, of daily marital life. It was an area that James Joyce explored later—with brilliant cohesiveness and much less prudery—in Molly Bloom's lyric soliloquy in *Ulysses*. But during the early years of World War I, Gertrude had already begun scouting the territory.

IV

Sequestered though they were on their calm Mediterranean island, Gertrude and Alice were not altogether removed from the war. They followed its progress eagerly, and anxiously, in the newspapers. When the crucial battle of Verdun began in the spring of 1916, they waited impatiently for word of its outcome, dismayed and discouraged when the early reports suggested it might be a debacle for the Allies. They noticed that the *Fangturm*, which had been lying idle and rusting in the harbor, was beginning to receive a new coat of paint. They studied the ship, unhappily, day by day, as the work progressed. Then, one day, the painting stopped. "They knew it before we did," Gertrude was convinced. "Verdun was not going to be taken. Verdun was safe." Within a day or two, they learned that the tide of battle had turned in favor of the Allies.

Throughout their stay, they had been reminded of the war by Mildred's letters. She was busy with relief work, visiting hospitals, cultivating her garden, writing a sequel to *A Hilltop on the Marne*. Her energy seemed boundless. They heard, too, from Florence Blood, whose casual life had been greatly changed by the war. She wrote to them from the Sachino in the Basses-Pyrénées, where she was running a hospital for convalescent soldiers: "forty-five beds, a resident doctor, four sisters, a chaplain & innumerable servants. I boss them too! & never have I had the feeling of doing a job as well. Every faculty I have is used to its utmost & all I do is absolutely within my line." Among the friendly sentiments of the letter, there was a subtle barb: "I wonder," Florence Blood added, "if you are serenely writing for a few initiated those extraordinary essays & portraits? You will have to add a postscript to mine, since this new phase of my career!"

In December they had had unhappy news from Picasso in Paris; Eva was critically ill with tuberculosis. "My life is a hell," he wrote Gertrude. "Eva has been continually sick and grows worse each day and she has been in a nursing-home for the past month. This is the end. My life is not very gay. I hardly work at all. I go to the nursing-home and I spend half the time in the metro. I have not had the heart to write you; I've thought of you—you know that—I even asked Beffa [the concierge] when I met him for news of you." The final word came on January 8. "My poor Eva is dead," Picasso wrote Gertrude. "A great sorrow to me. . . . She has always been so good to me. I would also be very happy to see you since we have been separated for so long. I would be very happy to talk to a friend like you."

Their apprehension over the fate of Verdun had made them feel isolated. By the time the outcome of the battle was assured, they had decided to return to France. Cook and his wife had already left. Gertrude and Alice followed soon after. They had some minor difficulties securing visas for re-entering France, and there was a comic but frightening incident when the coastal steamer they took from Palma landed at Cartagena. A suspicious police officer had asked them, rather brusquely, what they were doing there. He insisted on inspecting the canvas bag in which Gertrude kept the books from Mudie's Library. Finding that it contained books with military maps, he refused to let them go. It was only after Alice had repeatedly informed his superior that the books were history books and they were innocent travelers that they were allowed to take the train to Granada. By June 20 they were back in Paris.

The example of their friends had not been lost on them. Once established in Paris, Gertrude and Alice resolved to help the war effort in some manner. One day, while walking down the rue des Pyramides, they saw a young woman in uniform beside a parked Ford. They learned that she was working for the American Fund for French Wounded, an organization that distributed supplies to hospitals throughout France. They were taken to meet Mrs. Isabel Lathrop, the director of the fund in France. Mrs. Lathrop, wearing a pink dress with pearls and a garden-party hat that belied her efficiency, told them that they would have to provide their own vehicle, and for that it was best to write to friends in America. In the meantime, someone was needed to classify the supplies that were being sent out to the various hospitals; Alice could take charge of that while waiting for the truck to arrive.

Gertrude wrote to her cousin Bird Gans in New York. In mid-September Bird's husband, Howard, wrote that he had managed to solicit half of the $550 necessary to buy and ship the Ford van. He had just returned from a training camp for military preparedness in Plattsburg and hoped to get the remaining funds in a few weeks. Meanwhile, Gertrude was learning to drive. In the hot summer afternoons, she and Cook drove out beyond the fortifications of Paris, where Cook gave her lessons in his Renault taxi. She had a long wait, however, before she could take up her duties with the American Fund for French Wounded; her Ford did not arrive until the following February.

The cold, dreary winter of 1916–17 was made worse by a coal shortage in Paris. Gertrude and Alice were forced to close down the studio room, heating only the small room in the pavilion. The government was dispensing coal to needy cases, but neither Gertrude nor Alice felt they should send their servant to get coal without paying. With her customary directness, one cold, blustery day, when there was little coal left for their small room, Gertrude simply confronted a policeman on her corner and explained her problem. That evening the policeman arrived in civilian clothes, carrying two sacks of coal. Neither Gertrude nor Alice asked any questions.

They saw friends. Picasso had moved to Montrouge after Eva's death, and they went to visit him and admired the fancy pink silk counterpane on his bed, the gift of a Chilean society woman—one of the women he was consoling himself with. Often he stopped by the rue de Fleurus, "bringing Paquerette a girl who was very nice or Irene a very lovely woman who came from the mountains and wanted to be free." Occasionally he brought Erik Satie, who was composing the score for the Diaghilev ballet *Parade*, for which Picasso was to design the sets and costumes. He also brought the Princesse de Polignac and Blaise Cendrars.

They met Mary Borden Turner, a Chicago millionairess who was operating a hospital near the front. Mrs. Turner had taken a house near the Bois de Boulogne. Being invited to dinner there was a special pleasure; not only was Mrs. Turner an admirer of Gertrude's writings, but her house was well heated. Her husband was a captain in the British Intelligence Service. Mary Borden Turner was, in Gertrude's view, "very Chicago," a type that held a certain fascination for her: "They have to lose the Chicago voice and to do so they do many things. Some lower their voices, some raise them, some get an english accent, some even get a german accent, some drawl, some speak in a very high tense voice, and some go chinese or spanish and do not move the lips."

Finally their Ford van arrived and had to be driven to a workshop to have a special truck body made for it. They waited several more weeks. On trial runs, the Ford proved balky. The first day, when Gertrude drove it back from the workshop to the city, it promptly stalled in the middle of the tracks between two streetcars. A crowd of bystanders helped to push it out of the way. The next day, undaunted, Gertrude and Alice set out for the Fund headquarters. They got as far as the Champs Elysées, and the car went dead. A crowd gathered; Gertrude cranked; the bystanders cranked. The van would not turn over. Finally a chauffeur who had been standing nearby said, "No gas," and looking into the tank discovered there was none. Alice took a taxi to a store in their neighborhood that sold tins of gasoline. That mission accomplished, they proceeded on their way.

Gertrude was to display certain peculiarities as a driver; she could go forward admirably, but she shunned reverse. This necessitated an uncompromising attitude in the matter of parking—which frequently meant directly in the path of other parked vehicles. It was on the question of parking and refusing to back up that Gertrude and Alice had their only violent arguments on the subject of driving. There were those, however, who maintained that even Gertrude's forward driving could present certain hazards. She had the habit of conversation, and to her passengers it often seemed Gertrude did not pay sufficient attention to the road. This frequently made riding with her invigorating; her brisk turns could sometimes be hair-raising. She did not like to drive at night but often was obliged to because she did not always believe in road signs and thought road maps and predesignated routes hampering to her freedom of action. She preferred to trust to instinct.

Gertrude had, however, one unique gift as a driver. Anyone, anywhere would help her fix a flat, crank the car, or assist in any necessary repairs. This ability mystified other drivers, but Gertrude explained that others looked so efficient that no one would bother to help them. As for herself, she said she was good-humored and democratic. "One person was as good as another," and she knew what she wanted done. "The important thing," she claimed, "is that you must have deep down as the deepest thing in you a sense of equality. Then anybody will do anything for you."

Their Ford was christened "Auntie," after Gertrude's aunt Pauline, "who always behaved admirably in emergencies and behaved fairly well most times if she was properly flattered." Early in the spring Gertrude and Alice were ready to take Auntie on their first long trip away from Paris. Mrs. Lathrop had asked where they would like to open their first depot and Alice had promptly suggested Perpignan. They had friends there. Jo Davidson's wife, Yvonne, was running a hospital for wounded officers near Perpignan, and there were several more military hospitals in the area.

Either in late March or early April, they headed south, "armed with a Michelin guide and innumerable maps." They encountered a snowstorm going through a mountain pass, and several times Alice was convinced they were on the wrong road. Gertrude, however, would not turn back; straight ahead was the only direction she would consider. But the trip had its pleasurable aspects, for they made it something of a gastronomical tour. At Saulieu, they stayed at the Hôtel de la Côte-d'Or, where they lunched on *panade veloutée*, ham croquettes, and *pêches flambées*. Alice, however, was suspicious of the proprietor of the hotel, the cut of whose clothes looked German. There had been reports of escaped German prisoners of war. When she inquired of the *maître d'hôtel*, she learned that the proprietor had only recently been released from Germany, where he had been a civilian prisoner. He had, for several years, been the Kaiser's chef at Potsdam.

It was not the first, nor the last, time that Alice became concerned about lurking Germans. After war had been declared, Alice had come across a portfolio of photographs that had been given to them by Arnold Rönnebeck, Hartley's German sculptor friend. They were aerial views of a number of French cities, taken in the manner of a Delaunay painting, usually from the tallest vantage point Rönnebeck could find—the cathedral spire. Alice tore them up in a rage, convinced that Rönnebeck, with his Prussian connections, had been a German spy all along.

At Lyon, Gertrude and Alice dined in the tiny restaurant of La Mère Fillioux, one of the great chefs of the time. They had Mother Fillioux's finest lunch—*lavarets au beurre*, hearts of artichokes with truffled *foie gras*, steamed capon with *quenelles,* and *tarte Louise*. Alice was fascinated with the compact little woman who padded up to their table in carpet slippers, brandishing a carving knife, and finished off the steaming white capon with absolute dispatch: "She was an expert carver. She placed a fork in the chicken once and for all. Neither she nor the plate moved, the legs and wings fell, the two breasts, in less than a matter of minutes, and she was gone."

When they arrived at Perpignan, early in April, there was a hearty letter from Mildred awaiting them: "Well I am proud of you. Think of you two rushing through the passes in a snowstorm. Now I feel as if there were nothing you could not do." They settled in a hotel in Perpignan and were allotted a small ground-floor room for storing the hospital supplies that had already arrived at the train station. They visited neighboring hospitals, took note of the needed supplies, and telegraphed headquarters for additional ones. They distributed comfort bags to the wounded soldiers. Yvonne Davidson had warned Alice about the military director of the hospital at Perpignan; he would ask for more than he really needed. He had already requested, from Alice, a pair of silk pajamas. Alice husbanded her supplies, doling them out carefully. She took charge of the paper work; Gertrude did the driving.

Gertrude and Alice visited Rivesaltes, the birthplace of Marshal Joffre, and had themselves photographed with Auntie in front of the dilapidated house where the marshal had been born. The photograph was made into postcards, which they sent to friends and which were sold for the benefit of the American Fund for French Wounded.

In her spare moments, Gertrude wrote. Her long, conversational

poem "Work Again" appears to refer to the Perpignan-Rivesalte period.
There are references to Auntie—"Fasten it fat we say Aunt Pauline./
Not snow now nor that in between." And the exclamation "Hurrah for
America" may be the author's response to America's entry into the
war in April, 1917. Gertrude and Alice celebrated by cutting up ribbons
printed with the stars and stripes and distributing them among the
soldiers. In her poem her experiences with the French soldiers were also
recounted. "Soldiers like a fuss," one of her lines reads. "Give them
their way." Another reports:

It is astonishing that those who have fought so hard and so well should
pick yellow irises and fish in a stream.

But the idyllic moments in the midst of the war and their service duties
were rare. The summer in Perpignan proved unbearably hot. Gertrude,
who normally enjoyed the heat, complained that it was like being a
"pancake" with the heat above and the heat below. And Auntie had
become balky. Trying to crank the car in the sweltering heat, Gertrude
would curse it out heartily, then swear that she was going to "scrap it."
    In the fall, much to their relief, they were recalled to Paris for re-
assignment. They spent only a few days at the rue de Fleurus, while
Auntie was undergoing necessary repairs at a garage. They learned that
their new assignment would be more extensive. They were to open a
depot at Nîmes that would serve the three departments of the Gard,
the Bouches-du-Rhône, and the Vaucluse. On the Monday before they
were to leave, they had a surprise visit from Mildred, who was in Paris
to see friends. They told her that their new assignment would keep
them away from Paris for some time. They remained at Nîmes, in fact,
until after the war. Mildred wrote them on October 12: "I do hope
that you ran little Aunty Pauline right out of this weather. . . . I was
so glad that I risked that late call on Monday. I should have been sorry
if you *had* got away for so long a time without my seeing both of you
for a moment."
    It was at Nîmes that they began to strike up friendships with Ameri-
can doughboys. An American regiment was stationed at Nîmes, and
occasionally an American would turn up in one of the French hospitals
that Gertrude and Alice visited regularly. On the road, Gertrude would
always stop and give a soldier a lift if there was room in Auntie. Always
inquisitive, she would query them about their families, what state they
came from. She and Alice seldom remembered the names of the doughboys they met; Gertrude would frequently nickname them California
or Iowa, after the states they came from.
    There was, for instance, Duncan, whose last name they never learned.
Duncan was a Southern boy, a supply sergeant stationed in Nîmes. He
frequently traveled with them on their trips to outlying hospitals. He

could be counted on to help load and unload the supplies, and there was always the danger that Auntie might break down somewhere in transit. Gertrude appreciated Duncan's laconic view of the world. One day, not long after the Americans had captured forty villages at Saint Mihiel, they were driving to Avignon. As they passed a cluster of houses, Duncan asked what it was. "Oh, just a village," Gertrude answered. Farther on, they passed another cluster of houses, and Duncan asked once more. Gertrude answered that it was another village. There was a long, contemplative silence. Finally, Duncan sighed, "Forty villages ain't so much."

Duncan, however, had his problems. His skills as a supply sergeant were such that he was never allowed to see action. Occasionally he could become mournful about the prospect of returning to America without ever having been at the front. On those occasions Gertrude and Alice would try to console him. But once, while Duncan was visiting them at the Hotel Luxembourg, where they were staying in Nîmes, he had become quite drunk and had fallen asleep at the table. Gertrude and Alice were worried. There were American officers in the front room, and they did not want the officers to see Duncan in such a condition. Gertrude roused the soldier. "Duncan," she said sharply, "listen Duncan. Miss Toklas is going to stand up, you stand up too and fix your eyes right on the back of her head, do you understand." Duncan muttered yes. "Well then," Gertrude said, "she will start to walk and you follow her and don't you for a moment move your eyes from the back of her head until you are in my car." The procession filed past the officers and out the front door of the hotel. Duncan, glassy-eyed, trailed behind the small, slight figure of Alice, and Gertrude blocked out the view from the rear. They hustled Duncan into Auntie and drove him out to the camp.

As an American with a medical background who knew French, Gertrude was often called in as a translator when an American soldier was taken to a French hospital. One day she was asked to assist at the funeral of a young American who had fallen off a train and died of his injuries. Duncan and two of his comrades were to attend. The French pastor had asked Gertrude about the dead man "and his virtues," so that he might say a few words. But when Gertrude asked the soldiers, no one could think of any virtues. "Apparently," Gertrude surmised, "he had been a fairly hard citizen." In desperation, she asked again for some redeeming quality she could pass on to the pastor. One of the soldiers obliged, saying: "I tell you he had a heart as big as a washtub."

In the Hotel Luxembourg they met the soldier William G. Rogers, whom they remembered only as "the Kiddie," the nickname they had given him. Rogers was on furlough at the time and had gone to Nîmes to see the Roman ruins in the region. In the dining room of the hotel, Gertrude and Alice had studied him carefully for several days and then introduced themselves. He was invited to have tea with them that afternoon in the hotel dining room. There, after being informed that "Miss Stein writes," he was questioned. "They pumped me," Rogers recalled, "for all they were worth."

Where I was born, who were my parents, what did my father do, where did I go to college, who were my professors, how did I happen to be in the army, was this my first visit to France, what would I do when the war ended? One spelled the other, like police grilling a prisoner for hours on end, until they dragged my whole history out of me.

After the interrogation, Rogers was "propositioned" by Alice. He was told that, if he liked, he might ride with them in Auntie, as a means of visiting the historic sites in the region. There were certain regulations that had to be observed. If anything went wrong with the car, he would, of course, attempt to fix it. He must not crowd "Miss Stein"; he would sit on the floorboards next to Alice. They would never make any trips that would not allow them to return to the hotel by nightfall. "Miss Stein" did not like to drive at night.

During the next ten days of his furlough, Rogers was given a guided tour of the region. They visited Romanesque churches and Roman ruins, the battlefields where Caesar had fought. They traveled south toward the Mediterranean, visiting Aigues-mortes and Arles. They stopped at Avignon and Orange. Often they picnicked on lunches that Alice had ordered from their hotel, or they dined at inns and hotels along the way. Only once did Gertrude and Alice allow the Kiddie to pay, and then Alice had cautioned him about paying for their modest eighteen-franc lunch with a fifty-franc note. It was inviting the waiter to cheat him, Alice told him. Although Alice's list of prohibitions may have been necessary, Rogers noted that Gertrude usually broke most of them. The two women waited patiently until he had seen everything he wanted; Gertrude would suddenly veer off their route to show him some sight that had not been scheduled. Once they returned so late that Rogers was obliged to shinny up a signpost and strike a match to see in what direction they were headed.

Back at his post, the Kiddie had written to thank them. He also reciprocated by sending some "expert" advice on the care of Auntie: "I asked our mechanic about the knock in your Ford. He said that if it wasn't due to the carbon, it was probably a broken bearing in your driving rod. Get the car going fast, and then, leaving it in gear, put on your foot brake. If that makes it knock, it is one of the afore-mentioned bearings, and ought to be fixed—in Paris. Also, you absolutely should *not* touch the carburetor. Put it in one place and then leave it alone."

Gertrude and Alice were as obliging to the French soldiers that they met. It was at Nîmes, shortly before Christmas, that Alice lost her purse and thereby acquired their favorite French military godson. The purse, which contained a considerable sum of money, was returned to them at the hotel. Alice gave the man a reward. They learned that he and his family were evacuees from the Marne. They were asked if they would act as military godmothers for his son, Abel Leglaye, who was seventeen and garrisoned at Nîmes. Gertrude thought that Abel, who presented himself at their hotel the following evening, was "the youngest, the sweetest, the smallest soldier imaginable." It was the duty of a military godmother to write to her godson every time she had received a letter from him and regularly to send him packages of food and clothing. Gertrude and Alice had already acquired several French godsons, but Abel was the one of whom they became fondest. They wrote to him frequently and sent him presents. Not long after they met, Abel was assigned to the front. He wrote to them from there, assuring them that although the cannon balls were whistling overhead and his two comrades had been wounded the day before, he was not afraid. He was detailed to carry munitions at night. The next time they saw him, he was wearing the Legion of Honor; his regiment had been decorated. Gertrude and Alice were proud of their *fileul*.

They were cut off from many of their friends during their wartime tours at Perpignan and Nîmes. Marsden Hartley, Gertrude learned, had returned to the States safely. But incredibly, Claribel Cone had remained in Germany. Apparently unwilling to face the discomforts of wartime travel and the possible indignities of a thorough physical search at the border, she had stayed in Germany until it was too late and America had entered the war. Her family had not heard from her since early in 1917—all of her letters had been returned to her. It was only after the war that Gertrude and Alice learned that Claribel had managed to survive, an enemy alien, living in a room in the luxury Regina Palast Hotel in Munich.

Leo, Gertrude knew, was in New York. Howard Gans had written her in June: "Leo . . . is psycho-analyzing and being psycho-analyzed, philosophizing and perambulating; also he is writing things that are being published. . . . He says that his great ambition is to say what he has to say in such manner as to get it published in the Saturday Evening Post."

They had seen Apollinaire, the year before, in Paris. He had been badly wounded in the head. They had met him briefly at a party. In his military uniform, his head still bandaged from the trepanning, Gertrude thought he looked dashing and heroic. Early in the spring of 1918 she and Alice went to pay a visit to Braque, who had also received a serious head wound and was convalescing at Sorgues, near Avignon.

They drove him to Avignon, and along the way, they gossiped. Apollinaire, so Braque told them, had recently married "a real young lady," Jacqueline Kolb, and the couple were living in a small apartment on the boulevard Saint-Germain. Braque, however, had been acutely embarrassed by their visit. The official uniforms that Gertrude and Alice had adopted were somewhat peculiar. In pictures taken at the time, Alice wears something like a British officer's jacket, with many pockets, and a pith helmet. Gertrude's getup looks somewhat Russian—a Cossack-type hat and a greatcoat that emphasizes her already massive bulk. Braque's recollection of their visit, written many years later, may have confused the details of their outfits. "They looked extremely strange," the painter recalled, "in their boy-scout uniforms with their green veils and colonial helmets. When we arrived at Avignon, on the Place Clémenceau, their funny get-up so excited the curiosity of the passers-by that a large crowd gathered around us and the comments were quite humorous. The police arrived and insisted on examining our papers. They were in order alright, but for myself, I felt very uncomfortable."

They heard of another marriage, as well. Picasso wrote them that he was intending to marry a young ballet dancer, Olga Koklova, whom he had met in Rome when he was designing the sets for *Parade*. Olga, the daughter of a Russian army officer, was not one of the major dancers in Diaghilev's troupe, having taken up the profession too late in her young life. She was, however, attractive, with regular, classical features that seem to have inspired some of Picasso's paintings at the time. She was, as well, somewhat bourgeois in her attitude. The civil ceremony for their marriage took place in July, 1918. Olga insisted that it be followed with all the proper rites in a Russian Orthodox church on the rue Daru. The bohemian life of the *avant-garde* years was now in the process of being legitimatized. In honor of the celebration, Picasso sent Gertrude a "lovely little painting," which many years later Alice copied in petit point to cover a small footstool.

The Michael Steins had settled at Montigny-sur-Loing, in the department of Seine et Marne. Michael wrote Gertrude about a subject that had been of some concern to her. Early in the year, the Germans had begun bombarding Paris with their mammoth cannons, the Big Berthas. One of the shells had fallen into the Luxembourg Gardens, not far from the rue de Fleurus, and Alice had become extremely apprehensive about the report. She was frightened, she moaned, of becoming "a miserable refugee." Michael wrote Gertrude in April, saying that he had gone to Paris for the first time in a month. The cannons were mercifully silent for several days and did not start up until he took the train home. In the meantime, he had given Beffa, the concierge, instructions to place all of the paintings in the pavilion stacked against the joint wall against the main building, which would be stronger. "Then I did a thing which I had been pondering over for several days before going to Paris," Michael continued, "and which I weighed carefully in all its respects. I took the [Cézanne] *Baigneurs,* the [Cézanne] *Fumeur,* & the Manet, made a good package of them and on our way to the Gare left them at the Am. Ex. Co who will place the package in a wooden box and send it to you—insured for forty thousand francs. At Nîmes you can have it stored in the safe of the branch of the Credit Lyonnais and at least you will have them where they need cause you no anxiety."

Gertrude and Alice were at Nîmes when the Armistice was declared. Alice, overjoyed, wept with relief. Gertrude, in a jocular mood, warned her: "Compose yourself, you have no right to show a tearful countenance to the French whose sons will no longer be killed." But she also remembered the remark a wounded French soldier had made when she had told him, "Well here is peace." "At least for twenty years," the soldier had answered.

The end of the war, however, did not signal the end of their relief services. A wire from Mrs. Lathrop arrived almost immediately asking if they spoke German and, if so, to close out their operations in Nîmes and return to Paris. They would be needed to open a depot for civilian relief in Alsace. They turned over their supplies to the nuns in one of the hospitals in Nîmes and went back to Paris.

Preparing themselves for a winter in Mulhouse, where they were to be stationed, they had Auntie serviced again and bought themselves aviators' fur-lined jackets and knitted sweaters. The trip to Alsace was eventful. On the road to Nancy, Aunt Pauline collided with a horse-drawn kitchen wagon, which bent the steering wheel and tore off the tool chest on the running board. The car wandered all over the road until, fortunately, they passed an American ambulance unit. Gertrude presented her problem, and the gruff sergeant in charge told her to run the car into the garage. The mechanic took off his tunic and threw it over the radiator. Gertrude sat back in relief. "When any American did that," Gertrude maintained, "the car was his."

Beyond Nancy, where they had stayed overnight, they passed through the blighted landscape of no man's land; miles of trenches lining each side of the road and here and there a shabby hut. The weather was bleak and damp. Gertrude found the sight impressive in an odd way: "It was not terrifying it was strange. We were used to ruined houses and even ruined towns but this was different. It was a landscape. And it belonged to no country."

In the midst of the desolate landscape, the fan belt broke. Gertrude, in a moment of feminine inspiration, was trying to fix it with a hairpin when a French staff car with two generals passed. Gertrude hailed it. The driver asked permission to make the necessary repairs and was granted it. In a few minutes the fan belt was repaired and Alice dipped into her hoard of Red Cross cigarettes to give the driver a handful. They proceeded on to Strasbourg and then Mulhouse.

Their mission in Alsace was to distribute blankets and clothing and children's garments to the Alsatian refugees who were returning to their devastated homes. They set up their distribution center in the gymnasium of one of the larger schools in Mulhouse. Gertrude, according to Alice, "spoke a fluent incorrect German the Alsatians understood." Gertrude was delighted when she overheard one of the women say of Alice, "She is a Prussian."

Despite the lingering wartime conditions, Alsace was well-provisioned; there were quantities of real coffee and large hams and milk. The patisseries, Alice noted, were filled with Alsatian delicacies. Only once did they forgo one of the specialties of the region. Alice had spied links of tempting sausages hanging in a butcher's window and considered buying some. "Take care," Gertrude warned, "it might be Claribel." They made friends with an *abbé* in nearby Cernay and with the French families in Mulhouse. On Sundays they were often asked to lunch. They invited their military godson, Abel Leglaye, to spend a few days with them and drove him to Strasbourg so that he could have the pleasure and the pride of climbing to the top of the Strasbourg Cathedral.

After the long cold winter, the first spring of the peace arrived; the storks returned, the fruit trees began to bloom. Their relief work was over. Gertrude had begun writing again, and the mood of bourgeoning spring crept into the final segment of her play poem "Accents in Alsace":

Sweeter than water or cream or ice. Sweeter than bells of roses. Sweeter than winter or summer or spring. Sweeter than pretty posies. Sweeter than anything is my queen and loving is her nature.

Loving and good and delighted and best is her little King and Sire whose devotion is entire who has but one desire to express the love which is hers to inspire.

In the photograph the Rhine hardly showed.

In what way do chimes remind you of singing. In what way do birds sing. In what way are forests black or white.

We saw them blue.

With for get me nots.

In the midst of our happiness we were very pleased.

They returned to Paris by way of the battlefields at Verdun and went out of their way to inspect a military tank that had been left on the road to Rheims. They stopped overnight at Mildred's farmhouse at Huiry. It was a joyous reunion of old friends, clouded only by the fact of learning from Amélie, Mildred's housekeeper and neighbor, that Mildred was once more hard up. She had spent all the money earned from *A Hilltop on the Marne* on wounded soldiers in the nearby hospitals and on the local families whose husbands had been wounded or killed in the war. As Alice observed, "She had given it to the hilltop from which she said she had earned it." They talked that evening of the devastation they had seen in their travels—Mildred had just returned from a trip to Château-Thierry. Still, Gertrude was philosophical. "Terrible as it all is," she remarked, "it gets less terrible every day. Time is doing its work, and time is such a healer." That evening, in Mildred's garden, Alice wrote out her last report for the American Fund.

The next morning they drove on to Paris, which was, in Alice's words, "more beautiful, vital and inextinguishable than ever."

BOOK II
The Literary Life

And so I am an American
and I have lived half my life in Paris,
not the half that made me but the half
in which I made what I made.
　　　　　　　—Gertrude Stein,
　　　　　　"An American and France"

CHAPTER NINE

The Old Door, a New Bell

I

The sight of Gertrude Stein, perched high atop the driver's seat of her Ford runabout, gripping the steering wheel, peering intently ahead and proceeding down Parisian streets, like some comically large goddess of the machine, was a vision many expatriates of the twenties recalled. Gertrude had been obliged to retire Auntie, which had seen hard duty during the war; moreover, only "civilian" vehicles were allowed in the Bois de Boulogne, which she and Alice favored as the scene of their drives. Although Auntie had been renovated and repainted black, she did not qualify as a civilian vehicle; she looked, so Frank Jacot told them, like "a second-class hearse." Gertrude ordered a new Ford, a two-seater, which arrived in early December, 1920, stripped of all the amenities. Riding in the car for the first time, Alice remarked that it was nude. "There was nothing on her dashboard, neither clock nor ash-box nor cigarette lighter." Gertrude answered, "Godiva," and that became the name of the car. It was in Godiva, parked at the curbside, that Gertrude often scribbled at her poems on odd scraps of paper. She had discovered, while waiting for Alice to attend to errands, that her lofty position in the driver's seat was an inspiring spot in which to write.

Winifred Bryher, the English poet and novelist, had her first glimpse of Gertrude riding in Godiva. She was walking with her newly acquired husband, Robert McAlmon, the American writer and editor. Bryher (that was her professional name) was the daughter of the wealthy shipping magnate John Ellerman, reputedly the heaviest taxpayer in England. Her marriage to McAlmon, whom Gertrude knew, was strictly a matter of convenience. It enabled her to escape from a tiresome family situation and conduct her own career, unhampered either by family or husband, for she chose to live much of the time in Switzerland, while McAlmon preferred Paris. The arrangement had proved advantageous for McAlmon, as well. With his father-in-law's backing, he was able to launch an ambitious publishing venture, the Contact Editions of Joyce, William Carlos Williams, Hemingway, and Gertrude, as well. Gertrude's friendship with McAlmon was both profitable and troublesome: It was McAlmon who finally brought out the complete, unabridged edition of *The Making of Americans* in 1925. Gertrude's meddling with his handling of the distribution of the book, however, resulted in a bitter quarrel that was never reconciled, much to Gertrude's regret.

On the occasion of her first meeting with Bryher, however, Gertrude was on the best of terms with McAlmon, and spotting the couple as she rode along, she pulled over to the curb and lumbered down from the vehicle. Bryher recalled the meeting vividly: "Two penetrating eyes in a square impassive face seemed to be absorbing every detail of my appearance. 'Why McAlmon,' a puzzled voice remarked, 'you did not tell me that you had married an ethical Jewess. It's rather a rare type.' " Bryher's ancestors had all been English Protestants and German Lutherans, but as she observed, "You did not argue with Gertrude Stein. You acquiesced."

Ford Madox Ford, the urbane English novelist and the editor of the *Transatlantic Review*, had caught sight of Gertrude on one of her routine excursions. With characteristic inaccuracy he set the scene prior to World War I, when Gertrude neither had a car nor knew how to drive. "Years ago," Ford recalled in his memoir, *It Was the Nightingale*, "—I should say in 1913—I was on the top of a bus in front of the Bon Marché. I saw Miss Gertrude Stein driving with a snail-like precision her Ford car. It was a vehicle of the original model of my namesake and with its great height above the roadway gave to Miss Stein, driving, the air of awfulness of Pope or Pharaoh, borne aloft and swaying on their golden thrones." Ford got off the bus and proceeded after Gertrude, but lost her as the car proceeded majestically along the avenue, while he was blocked by a crowd of pedestrians. He had wanted to air some disagreement with Gertrude, but could not recall what: "I have had so many and such long arguments with that old friend—or enemy—that they seem to fuse, the one into the other in an unbroken chain of battle."

The twenties were, indeed, to be a querulous decade. Old friendships had been dissolved by the war. Gertude felt that it was the loss of Apollinaire that had contributed to the "disaggregation." The poet had been a victim of the Spanish influenza epidemic and had died two days before the Armistice, his last hours troubled by the shouting crowds in the streets below his apartment. In his delirium, he thought that the hoarse cries of "*A bas Guillaume*," directed at the Kaiser, had been intended for him. Gertrude and Alice were in Nîmes then. Picasso heard the news by telephone at the Hotel Lutétia, where he was staying. As if to confirm his own existence, he drew a morose portrait of himself, staring into the bathroom mirror. "Guillaume would have been a bond of union," Gertrude felt. "He always had a quality of keeping people together, and now that he was gone everybody ceased to be friends."

The *Autobiography* summed up the immediate postwar period: "The old crowd had disappeared. Matisse was now permanently in Nice and in any case although Gertrude Stein and he were perfectly good friends when they met, they practically never met. . . . Braque and his wife we saw from time to time, he and Picasso by this time were fairly bitterly on the outs." For Gertrude the period had begun with a quarrel with Picasso, the cause of which neither she nor Picasso could afterward remember, but the effect of which was to keep them apart for a few years. He and Olga were then living in a fashionable Right Bank apartment on the rue La Boètie, with a drawing room and dining room that Olga furnished in correct bourgeois taste, expecting to entertain all the right people. Picasso had his studio on the floor above. The painter now dressed in sedate business suits with vest and tie; he and his wife saw few of their old bohemian associates. Gertrude clearly thought the marriage between the Spanish painter and the Russian ballerina was a mistake and later evolved the queer theory that it was due to the superficial attraction of a similar orientalism in both nationalities. "Scratch a Russian and you find a Tartar. Scratch a Spaniard and you find a Saracen," she maintained. She avoided the painter, and once when the two had met at a party one evening, Picasso had asked her to come and see him. Gertrude had answered with the gloomy reproach, "No I will not." Picasso sought out Alice: "Gertrude says she won't come to see me, does she mean it?" Alice said, "I am afraid if she says it she means it." It was only after the birth of Picasso's son, Paulot—on February 4, 1921, a day after Gertrude's birthday—that they were reconciled. They happened to be in a picture gallery together. Picasso, putting his hand on Gertrude's shoulder, had said, "Oh hell, let's be friends." Gertrude said, "Sure," and they embraced. Picasso and Olga came to dinner on the following evening.

The end of the war brought a truce of sorts in Gertrude's relationship with Leo. He had spent the war years in America, undergoing a period of psychoanalysis first with A. A. Brill and then Dr. Smith Ely Jelliffe, both of whom were dropped when Leo decided he could perform the service for himself. He seems to have regarded his attitude toward Gertrude as one index of his mental progress. Another was the continuation of his long-distance affair with Nina, whom he had been obliged to leave behind in Europe. When he arrived in the United States in 1915, he had attempted to send for her, but Nina's difficulties in getting the proper papers—and, perhaps, her reluctance—had made this impossible. In the meantime, he wrote Nina ardent letters and sent her money for her voice lessons.

On his own, Leo had had another of his epiphanies—this one apparently sexual. He wrote to Mabel Dodge about it in an odd vein: "I have circumvented many mysteries, anal eroticism, and 'why nature loves the number five' (what a poor innocent Emerson was not to know that the mystic number was not five but sixty-nine. Such are the tragedies of a life that ends before the great enlightenment)." Even his love letters to Nina gave glowing reports of his new sexual prowess. It seemed to be "raining women" he told her. His analysis had also widened his sexual horizons, for after telling Nina about his affair with X, "the most androgynous woman who has ever known love," he went on to claim: "If I had more skill in this sort of thing, I could compile a classified catalogue of about fifteen women and about an equal number of men who interest me for the moment, but that would take too long, especially since in spite of all this galaxy I always return to you, my beloved, as the only one that I love, I love, I love."

Leo had written to Gertrude twice while in America. In his first letter, written from New York in February, 1916, he admitted that he had intended to write before but had been annoyed with her. He had learned that Nina had written to her—it seems to have been when Gertrude and Alice were in Majorca—and that Gertrude had not bothered to reply. "That froze the genial currents of the soul and my intention dried up and was very thoroughly thawed since. However, it's cold enough over here these last few days to thaw most anything," he told Gertrude in a highly ambivalent confusion of thawing and freezing episodes.

The primary intention of his letter, it seemed, was to inform Gertrude that he had "broken into authorship of late to the extent of a couple of articles in a new review, one on Cézanne and one a criticism of a book. They want me to write regularly for them, and I am trying to get into the habit." For the rest, his letter conveyed news about mutual friends: He was paying weekend visits to Mabel Dodge at her farm at Croton-on-Hudson; Marsden Hartley had finally returned from Germany; New York was full of old acquaintances of Parisian days, "Pascin, Picabia, Nadelman, Duchamps, Gleizes—everybody who isn't in the trenches."

His next note, written from Nantucket in October, 1917, passed on an item he had found among some old family papers: "In a letter of Rachel's dated Vienna, Nov. 28, 1875: 'Our little Gertie is a little Schnatterer. She talks all day long and so plainly. *She outdoes them all.* She's such a round little pudding, toddles around the whole day & repeats everything that is said and done.' " Despite the cordiality of the gesture, one wonders if Leo, still unable to accept Gertrude's literary reputation, did not want to convey his impression that her adult literary activities were little more than a continuation of her childhood practices.

Gertrude evidently did not bother to reply to her brother. For when he next wrote her—from Settignano, when he returned to Europe in December, 1919—Leo went back over old ground. He found, he said, "that the antagonism that had grown up some years ago had gotten

Picasso caricature of Leo Stein walking, *circa* 1905–6. (Collection Mrs. Jerome B. Rocherolle, Stamford, Connecticut.)

dissipated and that I felt quite amiable, rather more so even than I used to feel before that strain developed. . . . The 'family romance' as it is called is almost always central in the case of a neurosis, just as you used to get indigestion when we had a dispute. So I could tell pretty well how I was getting on by the degree of possibility I felt of writing as I am doing now." The tone of his letter was reflective and amiable: "It's a curious thing to look back upon one's life as I do now as something with which I have nothing to do except to stand for the consequences, because it was really a prolonged disease, a kind of mild insanity." He also informed Gertrude about his difficulties in writing: "There was a large demand for my writing, and speaking too, but unfortunately almost every expression was followed by a corresponding repression. I may get out of it now, though some teaching I should like to have done is no longer possible on account of my deafness." Leo's candid admissions, however, did nothing to bring about a reconciliation. Gertrude apparently welcomed the estrangement and made no serious effort to repair the break.

One day, soon after acquiring Godiva, Gertrude and Alice were momentarily stalled in traffic near the church of Saint-Germain-des-Prés. Gertrude rose from her seat and bowed solemnly to a man who had doffed his hat in passing. "Who was that?" Alice asked, having caught sight of the man out of the corner of her eye. "Leo," Gertrude answered. "Not possibly," Alice said in astonishment, turning to watch Leo stroll down the boulevard with the light, springing stride she had always admired.

II

Old friends and new visitors stopped at the rue de Fleurus. "You can tell that the war is over," Gertrude had written to Henry McBride in December, 1919. "So many people knock at the old door instead of ringing the new bell. The other day Duchamp and Roché turned up." Jessie Whitehead, Professor Whitehead's daughter, arrived in Paris to work as a secretary to one of the delegations at the peace conference. Her accounts of events at the conference provided the inspiration for a number of Gertrude's poems and prose pieces, including "League," "More League," and "Woodrow Wilson," which purportedly dealt with current events and world affairs, but which were really continuations of Gertrude's then-current writing style. Gertrude and Alice had watched the victory procession from Jessie Whitehead's hotel room, where they had a good view of the Allied armies marching down the Champs Elysées and through the Arc de Triomphe—the wounded in their wheelchairs starting off the procession and followed by the various armies, with General Pershing leading the American doughboys. It was a stirring event, but like the peace, it left Gertrude and Alice somewhat restless and dissatisfied. After the parade they walked up and down the Champs Elysées: "The war was over and the piles of captured cannon that had made two pyramids were being taken away and peace was upon us."

For a time they were "still in the shadow of war work," visiting wounded soldiers in the nearby hospitals, most of whom, Gertrude observed, were "now pretty well neglected by everybody." The Saturday evenings had been a casualty of the war and were not reinstated. They were forced to economize, having used up a good deal of their funds during the war: "We were economising," Gertrude remembered. "Servants were difficult to get if not impossible, prices were high. We settled down for the moment with a femme de ménage for only a few hours a day." Gertrude was the chauffeur and Alice served as cook; they did their marketing each morning.

During Auntie's declining days, they took short trips to the country, driving out to the forests of Saint-Germain and Fontainebleau to pick wildflowers. For these excursions Alice would prepare one of two standard picnic lunches: a cold chicken, mushroom sandwiches, a dessert of cream-puff shells to be filled with crushed strawberries, or roast-beef sandwiches accompanied by sweetbreads and truffles rolled in lettuce leaves. They made regular monthly visits to Mildred Aldrich and once took her on an excursion to nearby Rheims to visit the cathedral, which had been shelled during the war.

In recognition of their war efforts, Gertrude and Alice were awarded the Médaille de la Reconnaissance Française. It was an official honor, more or less routinely awarded to those who had taken part in the French war effort, but both were pleased and proud. Alice was amused by the fact that while each of their citations was practically identical, hers stated that she had performed her duties, "sans relâche"—without respite—Gertrude's did not. As a result of the award, they began a campaign to see that Mildred Aldrich was given the Legion of Honor. It was Gertrude's contention that Mildred's services and her propaganda efforts in America through the popularity of her books, which depicted the bravery of the Allied soldiers and French civilians, were well deserving of the honor. However, the task was made difficult by the fact that Mildred had not been associated with any official organization. Gertrude and Alice drew up a list of prominent Americans and circulated a petition, but the list in itself proved ineffectual. They discovered that most of the people they approached had other, more official, candidates whom they wished to promote. As the affair dragged on, they tried various French officials as well as members of the American Legion. Nearly everyone was sympathetic, but no action resulted. They consulted a French senator who was equally sympathetic, but with similar results. Their break finally came in the form of the senator's secretary. Gertrude offered her a lift home in Godiva one day. It turned out that the senator's secretary had been taking driving lessons but without success. Gertrude's confidence behind the wheel was sufficiently inspiring so that when the senator's secretary got out of the car, she assured Gertrude that Mildred's papers would be pushed through the maze of French bureaucracy. Not long after—at the end of August, 1922—the official ceremony awarding Mildred the Legion of Honor was held at the *mairie* at Huiry. Mildred, standing erect and proud, received the decoration with all the dignity proper to her sixty-eight years. She wrote to Gertrude and Alice, who were traveling at the time, saying that she was "for the moment overwhelmed and terribly timid." But she vowed, "I'll try to get used to it before you return and to recover from the impulse I have when any one looks at me to cover it with my hand." Nevertheless, she pinned the red ribbon to her nightdress every evening. From their campaign on Mildred's behalf, Gertrude concluded that whenever one wanted to get something official done, the safest course was not to depend upon senators or generals, but to get "a pleasant female clerk or an amiable sergeant" to do it for you.

The friendships Gertrude made during the volatile twenties seemed to develop in a series of chain reactions. In 1920 she became the first annual subscriber to Sylvia Beach's Shakespeare & Company, the vital library service that the American woman initiated in Paris for the benefit of American and English writers. It was in Sylvia Beach's shop on the rue de l'Odéon that Gertrude encountered a group of young Oxford men whom she was delighted to find were admirers of her work. They arranged to publish "More League" and the "Portrait of Harry Phelan Gibb," an English painter friend, in the May 7, 1920, issue of the *Oxford* magazine. It was through Sylvia Beach that Gertrude and Alice met Adrienne Monnier, a quiet, unassuming Frenchwoman and Sylvia Beach's lifetime friend, who ran a French bookstore across the street from Shakespeare & Company. Adrienne Monnier was sponsoring a group of young French writers, such as Valéry Larbaud and the Dada poet Tristan Tzara, whom she introduced to Gertrude. For a time Larbaud planned to translate *Three Lives* into French, but the project, unfortunately, fell through.

Gertrude's relationship with Sylvia Beach began cordially, but suffered periods of estrangement in later years. Gertrude, Sylvia Beach recalled, had "so much charm" that others forgave her the "monstrous absurdities" she sometimes uttered. One evening, at the rue de Fleurus, Gertrude announced to Adrienne Monnier: "You French have no Alps in literature, no Shakespeare, all your genius is in those speeches of the generals: fanfare. Such as '*On ne passera pas!*'" Adrienne was not amused, but remained tolerant.

In 1921 Sylvia brought Sherwood Anderson to the rue de Fleurus. The writer was making his first trip to Paris. In the following year Anderson sent the young Ernest Hemingway, then beginning his career as Paris correspondent for the *Toronto Star*. Hemingway, in turn, brought F. Scott Fitzgerald, then at the height of his fame. But Sylvia observed that her own friendship with Gertrude cooled considerably after Shakespeare & Company had published James Joyce's *Ulysses* in 1922. Gertrude had even come to the shop to inform her that she would now be subscribing to the American Library, on the Right Bank. Gertrude clearly viewed Joyce as her principal rival as a literary inno-vator, and she was fond of quoting Picasso's remark: "Yes, Braque and James Joyce, they are the incomprehensibles whom anybody can understand." Sylvia Beach's sponsorship of a major work by Joyce was evidently regarded as a form of disloyalty. Although the names of the two literary experimenters were inevitably linked throughout the 1920's, Joyce and Gertrude did not actually meet until the mid-1930's at a tea at Jo Davidson's studio. Sylvia Beach introduced the pair, who dis-covered that neither had much to discuss with the other except the odd circumstance that they should both be writers who had been living in the same quarter of Paris for years and yet had never before met.

Throughout the early 1920's, Gertrude renewed old acquaintance-ships. One day, in 1920, she had encountered the sculptor Jacques Lipchitz acting strangely on the street. Lipchitz, whom she had known before the war, when he was associated with the Cubist group, was pacing back and forth in front of a shop window, studying an iron cock that he was thinking of buying and finally did. Lipchitz asked Gertrude to come to his studio and pose for him, and she agreed. Lip-chitz found her an interesting subject, and her egotism memorable. He recalled Gertrude's telling him, once, very solemnly, "Jacques, of course you don't know too much about English literature, but besides Shake-speare and me, who do you think there is?" Lipchitz's bust of her, ex-ecuted in 1920, was one of his most effective portrait sculptures. He portrayed her as a sleek Buddha with a topknot. The eyes, however, gave him difficulties, a problem he solved by hollowing them out rather than attempting to render them. This gave Gertrude's face an in-scrutable look.

Ordinarily Gertrude liked to pose, and she enjoyed Lipchitz because he was an "excellent gossip." He could always be counted on to "sup-ply several missing parts of several stories" she already knew. But it was a hot spring, and Lipchitz's studio was sweltering. Gertrude liked the portrait when it was finished but, much to the sculptor's regret, did not offer to buy it. Lipchitz, however, agreed to bring her photographs of the bust. Weeks went by and she did not hear from him. Finally she wrote, asking him to bring the photographs. When Lipchitz arrived, she asked him what the trouble was. Lipchitz told her that he had heard from a mutual friend that she had found the sittings boring. "Oh hell," Gertrude said. "Listen I am fairly well known for saying things about any one and anything, I say them about people, I say them to people, I say them when I please and how I please, but as I mostly say what I think, the least that you or anybody else can do is to rest content with what I say to you." Strangely, Gertrude concluded that Lipchitz had been content with this explanation, and she wondered why she did not see the sculptor again for several years.

It was through Lipchitz, who had just completed a bust of Jean Cocteau, that Gertrude became reacquainted with the young French poet. Picasso had brought him to the rue de Fleurus, "a slim elegant youth," leaning on the painter's shoulder, one day in 1917, just before the pair were to go to Rome. Cocteau had written the scenario and verbal segments of the ballet *Parade*, for which Picasso was to design the scenery and settings. Lipchitz had alerted Gertrude to the fact that Cocteau was an admirer of her writing and that he had even claimed that one of her lines had provided the inspiration for his *Le Potomak*, written in 1913 but which had not been published until 1919. Gertrude, evidently, never consulted Cocteau's strange tale of a monster, the "Potomak," which lived in a subterranean aquarium on a diet of olive oil, spelling mistakes, and other curious items provided by "an American gentleman," for she was never disabused of the notion that Cocteau had quoted from her "Portrait of Mabel Dodge," when, in fact, he had referred to her three-word line, "Dining is west," from *Tender Buttons*.

The circumstances of Gertrude's having been one of the inspirations for Cocteau's book are curious. "One night," the poet maintained in the "Prospectus" to *Le Potomak*, "I heard friends laughing over a poem by an American woman. But her telegram went straight to my heart. 'Dining is west,' Gertrude Stein decides, quite simply, in the middle of a blank page. A single epithet should be enough to set off a dream—a light touch on the shoulder, the arrow on a road sign. What offended my friends—the American joke—seemed to me on the contrary, a proof of confidence." The problem is that *Tender Buttons* was not published until 1914, and the only possibility of Cocteau's having seen Gertrude's words in "the middle of a blank page" would seem to have been a typescript version.

Despite Gertrude's lack of interest in precisely what Cocteau had said or quoted, she was grateful for this first mention of her work by a French author. In the early twenties she set out to cultivate him, but had to admit, after an initial meeting or two, that their friendship was to consist in their "writing to each other quite often and liking each other immensely and having many young and old friends in common, but not in meeting." Cocteau seemed to be chronically ill early in their friendship. To an early invitation, he sent his excuses by way of Lipchitz, saying that he was suffering from a bad toothache, but signing himself, "your old admirer and, I hope, your future friend." In February, 1922, she sent him a copy of her word portrait of Picasso and complimented him on his poem "The Cape of Good Hope," which had appeared in the autumn, 1921, issue of *The Little Review*. Cocteau replied on the twentieth, in English, apologizing for having to dictate the letter to a friend. He had been quite ill, he said, with *"la grippe rheumatismale,"* and was not yet strong enough to sit up. "Your Picasso is a beautiful thing which resembles his photograph with the dog. If the poem in *The Little Review* pleases you, you will lend me your copy so that I may correct the mistakes which are to be found on every page."

Later that year, Gertrude wrote him while she was on vacation in southeastern France, blatantly asking for a literary favor to which he did not respond. He had sent her a copy of his book *Le Secret Professionel*. "My dear Cocteau," Gertrude wrote him:

Thanks so much for your little book. It looks like a nice little book. And how are you, all well again I hope. We have been wandering around everywhere a bit and have finally settled in St. Remy. Gounod was here before us but not in the same hotel. We will be staying a month, I have been writing a lot, a little story of Avignon that I think would please you. I expect my book [*Geography and Plays*] will be out in October. I will send it to you then. I [would] like you to do a review of it. That would please me very much.

Gertrude had, perhaps, written him as soon as his book arrived, thus avoiding the necessity of commenting on it. Cocteau was apt to respond in kind when she sent him her literary efforts. Early in 1926 she sent him a copy of *The Making of Americans*, together with a typescript copy of her word portrait of Cocteau. "*Gertrude l'admirable*," he wrote back, "*J'ai reçu ce soir votre grand sourire grammatical.*" He commented on their special relationship, despite the fact that they seldom saw one another: "*Je ne vous vois mais je vous aime, vous le savez, et j'habite avec vous le pays perdu.*" Then he confessed that he did not completely understand her portrait: "*Hélas, je comprends mal seulement a moitié* [When half is may how much is may]." His letter was signed with a heart. As for her mammoth novel, Cocteau noted in a postscript that he was waiting "daily" for friends who would translate it for him.

Their largely epistolary friendship trailed off in good feeling. At one point, presumably after a long period of noncommunication, Cocteau wrote her reassuringly, *"le silence n'existe jamais entre nous."* As late as 1934, when *The Autobiography of Alice B. Toklas* was in its third printing, and her opera libretto *Four Saints in Three Acts* had been published—it is not clear which of them Gertrude sent him—Cocteau wrote her one of those letters authors are sometimes obliged to write one another. "The book came in one of those periods when life was making only nightmare gestures and grimaces at me," he explained. "Since then I have read it as I like to read you, in detail, here and there, as the bird flies—before plunging into the soul of the matter." He countered by asking if she had received his *Enfants Terribles* and concluded: "Dear Gertrude I embrace you, I feel myself nearer to you than to all those who come around me and our hearts are united by a special thread." Despite that "special thread," neither of them seems to have made any profound assessment of each other's talents. They were, it appears, more impressed with each other's reputations.

Jo Davidson and his wife, Yvonne, had returned to Paris after the war. In 1922 Davidson, too, decided to make a portrait sculpture of Gertrude. She sat for him in his studio on the avenue du Maine, raised on a low platform, her shoulders hunched forward, her hands resting in her ample lap. The pose made her look like an Egyptian scribe or a burly workman resting on his lunch hour. During the course of the sittings, Gertrude wrote a word portrait of the sculptor, and when he was in New York in the fall, he reported that he was "hammering at the Century Magazine to publish your portrait of me, and illustrate it with my portrait of you. I hope to succeed—they are so damn timid—that it's awful. If they should turn me down, I'll try elsewhere." The two portraits eventually appeared in the February, 1923, issue of *Vanity Fair.*

Among the celebrities that the Davidsons introduced to Gertrude was the muckraking journalist Lincoln Steffens. Steffens included a flattering "portrait" of Gertrude in his lengthy *Autobiography,* published in 1931. He was sympathetic and admiring of the vigor and seriousness he found among the experimental artists and writers of the Parisian milieu when he visited there in July, 1922. "Gertrude Stein," he said, "was another powerful revolutionary leader who was content to be herself, do her own work, but when the young men and women came to her, she gave them all they would take." Gertrude struck him, Steffens went on, not only "as a genius, but as a wise woman." He had heard Gertrude's portrait of Davidson read aloud one evening, although from a distance, and "unable to hear distinctly all the words, the reading sounded like the sculptor monologuing at his work—but exactly." Coming from a man whose principal interests were social and political, Steffens's description and his favorable glimpse of the Stein salon did no harm to a writer known as a literary eccentric, a coterie figure living in an ivory tower.

Not all of the new arrivals at the rue de Fleurus were as well received as Steffens. Shortly after the war, Gertrude had met the poet Ezra Pound at Grace Lounsbery's salon. For a time Pound was a regular visitor at her studio. Gertrude, rather disingenuously, claimed that she liked him but did not find him amusing. He was "a village explainer," a type she found wearying. Furthermore, she did her best to discourage the long flirtation that her friend and admirer Kate Buss, a journalist and sculptor from Medford, Massachusetts, who had turned up in Paris after the war, was conducting with the poet.

Gertrude's antipathy toward Pound, however, probably had deeper and more personal causes. Brilliant, opinionated, generous with those he liked, vehement in arguments, Pound was a tireless promoter of young writers whose works he pushed in the pages of *Poetry* and *The Dial*, and in *The Little Review*, for which he served as Parisian literary editor and agent. It was Pound, Gertrude recalled, who had first mentioned T. S. Eliot to her. In any aesthetic argument, Pound was apt to be crusty and frank; he would hardly have been deferential to Gertrude's opinions. Moreover, she probably sensed in him a formidable rival to her own role as a mentor to the young.

Her break with Pound resulted from a minor accident. He had brought the editor of *The Dial*, Scofield Thayer, to the rue de Fleurus one evening, and a spirited argument ensued. The discussion became more violent as the evening progressed—so heated, in fact, that at one point Pound fell out of one of the little armchairs that stood on either side of the fireplace. Gertrude could barely conceal her scorn. "Finally," as she recorded it, "Ezra and the editor of the *Dial* left, nobody too well pleased." She decided that she did not want to see Pound again. When, sometime later, the poet met her in the Luxembourg Gardens and asked to come around and see her, Gertrude excused herself, saying that Alice had a bad toothache and that they would be busy "picking wildflowers." Pound's pronounced anti-Semitism would never have endeared Gertrude to him to begin with, but for the most part it was on literary grounds that he later dismissed her.

At the Willie Dunbar Jewetts' Parisian hotel suite—the Jewetts were an American couple Gertrude and Alice had met during their wartime service in Perpignan—they were introduced to two other interesting young Americans, the photographer and Dadaist painter Man Ray, and the writer Robert Coates. Man Ray, who was photographing all the cultural celebrities of Paris, had asked Gertrude to come and pose for him in his tiny rue Delambre studio. Gertrude was immensely pleased with the results, and he became something of an official photographer at the rue de Fleurus. Although Gertrude was to speak admiringly of

Man Ray in later years, the photographer was not so kindly disposed toward her. In an interview many years later, he pronounced her an "idiot" whose attitude as a "dictator of art" he resented. In his auto-biography, *Self-Portrait*, he remembered a painful domestic scene at the rue de Fleurus. It was Alice's function to talk with the less important visitors and keep them off Gertrude's hands. One afternoon, while he was having an animated discussion with Gertrude, they became aware of Alice carrying on a lively discussion with one of the women visitors. Gertrude turned toward Alice and "shouted belligerently for them to lower their voices." For the rest of the afternoon there was mortified silence in Alice's corner.

Coates, who later became art critic for *The New Yorker*, impressed Gertrude as a writer. He was, she claimed, the one younger writer she had met "who had an individual rhythm, his words made a sound to the eyes." She was particularly impressed with Coates's early novel, *The Eater of Darkness*. Of an adventurous disposition, Coates and a friend made the only known canoe trip through France in the early twenties, traveling down the Seine and the Epte, carrying the canoe overland when necessary, much to the amazement of French farmers. Along the way, an old postman had cheered them on with cries of "*Vivent les Peaux-Rouges!*" Gertrude became "quite attached" to the young red-headed writer, and Alice admired his "pretty, velvety voice and gentle ways." In later years Coates felt that Gertrude had never received the recognition that was properly due her for introducing "an almost mathematical lucidity . . . into the treatment of the English language." He recalled the "genial feeling of artistic equality" that he had had on his visits to the rue de Fleurus.

Janet Flanner, who became *The New Yorker*'s famed Paris correspondent, Genêt, for nearly a half-century, also arrived in Paris, just after the war, in 1921. Brisk, alert, peppery, with a sense of personal style and great flair that was to sustain her as one of the shrewdest and most entertaining observers of the French political, social, and artistic scene, she met Gertrude, "not the first minute I arrived in Paris, but shortly thereafter." She was never to become a great admirer of Gertrude's hermetic style of writing, but she remained loyal in her appreciation of Gertrude's personality and the integrity of her literary ambitions. As an active correspondent covering the French scene, she was not as frequent a guest at the rue de Fleurus as some of the other Americans in Paris, and her absences were often a subject of complaint. "You say you love us," Gertrude told her on one of her visits, "but you never come to see us—and when you do, you bring white flowers so we can't be mad at you." In truth, Janet Flanner's great friendship was with Ernest Hemingway, but she remained open to certain of the virtues of the ménage at the rue de Fleurus.

III

In midsummer, 1922, Gertrude and Alice made their first long trip in Godiva. An American friend, the sculptor Janet Scudder, and her friend Camille Lane were driving, in *their* new Ford, to Grasse in Provence, where they planned to buy a house. Gertrude and Alice accompanied them in Godiva.

Janet was a friend from prewar days, though Gertrude's closest relationship with her developed during the twenties. Before the war, Janet had shuttled back and forth between New York and Paris, studying sculpture with MacMonnies in Paris, attempting to make a career for herself in America. Her forte was pleasant and inoffensive garden statuary—prancing fauns, nubile girls, boys on dolphins. For a time one of her principal clients had been the architect Stanford White, who commissioned a number of garden pieces for the Long Island estates he was then building. In Paris, Janet held "afternoons" on Saturdays in her studio on the rue de la Grand Chaumière. There one might meet Gordon Craig and, occasionally, the aged Henry Adams.

Gertrude maintained that "there were only two perfectly solemn things on earth, the doughboy and Janet Scudder." Her friend was consequently nicknamed "The Doughboy," because she had "all the subtlety of the doughboy and all his nice ways and all his lonesomeness." Gertrude, however, did not approve of Janet's plans to buy a house because she felt that Janet also had "the real pioneer's passion for buying useless real estate." All along the route there were conferences, with Gertrude firmly disapproving, when Janet earnestly seemed ready to buy property in every little town they traveled through rather than in Grasse, which had been her original intention. For the moment, Gertrude's judgment prevailed.

At Saint Rémy, however, Gertrude and Alice decided to put up in a hotel and stay, while Janet and Mrs. Lane went on to Grasse. The landscape and scenery around Saint Rémy were not spectacular, but they seemed to have a certain fascination for Gertrude. The low foothills, the shepherds leading their flocks up into the mountains, the Roman ruins in nearby Les Baux figure in the poems and plays she wrote during their stay. She was having a productive period—the primary reason that their brief vacation lengthened into a stay of several months. "Lend a Hand or Four Religions," "Saints in Seven," and "Talks to Saints in Saint Rémy" were all written there, as well as the long meditative piece "An Elucidation," ostensibly about style and grammar. The saint poems and plays were notably earlier, more comprehensible versions of her later opera libretto, *Four Saints in Three Acts*, and "An Elucidation" was the harbinger of a theme—grammar and creative writing—which she was to develop in the several later pieces that make up *How to Write*. Their stay in Saint Rémy was to be remembered more for literary reasons than for the pleasures of the spot.

Meanwhile, Janet, after an unsuccessful search for a house in Grasse, had gone to Aix-en-Provence, where she found property that she decided to buy. Gertrude telegraphed her and wrote her advising against it, but she was not successful. In this case Gertrude was proved right, for after a hard winter and a hot summer, Janet concluded that she had made a mistake and fortunately was able to sell the house. Periodically throughout their stay, Gertrude and Alice had visited Janet and Mrs. Lane in Aix, and they went regularly to Avignon. Otherwise they kept to themselves. In the end, Gertrude came to feel that there was something especially dismal about the Provençal region in the wintertime with the mistral blowing. As she later told a friend, "If you go to Provence you'll find you're getting nervous down there. You'll find yourself having a big fight with your best friend. You just can't help it."

They had remained until the weather grew cold and the wind blustery. The hotel was uncomfortable. Alice, with little to do, was miserable. One day, as they were walking across a plowed field on their way to a little village in the hills, she broke down and cried. Gertrude asked her what was the matter. "The weather," Alice said forlornly. "Can we go back to Paris." "Tomorrow," Gertrude said.

Gertrude, however, regarded their stay as a turning point. "This long winter in Saint-Rémy," she observed in the *Autobiography*, "broke the restlessness of the war and the after war. A great many things were to happen, there were to be friendships and there were to be enmities and there were to be a great many other things but there was not to be any restlessness."

CHAPTER TEN

All Honorable Men

I

Tender Buttons, that problematic book, had brought Sherwood Anderson to Gertrude's door. Anderson was forty-four when he first met her in the summer of 1921. His early career had been spent first in the mail-order business, then as an advertising copywriter. Anderson liked to promote the legend that he had decided to chuck it all one day and become a writer. But he was still carrying a few of his advertising accounts when he met Gertrude; he did not give them up until the following year. And he was already an established author. He had, in fact, been notified that he was to receive the first of the annual *Dial* awards, acknowledging his "service to letters" and carrying with it a stipend of $2,000.

Anderson had come upon *Tender Buttons* in 1914, not long after he had begun contributing stories and articles to the little magazines. Although the book had been widely ridiculed in the press, he had found something tonic in its use of words: "It excited me as one might grow excited in going into a new and wonderful country where everything is strange—a sort of Lewis and Clark expedition for me." His mind, he claimed, "did a kind of jerking flop," and for several days he carried around a notebook on which he made new combinations of words.

"The result was I thought a new familiarity with the words of my own vocabulary. I became a little conscious where before I had been unconscious. Perhaps it was then I really fell in love with words, wanted to give each word I used every chance to show itself at its best."

Sylvia Beach's note asking to bring Anderson to the rue de Fleurus on a Friday evening—"He is so anxious to know you for he says you have influenced him ever so much & that you stand as such a great master of words"—had delighted Gertrude. Anderson came with his second wife, Tennessee, and the music critic Paul Rosenfeld, who had financed their first trip abroad. "Sherwood's deference," Sylvia Beach observed, "and the admiration he expressed for her writing pleased Gertrude immensely. She was visibly touched." Tennessee Anderson, less manageable than many of the wives brought to the rue de Fleurus, seems to have wanted to take part in the conversation between her husband and Gertrude. But Alice soon took her in hand and away from the discussion. There was, Sylvia Beach noticed, one peculiarity to the ritual at the rue de Fleurus. "Curiously, it was only applied to wives; non-wives were admitted to Gertrude's conversation."

Anderson gave a fanciful account of his visit in a short article, "Four American Impressions," which he wrote for the October 11, 1922, issue of *The New Republic*. He likened her to a wholesome cook, working in a "kitchen of words." She was, he said, "an American woman of the old sort, one who cares for the handmade goodies and who scorns the factory-made foods." Gertrude was, he claimed, "laying word against word, relating sound to sound, feeling for the taste, the smell, the rhythm of the individual word. She is attempting to do something for the writers of our English speech that may be better understood after a time, and she is not in a hurry." For several years Anderson's letters to Gertrude bristled with similar compliments and flattering remarks that went beyond the call of necessity. Gertrude, too, had been complimentary to the author of *Poor White* and *Winesburg, Ohio*. "You sometimes write what is the most important thing of all to be able to write," she told him, "passionate and innocent sentences." The remark was guarded—not unqualified flattery—but one that held up the notion of fellow workers in a difficult métier. She had reason for being obliging to Anderson, for she was to ask him to provide an introduction to her new volume, *Geography and Plays*.

The idea of bringing out a new volume had been in Gertrude's mind for some time. The likelihood, however, was that she would have to publish it at her own expense. Shortly after the war, her English painter friend Harry Phelan Gibb had told her that she should bring out a book as a way of re-establishing her position in the postwar literary world. And in November, 1920, her friend Henry McBride had written her with the same advice. He and the collector Walter Arensberg and Marcel Duchamp had spent an evening discussing the possibilities of bringing out "a new book of your things and the best way to put it over." McBride's opinion was that she should print it privately at her own expense. "There is a public for you," McBride remarked, "but no publisher." Still he was sure that a writer with Gertrude's following would be able to realize her investment. "Only don't be impatient," he warned her.

Kate Buss, on a trip to the United States, had scouted up a Boston publisher, Edmund F. Brown of the Four Seas Press, who would undertake the work. "Honest-to-God" Brown, as Gertrude referred to him, offered her a contract that provided a first edition of 2,500 copies for a cost of $2,500, paying a 15 per cent royalty and $1.00 a copy on every copy sold as, hopefully, a return on her investment. A preface by Anderson, Brown assured her, would not only be helpful "as an aid to the general reader but also to us in marketing."

Gertrude agreed to the terms. She put together a selection of representative pieces, drawn from over a decade of her own work. It included rhythmic Spanish poems, such as "Susie Asado," and a selection of both her early and later word portraits, among them, "Ada," her first word portrait of Alice. She included, as well, domestic idylls, such as "Sacred Emily" whose line "Rose is a rose is a rose is a rose" was to become her most famous and most frequently quoted line, and a representative gathering of her plays and monologues, such as "He Said It," and "Turkey and Bones and Eating." *Geography and Plays*, which appeared in December, 1922, was to remain one of the most balanced and satisfying volumes of her "difficult" writings.

Anderson, however, had been delayed in getting to the introduction. He had written to Gertrude in February from New Orleans: "I was afraid you might have changed your mind about having me write the introduction and had you done so I should have been quite upset. It's a literary job I'd rather do than any other I know of. I'll get at it very soon and send it along." He had heard, he said, that she was "off Americans" and that "frightened me too." Anderson finished the introduction shortly afterward. It was amiable and conversational in tone, beginning with Anderson's recollection of a winter evening in Chicago when his brother Karl, a painter, had brought *Tender Buttons* to his apartment. Anderson recorded his brother's impressions: "It gives words an oddly new intimate flavor and at the same time makes familiar words seem almost like strangers, doesn't it."

In his introduction, Anderson forswore any discussion about the problems of meaning or the associational context of Gertrude's writing. He chose, instead, to deal with the experimental vitality of her work, her ability to give words a kind of renewed vigor. He put the discussion in charming terms:

There is a city of English and American words and it has been a neglected city. Strong broad shouldered words, that should be marching across open fields under the blue sky, are clerking in dusty dry goods stores, young virgin words are being allowed to consort with whores, learned words have been put to the ditch digger's trade. Only yesterday I saw a word that once called a whole nation to arms serving in the mean capacity of advertising laundry soap.

Against this corruption of language, he commended Gertrude's efforts:

For me the work of Gertrude Stein consists in a rebuilding, an entirely new recasting of life, in the city of words. Here is one artist who has been able to accept ridicule, who has even forgone the privilege of writing the great American novel, uplifting our English speaking stage, and wearing the bays of the great poets, to go live among the little housekeeping words, the swaggering bullying street-corner words, the honest working, money saving words, and all the other forgotten and neglected citizens of the sacred and half forgotten city.

Anderson's praise, however, was not totally unqualified. A short time after, he wrote to his brother Karl, claiming: "As for Stein, I do not think her too important. I do think she had an important thing to do, not for the public, but for the artist who happens to work with words as his material."

Nevertheless, in the spring of 1923, Anderson was still writing to Gertrude in a complimentary vein. He was in Reno, waiting out a divorce and attempting to finish an autobiographical book in which, so he informed Gertrude, she was to figure. "I am trying to make a kind of picture of the artist's life in the midst of present-day American life," he told her. Anderson's *A Story Teller's Story* was to be a somewhat long-winded and repetitive piece of writing, but it sketched out his early life and his dissatisfactions, and the queer, crabbed lives he had encountered. It was redolent of homespun Americanism and his general distrust of big-city intellectual types. But in the book he honestly tried to set down, as he informed Gertrude in his letter, the "things and people that have meant most. You, Jane Heap [the co-editor of *The Little Review*], Dreiser, Paul Rosenfeld, Van Wyck Brooks, Alfred Stieglitz. That about nails the list."

"It was a vital day for me when I stumbled upon you," he told her. "But also there was and is something else. There was not only your work, but also your room in the house there in Paris. That was something special too. I mean the effect on myself. You would be surprised to know just how altogether American I found you."

Gertrude's heartfelt appreciation for Anderson flowed out in one of her poems, "A Valentine to Sherwood Anderson: Idem the Same," which appeared in the spring, 1923, issue of *The Little Review*. In its more comprehensible passages, the portrait poem luxuriated in old-fashioned sentiment:

Very fine is my valentine.
Very fine and very mine.
Very mine is my valentine very mine and very fine.
Very fine is my valentine and mine, very fine very mine and mine is my valentine.

But it is difficult to locate precisely those passages that might have prompted Anderson to write about it: "I like it because it always stirs me and is full of sharp criticism too."

And when Anderson's *A Story Teller's Story* was published, she reviewed it appreciatively in the March, 1925, issue of *Ex Libris*. The title of her review was somewhat antic: "A Stitch in Time Saves Nine. Birds of a Feather Flock Together. Chickens Come Home to Roost." Gertrude had a penchant for homely, old adages and collected them, after a fashion. But she came to the conclusion that few of them had any real truth. Her appraisal of Anderson's book, however, was more pertinent:

There are four men so far in American letters who have essential intelligence. They are Fenimore Cooper, William Dean Howells, Mark Twain and Sherwood Anderson. They do not reflect life or describe life or embroider life or photograph life, they express life and to express life takes essential intelligence. Whether to express life is the most interesting thing to do or the most important thing to do I do not know, but I do know that it is the most permanent thing to do.

Gertrude acknowledged that like all long books, *A Story Teller's Story* was "uneven, but there is no uncertainty in the fullness of its quality." She was particularly impressed with Anderson's treatment of youth. No one, she felt, "can hesitate before the reality of the expression of the life of the Anderson boys . . . and the being of the girl who has to have and to give what is needed is without any equal in quality in anything that has been done up to this time by anyone writing to-day."

Anderson wrote her gratefully, saying that he loved the review. "You always manage to say so much and say it straighter than anyone else I know. Bless you for it." He also told her that he had finished a new novel that he thought was good. It was called *Dark Laughter*, and Liveright would be publishing it in the fall.

That issue of *Ex Libris* was also notable for a seconding review of Anderson's book—this one by Ernest Hemingway. Hemingway, who had known Anderson since 1921, in Chicago, was already regarded, in certain quarters, as a protégé of the older writer. It was a characterization of his talent that Hemingway was unhappy about. His review, nevertheless, was cordial. There were "very beautiful places" in the book, Hemingway noted, "as good writing as Sherwood Anderson has done and that means considerably better than any other American writer has done. It is a great mystery and an even greater tribute to Sherwood that so many people writing today think he cannot write." Hemingway went on to give a reasoned assessment:

He is not a poor scribbler even though he calls himself that or worse again and again. He is a very great writer and if he has, at times, in other books been unsuccessful, it has been for two reasons. His talent and his development of it has been toward the short story or tale and not toward that highly artificial form, the novel. The second reason is that he has been what the French say of all honest politicians *mal entouré.*

Hemingway's book of early stories, *In Our Time,* was scheduled for publication by Liveright that fall. It was to carry a laudatory blurb by Anderson. Anderson, in his letter to Gertrude, said he had written a "crackerjack review" as a blurb for Hemingway's book and that he had already made arrangements to review it in "one of the bigger reviews." It was one of the last amiable occasions for the three writers. The mutual admiration that existed between the two older writers and Hemingway, whom they regarded as a "favorite pupil," was soon dispelled. The precipitating cause for the quarrel that developed was Anderson's novel *Dark Laughter.*

II

Ernest Hemingway was twenty-two, newly married, and a promising young correspondent for the *Toronto Daily Star* when he met Gertrude in March, 1922. When Hemingway took an assignment as the European correspondent for the Canadian paper, Anderson wrote a letter of introduction to Gertrude. He spoke of the young writer as "instinctively in touch with everything worth while going on here." Gertrude took to Hemingway immediately when he visited the rue de Fleurus with his young wife, Hadley. Alice did not. She was never to develop anything more than an appreciation of Gertrude's professional interest in the budding writer.

Gertrude, who was then forty-eight, thought Hemingway "extraordinarily good-looking," with "passionately interested, rather than interesting eyes." Handsome, dark-haired, with a self-conscious manliness, he had an immediate attractiveness to women—a trait that Gertrude responded to readily among her male friends such as Picasso, Picabia, Juan Gris. For his part, Hemingway was impressed with Gertrude's physical bearing: "She had beautiful eyes and a strong German-Jewish face that also could have been Friulano." She reminded him of a "northern Italian peasant woman with her clothes, her mobile face and her lovely, thick, alive immigrant hair." Alice, he thought, had a pleasant voice. He was struck by her small, sharp features and her haircut, which looked like that of Joan of Arc in the conventional illustrations. But while Alice appeared hospitable, working quietly at her needlepoint or serving little cakes and liqueurs, both he and Hadley had found her a little frightening.

Hemingway was impressed with the studio which was like "one of the best rooms in the finest museum," but warmer and more comfortable. He especially recalled the liqueurs—"fragrant, colorless alcohols," that tasted of raspberries and black currants and that seemed to be converted "into a controlled fire on your tongue that warmed you and loosened it." The talk was always good, although in the beginning it was Gertrude who monopolized the conversations. "There were almost never any pauses in a conversation with Miss Stein," Hemingway noted.

Hadley invited the women to tea at the apartment on the rue Cardinal Lemoine, and Gertrude and Alice accepted. In those cramped quarters, Gertrude sat on the bed, reading the stories and poems that Hemingway brought out to show her. He had started an "inevitable" first novel. Gertrude had liked the poems; they were "direct, Kiplingesque," but she found the novel unsatisfactory. "There is a great deal of description in this," she told him, "and not particularly good description. Begin over again and concentrate." He also showed her some recently completed short stories. She liked them all except the story "Up in Michigan," which contained a graphic sexual scene. Hemingway was a bit surprised by her nineteenth-century prudery, but Gertrude couched her criticism in terms of the impracticality of writing about such things. The story was good, she said. "That's not the question at all. But it is *inaccrochable*," meaning that it was like a painting that an artist might paint but could never exhibit because it was too salacious. No collector would buy it either, because he could not hang it. When Hemingway protested, mildly, that it was an attempt to write about the facts of life in an honest way, Gertrude told him bluntly that he should avoid the *inaccrochable*: "There is no point in it. It's wrong and it's silly." The remark casts some light on her own euphemistic handling of such subjects. But she may also have sensed that at certain moments in the story—as when the heroine complains about the size of the hero's penis—the writing was more involved in satisfying the author's ego than his sense of the literary requirements.

In the early stage of their friendship, Gertrude and Hemingway got on famously. He was invited to stop by the rue de Fleurus in the afternoons after five. He would sit by the fire, sipping on an *eau de vie*, his eyes casually wandering to the Picassos hanging on the walls. Gertrude would tell him about the modern painters—"more about them as people than as painters," Hemingway recalled—and about her own writing, showing him the stacks of copybook manuscripts that were piling up in the Henri IV cabinet. He was aware then of the happiness that the daily writing stint brought Gertrude. It was only later that he sensed the bitterness she sometimes felt about her lack of recognition. In the early years of their friendship, Gertrude's dissatisfaction had not become "acute."

Hemingway admired her forceful character. She had, it seemed, a personality that could "win anyone over to her side" when she chose to make the effort. Critics, he felt, took a good deal of her writing on faith, persuaded by her formidable personality. But he also remembered the validity of Gertrude's discussions about the use of rhythm and repetition in writing.

Gertrude maintained that she did not discuss particularities with young writers, nor would she critically edit their work. She preferred to stick "strictly to general principles, the way of seeing what the writer chooses to see, and the relation between that vision and the way it gets down." "When the vision is not complete," she insisted, "the words are flat, it is very simple, there can be no mistake about it." Unlike Anderson, whose writing style already exhibited a tendency to the discursive and the emotionally vague, and who found in Gertrude's writing an authority for the repetitions and prolixity that only emphasized the weaknesses of his own style, Hemingway had fixed upon her strengths. In his early journalism, he had already developed the terse, declarative style for which he was to become famous, and the insights he picked up from Gertrude pointed up his virtues.

Gertrude seems to have blossomed under the attentions of the young writer. He listened well, was attentive, and had a persuasive gift of flattery when the occasion suited him. She took him under her wing, instructed him on how to conduct his personal life in order to further his writing career, even advised him on how he might acquire paintings by limiting his purchase of clothing, particularly his wife's clothing. Hadley Hemingway, glancing at Gertrude's "steerage" outfit, listened with dismay. Gertrude told the couple that they should pay no attention whatsoever to the fashions. They should buy their clothes "for comfort and durability" only. That way, they would be able to buy paintings with the money they saved. For the Hemingways, living on a meager income, Gertrude's economic advice was not particularly enlightening.

On one occasion she seems to have instructed Hemingway on the mysteries of sex. In *A Moveable Feast*, Hemingway reported that one afternoon, while sitting in the quiet of her studio, Gertrude had elected to put him straight on the question of homosexuality. She regarded him as "too uneducated" on the subject and apparently wanted to soften the prejudices he had picked up in his youth and during his war service in Italy. She was noticeably patronizing on the subject of male homosexuals.

"You know nothing about any of this really, Hemingway," Gertrude told him. "You've met known criminals and sick people and vicious people. The main thing is that the act male homosexuals commit is ugly and repugnant and afterwards they are disgusted with themselves. They drink and take drugs, to palliate this, but they are disgusted with the act and they are always changing partners and cannot be really happy." Male homosexuals, as Hemingway reported Gertrude's view, were to be pitied rather than scorned.

"In women," she went on, "it is the opposite. They do nothing that they are disgusted by and nothing that is repulsive and afterwards they are happy and they can lead happy lives together." It was a sunny simplification, and perhaps one that Hemingway simplified even further in the retelling, for he was recalling the incident long after they had had a bitter falling out, but it has the strangeness of some of Gertrude's generalizations about life.

Although Hemingway was not prepared to go along with Gertrude's explanations of sexual matters, he did, on one occasion, turn to her for consolation. He showed up, one morning, alone, at the rue de Fleurus, soon after he and his wife had gone off on a trip together. Gertrude had been urging him to give up newspaper work, to live quietly on the little money they had been able to save, and to concentrate on his writing. "If you keep on doing newspaper work," she had told him, "you will never see things, you will only see words and that will not do, that is of course if you intend to be a writer." On the day that he came to the studio, Hemingway acted strangely. "He came to the house about ten o'clock in the morning," Gertrude noted in the *Autobiography*, "and he stayed, he stayed for lunch, he stayed all afternoon, he stayed for dinner and he stayed until about ten o'clock at night and then all of a sudden he announced that his wife was enceinte and then with great bitterness, and I, I am too young to be a father. We consoled him as best we could and sent him on his way."

One of the consequences of Hemingway's coming fatherhood was that he and Hadley decided to return to America for the baby to be born. Hemingway planned to work on the *Star*, hopefully saving enough money to guarantee their return to Paris. But before leaving, Hemingway planned a trip with Hadley to Spain to witness the bullfights at Pamplona. Gertrude had recommended the Spanish city, telling him that early in July every year there was a grand fiesta, which attracted all the most famous matadors. Hemingway had a precocious interest in the bull ring, which became an important theme in his writing. Purely on the hearsay accounts given him by Gertrude and Alice and his painter friend Mike Strater, Hemingway had written a vivid account of the goring of a matador for a vignette that was published in *The*

Little Review. Shortly afterward, he had taken a trip to Spain to witness an actual bullfight, accompanied by the publisher William Bird
and Robert McAlmon, who had generously offered to pay Hemingway's
expenses. But the weather had proved disagreeable, and Hemingway,
who often took a dislike to people who were doing him a good turn,
became insulting toward McAlmon. His trip to Pamplona with Hadley, in July, 1923, had an odd motivation: He thought it would be a
good prenatal influence on his unborn child. Hemingway was impressed
with the bullfights and developed a great admiration for two of the
matadors, Manual Garcia and Nicanor Villalta. He and Hadley vowed
that if they had a son, they would name him after the latter. In mid-
August, after their return to Paris, they paid a final visit to Gertrude
and Alice just before sailing on the *Andania*.

Their son, John Hadley Nicanor Hemingway, was born on October
10, but his mother's nickname for him, Bumby, was the name he was
to have throughout childhood. A month after the event, Hemingway
wrote Gertrude, "I am getting very fond of him." He also wrote her
that he was still seriously thinking of giving up journalism, as she had
urged him, and that as soon as the baby was three months old, they
were planning to return to Europe. It was shortly after New Year's that
the Hemingways arrived in Paris. They took an apartment in Montparnasse, not far from the Closerie des Lilas. The parents asked Gertrude and Alice to be godmothers to Bumby. An English friend, Chink
Smith, was to be godfather. "We were all born of different religions
and most of us were not practising any," Gertrude recalled, "so it was
rather difficult to know in what church the baby could be baptised. We
spent a great deal of time that winter, all of us, discussing the matter."
Finally, the Episcopal church was elected as the most suitable for the
christening. Alice knitted Bumby some baby clothes and embroidered a
tiny chair cushion for him.

III

Hemingway's appreciation of Gertrude's maternal interest took concrete form after his return to Paris. It was a gesture Gertrude always
remembered. At Ezra Pound's urging, Hemingway had agreed to become assistant editor of *The Transatlantic Review*, which Ford Madox
Ford was then publishing in Paris. The money for this literary venture
had been put up by John Quinn, a wealthy American lawyer and art
collector, and by Ford and his current mistress, Stella Bowen, a painter.

Ford was an erratic editor, pompous and overbearing, fumbling in his
management of finances, but generous in his support of younger men.
The first issue of the *Transatlantic*, in January, 1924, had included

works by Pound and e e cummings. Nor was Ford above puffing his own work in his own pages, printing one of his earlier, minor collaborations with Joseph Conrad, "The Nature of a Crime." The young expatriate writers in Paris felt that Ford was too tradition-bound, that his editorial direction was an uneasy compromise between the vanguard and the safe and conventional. Nor were they particularly kind about Ford himself. Portly, officious, with vague blue eyes and a drooping mustache, he reminded Robert McAlmon of Lord Plushbottom in the *Moon Mullins* comic strip. Hemingway, who caricatured Ford and his mistress as Mr. and Mrs. Braddock in *The Sun Also Rises* as a pair of gullible expatriates, referred to Ford, in private, as the "golden walrus." Ford, who was open in his praise of Hemingway's talents, was under no illusions about the gratitude an editor might expect from temperamental and competitive contributors. He once described himself in a letter to Gertrude as "a sort of half-way house between nonpublishable youth and real money—a sort of green baize swing door that every one kicks both on entering and on leaving."

It was not long after joining the staff of the *Transatlantic* that Hemingway turned up excitedly at the rue de Fleurus, announcing that Ford had agreed to publish something of Gertrude's. Hemingway wanted to run *The Making of Americans* as a serial. Gertrude was overwhelmed. Hemingway needed the first fifty pages right away. Unfortunately Gertrude had only a bound copy of the manuscript—the typescript had been sent to Carl Van Vechten, who was trying to sell his publisher, Knopf, on the book. Hemingway offered to copy out the installments with Alice's help and further took on the job of correcting the proofs, a task that Gertrude did not find congenial at all. "Hemingway did it all," she acknowledged gratefully in the *Autobiography*, years later. But she also recorded Alice's instinctive suspicion that there had been more to the story than Hemingway had told them.

A short time later, Hemingway wrote her enthusiastically: The first installment of *The Making of Americans* would appear in the April issue. "Ford alleges he is delighted with the stuff," Hemingway informed her, "and is going to call on you. . . .

I told him it took you 4½ years to write it and that there were 6 volumes. . . . He wondered if you would accept 30 francs a page (his magazine page) and I said I thought I could get you to. (Be haughty but not too haughty.) I made it clear it was a remarkable scoop for his magazine obtained only through my obtaining genius. He is under the impression that you get big prices when you consent to publish. I did not give him this impression but did not discourage it.

He advised her to treat Ford "high wide and handsome." He had told him that the book got better and better as it progressed and that the *Transatlantic* could print as much of the six volumes as it wished.

Hemingway's impressions of *The Making of Americans* and of Gertrude's writing were to change noticeably during the course of his transcribing and proofreading sessions. His early letters to Gertrude were those of an eager protégé. He had tried to persuade Harold Stearns, the agent for Liveright, to take on the book, and when that possibility had fallen through, he wrote to Gertrude that it was "a rotten shame." He added comfortingly: "It is up to us, i.e. Alice Toklas, me, Hadley, John Hadley Nicanor and other good men to get it published. It will all come sooner or later the way you want it. This is not Christian Science." Later in the year, discussing his own efforts at writing, he had commented: "But isn't writing a hard job though? It used to be easy before I met you. I certainly was bad, gosh, I'm awfully bad now but it's a different kind of bad." Gertrude, with a somewhat benign egotism, thought that Hemingway's proofreading of the book had given the younger writer a finer appreciation of her style. In correcting the proofs, she claimed, "Hemingway learned a great deal and he admired all that he learned." But Hemingway's later and considered opinion was somewhat different. *The Making of Americans*, he contended, "began magnificently, went on very well for a long way with great stretches of great brilliance and then went on endlessly in repetitions that a more conscientious and less lazy writer would have put in the waste basket."

The serialization of *The Making of Americans* continued through nine installments, from April to December, 1924, in the precarious life of Ford's magazine. Ford had little facility for business and early on in its life, *The Transatlantic Review* was in financial difficulties. Ford, rather disingenuously, thought the problem lay in America. "Over twenty thousand copies of the review," he claimed, "have vanished into the American scene." A brief trip to New York in the spring of 1924 was of little use; John Quinn, dying of cancer, was not interested in reviving the project. In Paris, Ford tried to find backers. He hit upon a scheme of issuing stock in the flagging enterprise. Gertrude, anxious to have *The Making of Americans* continue, bought shares, as did her friends Natalie Clifford Barney and Elizabeth de Gramont, the Duchess of Clermont-Tonnerre. Ford made a great show of carrying on the enterprise in an efficient manner, issuing fancy stock certificates and calling stockholders' meetings, a few of which were held at the rue de Fleurus. Hemingway, too, searched for backers. He induced a wealthy acquaintance, Krebs Friend, to put capital into the magazine, and for a time the *Transatlantic* continued publication. But with the financial difficulties and Ford and Friend not always seeing eye to eye, Hemingway worried that Gertrude would not receive payment for the serialization. He warned Gertrude to write to them for her money: "It is evidently the old American game of letting a debt mount until you can regard any attempt to collect it with righteous indignation." He was still among her loyal supporters: "The only reason the magazine was saved was to publish your stuff. . . . If they try to quit publishing it I will make such a row and blackmail that it will blow up the show. So take a firm tone."

Gertrude's relationship with Ford was ordinarily amicable. She and Alice had known him before the war, when his name had been Ford Madox Hueffer and his affair with Violet Hunt, the writer, had caused a scandal in English society. An English paper had mistakenly identified Violet Hunt as Mrs. Hueffer, and Ford's first wife had brought suit against the publication. The result was that they were socially ostracized; Henry James, who knew them both, had regretfully felt obliged to avoid their company. Ford's wife refused to divorce him. After the war, living with Stella Bowen, who bore him a daughter, Julie, Ford had changed his name to Ford Madox Ford, in order to avoid a repeat of the same mistake.

Gertrude and Alice had been kind to Stella and were particularly fond of Julie. Stella was often invited to the rue de Fleurus for what Ford's mistress referred to as "a spot of cosy low-brow conversation," and both Gertrude and Alice made a point of attending the Christmas parties that Ford and Stella gave for the neighborhood children. They often stopped by Ford's offices on the Quai d'Anjou, where, on Thursday afternoons, Stella served tea to a mixed gathering of literary expatriates. Ford was genuinely pleased when Gertrude attended these occasions and took pride in introducing her around. Once he asked Gertrude how many of the young men she knew. Gertrude, who at that time sported a walking stick, raised it. "Up to there," she said. "Get up and bow to Miss Gertrude Stein," Ford said dictatorially. The none-too-pleased young man was Harold Loeb, the publisher and editor of *Broom*. Ford longed to be addressed as *cher maître*, a term he had himself used with Henry James, and one that, in his mistress's words, "filled his heart with simple pleasure." But his officious manner with the young was hardly calculated to have the desired effect.

Gertrude, with a modern's prejudice, had little interest in Ford's somewhat conventionally structured but beautifully realized novels. Instead, she preferred his travel writings. Ford was to dedicate one of these to her, *A Mirror to France*, a collection of travel notes and opinions on French life and cuisine. The announcement of his intention was typical of his social manner. At a party in the quarter, he had come upon Gertrude and Hemingway in conversation. He stepped up to the couple and, brushing Hemingway aside, said, "Young man, it is I who wish to speak to Gertrude Stein." He asked if he might dedicate his new book to her. Gertrude was delighted.

When Gertrude wrote to Ford about the delinquent payments for the July and August installments of *The Making of Americans*, she received one of Ford's disingenuous replies. "The business management," he told her, "has passed, to my immense relief, out of my hands into those of a capitalist who is a little slow in parting with the money but who *will* part immediately." He also informed her that he had understood, from Hemingway, that *The Making of Americans* was a long short story. He admitted that it was "probably my fault that I had that impression." Had he known it was a long novel, he would have offered her a lump sum, the usual arrangement with serials. The magazine, he mentioned, was "just beginning to run smoothly again" and looked as if it "might really pay."

Hemingway's next letter, on October 10, 1924, disabused Gertrude of several notions: "By the way did you ever, speaking of honesty," Hemingway wrote her, "get a letter from Ford marked private and confidential and not consequently to be revealed to me in which he said I had originally told him that the Makings was a short story? He had a number of other lies in this letter which he hoped I would not see and the gist of it was that he wanted you to make him a flat price." Things were not going well with the review. He was having a constant fight to keep it going since "Mrs. Friend conceived the bright idea of reducing the expenses of the magazine by trying to drop everything they would have to pay for. Krebs' latest idea is to have all the young writers contribute their stuff for nothing and show their loyalty to the magazine by chasing ads during the daylight hours." Hemingway's prediction was that "the magazine is going to Go to hell on or about the first of Jan and in that case I want you to get your money fairly well up to date and to have had the Makings appear regularly straight through the life of the review." The last installment of *The Making of Americans* appeared in the final, December, issue of *The Transatlantic Review*.

IV

Hemingway's recollections of his early friendship with Gertrude were understandably colored by his bitterness over Gertrude's later published remarks about him. In *A Moveable Feast*, written more than thirty years later, he described an idyllic Paris, projecting himself as a figure of wounded innocence and special integrity—a figure much like that of Jake Barnes, the protagonist of his celebrated novel *The Sun Also Rises*. In those idyllic years, Hemingway recalled, Gertrude never spoke of Anderson as a writer; she spoke "glowingly" of him only as a man. What she found charming about him was his "great, beautiful, warm Italian eyes." It was only after Anderson had cracked up as a writer, Hemingway contended, that Gertrude began to praise him lavishly. Gertrude, he implied, was jealous of Anderson, was jealous of any writer who might be considered a threat to her own position. At the rue de Fleurus, he maintained, "If you brought up Joyce twice, you would not be invited back."

Hemingway's account of those early years may have been a direct refutation of Gertrude's version in *The Autobiography of Alice B. Toklas.* There, Gertrude had related not only their discussion of Anderson as a writer but also their basic disagreement about Anderson's merits. Anderson, Gertrude maintained, rephrasing the remark she had made to Anderson himself, "had a genius for using a sentence to convey a direct emotion, this was in the great american tradition, and that really except Sherwood there was no one in America who could write a clear and passionate sentence." Hemingway had disagreed: He admired Anderson's short stories, but found his novels "strangely poor." Furthermore, he objected to Anderson's taste. "Taste," Gertrude contended, "has nothing to do with sentences."

As early as 1923, Hemingway had attempted to disown Anderson's influence. When the critic Edmund Wilson wrote him that he might do a note on Hemingway's *Three Stories and Ten Poems* for *The Dial,* Hemingway replied with an attempt to disengage himself from any comparison with Anderson's style. His letter was very Steinian:

No I don't think *My Old Man* derives from Anderson. It is about a boy and his father and race-horses. Sherwood has written about boys and horses. But very differently. It derives from boys and horses. Anderson derives from boys and horses. I don't think they're anything alike. I know I wasn't inspired by him.

He added, further, that he thought Anderson's work "seems to have gone to hell, perhaps from people in New York telling him too much how good he is." But he concluded: "I am very fond of him. He has written some good stories." In the same letter, he was far more open in acknowledging Gertrude's influence: "Her method," he told Wilson, "is invaluable for analysing anything or making notes on a person or a place. . . . She is where Mencken and Mary Colum fall down and skin their noses."

Wilson's review did not appear until the following year, in the October, 1924, issue of the *Dial,* when the critic also discussed the Paris edition of Hemingway's *In Our Time.* There, Wilson noted that Hemingway was "the only American writer but one—Mr. Sherwood Anderson—who has felt the genius of Gertrude Stein's *Three Lives* and has evidently been influenced by it. Indeed, Miss Stein, Mr. Anderson and Mr. Hemingway may now be said to form a school by themselves." The characteristic of this school, Wilson found, was "a naïveté of language, often passing into the colloquialism of the character dealt with, which serves actually to convey profound emotions and complex states of mind." Wilson thought it "a distinctively American development in prose." Although Hemingway wrote the critic that he liked the review very much, and thought that Wilson was "the only man writing criticism who or whom I can read when the book being criticized is one I've read or know something about," he could hardly have been altogether pleased at being so firmly linked to two writers from whom he was now trying to distance himself.

Hemingway's opportunity to break publicly with Anderson came with the publication of *Dark Laughter* in 1925. Hemingway claimed that Anderson's book was "so terribly bad, silly and affected" that he "could not keep from criticizing it in a parody." It was a response he sometimes felt to those who represented some threat to his image. When Ezra Pound first befriended him, Hemingway had promptly written a parody of the poet, satirizing his bohemian life-style. Only the argument of a friend, Lewis Galantiere, had dissuaded him from turning the satire over to Margaret Anderson and Jane Heap, the editors of *The Little Review*, who were then in Paris and had asked to publish something of his. Galantiere pointed out that it was unlikely that the editors of the *Review* would accept a piece that ridiculed the man who had persuaded John Quinn to invest in their magazine and who also served as their literary editor in Paris.

Hemingway's parody of Anderson took the form of a mock novel, *The Torrents of Spring*, an offhand literary job, written in ten days, that pilloried the American writer for what Hemingway felt was his affected and sentimental treatment of his American subjects. Its fourth chapter neatly joined two themes—Hemingway's dissatisfaction with Anderson and his disillusionment with Gertrude's major novel. It was entitled "The Passing of a Great Race and the Making and Marring of Americans." Gertrude, it appears, did not mind the joking at her expense, but Hemingway remembered that she was "very angry" about his treatment of Anderson. He had "attacked someone that was a part of her apparatus."

With Anderson, Hemingway added insult to injury. He offered the book to Liveright. Liveright was both his and Anderson's publisher; Anderson, in fact, had encouraged the firm to take on the younger writer. There was little likelihood that Liveright would publish the attack, a result that Hemingway anticipated. But he was anxious to make a move to Scribner's, particularly for his novel *The Sun Also Rises*, which he was then in the process of revising. If Liveright refused *The Torrents of Spring*, he reasoned that he would be free to break his contract and offer both books to Scribner's. When Liveright rejected *The Torrents*, Hemingway wrote to F. Scott Fitzgerald, whom he had met in Paris that year and who had encouraged him to make the change to Scribner's, about the success of his tactical maneuver. "I have known all along that they could not and would not be able to publish it as it makes a bum out of their present ace and best seller Anderson. . . . I did not, however, have that in mind in any way when I wrote it."

The Anderson affair did not create an immediate break with Gertrude, only a cooling of their relationship. For his important new novel, in fact, Hemingway had used a recent remark of Gertrude's—"You are all a lost generation"—as an epigraph. For a time, he had even thought of using the "lost generation" phrase as a title. Hemingway's different versions of the incident that had prompted Gertrude's remark cast some light on the progress of their friendship. In an unpublished foreword to the book, written in September, 1925, after he had finished revising the manuscript, he gave a relatively straightforward account of the episode. Gertrude had been traveling in the department of Ain during that summer and had had to take her car to a garage in one of the smaller villages. The young mechanic had been particularly efficient. Gertrude had praised him to the garage owner and had asked how he managed to get such good workers. The garage owner answered that he had trained him himself; young men of his age took training very readily. It was the young men between the ages of twenty-two and thirty, those who had served in the war, who could not be trained. They were "*une génération perdue*," the garage owner claimed. In his foreword, Hemingway seemed to imply there was something distinctly "lost" about his own generation that was not true of the "lost generations" of times past.

Hemingway's second version of the incident, written more than thirty years later in *A Moveable Feast*, was more maliciously contrived, and he seems to have disavowed the term completely. In the later version, the young mechanic is a member of the "lost," war generation, having served in the final year of the war. He was not "adept" at his trade and Gertrude had complained about him to the *patron* of the garage— perhaps, Hemingway suggested, because he had not serviced Gertrude's car before other standing orders. The *patron* had reprimanded the young mechanic, saying, "You are all a *génération perdue*." In this version Gertrude accused the lost generation—Hemingway included—of having no respect for anything and of drinking itself to death. Hemingway countered that the boy's *patron* "was probably drunk by eleven o'clock in the morning. . . . That's why he makes such lovely phrases."

"Don't argue with me, Hemingway," was Gertrude's retort, "It does no good at all. You're all a lost generation, exactly as the garage keeper said." On his way home that evening, so Hemingway reported in his second version, he mused about Gertrude and Anderson and the question of "egotism and mental laziness versus discipline." He wondered "who was calling who a lost generation?" He dismissed Gertrude's "lost generation talk and all the dirty, easy labels," but he thought of her warm and affectionate friendship. He decided that Gertrude was "nice" but that she did "talk a lot of rot sometimes."

Hemingway's later version has an air of plausibility. Gertrude did have the notion that, in France, creative artists and professionals were commonly granted special privileges. They were entitled to be served promptly, to be given special parking places when parking places were difficult to find. She was never disabused of that notion for the remainder of her life. She might easily have complained, therefore, if a garage mechanic had kept her waiting. Nor did she approve of the young expatriates she saw crowding the cafés in the twenties. She felt it was dangerous for artists and writers to court the bohemian life. One had to hold oneself in readiness, she believed, for the act of writing, for the "daily miracle." Drinking, drugs, the hunt for unwarranted "excitements" were all destructive to the creative process. But she knew many drunks in her lifetime, and she was fond, she maintained, of "a number of people who are always more or less drunk. There is nothing to do about it if they are always more or less drunk." Her rule, learned from experience, was to treat them "as if they were sober." About men and drunkenness, she had come to some odd conclusions: "It is funny," she claimed, "the two things most men are proudest of is the thing that any man can do and doing does in the same way, that is being drunk and being the father of their son. . . . If anybody thinks about that they will see how interesting it is that it is that."

Gertrude's account of the "lost generation" story was less elaborate than Hemingway's. She had first heard the phrase from the proprietor of the Hôtel Pernollet in Belley, a city in the department of Ain: "He said that every man becomes civilized between the ages of eighteen and twenty-five. If he does not go through a civilizing experience at that time in his life he will not be a civilized man. And the men who went to war at eighteen missed the period of civilizing, and they could never be civilized. They were a lost generation." The circumstances seem to accord with Hemingway's first version. As it happened, there was a young garage mechanic at the Hôtel Pernollet. According to one of Gertrude's guests at the hotel, the writer Bravig Imbs, the young mechanic was "cross-eyed and really very sweet" and Gertrude had "interminable" conversations with him, while Alice fretted, waiting in the courtyard. Hemingway's second version of the "lost generation" story, it appears, was recollected not in tranquillity but in the special bitterness of an old feud.

Gertrude and Hemingway were still on amicable terms in 1925, when Hemingway first brought F. Scott Fitzgerald to the rue de Fleurus. It was a summer of "1000 parties and no work," so Fitzgerald confided to his ledger book. He was at the height of his success, catapulted into extraordinary fame by his first novel, *This Side of Paradise*, published in 1920, when he was not quite twenty-four. He and his wife, Zelda, both handsome and self-indulgent, seemed to be on a perpetual binge. In his soberer moments, Fitzgerald had already begun to worry about their spendthrift life, the drunken sprees that had made them international celebrities of a dubious kind.

Gertrude had read *This Side of Paradise* when it first appeared and before she had met any of the young writers of the period. She was of the opinion that Fitzgerald's novel had "really created for the public the new generation." Moreover, she felt that Fitzgerald was "the only one of the younger writers who wrote naturally in sentences." Like many of her more durable friendships, Gertrude's relationship with Fitzgerald did not encompass many meetings, but they wrote admiringly to each other. Later, she made a special point of spending an evening with him at Christmastime in Baltimore during her 1934 American trip. By then, Fitzgerald's fortunes were far different; his wife was institutionalized in a sanatorium, and Fitzgerald himself was suffering through the dreary hangover of his meteoric success. Gertrude remained convinced that Fitzgerald, who had created his age as Thackeray had created the age of *Vanity Fair*, would still be read "when many of his well known contemporaries are forgotten."

A brilliant and subtle writer, Fitzgerald was, it seems, a poorly educated man, despite his Princeton sojourn. Insecure in his talent, he was deferential to writers with established reputations or those in whom he readily recognized talent. His friendship with Hemingway—more sought after by Fitzgerald, it appears—was an uneasy one. When the two drank together, Fitzgerald became sometimes maudlin, sometimes vindictive. "I half bait, half truckle to him," Fitzgerald admitted.

Fitzgerald's visits to the rue de Fleurus were usually made in a condition of sobriety. "There used to be a good deal of talk about his drinking," Alice recalled, "but he was always sober when he came to the house." He was to treat Gertrude as something of a mentor. Even before he had met her, he recognized her importance as one of the "real people" in literature and had even attempted to persuade his Scribner's editor, Maxwell Perkins, to consider publishing *The Making of Americans* on the basis of the installments that had appeared in *The Transatlantic Review*. When Perkins declined, Fitzgerald wrote him: "But I am confused at what you say about Gertrude Stein. I thought it was one purpose of critics and publishers to educate the public up to original work." His later view of Gertrude's novel, when it was issued in book form, paralleled Hemingway's. As he wrote Perkins, admitting his mistake, only the early portions of the book were "intelligible at all."

Gertrude had complimented him on his new novel, *The Great Gatsby*, a copy of which Fitzgerald had given her on their first meeting. Fitzgerald wrote Perkins that both Hemingway and Gertrude were "enthusiastic" about his new book. "The real people, like Gertrude

Stein (with whom I've talked) and Conrad (see his essay on James) have a respect for people whose materials may not touch theirs *at a single point.'*

To Gertrude, shortly after their meeting, he wrote in a complimentary vein: "My wife and I think you a very handsome, very gallant, very kind lady and thought so as soon as we saw you." His letter, in fact was magnanimous:

You see, I am content to let you and the one or two like you who are acutely sensitive, think or fail to think for me and my kind artistically (their name is not legend but like it) much as the man of 1901, say, would let Nietche (sp?) think for him intellectually. I am a very second-rate person compared to first-rate people—I have indignation as well as most of the other major faults—and it honestly makes me shiver to know that such a writer as you attributes such a significance to my factitious, meritricious (metricious?) *This Side of Paradise.* It puts me in a false position, I feel. Like Gatsby, I have only hope.

Gertrude's compliments to the young writer were, in fact, to become something of a ritual joke between them whenever they met. Fitzgerald claimed that she said such things only to annoy him by making him feel that she meant them. Her doing it, he added, "is the cruellest thing I ever heard." One afternoon—it was his thirtieth birthday—he was visiting Gertrude and Alice and was in a restless state. He felt that he had arrived at a tragic stage in his career—the end of his youth. What was to become of him, he asked, what was he to do. Gertrude told him not to worry; he had been "writing like a man of thirty for many years." She told him that he should go home and write a novel greater than any he had done so far. She had even drawn a line on a piece of paper and told him his next book should be that thick. When Fitzgerald's *Tender Is the Night* was published, eight years later, he sent Gertrude a copy, inscribed, "Is this the book you asked for?"

There were occasions, however, when Gertrude's compliments put him on the defensive. In 1929, visiting the rue de Fleurus with Hemingway, Fitzgerald began baiting Hemingway, whose *A Farewell to Arms* had recently been published and was selling well. Fitzgerald was in a fallow period and irritable. Sidling up to Alice, whose dislike of Hemingway he probably had sensed, he said to her, "Miss Toklas, I am sure you want to hear how Hem achieves his great moments."

Hemingway, suspicious, said, "What are you up to, Scotty?"

"You tell her," Fitzgerald answered.

"Well you see, it is this way," Hemingway explained, "When I have an idea, I turn down the flame, as if it were a little alcohol stove, as low as it will go. Then it explodes and that is my idea."

With that, Fitzgerald had turned and walked away. Alice, whose compliments to Hemingway were rare, remarked that the retreat from Caporetto had been very well done.

Probably to bolster Fitzgerald's ego, Gertrude had said that Fitzgerald's "flame" and Hemingway's were not at all the same.

Fitzgerald brooded over the incident, finally convincing himself that Gertrude had meant that Hemingway's "flame" was superior. He wrote Hemingway a bitter and complaining letter, taking him to task for his superior attitude. Hemingway was obliged to answer him cautiously, reassuring him that Gertrude had meant no such comparison and that anyway the comparison of hypothetical flames was all nonsense.

V

On Sherwood Anderson's second visit to Paris, in December, 1926, he was accompanied by his new wife, his third, Elizabeth Prall, the manager of a Doubleday bookstore, whom he had met in New York. With him also were one of his sons, John, and his daughter Mimi, both children of his first marriage. The Andersons saw very little of Hemingway. The younger writer seems to have avoided meeting them even though mutual friends had tried to effect a reconciliation. Gertrude's opinion was that Hemingway "naturally was afraid" of such a meeting.

The Andersons were frequently invited to the rue de Fleurus. Elizabeth Anderson had been forewarned about the protocol and on her first visit had felt somewhat intimidated, only to find that Gertrude and Alice were both extremely cordial and that the stories about wives being obliged to keep their places had been overemphasized. It was only when her husband and Gertrude became involved in a lengthy discussion about the Civil War, in which she had no interest, that Elizabeth Anderson settled down to discussing cooking and domestic subjects with Alice.

In the course of their discussions about the Civil War, Gertrude and Anderson discovered that their mutually admired hero was General Grant, rather than Lee or even Lincoln. Half seriously, half jokingly, they had even talked about collaborating on a life of Grant. Gertrude had more than entertained the idea and was disappointed when Anderson, later, let the idea drop. Eventually she made Grant one of the principal subjects in her series of long biographical perorations on American figures, *Four in America*—the other heroes being George Washington, Henry James, and Wilbur Wright.

The principal subject of discussion between Gertrude and Anderson that winter, however, was Hemingway. Both regarded him patronizingly as a "good pupil," and both were "a little proud and a little ashamed" of their product. Alice protested that Hemingway was a "rotten" pupil, but they argued that it was flattering "to have a pupil who does it without understanding it, in other words he takes training and anybody who takes training is a favourite pupil." Anderson found it difficult to understand Hemingway's behavior toward a friend who had helped further his career. He was particularly upset by a twist-of-the-knife letter Hemingway had sent him just before *The Torrents of Spring* was published. In it, Hemingway explained that his parody was not a personal attack but that Anderson had written a poor book and he (Hemingway) had been obliged to call him on it. Serious writers, Anderson was to understand, should not be obliged to pull punches with one another. Anderson thought the letter was "a kind of funeral oration delivered over my grave. It was so raw, so pretentious, so patronizing, that it was amusing but I was filled with wonder." Gertrude claimed that Hemingway's character was such that he had to kill off his rivals. (She later made the same claim to Hemingway and Hemingway denied that he had ever done so intentionally.) She told Anderson that there were two of his stories, "I'm a Fool" and "I Want to Know Why," that Hemingway "could not bear the thought" of Anderson's having written. Hemingway, she said, had "staked out the whole field of sports for himself."

More than that, Gertrude claimed that Hemingway was "yellow." He was, she said, "just like the flat-boat men on the Mississippi River as described by Mark Twain." There was a real story to be written about Hemingway, one that he should himself write, "not those he writes but the confessions of the real Ernest Hemingway. It would be for another audience than the audience Hemingway now has but it would be very wonderful." But Hemingway, she was sure, would never write it. As Hemingway himself had told her, "There is the career, the career." In her discussions with Anderson, Gertrude was particularly hard on Hemingway as a writer. He was like the painter Derain, she maintained. "He looks like a modern and he smells of the museums." Despite all this, Gertrude continued to insist that she had "a weakness" for Hemingway.

It was during Anderson's Parisian visit that Gertrude made a remarkable change in her appearance. Her friend Elizabeth de Gramont, the Duchess of Clermont-Tonnerre, had arrived late one evening. Taking off her hat, she had turned around for Gertrude's approval. She had had her hair bobbed in the style that was just then coming into fashion. Gertrude thought it looked extremely attractive. At the end of the evening, Gertrude told Alice, "Cut off my braids." On the following day, Alice was still clipping gradually. The more she cut, the better Gertrude seemed to like it. Finally there was only a short cropping of hair like a crew cut. The doorbell rang; it was Sherwood paying a visit. Alice let him in, then asked nervously, "Well, how do you like it?" Gertrude waited, smiling, embarrassed. "You look like a monk," Anderson said approvingly.

Throughout his Parisian visit, Anderson was mildly lionized. He was invited to a poetry reading at Natalie Clifford Barney's. Miss Barney, a wealthy American dedicated to intellectual pursuits, was an ardent feminist who maintained one of the most durable Parisian salons, a gathering place for French academicians and American writers. One could encounter there Paul Valéry, André Gide, Ezra Pound, and, in the earlier days, Remy de Gourmont. It was to Miss Barney, an accomplished horsewoman, that Gourmont had dedicated his *Lettres à une Amazone*. A tall, impressive woman, she held court in her home on the rue Jacob, where there was a small garden of shrubs and trees. Beyond it was a small Greek temple that was variously referred to as a temple of love or friendship. Miss Barney was the leader of a group called *L'Académie des Femmes*, intended to be the female counterpart of the all-male French Academy, and she frequently devoted evenings to women in the arts. There was always a large group of women at any of Miss Barney's "evenings," and the evenings usually ended with the women dancing solemnly with one another. A rude story had it that on one of these occasions, a gentleman visitor had become so exasperated by the dancing women that he had stood in the middle of the dance floor, pulled out his penis, and shouted, "Have you never seen one of these?"

On the evening that Anderson attended, he and Gertrude sat down front together—Alice seems to have avoided the affair—in a row of rickety chairs facing the temple. Elizabeth Anderson and Ralph Church, a friend of Anderson's, sat farther back. As one tall, waistshirted and monocled woman after another came forward to deliver, in English and French, their poems in praise of "some mystical complicated concept of love" or a lyric about the Isle of Lesbos, Elizabeth and Church found it more and more difficult to suppress their laughter. They were relieved that the program was mercifully short. It was through Miss Barney, however, that Anderson was invited to attend a meeting of the P.E.N. Club, the international literary society. Anderson had pleaded with Gertrude to go with him. Gertrude told him that while she loved him very much, it did not encompass the P.E.N. Club.

Despite the attention he was getting, Anderson was gradually settling into a mood of depression. His mornings were reserved for writing in his hotel room, and his writing was not going well. Moreover, his marriage was beginning to exhibit the warning symptoms of his previous marriages, and in three years' time, Elizabeth Anderson was to become another of the discarded women in his career. Although they shared a mutual interest in literature, Anderson and Elizabeth were temperamentally unsuited. There were periods of bickering followed by prolonged silences. In the end, the separation was effected after their return to the States. Elizabeth was visiting her family in California. Anderson sent her a letter saying, simply, "I just wish you would not come back."

Gertrude did her best to entertain the Andersons while they were in Paris. She arranged an evening party especially in Sherwood's honor. Anderson had seemed agreeable to it, but on the evening of the party, he had remained behind in the hotel, sitting in his chair drinking—convincing himself, his wife claimed, that he had the flu. He sent Elizabeth to the rue de Fleurus to make his apologies. When Elizabeth made her excuses, Gertrude had simply told her, "My dear, you don't have to explain to me. I know exactly what happened." Alice explained to the other guests that Sherwood was sick.

Anderson did, however, attend the Christmas Eve party at the rue de Fleurus. Gertrude thought he looked extremely handsome, wearing a bright scarf tie. She had had new electric radiators installed in the studio, and it was "terrifically hot" and the radiators had smelled, but the evening seemed to have gone off well. She had taken a fancy to young John Anderson, who planned to stay behind in Paris after his parents left. He was considering a career as a painter and intended to study at the Académie Julian. Gertrude had noticed that young John, in the company of his father, seemed to be a shy and awkward boy. But on the day after Sherwood and his stepmother left Paris, he had turned up at the rue de Fleurus, sat nonchalantly on the arm of the sofa, and talked readily and easily. He was, Gertrude observed, "beautiful to look upon and he knew it. Nothing to the outward eye had changed but he had changed and he knew it." The moment of one's coming of age seemed to be a special moment for her and one that she was responsive to in others.

It was not until just before the Andersons left Paris that Sherwood and Hemingway finally confronted each other. Hemingway seems to have been prodded into making the gesture by friends. In his *Memoirs*, Anderson gives a deadpan account of their meeting. It was on his last day in Paris, and Hemingway had come to the hotel. Standing in the doorway, he said, "How about a drink?" Anderson followed him to a bar across the street. They both ordered beer. Hemingway, lifting his glass, said, "Well, here's how." Anderson responded, "Here's how." Hemingway gulped down his beer, then "turned and walked rapidly away." Hemingway, however, wrote to Max Perkins about the meeting, saying that Anderson was "not at all sore" about *The Torrents of Spring*, claiming that they had had a "fine time" together. Elizabeth Anderson adds to the confusion by describing Hemingway's visit in quite different terms, without mentioning the drinking incident. Hemingway had spent some time in their room, making fun of the hotel and the way it was run. She snapped at him: "Keep in mind that they're very nice to us here. That's why we came here and that's why we're staying here." When Hemingway left, Anderson scolded her for being rude. That, she admitted, had been her intention.

The real break between Gertrude and Hemingway occurred a good deal later, in 1933, when she published the substance of her remarks about Hemingway in *The Autobiography of Alice B. Toklas.* Following Sherwood Anderson's visit in 1926, she and Hemingway saw each other less frequently. Alice was in the habit of telling Gertrude, when she went out on her afternoon walks, "Don't you come home with Hemingway on your arm," and, of course, one day she did. They had had a long discussion, and Gertrude finally said, "Hemingway, after all you are ninety percent Rotarian."

"Can't you make it eighty percent?" Hemingway asked.

"No," Gertrude answered, "I can't."

Hemingway's definitive version of their break was written much later, in 1957, when he began writing a series of memoirs on his early years in Paris. He set the time as early in their friendship, when Gertrude had given him the run of the house. She told him that he was welcome at any time, even if she were not at home. The maidservant would take care of him and he should make himself comfortable and wait until she returned. Without specifying the year, Hemingway described an incident that had happened, one morning, when he had gone to bid them good-by. Gertrude and Alice were leaving on a trip to the south, and she had asked him to stop by. It was during that still-happy time when he was in love with Hadley. Gertrude had asked them to come and visit them that summer, but Hemingway and Hadley had other plans.

It was a lovely spring day, Hemingway recalled, and he had walked through the Luxembourg Gardens with the chestnuts in bloom and the children playing while their nursemaids looked on. At the rue de Fleurus, Gertrude's maid had opened the door even before he had knocked. Gertrude and Alice were upstairs, and the maid had poured him a glass of *eau de vie* even though it was before noon.

As he waited, he heard the sounds of a particularly vicious argument between Gertrude and Alice. Alice was speaking to Gertrude in a way that Hemingway "had never heard one person speak to another; never, anywhere, ever." Then he heard Gertrude, pleading and begging, "Don't pussy. Don't. Don't, please don't. I'll do anything, pussy, but please don't do it. Please don't. Please don't, pussy."

"It was bad to hear and the answers were worse," Hemingway felt. He swallowed his drink and started to leave. When the maidservant wagged her finger at him and asked him to wait, since Miss Stein would be down any moment, Hemingway said that he had to leave. He told the maid to say that he had met her in the courtyard, that he could not wait because of a sick friend. He would write to Gertrude.

That was the way it had ended for him with Gertrude, Hemingway contended, "stupidly enough, although I still did the small jobs, made the necessary appearances, brought people that were asked for and waited dismissal with most of the other men friends when that epoch came and the new friends moved in." In the end, he admitted, he had, like most people, made friends with her again "in order not to be stuffy or righteous." But he had never "truly" been able to make friends with her again either in his heart or his head.

It is a vivid, acid account, with all the detailing of the truth. It is entirely possible that he had overheard a particularly bitter quarrel between Gertrude and Alice, one that established the Lesbian nature of their relationship beyond doubt for him, and one in which the steely character of Alice's will was revealed, privately, as it had never been revealed in public. But it is also possible that the incident, like the story of the garage mechanic, has been recast for better effect. In any event, Hemingway had predated his disillusionment with Gertrude, moving it back from its more probable cause—the caustic remarks she had made about him in the *Autobiography*.

With unerring instinct, Gertrude had wounded him where he was most vulnerable—in that image of untarnished courage and masculinity that he wished to project. He countered it, very effectively, by exposing her lack of "manliness." In his quarrel with Gertrude, Hemingway was to have the last word, when *A Moveable Feast* was published in 1964. But by then it mattered little; both were dead.

CHAPTER ELEVEN

Entrances, Exits

I

Throughout the twenties, Gertrude's literary reputation was based on her contributions to the always-precarious "little magazines." She published only three books during the decade, discounting the specially produced and illustrated volumes brought out by her art-dealer friend, D.-H. Kahnweiler—"A Book Concluding with As A Wife Has a Cow. A Love Story," a luxury edition with lithographs by Juan Gris, brought out in 1926, and "A Village. Are You Ready Yet Not Yet," subtitled "A Play in Four Acts," published in 1928, with illustrations by Elie Lascaux. Kahnweiler had planned another book, to be illustrated with engravings by Picasso. Gertrude had supplied the text, "A Birthday Book," with entries for each day of the year. It had been written for Picasso's son, Paulot, whose birthday, February 4, fell on the day after her own. But Picasso delayed and procrastinated and the illustrations were never done. Gertrude was disappointed. Picasso, she decided, had entered into a "period of unreliability."

Two of the three books were collections: *Geography and Plays*, published in 1922 at her expense, was a selection of poems and plays, most of which had been written during the war and immediately afterward. *Useful Knowledge*, published in 1928, by the small New York firm of

Payson & Clarke, was another collection of short and long pieces, including her "Valentine" for Sherwood Anderson, a number of geographical considerations such as "Wherein Iowa differs from Kansas and Indiana," prompted by her discussions with American doughboys, and her lengthy domestic idyll, "Farragut," written during her wartime sojourn in Majorca. The book that Gertrude considered her major publication, *The Making of Americans*, brought out by Robert McAlmon's Contact Editions in 1925, had been completed in 1911.

The little magazines were a feature of the twenties. Most of them were short-lived; they came into being with the twenties boom and disappeared with the bust—or even before. They existed for a month or two, a year or two, financed by the wealthy, who usually lost interest when the debts began to mount after the first few issues. Their names were plain or fanciful—*The Little Review, Larus, or The Celestial Visitor, transition, This Quarter, Black & Blue Jay, Broom, Close-Up, Pagany*. Each claimed some special viewpoint as their reason for being; most courted the *avant-garde* writers and poets of the period. The same names—Joyce, Pound, Stein, William Carlos Williams—appeared from one issue to the next, crossed over from one magazine to another. They were names that survived the decade; others—Harold Loeb, Lola Ridge, Mina Loy, Evan Shipman, Mary Butts, Ernest Walsh—were to drift out of sight. For most of the writers concerned, the little magazines were a means—an ephemeral means—of keeping themselves in view, albeit for the special audience they served. For Gertrude, they were often the only outlet for her writing.

"The *Little Review* will be in Paris for a short time—are you disposed to see enthusiastic admirers?"—the letter, from Jane Heap, in May, 1923, was not to remain strictly accurate. Of the two editors of that peripatetic review, published at various times in Chicago, in Muir Woods, California, in New York, in Paris—published as a quarterly when the always-unpredictable finances allowed and as an annual when they did not—only Jane Heap was to display a continuous degree of enthusiasm for Gertrude Stein as a person and a writer. Margaret Anderson, who had founded the review as a vehicle for new ideas, which she cultivated strenuously and with the express purpose of shocking her readers, was to be less than enthusiastic after meeting Gertrude in Paris.

As the most famous of the American expatriate writers in Paris in the early twenties, Gertrude had already appeared in the pages of *The Little Review* before she met its editors. Her "Vacation in Brittany" had run in the spring, 1922, issue, followed that fall by "B.B. The Birthplace of Bonnes." In the spring before their arrival in the French capital, *The Little Review* editors had published Gertrude's recent valentine to Sherwood Anderson.

Margaret Anderson was a woman of pronounced and sometimes prolonged enthusiasms. Attractive, usually swaddled in fur and trailing perfume, she lived for the art of living. To charges that she was arrogant, she pleaded innocent on the grounds that "no one can feel arrogant who must live for months without her favorite perfume." Even her periods of relative poverty were lived through with a unique flair. One summer, finding herself without funds for the offices of *The Little Review*, she set up a squatters' colony for the staff on the shores of Lake Michigan; she borrowed tents with wooden floors, an army cot, a deck chair, and an oriental rug for each unit.

When she met the mannish, blunt-spoken Jane Heap in Chicago in 1916, she decided that Jane was the "world's best talker" and that Jane's views on art and life must be "presented" to the world by way of the pages of her review. It took considerable cajoling and nagging persistence, since Jane was wary of the combatant's role she was supposed to play in public and especially in print. Jane claimed, "Margaret carries me about under her arm like a fighting cock and throws me into every ring she sees. And she sees nothing but rings."

Their pugnacity in presenting the new literature landed them in difficulties with the New York Society for the Prevention of Vice. In 1918 they began publishing installments of Joyce's *Ulysses*. Four issues were burned by order of the U.S. Post Office on the grounds that they contained "obscene" material. In September, 1920, papers were served on *The Little Review*, which had published episode XIII of Joyce's book—Bloom's orgasmic reveries about Gerty MacDowell—and on the Washington Street Book Store, which had sold the issue.

Their case was argued by the able New York lawyer John Quinn, friend and patron of the Irish writer, who had donated sixteen hundred dollars to *The Little Review* expressly for the purpose of publishing Joyce's book. Sensing the imbroglio that might develop if he allowed the two outspoken women to testify, he had them appear in court and sit, meek and mild, surrounded by "window trimmings"—a group of conservatively dressed women friends. When it became a question of reading aloud some of the "obscene" passages, the judge objected to having such words read in front of Miss Anderson, who looked the perfect figure of a sedate society woman. "But she is the publisher," Quinn answered, winning a point. The verdict was nevertheless against them; a fine of one hundred dollars. "And now for God's sake," Quinn told the two women, "don't publish any more obscene literature."

Jane Heap, so Gertrude remembered, "turned up one afternoon" at the rue de Fleurus—apparently unaccompanied by Margaret Anderson. The round of talk that she, Gertrude, and Alice began that afternoon lengthened into the evening, through dinner, past midnight, and well into the dawn. Godiva, parked outside, with lights burning, to take the guest back to her hotel, would barely start when the marathon talk was ended in the early dawn. Gertrude, following that first encounter, had liked Jane Heap "immensely." Margaret Anderson, whom she met later, "interested her much less."

Margaret Anderson's first encounter with Gertrude, published in the opening volume of her autobiography, *My Thirty Years' War* (1930), was interested but not wholehearted. It may account for Gertrude's brief dismissal of Margaret Anderson in the *Autobiography*, published three years later. While Margaret Anderson responded to the nonconformity of Gertrude's life-style, she was not wholly approving of the Stein prose style. Gertrude, when they first met, had been reading the memoirs of an American congressman. "Good prose, by the way," Gertrude had said. About the younger generation, she had informed Margaret Anderson: "There is of course, no one who has any difficulty reading me." Margaret Anderson was to have grave doubts about this optimistic statement. And in her autobiography she expressed her dissatisfaction with Gertrude's writing, particularly with the endless repetitions in *The Making of Americans*, which she found unnecessary and boring. She even attempted a mild parody of the Stein manner in explaining her contention that people like Gertrude, "with heavy physical vibrations," seemed to rule the world, particularly the world of literature and art. In what seems to be a comparison between her own quick intelligence and Gertrude's slower ruminations, she complained: "If anyone has a delicate and quick way of living, it is always not so important to people as if he had a strong and heavy way of saying." Gertrude, she concluded, was "full of homely important knowledge of simple vital people," but she lacked "knowledge of many of the human masks." She was not convinced that Gertrude's imagination would measure up to "even a preliminary examination of what I would call significant singularity."

During the later years of *The Little Review*, it was Jane Heap who assumed the burdens of editorship. Margaret Anderson had discovered a new devotion, the singer Georgette Leblanc, Maeterlinck's ex-wife, with whom she lived for twenty years as a companion and sometimes piano accompanist. While she remained titular editor and publisher of the magazine, it was Jane Heap who shuttled back and forth between New York and Paris, putting out the magazine and, for a time, managing The Little Review Galleries in New York. It was for a special issue of the magazine, devoted to the work of the Spanish painter Juan Gris, whom both she and Gertrude admired, that Jane Heap asked Gertrude to write an appreciation of the painter that appeared in the autumn and winter issue of 1924–25. But Gertrude contributed to *The Little Review* less frequently in the later years—the magazine ended publication in 1929—probably because it was the magazine's policy not to pay contributors and she could command, at least, minor fees from other publications.

Gertrude and Jane Heap corresponded frequently, and when Jane was in Paris, they saw each other often. Jane acted as an unofficial agent for her in New York, trying to induce B. W. Huebsch, then, later, Boni and Liveright, to publish *The Making of Americans*. When it appeared that the *Transatlantic* might fold, Jane tried to persuade Lady Rothermere, the sponsor of *The Criterion*, T. S. Eliot's magazine, to continue the publication of *The Making of Americans* in its pages.

Eliot was not responsive to printing *The Making of Americans*. But he did make Gertrude another offer. The poet was in Paris in the late fall of 1924. Gertrude had been invited to meet him at a party to be given by Lady Rothermere. It was one of the few times when she was reluctant to meet another writer, particularly a celebrated writer. Alice finally persuaded her that she must go. One afternoon, while Alice was sewing a new evening dress for the occasion, Eliot and Lady Rothermere paid an unexpected visit. It was not a memorable meeting. Eliot, for some reason, refused to give up his sturdy English umbrella throughout the visit. He sat, so Alice recalled, "clasping its handle, while his eyes burned brightly in a noncommittal face." Eliot asked Gertrude—perhaps baiting her—who was her authority for a consistent use of the split infinitive. Gertrude promptly replied, "Henry James." Before he left, Eliot suggested that *The Criterion* would be agreeable to publishing something of hers, but he cautioned her that it would have to be her "very latest thing."

As soon as the company had left, Gertrude turned to Alice. "Don't bother to finish your dress," she told her, "now we don't have to go." That evening she wrote out a word portrait of Eliot, titled, "A Description of the Fifteenth of November," wryly commemorating her meeting with the poet and the fact that it was her "latest thing." The piece was cast in her usual poetry and prose merger, with repetitions, word plays, sentences that read like demonstrations of grammatical practice—mentions of wool and silk might refer to Alice's dressmaking—otherwise there was little that alluded to Eliot's visit itself.

Although Eliot had wanted a recent example of her work, he delayed in publishing it for more than a year. There was some correspondence back and forth, with Alice, serving as Gertrude's secretary, writing to Eliot's secretary. Finally Eliot wrote Gertrude, apologizing "most humbly for the long delay." He proposed to publish her piece in the October issue. Gertrude answered that nothing would be more suitable than to have the "Fifteenth of November" appear on the fifteenth of October. There was, however, a further unexplained delay, during which Gertrude made certain that every English visitor was told the story of her contribution to *The Criterion*, and her conclusion that Eliot was "afraid" to publish her. The "Fifteenth of November" was finally printed in the January, 1926, issue of *The Criterion*. On a later visit to England, Gertrude learned that Eliot had remarked that "the work of Gertrude Stein was very fine but not for us." It had a Steinian ring that pleased her.

II

Robert McAlmon was the son of a Presbyterian minister, a type that Gertrude felt she knew quite well. "Preachers' sons," she claimed, "will when they begin will drink a lot and it wears them out." McAlmon was in his midtwenties when he met Gertrude in 1924. He was slight in stature, with a lithe body, not exactly handsome, but nevertheless attractive to both sexes. He had hard blue eyes and a vindictive tongue. McAlmon had done a stint in Greenwich Village before settling down to a bohemian life in Paris. His marriage to Bryher had pulled him out of a hand-to-mouth existence; the Ellerman money enabled him to assume at least the respectable position as the publisher of the Contact Editions, bringing out Hemingway's first volume of stories and poems, as well as works by Pound and William Carlos Williams. The Contact Editions were limited to three hundred copies of books that, as McAlmon announced in the *Transatlantic*, were "not likely to be published by other publishers for commercial or legislative reasons." The books had no adequate distribution in the United States, which meant that the Contact Editions, as a business proposition, were very likely doomed to failure. Moreover, McAlmon was very diffident about business methods; he frankly found such details boring.

He was a heavy drinker and liked the night life of the Parisian cafés. Bryher had no interest in drinking at all and disliked the seedy casualness of Parisian life. The result was that they lived separated from each other much of the time until their marriage ended in 1927. The divorce reportedly brought McAlmon a handsome settlement from the Ellerman family. For a time pundits in the Parisian cafés referred to him as Robert McAlimony. His sexual tastes, as he once informed the Canadian writer Morley Callaghan, encompassed both sexes. His nights were spent drifting from the bars like Jimmy's, where the literary set gathered, to the haunts of homosexuals and drag queens.

Pugnacious and frank, McAlmon's remarks about his acquaintances, particularly during his drinking sessions, were apt to be malicious and destructive. In New York, once, annoyed with Hemingway's hairy-chested masculinity, he rumored it about that Pauline Hemingway, the writer's second wife, was a Lesbian, and Ernest himself, a homosexual. Hemingway's response was that McAlmon was "too pitiful" to beat up, though he supposed that it would be necessary to do so, since his kind only responded to physical correction. James Joyce, who knew both men—and drank with both—thought it all a mistake, "Hemingway's thinking himself such a tough fellow and McAlmon trying to pass himself off as the sensitive type." It was the other way around, Joyce thought.

McAlmon had not been eager to meet Gertrude when he came to Paris. He had seen her, in her odd clothes, "driving about Paris mounted on the high seat of her antiquated Ford. There was no doubt that Miss Stein knew how to stage-set herself to become a character and a celebrity." But when he was visiting his wife in Switzerland in the summer of 1924 and was planning to bring out a volume to be called the *Contact Collection of Contemporary Writers*, he wrote to her. He had, in the meantime, read *Three Lives* and had been impressed by the Melanctha story, which, as he wrote Gertrude, he found "amazing: *a clarified* Dostoevskian depiction of niggers. It gave me an entirely different and larger view of your work." He asked her to send "something—or even several things—for the book," and added that even a later segment from *The Making of Americans*, which he had been reading in the *Transatlantic*, would do, since the "expected death" of the *Transatlantic* seemed imminent. Gertrude sent him "Two Women," her early word portrait of Claribel and Etta Cone, which appeared in the volume when it was issued in 1925, along with contributions by Hemingway, Joyce, Pound, and Ford Madox Ford.

On his first meeting with Gertrude, McAlmon had found her "almost shy." He had expected a type like Amy Lowell. "But she was much more human, indeed, a much better specimen than Amy Lowell, although the species were of the same family," which meant, "a pronounced example of the protected child, never actually allowed to face real hardship." McAlmon discovered that he and Gertrude had "a mutual passion" for Trollope as well as a confirmed interest in documentary and autobiographical writing. She had recommended Queen Victoria's *Letters*, while he promoted those of Cardinal Manning.

McAlmon, in 1925, wrote a brief "profile" of Gertrude that he claimed he did not intend to publish. But he sent a copy to Ezra Pound, and Pound had forwarded it, as an anonymous piece of writing, to Eliot at *The Criterion*. Eliot commented that it was "the best criticism of Gertrude Stein" that he had seen and that he would like to publish it. McAlmon delayed for a time, since he did not want it published anonymously, and in the meantime, Eliot finally decided against using it, claiming—according to McAlmon—that it was "too intelligent for his public." It seems probable that Eliot's delay in publishing Gertrude's "Fifteenth of November" may have been prompted by his uncertainty about publishing a critique of her as well, and which should take precedence.

That Eliot would have found McAlmon's portrait "too intelligent" for his public seems unlikely. It is a heavy-handed piece of writing, mainly taken up with an imitation of Gertrude's *The Making of Americans* style. McAlmon spoke of her as a writer with "the elephant's sensibility" rather than "the humming bird's," and his Steinian attempts to convey the image lumber on rather ponderously: "The aged elephant mastadonically heaves to being, breathing in the slow slime, slowly with aged hope, breathing." But it is interesting at points for occasional observations of the author and for some of the oracular pronouncements that he attributes to Gertrude. "No," he records her as saying, "nobody has done anything to develop the English language since Shakespeare, except myself, and Henry James perhaps a little." Or, even more grandiosely, "Yes, the Jews have produced only three originative geniuses; Christ, Spinoza and myself."

McAlmon found that she was pleased by his very patent flattery—without even recognizing it as such. He told her, "Of course you are not touched by time, so you need not think of your generation. Even the youngsters have not the sense of modernity which you had before the war." But Gertrude responded with a bit of uncharacteristic uncertainty: "I sometimes wonder how anybody can read my work when I look it over after a time. It seems quite meaningless to me at times. Of course, when I write it it seems luminous and fine and living, and as you say it has a tremendous pulsation."

For her part, Gertrude thought McAlmon rather "nice" in the early period of their relationship—"very mature and very good-looking." As a writer, she felt, McAlmon had one quality that appealed to her: "abundance, he could go on writing." But her opinion of McAlmon's writing was no different from that of many of McAlmon's associates: It was "dull." Of McAlmon's wife, Gertrude had almost nothing to say, although Bryher often visited the rue de Fleurus when she was in Paris.

Unlike her husband, who thought that when Gertrude talked she lost herself "in the labyrinthine undergrowths of her jungle-muddy forestial mind, naively intellectualizing," Bryher was impressed with Gertrude's conversational abilities. In her autobiography, *The Heart to Artemis*, published in 1962, Bryher "bitterly" regretted that the tape recorder hadn't been invented when she first visited the rue de Fleurus. Gertrude, in conversation, "would pick up a phrase and develop it, ranging through a process of continuous association until we seemed to have ascended through the seven Persian heavens and in the process to have turned our personalities inside out. Make no mistake, however, it was not an ego selfishly seizing the stage, it was rhetoric, spare and uncolored by emotion." But Bryher seldom took part in those conversations; she found Gertrude a bit frightening and much preferred sitting with Alice, talking about gardening and the servant problem. Alice, Bryher felt, had "subordinated her own gifts to looking after her friend, yet they never grew to resemble each other as often happens in such cases. Her personality was intact." Looking back over the intervening years, Bryher gave a considered estimate of Gertrude as a writer. She had been reading over the magazines of the period and found that it was "Gertrude's work that now seems the most alive. It is not dated. . . . Her attack on language was necessary and helped us all, even if we did not follow her. Some of her books are so simple and so profound that we can read them whether we are eighteen or eighty. The rest of her work is experimental, highly technical and should be reserved for specialists. It is a measure of the decline of real learning that some people today have questioned her genius."

In 1924 William Carlos Williams was traveling in Europe with his wife, Flossie, taking an extended vacation from his Rutherford, New Jersey, medical practice. McAlmon introduced the couple to the local celebrities in Paris. The meeting with Gertrude—as recorded in both Williams's *Autobiography* and McAlmon's 1925 "profile"—was hardly auspicious. Williams, forty-one, outspoken, brusque, and aggressive as a personality, was not one of the deferential young men likely to sit at Gertrude's feet. There had been at first some genial discussion of medical training, for Williams came away with the impression that Gertrude's medical education had been a more deliberate process than it actually was. Gertrude, he felt, had studied the "psychic factors" of man under William James at Radcliffe, and the "somatic factors" at Johns Hopkins, all in preparation for her later career as a writer.

After tea Gertrude had gone to her pile of manuscripts in the cabinet and, taking them out a few at a time, read over the titles, saying that she hoped that some day they would be printed. Turning to Williams, she asked what he would do if he were faced with the same situation.

In his *Autobiography* Williams acknowledged that his reply had been abrupt and hardly tactful. He had been influenced, he thought, by the cynical opinions of Pound and others. He said, bluntly, "If they were mine, having so many, I should probably select what I thought were the best and throw the rest into the fire.

"The result of my remark," Williams continued, "was instantaneous. There was a shocked silence out of which I heard Miss Stein say, 'No doubt. But then writing is not, of course, your métier.' That closed the subject and we soon left."

McAlmon's account of the incident was more expansive: Gertrude's reply had been a nearly torrential outpouring. "No, oh no, no, no, no," Gertrude said emphatically in the McAlmon version, "that isn't possible. You would not find a painter destroying any of his sketches. A writer's writing is too much of the writer's being; his flesh child. No, no, I never destroy a sentence or a word of what I write. You may, but of course, writing is not your métier, Doctor."

According to McAlmon, Williams answered, "But Doctor Stein, are you sure that writing is your métier? I solve the economies of life through the profession of doctoring, but from the first my will was towards writing. I hope it pleases you, but things that children write have seemed to me so Gertrude Steinish in their repetitions. Your quality is that of being slowly and innocently first recognizing sensations and experience."

Either version would have been a blow to Gertrude's self-esteem, no matter how impregnable her ego seemed to others. According to McAlmon, the break with Williams was final. On some later occasion, she told McAlmon, "I could not see him [Williams] after that. I told the maid I was not in if he came again. There is too much bombast in him."

The last remark was not quite accurate. Williams later made a more thorough study of Gertrude's writing and was particularly impressed with the slow, ruminative, colloquial style of *Three Lives*. In the winter, 1930, issue of *Pagany*, he devoted an essay to "The Work of Gertrude Stein," and in the course of it asked, "Why, in fact, have we not heard more generally from American scholars upon the writings of Miss Stein? Is it lack of heart or ability or just that theirs is an enthusiasm which fades rapidly of its own nature before the risks of today?" He offered a partial explication of her method and intention, based upon a reading of her work, notably *Geography and Plays*, which he compared with Laurence Sterne's *Tristram Shandy*. He was not, it seems, a man to hold grudges. Gertrude, flattered and pleased, had written to thank him and, on several occasions, sent him copies of her later books, including *The Autobiography of Alice B. Toklas*. It was, it appears, the poets and writers interested in revitalizing the language—individualists of style—who were to make the most careful estimates of her style and influence.

III

Although Gertrude had learned in Sylvia Beach's bookstore that she had a following at Oxford, it was from rival Cambridge that she received her first invitation to lecture in England. The offer, coming late in 1925, had thrown her into some consternation. It represented an opportunity to present her case before a new generation, but she was plainly frightened by the prospects of addressing a large audience. She promptly declined.

The Cambridge invitation had been promoted by Edith Sitwell, whom Gertrude had met earlier in the year, when the English poet and her companion, Helen Rootham, had come to Paris for a lengthy stay. Both Gertrude and Alice had been struck by Edith Sitwell's appearance; she was tall, birdlike, and hesitant in her movements, with a long, aristocratic nose that was the most prominent feature in the long oval of her face. Alice thought she looked like a gendarme in her double-breasted coat with large buttons. Gertrude and Edith Sitwell discussed poetry, and Gertrude remembered the "delicacy and completeness" of the English poet's understanding of the subject. Edith Sitwell, who went often to the rue de Fleurus during her stay in Paris, remembered the pleasure of her visits. Gertrude, she thought, was "verbally very interesting, the more so as she invariably got everybody wrong." Gertrude's appearance reminded her of "an Easter Island idol," and she found her "immensely good humored."

As writers, Gertrude and Edith Sitwell had much in common: an intense preoccupation with the language, a willingness to experiment, particularly in the use of rhythm and with the texture and color of words. Edith Sitwell had already demonstrated her ability to treat words abstractly in *Façade*, her early group of poems, many of them based on the rhythms of popular songs—fox trots, waltzes, polkas. The first public performance of that work, given at the Aeolian Hall in London, in July, 1923, with a musical score by William Walton, and the poet herself reciting her words through a megaphone from behind a curtain, had created a *succès de scandale*. As a poet, Edith Sitwell had a reputation for eccentricity that was comparable to Gertrude's.

She had been acquainted with Gertrude's work before they met and had formed a high opinion of *Geography and Plays*. Her considered estimate of Gertrude's work was that it was "an illustration of the success and also the dangers of revolution. She is the last writer in the world whom any other writer should take as a model; but her work, for the most part, is very valuable because of its revivifying qualities, and it contains, to my mind, considerable beauty." Since she was lecturing on poetry, Edith Sitwell—so she informed Gertrude—lost no occasion to propagandize on behalf of the American writer.

She was, therefore, "bitterly disappointed" when she learned that Gertrude had turned down the offer to lecture at Cambridge. "I do feel your actual presence in England would help the cause," she argued. "It is quite undoubted that a personality does help to convince half-intelligent people." She suggested that she would "work up" Oxford and the University College, London, if Gertrude would change her mind and agree to lecture at Cambridge sometime in the summer. She was still "working hard at propaganda," she told Gertrude, but confessed it was "miserably disappointing" that Virginia and Leonard Woolf, whom she had tried to interest in bringing out an English edition of *The Making of Americans*, had turned down the proposal. "However," she added, ". . . a great writer like yourself is absolutely bound to win through. There can't be any question about it. . . . Do, if you can, reconsider this question of coming over here." In a post-script she added: "There are *many* fresh admirers."

Gertrude brooded over the situation: "Peace," she told Alice, had "much greater terrors than war." Finally she wrote the Cambridge literary society, agreeing to lecture, but putting off any firm date other than to suggest sometime in the spring or early summer. That deci-sion having been made, she became anxious and gloomy about the sub-ject of her lecture. It was still early in January. Her six-year-old Ford, Godiva, was in need of repairs: It seemed to have "everything the mat-ter with it." The local garages were not helpful, and Gertrude was obliged to take Godiva out to a shed in Montrouge, waiting while the mechanics worked at it. It was on one of these trips, on a gloomy after-noon, sitting in another decrepit Ford while the garagemen disassem-bled her car, that Gertrude wrote out her lecture. It was a rambling exposition of her own development as a writer and the stylistic methods she had used in overhauling the English language in an attempt to ar-rive at what she termed "the modern composition." She titled the lec-ture "Composition as Explanation."

Early in March she received a second invitation to lecture—this one from Oxford. The writer was Harold Acton, the president of a literary society at the university. Gertrude had known Acton as a boy, during her years of summering in Italy. His father, Arthur Acton, owned the Villa La Pietra in Florence and had restored its gardens in the English manner, making it one of the showplaces in the city. Young Acton's letter was ingratiating. "Granted that there are more intelligent young men in Cambridge than in Oxford at present," he conceded, "there are still more than a few who would be more than disappointed, seriously grieved, if you paid such an honour to a rival university while leaving Oxford to wallow in an almost-deserved oblivion." Gertrude capitu-lated.

There were other worrisome details: Gertrude was nervous about the delivery of her lecture. Friends were pressed into service to hear her read it or to read it themselves, while Gertrude listened. At Natalie Clifford Barney's, an old French professor advised her to "talk as quickly as you can and never look up." At the rue de Fleurus, an old Boston friend, Prichard, an experienced lecturer, told her to speak "as slowly as possi-ble and never look down." Gertrude confessed that she was "too wor-ried to have any manner." She would also need a new dress in which to give her lecture. That problem was solved when Yvonne Davidson, the Parisian *couturière*, designed a long, flowing robe in a rich blue Chinese brocade.

Early in May, Gertrude and Alice crossed the Channel. Gertrude, in a growing state of fear, refused to go through the fuss of presenting her passport, sending Alice to do it instead. At their hotel Gertrude's growing case of stage fright showed no signs of abatement. The Sitwells— Edith and her brothers Osbert and Sacheverell—had arranged a dinner party in her honor. As it happened, the trio were scheduled for a reading of their own poetry and invited Gertrude to sit with them on the platform. Perhaps to acclimate herself to her coming ordeal, Gertrude agreed. She developed a special affection for Osbert, who reminded her of "an uncle of a king. He had that pleasant kindly irresponsible agitated calm that an uncle of an english king always must have." Together they discussed "all the kinds of ways that he and she could suffer from stage fright," with the result that Gertrude felt "quite soothed."

The Cambridge lecture was scheduled for an evening performance— preceded by an afternoon tea and a small dinner party given by the president of the literary society. Gertrude's account of it in the *Autobiography* is skimpy in detail, perhaps because the Oxford lecture, delivered on the next afternoon, proved to be more successful. The Cambridge lecture, however, had gone well, and she had felt "at ease" once she began to speak. The questioning, afterward, had been "very enthusiastic." But she did wonder why it had been only the men who had asked questions, while the women remained silent.

That first public appearance had evidently drained away the worst of her anxiety. On the following day, she felt rather like a "prima donna." Osbert Sitwell, who drove with her to Oxford, detected that she was somewhat nervous. All three Sitwells gave her moral support by sitting on the platform with her in the large lecture hall. On the platform, Osbert recalled, Gertrude sat with monumental calm, "as if she were sitting to a painter who was making a record for posterity." When Gertrude stood up, he remembered "—and always because of the latent force to be divined in her, one expected her to be taller than she was— she showed a mastery of her audience, and her address, though couched in her accustomed style, proved a consummate piece of lucidity." He remembered, however, that there had been a slight ripple of laughter when, midway through her reading, Gertrude announced: "Everything is the same and everything is different."

Gertrude's reputation as an eccentric writer had drawn large audiences for both lectures. But at Oxford she read to a standing-room audience—larger than Harold Acton had expected. The audience, Acton recalled in *Memoirs of an Aesthete*, had been somewhat "deflated" by the famous author's appearance—it had expected an "eccentric visionary, a literary Madame Blavatsky in fabulous clothes." "Nobody," he maintained, "was prepared for what followed, a placid reading of 'Composition as Explanation.' . . .Though we had heard dozens of lectures, nobody had heard anything like this before. There was no nonsense about her manner, which was in deep American earnest, as natural as could be." Following the lecture, Gertrude read aloud several word portraits, including one of Edith Sitwell, who, according to Acton, tried to look unembarrassed, while Sacheverell "looked as if he were swallowing a plum." Osbert "shifted on his insufficient chair with a vague nervousness in the eyes."

The question period following was lively. Throughout the lecture some members of the audience had been taking notes. Gertrude was asked why she thought what she was doing in literature was right. She explained that it "was not a question of what anyone thought," but that she had, after all, been writing as she had for about twenty years and now they had asked her to lecture. While that might not prove anything, "on the other hand it did possibly indicate something." Two young men, who had obviously come to bait bear, popped up and took turns engaging her with questions. Finally one of them asked: "Miss Stein, you say that everything being the same, everything is always different, how can that be so?" Gertrude observed them both for a moment, then said, genially, "Consider, the two of you, you jump up one after the other, that is the same thing and surely you admit that the two of you are always different." "*Touché*," one of them answered, bringing the lecture to a close.

The Sitwells, Gertrude noted, had been delighted with her handling of the hecklers. They tried to persuade her to stay on in London for a few days more, in order to be interviewed and to capitalize on the success of the lectures. But Gertrude beat a hasty retreat. She had had "enough of glory and excitement." She and Alice returned to Paris on the following day.

It was to Gertrude's credit that her lecture, "Composition as Explanation," made no concessions to popular taste or, even, to the limitations of her audience. Although her delivery may have been plain-spoken, her ideas on "the modern composition" and her attempts to achieve it were spelled out in the literary style she had evolved for herself. The lecture had its epigrammatic moments, sentences that were well rounded and succinct, but her habits of generalizing, of reinforcing an idea through repetition, and of running her sentences together for cumulative effect undoubtedly played havoc with listeners who had grown used to lecturers who put their ideas before an audience in the easiest and most convenient terms. Gertrude had stood her ground.

Literature, and her own writing in particular, was the subject of her lecture. She explained the progress of her own work from *Three Lives*, in which she had attempted to break out of the usual narrative conventions of a beginning, a middle, and an end, by creating what she termed a "prolonged present." With *The Making of Americans* she had moved into a "continuous present," and the progress of her "conceptions," she was sure, was "entirely in accordance with my epoch." But the unspoken example of the success of the modern artist in her lecture was the modern painter, Picasso, and the Cubists, whose works she could now no longer afford. The fact that she had been asked to lecture in academe—as she pointed out to her audience in the question period—made it plain that her method, and that of Picasso, had now become interesting and acceptable to the academy, if not to the broad public.

Gertrude did not posit the artist as someone apart from the rest of the world, but as someone more sensitive, more receptive to the wave of the future that would inevitably inundate the rest of the public. "No one," she said, early in the lecture, "is ahead of his time, it is only that the particular variety of creating his time is the one that his contemporaries who also are creating their own time refuse to accept. And they refuse to accept it for a very simple reason and that is that they do not have to accept it for any reason." The rule of art, in other words, was not the rule of law—except for the genuinely contemporary artist.

She paused, in her lecture, to consider the odd fact that: "Those who are creating the modern composition authentically are naturally only of importance when they are dead because by that time the modern composition having become past is classified and the description of it is classical." And the odder fact: "That is the reason why the creator of the new composition in the arts is an outlaw until he is a classic, there is hardly a moment in between and it is really too bad very much too bad naturally for the creator but also very much too bad for the enjoyer, they all really would enjoy the created so much better just after it has been made than when it is already a classic." Behind these plain observations, there were her own experiences with modern painting—that moment, in the Autumn Salon, in 1905, when she had recognized the struggle inherent in Matisse's *Woman with a Hat*, tempered by her recognition, too, that she had found Picasso's *Young Girl with a Basket of Flowers* too ugly on first appearance and had learned to appreciate the artist's qualities only in time.

But as her lecture made clear, she realized that Picasso's situation, and her own, were not quite the same as the rejected artists of the past. She had considered that difference, as well. She had recently been reading the memoirs of Lord Grey, the English statesman and foreign secretary during the early years of World War I, and she noted that "Lord Grey remarked that when the generals before the war talked about the war they talked about it as a nineteenth century war although to be fought with twentieth century weapons. That is because war is a thing that decides how it is to be when it is to be done. It is prepared and to that degree it is like all academies it is not a thing made by being made it is a thing prepared." She went on to observe, referring to Lord Grey, that "it is quite certain that nations not actively threatened are at least several generations behind themselves militarily, so aesthetically they are more than several generations behind themselves." But it was, she concluded, the war that had catapulted artists such as herself and Picasso into recognition "before we were dead some of us even quite a long time before we were dead." The war, she claimed, made everyone "not only contemporary in act not only contemporary in thought but contemporary in self-consciousness." It "advanced a general recognition of the expression of the contemporary composition by almost thirty years."

The insight for that observation, it appears, had been drawn from personal experience. Not long after the outbreak of World War I, she and Picasso had been standing on a street corner in Paris, watching a procession of camouflaged lorries passing, the sides of vans disguised by blotches of gray and green paint. Picasso, in his amazement, had blurted out, *"C'est nous qui avons fait ça*—It is we that have created that."

One of Gertrude and Alice's first duties, once they had returned to Paris, was to drive to Huiry to visit Mildred Aldrich, who wanted to have the lecture read to her again. Gertrude had made a special trip to read her the lecture before their English journey, and now Mildred wanted to hear it once more and to be told the details of the Cambridge and Oxford triumphs. Mildred was enormously proud of Gertrude's accomplishment, and while it was not an appearance in the *Atlantic Monthly*, which was one of Mildred's greatest ambitions for Gertrude, lecturing at the two most important English universities was decidedly comparable.

Mildred's advanced age—she was now seventy-two—and her living alone were subjects of some concern for both Gertrude and Alice. She was, of course, being looked after by Amélie and Père Abélard, who lived on the neighboring farm. But ever since the war, Gertrude and Alice had made it a practice to visit her at least once a month, and occasionally they brought friends, such as Sylvia Beach or Hemingway, who thought her "a fine old femme." They also tried to spend American holidays, like Thanksgiving, with her. On other holidays, like Christmas or New Year's, she was invited to the rue de Fleurus. But on those occasions, Gertrude's friend William Cook drove out to get her and she stayed over with the Cooks. She had always been frank in her conversation; in her old age, she had become a bit cantankerous. William Cook claimed that Mildred was an interesting old woman, but "a difficult guest."

For two years Mildred had been living on a fund that Gertrude and Alice had initiated with the help of Janet Scudder. In 1924, they had heard, one day, from Dawson Johnston, the librarian of the American Library in Paris, that Mildred had written to him to come out and take her library, which contained a number of valuable first editions and autographed copies of books by writers she had known during her long career as a journalist. Gertrude and Alice drove out to Huiry immediately. The small annuity that Mildred had been living on, they learned, had been stopped. It had come by way of one of Mildred's old beaux, whose wife, unfortunately, held the purse strings. The wife, "suffering from an attack of parsimony," so the husband claimed, had told her lawyer to cancel all such charities.

Gertrude and Alice and Janet Scudder had set about initiating a fund called the Mildred Aldrich Memorial. Janet had objected to calling it Amies Mildred Aldrich, since it was not American and America presumably would be their greatest source of funds. They hoped to collect enough money to insure Mildred's living expenses during her last years. Alice had been asked to do much of the secretarial work. The three women drew up a list of prominent Americans and the usual charitable sources. They had hoped to spare Mildred any embarrassment and did not tell her about it. Gertrude, however, had sent a letter to the *Atlantic Monthly*, to which Mildred had once been a contributor, and the magazine, unfortunately, had printed a paragraph about the appeal. The money for the fund came from various sources; among them old friends and people who had read the *Atlantic Monthly* appeal. Kate Buss approached the Carnegie Fund, which contributed five hundred dollars.

As the money came in, the funds were made available to Mildred by way of a local bank. In December, 1924, Mildred had written Gertrude, complaining that she was "all at sea." "The bank," she said, "sent me out 520 francs in bills this morning and no sign of the source, and that upsets me. I know by experience with Morgan and Harjes Co. two months ago that I shall gain nothing by asking who sent it—so there I am." Her grandmother, she said, had taught her that it was more blessed to give than receive: "Life taught me that it was a darned sight easier & my mother taught me that grace was a prettier virtue than gratitude, so—God give me grace to accept—gracefully, as I am rather weak in gratitude." She had, nevertheless, learned something that had given her a "wonderful uplift—that people were to live on the place when I was gone. . . . I should love to think of young people enjoying what I have loved—especially young painters, for the country is paintable."

By July, 1925, Gertrude had been able to write Henry McBride, thanking him for his check to the Mildred Aldrich Memorial, saying, "Really, Henry, things are doing quite well. We have about $3500 now and enough to keep her going a bit. . . . I can't tell you what a relief it is to know she is safe."

Mildred, of course, had long since made up her mind about Gertrude and Alice's charitable efforts on her behalf. In her later years she was in the habit of reprimanding Gertrude, saying: "You would not let me go elegantly to the poorhouse and I would have gone elegantly, but you have turned this into a poor house and I am the sole inmate." Gertrude comforted her as best she could, suggesting that she could be just as elegant at Huiry. "After all, Mildred," Gertrude would tell her, "nobody can say that you have not had a good run for your money."

IV

Gertrude's appreciation of music was strictly limited. From her childhood she could remember the performances of the "twenty-five cent" opera in San Francisco, or the strains of Chopin's Funeral March, played by a military band as she sat reading in the Mercantile Library. During her undergraduate years at Radcliffe, she was mildly addicted to Wagner and the German opera. And in her English 22 composition class, she was once moved, somewhat out of season, to describe the sound of the wind blowing through trees covered with snow as like "the soft murmur of the spring song from the Walküre." And then, gradually, she came not to care for music at all, "having concluded that music was made for adolescents and not for adults and having just left adolescence behind me."

The young American composer Virgil Thomson, whom she first met in the winter of 1925–26, was to change her prejudice against music slightly. Thomson was thirty when their friendship began in earnest. Born in Kansas City, Missouri, he had had a precocious musical development. Before the age of five, he began pounding out improvisations on the piano, "always with the pedal down and always loud." The improvisations were invariably descriptive and narrative, named after "the Chicago Fire and similar events." Like Gertrude, Thomson had a deep interest in "family living." He came from a large, sociable family of Scottish, Scotch-Irish, and Welsh forebears, most of whom were Southern Baptist. The men had served in the Civil War on the Confederate side.

While studying at Harvard, he had become acquainted, through S. Foster Damon, the Blake scholar, with the music of Erik Satie and with Gertrude's *Tender Buttons*, both of which, he wrote later, "changed my life." Although he met Satie on his first trip to Europe in 1921, when he was studying in Paris with Nadia Boulanger, he had not become friendly with that erratic and elusive musical genius. Nor had he met Gertrude on that occasion. When he returned to Paris again, in 1925, he was already something of an established authority on modern music, having written for *The Dial*, Mencken's *American Mercury* and

The New Republic. But his second sojourn was strictly for the purposes of creating his own work rather than studying or writing about the music of others.

In Paris he was befriended by the brash young American composer George Antheil, the protégé of Ezra Pound and Sylvia Beach, who was being much talked about at the time. Gertrude, according to Thomson, had invited Antheil to the rue de Fleurus in order to inspect the new sensation. Antheil, in turn, brought Thomson with him. Gertrude had liked Antheil well enough, but did not find him "particularly interesting." But the evening had gone well for Thomson; he and Gertrude had gotten on like a pair of "Harvard men." As they were leaving, Gertrude gave a friendly good-by to Antheil, but she shook hands with Thomson and pointedly remarked, "We'll be seeing each other." Alice, Thomson concluded, "did not on first view care for me." Their friendship, however, was to develop into a cordial one.

Thomson had not pursued the friendship with Gertrude even then. But he wrote to her from Savoy that summer, and Gertrude had replied with a friendly letter. The following Christmas, he was invited to a Christmas Eve party at the rue de Fleurus—it was the party at which the visiting Sherwood Anderson and his family were guests of honor. It was a festive occasion, with a Christmas tree, the singing of carols, and a great Christmas cake bedecked with ribbons and candles. On New Year's Day, Thomson called at the rue de Fleurus, only to be told that Gertrude and Alice were not at home. But he left a gift, the manuscript for his piano and vocal setting of one of Gertrude's early poems, "Susie Asado." Gertrude wrote him promptly, confessing that they had been "[e]xhausted by the week's activities" and had told the maid that they were not at home to anyone. If they had known it was Virgil, they would have made an exception. She admitted her inability to read the musical score, but was nonetheless gratefully enthusiastic: "I like its looks immensely and want to frame it and Miss Toklas who knows more than looks says the things in it please her a lot and when can I know a little other than its looks, but I am completely satisfied with its looks."

It was the beginning of a secure but not untroubled friendship and a series of artistic collaborations. Thomson was to compose vocal settings and scores for a number of Stein works: *Preciosilla*, *The Portrait of F. B.*, and *Capitals Capitals*—the last a lengthy dialogue for four provincial capitals (Arles, Les Baux, Aix, and Avignon), which Gertrude had written during her winter at Saint Rémy and which Thomson scored for four male voices and piano. He also wrote the score for the only film scenario Gertrude wrote, *Deux Soeurs Qui Sont pas Soeurs*, never produced as a film, however. And he began composing a lengthy series of musical portraits, including one of *Miss Gertrude Stein as a Young Girl*, most of them written in the presence of the sitter. "My portrait trick is developing nicely," he acknowledged early in the practice, "and seems to be quite new. That is, for music, since the idea of it comes obviously out of you."

But before most of these developments—early in the new year, in fact —he had proposed what was to be their most important and direct collaboration. He asked her to write the libretto for an opera, the subject of which they worked out in the late winter and early spring, when they were seeing a good deal of each other. The theme that Thomson initially proposed was the working life of the artist with the additional observation that since good things came in pairs—"in letters, for instance, there were Joyce and Stein, in painting, Picasso and Braque, in religion Protestants and Catholics"—it would be possible, "without going in for sex unduly," to have both male and female leads with secondary characters and choruses, "for all the world like Joyce and Stein themselves holding court in the rue de l'Odéon and the rue de Fleurus." The structure of the opera, he decided, should be in the classical Italian tradition, the "eighteenth century *opera seria*," carried on chiefly in recitative, with the usual mythological subject with tragic ending expanded to include both political history and the lives of the saints.

They had not been able to come to any agreement on a subject from American history, one of Gertrude's then-current enthusiasms. Her suggestion of an opera about George Washington was vetoed by Thomson, who disliked eighteenth-century costumes, in which, he felt, "everybody looks alike." They eventually discarded the idea of historical subjects and agreed upon the lives of the saints, though neither had a taste for medieval or Italian saints. When they finally opted for Spanish saints, Gertrude was pleased. She had a particular affection for Spain and Saint Teresa, whose city of Avila she had visited with Alice.

Gertrude's interest in the project and the closeness of her working arrangement with Thomson crept into one of the longer poems she was writing at the time, "A Diary." From the textual evidence, it seems to have been written during the early months of their collaboration. One episode, since the piece seems to consist of daily entries, suggests the day on which Thomson had called, leaving the manuscript for "Susie Asado": "I like to be told not to go to the door. It is very nice to have words and music and to see them at the same time when by accident it is where they need it best. Most and best." Another entry reads, "Every day a little greeting from Virgil." In another moment Gertrude observes, "Besides that an opera should have been named gradually," which was to be the case with *Four Saints in Three Acts*, the opera that finally evolved out of her collaboration with Thomson. In the course of their friendship, Gertrude was to develop great respect for Thomson's musical judgments. If she had little knowledge of musical matters, she was at least able to recognize someone who did. In later years,

Thomson became one of the most astute critics of the musical scene, writing regularly for the *New York Herald Tribune.*

It was through Thomson that she developed an appreciation for the music of Erik Satie. Early in their friendship, he had invited Gertrude and Alice to his tiny room in Montmartre, where he played and sang for them, in his reedy tenor voice, the entire score of Satie's *Socrate.* It was then, Gertrude claimed, that she had "really become a Satie enthusiast." She had met the eccentric French composer years earlier; Picasso had brought him to the house when he and Satie were engaged in creating the ballet *Parade.* Gertrude had not seen its performance in May, 1917, nor heard Satie's music—she and Alice had already begun their wartime service with Auntie. But they had become reacquainted with Satie, after the war, when he was invited to the rue de Fleurus on several occasions. With his pince-nez, straggling mustache, and goatee, he looked rather like some petty French official—but he was, in reality, an embattled foe of the musical establishment who wrote scathing letters, studded with gutter insults, to critics with whom he disagreed. Gertrude remembered him only as a "charming dinner guest" who told witty and usually biting stories. He had died in 1925—an innovator with a following among young composers like Thomson, but one whose music had been seldom performed.

The writing of *Four Saints in Three Acts* occupied Gertrude for nearly three months, beginning early in the spring of 1927 and continuing until mid-June, when she was able to send Thomson the completed manuscript. By March 26, she wrote him that she had made a start on the libretto, adding, "I think it should be late eighteenth-century or early nineteenth-century saints. Four saints in three acts. And others. Make it pastoral. In hills and gardens. All four and then additions. We must invent them. But next time you come I will show you a little bit and we will talk some scenes over." She had, at least tangentially, arrived at the title of the opera. Within a few days, she and Thomson had determined that the two principals were not to be eighteenth- or nineteenth-century saints, but Saint Thérèse—Gertrude favored the French spelling, but Thomson opted for the Spanish, Saint Teresa, in his score—and Saint Ignatius Loyola, Saint Thérèse's sixteenth-century contemporary. She reported to Thomson: "I think I have got St. Thérèse onto the stage, it has been an awful struggle and I think I can keep her on and gradually by the second act get St. Ignatius on and then they will be both on together but not at once in the third act. I want you to read it as far as it has gone."

Saint Thérèse had been, after all, an expectable choice. Gertrude and

Alice were familiar with the Carmelite saint's native city, and Gertrude knew some of the Thérèsian literature, perhaps the saint's autobiography or *The Interior Castle,* and had decided that Saint Thérèse's mysticism was "real and practical." Her associations with Saint Ignatius dated back to her California childhood. She had visited the Church of Saint Ignatius in San Francisco and claimed that later she had read his "confessions."

The theme of the saintly life was a happy choice. Gertrude had already, in Saint Rémy, written several poems in which saints provided the titular theme, if not the substance, of the poems. In her libretto the dramatic incidents—a glimpse of the Heavenly City, a vision of the Holy Ghost, a combined wedding and funeral march—are merely hinted at, textually, and considerably reinforced by Thomson's score. Gertrude cast the opera almost entirely in a conversational idiom, without very explicit suggestions for dramatic action. For the staging of *Four Saints* it was necessary to resort to a working scenario, and this was developed by Maurice Grosser, Thomson's painter friend, with Gertrude's consent and collaboration. In the play itself, language .provides the important over-all surface of the work—not as depicting episodes and incidents out of life, but as language set free from argument and rhetoric, words at play, language in a state of beatitude.

Even the creation of the opera itself became a subject of the opera. *Four Saints* opens with a meandering preamble in which the author announces her general intention—"In narrative prepare for saints"—although she was to dispense with any consecutive narrative action. Gertrude next introduces what appears to be a personal digression, a fragment that might almost have broken free from her poem "A Diary":

What happened to-day, a narrative.
We had intended if it were a pleasant day to go to the country it was a very beautiful day and we carried out our intention. We went to places that we had been when we were equally pleased and we found very nearly what we could find and returning saw and heard that after all they were rewarded and likewise. This makes it necessary to go again.

Attempts to start the opera moving are only slowly successful. What appear to be bits of scenic description, tentative proposals for action, are suggested—"Imagine four benches separately," "A croquet scene and when they made their habits." Finally, in her attempts to conjure up the figure of her principal lead, there is a flurry of patriotic sentiment and a comparison:

My country 'tis of thee sweet land of liberty of thee I sing.
Saint Therese something like that.
Saint Therese something like that.

There are momentary reflections about Saint Thérèse, among them an image of her "half in doors and half out out of doors." The subject of Saint Ignatius is broached: "Saint Ignatius. Meant and met." Then the preamble concludes with a roll call of twenty-one saints, with Saint Thérèse heading the list of women saints and Saint Ignatius leading the men.

With Act One, the opera ostensibly begins. Saint Thérèse is introduced "in a storm at Avila there can be rain and warm snow and warm that is the water is warm the river is not warm the sun is not warm and if to stay to cry." The end of the passage, repeated and varied—"If to stay to if to stay if having to stay to if having to stay if to cry to stay if to cry stay to cry to stay"—is an oblique autobiographical recollection of her visit to Avila with Alice in 1912, when Alice had been so charmed she pleaded to stay longer. A few lines later, there is another autobiographical instance. The question is asked: "If it were possible to kill five thousand chinamen by pressing a button would it be done." And the response is given: "Saint Therese not interested." The passage refers to an incident earlier in her life, during her friendship with Hutchins Hapgood. Hapgood liked to pose philosophical and ethical questions, and he asked Gertrude, once, if she could save her brother by pushing a button that would kill five thousand Chinamen, would she do it. Gertrude answered that she was extremely fond of her brother and could "completely imagine his suffering," whereas "five thousand Chinamen were something I could not imagine and so it was not interesting." She had, it appears, identified herself with the heroine of her opera.

Throughout *Four Saints*, Gertrude plays havoc with scenic conventions. Following the opening of Act One, when the action has gotten under way, the stage directions announce "Repeat First Act," and then "Enact End of an Act." The material in these two segments of the opera are much the same as in the opening section, introducing a few scenic possibilities. Saint Thérèse is presented as "visited by very many as well as others really visited before she was seated." It was Thomson's notion to introduce two Saint Thérèses, allowing him to score the role for both a soprano and a contralto. But there is, at least, a hint for this device in one of the later lines in the text: "Can two saints be one."

The opening line of the "repeat" of the first act—"A pleasure April Fool's day a pleasure"—may well refer to the date on which Gertrude began writing that segment of the opera. Thomson was to score it as a long, lovely aria against a choral background. A homely conversation, which Thomson scored for the two Saint Thérèses, then ensues. "How do you do. Very well I thank you. And when do you go. I am staying on quite continuously. When is it planned. Not more than as often." Gertrude's image of the saintly life was more the idea of a state of celestial harmony rather than the activities and trials of the real world.

She discarded entirely any dependence upon the factual lives of either Saint Thérèse or Saint Ignatius. Saints, as she explained in a later interview, "exist and converse," but "they don't do anything." The notion of saintly conversations—the *sacra conversazione* that was a familiar motif in Italian Renaissance painting—dominates her libretto.

In a lecture on her dramatic methods, "Plays," delivered several years later in America, she also explained that she had wanted to make the saints a "landscape." As she claimed then: "A landscape does not move nothing really moves in a landscape but things are there, and I put into the play the things that were there." She had, in her word portraits, "tried to tell what each one is without telling stories," so, in her plays, she "tried to tell what happened without telling stories." Her conception of the play as a landscape, a peculiar innovation, had evolved from a curious logical progression:

The landscape has its formation and as after all a play has to have formation and be in relation one thing to the other thing . . . then the landscape not moving but being always in relation, the trees to the hills the hills to the fields the trees to each other any piece of it to any sky and then any detail to any other detail, the story is only of importance if you like to tell or like to hear a story but the relation is there anyway. And of that relation I wanted to make a play and I did.

The purpose of this odd conception of the drama was to avoid something that Gertrude said she had noticed about playgoing during her childhood, when she attended the touring performances of Sarah Bernhardt and Edwin Booth. What troubled her then, she claimed, was her sense that the audience's emotional reactions—and her own—were in "syncopated time" to the action on the stage. Unlike real life, where one was caught up directly in the emotions of a situation, Gertrude felt that sitting in a theater, watching a play, "Your emotion concerning the play is always either behind or ahead of the play at which you are looking and to which you are listening." The notion seems subjective, yet it has its basis in fact, in the conventional structuring of a play that allows the audience to be privy to information that is denied to the characters in the play. In Shakespeare's *Julius Caesar*, for example, the brief scene between Calpurnia and Caesar, in which Calpurnia warns her husband of her forebodings, is played out against the audience's knowledge of Caesar's assassination. It was that sense of theatrical anticipation, of being "ahead" of the action of the drama, that Gertrude wanted to eliminate in her plays. What she wanted to replace it with was the heaven of continuous immediacy, of actors and audience held together in that "complete actual present" that she considered the hallmark of a modern work.

Four Saints is a paradigm of Gertrude's difficult plays. Its presentation of language as the hero of the drama—language relieved, like the saints in paradise, of quotidian functions, mundane associations; its general disruption of theatrical conventions—the jumble of scenes and acts, repeated or reduced to a mere line or two; its lovely and evocative fragments of description—"Pear trees cherry blossoms pink blossoms and late apples and surrounded by Spain and lain"; its confusions of bits of dialogue and what might be stage directions, announce a new concept of drama, a preview of the Theater of the Absurd, which became popular decades later. Certain of its dramatic events—the funeral and wedding procession in Act III, recalling, probably, the Catholic custom of viewing the death of a woman saint as a wedding day, when she espouses the Heavenly Bridegroom—are suggested in the text, as in the lengthy "in wed in dead in dead wed led" passage. Others—a sudden storm and its departure, Saint Ignatius's vision of the Last Judgment— were introduced into the actual production by Maurice Grosser with Gertrude's approval. Since there was no rigidly planned plot to the opera, it was open and adaptable to staging. As a final and playful contradiction, the opera did not end with Act III, but continued on with a discussion of the advisability of a further act in Act IV itself:

How many acts are there in it. Acts are there in it.
  Supposing a wheel had been added to three wheels how many acts how many how many acts are there in it.

Then, after a few brief scenes, the saints and chorus make the rousing announcement, "Last Act. Which is a fact," bringing the proceedings to a close.

Virgil Thomson's intentions in setting his first Stein text, *Susie Asado*, to music had been remarkably deliberate. In his autobiography, he acknowledged that he had wanted "to break, crack open, and solve for all time anything still wanting to be solved, which was almost everything, about English musical declamation." He had, even at this early phase of his career, arrived at the conclusion that if a text were set sensibly, according to sound, its meaning would "take care of itself." The Stein texts he regarded as "manna" for this type of prosodizing: "With meanings already abstracted, or absent, or so multiplied that choice among them was impossible, there was no temptation toward tonal illustration, say, of birdie babbling by the brook or heavy heavy hangs my heart."
  He began composing the score in November. Gertrude had sensibly

offered him the liberty of cutting where he felt it needed, but Thomson, capitalizing on the unconventionality of the libretto, set everything to music, "every word of it, including the stage directions," which he considered "so clearly a part of the poetic continuity" that he did not feel it proper to cut them. He did, however, introduce the two Saint Thérèses, "not alter egos, just identical twins," and further invented a *compère* and *commère*, to serve as "end men," a kind of liaison between the audience and the difficult text. Whatever cuts were made in the text were made later, to facilitate Maurice Grosser's scenario and the introduction of a ballet, which was intended to give variety to the production. The musical inspiration for the score came not from Spain —which Thomson had not then visited—but from his own Missouri childhood and his Southern Baptist upbringing, the hymns and Sunday School ditties that provided a perfect foil for Gertrude's strange but plain-spoken text.

By mid-December—Thomson was then living in the studio apartment on the quai Voltaire that was to become his permanent residence in Paris—a performing score for the first act of the opera had been completed. A friend sent a Christmas gift box containing a large *foie gras en croûte*, a Stilton cheese, and a plum pudding. It was the occasion for a Christmas-night champagne party for a dozen friends at which Thomson performed Act I. The opera appeared to be a success. Gertrude and Alice were visibly pleased, while "everybody, in fact, seemed buoyed up by the opera's vivacity." Both Tristan Tzara and the French poet Georges Hugnet were among the guests, and Tzara later commented to Hugnet on how impressed he had been with a music "at once so 'physical' and so gay." Throughout the winter, usually in the mornings, Thomson worked solidly on the opera. By February, Act II was completed; by July, Acts III and IV were finished and a first working score written out.

During this period, Gertrude tried to be helpful in the matter of Thomson's finances, attempting to find, among former friends, a patron who would back Thomson's venture. She consulted a Chicago millionairess, Emily Chadbourne Crane, who, in time, contributed $1,000 to the cause. Gertrude's efforts with the Cone sisters, who were in Paris, were less successful. She had arranged for Thomson to play for them, but with "no great cash result," Thomson admitted. Through the sculptor Jo Davidson, a meeting was arranged with the international hostess Elsa Maxwell, who was then promoting Monaco as a summer resort for the rich. Miss Maxwell made large promises—among them a production of *Four Saints* at Monte Carlo, in the spring of 1929—but after one luncheon discussion at the Ritz, she left for the south, leaving behind a trail of broken engagements and no explanation. It was to be six years, and largely through Thomson's perseverance, before the opera was produced.

V

In his later years, Juan Gris had suffered from a variety of ailments. By the end of 1926, the state of his health had become especially worrisome. On December 28 he wrote to Gertrude: "I'm suffering now mostly from attacks of asthma which come the moment I lie down and force me to sit in an armchair for two or three hours. As you see, I have actually all that is necessary for happiness." He was still working regularly each day, he told her. "I am not dissatisfied but as yet there is too little." He had not realized he would be "capable of leading such a sober, regulated and solitary existence. Save for a short daily walk after lunch, I have no other distraction. And the worst of all is that I am getting used to this and am going to become a savage." Within a month, Gris was in the hospital at Puget Théniers, where his condition was diagnosed as uremia. In two days, Gris and Josette returned to Paris, where his condition became progressively worse.

Since the war, Gertrude had developed a special affection for the Spanish painter. They saw each other regularly, and Gertrude regularly kept watch over the progress of his work. Gris valued her judgment. If for some reason she delayed her response, he would express his disappointment to Kahnweiler, his dealer. In a February, 1922, letter to Kahnweiler, Gris wrote: "Gertrude Stein has not written to me as you said she would. Yet I would have liked to know what she thinks about the pictures." On other occasions he was heartened. When Gertrude and Alice visited him in Monte Carlo in 1923—Gris was supervising the execution of his designs for Diaghilev's ballet *La Colombe*—and Gertrude commented that she thought his latest paintings "very pretty," the painter was pleased. He wrote to his dealer: "That has encouraged me because I wasn't sure of them."

She had begun acquiring several of Gris's paintings after the war, beginning in 1921, with *The Table in Front of the Window*, a relaxed and handsomely structured Cubist still life. Over the next few years she bought sparingly, as her means would allow, since Kahnweiler was maintaining his prices, as a measure of support at a time when Gris's reputation and prestige were flagging. In 1924 Gertrude bought Gris's *Seated Woman*; in 1925 *The Green Cloth*, for which she traded an André Masson still life and a thousand francs; and in 1926, *Dish of Pears*. In the meantime, Gris was to present her with two drawings, *The Clown*, of 1924, signed "À Gertrude Stein, très amicalement, Juan Gris," and a watercolor sketch for an unrealized theatrical project, *Boat Deck*, of the same year. All of these, together with the three Cubist pictures she had bought before the war, remained in her collection until her death.

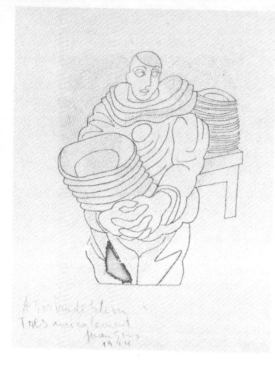

Gris, *The Clown*, 1924. (Collection of Mr. and Mrs. Lionel Steinberg, Palm Springs, California.)

Gertrude tried, too, in other ways to support and promote him. In August, 1922, she had sent Kate Buss to visit Gris in his studio at Boulogne-sur-Seine, hoping that she might write about the artist for a Boston newspaper. And she had actively promoted the Juan Gris issue of *The Little Review*, promising an article of her own on the painter. Gris was delighted. "No one," he wrote her, "will write better about my painting than yourself."

Considering some of the more abstruse writings of this period, Gertrude's article on Gris in the autumn–winter, 1924, issue of *The Little Review* was a model of lucidity. Her essay began: "Juan Gris is a Spaniard. He says that his pictures remind him of the School of Fontainebleau." The opening sentence was more than a flat-footed announcement of Gris's nationality; it conveyed Gertrude's notion that Cubism was properly a Spanish invention. The second sentence was intended to convey the seduction that French culture—the sixteenth-century school of Fontainebleau, and even that elegant, eighteenth-century court painter Boucher—had exercised over Gris. She was fond of quoting Gris's remark: "It seduces me and then I am seduced over again."

Gertrude's friendship with Gris evidently produced some jealous repercussions with Picasso. After an exhibition of Gris's paintings at the Galérie Simon, Gertrude recalled, Picasso had said to her with some violence, "Tell me why you stand up for his work, you know you do

not like it." Gertrude refused to answer him. "Juan Gris," she concluded, "was the only person whom Picasso wished away. The relationship between them was just that."

Her understanding of Gris, Gertrude felt, was based upon a similarity in their respective works. They shared, she thought, a "passion
for exactitude," while Picasso, "by nature the most endowed had less
clarity of intellectual purpose." In her own work, Gertrude claimed, she
had achieved the "destruction of associational emotion in poetry and
prose." She had arrived at the knowledge that "beauty, music, decoration, the result of emotion should never be the cause, even events
should not be the cause of emotion nor should they be the material of
poetry and prose. . . . They should consist of an exact reproduction of
either an outer or an inner reality." In Gris's cool and carefully structured paintings, she sensed a similar concern. In Gris, however, she was
convinced that this passion for exactitude had "a mystical basis." "As a
mystic," she maintained, "it was necessary for him to be exact." In
herself, "The necessity was intellectual, a pure passion for exactitude."
It was, perhaps, a strange conception to have arrived at about Gris's
later works, which tended to be softer and more sentimental in coloring.
It was probably more indicative of his early, rigorously conceptual
Cubist paintings. Even in 1915 Gris worried about the austerity that
was a marked stylistic trait of his painting. He complained: "I can't
find room in my pictures for that sensitive and sensuous side which I
feel should always be there."

On May 11, 1927, Kahnweiler sent Gertrude a warning note: "Poor Juan
is very low. The doctor believes the end very near." Gris died later that
day; he was forty. Gertrude was "heartbroken." Picasso, on learning of
his colleague's death, came to the rue de Fleurus and spent the day with
her. It was an occasion for bitter reflections. At one point she turned
on him, saying, "You have no right to mourn." Picasso replied, "You
have no right to say that to me." Gertrude answered, angrily, "You
never realised his meaning because you did not have it." "You know
very well I did," Picasso said.

Over the next few days, Gertrude wrote a final tribute to her painter
friend whom she felt had died without proper recognition. "The Life
and Death of Juan Gris," which was printed in the July issue of *transition*, she regarded as "the most moving thing" she had written. In the
most straightforward manner, she described Gris's life, his arrival in
Paris, his character, his love of French culture, which seduced him over
and over again and which, in a strange way, she merged with Gris's
affection for his wife: "Josette equable intelligent faithful spontaneous
delicate courageous delightful forethoughtful the school of Fontaine-

bleau delicate deliberate measured and free all these things seduced."
Gertrude had, it seems, a high estimate of Josette's qualities as a wife.
Buried among the adjectives was one that she quite evidently felt was
admirable in a wife—"forethoughtful." It was a word she used about
Alice in several of her poems.

In the course of her elegy on Gris, Gertrude also took note of Kahnweiler's loyalty to the painter: "No one can say that Henry Kahnweiler
could be left out of him. I remember he said, Kahnweiler goes on but
no one buys anything and I said it to him and he smiled so gently and
said I was everything."

"As a Spaniard," Gertrude wrote of Gris, "he knew Cubism and had
stepped through into it. He had stepped through it. There was beside
this perfection. To have it shown you. Then came the war and deser-
tion. There was little aid. Four years partly illness much perfection and
rejoining beauty and perfection and then at the end there came a definite creation of something. This is what is to be measured. He made
something that is to be measured." It was her standard of the artist; he
made something "to be measured."

On the morning of May 13, Gertrude and Alice attended Gris's funeral
at Boulogne-sur-Seine, following after the hearse as it moved down the
avenue de la Reine toward the old cemetery. The chief mourners were
Kahnweiler, Gris's son Georges, Picasso, Lipchitz, and Maurice Raynal.
At the graveside Gertrude stood next to the tall figure of Braque. There
were neither speeches nor a religious ceremony. As she looked out into
the crowd of mourners that had gathered, Gertrude felt that they all
looked, somehow, familiar, though she could not place them. She asked
Braque afterwards: "Who are all these people, there are so many and
they are so familiar and I do not know who any of them are." Braque
said: "Oh, they are all the people you used to see at the vernissage of
the independent and the autumn salon and you saw their faces twice a
year, year after year." Imperceptibly, it seemed, a chapter of her life
had closed, had become distant and unrecognizable.

CHAPTER TWELVE

The Good Life at Bilignin

I

Every year, since 1924, Gertrude and Alice had spent their summers in the department of Ain, a rural province in eastern France, bordering on Switzerland. They had come upon the region by chance. In August, 1924, they had decided to drive Godiva to the French Riviera, planning to stop at Nice and then pay a visit to Picasso, who was staying at Juan-les-Pins. They planned to take the trip slowly, stopping off at Chablis and Dijon, then make a detour to Bourg-en-Bresse, the principal marketing city in Ain. Alice had recently subscribed to a series of *guides gastronomiques* recommended by Hemingway, and the region around Bourg-en-Bresse seemed particularly fascinating. It was a farming region, noted for its thick-breasted chickens, the famous *poulardes de Bresse*, for its dairy products and vegetables, as well as its abundant supply of local fish and game. The presiding deity of the region was the renowned nineteenth-century gastronome, Jean-Anthelme Brillat-Savarin, author of *The Physiology of Taste*, who had been born in the small town of Belley and, for most of his life, maintained a country house at nearby Vieu-en-Valromey. Originally, Gertrude and Alice had intended to make an overnight stop at Bourg, then drive south to

Belley, where they planned to stay a day or two at the Hôtel Pernollet —especially recommended by the guide.

Gertrude was apprehensive about the trip; she disliked heights and was fearful of mountain roads. Maps of the region made it appear especially mountainous, cradled, as it was, between the Jura Mountains on the north and the Alps to the east. When they encountered precipitous cliffs along the roadside, Gertrude began to protest and Alice was afraid that her idea had been a mistake. Fortunately the country opened out into rolling green farmlands and occasional deep valleys. At Bourg they had had a delicious dinner at the local hotel and had toasted their good fortune and the guide book. The next morning they visited the market place, bustling with activity, the stalls stocked with fresh produce. They rather wished that they lived in the region. That afternoon they drove to Belley.

The Hôtel Pernollet proved to be something of a disappointment. It was situated in the middle of Belley, on the avenue d'Alsace-Lorraine, its lengthy ivy-covered façade fronting directly on the street, across from a public mall. They had both expected gardens, but there was only a small vegetable garden that could be seen from the rear of the hotel. The Pernollet may well have seemed familiar; it was like a smaller version of the rue de Fleurus, with a street façade and a small archway leading to a tiny courtyard. Madame Pernollet, a small and amiable woman, the proprietess of the hotel, was exceptionally pleasant. On their first day she brought a huge bouquet of flowers to their room. The ground-floor dining room, paneled in light brown wood, was extremely cosy. They were so charmed by the hotel and their accommodations that it was not until two or three days later that they came to the conclusion, despite the guide book, that the meals at the Pernollet were only mediocre. Consequently they dined, each evening, on poached lavaret, a local fish, served in brown butter; they considered it the most carefully prepared item on the menu. Alice was later to conclude that the proprietor and chef, Monsieur Pernollet, was more interested in reading Lamartine than in attending to his duties in the kitchen. A man with a decided literary and philosophical bent, it was Monsieur Pernollet who had coined the phrase *"une génération perdue."*

Despite the meals at the hotel, Gertrude and Alice found the region so attractive that they lingered on from one day to the next, driving around the countryside, charmed by everything they discovered. Even thirty years later, Alice's recollections of that first summer in Belley remained vivid. "The country was beautiful and diversified," she wrote in *The Alice B. Toklas Cookbook,* "The people on the roads and in the fields were upstanding and had an air of well being. The children were charmingly pretty. In the hills there were lakes and in the valleys there were streams. It was too good to be true."

At first they wired Picasso that they would be delayed for a week;

finally they were obliged to write him that they would not be going to the Riviera at all. In the meantime, early in September, Gertrude wrote Henry McBride about their discovery of Belley, making a feeble pun: "We are on our way to Nice but don't seem to get there. We have found this charming spot which does in no way belie its name and we rest and are rested. Perhaps later we will get to Nice." They remained on, however, day after day, exploring the countryside, sampling the regional cuisine in small hotels and inns along their daily routes—chicken served in thick cream sauces, pungent with the flavor of the local black morels, trout and salmon trout brought to the table bubbling and crackling in buttery sauces, good local wines and cheeses. They traveled to Aix-les-Bains on the lac du Bourget, a famous thermal spa that had, for years, catered to wealthy English and American tourists, and to the town of Annecy, with its medieval quarters and ancient canals situated on the crystal-clear lac d'Annecy. Along the lakefront, they discovered restaurants where they lunched on *omble chevalier*, a rare local fish, and *écrevisses*, the tiny crayfish that were a delicacy of the region.

Their two favorite restaurants, however, which they visited often that summer and to which they always brought their guests in later years, were the hotels Berrard and Bourgeois. The Berrard, located at Artemare, several minutes north of Belley, was a thoroughly unpretentious country hotel, with a shaded dining terrace and two dining rooms. The *maître d'hôtel*, Monsieur Berrard, was a short, stocky man with a full mustache and goatee, a provincial version of Napoleon III. His wife, tall, sturdy, with deep-set eyes, had a peasant-like reserve, compared to her affable husband. Alice was to feel that the quality of the cuisine at the Berrard was to deteriorate, later, when it became popular with the Swiss. But she was friendly with Monsieur Berrard, who often gave her his recipes. She was much more impressed with the food at the Hotel Bourgeois. Madame Marie Bourgeois—later twice-decorated as the best chef in France—was, Alice claimed, a "genius" of the kitchen. It was from Madame Bourgeois that she learned "much of what great French cooking was and had been."

Each evening, after their excursions, they returned to the Pernollet, where Madame Pernollet had given them better rooms on the top floor, with a view looking out over the mall and toward the distant hills. They lingered on through the vintage days and after. It was only with the first crisp, cold days of early fall that they reluctantly returned to Paris. Vacations in Belley, thereafter, became an established routine in their lives. They returned each year, leaving Paris early in the spring, remaining on, it seemed, later into each fall.

Their summers in the country were not all leisure, however. Gertrude found it well suited to her writing habits, and she was able to dispose of other work, there, as well. The summer of 1925, for example, was devoted to reading and correcting the proofs of *The Making of Americans*. Earlier in the year, Gertrude had, using considerable charm, persuaded Robert McAlmon to publish the book as one of his Contact Editions. Considering her reputation and her friends, Gertrude argued, McAlmon could reasonably expect to sell fifty copies. McAlmon planned to bring out a one-volume book, in an edition of five hundred copies, including five deluxe copies to be printed on vellum. The type was to be set by the firm of Maurice Darantière, then located at Dijon, not far from Belley.

Given the prolix nature of the book, its repetitive sentences, and the difficulties the French compositors had in setting it in English, the task of reading the proofs was formidable. Each day Gertrude and Alice, taking lunches and folding camp chairs, drove out to some pleasant spot in the countryside and set to work. It was a tedious job, and in the process, according to Gertrude, Alice broke her glasses; then her eyesight gave out, and Gertrude herself was obliged to finish the task alone.

In August, Gertrude sent a copy of the cover and title page to Sherwood Anderson, reporting that the book had come to 925 pages. She cautioned Anderson: "Lots of people will think many strange things in it as to tenses and persons and adjectives and adverbs and divisions are due to the French compositor's errors but they are not it is quite as I worked at it and even when I tried to change it well I didn't really try but I went over it to see if it could go different and I always found myself forced back into its incorrectnesses so there they stand. There are some pretty wonderful sentences in it and we know how fond we both are of sentences."

It was dim praise for a book whose claim to being the great literary masterpiece of her generation she would never quite relinquish. Gertrude did not give up hope of having the book adequately distributed and promoted in America. Even while Gertrude was negotiating her contract with McAlmon, who seems to have wanted to keep it on a gentlemen's-agreement basis, Jane Heap was trying to interest New York publishers in publishing an edition from the sheets of McAlmon's printing. The Dial Press and B. W. Huebsch had turned the offer down. For a time, however, Charles and Albert Boni considered buying up McAlmon's edition. When those negotiations broke down, in September, McAlmon wrote to her from London, where he had discussed the deal with Boni's London agent:

I'm sorry Boni's did not take the book in a way as they could give it more general publicity, but the cost of it is well over three thousand dollars, and if we are to lose most of that I prefer doing it with our imprint on the book, to losing it as a gift to a commercial publisher whose interest in books is that of grocers in a stock they don't themselves test. They however could not be safe, since for two months they have written letters that declared directly they would buy the book and I did not change my terms in any way. It was only when I requested a part payment on shipment, and the remainder in thirty days as would an American printer had the work been set up there, that another partner assured me that Mr. Baer had misunderstood.

Gertrude was confused and disappointed. McAlmon had originally quoted a different estimate on the printing costs. On the back of his letter, she drafted a reply:

What the dickens is the matter with you. You have not paid any 60,000 francs for the book. You said after you made the contract with Darantière that it would cost you 30,000 francs. The big expense of proofreading a work like that I undertook and did, you have had no expense . . . except the Darantière bill which is a sum that is definite.

In the meantime, she had had another offer by way of Jane Heap, this one from a "syndicate" whose names she was not at liberty to divulge at the moment. The principal in the syndicate, as Gertrude learned later, was Stanley Nott, the English publisher. She wrote to McAlmon about the offer:

There is a syndicate which very seriously wants to put all my books on the market, Three Lives, the long book and several later and newer ones. It is for me an important opportunity. Their proposal is to buy the Making of Americans from you that is the 500 copies minus the 40 copies already ordered, for a thousand dollars which really means 1620 dollars a 1000 dollars for the 460 books and 40 ordered at 8 dollars and the five bound in vellum at $60. They would pay for the unbound sheets and covers upon delivery that is as soon as they are delivered in France.

Will you wire me your answer within 24 hours. You will realise how much this opportunity means to me.

McAlmon wired her that the offer was "too low and vague," then wrote her a long letter, mentioning the $3,000 printing fee and explaining that the sale of books already ordered had been mostly through bookstores, where he was obliged to give a 40 per cent discount.

Gertrude answered, expressing her confusion, referring to McAlmon's earlier estimate. McAlmon was obliged to admit he had made a mistake; the $3,000 printing fee was an earlier estimate, when he thought Darantière had run off 1,000 copies, rather than the original 500 that had been planned. In response, Gertrude escalated her tone to one of self-righteousness:

You know perfectly well that it was not I who suggested to you selling the Contact edition. . . . when you, not I mind you, suggested selling your edition to Boni I agreed because I thought if you felt that way about it you would not sell the edition and that I did not want for obvious reasons.

Even now, she confessed, she was afraid that after the first orders had been bound, McAlmon would lose interest and then it would be "too late to sell." "After all," she wrote him, "you know I want it to go big and I want to get my royalties, that is only fair. Of course my book has big publicity but that if I may [say] so is because of me."

The debacle followed soon after. Nott wrote Jane Heap that Mc-Almon had agreed to the transaction and gave her instructions for having the 400 sheets sent to his Paris shipping agent. Jane Heap informed Gertrude, who, in turn, called Darantière at Dijon, passing on the instructions. The printer, however, took the precaution of writing to McAlmon first. McAlmon told him emphatically to take instructions from no one but himself. McAlmon then wrote Gertrude telling her she had no authority for her action. He would ship 200 sets of sheets to Nott's agent, provided he heard from Jane Heap on the following day; otherwise, he would direct Darantière to bind the entire edition. The tone of his letter was acrid.

Gertrude exploded: "What are you talking about. You wrote a letter to Jane Heap telling her you accepted her offer which letter she showed me. . . . Will you tell me why you changed your mind and when."

Her letter apparently crossed with another from McAlmon, this one full of rancorous afterthoughts:

Had you wished to give arbitrary orders on the book you could have years back had it printed yourself. . . . I have a letter from Miss Heap which shows that she understood my letter to her, also understood that I felt a passing of the buck between her in which I said 200—not 400 as you told M. Darantière. She and Mr. Nott, and she knew I asked her to send ME the address of the Paris shipping agent. . . .

However the book is now complete, stitched, and will be bound. You will get your ten copies which will be sufficient for your friendly gifts, and at least more than commercial publishers give authors. Whatever others you want you can have at the usual author's rate of 50% on the sale price of eight dollars. We will send out review copies to some special reviewers if you choose to send us a list of names and addresses. Further panic and insistence, and "helping" us will not delight me.

Gertrude answered tartly:

You do forget from one letter to the next the figures you mention. . . . and also my dear publisher you are not giving me ten copies even John Lane always gave the author 10 copies and mine were called for in our contract so you are doing no more than is customary but all of this is only repetition and there has been enough of that. I am inclosing the list of reviewers for you to send. Decide your 400 your 300 your 200 as you will. All I am interested in naturally as we agreed when we talked is distribution and I repeat I was requested to do as I did in accordance with your letter, one of your letters.

At this embittered stage, the negotiations with Nott broke down, and the 200 sets of sheets were apparently never delivered. The British censors had seized copies of Gertrude Beazely's frank autobiography, *My First Thirty Years*, on charges of obscenity. The book had been published by McAlmon in his Contact Editions and was being distributed in England by Nott. The shock seems to have curtailed Nott's interest in a further project with McAlmon.

The reviews of *The Making of Americans* were discouraging. William Rose Benét, writing about it in the *Saturday Review of Literature*, compared it to conversations in the Tower of Babel; Edmund Wilson, reviewing it for *The New Republic* confessed that he had been unable to read it to the end and doubted that anyone else could:

With sentences so regularly rhythmical, so needlessly prolix, so many times repeated and ending so often with present participles, the reader is all too soon in a state, not to follow the slow becoming of life, but simply to fall asleep.

A reviewer in *The Irish Statesman* confessed to boredom, claiming "it must be among the seven longest books in the world." Only Marianne Moore, writing about it in *The Dial*, saw in it a "picture of life which is distinctively American, a psychology which is universal." She compared it to Bunyan's *Pilgrim's Progress*.

By December, 1926, only 103 copies of the book, including 1 deluxe and 28 leather-bound copies, had been sold and paid for. In the following spring, McAlmon wrote her with a curt summing up on the situation of the book:

Contrary to your verbal statements that you would help rid us of the volume, you have done nothing. The Dial review I got for you. The Irish Statesman review, came from a book sent them at my instructions. Books were sent to people you asked to have them sent to. Ten books were GIVEN you. You *asked* me to take on the book. You knew it was a philanthropic enterprise as the Ms. had been some twenty years on your hands. There is no evidence of any order having come in through your offices except from your immediate family.

McAlmon informed her that she could bid on the remainder of the books if she wished to do so. It had been on the market for six months, he noted, and there was no evidence that it would sell. He had no intention of storing a book of that size, "when its author so warily fears we might get back a portion of the amount paid for it." Gertrude willingly admitted that McAlmon's anger was "not without reason." She attempted to restore the break, but McAlmon would have none of it. The tone of his letter makes it clear that he was not likely to change his mind. It was charged with anger:

Incidentally the whole publishing of the book was GIVEN you, at your request, quavering. No attitude on your part will delude me into believing that you did not know at the time it amounted to that. Incidentally you have never been financially incapable of putting your book before the public if *your* art is of prime importance to you. If you wish the books retained, you may bid for them. Otherwise, by Sept.—one year after publication—I shall simply rid myself of them en-masse, by the pulping proposition.

McAlmon, in his anger, seems to have overlooked the fact that it was precisely Gertrude's efforts to unload the edition that had caused the break. Gertrude, in the matter of the Nott offer, seems to have felt that McAlmon, who had gone to the trouble of printing the book and assuming the expense of it, would sell the edition for a very meager profit —if there was a profit at all. She had, moreover, been peculiarly insistent on the matter of her 10 author's copies. That was one of the points she stressed in her contract negotiations. And when it seemed that Boni might buy up the edition, she made it clear that she expected her 10 copies from McAlmon and 10 more from Boni. When McAlmon failed to answer her on this point, she became quite peremptory: "Will you without fail answer this by return mail telling me definitely that if, the edition is sold to Boni brothers and you deliver any volume whatsoever from yourself to any purchaser that of that delivery I am to have 10 copies for myself. I want you to confirm this to me." She made no move to buy up the edition from McAlmon. Nor did McAlmon, as he threatened, destroy the books. Under the circumstances, Gertrude's fixation on the matter of her copies makes it seem plausible that despite her hopes for *The Making of Americans,* she had a suspicion that she might have only her author's copies and a few reviews as her reward for her effort.

II

In Paris, Gertrude was surrounded by the young. It was a time when she referred to all the young men as being twenty-six. Virgil Thomson, who was not twenty-six, had developed a circle of young friends—the French poets Georges Hugnet and René Crevel, and the group of Neo-Romantic artists that included Christian (Bébé) Bérard, the brothers Eugène and Leonid Berman, the Russian emigré painter Pavlik Tchelitchev, and the Dutch painter Kristians Tonny—most of whom he introduced to the rue de Fleurus. Gertrude had seen the paintings of most of these artists in the Parisian galleries. But she was cautious in her evaluation of their work. Her allegiances were still with Picasso, whose paintings she could no longer afford. Moreover, she felt some dissatisfaction with the artistic scene in Paris after World War I. "Painting now after its great moment must come back to be a minor art," she observed at the end of the decade. It was one of the scattered reflections she introduced into her volume *How to Write*.

Still, she confessed that she was interested in knowing who was the leader of the group. She felt that at the center of any creative movement there had to be "a very dominant creative power," and she was hard pressed to find one among the five artists who constituted the group. But she had seen one of Tchelitchev's paintings, *Basket of Strawberries*, in the Autumn Salon and had been impressed with it. She had met Tchelitchev through Jane Heap, who was promoting the artist. Edith Sitwell, who developed a long and tempestuous friendship with the Russian artist—having met him at the rue de Fleurus—liked to relate the apocryphal story that Gertrude had gained access to Tchelitchev's studio one day when the artist was absent and had bought out his work. But Gertrude's interest in Tchelitchev was measured. She thought his work was the most "vigorous" and the most "mature" among the group, but she felt that he was hardly the forceful creative intelligence she had expected to find at the center of the movement.

Gertrude had long since reached that point of self-assurance in her judgments about painters and painting where she could afford to admit to uncertainty when the case required. She was, as she acknowledged, fond of telling the story of her uncertainty to "any one who would listen." Among the temperamental, highly competitive young Neo-Romantics, eager for her approval, her ambivalence promoted a lively sense of rivalry that she thoroughly enjoyed. When Tchelitchev, who had a "passionate enmity" for Bébé Bérard, complained that Bérard "copied everything," Gertrude beamed.

She had no interest at all in Leonid Berman's moody seascapes, but for a time she courted his brother, Eugène. Genia Berman, as she called him, had, like his brother, fled from Russia after the Revolution. In Paris he had studied at the Académie Rançon under Bonnard and Vuillard. His classmates were his brother, Leonid, and Bérard. Gertrude had first seen the brooding, romantic views of ruined architecture Berman was then painting at the first Neo-Romantic exhibition at the Duret Gallery in 1926 and had come to the conclusion that she was "not uninterested" in Berman's painting. She visited his studio and looked patiently at his work. Berman, she decided, had a "purer intelligence" than the others. It seemed just possible that he might be the originating intelligence behind the movement. With disarming frankness, she told him about her doubts, then asked him point blank if he were the creative influence in the group. Berman gave her an "intelligent inner smile" and with uncharacteristic modesty acknowledged that he thought he might be. She was to acquire only a few of his works, however, watercolors, chiefly, and portrait sketches of herself and Alice for portraits that were never executed. Her final evaluation of Berman was that he was "a very good painter" but he was "too bad a painter to have been the creator of an idea."

Her feelings about Christian Bérard were equally mixed. She and Thomson, who had begun acquiring Bérard's paintings, held lengthy discussions about the painter's virtues. Thomson was inclined to feel that Bérard was the real leader. But Gertrude, whose train of argument had taken an ecclesiastical turn while working on the opera, claimed that the Church made a distinction between a true mystic and a "hysteric." She felt that Bérard was the latter. Nonetheless, she and Thomson entertained the idea of Bérard's doing the sets and costumes for *Four Saints*. Gertrude had written to Henry McBride, at the time, mentioning their plans: "And then my opera about Saint Therese and Saint Ignatius that Virgil Thomson is to write the music and Baby Berard with the direction of Jean Cocteau to do the decor and to be published we do not know how or where or when." But although she saw Bérard often and was cultivating Cocteau assiduously—if only by letter—the plans never materialized.

Gertrude acquired only a few works by these artists; many of them were gifts and personal in nature, like Berman's portrait sketches. "Baby" Bérard, early in their acquaintance, made two wash impressions of Gertrude, both of which remained in her collection until her death. From Kristians Tonny, the youngest in the group—Tonny was twenty, not the usual "twenty-six"—she acquired an oil, *Le Bateau Ivre*, a hallucinatory image inspired by one of Rimbaud's poems. Most of these works had a transient life in her collection. Toward the end of the decade they were consigned to the *salon des refusés* and then, by one means or another—either as gifts to friends or through exchanges—discarded. When the painters complained that she had changed her mind about their work, Gertrude responded by saying that this was not true at all; their pictures had begun disappearing into the walls and she no longer saw them. When they did that, she countered, "They go out of the door naturally." She had discovered in the Neo-Romantics, it seems, a movement that had no vital center. It was perhaps indicative of the group that three of the artists—Tchelitchev, Bérard, and Eugène Berman—were to become internationally famous as theatrical designers.

For about five years Gertrude was the center of this rivalrous group, which included not only the painters but also Georges Hugnet, the French surrealist poet René Crevel, and a young American writer,

Bravig Imbs. Among these young men she was a kind of mothering figure and sometime muse; for the painters, she was an occasional patroness whose reputation as a discoverer of genius could be useful to their careers. From one month to the next, fortunes rose and fell at the rue de Fleurus. Among themselves, the young men vied for her attention, and she found it flattering. At first it was Pavlik Tchelitchev and his friend the American pianist Allen Tanner who were in favor. When, at an afternoon tea, Tchelitchev, waiting for the most effective psychological moment, blurted out that Edith Sitwell had agreed to sit for a portrait, Gertrude was enthusiastic. "The boy needs some tea," she told Alice. "It isn't every day he secures such a commission." Tchelitchev, jealous of his position, reported all his small victories. On his way to North Africa, he had encountered Berman and Bérard in Marseille. "Bébé almost died of astonishment when I was nice to him; he couldn't understand it at all. I had a good laugh."

Gertrude, as Bravig Imbs noted in his memoir, *Confessions of Another Young Man*, was practiced in the art of *"brouille."* She enjoyed "setting people at sixes and sevens," while remaining, herself, beyond reproach. Alice would sometimes quietly reprimand her when she went too far, but Gertrude would respond by quoting Juan Gris's dictum: "One must always yield to temptation." In the company of Thomson and Tchelitchev, she might draw Thomson out on the subject of Bérard's painting and watch Tchelitchev's silent displeasure with some amusement. Then she would turn the tables, reprimanding Thomson for using, in the heat of an argument, an indelicate phrase in front of Tchelitchev's sister, Choura. But whenever arguments got out of hand, Gertrude was likely to pull the participants up short, pretending to a "deep displeasure" in their conduct.

With Georges Hugnet, whom Thomson had introduced to her, Gertrude formed a quite special relationship. Hugnet, backed by his father, a furniture manufacturer, had embarked on a publishing venture, the Editions de la Montagne, bringing out limited editions of his own poetry and the works of other young writers, such as Tristan Tzara and Pierre de Massot. He brought out two books by Gertrude; the first, published in 1929, was a selection of passages, in French, from *The Making of Americans*. Thomson had begun the translation with Hugnet but was obliged to leave it to the poet and Gertrude to work out together when he returned to the United States for several months in November, 1928. Gertrude wrote Thomson about their progress in December: "We are peacefully and completely translating, it goes, I go alone and then Alice goes over me and then we all do it with Georges and then he goes alone and really it all goes faster than anyone would think." "Otherwise," she reported, "life is peaceful, that is with the usual gentle [e]xplosions."

The second was *Dix Portraits*, a series of Gertrude's word portraits, most of them recent, including a new portrait of Picasso, "If I Told Him: A Completed Portrait of Picasso," as well as sketches of Apollinaire, Satie, Thomson, Hugnet, and the Neo-Romantic artists, Tchelitchev, Bérard, Tonny, and Eugène Berman. Thomson and Hugnet translated the series, and both the French and English versions were printed, accompanied by portraits and self-portraits by the artists involved. It was issued in 1930.

Working with Hugnet evidently aroused the collaborative instinct that seemed peculiarly active in Gertrude throughout the twenties. She began a "translation" of Hugnet's poem sequence, *Enfances*. Her work was not, in fact, to be a literal translation. As she wrote Thomson, what she was making of Hugnet's poem sequence was "a mirroring of it rather than anything else, a reflection of each little poem." This, among other things, was to be the cause of a later serious quarrel between her and Hugnet—and with Thomson as well. Hugnet regarded it as "more than a translation" and wrote Thomson, "Really I have friends too strong for me." When Gertrude's version was published without Hugnet's accompanying text, she archly titled it "Before the Flowers of Friendship Faded Friendship Faded."

Bantam-like and combative, Hugnet had a flair for randy insults that he must have held in check in Gertrude's presence, since Gertrude frowned on anything that smacked of vulgarity in her salon. She was, apparently, enthralled by his dark good looks and his literary talent. Her translations of Hugnet's nostalgic and introspective poems, Thomson noted, opened up a new, more romantic vein in her own difficult poetry, and Gertrude took to the poet himself in a headstrong fashion that Alice could eye only warily, while biding her time.

Alice, however, "adored" René Crevel. Small, blue-eyed, and blondish, he had, so Alice thought, the look of a sailor. In the parlor, Crevel was effusive and lively, politely kissing Gertrude's and Alice's hands on arrival. Although Gertrude belittled the poetry of the French surrealists —"girls' high school stuff," she once commented about it—she had a particular fondness for Crevel, whom she regarded, like Marcel Duchamp, as the complete exemplar of "French charm." Crevel, who was tubercular, was frequently away on cures or in sanatoriums. His letters to Gertrude were written in a comic and exuberant English. On one occasion, after a visit to Antibes, he told her of meeting Scott Fitzgerald: "Curious and poor fellow. A boy. He has a wonderful wife, you know her, I think, but what this young charming and spirituel people has in the hed (tête)? I cannot say, but I want [to] speak about that with you and Miss Touclas." Gertrude described Crevel as "young and violent and ill and revolutionary and sweet and tender." Although she claimed little acquaintance with French writing, Gertrude had guarded praise for Crevel's earlier writing. But she felt that his last book, *The*

Clavecin of Diderot, had the "brilliant violence" she regarded as his special quality.

She especially recalled meeting Crevel once after a *vernissage* of one of the painters in the group. The poet was "exhilarated with exasperation" and began a violent denunciation of his painter friends. These painters, he told her, were selling their paintings for several thousand francs apiece, and "They have the pretentiousness which comes from being valued in terms of money." Writers such as himself and Gertrude, he said, had "twice their quality and infinitely greater vitality," but could not earn a living at their trade. The time was coming, Crevel announced, "when these same painters will come to us to re-create them and then we will contemplate them with indifference." His views seemed to mirror Gertrude's growing dissatisfaction.

But she continued seeing all the young men, visiting their exhibitions, scolding them about their life-styles. They wrote her faithfully when she went to the country in the summer, keeping her informed about their activities in Paris, the constant squabbles and bickering among themselves. Hugnet's letters might deal with some element of their publishing ventures, but then go on in a mood of despondency: "I am unhappy just now—without an incentive, even a futile one. Ah, how I wish you were here: you could say the right things without my telling you what the trouble is, by intuition and true friendship." Tchelitchev's letters, on the other hand, long and flattering, outlined his latest successes—an exhibition of his paintings, arranged in London by Edith Sitwell, the success of his latest theatrical designs for Diaghilev, a momentary reconciliation with Bérard, who told him "with tears in his eyes how astonished and touched he was by the spectacle, how it had surprised him." Bravig Imbs wrote her about the latest fight in a Montparnasse bar, which had begun with Tonny shouting insults at Bébé Bérard, sitting at a nearby table with two millionaires and Diaghilev's secretary, Boris Kochno. When Bérard tried to be placating, Hugnet—with a dislocated shoulder from the week before—hurled a chair at him. The entire group had to be ousted by the gendarmes, "to the accompaniment of some of the most magnificent Billingsgate I have ever heard."

On the first afternoon that he went to tea at the rue de Fleurus, in the spring of 1926, Bravig Imbs successfully passed his screening test with Alice. He had gone with Choura Tchelitchev and had been turned over to Alice while Choura related to Gertrude the details of her brother Pavlik's recent departure for Tunis, accompanied by Allen Tanner. Gertrude, at first, had some difficulty in making Imbs out, and

promptly invited him again so that she could study him further. She
told him later that she had suspected he was "just another YMCA
secretary," a type that she had met frequently during the war and a type
that she wanted to see no more of. Imbs soon showed her some of his
short stories, and Gertrude gave him a bit of practical advice. "You
have the gift of true brilliancy," Imbs reported Gertrude as saying, in
his memoirs, "and less than anyone should you use crutch phrases.
Either the phrase must come or it must not be written at all. I have
never understood how people could labor over a manuscript, write and
re-write it many times, for to me, if you have something to say, the
words are always there. And they are the exact word and the words that
should be used." If the story did not succeed, she informed him, "*tant
pis*, it has been spoiled, and that is the most difficult thing in writing,
to be true enough to yourself, and to know yourself enough so that
there is no obstacle to the story's coming through complete." "You
see," she added, "how you have faltered, and halted, and fallen down
in your story, all because you have not solved this problem of communication for yourself. It is the fundamental problem in writing and
has nothing to do with metier, or with sentence building, or with
rhythm." The language is stilted—the problem may have been Imbs's,
for his writing style was distinctly self-conscious—but the ideas ac-
curately reflect Gertrude's views, part shrewdness and part rationaliza-
tion for her diffident writing habits.

Both Gertrude and Alice admitted to liking Imbs, even though, as
Gertrude said, "His aim was to please." She seems to have taken his
professional career under her wing, for once when they were at a tea
party for the Dayang Muda of Sarawak, given by her cousin, Sir Archi-
bald Craig, in his apartment in Passy, Imbs was asked to collaborate on
a history of Sarawak, based on documents in the possession of the
Dayang Muda. Imbs, who was out of work at the moment, and desperately in need of a job, said that he would think it over. As he and
Gertrude rode back to the quarter in Godiva, Gertrude confronted
him. "Don't," she said, "don't get mixed up with those people. They're
not professionals. If you don't make the distinction now between ama-
teur and professional, there'll be confusion later. That would be most
unfortunate because you are a professional writer." Imbs also made an
impression on Hélène, who had come back to service at the rue de
Fleurus, though only for a year, and, so Gertrude claimed, "to give the
young generation the once over." As one of the items in her poem "A
Diary," Gertrude recorded: "Helen is very pleased with Bravig and
wonders why it is not he rather than Virgil who is asked to stay."

Imbs's relationship with Gertrude was characterized by a certain
brassiness. Early in their friendship, he had once brought a taciturn co-
worker from the Paris edition of the *Chicago Tribune*, where he worked
as a proofreader. The friend, stunned by the pictures, had remained

silent throughout the visit. The next day, Tchelitchev communicated Gertrude's displeasure: "Gertrude does not like silent men. Silent men are, more often than not, second raters. And you simply must not bring people to the salon." Not liking to be told what to do, Imbs had brought another friend a few days later. This time, however, he redeemed himself, for the friend was Elliot Paul, whose reputation as an important writer and whose flattering interest in Gertrude had thoroughly pleased her. Imbs noted, too, that Alice "was quite swept off her feet" by Paul's suave manner. Usually a reserved New Englander, Paul had a penchant for irony; he was one of the few people who could mention Joyce to Gertrude without creating a chill. Not long after their meeting, Paul became one of the editors of the new literary magazine *transition*, published in Paris. It was a position Gertrude had urged Paul to take. "After all," she said, "we do want to be printed." She told him that he would make a good editor: "You are not egotistical and you know what you feel." Over the next few years, *transition* published her work regularly. Aside from shorter pieces, such as "An Elucidation," "As a Wife Has a Cow: A Love Story," and her "lament" for Juan Gris, the magazine reprinted *Tender Buttons*, a bibliography of her works until 1929, and the text of *Four Saints in Three Acts*. Although she was cordial to the publishers, Eugene and Maria Jolas, Gertrude always acted as if Paul were the operative intelligence on the staff. It was an attitude that other writers took, as well, and the Jolases were somewhat jealous. When Paul left the magazine, Gertrude appeared less frequently in its pages. She summed up her dealings with *transition* with blunt solipsism: In the last number of the magazine nothing of hers had been printed—"Transition died."

Like many of the especially favored young men, Bravig Imbs was invited to visit Gertrude in Belley for a few days. His account of his short visit with them, in the summer of 1928, has the air of a provincial idyll. He had arrived at dusk; Gertrude and Alice were waiting for him at the small railroad station. The countryside charmed him; Lombardy poplars silhouetted against the evening sky and, in the village, a group of boys playing *boules* in the square. At the hotel Gertrude had opened the door to his room with a flourish; they had arranged for a bouquet of gladiolas and a plate of apricots and pears placed next to his bed. At dinner that evening, despite Alice's dissatisfaction with the food at the Pernollet, Imbs found the meal of salmon trout followed by roasted chicken, accompanied by a refreshing local white wine, so delicious he wanted it to last as long as possible.

Imbs had just completed a second novel, *A Parisian Interior*, and was anxious for Gertrude's opinion. He was rewarded the next morning, when, passing by their room, he overheard Gertrude reading aloud portions of it to Alice with evident satisfaction. Throughout the remainder of his stay, Gertrude "piled compliment upon compliment and at last,

if I had not taken the train, I should probably have floated away." Both
Gertrude and Alice were in an expansive mood, eager to show him the
countryside and have him sample the regional cuisine. They drove to
Artemare, to dine on *écrevisses*, with Alice staying at the Hotel Berrard to arrange the luncheon while Gertrude and Imbs drove out
through the countryside. Gertrude told him that she thought his book
was as "fine an exposé of Russian characters" as she had ever read.
"And you needn't be worried about the end," she added. "It comes
plumply and falls just right."

On the following day they drove to Aix-les-Bains, where they dined
on *omble chevalier* at a lakeside restaurant. They had visited the spa
first, sitting in the shaded park, watching the "ancient British fossils"
sipping at their glasses of spring water. Gertrude, musing over the scene,
observed: "I can't see why anyone should go to the trouble of starting
a revolution with the view to demolishing the class represented here.
They're so perfectly harmless. Did you ever see so many dead-from-the-
neck-up people gathered in one place?" After lunch, they took a boat
trip to the Abbey of Hautecombe on the other side of the lake, the setting of Lamartine's romantic poem *Le Lac*. There Alice renewed their
supply of the delicious honey sold by the monks.

On his last evening, Imbs was taken to view the ruins of an old castle
near Saint-Germain-les-Paroisses. It was a spot Gertrude wanted him to
see and best viewed by moonlight. As they drove along the dark, winding country road—Alice had remained at the hotel—Gertrude had expounded on one of her recent theories: that America was now the
oldest country in the world, having entered the twentieth century earlier than other countries. Its problems, she explained, were "the troubles of senility rather than of youth." Imbs listened drowsily, enjoying
the fragrant night air. The car came to an abrupt halt. The castle watch
tower stood atop a hill bathed in moonlight; the ruined castle walls
were shadowed with dark poplars. They climbed slowly to the top of
the hill and stood, surveying the scene. Gertrude pointed to a moonlit
ribbon of roadway: "It dates back to the Crusaders. They had to pass
it to cross the Rhone." For several moments they looked out over the
darkened valley. Then Gertrude said quietly, "We must be getting back
to Alice. If I'm away from her long I get low in my mind."

Among the young, Gertrude had reason to remember her own age. The
death of Juan Gris had affected her. And early in 1928 she had had
equally sharp reasons for recalling the passage of time; Mildred Aldrich
had died. Amélie, Mildred's maidservant, had called, one morning, to
say that she had found her mistress on the floor when she arrived for
work; Mildred had had a stroke. Amélie had sent for the local doctor.

Gertrude had hurriedly called William Cook—she was too nervous to drive out to Huiry herself. She and Alice and Cook had ridden out to La Creste, Mildred's little farmhouse. Mildred's condition did not seem hopeful. Cook felt that she would be better cared for at the American Hospital in Neuilly, and as soon as she was able to be moved, Mildred was taken there. It was from the hospital, on February 19, that Gertrude and Alice had word that Mildred had died. She was seventy-five.

Gertrude had known Mildred since the early days in Paris; she was another friend gone, now, from that crowded canvas. She was a figure connected with the American past that Gertrude was fond of thinking about. Mildred had remembered the Civil War; as a small girl, she had shaken hands with Abraham Lincoln in Boston. Gertrude admired her fine spirit, her courage, and her love of her adopted France. Mildred had led a life dedicated to the literary profession. Even in her last years, when she was no longer active, she had maintained a lively interest in the younger generation. In December she had written to Gertrude about her reading: Carl Van Vechten's new novel, *Peter Whiffle*, which Gertrude had sent her, and the *Cahiers de Marcel Proust*. The latter had especially impressed her: "When I put it down I felt that I should throw a fit if I could not talk to some one about it. I was as full of words that I wanted to throw off as I used to be in the old days when I earned my living doing .it."

One of Mildred's last letters to Gertrude and Alice had been written on Christmas Day. She was as alert as ever:

I got up quite early this morning and dolled myself all up. I went down to my coffee, in my best mauve kimono and my best sandals, with my Christmas cap—very becoming—on my head. . . . and my nose powdered and my eyebrows pencilled, and before I went in to my coffee I had a praise service —"Come all ye faithful"—a new disk . . . sung in the Metropolitan Opera House by the United Glee Clubs of America (850 voices), with the audience of 4000 singing the refrain. It shook the rafters—I have rafters to shake.

It was rather a pity no one saw me. I am not sure whether I looked like a perfect lady, or a perfect rip, but I knew I was feeling better.

Gertrude and Cook had made the arrangements for the funeral. It took place in the village of Huiry, where, during the war, Mildred had lived out the great adventure of her life. She was buried with a simple ceremony, in the local cemetery. The mayor attended and Amélie and Père Abélard—a few of her neighbors, perhaps. Alice remembered the many flowers and a much-beribboned officer—the delegate from the Légion d'honneur.

There were details to be attended to; Mildred's family had to be told the details of her burial. Among the papers in the Stein archives at Yale, there is a testy letter to Gertrude from Mildred's sister in the United States, resentful of the fact that Mildred had chosen to give her books to the American Library in Paris, when she had so little else to leave; her family plainly disapproved of her expatriation, of her choosing to die among foreigners.

Mildred had destroyed some of her correspondence—probably the more personal items—but she had intended that the rest of her papers would go to Gertrude. It was surely an intriguing collection, for among her correspondents were figures such as Maeterlinck, for whom she had served as an American agent, and friends like Henry McBride and the Irish poet James Stephens. Judging from the extensive number of letters Mildred had written to Gertrude—there are 487 letters and notes —Mildred had been a faithful correspondent during the fourteen years she lived at Huiry. There must have been a correspondingly large number of letters to her from Gertrude and Alice. But Gertrude never made the trip to Huiry to collect Mildred's papers and they were, evidently, destroyed.

III

With each passing summer Gertrude and Alice became more determined to have a country house in the area around Belley. They had given serious thought to buying land and building a house, probably inspired by the examples of Gertrude's brother Michael and William Cook, both of whom had had new houses built, designed by the young architect Le Corbusier. But they had not been able to find a suitable property; the land they wanted to buy was either not for sale or had no water. They looked at houses for rent, but there were none that they would have moved into. One afternoon, driving out from Belley, they caught sight of a house perched on a hill above a steep retaining wall. It looked like the perfect house, ample and old, with many windows, commanding a fine view across the valley.

With that right of eminent domain that she felt accrued to her genius, Gertrude decided, on the spot, that it would be their summer home. "I will drive you up there," she told Alice, "and you can go and tell them that we will take their house."

"But it may not be for rent," Alice protested.

"The curtains are floating out the windows," Gertrude said, by way of explanation.

"Well, I think," Alice said, resorting to logic, "that proves someone is living there."

The most Alice would do, reluctantly, was ask a farmer they met on the road if he knew to whom the house belonged. They were told that it was being leased by a French army officer garrisoned at Belley and were given the name of the agent.

Both Gertrude and Alice constructed simple and complicated versions of how they acquired their dream house. The most economical account, offered by both, was that the officer—a lieutenant in Gertrude's version, a captain in Alice's—was due to be transferred and that they simply had to wait. "Allez doucement," the old farmer had told Gertrude, and they had done just that. Gertrude's more elaborate version, given in *Everybody's Autobiography*, has them turning to a friend, Georges Maratier, a Parisian picture dealer who formerly had been a clerk in the war office. Maratier came from a conservative, well-connected family, and Gertrude often turned to him for advice. He had one peculiarity, so she thought; he believed in the Napoleonic dynasty —he was a Bonapartist. Gertrude found it odd: "It does seem very foolish as the Bonapartists never did anything except bring disaster upon France and George loves France." They told Georges their problem. There followed months of waiting, in which, it seemed, one was obliged to "look anxious but ask no questions." Finally Maratier informed them that the lieutenant was scheduled to retire in two to three years and that it was not likely that he would be promoted to the rank of captain only to be pensioned off at a captain's salary. He could, however, be transferred to Morocco and would receive active-duty pay that would be comparable to a promotion. Gertrude's answer had a touch of old-fashioned melodrama: "No no said we as good Americans and George went off and said nothing." A month later, they were informed that the lieutenant was being transferred to Morocco for two years and they could now sublet the house. According to Gertrude's version, they never knew whether Maratier pulled strings or whether it was pure coincidence.

Alice's account in *The Alice B. Toklas Cookbook*, however, has them both directly involved. When they learned that the officer was a captain and that there were too many majors in his battalion, a way seemed clear: "We would get two influential friends in Paris to have him promoted, he would be ordered to another garrison and the house would be free for us." The captain, unfortunately, failed twice in his examinations, and they were "despondent." Then someone suggested that the captain might be transferred to Africa with more pay: "The captain accepted, the friends became active again and soon we were ecstatically tenants of a house which we had never seen nearer than two miles away." It was not the last they heard of the French officer, however. Shortly after he had been transferred to Morocco, war broke out there and Gertrude and Alice were told he had been taken prisoner. "Alice Toklas' conscience troubled her," Gertrude noted. "Mine did not trouble me but hers troubled her and then later came the news that he was not a prisoner and nothing happened to him."

Gertrude and Alice moved into their dream house early in the spring of 1929. It was located at Bilignin, a small farming community, nothing more than a few houses and barns, on a winding dirt road a few miles from Belley. The house was separated from the road by a high wall with a large iron gate. There was an ample courtyard formed by the manor house itself and a series of fine old, broad-roofed outbuildings. To the right of the gate, built into the wall, there was a fountain with a spigot and basin. A huge plane tree, standing off center in the courtyard, screened the upper stories of the building from view.

To the left there was a passageway between the house and its outbuilding. This led to the terrace garden, which overlooked the valley. A small garden house with a quaintly peaked roof stood in the center of the retaining wall. The terrace was wide and long with flowerbeds shaped in geometric patterns by low boxwood hedges. At one end of it a tall, unkempt pillar of boxwood rose to the height of second-story windows. The house itself, sturdy and solid, was of stone covered with ancient, yellowing stucco. Two tiers of tall, shuttered windows took in the view across a broad green valley with hazy mountains in the distance.

Built in the seventeenth century, the house, so Gertrude learned, had always belonged to the same family—a family that was regarded as somewhat miserly. Little had been done to change it over the years. When Gertrude and Alice first took it, there was no inside plumbing; water had to be brought in from the fountain. The wallpapers in the high-ceilinged salon and in the bedrooms upstairs—so one of her guests discovered by applying dampened cotton—went back, layer by layer, through the Empire and the Directoire to the age of Louis XVI. The kitchen was old and antiquated; it was not until they acquired their own lease that they began to make the necessary improvements.

That first summer had been one of settling in. Just before leaving Paris, Gertrude bought her first dog, a white caniche, a puppy they had seen in a dog show and that had jumped into Gertrude's arms. Alice had wanted a white French poodle ever since she had read Henry James's *The Princess Casamassima*, and the puppy was named Basket because Alice fancied that when it was grown, it would carry a basket of flowers in its mouth. Basket never mastered the trick, however.

Gertrude's regimen at Bilignin followed much the same pattern as her winters in Paris: She arose late in the morning and spent a leisurely day, with a certain portion of her time set aside for writing. In her afternoon walks with Basket, she liked to gather nuts and seek out mushrooms, bringing them back in her capacious pockets. If there were guests at Bilignin—as there frequently were—Gertrude was apt to greet them in the morning from the second-story window of the bathroom, while they waited below on the terrace for the breakfast trays that were Alice's pride. While Alice managed the household, Gertrude, a conscientious hostess, took the guests for long drives in the country, show-ing them the historic sites of the region, and to lunches in the restaurants they had discovered. She became restless, however, if guests stayed beyond their welcome; she did not like them to settle too comfortably into the daily routine of her life.

From their first year at Bilignin until World War II, there was never a summer without its roster of guests at Bilignin. At first she invited the young writers and painters of her acquaintance for brief stays—Bravig Imbs, Eugène Berman, Georges Hugnet. One summer day, in 1930, Picasso and Olga and young Paulot arrived in their chauffeured limou-sine, stepping out of the car, to Gertrude's delight, in their modish Riviera costumes of brightly colored shirts and shorts. During the thir-ties, there were visits from the French historian and writer Bernard Faÿ, Cecil Beaton, Carl Van Vechten, Thornton Wilder—fresh from a meeting with the eminent Dr. Freud—Clare Boothe Luce and her hus-band, on their way home from a tour of the European capitals on the brink of war. If the guests were less favored or the accommodations at Bilignin were overstrained—as happened with Francis Picabia and his wife—they were expected to put up in the Hôtel Pernollet at Belley.

Virgil Thomson, who spent ten days at Bilignin in August, 1930, has given a lively account of Gertrude's regimen—both at the rue de Fleurus and at Bilignin—during this period:

In the morning she would read, write letters, play with the dog, eventually bathe, dress, and have her lunch. In the afternoon she drove the car, walked, window-shopped, spent a little money. She did nothing by arrangement till four. . . .

Year round, these routines varied little, except that in the country, if there were house guests, excursions by car might be a little longer, tea or lunch taken out instead of at home. When alone and not at work, Gertrude would walk, read or meditate.

At Bilignin, books were sent to her from the American Library in Paris. Thomson noted her reading preferences at the time: "English and American history, memoirs, minor literature from the nineteenth century, and crime fiction, rarely modern art-writing and never the commercial magazines." He also noted her penchant for engaging in conversation at every opportunity: "She talked with anybody and every-body. When exchanging news and views with neighbors, concierges, policemen, shop people, garage men, hotel servants, she was thoroughly interested in them all. Gertrude not only liked people, she needed them. They were grist for her poetry, a relief from the solitudes of a mind essentially introspective." At some point in every day, she wrote, "and since she waited always for the moment when she would be full of readiness to write, what she wrote came out of fullness as an over-flowing."

In her midfifties, Gertrude had pared down her schedule of writing to a minimal daily effort. "They talk a great deal these days about only working a half hour a day and so the work of the world will be done," she confessed in *Everybody's Autobiography*. "Well I have never been able to write much more than a half hour a day. If you write a half hour a day it makes a lot of writing year by year. To be sure all day and every day you are waiting around to write that half hour a day." Her days, therefore, were organized around the regimen of her writing, with Alice seeing to it that the possibly irksome details of daily living were spared her. The muse, however, could overtake her in odd situations and in odd places. Bravig Imbs reported, from a visit to Belley, that he had seen the writer at work, sitting on a camping stool in the middle of a pasture. Alice, on command, was driving a cow around the field. Gertrude's inspiration often came from odd sounds and eccentric rhythms, and that day she had taken a fancy to the clunking of the cowbell as that ungraceful, ruminative animal was forced to jog, udders swaying, around the pasture.

It was from her own artistic compulsions that Gertrude had evolved the dictum, "It takes a lot of time to be a genius, you have to sit around so much doing nothing." Bilignin proved conducive to the kind of leisurely meditations that prompted Gertrude's writing. Dawdling in her bath one morning—"I like moving around in the water in a bathtub"—she found herself drumming out the rhythm of Chopin's Funeral March on the side of the tub. That unconscious recollection of the music she had heard during her adolescence in San Francisco, when she brooded about the death of ancient civilizations, had accompanied her bathtub meditations on "identity and memory and eternity"—themes that occupied her writing for several years. Her ideal spot for reflection, however—when there were no guests—was on the terrace, overlooking the garden. Sitting in a deck chair, Basket in her lap, she meditated on two of her favorite subjects, the English language and American history. Both were interwoven into the fabrics of two of her most difficult and cryptic books of the period, *How to Write* and *Four in America*, considerable portions of which were written at Bilignin.

"I am writing a lot, grammatically speaking," Gertrude informed Henry McBride in September, 1928. Again, in the following spring from Bilignin, she told him: "I am writing a lot about sentences. I have made some very good ones." The question of her identity had begun to nag her, as well: "Anyway what am I an American, Alice says a civil war general in retirement, perhaps." Inspired by her Cambridge and Oxford lectures, Gertrude had taken up the subject of language in a series of pieces—"Saving the Sentence," "Arthur a Grammar," "Regular Regularly in Narrative," "A Vocabulary of Thinking"—which formed her book *How to Write*, published in 1931. The book is one of Gertrude's most gnomic productions, a sequence of seven meditations on sentences and paragraphs, grammar, narrative, vocabulary, and forensics. The epigraph for the second section, "Sentences and Paragraphs," reads: "A sentence is not emotional a paragraph is"—an insight into the mystery of language, which Gertrude claimed she had discovered while listening to the eccentric rhythm of her dog lapping up water. In large part, *How to Write* is a kind of chapbook, with demonstration sentences and paragraphs, followed by the author's evaluation of their success or failure: "Way-laid made it known as quince cake. This is a perfect sentence because it refers to regretting." Or: "Dogs get tired and want to sleep. This is not a sentence to be abused."

The opening segment, "Saving the Sentence," was written early in Gertrude's tenancy of the house at Bilignin, and it contains some of the more lyrical and personal references that thread their way through her linguistic meditations. There are several references to Basket and to gardening—"A rain makes transplanting following easy. Thank you for thinking of the rain." Questions of grammar and the problems of identity are merged: "What is a sentence for if I am I then my little dog knows me." Mentions of tapestries probably refer to the needlepoint chair covers, designed by Picasso, that Alice was working, during this period, and that were destined for the two small Louis XV armchairs stationed by the fireplace at the rue de Fleurus. There are also amiable references to a new pride of ownership—in husband-and-wifely terms—and a sense of standing in the community:

Hers and his the houses are hers and his the valley is hers and his the dog named Basket is hers and his also the respect of the populace is hers and his.

The section "Regular Regularly in Narrative," written predominantly in paragraph form, contains two noteworthy references. The first is a lengthy paragraph devoted to the subject of Mabel Haynes: "What happened to Mabel Haynes American four Austrian children." This recollection of one of the protagonists in her early novel *Quod Erat Demonstrandum* seems to have been prompted by an incident from life. Rummaging through her cupboardful of unpublished manuscripts one day at the rue de Fleurus, she had come across the two copybook volumes of the novel. Slightly embarrassed by her early literary effort, she had handed the book to Louis Bromfield, the novelist who was visiting her at the time, asking him to look it over. Bromfield wrote her early in 1931 that he found the book "vastly interesting." Considering the Lesbian nature of the relationship described in the book, he thought there might be "great difficulties" involved in publishing it but that these might be overcome.

Gertrude had met Bromfield several years before, but had not been particularly impressed with him or his writing. But after 1929 she had reasons for cultivating his friendship. One afternoon, at the rue de

Fleurus, she had returned from her walk and informed Alice that they would be having lunch, the next day, with Bromfield and his wife. Alice, puzzled, had asked why. "Because," Gertrude answered, radiantly, "he knows all about gardens."

Bromfield did, in fact, "know all about gardens and all about flowers and all about soils." At Senlis he operated a small farm and menagerie —several dogs, cats, and a mongoose picked up in his travels in India. When he returned to America at the outset of World War II, Bromfield took up farming in the Ohio Valley and produced a series of books, beginning with *Pleasant Valley*, that were early tracts on organic farming. Gertrude thought Bromfield "as American as Janet Scudder," though a good deal less "solemn." Her interest in him is frankly stated in the *Autobiography*. They had first "liked each other as gardeners, then they liked each other as americans and then they liked each other as writers." Still in a collaborative mood, Gertrude had hoped to interest Bromfield in collaborating on a mystery story, a genre they were both interested in, but the writer had never shown any great enthusiasm for the project.

The other reference, in "Regular Regularly," is to her proposed collaboration with Sherwood Anderson on a biography of General Grant. "Collaborators tell how in union there is strength," reads one of the lines in Part II, which opens with the peculiar observation:

I often wondered whether I would have liked it better if he had not taken the name Ulysses Simpson which made U.S. Grant United States Grant Unconditional Surrender Grant but had kept the name Hiram Ulysses which could not have been used in that way.

The passage is the germ of an interminable disquisition on the subject of names and the problem of identity that occupies much of her time in her later volume, *Four in America*.

Country life at Bilignin, it seems, gave rise to a long series of speculations on her craft as a writer and her feelings about America. The latter were to result, after years of self-imposed exile, in a celebrated and sentimental journey to her native land.

In that first summer of 1929, Alice had attacked the problem of the vegetable gardens. There were two at Bilignin; one on the level of the terrace garden behind a thick stone wall with a heavy wooden door; the other on higher ground, some distance from the courtyard. It was her dream to plant fifty-seven varieties, "like the Heinz pickles," and in the fourteen years in which they had the house, she often came close to realizing her ambition. In that first summer the ground had had to be cleared of a jungle growth of weeds; potatoes had been the only crop planted the year before. In the process a respectable strawberry patch and rows of blackberry bushes had been discovered. It had taken seven hired men a full six days to clear away the accumulation of rubbish and weeds; then the fields were manured and raked. Gertrude hired a young village boy to do the heavier work, and when the fields were ready, they planted the seeds they had brought from Paris and the slips and seedlings that had been bought at the farmers' market in Belley—early salad greens, peas and pole beans, radishes, tomatoes, melons.

At first, Alice had scoffed at the superstitions of the local farmers: Never plant seeds on the new and full moons, never transplant parsley or plant it on Good Friday. But after several seasons and a few errors —peas and beans ruined by late spring frosts—she became a successful and "weather-wise" gardener. The Widow Roux, who came to do the washing and ironing, supervised her efforts. She advised Alice that the spinach she was planting would need a good deal of fertilizer. "*La crème de la crème,*" the Widow Roux had said, and the next morning came with a wheelbarrow full of pig manure. In time, the gardens began to produce abundantly—early salad greens and spinaches, the small pink radishes that Alice liked to serve as hors d'oeuvres, globe tomatoes, artichokes and eggplants, the green beans that were served, plain, with butter, when young and succulent, then with cream sauces as the summer advanced. The gardens supplied the table at Bilignin—the surplus was given to neighbors and friends in Belley. But their farmer neighbors were never tempted to try the young ears of corn, planted by seed sent to them from America each year—corn was strictly for fodder. The strawberry patch yielded jars of preserves. At first, Alice had tried to pick enough of the tiny *fraises de bois* for her guests' breakfasts when the fruit was in season. But it became too tedious a job. Their guests were told that if they wished strawberries for their breakfast trays, they would have to pick them for themselves. But Alice picked a supply for Gertrude each morning. The raspberry bushes—pruned like French vines and trained on wires—produced ruby-red berries for dessert from May until the end of the season. With black and red currants, Alice made the liqueurs that were served to the winter guests at the rue de Fleurus.

In the cold, crisp days of October, they harvested the winter vegetables and the last ripe tomatoes, which were packed and crated for the return to Paris, the leaves turned onto the compost heap. Alice confessed that her proudest days as a gardener were those last days in October each year, when she stood in the yard with the crates and baskets of orange squashes, yellow turnips, and purple eggplants surrounding her. Gertrude, stepping out into the wet garden, would survey the results of the bountiful summer and declare that if all that were being sent to Paris, the *expressage* would ruin them. It was enough to feed "an institution," Gertrude observed. "There was no question," Alice confessed, "that, looking at that harvest as an economic question, it was disastrous, but from the point of view of the satisfaction which work and aesthetic confer, it was sublime." Her winters in Paris were spent in planning and dreaming of the next year's crops.

IV

Around 1930 the purge began. The first rumblings may have occurred a year or two earlier, when Gertrude began to lose interest in Tchelitchev and his paintings. By 1932, however, she had divested herself of the circle of young men that had crowded her salon, courted her, sought her imprimatur, run errands for her. The means were various: Some were given such chilly receptions at the rue de Fleurus that it was clear their presence was no longer welcome; others were informed by curt notes of dismissal or by way of the telephone that had recently been installed. The reasons for the purge are not altogether clear. Some of the painters of the Tchelitchev-Berman-Bérard group were beginning to receive a certain *réclame* as theatrical designers, and there may have been a taint of that professional jealousy that had brought about Gertrude's estrangement from Hemingway. The future was opening up for her young protégés in a way that seemed closed to Gertrude. She quarreled with their success—and later frankly admitted it in an article for *Vanity Fair*. She had, she said, quarreled with a great many young men: "And one of the principal things that I have quarreled with them about was that once they had made a success they became sterile, they could not go on. And I blamed them. I said it was their fault. I said success is all right but if there is anything in you it ought not to cut off the flow not if there is anything in you."

Virgil Thomson recalled that Tchelitchev's dismissal had occurred in the spring of 1928. The precipitating factor had been a dispute that Gertrude herself had brought about one evening when Thomson dropped by the rue de Fleurus. Tchelitchev and his sister Choura were also paying a visit. Thomson had recently undertaken to coach a young American singer, a woman, in Satie's *Socrate*. But the woman had never returned for further appointments. Since Allen Tanner, Tchelitchev's roommate, was the woman's regular accompanist, Thomson thought it best to clear the air by mentioning the subject. At the mention of her name "Pavlik's long face froze, and I realized that his household suspected me of trying to win away a paying customer." Thomson decided, therefore, to drop the subject altogether.

Gertrude, however, seemed to be spoiling for a fight and perversely began questioning Thomson—how had he met the woman, how had he come to know her. Finally, Thomson blurted out, "Through her having slept with one of my friends." There was a hushed silence, in which Alice gently murmured, "One doesn't say that." When Tchelitchev left with his sister shortly after, he gave Thomson a chilly, *"Bon soir, monsieur,"* and no handshake. As soon as the pair had left, Gertrude and Alice eagerly cross-examined him about the details and supplied him with information about the financial situation in the Tchelitchev household. He was reprimanded for using the phrase *coucher avec* in front of Choura, and Gertrude, blandly overlooking her part in the affair, informed him that while he had "a perfect right" to quarrel with Pavlik, he shouldn't have chosen her parlor for doing it. There were, it seems, rules to the game. Thomson's reinstatement, however, was' prompt. After the arrival of a bouquet of yellow roses he had sent to Gertrude and a meeting with the two women on the street, he was invited to call.

Having now taken Thomson's side, Gertrude informed Thomson "by inference that she found it intolerable of Pavlik to have first suspected me of an intrigue against him and then to have initiated one against me by asking her in effect to choose between us. And though she did not exactly offer me his head, it came off in the spring of '28." There were those, however—Bravig Imbs was one—who suspected Alice of maneuvering the break with the Russian painter because of an unflattering portrait he had painted of her, one that, so Imbs thought, gave her "a sleepy vulture look which was very strange." Another reason may have been the fact that Tchelitchev had taken up very heartily with Edith Sitwell, and although Gertrude had brought the two together, she may have regarded Tchelitchev's attentions to another woman writer as a gesture of disloyalty.

Gertrude's break with Eugène Berman was equally abrupt and no less final. Gertrude put down the cause as her lack of interest in Berman's work, following a visit he made to Bilignin in September, 1929. It was then, she maintained, that she decided Berman was not original enough to be the "creator of an idea." Berman, who could bristle at the mention of her name even forty-three years later, pronouncing her "an *impossible* woman, an *impossible* woman," attributed the break to Gertrude's overweening ego. During his stay at Bilignin that summer, he had made a sketch of Alice and several sketches of Gertrude in preparation for a portrait. Gertrude had been "a splendid and most attentive hostess" during the two or more weeks he stayed there. He had, however, been irritated on a few occasions, during Gertrude's posing sessions, when she broke off the sessions, saying that the artist was evidently not working well and that it would be better to postpone it for the next day. The break, however, had come when Gertrude gave him a copy of her word portrait "More Grammar, Genia Berman" to read. Berman knew very little English at the time and knew even less about Gertrude's writing style. He told her that flattering as her portrait was, he was not really in a position to understand or appreciate it. The next morning Gertrude asked him when he intended to return to Paris, since she had other guests arriving and would need his room. The request, Berman recalled, was so abruptly presented that it was almost a matter of taking the next train out of Belley, even though Gertrude had previously planned to take him to Annecy that day to buy paints and canvas so that he might start the portrait.

Despite Gertrude's peremptory behavior toward him, Berman's bread-and-butter letter to her from Paris was unusually warm and flattering. "My holiday with you," he wrote Gertrude on October 1, "thanks to your invitation will have done me the greatest good. I speak not only of the physical well-being which the good life at Bilignin did me, the absolute quiet, calm of air and sun and all the attentions with which you surrounded me and for which I owe you my deepest gratitude, but also of a good of another order—new impressions, fine landscapes, perhaps even new subjects, new forms and above all the great impression made upon me by your words on the mixture of true and false, the need of separating them, of concentrating every effort on that." Not only did he write her in this fashion, but he subsequently made her a present of a self-portrait she had seen and liked in his studio. The gesture, he claimed, was "a sort of courteous revenge" for her "very dictatorial and mean behavior."

Gertrude's remarks about the "mixture of true and false" make it clear that she was beginning to have reservations about the Neo-Romantic painters. As she explained later about them: "I do not care about anybody's painting if I know what the next painting they are painting looks like." She used a curious analogy to explain her dissatisfaction—the connoisseurship of dogs taken out to pursue their natural functions: "I am like any dog out walking, I want it to be the same and I want it to be completely unalike. The painting anybody was painting just then was not the same and it was completely alike."

The one exception was Francis Picabia, with whom she had resumed her friendship. In the early days she had thought him "too brilliant" and too talkative. She had not liked his painting then: "I did not care for the way it resembled Picasso and I did not care for the way it did not resemble him." But she began to take note of Picabia's exhibitions in the early thirties. Like most of the early Cubists, Picabia's manner changed considerably throughout the twenties—a difficult period for all the modernists—and by the thirties he was painting in a representational, somewhat surreal, style with fluidly drawn, transparent figures of humans, animals, and birds. What Gertrude seems to have appreciated in this pastiche of a style was the artist's attempt to solve "the problem that a line should have the vibration of a musical sound," with a way of "achieving the disembodied." She felt that Picabia, in a sense, did not have the "painter's gift," but that he was well on his way to solving the problem of "the vibrant line." Her observations about Picabia in

Alice and Gertrude at home, 1923. (Photo by Man Ray.)

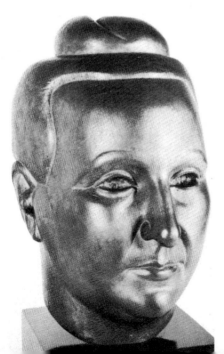

Lipchitz, *Gertrude Stein*, bronze, 1920. (Cone Collection, The Baltimore Museum of Art.)

Hemingway and his second wife, Pauline, on shipboard, 1934. (Courtesy the Bettmann Archive, Inc.)

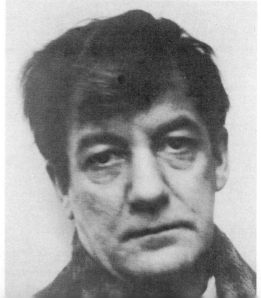

Sherwood Anderson, 1925. Photograph by Alfred Stieglitz. (Courtesy the Bettmann Archive, Inc.)

Zelda and F. Scott Fitzgerald. (Courtesy the Bettmann Archive, Inc.)

Virgil Thomson, Walter Piston, Herbert Elwell, and Aaron Copland, Paris, 1926. (Courtesy Yale Collection of American Literature.)

Juan Gris, 1922. (Photo by Man Ray. Courtesy Yale Collection of American Literature.)

Gris, *Flowers* (formerly *Roses*), oil and pasted paper on canvas, 1914. (Collection Mr. and Mrs. Harold Diamond, New York.)

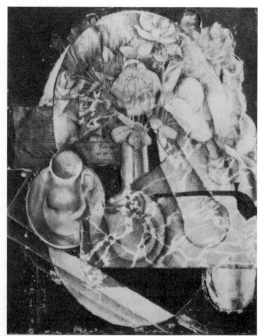

Alice and Gertrude in "Godiva," late 1920's. (Courtesy Yale Collection of American Literature.)

An outing with Pavel Tchelitchev, late 1920's. (Courtesy Yale Collection of American Literature.)

Berman, *Alice Toklas*, ink on paper, 1929. (Gilbert Harrison Collection of Gertrude Stein, Research Library, University of California, Los Angeles.)

Berman, *Portrait of Gertrude Stein at Bilignin*, pen and ink, 1929. (Collection of Georges Hugnet.)

With the poet Georges Hugnet at Bilignin, late 1920's. (Courtesy Yale Collection of American Literature.)

Taking the waters with Bravig Imbs at Aix-les-Bains, 1928. (Courtesy Yale Collection of American Literature.)

Following page: Greeting guests from the second-floor bathroom window at Bilignin, mid-1930's. (Courtesy Yale Collection of American Literature.)

the *Autobiography* when she tried to distinguish him from the surrealists, were somewhat stilted: "The surréalistes taking the manner for the matter as is the way of vulgarisers, accept the line as having become vibrant and as therefore able in itself to inspire them to higher flights. He who is going to be the creator of the vibrant line knows that it is not yet created and if it were it would not exist by itself, it would be dependent upon the emotion of the object which compels the vibration." That she could not pursue that line of generalization too much further seems to have occurred to her. "So much for the creator and his followers," she concluded.

With Georges Hugnet, Gertrude's quarrel—on the surface, at least—erupted over a question of equal billing. She had, herself, proposed the collaboration with Hugnet, her translation of his poem-sequence, *Enfances*, in March, 1930. During the summer months at Bilignin, she began work at her free-form adaptation, taking off from phrases and lines in Hugnet's text, to produce a compatible series of poems that nevertheless remained firmly entrenched in her own literary style. When she sent Hugnet a copy of her version in July—he was vacationing at Saint Malo in Brittany—the poet responded with a burst of enthusiasm and unusual affection:

Admirable Gertrude, what joy you give me in my solitude of sand and rock! I laugh at the sea which breaks out into white laughter all along the shore. This isn't a translation, it is something else, *it is better*. I more than like this reflection [of my poem], I dream of it and I admire it. And you return to me hundred-fold the pleasure that I was able to offer you. . . .

I love you with all my heart for so brilliantly translating me and I send you the last thought of my 23rd and the first thought of my 24th year.

The amity between them, however, was to be clouded when Hugnet visited Gertrude at Bilignin in September. While he was willing to speak of Gertrude's text as being something more than a "translation," in the practical matter of publication he wanted to refer to it as just that. The book was scheduled for publication in Paris by Jeanne Bucher, with both texts on facing pages and accompanied by illustrations by Picasso, Tchelitchev, Marcoussis, and Kristians Tonny. Hugnet proposed to refer to Gertrude's text as a *traduction*. Gertrude preferred "adaptation" or "transposition." When Hugnet suggested "free translation," Gertrude rejected it. The matter was left at a friendly impasse. In the meantime, it had been arranged that the two sets of poems would also appear in the literary magazine *Pagany*.

Gertrude and Hugnet had conducted one further piece of business during Hugnet's September visit. This was an edition of Virgil Thomson's music, for which Hugnet was to put up about $200, supplied by his father, with Gertrude supplying the remainder of the financing, a sum that might run as high as $800. Thomson had spent ten days visiting Gertrude the month before. Thomson had brought with him the newly composed Sonata no. 3 "for Gertrude Stein to improvise at the pianoforte." On leasing the house at Bilignin, Gertrude and Alice had acquired a piano, and Gertrude was in the habit, in the evenings, of improvising "sonatinas," on the white keys only, since she did not like the black keys or chords. While at Bilignin, Thomson had composed another score for one of her texts, this one for a film scenario, dealing with the acquisition of her dog, Basket, and titled *Deux Soeurs qui sont pas soeurs*, one of her rare ventures in writing in French. Thomson's visit had been remarkably enjoyable, and Gertrude's interest in promoting him by way of a volume of his music was clear evidence of her motherly interest in his career.

She had remained in Bilignin until late in November that year, and she kept in touch with the composer on the selection of the material for his forthcoming book. Thomson's plan was to publish three scores, a setting of a poem by the Duchess of Rohan, and *Le Berceau de Gertrude Stein*, the text for which had been written by Hugnet, as well as his recently composed score for Gertrude's film scenario. Hugnet, however, had objected to appearing between two women. In response to a letter from Thomson, outlining his difficulties in making up the book, Gertrude answered: "I am being quite thoughtful you see I want this book to do for you something like *Geography and Plays* did for me, make something definite and representative." She suggested he use the English text for his setting of her *Capitals, Capitals*, Bossuet's *Funeral Oration*, and Hugnet's *Gregorian Waltzes*. "Think this over very carefully," she added. "You see I want you shown at your best and want you saleable to those who are your natural audience."

When she returned to Paris, the matter was still stalled. Gertrude was still pumping for *Capitals, Capitals*, preferring to be represented by an English text, while Georges Hugnet, becoming somewhat truculent, was holding out for all French texts. In the meantime, Thomson had had a minor quarrel with Hugnet over not receiving a complimentary copy of a book by Pierre de Massot that Hugnet had published. When he came down with the grippe, following an argument with Hugnet, Thomson wrote Gertrude: "I'm afraid I have a *coeur sensible* after all. I thought I had won the little incident with Georges about Pierre's book and was proud of myself but I came home and went to bed of a grippe and so I guess I didn't after all."

Gertrude's reply was all motherly reasonableness:

Sorry about the grippe but look here I am not awfully anxious to mix in but you must not be too schoolgirlish about Georges and also after all he is

putting down his 5,000 francs of his father's credit for your book and hell it
is a gamble and he could do things with it that would be surer. . . . anyway
I love you all very much but I always do a little fail to see that anyone is
such a lot nobler than anyone else and we are all reasonably noble and very
sweet love to you.

Her own sweetness was to be tried within a few days when she
received the printed announcement for the forthcoming *Enfances*. Hugnet's name and the title appeared in large type, followed by the explanation, in much smaller type, "*Suivi par la traduction de Gertrude
Stein*." Gertrude objected strongly, and Hugnet responded with a letter
that was meant to be mollifying but that only irritated her more.
"Those whom I have questioned about the phrasing which you wanted
on the prospectus, both poets and publishers, have all said that your
name beside mine would give the impression of a collaboration, when,
don't you agree, there is no question of that." Hugnet went on:

You know, dear Gertrude, that I admire your translation, this "reflection"
as you call it of my *Enfances*, and nothing will take away the joy that I
felt in reading what you had written in the margin, if you wish, of my text,
still following it sufficiently so that I could make no objection, this summer,
to the translation which you read me page for page almost. . . .
I dare believe, my very dear Gertrude, that you will understand and even
approve of the importance which I attach to the responsibility for this work
living in me and to my prior right. . . . I dare believe also that an incident
of this kind will not affect our friendship which I wanted to be alive and
fresh.

Hugnet, however, had mistaken Gertrude's reasonableness, for it
seemed to be the case with her that on the eve of publication, or possible publication, she was apt to be her most temperamental. It was at
that stage that she had become peremptory and demanding with both
Mabel Dodge and McAlmon. Furthermore, it was hardly likely that
she would want her work considered in the marginal status to which
Hugnet referred. Hugnet, according to Virgil Thomson, was clearly
worried that he might be overshadowed by Gertrude's celebrity if the
matter were not made typographically plain.
Gertrude's response was simply to withhold her text from publication,
leaving the publisher, Jeanne Bucher, hanging. And when she encountered Hugnet in the Bucher Gallery, she pointedly refused to shake the
poet's hand. As she wrote to Thomson, following this incident: "The
last act of the drama was played this aft. you have been very sweet
about not saying I told you don't imagine I don't appreciate it."
Hugnet enlisted Thomson's help in arranging some settlement of the
matter, and Gertrude appeared obliging, on the condition that what-

ever typographic solution was arrived at, the two names were to appear in the same type size and there was to be no mention of a translation. Thomson worked out a version with Hugnet's name on top and Gertrude's on bottom, with the title equidistant between them. But in the meantime he had received a *petit bleu* from Alice, requesting that he telephone her immediately. She told him that whatever solution was arrived at, it would have to be "distinctly understood that it comes from Georges." Placed in the uncomfortable position of middle man between two temperamental authors, Thomson showed his typographical solution to Hugnet, who simply scribbled, "I accept" on it.

The proposed title page was presented to Gertrude at a Christmas Eve party at the rue de Fleurus. Thomson had waited until after the festivities—a dinner of venison, gifts of silk scarves and ties from Charvet for himself and Maurice Grosser—before bringing out the title page. Gertrude, looking it over, said simply, "This seems to be all right." She handed it to Alice, asking, "What do you think, Pussy?" Alice glanced at Hugnet's two words scrawled upon the page and said firmly, "It isn't what was asked for." The remainder of the evening passed without incident and no further mention of *Enfances*.

For some days after that evening, Thomson was ill and then busy practicing for a forthcoming concert. When he finally presented himself at the rue de Fleurus one evening, two weeks later, he was met by Gertrude at the door. "Did you want something?" she said very coolly. "Merely to report on my absence," Thomson answered. "We're very busy just now," Gertrude told him. Thomson next sent her an invitation to his concert, which included several pieces written to her texts, hoping that she and Alice would attend. He received one of Gertrude's cards, engraved "Miss Stein." Underneath the name were the words, written in Gertrude's hand, "declines further acquaintance with Mr. Thomson."

Bravig Imbs's head was the next to roll. Following the Hugnet-Thomson break, he was briefly excommunicated. (Both Gertrude and Alice, it appears, had suspected Imbs of influencing Thomson to take Hugnet's side in the affair.) But in January he wrote Gertrude and Alice a letter that was a blanket apology, without precisely knowing the reasons for his having been dropped:

Losing friends is a sad matter for me, as I have so few of them, and to lose such friends as you and Alice have been, is doubly hard. I remember you said once that all the young men went away, and I wondered at your statement, for I could not believe it possible. Perhaps the young men should go away for their own sakes, but I do not feel or care to be one of them.

Imbs concluded in a nearly abject tone: "Still, I should like to thank you for all the kindnesses you and Alice have shown me in the past, and to assure you of my loyalty. I am really deeply grateful, and my admiration and respect for you is limitless."

Imbs's reinstatement lasted only a brief time. In 1928, while traveling in Latvia, he had met a young girl whom he had brought back to Paris and married. Neither Gertrude nor Alice had taken warmly to Imbs's young bride, Valeska, but they had been invariably polite and helpful to her. And they had attended the christening of the couple's first child, a girl, bringing gifts of a silver mug and a jar of the honey from the monks at the Abbey of Hautecombe. One evening, in the spring of 1931, while visiting with Valeska at the rue de Fleurus, Imbs announced that Valeska was again pregnant and that their plans were for Valeska to spend the summer quite near Belley, where they had sometimes vacationed before. Imbs would join her, later in the season, when his vacation fell due. Gertrude, Imbs recalled, had taken his announcement matter of factly. But he had the impression that Alice, working on her needlepoint in the corner, may have glowered.

The next morning he received a telephone call. It was Alice. "Miss Gertrude Stein," Alice said, "has asked me to inform you that she thinks your plan of sending Valeska to Belley, considering Valeska's condition, a colossal impertinence, and that neither she nor I ever wish to see either you or Valeska again."

Imbs listened, stunned.

"Miss Gertrude Stein," the steely voice at the other end of the phone went on, "was polite enough to restrain herself last evening, owing to the presence of Valeska, but she thinks your announcement of sending Valeska to Belley without any other friend in the region than ourselves was the coolest piece of cheek she has ever encountered." Imbs was further informed: "Your pretension is unpardonable. You must not come to the house or write, for neither visit nor letter will be accepted. We want never to see you again." And with that, there was the loud bang of the receiver. The years of all the young men of twenty-six were over.

V

In 1930 Gertrude was fifty-six. She was a celebrated personality, interviewed, quoted, and lampooned, yet, except for her contributions to the short-lived literary magazines, seldom published. She had reason to believe Henry McBride's dictum: "There is a public for you but no publisher." In her late middle age she had begun to brood about eternity, identity, her unpublished manuscripts. She had cause for thinking about death. Juan Gris had died, cut off in his prime, without having achieved the success she felt he had deserved. After a long career as a writer and journalist, Mildred Aldrich had died with only a brief success that had not lasted into her final years. Gertrude's circle of old acquaintances was narrowing. In September, 1929, she had learned of the death of another old friend. Michael had written to her that Claribel Cone had died suddenly of pneumonia at Lausanne. Etta had been with her—the pair had spent the summer in Europe—and Etta was making the journey back to America with her sister's body. A special train had been hired to bring the coffin from Lausanne to Paris— even in death, Claribel was to travel first class.

Gertrude had seen the two sisters only infrequently during the twenties. On their stops in Paris, Claribel and Etta had visited at the rue de Fleurus. Gertrude had arranged to sell them various items from her collection—the Cone sisters had bought the Marie Laurencin group portrait in the summer of 1925 for $2,150—as well as various items of antique furniture for which she and Alice no longer had room. Earlier, in 1924, she had tried to interest Etta in buying the manuscript of *Three Lives*. Gertrude had heard that John Quinn's collection of modern authors, including Joyce, had brought large sums in a recent auction. In a somewhat embarrassed letter, Gertrude wrote Etta that she was offering her first refusal on the manuscript, considering Etta's personal association with the book. She was asking $1,000 for it, and she didn't "suppose" that Etta would be interested in paying "any such price." She confessed that she thought it "kind of foolish," but she wouldn't have wanted Etta to think she would sell it to someone else first. Etta had declined, pleading poverty. She said she was "putting all I can spare of what I have left of my income in a Renoir painting."

Gertrude had had occasion to remember Claribel during that summer of 1929 in Bilignin, for Dr. Marian Walker and her family had paid her a visit. They had talked about Claribel and their medical-school days. When she learned of Claribel's death, she wrote immediately to Etta, who was staying at the Hôtel Lutetia in Paris, waiting for the ship that would transport Claribel's body to America:

My very dear Etta:
    I have just had word from Mike of the death of Claribel and it has saddened me terribly, I was awfully attached to her . . . everything she did had an extraordinary quality all her own. I had not seen so much of her in recent years but she made a very important and rather wonderful part of my Baltimore past and Dr. Marian Walker and I were talking of it all and of her when she was here just a couple of months ago, and so strangely enough Claribel had been very near me this last summer, and now Etta you know how I understand your loss and feel for it, do take my love and my fondest thought of Claribel.

Etta's reply was brief—she was quite possibly still stunned by the loss of her elder and clearly dominant sister. She thanked Gertrude for her "understanding sympathy" and remarked that she would "like so much to hear you talk of my sister some day when I am more calm within."

In 1932 Gertrude. was to make a gift of the typescript of "Two Women," her word portrait of Claribel and Etta, to the Cone collection. For Claribel had left her five rooms of art—her collection of Picassos, Matisses, and Cézannes—to the Baltimore Museum of Art, but with the provision that "the spirit of appreciation of modern art in Baltimore becomes improved." In the meantime the collection was to remain in Etta's custody until her death, unless Etta deemed that the "spirit of appreciation" had improved sufficiently before that.

"When a Jew dies he's dead" was Gertrude's maxim; there was no solace in ideas of eternity. In her late middle age the sight of her manuscripts mounting up in the cabinet seemed a reproach that could, on occasion, as it had with William Carlos Williams, bring on an attack of ill temper. Although she was to deny that she wanted to be a popular success in America, she did want official recognition there. She had never realized Mildred Aldrich's great ambition for her—to appear in the pages of the staid *Atlantic Monthly*—though she had at times submitted manuscripts to the magazine with the usual results. "My dear Miss Stein," the editor, Ellery Sedgwick, had replied, in 1919, "Your poems, I am sorry to say, would be a puzzle picture to our readers. All who have not the key must find them baffling, and—alack; that key is known to very, very few." In another letter, the bedeviled *Atlantic* editor had suggested that she had misjudged the American public: "Here there is no group of *literati* or *illuminati* or *cognoscenti* or *illustrissimi* of any kind, who could agree upon interpretations of your poetry. More than this, you could not find a handful even of careful readers who would think that it was a serious effort." In 1927, when Gertrude, still trying, submitted her "Portrait of Cézanne," Sedgwick confessed that although he was not "unsympathetic with the present and the future," he had read her "Impression" of the French painter a dozen times with unsatisfactory results. "The little rhythms which ripple through your picture do not, to my heavy wit, call up the faintest suggestion of the exciting impression of a Cézanne." He even expressed a certain wary gratitude for Gertrude's efforts on his behalf: "You have taken a friendly interest in my training, and as an example of adult education it is an experiment worth trying! Perhaps you would some day write me an entirely intelligible comment upon these paragraphs of yours. I ask this in all seriousness, for as I near my second childhood, I yearn increasingly to be educated."

After a decade Gertrude became defensive on the subject of her lack of success in America. Interviewed by Eleanor Wakefield, a reporter for the *New York World* in May, 1930, she claimed: "Lack of popular success in America is the last of my worries. I am working for what will endure, not a public. Once you have a public you are never free. No one who is ever to be really great succeeds until he is past forty, be he inventor, painter, writer or financial genius. The early setbacks aid the eventual greatness. Quick success is killing." At fifty-six she had long since passed the threshold age to greatness.

Charges that she was incomprehensible rankled her still. "All this foolishness about my writing being mystic or impressionistic is so stupid," she told Miss Wakefield. "Just a lot of rot. I write as pure, straight, grammatical English as any one, more accurate, grammatically than most. There isn't a single one of my sentences that a school child couldn't diagram." What irritated her even more was her reputation as an "expatriate." She recalled an "East Side New York youth" who had interviewed her previously and had made the mistake of asking her about "this expatriate business." "I turned on him," she told Miss Wakefield, "and nearly scared him to death."

I said: "Listen to me young man; you don't know anything about it. Don't you dare call me an expatriate. I am more American than you could ever hope to be. You weren't even born in America; you've never been any place in America but New York. I know all about it. I have generations of Americans behind me. Americanism is born in me." Well that poor boy was so confused when I got through with him he forgot everything else he wanted to ask me. But I couldn't help it. I was furious. My patriotism is fundamental, instinctive.

The charge that she was a coterie writer, nurtured in exile by a group of *literati*, had been a burden for Gertrude throughout the twenties. She and Alice bemoaned the fact that there were no publishers adventurous enough to publish her work steadily and thereby create a public for her —as dealers such as Kahnweiler had done for Picasso and even Gris. As a possible measure, Alice had begun to think seriously about bringing out an edition of Gertrude's unpublished works. She had even asked Gertrude to think of a name for the edition, and Gertrude laughingly suggested, "Call it Plain Edition,"—which was the name they eventually decided upon. Gertrude took the venture seriously; it was obvious that she was not going to find the adventurous publisher she had been seeking. Perhaps, too, she had been nettled by Robert McAlmon's charge that if she had such faith in her own writing, she could well have afforded to publish it herself, rather than expect others to assume the risks. In order to finance the Plain Edition, Gertrude was obliged to sell one of her loveliest early Picassos, the 1905 *Woman with a Fan*, to the New York art dealer Marie Harriman. Alice had been upset by

Gertrude's decision. It broke her heart, she said. "And when she told Picasso it made me cry. But it made it possible to publish the Plain Edition."

Alice assumed management of the new venture; Gertrude was to be its sole and honored author. They asked friends for advice on business details. William Aspenwall Bradley, the Parisian literary agent—later to become Gertrude's agent—advised Alice to subscribe to *Publishers Weekly*; Ralph Church, Sherwood Anderson's friend, warned her to "stick to the booksellers, first and last." Through another friend, Alice acquired an old publisher's list of booksellers in the United States and began sending out circulars for the first volume, *Lucy Church Amiably*, a meandering romantic novel that Gertrude had begun in 1927, her first attempt in the genre since completing *The Making of Americans* in 1911. Like most of her later novels, it is aimless in structure and somewhat puerile in style—a charming, picaresque adventure in language, perhaps, but a poor choice, it would seem, for building a new public for her work. The book was printed in an edition of a thousand copies, bound in blue boards, carrying the title page, in black letters, on its cover: *Gertrude Stein A Novel of Romantic beauty and nature and which Looks Like an Engraving Lucy Church Amiably*. Inside there was a brave announcement: "The Plain Edition an edition of first editions of all the work not yet printed of Gertrude Stein." The publication date was January 5, 1931.

Gertrude, who had wanted the book to look like a child's schoolbook, had been satisfied with the results; she was even more pleased when she saw it in the windows of Parisian bookstores. Each day she reported back from her walks with new sightings. Alice, more practical-minded, was dissatisfied with both the printing and binding, which had been done by the Imprimerie "Union" in Paris. The spine of the book, she found, broke easily, and the covers did not close properly. For their second choice, *How to Write*, they decided to take the book to the Darantière firm in Dijon, the printer who had done McAlmon's edition of *The Making of Americans*. Gertrude wanted the book to look like an eighteenth-century copy of Sterne she had picked up in London, and Alice chose a light-gray laid paper and dove-gray binding that, if it did not match the blue and white paper of Gertrude's Sterne, did give the small-format book a period look. *How to Write* was also printed in an edition of a thousand copies and was issued in November, 1931. Earlier, in May, Alice had also brought out a limited edition of Gertrude's ill-fated "translation" of Georges Hugnet's *Enfances* under Gertrude's title, *Before the Flowers of Friendship Faded Friendship Faded*. It was printed in an edition of 120 copies by Durand, printer at Chartres.

None of these productions quite satisfied Alice, however. *How to Write*, she felt, was better produced, but she was not happy with the binding. When she complained to the printer, he told her, "What do you expect, Madame? It is machine made, it is not done by hand." It became, for both Gertrude and herself, "a classic answer" for the supposed benefits of the machine age.

It was not until she met Maurice Darantière, however, that Alice produced the editions she wanted. Darantière had left the Dijon firm and had opened his own printing establishment on the outskirts of Paris. They had met the printer at a party one evening, and Alice told him: "You must get me out of a mess, I have two books to print for Gertrude and I need you to help me. I want them to be inexpensive so that they can be sold in the United States for two dollars and a half and leave me with postage and duty and a possible profit." Darantière said he could print the books in monotype, a less expensive process, and he came up with the idea of binding the books in the usual French paper covers but placing them in cardboard slip cases. The next two Plain Edition volumes—*Operas and Plays*, a collection of Gertrude's theatrical pieces, and *Matisse Picasso and Gertrude Stein*, a lengthy early word portrait of herself and her painter friends—were printed by Darantière and issued in 1932 and 1933, respectively. The latter volume also included two more early unpublished works, *A Long Gay Book* and *Many Many Women*. Alice now had a more up-to-date list of booksellers, but she had cut back the print run for her last two volumes to 500 copies each —a sure indication that the books were not moving as readily as they had hoped.

The Plain Edition was a brave venture and, possibly, an act of self-gratification by an author who had, for years, been frustrated in her attempts to get her work before the public by means of the established publishing houses. It turned out to be a stop-gap measure, for by 1933 Gertrude had written the book that was to make her a best seller.

CHAPTER THIRTEEN

The Last Touch
of Being

I

"If there had not been a beautiful and unusually dry October at Bilignin in France in nineteen thirty two followed by an unusually dry and beautiful first two weeks of November would The Autobiography of Alice B. Toklas have been written. Possibly but probably not then." Gertrude's question and answer about her best-selling book was largely a rhetorical game. She recalled Victor Hugo's remark that if it had not rained on June 17, 1815, "the fate of Europe would have been changed." But Hugo's remark, she observed, was not true. "If you win you do not lose and if you lose you do not win." Still, she did have the feeling that, somehow, time and the season had conspired to produce *The Autobiography of Alice B. Toklas*, the book that changed her fortunes.

Her long years in Paris, her friendship with artists and writers who were now international celebrities, and her own eccentricities would have made her memoirs of interest to many publishers. Friends had often suggested that she write them, but Gertrude's answer had always been, "not possibly." There were several reasons why the subject would have appealed to her at this point in her career. She had come to some natural break in the routine of her life; she had severed connections with the young writers and artists who had surrounded her, her older acquaintances were dying—it was a time for taking stock of herself. The question of her identity as a writer and an American was much on her mind during these years; "I am I because my little dog knows me," a nursery rhyme answer, was a persistent leitmotiv in her poetry during this period. She had long been aware of that "last touch of being that a history of anyone can give." And she seemed to view the subject of personal identity as irrevocably fixed in one's daily life. "Except in daily life nobody is anybody," she claimed. What she was to write in *The Autobiography of Alice B. Toklas* during the six weeks of an unusually temperate fall season at Bilignin was a monument to her daily life with Alice, a history of their salon and of their adventures with the great and near great. At first she had suggested that Alice write such a book. "Just think," she would tease Alice, "what a lot of money you would make." Gertrude had even begun to make up titles: *My Life with the Great, Wives of Geniuses I Have Sat With, My Twenty-Five Years with Gertrude Stein*. In the end, Gertrude wrote the book herself.

The form of the autobiography was an unusual one. Gertrude cast it as a personal history written from Alice's viewpoint and, as closely as possible, in Alice's words. Alice's voice, both real and imagined, had been a perennial voice in Gertrude's poetry over the years, her terse declarative sentences cutting through Gertrude's sometimes numbing repetitions and word-playing like a call back to reality. The form of the book, therefore, was a natural. And there was, too, a certain malicious advantage in Gertrude's adoption of this alter-ego device. In her handling of Hemingway, when she reported her conversations with Sherwood Anderson, branding the younger writer as "yellow," she could present her own tempered appreciation of his gifts, her "weakness" for Hemingway, together with Alice's suspicious dislike. She could have it both ways.

The *Autobiography* presented a crowded canvas, dense with personalities, ranging from figures such as Picasso, Matisse, Hemingway, Fitzgerald, Anderson, who had become world famous, to all the minor but interesting people who had ever moved into Gertrude's orbit—Constance Fletcher, the author of *Kismet*, their Moroccan guide Mohammed, their maidservant Hélène. They were all sketched in rapidly, surely, and humorously, their queer observations about life, about others, reported. And since the book was written from Alice's viewpoint, Gertrude could treat of her own personality, though in milder terms than she accorded Hemingway, exposing a few of her quirks—her dislike of Picasso's painting on first sight, her peculiarities as a driver, her claims to genius. The book did more than present a gallery of personalities, it chronicled a quarter of a century of the Parisian art world and the literary world in a historic period; the revolutionary exhibitions of the

Fauves and the Cubists, the always intemperate and volatile world of the little magazines during the twenties, the lives and hard times of exiles and expatriates after the Great War. The *Autobiography* became, in fact, a masterpiece of the genre—a history of the period, written, as with most things Gertrude wrote, from a vantage point unique to herself. When the book was published, there were to be many charges of misstatements of fact, misdating, misquoting; but considering that it was written at Bilignin in a six-week period, away from the corroborating evidence of letters and documents, it is amazing that it proved to be as accurate as it was—as accurate, say, as the also-inaccurate memoirs of others who wrote about the period, some of them in response to her book.

In mid-November, Gertrude had alerted her agent, William Aspenwall Bradley, to the existence of the book; she had taken him on the year before. Bradley, alert to the possibilities of the book, had written her enthusiastically: "Of course I shall be *delighted* to see Miss Toklas' Autobiography and hope you will send it to me as soon as it is completely typed. Or, better still, you might send it in two instalments, so that I can get on with the reading as fast as possible." By November 26 he had received the second installment and had replied immediately that "wild horses couldn't keep me from reading it at once! I am now looking forward to seeing you both as soon as you return to Paris, next week."

Bradley placed the book with Harcourt, Brace for publication in America, with no difficulties at all. And within a few months Gertrude received word that one of her lifetime ambitions was to be realized—the *Atlantic Monthly* would be publishing an abridged version of the book, prior to publication. On February 11, 1933, Gertrude's old nemesis, Ellery Sedgwick, wrote her heartily: "There has been a lot of pother about this book of yours, but what a delightful book it is, and how glad I am to publish four installments of it! During our long correspondence, I think you felt my constant hope that the time would come when the real Miss Stein would pierce the smokescreen with which she has always so mischievously surrounded herself. . . . Hail Gertrude Stein about to arrive!"

A month later the assistant editor, Edward Aswell, who had been assigned the task of editing the book down to the "sixty percent" that Bradley had allowed for magazine publication, wrote her in even more glowing terms. Aswell told her that he had begun reading her book at ten o'clock one morning and continued reading until he noticed that it had become dark in the room. Thinking that a storm had come up, he glanced out the window and discovered that it was five o'clock in the evening. "I had forgotten time, forgotten my lunch, forgotten a dozen things I had meant to do that day, so entirely had I been caught up by

the spell of your words. . . . If you could do this to an editor, of all people the least susceptible to the magic of print, what, I wonder, will be
the effect of your story on the general public?"

Gertrude was about to become a popular author. She had achieved
one of the ambitions that had dogged her throughout the twenties:
a perfect collaboration. And she had achieved it by collaborating with
herself.

The success of *The Autobiography of Alice B. Toklas,* however, was to
be a mixed blessing. The financial success of the book was more than
welcome. For the first time, Gertrude was to realize a considerable income from her writing. Bradley's arrangements with Harcourt, Brace,
which brought out the book in the late summer of 1933, had included
a $500 advance against royalties, with royalties of 10 per cent for the
first 5,000 copies and 15 per cent thereafter. The book ran to four
printings by 1935, with 11,400 copies. The first printing of 5,400 copies
was sold out by August 22, 1933, nine days before the book was officially published. In addition, the Literary Guild offered it as its September selection to subscribers, printing its own independent edition. Gertrude had asked Bradley expressly to place the English edition with
John Lane's Bodley Head Ltd., "for sentimental reasons, after all John
Lane was the only real publisher who had really ever thought of publishing a book for me, and you have to be loyal to every one if you do
quarrel with anyone." In 1934, there was a French edition, translated
by her friend Bernard Faÿ, issued by Gallimard, under the prestigious
Nouvelle Revue Française imprint. And in 1938 an Italian edition,
translated by the novelist Cesare Pavesi, was published by G. Einaudi.
The serialization of the book in the *Atlantic Monthly,* which she had
also asked Bradley to arrange, had brought only a modest $1,000 for the
four installments, but it was the success of having achieved a long-held
ambition that counted there. Gertrude's royalties from Harcourt, in all,
had amounted to $4,495.31. The sale to the Literary Guild brought her
$3,000 more.

In a burst of enthusiasm, Gertrude had bought a new eight-cylinder
Ford and "the most expensive coat made to order by Hermes" for her
poodle, Basket, as well as two studded collars. For the first time, she
and Alice engaged two servants, a couple, Mario and Pia, who insisted
on giving both the studio and the pavilion a thorough cleaning, as well
as repainting the studio. "There is no doubt about it," Gertrude commented, "there is no pleasure like it, the sudden splendid spending of
money and we spent it."

The success of the book and its serialization, beginning in the May,
1933, issue of the *Atlantic Monthly,* gave her a certain leverage with

publishers. She had authorized Bradley, optimistically, to arrange for the publication of her other manuscripts, languishing in her studio cabinet. During a trip to the United States, Bradley had persuaded Harcourt to bring out an abridged version of *The Making of Americans*. The editing had been done by Faÿ, who had earlier made a French translation with the Baroness Seillière for publication by the Librairie Stock. Gertrude was to regret having hastily signed the Harcourt contract for *The Making of Americans*. Within a few days Bennett Cerf cabled her, offering to publish both *Three Lives* and *The Making* in his Modern Library editions, proposing to publish the complete version of the latter in a Modern Library Giant. Gertrude agreed to the publication of *Three Lives*, which was issued in 1933, and proposed a collection of some of her recent and older pieces, to be titled *Portraits and Prayers*, which Cerf accepted and published the following year.

From America came word of the *Autobiography*'s runaway success. Carl Van Vechten, who had followed the serialization and then read the book, had "nothing but words of praise for it. It seems to me, indeed, that I have talked about nothing else since the first part appeared in the Atlantic. What a delightful book it is! I am showering copies on my happy friends." "I think," he concluded, "you'd better come over and take the tribute due you and be photographed."

Van Vechten's was but one of a chorus of voices that suggested that Gertrude come to America and be lionized. Sherwood Anderson expressed his "joy" on reading the serialization, though he was aware of the book's caustic moments, and felt "a bit sorry and sad on the night after that number when you took such big patches of skin off Hemmy with your delicately held knife. But great joy in the whole performance." He added: "Why don't you and Alice come to America as a great adventure next summer, Ford around, come see us and others?" There was another book in it for her, Anderson suggested: "Do another all about people seen and felt, as you see and feel them, all kinds of people, their talks, your talks with them, impressions—well, you'll know." It would be an opportunity for her to have "one big taste, square meal of America again."

Henry McBride wrote her about someone who had been displeased. He had been lunching with Matisse in New York—the painter had made a trip to inspect his murals in Dr. Albert Barnes's museum in Pennsylvania. When McBride suggested that the painters ought to be pleased at the *"bonne réclame"* Gertrude's account would give them in America, Matisse had shuddered visibly. McBride added: "He would prefer, it seems to be spoken of sepulchrally, as though he were Poussin and you were Bossuet."

Gertrude was already aware that the book might cause consternation among some members of her Parisian circle. When she returned to Paris after writing it, she had telephoned Picasso, who was eager to have it read to him in translation. He and Olga had come to the rue de Fleurus one afternoon. Gertrude and Picasso sat on the sofa while Gertrude read aloud the early descriptions of the studio and her meetings with the artists and the bohemian life-style at the Bateau Lavoir. Picasso, listening avidly, corrected her description at one point, saying that there had been three swords hanging on the studio wall. When Fernande came into the story, Olga became noticeably disturbed and then stood up, announcing that she did not know "that woman" and that she intended to leave. Picasso did not follow her out, but motioned Gertrude to go on reading. Gertrude told him that he must go after his wife. Picasso said, "Oh." Gertrude answered, "Oh," and Picasso left. It was not until two years later—when Picasso and Olga had separated—that Gertrude saw the painter again.

Leo Stein, living in Settignano, wrote to his old friend and confidante, Mabel Weeks, about the book. He thought it "maintained very well the tone of sprightly gossip rising at times to a rather nice comedy level. But God what a liar she is!" Most of his corrections, however, consisted of emending Gertrude's vague recollections of childhood events. Gertrude was four and a half, not three, when their parents took them to Paris. She was fourteen and not eight when she had attempted to write a Shakespearean play with such bits of stage direction as "The courtiers make witty remarks." Leo seemed concerned that even that minor adolescent adventure should be credited to him. He had made the suggestion of writing the play in the first place, having recently bought a volume of Elizabethan plays. "Practically everything that she says of our activities before 1911," Leo maintained, "is false in fact and implication, but one of her radical complexes, of which I believe you knew something, made it necessary practically to eliminate me."

The reader who was most justifiably disturbed by the book was Hemingway. He had been the target, as well, for a malicious remark in Margaret Anderson's recently published memoir, *My Thirty Years' War*, in which he was characterized as a pink and white rabbit. Hemingway branded both assaults as menopausal phenomena and mentioned, disdainfully, the "feathered friends" with whom Gertrude had taken up after her break with him. Writing to Ezra Pound in July, 1933, he magnanimously acknowledged that he had gotten some good advice from Gertrude as well as a lot of rubbish. He threatened that it would be a big day when he came to write his own memoirs.

While she was writing the *Autobiography* during that dry October in Bilignin, Gertrude often asked Alice if she thought it would be a best seller. Alice had always responded that she did not think it was "sentimental enough." Now Alice had been obliged to revise her opinion. It was, after all, "sentimental enough." The success of the book had brought with it a flurry of social activities; where before they had entertained their friends at the rue de Fleurus, they were now invited out. They attended evenings, for example, at the salon of Marie Louise Bosquet, who made a point of bringing together figures from the older French literary establishment and the young men such as René Crevel. Gertrude and Alice were now making engagements a week in advance, sometimes two a day. As Gertrude observed, comparing her new celebrity with that of the young men she had recently purged from her circle: "We did not yet use a tiny engagement book and look at it in a nearsighted way the way all the young men used to do as soon as they were successful but we might have."

The book had received warm critical notices. Edmund Wilson, reviewing it in *The New Republic*, praised its "wisdom, its distinction and its charm." He sensed Gertrude's suspicion of popular success: "Success, for her seems to imply some imposture and deterioration." And he noted the change her new book seemed to have brought about with the broad public. "Hitherto, though her influence has always been felt at the sources of literature and art, her direct communications with this public have been intermittent and blurred, and, on the whole, neither the readers of modern books nor the collectors of modern painting have realized how much they owe her." William Troy, writing about her position in American literature in *The Nation*, discussed her with unusual seriousness, finding that she was "not nearly so isolated and eccentric a figure in American letters as is often believed." He placed her within the tradition of esteemed American authors such as James, Poe, Hawthorne, and Melville, who had "an orientation from experience toward the abstract, an orientation that has been so continuous as to constitute a tradition, if not actually *the* American tradition." It was a judgment that, more or less, concurred with Gertrude's estimate of herself.

Having claimed that "lack of popular success" was the least of her worries, Gertrude was now obliged to worry about it. She was being pressed to revisit America and harvest her new-found popularity. Bradley had been pressing her to accept a series of lecture engagements in America, as a means of furthering the sales of her book. But it was a move that left Gertrude reluctant and indecisive. She had never cared much about public lecturing, and while her English lectures had gone well, they had been held before smaller college audiences. Jo Davidson had once told her that one had to "sell one's personality" in order to succeed, and she had countered by saying, "only insofar as that personality expressed itself in work." It bothered her that the American public was more interested in her personality than in her work when, she reasoned, it was her work that had made her interesting in the first place. She did not want to be exhibited as some kind of literary curiosity.

Nonetheless, Bradley had gone to the trouble of bringing an agent from an American lecture bureau around to the rue de Fleurus. Gertrude found the man exceedingly solemn. In America he was a publisher of religious books and school texts. During his European trips, he engaged celebrities for the American lecture circuit. His most recent prize was an international celebrity, the Princess Bibesco. When Bradley told him that Gertrude would undoubtedly be a popular lecturer because of her forthcoming autobiography, the man had nodded solemnly and commented, "Interesting, if true." Gertrude, who was looking for any excuse to relieve her indecision about an American trip, decided then and there that "if lecture agents were like that" she would definitely not go. Asked what she would require if she agreed to lecture, she made the conditions difficult. She told the man that Miss Toklas, of course, would have to go and their two dogs, Basket and Pépé, the latter a Mexican chihuahua, which had been given to them by Picabia. But she added that she did not think "any of us will really go over." Bradley was clearly disappointed. He told Gertrude she was making a mistake. Gertrude, however, held firm. For the moment, at least, the worrisome problem of an American trip was shelved.

II

The most disturbing problem connected with Gertrude's success, however, was that she began to develop a writer's block. After completing the *Autobiography*, she had become restless and uncertain. In Paris she began to take lengthier walks than usual. At night, accompanied by Basket, she would wander up one street and down the next, conversing with neighbors, observing the life of the quarter. In the summer of 1933, spent as usual in Bilignin, the problem became particularly acute. She was unable to write anything. She spoke of this period ruefully: "I had written and was writing nothing. Nothing needed any word and there was no word inside me that could not be spoken and so there was no word inside me." Her explanation of her dilemma in an article for *Vanity Fair* was diffident and even lighthearted, but the problem was real. There was, too, an element of chagrin, for having told all the successful young men that success had spoiled them, she was now facing the same problem. "What happened to me was this," she explained. "When the success began and it was a success I got lost completely lost. . . . I did not know myself, I lost my personality. It has always been completely included in myself my personality as any personality naturally is, and here all of a sudden, I was not just I because so many people did know me. It was just the opposite of I am I because my little dog knows me. So many people knowing me I was I no longer and for the first time since I had begun to write I could not write and what was worse I could not worry about not writing and what was also worse I began to think about how my writing would sound to others, how could I make them understand, I who had always lived within myself and my writing."

The summer at Bilignin was hectic and tiresome: a succession of new servants, a succession of house guests and visitors. The Italian couple, Mario and Pia, whom they had engaged in Paris, felt that the house in Bilignin was too big. Having just cleaned the smaller pavilion and studio, they did not look forward to attacking the large manor house with the same thoroughness. Moreover, the move to Bilignin had taken place in the late spring—a period of drenching mountain rains—and Mario and Pia had become depressed. They left, complaining that they had been "deceived" by their mistresses.

Next Gertrude and Alice engaged a mountain couple recommended by the local priest. The marital status of the various servants who passed through their lives that summer was a subject of constant interest to Gertrude, who suspected that, even though recommended by a priest, the mountain couple were not married. They did not remain long: "She had everything the matter so the doctor said whom we finally called in to see her and he [the doctor] took her to the hospital . . . and he the husband went out in the hallway and fell and so he decided he would leave us and her." They next engaged a Portuguese woman and her Alsatian mate. This couple had been found for them, in Paris, by their friend Georges Maratier. The new couple arrived, unexpectedly, with a little girl, who, according to Gertrude, climbed the stairs very "gracefully." The wife was an extremely good cook, but she suffered from a kidney ailment. The husband, who loved "automobiles and poetry," vowed that he would serve Gertrude and Alice for the rest of their days, but first extracted from Gertrude a promise that if anything should happen to him, she and Alice would undertake the future care of his family. Everyone in the family became an object of suspicion for sleeping out under the trees at night, a habit that the conservative villagers thought distasteful. Gertrude, however, felt it was dangerous for the ailing wife who was such a good cook. They soon left, as well, after the country doctor had had to be called in for the wife. They left separately, the wife taking the little girl with her. The husband hung around the village for a few days and then disappeared.

Still in need of servants—and with guests arriving—Gertrude and Alice rode to Lyon, where they secured a Polish woman and her Czechoslovak husband. The wife, although somewhat mournful in appearance—she claimed she could never be happy anywhere—turned out to be a very good cook. The husband was presumably a good mechanic—a talent certified to Gertrude when he promptly fixed their newly installed water closet, which had flooded. But he preferred to be a *valet de chambre,* feeling it was somehow undignified to lie under an automobile with one's legs sticking out. For a time, at least, the servant problem had abated.

In July they had a visit from Picabia and his current companion, Olga Mohler, whom Gertrude referred to as Picabia's Swiss wife. Gertrude felt that Picabia's virtue at that moment was that he kept on painting while many others seemed to be stalled. She and Picabia had discussed Cézanne during his visit, and Gertrude was surprised to hear Picabia deny the importance of Cézanne, whom he felt—at least in his own early work—was a distraction. Everyone of that period, Gertrude felt, had been influenced by Cézanne, and here was Picabia denying it. It was one more element of uncertainty in that summer: "I thought I understood all about what we had done and now understanding Picabia made me start all over again."

A few weeks after the Picabias left, Janet Scudder announced that she was driving to Bilignin with a friend for a few days' visit. Gertrude did not mind, because Janet would only stay a few days on any visit. Moreover, she enjoyed Janet's rough-and-ready seriousness. But Gertrude had advised her to take two days to come from Paris, and Janet, having made up her mind to do it in one day, had arrived quite late for dinner, causing the Polish cook to look even less happy than usual. Janet's view of the servant problem was that it was difficult to find one person who would be "both useful and pleasant," and next to impossible to find two such people and those two married to each other. "Better give it up," she advised Gertrude.

For lunch on the following day, Gertrude had invited a pair of neighbors, Madame Caesar and her English womanfriend. Madame Caesar was a "big good-looking woman," who wore trousers. Her English friend wore trousers as well, and, usually, a Basque cap. The pair raised chickens and ducks on a nearby farm. Since Madame Caesar had a passion for things electrical, they had acquired an electric incubator. Having raised an extraordinary number of chickens and ducks by means of this device, they built "a very pretty little village" for the chickens and ducks to live in. So far as Gertrude knew, she and Alice were the only ones who were on friendly terms with Madame Caesar and her friend—except for another neighbor, Madame Steiner, who had lived with Madame Caesar before the arrival of the English friend. The ménage, it appears, was considered somewhat irregular in the region of Belley.

The day of the luncheon proved to be a progression of events that puzzled and amused Gertrude for several years and that she was never to resolve satisfactorily in her writing. Janet had wanted to paint, and her friend, worried about the state of Janet's Ford, had thought it should be looked at by a mechanic. When she attempted to start the car, however, it would not turn over; the motor was dead. Gertrude said she would take her own car and drive to Belley to get Monsieur Humbert, the garage man. But when Gertrude attempted to start her own Ford, she found that it was dead, too. Gertrude said she would telephone the garage man. But the phone was mysteriously dead as well. "Then I went out to speak to every one," Gertrude recalled in *Everybody's Autobiography*. "The Polish woman was there and I said well and she said yes and she said Jean is always like that when anything like that can happen. What I said. Blood on the dining room floor she said." The meaning of that cryptic phrase was never to be explained. There was another phone in the village, "but nobody in the house had known about that," Gertrude added ominously. She telephoned Monsieur Humbert, who came to repair the cars. When he examined them, he found someone had put water in the gas tank of Janet's car. In Gertrude's he found a piece of dirty cloth in the distributor cap and several of the spark plugs broken. "Who is that man?" he asked Gertrude, gesturing at Jean the valet. Gertrude explained. Monsieur Humbert motioned the valet over to the car and pointing down, said, "Well." Jean didn't answer. "I guess you better get rid of him and say no more about it," the garage man told Gertrude.

Just at that moment, Madame Caesar and her friend arrived. And when Gertrude walked into the dining room, she found Francis Rose, the English painter, standing there with a painting in his hand. She had known Rose for only a few years, and their relationship had been a testy one, interrupted by frequent quarrels. He was acquainted with the Neo-Romantics and painted romantic landscapes in a too-obvious primitive vein. Gertrude had seen his work in the galleries and had not liked it, but, still, could not forget it. Then, one day, in a fit of indecision, she asked the dealer the price of one of his paintings, a picture of a poet by a waterfall, and bought it. Picasso, when he saw her purchase, asked how much she had paid for it. Gertrude told him that she had paid three hundred francs. Picasso's comment was blunt: "For that price one can get something quite good." Thereafter, Gertrude bought his work steadily; by the time of her death, she had acquired nearly a hundred of Rose's paintings. In Gertrude's theory of names: "Anybody called Francis is elegant, unbalanced and intelligent" and Francis Rose "was all that." Alice found him a "difficult guest" when he visited Bilignin, as he often did. But they had recently quarreled with Rose, and more particularly with his friend Carley Mills, a young Californian. So Rose's arrival, in the midst of that day's confusion, was a complete surprise.

Rose was driving from Cannes to Paris and had brought the painting as an impromptu peace offering. Gertrude kissed him and asked how he had gotten there. Rose told her that Carley was waiting outside in the car. Since she and Alice had "completely quarreled" with Mills, Gertrude did not invite Rose to stay. She walked him to the car, kissed him and thanked him, shook hands with Mills, and saw them off. The interrupted lunch was finally served. Then Jean and his Polish wife were dismissed. Once more Gertrude and Alice were faced with the servant problem. This time they hired "a very serious old pair" from Lyon. The man was an old soldier who seemed to polish the furniture quite well; his wife was an old French cook.

Gertrude's most welcome guest, during that troubled summer of 1933, was Bernard Faÿ. Of all the young men she had met in the late twenties, Faÿ was one of the few with whom she had no serious arguments. A professor of history, a student of American history and culture—he had studied at Harvard—Faÿ lectured weekly at the University of Clermont-Ferrand, which was not far from Bilignin. René Crevel had spoken of him as an admirer of Sherwood Anderson's writing, and Virgil Thomson had known him for several years before Gertrude met him. A member of an ultraconservative Catholic family with connections, Faÿ smoothed Thomson's way, as a journalist, to the principal musical events of the Paris season. Well placed in literary and social circles, Faÿ became an indefatigable promoter of Gertrude's reputation in the publications to which he had access and with French publishers. An author himself, he produced a long, evocative biography of Benjamin Franklin and another on George Washington. Gertrude spoke of her relationship with Faÿ as one of "the four permanent friendships" of her life.

She had not been immediately impressed with the French historian, however, when she first met him in May, 1926. Faÿ had invited her to tea at his apartment on the rue Saint-Florentin in Paris. Gertrude felt, then, that they "had nothing in particular to say to each other." The situation changed when Sherwood Anderson visited that winter and Gertrude had several occasions to meet Faÿ again. She then found him "stimulating and comforting." Faÿ became a frequent visitor to the rue de Fleurus and a favored guest at Bilignin, where he was usually invited to stay. On other occasions, when he was working at his own writing, he usually put up in the Benedictine monastery in the nearby Abbey of Hautecombe.

Gertrude's change of heart probably resulted from the fact that in the interim between their first meetings, Faÿ had boned up on her writing. In his first invitation, asking Gertrude to tea, he had claimed to have "read eagerly everything" that she had written. But his later preface to the abridged French edition of *The Making of Americans*, which he had translated, told a somewhat different story. What had impressed him, on their first meeting, was Gertrude's laughter in the midst of a crowded and noisy room: "It came after a joke made by a young man to whom I wasn't listening, but this sudden burst of laughter suddenly seemed to give brilliancy to the words of the young man and make them exceedingly amusing. These few seconds suddenly became like a gem, brilliant, hard, real." It was then, Faÿ admitted, that "I began to feel for her this deep friendship which I have for her, together with great admiration." After this meeting he had "wanted to read her books. I had been told that she was modernistic and that she was the only Anglo-Saxon writer of today who had the sense of the modern as we have it in France. I found out right away that I hadn't been misinformed, her books had a flavor which was unique, and even when I didn't understand all their words I always enjoyed their tempo."

Faÿ's preface was that of an ideal disciple, dipping into the Steinian stream of repetitions and run-on sentences, presenting the Stein case, as it were, straight from the horse's mouth, comparing Gertrude's search for a "continuous present" in her writing to the inferior, dead styles of other contemporary writers: "As our food is made up only of dead animals (the best being somewhat rotted), in the same way death rules in literature and rotted things are the most agreeable to the reader's mind." He dealt out praise: "Amongst all the English writers of today, she is the freest, the one who has been able to dismiss most cheerfully the habits of yesterday and the empty dreams of tomorrow, and to ignore the silly tricks of today." And he dealt with Gertrude's personality as flatteringly as he dealt with her prose, declaring, "The greatest and most beautiful of her gifts is her presence." Faÿ's visit in the summer of 1933 was more welcome than usual, since he was in the process of translating *The Autobiography of Alice B. Toklas* for publication by Gallimard.

That summer, in Bilignin, there were two tragedies—one of which occurred during Faÿ's visit—which fixed it in Gertrude's mind as a "queer summer." The first involved the illustrious Hôtel Pernollet, where, one morning, Madame Pernollet was found lying on the cement courtyard, barely alive. She died five days later in the hospital; local rumor had it that she had been sleepwalking when she fell. Gertrude was prepared to accept this version, but she also felt that it might have been suicide: "Once in a while she said to us, well she did not say it, but once in a while she did say it as if it was, not the work, but something was overwhelming." The mystery was never solved for Gertrude.

The second tragedy involved Madame Caesar and her English friend. One morning, Gertrude received a call from a neighbor saying that Madame Caesar's friend had been found dead in a ravine and would she go to their house. Bernard Faÿ went with her. There were various people at the home of Madame Caesar, including the electrician who had installed the incubator, his wife, and his mother-in-law, "a very large woman who was not moving and she was all in black as if it might be evening."

The Englishwoman, they learned, had just returned from a vacation in England. On the previous evening, she and Madame Caesar had discussed plans for the following day. That morning, she had been found dead with two bullets in her head, her Basque cap laid very carefully on a rock beside her. Gertrude, playing detective, was to investigate this point carefully. The local doctor, whom she queried, thought it impossible for someone to shoot himself twice in the head; but from veterans of the war she learned that if a man at the front "wanted to kill himself he did shoot himself twice." At Madame Caesar's, Gertrude had attempted to puzzle out the Englishwoman's motivation, saying rather callously that if Madame Caesar's English friend had wanted to kill herself, "she should have done it on the boat coming over and not waited until when she did do it it was most inconsiderate of her." And Madame Caesar had concurred, saying, "And she always had been so considerate of me."

After the tragedy, Gertrude and Alice saw little of Madame Caesar. She came once to Bilignin, to pay a call, but as Gertrude noted, "Any one was frightened of her and about her." Madame Caesar lived, after that, as a recluse in her house with the "pretty little village" for the ducks and chickens. Madame Steiner never called on her anymore; no one visited her—except the electrician's wife.

Gertrude wrote about the strange events of that summer twice; once in her first attempt at a detective story, *Blood on the Dining Room Floor,* and again in *Everybody's Autobiography. Blood on the Dining Room Floor* is something of a nonbook. It purports to deal with the strange and antic events of that summer of 1933, chiefly the Pernollet tragedy, the servant problem, and a few related local matters, but in its bare declarative manner, it tells little more than the events themselves, with a few hints and guesses. Gertrude appears to have begun it late in the fall at Bilignin, thus breaking through the writing block from which she had been suffering. The aimless and distracted style of the book suggests that her difficulties in writing may have been very real. Like *Lucy Church Amiably, Blood on the Dining Room Floor* reads, at times, like a child's reading exercise: "How many houses and families do you know about now. One two three four five. And how many crimes. One two three. And how many possible crimes. Six." It was a meager production and was not published until 1948, two years after Gertrude's death, in a very handsome limited edition by the Banyan Press.

That Gertrude herself was not entirely satisfied with her initial effort at recounting the events of that summer, one can judge from the fact that she felt the need to relate them once more in *Everybody's Autobiography,* written in 1936. "It was a funny thing that summer so many things happened and they had nothing to do with me or writing," she noted. "I have so often wanted to make a story of them a detective story of everything happening that summer and here I am trying to do it again." This time she dealt with the events of the summer, including the strange tale of Madame Caesar and her friend, in a more satisfying reportorial fashion. But they are, chiefly, local mysteries that derive their interest largely from the fact that they reflected her own unsettled state of mind.

III

The break between Gertrude and Virgil Thomson was mended for eminently practical reasons. Thomson had found prospective backers for a production of their opera, *Four Saints in Three Acts*. A. Everett Austin, Jr., the director of the Wadsworth Atheneum in Hartford, had offered the museum's soon-to-be completed auditorium for a production in the 1933–34 winter season. And Austin was eventually to secure financial backing for it from among a group he had formed earlier with the quaint name The Friends and Enemies of Modern Music. Early in 1933 Thomson was already at work preparing the orchestration of his score.

Gertrude, who had heard about the forthcoming production indirectly, had advised her agent. Bradley, in turn, wrote Thomson in January, saying that Miss Stein "would be happy to have further particulars concerning the production itself, your arrangements with the director, Mr. Austin etc. etc." Thomson, as a generous gesture, because their collaboration had been a close one, had at first offered, through Bradley, a fifty-fifty split on the royalties between the composer and librettist, an offer that Gertrude happily accepted. By May they were corresponding with each other directly—Gertrude being then in Bilignin —since working out details by way of a third party had proved cumbersome. But Thomson had reason to regret the generosity of his offer on the contract and brought up the subject again, pointing out that it was a far from standard arrangement. "It has since been called to my attention by the *Société des Droits d'Auteurs*," he wrote Gertrude on May 30, "that such an arrangement defeats its own end and that the contract commonly made in France allowing two-thirds to the composer and one to the author is designed to establish that very equality." This was the new arrangement he wanted to propose.

Gertrude, answering promptly, held firm to their original arrangement, justifying it on her reputation:

My dear Virgil,
Have just received your letter. I think, in fact, I wish to keep to the original terms of our agreement, half share of the profits. It is quite true

that upon you falls all the burden of seeing the production through but on the other hand, the commercial value of my name is very considerable and therefore we will keep it 50–50.

On other points about the production she was more amenable, agreeing to the out-of-door setting and hoping that they might be able to have a procession. "It all sounds very hopeful and about all these things," she wrote, "I am quite ready to accept what seems best to those who are doing it."

Thomson's reply was a tart litany of his efforts on behalf of the opera and the lack of support from her quarter, with the exception of Mrs. Crane, "who began very practically indeed but didn't continue very long." He set about enlightening her:

And dear Gertrude, if you knew the resistance I have encountered in connection with that text and overcome, the amount of reading it and singing it and praising it and commenting it I have done, the articles, the lectures, the private propaganda that has been necessary in Hartford and in New York to silence the opposition that thought it wasn't having any Gertrude Stein, you wouldn't talk to me about the commercial advantages of your name. Well they *are* having it and they are going to *like* it and it isn't your name or your lieutenants that are giving it to them.

"If you hadn't put your finger on a sensitive spot by mentioning this to me," the composer added, "I should never have done so to you. However, I've got it off my chest now and the fact remains that even were the situation reversed, a 50–50 contract would be, as far as I know, absolutely without precedent."

Flush with her newly begun success from the *Autobiography*, Gertrude chose to answer in a mood of sweet reasonableness, wishing, evidently, to avoid another break, but remained fixed in a Steinian repetition on the question of the contract:

My dear Virgil,
    Yes yes yes, but nous avons changé tout cela, however the important thing is this, the opera was a collaboration, and the proposition made to me in the agreement was in the spirit of that collaboration, 50–50, and the proposition that I accepted was in the spirit of that collaboration 50–50 and the proposition that I continue to accept is the same.

Gertrude continued to remain reasonable when Thomas later asked to make some cuts in the text in order to introduce some needed instrumental passages: "Yes, of course, you are to make the cuts, the burden of making it a successful performance lies upon you. I am very pleased that everything is arranged, Bradley will be sending me the agreement and I will sign it, and I hope it will all be as successful as possible, we certainly deserve it, do we not."

Well before the actual production, *Four Saints in Three Acts* became the object of speculation and interest in the press. The popularity of Gertrude's *Autobiography*, as Gertrude had suspected, had stirred up a good deal of curiosity about the forthcoming opera. But so, too, had Thomson's decision to use an all-Negro cast. It was a point raised by an interviewer from the New York *World Telegram*, to whom Thomson explained that "Negro singers have the most perfect and beautiful diction," a quality he deemed necessary for the difficult Stein libretto. "I have never heard a white singer," he added, "with the perfect diction and sense of rhythm of a Negro." To another reporter, Thomson commented that Negroes had "a more direct and unself-conscious approach to religious fantasy." The *New York Herald Tribune* sent Joseph Alsop, Jr., to the rehearsals held in a church basement in Harlem. Alsop, presumably expected to do a humorous piece on the entertaining subject of Gertrude Stein, reported that "it begins to look as if the mysterious woman so long laughed at would at last be justified to the world—and by Harlem." Listening to a lyric passage, "A scene of changing from the morning to the morning," the young reporter imagined that it brought "a whole dawn into the Sunday school room."

The idea of a Negro cast apparently at first troubled Gertrude, who felt it might introduce a sensual element that might be out of character with the opera, particularly in a Maypole dance in the second act, when it was planned to have the Negroes appear in transparent gowns. But Thomson allayed her fears, telling her that "the movements would be sedate and prim," assuring her that if the effect was more emphatic than intended, "petticoats would be ordered immediately for everybody."

The black and brown bodies were a matter of concern, too, to the production's scene and costume designer, Florine Stettheimer. Miss Stettheimer, who with her sisters Ettie and Carrie ran an intellectual salon in New York's Alwyn Court—Marcel Duchamp and Carl Van Vechten were among their regular visitors—was an eccentric painter whose style was at the same time amateurishly primitive and chic, who seldom, if ever, exhibited during her lifetime. For the opera, she had devised an extravagant setting with a sky of cellophane looped and draped like an opera curtain, with palm trees whose foliage was made of huge bows of pink tarlatan. For the principals' costumes, she had chosen liturgical colors—cardinal reds, purples, and greens, and for the combined funeral and wedding march a black-canopied baldachin with ostrich plumes, the whole production to be flooded with the whitest light possible. The designer was worried that the dark Negro skins would tone down the brightness she wanted, and for a time it was rumored in the press that she was considering whitening the Negro faces, an almost surreal touch, which did not come to pass. At the last moment, she did order dozens of white gloves, feeling that the bare hands were "inelegant."

For the producer, Thomson had engaged John Houseman, then an unsuccessful playright, later to become the producer, with Orson Welles, of the Mercury Theater. For choreographer he had suggested Frederick Ashton, a young dancer he had met in London. None of the principal shapers of the event, including Alexander Smallens, who conducted the orchestra, received salaries for their efforts; it was a labor of love. As early as two months before the production, Thomson was reporting enthusiastically to Gertrude. "Everything about the opera is shaping up so beautifully," he wrote her in December, 1933, "even the raising of money (It's going to cost $10,000), that the press is champing at the bit and the New York ladies already ordering dresses and engaging hotel rooms."

The invitational preview on February 7, 1934, and the official opening the following night were gala affairs. The New Haven Railroad ran special afternoon parlor cars to accommodate the New York society women and members of the art and theater worlds who entrained to Hartford to hear the opera and participate in the opening of the Wadsworth Atheneum's new wing and the large Picasso exhibition that opened concurrently. The audience arrived by train, plane, and Rolls-Royce. But the most unusual mode of conveyance was the bubble-shaped Dymaxion car from which Buckminster Fuller stepped, in dinner jacket, escorting Clare Boothe and Dorothy Hale.

As the houselights dimmed in the theater, there was a roll of drums. The red velvet curtain parted to reveal Beatrice Robinson-Wayne, Saint Thérèse I, kneeling in a full purple gown, with a double chorus of angels and saints, backed by the tufted blue cellophane cyclorama. There was a gasp of astonishment and delight at what appeared to be a huge valentine. From the moment the chorus intoned the opening lines,

To know to know to love her so.
Four saints prepare for saints.
It makes it well fish.
Four saints it makes it well fish.

there was a sense of mounting excitement. The various tableaux—Saint Thérèse and her alter ego being photographed, Saint Thérèse painting an Easter egg—brought occasional tittering, as did that moment in the third act when Edward Matthews as Saint Ignatius stepped forward and, with a male chorus, sang the passage "Pigeons on the grass alas."

The line, like Gertrude's famous observation about the rose, became the most popular and ridiculed line of the libretto. When, after some deliberation between the commère and compère and the assembled saints and angels, whether there would be a fourth act, the compère finally announced, "Last Act," and the chorus responded with an emphatic, "Which is a fact," the audience broke out into storms of applause. There were curtain calls after curtain calls. Henry Russell Hitchcock, the distinguished architectural historian, according to various newspaper reports, smashed his opera hat, tore off his collar and ruffled evening shirt, shouting huzzahs and calling for the composer. Carl Van Vechten, who had been in residence in Hartford during the run-throughs, cabled Gertrude immediately, then wrote her the next day: "Four Saints, in our vivid theatrical parlance is a knockout and a wow. . . . I haven't seen a crowd more excited since Sacre du Printemps. The difference was that they were pleasurably excited. The Negroes are divine, like El Grecos, more Spanish, more saints, more opera singers in their dignity and *simplicity* and extraordinary plastic line than *any* white singers could ever be. And they enunciated the text so clearly you could understand every word."

The superb diction of the Negro singers was to be a leitmotiv in the reviews of the opera, both in its Hartford run and in its later month-long engagement at the Forty-Fourth Street Theater in New York. Thomson's choice of the Negro cast, the *New York Times*'s reviewer reported, "seemed amply to have justified itself last night." "A spirit of inspired madness," the reviewer claimed, "animates the whole piece." Paul Bowles, then a young composer and only later a writer, whom Gertrude had met two summers before with Aaron Copland, sent her batches of notices after the opening of the New York run, but then conceding that "there were so many references to it" he stopped. *Variety* reported that *Four Saints* had received more coverage than any other opening of the season. Gertrude's publisher, Alfred Harcourt, who wrote her about the "thrilling evening and a really splendid performance" he had witnessed in March, went on to tell her: "Toscanini was in the orchestra chair behind me and I noticed that he seemed completely absorbed in the performance and applauded vigorously."

If the Negroes' superb diction had made the text plainly audible, it did not make it more comprehensible to the majority of the audience. There were a few who appreciated the libretto, like the gentleman who reportedly rose up during the premiere performance to shout, "It's like Grand Opera, only it's got more sense!" William Carlos Williams thought Thomson's music a "doubtful aid to Stein's prose." It showed up its weaknesses. He preferred the more revolutionary Stein, "smashing every connotation that words have ever had, in order to get them back clean." The critic Stark Young called it "The most important event of the season—important because it is theater and it flies off the ground, most important because it is delightful and joyous and delight is the fundamental of all art, great and small."

While kinder critics were inclined to view the text as some form of inspired nonsense like Mother Goose rhymes, there were those who thought it came close to madness. Lawrence Gould, a "consulting psychologist" interviewed by the *New York Evening Post*, compared Gertrude's passage about Saint Thérèse in a storm at Avila to the ravings of a patient printed in a recent medical text on insanity, suggesting that it was close to "Echolalia," a symptom of a particular form of psychosis known as "acute mania" in which the patient repeats "ad libitum, with slight variations, a word or phrase that frequently is meaningless except to the trained psychoanalyst."

Gertrude's old friend Henry McBride, who had sent regular dispatches about the opera's progress in Hartford, and who saw it several times more in New York, wrote her when it closed at the Forty-Fourth Street Theater. He regretted the closing, particularly since Gertrude herself had not seen it, "for positively you can have had no conception of the way it visualized itself for us." Recalling his earlier injunctions against success for her in America, he had had some second thoughts about his usefulness in promoting Gertrude Stein any longer. "I thought last autumn when the Autobiography made such a terrific success that I was finished with you and that I would have no further occasion to write about you (for all the population seemed delighted to have established contact with Gertrude Stein) but this confusion about the Four Saints shows me there is still some work to be done by somebody."

The irony connected with the spectacular success of *Four Saints* was that the person least involved with its production—Gertrude herself— reaped the major benefits. Although one dance critic had found it "the most interesting experiment that has been made here in many seasons and the most enlightening," Frederick Ashton received no interesting or worthwhile offers as a choreographer while he was in the United States. And Thomson was to receive little benefit from his fame at the moment. "No music publisher wished to issue *Four Saints* in score," he observed in his autobiography. "No lecture agent cared to take me on. And colleges were as silent as the clubs." For Gertrude it was a far different story. The fanfare surrounding *Four Saints* was to add immeasurably to what was to become her triumphant march across America.

IV

Early in January, 1934, Gertrude had a first taste of public lecturing, as distinct from the college lectures she had delivered at Oxford and Cambridge. Her friend Bernard Faÿ was scheduled to deliver a lecture on "Democracy and President Roosevelt" at a dinner meeting in Paris. But Faÿ had been detained in Copenhagen, and Gertrude had agreed to read the lecture in his place, although she was suspicious that Faÿ had prearranged the situation. After reading Faÿ's lecture, Gertrude had agreed to entertain questions from the floor. An American society woman, baiting bear, had stood up to denounce modern writers and painters, claiming that they were merely trying to "create a sensation," that "their inspiration comes from without instead of within." She touched a sensitive nerve.

"Don't be silly," Gertrude shouted. "Have you read my latest book?"

"No," was the defiant answer.

"Well, you better go and read it!"

"People today," Gertrude continued, "like contemporary comforts, but they take their literature and art from the past. They are not interested in what the present generation is thinking or painting if it doesn't fit the enclosure of their personal comprehension. Present day geniuses can no more help doing what they are doing than you can help not understanding it, but if you think we do it for effect and to make a sensation, you're crazy. It's not our idea of fun to work for thirty or forty years on a medium of expression and then have ourselves ridiculed."

The audience, slightly stunned by her mild outburst, discovered that she would also entertain questions along political lines. Politics became a subject that she attacked, as a celebrity, with a certain verve at first. But in time she became wary, conceding that on the subject of politics she was often wrong. But in the question period following Faÿ's lecture, she rendered a few political judgments. Republicans, she maintained, "are the only natural rulers" in the United States. "When a Democrat gets in, he only does so because of the singular seductiveness which he possesses." "Cleveland had it and Wilson had it," she claimed. She then went on to deliver one of those opinions that she would be obliged to reconsider: "Roosevelt was honestly elected, but he is not half as seductive as his predecessors, so I don't think he will be elected a second time."

Politics, particularly American politics, was still very much on her mind when she was interviewed later that spring by Lansing Warren, a reporter for the *New York Times Magazine*. Warren, who visited the rue de Fleurus shortly before Gertrude and Alice left for Bilignin, was admitted by Trac—the first and most memorable of the string of Indo-Chinese cooks and servants Gertrude and Alice were to hire. He was introduced to Alice, who he was pleased to discover was "a very real and efficient personality despite the doubts that were expressed as to her existence when the autobiography appeared." Readers, it seemed, thought that Alice was a fictional entity. Alice's duties as a secretary, Warren learned, had been "vastly increased." She was obliged to take care of the mail, "arriving in ever growing quantities."

The reporter had also been greeted by Basket, who made a show of "rather friendly hostility." Gertrude offered an explanation: "Basket is a great watchdog when he thinks about it. But he doesn't always remember and so he has to be all the more demonstrative when he does." Warren noted the air of order and sanity in the studio room. It seemed to be confirmed by Gertrude herself, although she turned impish when her more outrageous remarks seemed to stun him. The most outrageous was her contention that Hitler should have been given the Nobel Peace Prize. Gertrude claimed that Hitler was "removing all elements of contest and of struggle from Germany. By driving out the Jews and the democratic and Left elements, he is driving out everything that conduces to activity. That means peace." She reverted to an old line, one that she had given Bertrand Russell during World War I: "The Saxon element is always destined to be dominated. The Germans have no gift at organizing. They can only obey. And obedience is not organization. Organization comes from community of will as well as community of action. And in America our democracy has been based on community of will and effort."

She thought intellectuals were badly suited for governing: "They have a mental obliquity. By that I mean that they are diverted by their intellects, by their ideas and their theories, from responding to the instincts which ought to guide practical rule. The best governors are always the men who respond to instinct, and in a democracy this is more necessary than anywhere else." There were really only "two wholly sincere democracies," she told Warren, "and those are the American and the French."

In an expansive mood, settling back into the huge sofa in the studio, Gertrude also settled back into her role as an American. She didn't approve of the "stringent" immigration laws in America. "We need the stimulation of new blood. It is best to favor healthy competition. There is no reason why we should not select our immigrants with greater care, nor why we should not bar certain peoples and preserve the color line, for instance. But if we shut down on immigration completely we shall become stagnant." Then, as if she had already been transported across the Atlantic and were an American in residence, she told the reporter from the *Times*, "We have got rid of prohibition restrictions, and it seems to me the next thing we should do is to relax the severity of immigration restrictions."

Gertrude was near the breaking point with her agent, William Bradley. He wanted her to make an American lecture tour and was urging her to write another autobiography. She insisted that she wanted him to find a publisher for the book she was then working on, *Four in Amer-*

ica. Probably by way of getting advance publicity for the book, she informed Lansing that she was now engaged in writing a book, *Four in America*, dealing with Washington, Wilbur Wright, Grant, and Henry James, in which her ideas "about government and American democracy" would be expounded. It would not, she told her interviewer, with a blithe disregard for the book's numbing repetitions and non-sequitur arguments, be "difficult to read."

The American trip had been on her mind for months. There was no doubt about her curiosity about American life. She eagerly questioned every visitor from America—and her French friends who returned from visits there—about every detail of American life, from the meals they had eaten in restaurants and homes, to the look of American drugstores, a phenomenon she seems not to have seen but was very curious about. She had long since made up her mind that it was not practical for a writer or artist, on a limited income, to live in America. In answer to a questionnaire, "Why do you live abroad," published in *transition*, Gertrude had replied that "the United States is a country the right age to be born in and the wrong age to live in . . . a rich and well-nourished home but not a place to work." America, she contended, was "the most important country in the world—but a parent's home is never the place to work in." The question of a visit to her native land, however, seemed to be inextricably bound up with the practical advantages of making a lecture tour while she did so. And of that, she was clearly frightened. But with the perversity of the human species, having quarreled with her agent, who was causing her so much anxiety, she soon decided to accept a lecture engagement. It was during the crowded summer of 1934, at Bilignin, that she made up her mind.

It was a busy summer; there were to be several visitors—Bernard Faÿ, a new young American, James Laughlin, later the publisher of the vanguard New Directions Press, but then fresh from Harvard and the staff of the *Harvard Advocate*, and her old friend Carl Van Vechten. Van Vechten had developed a consuming passion for photography, and his visit, early in the summer, became a whirlwind session of portrait taking: Gertrude alone on the terrace; Gertrude sprawled out in her deck chair with Basket in her lap and Pépé couched above her head; Alice alone in the garden; Gertrude and Alice sitting together on the parapet wall beside the little garden house with its bower of roses. But the most important event, according to Gertrude, was the coincidence of a visit from "The Kiddie" and a flat tire. It was then that she made up her mind.

The Kiddie was William G. Rogers, a reporter for the Springfield, Massachusetts, *Union* and the former American doughboy whom Gertrude and Alice had befriended when he was on furlough in Nîmes in 1917. Gertrude had not seen or heard from him in the intervening years since the war, but she had mentioned the Kiddie and the trips they had taken to visit the Roman ruins during the war years in her *Autobiography*. Rogers had been told, then, that "Miss Stein writes," but it was not until the later twenties, when he had seen a photograph of Gertrude in the rotogravure section of a Sunday paper that he made the connection between the celebrated writer and the woman he had met years before. After the Hartford performance of *Four Saints*, which Rogers attended, he wrote Gertrude a long letter, recalling their trips to Arles and Les Baux and the "rather wild place supposed to have been the site of Caesar's defeat of Vercingetorix." Gertrude responded immediately:

My dear Kiddie: We always called you that you were so young and tender in those days. I don't know that you knew that we called you so, but we did. It was nice hearing from you and they were nice days. . . . Do you remember those cigarettes called Darlings with which you used to supply us. . . . It all does not seem long ago at all. . . . Do you remember we used to look out on the map for beauty spots, and make our duty coincide with them. The best wishes to you always and write again. Miss Toklas will write you very soon.

In April, Rogers renewed his acquaintance with them in Paris. Although they customarily left for Bilignin the last week in April, they had been delayed that year. Rogers was invited to dinner and to meet the guests who came to the studio afterward. Gertrude stood by him, beaming, at his elbow, each time he was asked to relate, in French and English, his account of the performance of *Four Saints*. They asked him to spend a weekend at Bilignin after they had settled in.

Rogers's weekend extended to four days. He was charmed by the atmosphere at Bilignin, the leisurely breakfasts on the terrace, the cups of steaming hot coffee served with freshly baked croissants and brioches. By the time the Widow Roux brought out the tray for another round of coffee, Gertrude would be up, throwing open the shutters of the second-floor bedroom that had been converted to a bathroom. With her close-cropped hair, dressed in a nondescript robe, sending her greetings to her guest on the terrace below, Gertrude looked like some papal figure conferring a blessing. During his stay, Rogers was driven to Aix-les-Bains, taken on shopping excursions to Belley. One afternoon they visited Gertrude's friend the aged Baronne Pierlot, who lived in an ancient chateau in Béon, across the valley from Bilignin. She had, once, as a young woman, been complimented by Anatole France, and was a friend of the poet Paul Claudel, of whose strenuous Catholicism she disapproved. The meeting with the aged but spry Madame Pierlot was to have humorous repercussions, for, as Gertrude wrote to

Rogers later, the old lady had been so taken with the young American she was proposing to marry him off to a cousin of hers, a young intellectual, who, so Gertrude maintained, "was very excited" about the prospect. Good-naturedly, Rogers answered that his only condition was that the young lady would have to be as charming as Madame Pierlot herself.

"Mme. Pierlot was much pleased at your answer," Gertrude informed him, "and she says but the young lady and myself have the same ideas, and I said, but Madame Pierlot it is not ideas but charm to which my young friend referred. Ah ça, she said." The young lady, Gertrude told him, had been present and wanted to be told about it again and again. "But Mme. Pierlot was right when she said Ah ça"—meaning that on the score of charm, the Baronne was not sure she could produce.

On the Tuesday that Rogers was scheduled to leave, they made a dash for the car in order to make the train at Virieu. One hundred feet from the gate at Bilignin, they had a flat tire. By the time they arrived at the station, the train had gone; there would not be another for two hours. Waiting in the tree-shaded stationyard, that summer afternoon, Gertrude and Alice began telling Rogers of their indecision about making the American trip and their dissatisfaction with the arrangements Bradley had proposed. In their on-again, off-again dealings with Bradley, so Gertrude informed Rogers, she had rejected a proposal for an over-all payment for lecturing, and they were now considering a tour for which Gertrude would be paid on a percentage basis. Gertrude opened up with a barrage of questions: "What did America think of her as a person and as a writer? What would America think of her as a lecturer? How would the press react? . . . Would six lectures offer enough variety?" Rogers assured her that she would "achieve a great popular success; newspapers would be friendly, or at least curious, which from one point of view amounted to the same thing." Gertrude was reassured: "We always believe everyone as we listen to them. We believed him." She was convinced that Rogers would see to it that things would be arranged as she wanted them. He had even suggested boarding the two dogs at his mother's farm in Springfield while Gertrude and Alice toured, a plan that he was grateful fell through, later, when Gertrude and Alice, deciding that the two dogs "might get sick from the change of climate," left them with a vet near the Bois-de-Boulogne.

On the train, Rogers had second thoughts, imagining Gertrude, after his optimistic predictions, "squeezed insultingly into half-inch fillers at the bottom of all the back pages. I was afraid I should have kept my mouth shut." Back in America, it was clear that Rogers was expected to do his part. Over the next four and a half months, Gertrude wrote him regularly, keeping him posted on the progress of the lectures she had begun writing, assigning him errands:

There have been so many alarms and excursions concerning the lectures. [Bradley's] proposition of a lecture bureau, disguised a little but still there, I had definitely refused before and have continued to refuse and we go on with what we talked about when you were here and had so pleasantly missed your train. Bernard Faÿ has suggested to me a young man Marvin Ross to do the clerical work and arrange the dates. He lives in Moriches, Long Island. As you do know very well what I want and how I want it, I would like it if you could that you would get into communication with him and help it all along.

She gave Rogers an account of her lecture writing thus far:

I am solemnly going on writing the lectures. I have finished one about pictures, one about the theater and am now doing the one about English literature. Then there are three about my work, Making of Americans, 2, Portraits and so-called repetition and what is and what is not, 3, Grammar and tenses. I get quite a bit of stage fright while doing them but if one must one must.

In her next letter she took up the subject of the young man from Moriches:

Do write again to Marvin Ross, I have split with Bradley he is not acting for me any more, we could not see eye to eye in this matter, I to I if you like. . . . I am writing now on my fifth lecture, I tried the English literature one on a private [group] that is to say on friends here last night and I guess it's pretty good.

Rogers had taken photographs of her while at Bilignin, and Gertrude commented on these in the course of their correspondence:

Bernard Faÿ is here and we talk lectures and plans all day long and things are getting quite nicely decided, and he likes your photos and so do we. . . . Faÿ suggests that you tell Ross that you have taken these photos and that he may use them, Faÿ thinks he will have need of quite a number. You have a weakness for taking two at a time but that I suppose is both New England efficiency and economy.

Gertrude had put her guest, James Laughlin, to work making abstracts of her lectures for the newspapers. For a novice, she was displaying considerable expertise, while blandly expecting others to get done what she expected to be done. "These abstracts," she wrote Rogers, "you would use as the basis of some articles and they would probably help a lot. As I say we all think that your plans are good plans and are looking forward to more. You must remember too about the traveling business that it is always [e]xpensive for two people that have to be considered and that also we have to be reasonably comfortable if I am not to get too tired."

Gertrude had some misgivings about her lectures, so she informed Rogers: "The lectures are good I have just been reading them to Fay and the Harvard boy but they are for a pretty intelligent audience and though they are clear very clear they are not too easy." As a result, she was to stipulate that she would not lecture before audiences of more than five hundred, a decision that was to be a source of disagreement later.

News of her impending lecture tour brought further offers. Her first lecture was scheduled to be given at the Colony Club in New York City, under the auspices of the Museum of Modern Art. And she was slated to deliver three lectures at Columbia University. She had agreed to lecture at Amherst College and at the Choate School as well. She turned down an offer, $1,000 a lecture, from a commercial lecture bureau that wanted her to lecture in the Midwest. As she explained to a reporter from the *Herald Tribune* in Paris a few weeks before her departure: "There is not enough money in the world to persuade me to stand up before a horde of curious people who are interested in my personality rather than my work." Even though her audiences would be limited, she conceded that she would "probably collapse from stage fright."

Bernard Faÿ, useful as ever, had booked passage for her and Alice on the *Champlain*, sailing from Le Havre on October 17. As a celebrity, she had been given staterooms at a reduced rate. In the meantime there had been other practical matters that had had to be attended to. Under Alice's supervision there were new dresses to be made—a dress for lecturing in the afternoons, one for lecturing in the evening, dresses for traveling. Gertrude ordered several pairs of new shoes at Chambéry. In Belley she had had a special leather case made to carry her six lectures. With all of the plans going forward irreversibly, she began to have moments of doubt. These were underscored by a letter from her old friend Janet Scudder, who thought the trip was a mistake. Janet wrote her: "I don't at all approve of your going to America. I think that you should follow your usual serene habits and allow America to come to you. In other words, the oracle on the mountain top should *stay* on the mountain top. Anyhow you have been away too long. You and Alice will be like two Rip van Winkles over there. It's too *late* to take this step."

Their departure, in Alice's words, was "prosaic." They were seen off at the boat train by Georges Maratier and James Laughlin. As Gertrude stepped up to the train, a button fell off one of her newly bought shoes. Seemingly from out of nowhere, Trac produced needle and thread and

sewed it back on. At Le Havre there was a drenching rain as they
walked up the covered gangway. In their room a huge bouquet of
flowers from Madame de Clermont-Tonnerre awaited them. Once
aboard, Gertrude felt the need to communicate. She penned a short
note to Rogers, even though he would not receive it until after they had
arrived: "I was awfully scared just at the last but now we are comfortable very comfortable and very peaceful." She had not seen America for thirty years.

CHAPTER FOURTEEN

Rediscovering America

I

On the morning of October 24 the *Champlain* pulled into New York harbor. Gertrude and Alice were already packed. They had been up since the unusual hour of 6 A.M.—unusual, that is, for Gertrude, who hated to see the dawn, but not for Alice, whose days at Bilignin regularly began before that hour. As the ship pulled into view of Manhattan, the pair stood on one of the upper decks, peering over the high railing. The New York skyline, Gertrude felt, was a disappointment. Although it had changed considerably in the thirty years since she had left America, it was familiar enough from photographs; in actuality, it seemed disappointingly low. She was to be much more excited, later, by the tall towers of Rockefeller Center under construction—with the thing-in-the-making rather than the already-made. Coursing through the harbor that morning, Gertrude was more impressed with Staten Island, shimmering green and white in the crisp morning light.

As the *Champlain* stopped for quarantine, a Coast Guard cutter approached, bearing a crowd of reporters to interview her and another writer celebrity from France, the Abbé Dimnet, whom Gertrude and Alice had met during the crossing. With the reporters were the Kiddie and Alan Blackburn, the executive director of the Museum of Modern

Art. Both Gertrude and Alice, apprehensive about the coming session with the reporters, gave Rogers a hearty embrace. His presence was reassuring.

The interview took place in the *Champlain's* lounge, with Gertrude seated in the middle of a circle of a dozen or more eager reporters. They had come, most of them, with their pat phrases—"the Sibyl of Montparnasse," "the matron saint of Paris art"—and they had boned up on some of her more enigmatic lines from *Four Saints* and *Tender Buttons*. They were surprised to hear her "speaking a language every one could understand." Gertrude, her confidence restored, assured them that she was "normal and intelligent and born legitimate of two respectable parents." She had come, she told them, "to tell very plainly and simply and directly, as is my fashion, what literature is." When one of the reporters asked her, "Why don't you write as you talk?" she turned to him. "Oh, but I do," she said calmly. "After all, it's all learning how to read it." The reporter—it was Joseph W. Alsop, Jr., with whom Gertrude was to have several interviews and carry on a correspondence on the subject of communication—looked unconvinced and sighed.

Although she had been highly vocal about politics on the other side of the Atlantic, in New York harbor—dissuaded, perhaps, by Alice—Gertrude refused to answer any questions on her political opinions. Nevertheless, her interviewers tried to draw her out on the subject. When the discussion turned to speech rhythms, one of them quoted from a recent speech by President Roosevelt. Gertrude, confused about the Roosevelt in question, gave her opinion that only Lincoln Steffens had "written correctly about Roosevelt." When it was pointed out that Theodore Roosevelt had died several years before, Gertrude answered firmly, "He may not be as dead as you think." She was less successful in avoiding a trap when another reporter, irritated by her refusal to discuss politics, asked her if she knew President Coolidge was dead. She hesitated a moment: "Of course he may have died while I was on the boat coming over." Coolidge, one of the stalwarts of her favored political party, had died only the year before.

Every reporter commented on the unusual attire of the two women. Gertrude was wearing an ample brown tweed suit with a cherry-colored vest. Her "sensible" shoes and thick "woolly" stockings were duly noted. What intrigued the reporters, however, was the odd hat fitted on her close-cropped, graying hair. They described it variously as a "Robin Hood" cap or a "deer-stalker's" cap. It was an old cap, copied from a Louis XIII cap that Alice had admired in the Cluny Museum, and Gertrude refused to be parted from it during most of her tour. Alice, who hovered in the background during the hour-long interview, was described as "thin, dark, nervous-appearing." Her Cossack cap and fur coat, it was reported, gave her a less conspicuous appearance than that of her companion.

In her interview, Gertrude discoursed on the writers who had influenced her—Shakespeare, Trollope, Flaubert—and disagreed about her repetitiveness as a writer: "No, no, no, no, it is not all repetition. I always change the words a little." She spoke about the "new bunch of youngsters" who were sending her manuscripts to read, saying she found them talented. She discounted any intentions of attempting to influence other writers: "If you can influence yourself it is enough." She pointedly mentioned the six lectures she would be delivering at colleges around the country. These lectures were now her favorite writings, she told the reporters, "because the last child is always most loved." The interview over, she consented to go out on deck and be photographed and to speak over a ship-to-shore radio hook-up. Everything was a blur of activities in which she only vaguely remembered being led about by the arm by various agreeable people. Then Alice intervened: It was time to go upstairs and pass through Immigration. When the boat docked, and Gertrude and Alice started down the gangway, they spotted Carl Van Vechten, with Bennett Cerf, waiting on the dock. Van Vechten, conspicuous in a bright purple and green shirt, was waving excitedly, several bracelets jangling on his arm.

If the Kiddie had been worried that Gertrude would be squeezed into half-inches on the back pages of the newspapers, he was soon reassured. Late that afternoon, as he left the Algonquin Hotel, where Gertrude and Alice had taken a three-room suite for their New York stay, he found the afternoon and evening papers already on the lobby newsstand. The arrival of the two expatriates was headline news. Gertrude was a front-page story in the *Sun, Post, World-Telegram,* and *Brooklyn Daily Eagle,* and there were lengthy feature stories in the *Times* and *Herald Tribune* the next day. The stories, Rogers discovered, were all much more straightforward than the headlines, which inevitably played on Steinian repetitions. "Gerty Gerty Stein Stein is Back Home Home Back," one of them blared.

On their first evening in America, Gertrude dined with Alice in their hotel room. The subject of American food had been much on her mind before the trip. She had cornered every visitor to America and pumped him for information. William Cook's wife, Jeanne, who had visited America in the twenties, told her that there was no lettuce to be found in the Midwest. A young French friend from the Bugey, who had recently returned from America, told her that American food was "moist" as compared with French food, which was dry and served with dry sauces. It was for this reason, he maintained, Americans did not care to drink wine with their meals. Gertrude rather favored this theory and, in time, enlarged upon it: American food was, indeed, "moist," and this was because American heating was dry, whereas in France, it was quite the other way round. Alice, who had a more profound interest in culinary matters, simply collected recipes for most of the foods they especially enjoyed—whether moist or not—and was to make a small garland of them, later, in her cookbook.

Gertrude, worried about her lecturing, had decided that they must dine lightly and alone before each of her lectures. In anticipation, for her first evening meal she chose a menu of oysters, corn bread, and honeydew melon. This proved eminently satisfactory, and the regimen was to be repeated, wherever possible, at every lecture date. But from the beginning, Alice noted, "the ubiquitous honeydew melon bored me." Melons, for Alice, were strictly a hot-weather refreshment. She preferred the nonlecture menus of T-bone steaks or soft-shelled crabs and the "ineffable" ice creams served at the Algonquin.

After dinner they took their first walk through the New York streets. They were stunned and surprised by the lights along Broadway. Alice, so Gertrude claimed, preferred that "anything should be American." Standing on Broadway, she complained: "Why do they call Paris la ville lumière?" Gertrude remarked, "You cannot blame them that they still think so although there are more lights here than anywhere." At Times Square, they saw the lights coursing around the Times Building, declaring: "Gertrude Stein has arrived in New York, Gertrude Stein has arrived in New York." "As if we didn't know it," Alice observed dryly. As they walked along the streets, people stopped, recognizing the pair. A few asked how they were enjoying themselves. Gertrude and Alice were impressed and excited. Then, Gertrude recalled, "after the thirty years we went to sleep in beds in a hotel in America. It was pleasing."

They were to be newsworthy celebrities throughout the duration of their trip. Her excited reports to Rogers in Springfield itemized events. "Have we had a hectic time," she wrote. "It is unbelievable, you know I did a news reel for the Pathé people, I think it goes on to-day, and everybody knows us on the street." In another letter she informed him that she was to broadcast "at the National Broadcasting." When she made a political contribution of five dollars to the campaign for Comptroller Joseph D. McGoldrick, a fusion candidate, it rated an item in the papers. When she wrote a last-minute essay for Dorothy Norman's *America and Alfred Stieglitz,* a volume of tributes to the art dealer, that fact was also noted in the news. Her dispute with Columbia University over the size of her lecture audiences there was certainly news. She was scheduled to deliver three lectures at Columbia in November. When she discovered that they had not taken her seriously when she had said she wanted her audiences limited to no more than five hundred, Gertrude, nervous before her first lecture for the Museum of Modern Art, blew up. "I lost everything, I was excited," Gertrude recalled. She gave Dr. Russell Potter, the dean of the Institute of Arts and Sciences at Columbia, twenty-four hours to settle the matter her way. Otherwise, she flatly refused to appear. Neither Gertrude nor her agent, Marvin Ross, was available for comment, but Dr. Potter informed a reporter from the *Herald Tribune* that Miss Stein had been "very pleasant but quite firm" when he tried to settle the matter. They were now revising their plans to hold the attendance within the "iron-bound" limits Gertrude had set. It was reported that "in some cases audiences ranging up to 1,700 were indicated for Miss Stein's lectures."

The result of this disagreement was that Ross was fired and Alice took over the management of the lecturing engagements. "Well, this is it," Alice wrote Rogers, later. "M. C. Ross who up to a certain moment was of the greatest use suddenly became a fearful nuisance. So about a week ago it was agreed that I should carry on alone. Since then I have spent considerable time attempting to get the papers & correspondence concerning the lectures."

Gertrude was faced with one more anxiety the day before her November 1 lecture. She became convinced that there was something wrong with her throat. She had had similar symptoms of stage fright while crossing the Atlantic and was sure that it was happening again. Fortunately, during the crossing, they had met a "nice" New York physician, a Dr. Wood, a throat specialist, who managed to talk her out of her symptoms. He had given Gertrude his telephone number in case she needed him. Dr. Wood was called. "Hearing his voice was already soothing," Gertrude remembered, "but having him come and feel my pulse was everything and he was there at the first lecture and so was my voice." To avoid any further causes of nervousness, Gertrude had decided against any introductions to her lectures whatsoever, although Carl Van Vechten had promptly offered his services. "Besides it was silly," Gertrude claimed, "everybody knew who I was if not why did they come and why should I sit and get nervous while somebody else was talking. So it was decided from then on that there would be no introduction nobody on the platform a table for me to lean on and five hundred to listen."

Her first lecture, given under the auspices of the Museum of Modern Art, was, appropriately, on the subject "Pictures." The museum had offered a limousine to take her to the lecture, but Gertrude refused. On the evening of the lecture, accustomed to country walks, she and Alice walked from the hotel on West Forty-fourth Street to the Colony Club at Park and Sixty-sixth. The audience that had gathered there was large and sophisticated, members of the new Museum of Modern Art, which had been swamped with requests for tickets. According to the news reports, there were considerably more than 500 people in the audience that evening, but Gertrude, who had been told that the seating capacity was 390, was unaware.

Promptly at nine o'clock, Gertrude marched out into the ballroom and took her position on the platform. She was wearing a voluminous brown silk dress, its only adornment a large Victorian diamond pin that glittered in the bright lights. In this solemn attire, her hair cropped, her face still tanned from the summer, she stood out in marked contrast to the fashionably gowned women in the audience. She bowed hurriedly in acknowledgment of the polite applause, then tested the carrying power of her voice, asking if she could be heard at the rear of the room.

The audience, expecting some complicated Steinian rigmarole, was disarmed by the conversational ease of her opening sentences. "It is natural that I should tell about pictures, that is, about paintings," Gertrude began. "Everybody must like something and I like seeing painted pictures." Reading evenly and slowly, in her cultured, eastern girls' school voice, she proceeded to list a few possible avocations: "Some people like to eat some people like to drink, some people like to make money some like to spend money," and then went on to state her own case. "I have not mentioned games indoor and out, and birds and crime and politics and photography," she added, "but anybody can go on, and I, personally, I like all these things well enough but they do not hold my attention long enough. The only thing, funnily enough, that I never get tired of doing is looking at pictures."

Her lecture was partly personal history, a recounting of her experiences with painting, from the moments during her childhood when she stood, awed, in the center of a huge painted panorama of the Battle of Waterloo and again when she had her first glimpse of a famous painting, Millet's *Man with the Hoe*, to her encounters with the radical young painters of Paris. There were ripples of laughter in the audience when she related her initial impressions of the Louvre, which, "at first was only gold frames to me gold frames which were rather glorious." Later, when she explained that there was something particularly satisfying about looking out of windows in a museum—"It is more complete, looking out of windows in museums than looking out of windows anywhere else"—the audience broke out in applause. But if her listeners had expected intimate accounts of her friendships with modern painters, she disappointed them. Instead, she recited brief passages from her word portraits of Matisse, Picasso, and Juan Gris.

Despite the homespun quality of the language, her discussion of art brooded over some thorny aesthetic issues. She talked about "the eternal question for painters"—the subject of the painting. She conceded that it was a "naturally pleasant human thing, to like a resemblance" in a painting, and that the relation between the painting and the thing painted was a perplexing one. Through Courbet and then Cézanne, she had grown to appreciate the autonomy of the painting.

She had come to realize—though hardly in conventional art-critical terms—that "the relation between the oil painting and the thing painted was really nobody's business. It could be the oil painting's business but actually for the purpose of the oil painting after the oil painting was painted it was not the oil painting's business and so it was nobody's business."

She discussed, too, the problem of "the frame." She had first encountered the problem when viewing Leonardo's *Virgin and Child with Saint Anne*, with its complicated internal rhythms: "Before this the moving in a picture was the effect of moving"—that is, the depiction of figures in more or less violent action—"but in this picture there was an internal movement, not of the people or light or any of these things but inside in the oil painting. In other words the picture did not live within the frame, in other words it did not belong within the frame." She had gone on to discover other "good attempts" to achieve that quality of movement: "Rubens in his landscapes, Picasso and Velasquez in their way, and Seurat in his way." With Cézanne, however, she made a distinction: "The Cezanne thing was different, it went further and further into the picture the life of the oil painting but it stayed put." "Modern pictures," she went on to say, "have made the very definite effort to leave their frame. But do they stay out, do they go back and if they do is that where they belong and has anybody been deceived. I think about that a great deal these days." She passionately hoped, she said, "that some picture would remain out of its frame." In a sense, Gertrude was anticipating the problem of Jackson Pollock and the American Abstract Expressionists, a decade later; for Pollock and his colleagues were to attempt to break out of the confines of the easel picture—the discrete, framed experience—and by opening up the scale of the picture to huge size, suggest that the edge of the canvas was merely a cutting-off point, that the activity within the canvas might be indefinitely extended.

At the conclusion of her lecture, she again dropped into the confidential tone with which she had begun. "I hope," she told her audience, "I have been making it slowly clear to you. I might have told you more in detail but in that case you would that is to say I would not have as clearly seen as I do now what an oil painting is." As she took off her horn-rimmed reading glasses, there was a prolonged, steady burst of applause.

The press, if it paid little attention to the ideas Gertrude had expounded, had watched the audience reaction from beginning to end. There had been, the *New York Times* reporter noted, "no unanimity of opinion among the audience," as to either the "meaning or significance of the lecture," but Gertrude's "straightforwardness and amiability" had disarmed those who had come to find fault. Aware of the peculiar lack of punctuation in her writing, some members of the audience were sur-

prised to find that she read her sentences "as if they had been punctuated precisely by a teacher of grammar." Joseph Alsop, covering the
event for the *Herald Tribune*, reported that Gertrude had "variously
pleased, mystified and infuriated her audience." Despite the puzzlement, there had been "rounds of delighted applause over and over again
all through the performance. The truth is that with Miss Stein there is
never a dull moment." Alsop noted that her repetitions were only
"mildly eccentric" and commented on the Stein delivery. Gertrude's
reading, he said, was given in "the same slightly monotonous voice that
mothers use to read to sick children."

Gertrude's second lecture was given the next evening at the McMillin
Theater at Columbia. Again she and Alice walked to the lecture, this
time a matter of seventy-two city blocks from the hotel to 116th Street.
It was a less successful affair. The audience comprised five hundred
members of the university's Institute of Arts and Sciences. According to
one press report, some twenty-five members of the audience walked out
on the speaker. Gertrude spoke that evening on "The Gradual Making
of the Making of Americans," a difficult exposition of her literary
method, as well as, incidentally, a promotion of her book, which had
been published in the abridged Harcourt, Brace edition in February.
Her talk included lengthy and soporific passages from the novel, with
its rolling, repetitive sentences, followed by similar passages from *A
Long Gay Book*. During the question-and-answer period, one perplexed
man stood up to complain that he hadn't understood what she was
talking about. Gertrude shook her head and waved her hands in the air.
"You don't need any special preparation to understand," she moaned.
"A child could understand it. Some children read my work and like it.
Some adults like it. I like it." Despite this minor difficulty, she had
experienced no stage fright after her initial lecture. "After all," she decided, "once you know an audience is an audience why should it make
any difference."

Their suite at the Algonquin was the base for their heavy schedule of
lectures and social engagements throughout November. They traveled
to Princeton by train, to deliver her lecture on *The Making of Americans* in McCosh Hall, on November 5. It was then that Gertrude
discovered that rail travel was no better than it had been thirty years
before. After that she avoided it whenever possible, preferring the automobile or, later, air travel. She lectured, too, in Philadelphia and at
nearby Bryn Mawr. En route to Philadelphia, Gertrude discovered one
of her continuous excitements in America, American wooden houses—
"There are so many of them an endless number of them and endless
varieties of them. It is what in America is very different, each one has

something and well taken care of or neglect helps them, helps them to be themselves each one of them. Nobody could get tired of them." She was also intrigued with the windows in the wooden houses: "That is one thing any American can do he can put windows in a building and wherever they are they are interesting." At Bryn Mawr they stayed overnight at the Deanery, the former residence of Carey Thomas, the spinster president of the college and the disguised purposeful head-mistress of the Redfern episode in *The Making of Americans*. Gertrude was amused to find, hanging in her room, the same sepia photographs of "capital works of art" that she remembered from her college years at Radcliffe.

Four Saints was scheduled for a week-long run, early in November, at Louis Sullivan's auditorium in Chicago, with Virgil Thomson con-ducting. Gertrude wrote excitedly to Rogers about it: "And we are flying to Chicago the 7th for the opera, the Curtis Air people are giving us free transportation *aller et retour* which is well its all mad but most pleasurable." The plane trip, the first Gertrude and Alice had ever taken, had filled them with fear. Carl Van Vechten, who had per-suaded them to make the flight in order to see the opera and return in time for their scheduled lectures, had agreed to accompany them. In flight, Gertrude looked down at the changing landscape and was amazed at the Cubist topography: "The wandering line of Masson was there the mixed line of Picasso coming and coming again and following itself into a beginning was there, the simple solution of Braque was there and I sup-pose Leger might be there but I did not see it." At the opera, she sat in Colonel McCormick's private box. Her Chicago hostess, Mrs. Charles ("Bobsy") Goodspeed, had also engaged orchestra seats down front, to which Gertrude moved for the second act. She had been less excited than she expected to be, but it "looked very lovely and the movement was everything they moved and did nothing, that is what a saint or a doughboy should do." While in Chicago, she also delivered her lecture on "Poetry and Grammar," at the University of Chicago, then under the direction of Chancellor Robert Hutchins and his assistant Mortimer Adler. The reading went so successfully she was asked to return at a later date for more lectures.

Back in New York, Alice wrote to Rogers, brimming with enthusiasm for this new mode of travel: "Everything has been wonderful, we are making plans for a leisurely tour of the whole country, by air of course. . . . I want to stay in U.S.A. forever. And I'm not discovering it, it's always been like that only now it's more so."

Their social life was strenuous. They attended the Yale-Dartmouth football game in New Haven, as the guest of her publisher, Alfred Har-court. In New York she addressed the Dutch Treat Club, a men's or-ganization, and was amused to find that the master of ceremonies, who was to introduce her—it was the one occasion when she allowed it, since it was a rule of the club—suffered from stage fright and could not eat. Carl Van Vechten, an inveterate partygoer and party giver, gave several parties in her honor. A promoter of Negro writers, singers, and dancers, Van Vechten had, in the 1920's, sent the Negro novelist Nella Larsen and singer Paul Robeson to the rue de Fleurus, armed with letters of introduction. In New York he arranged a party of "all the Negro intellectuals that he could get together," including Walter White, the head of the NAACP, and the poet James Weldon Johnson. Alice was rather shocked by their "outspokenness." Gertrude noted the preference of Negro intellectuals to refer to themselves as "colored," a practice with which she disagreed: "I know they do not want you to say Negro but I do want to say Negro. I dislike it when instead of saying Jew they say Hebrew or Israelite or Semite, I do not like it and why should a Negro want to be called colored. Why should he want to lose being a Negro to become a common thing with a Chinaman or a Japanese or a Hindu or an islander or anything . . . a Negro is a Negro and he ought to like to be called one if he is one, he may not want to be one that is all right but as long as he cannot change that why should he mind the real name of them. . . . Well its name is Negro if it is a Negro and Jew if it is a Jew and both of them are nice strong solid names and so let us keep them."

At another party Gertrude met "America's Sweetheart," Mary Pickford. The meeting was to pique Gertrude's curiosity about what was and what was not good publicity. She and the film star held a brief conversation about the value of speaking French. Mary Pickford "said she wished she knew more French and I said I talked it all right but I never read it I did not care about it as a written language she said she did wish she did know more French." Then it was suggested that the two of them should be photographed together. Mary Pickford at first seemed enthusiastic and agreed, saying it would be easy to get a photographer from the *Journal* to come. The photographer was called. Meanwhile a new acquaintance of Gertrude's, Belle Greene, the librarian of the Pierpont Morgan library, was saying to her, "You are not going to do it." "Of course I am going to," Gertrude answered emphatically. "Of course we are." She turned to Mary Pickford, who seemed, quite visibly, to be backing away. "Perhaps I will not be able to stay," the film star was saying. "Oh yes, you must," Gertrude said. "It will not be long now." She imagined that they might be photographed shaking hands. Mary Pickford retreated further. "No, no, I think I had better not," she answered. With that, Gertrude observed, Mary Pickford "melted away." Gertrude, nonplussed, asked everyone "just what it was that went on inside Mary Pickford. It was her idea and then when I was enthusiastic she melted away." The consensus of opinion was that, because Gertrude had been so ardent, Miss Pickford had felt the publicity would do Gertrude more good than it would do her; she retired from the field.

For the most part, her social engagements throughout the tour were to prove an enormous pleasure. She and Alice were surprised that they encountered no unpleasantness, received no crank calls or abusive letters, despite the continuous spate of publicity. The only unsettling incident occurred with a young man whom Alice had met. He professed great admiration for Gertrude Stein. Taking pity on him, Alice had invited him to a cocktail party being given that afternoon in their honor. There, with the aid of several cocktails, his admiration turned to adulation and he knelt down on the floor and kissed the hem of Gertrude's gown, much to her embarrassment.

Gertrude's lecture schedule continued unabated. On November 9 she lectured at the New School for Social Research. On a particularly busy Friday, November 16—just after her Philadelphia and Bryn Mawr lectures—she agreed to deliver a few extemporaneous remarks at a charity luncheon and musicale at the Ritz Tower Hotel, at which Virgil Thomson played excerpts from *Four Saints*, with Beatrice Robinson-Wayne and Edward Matthews singing the arias. That afternoon she arrived late and somewhat breathless for a lecture on "Poetry and Grammar" at Columbia, repeating the performance again that evening in the McMillin Theater. That weekend she and Alice took the train to Boston, where Gertrude was scheduled to deliver two lectures, one at the Signet Club at Harvard and another for Radcliffe students in the Agassiz Theatre. Gertrude found Cambridge more changed than any place she was to recall in America. It was "so different that it was as if I had never been there. . . . I lost Cambridge then and there." In Brooklyn she delivered three lectures at the Academy of Music. It was in Brooklyn, as the result of an accident, that she became acquainted with the American drugstore. A too attentive young man had closed a door on her finger as she was leaving the academy, and she was taken to a nearby drugstore to have it attended to. "It was dirty the drug store," Gertrude remembered, "one of the few things really dirty in America are the drug stores but the people in them sitting up and eating and drinking milk and coffee that part of the drug store was clean that fascinated me. After that I was always going in to buy a detective novel just to watch the people sitting on the stools. It was like a piece of provincial life in a real city. . . . I never had enough of going into them." Other features of American civilization were not so rewarding. The five and ten cent stores were definitely a disappointment; she had looked forward to going into them and buying something, but "There was nothing that I wanted and what was there . . . was not there for ten cents." And American radio was not satisfying either; all that seemed to come out of it was "crooning."

II

Chicago became Gertrude's favorite city during her American tour. The success of her first lecture there, early in November, had encouraged a return engagement, arranged by Mortimer Adler, the vice-president of the university. Gertrude and Alice returned late in the month for a two-week stay. Gertrude had not seen a real old-fashioned winter in years, and, from her windows in the Drake Hotel, she was more than satisfied with the wintry cityscape, with its drifts of snow and blustering winds. She liked the strange light of the tall buildings at night and the repetitive movements of an animated sign advertising a ballroom that she could see from her room: "I never tired of seeing them, the sombre gray light on the buildings and the simple solemn mechanical figures dancing, there were other things I liked but I liked that the most." When she was told that the skyscraper had been invented in Chicago rather than New York, she found it interesting "that it should have been done where there was plenty of land to build on and not in New York where it is narrow and so must be high of necessity. Choice is always more pleasing than anything necessary."

She was royally entertained by the Goodspeeds during her second visit, taken to concerts and the opera—she saw *Lohengrin* and *Salomé* —and it brought back memories of her college years. "It seemed as if Europe had not been." Gertrude saw a good deal of Fanny Butcher, the book reviewer for the *Chicago Tribune*, and, through Mrs. Goodspeed, met Thornton Wilder, then an instructor at the university, who became a close and loyal friend. Wilder, a writer with considerable prestige in the profession, served her loyally over the years, producing prefaces and introductions for her later books—*Narration*, her four Chicago lectures, *The Geographical History of America*, and the posthumously published *Four in America*. After Gertrude's death, he lectured on her ideas on the creative process, a subject with which he was thoroughly conversant by way of their lengthy talks in Chicago and, later, in Bilignin and Paris. In his lecture, Wilder likened her manner of writing to that of Emily Dickinson: creating her work in isolation— as Gertrude had in her earlier years—keeping the idea of an audience at bay.

It was at a dinner party at the home of Robert Hutchins that Gertrude was challenged to teach the students rather than merely lecture to them. Hutchins and Adler had initiated the Great Books program at the University of Chicago, concentrating on the books and writers that had introduced the most important ideas in the history of mankind. Gertrude was shown the list of books that were discussed in the special seminar. She noted that few had originally been written in English and

asked Hutchins if that had been intentional. Hutchins's answer that it
had not been intentional but that "in English there have really been
no ideas expressed"—so Gertrude recalled in *Everybody's Autobiography*
—set off a violent argument:

Then I gather that to you there are no ideas which are not sociological or
government ideas. Well are [there] he said, well yes I said. Government is
the least interesting thing in human life, creation and the expression of that
creation is a damn sight more interesting, yes I know and I began to get
excited yes I know, naturally you are teachers and teaching is your occupation and naturally what you call ideas are easy to teach and so you are convinced that they are the only ideas but the real ideas are not the relation of
human beings as groups but a human being to himself inside him and that
is an idea that is more interesting than humanity in groups, after all the
minute that there are a lot of them they do not do it for themselves but
somebody does it for them and that is a darn sight less interesting.

Her explosion turned into a personal attack on Adler, who interrupted
to take exception to what she was saying. Anyone, Gertrude barked,
could tell by looking at him that he "was a man who would be singularly unsusceptible to ideas that are created within oneself that he
would take to either inside or outside regulation but not to creation."
Hutchins then interrupted to say that, if she could improve on what
they were doing, then she should take over one of their seminars. Gertrude, in the heat of the argument, promptly said, "Of course I will."
   It was at that moment, Gertrude recalled, that a flustered maid entered and announced, "Madame the police." There was a moment of
stunned silence, then laughter. Fanny Butcher had arranged for Gertrude and Alice to ride around Chicago that evening in a squad car with
two detectives from the homicide department. The policemen had come
to pick them up.
   It was a rainy evening, and their ride with the two detectives took
them to the drabber precincts of the city, areas they had not yet seen.
It was the night, so Gertrude remembered, that Baby Face Nelson was
trapped by federal agents. There were frequent interruptions over the
police radio detailing the progress of the capture taking place twenty-five
miles away. Because of the weather, one of the detectives explained, it
was unlikely that there would be any homicides—people moved around
little on rainy nights. If there was any action it was likely to be a "family affair." In the Negro slums the sergeant in charge callously took
them into an apartment house on the pretext that they were to identify
a one-eyed man who had stolen one of their purses. The ten to twelve
occupants of the apartment they stopped in were, at first, plainly uneasy, then relieved when they learned it was a hoax. Gertrude asked
each of them where they had come from and discovered that they
were "mostly from somewhere in the South one was a Canadian and

now they were here and anyway they had no plans about anything."
She had had a glimpse of the misery to be found in a large American
city, but the sight had not moved her to anger, only to a benign kind
of pity and understanding. She was to remain something of a fatalist
about human affairs.

Later that evening, accompanied by the detectives, they witnessed a
walking marathon, a surreal event, like a scene from Dante's *Inferno*:
"They were all young ones and they were moving as their bodies were
drooping. . . . Some no longer had another one with them they were
moving and drooping alone but when there were two of them one was
more clinging than moving and the other one was supporting and moving. There was plenty of light and a little noise." It was out of such
disjunctive visions that she was harvesting her impressions of her native
land.

Within a few days her teaching assignment had been arranged. She
was apprehensive about the seminar; lecturing was something she had
now become used to; teaching was another thing. At the outset of the
class, Gertrude suggested that they should discuss epic poetry. The students, she said, might begin by asking her questions and in that way
they would bring out one another's ideas. The give and take of the
process became particularly lively, and Gertrude warmed to the task:
"Pretty soon we were all talking about epic poetry and what it was, it
was exciting we found out a good deal." After the discussion, as she and
Hutchins were leaving, Hutchins graciously conceded that Gertrude had
managed to get the students involved and talking much more than was
usually the case. Even students who had never talked before had been
drawn into the discussion. He asked her if she could arrange to return to
Chicago later in her tour and conduct a series of classes. They would
work out the details in the meantime. Gertrude agreed. "You see," she
recalled telling Hutchins, "why they talk to me is that I am like them
I do not know the answer, you say you do not know but you do know if
you did not know the answer you could not spend your life in teaching
but I I really do not know, I really do not, I do not even know whether
there is a question let alone having an answer for a question."

After their Chicago sojourn Gertrude and Alice had planned to spend
Christmas week in comparative seclusion, visiting Gertrude's cousin
Julian Stein and his family at Pikesville, near Baltimore. Julian, the son
of her uncle Samuel, had visited her at the Hôtel Pernollet in 1927. He
had been accompanied by his wife, Rose Ellen, and her two daughters
by a previous marriage, as well as their young son, Julian, Jr. Rose
Ellen, during the visit, had made the first home movies of Gertrude,

showing her with her new brush cut, walking down the marble steps of the soldiers' memorial across the street from the hotel. She had also photographed—at Gertrude's insistence—young Julian ceremoniously shaking hands with the three young sons of Monsieur Pernollet, all dressed in their Sunday best.

Christmas week was to be a somewhat bittersweet experience. Julian Stein, Sr., was bedridden, recuperating from a recent heart attack. But the family had contrived to make the festivities as joyous as possible. The Christmas stockings were a hit—Gertrude and Alice had been obliged to hang theirs. On Christmas morning the children and the two elderly celebrities had trooped into Julian's bedroom to open up their gifts, all dime-store trinkets, which brought guffaws of laughter. Gertrude especially appreciated a little poem written by Rose Ellen, in which she had enclosed a packet of bobby pins for Gertrude's close-cropped hair. But she was even more impressed with the small bound copies of comic books that had been bought at the five-and-ten. She liked their solid, square format. As she later explained to the French painter Elie Lascaux, "The romantic thing about America" was that "they do the best designing and use the best material in the cheapest thing, the square books and the old Ford car." The visit of Gertrude and Alice gave rise to a family joke, involving the three-year-old daughter of Julian's stepdaughter. The child had sat on Gertrude's lap frequently, and Gertrude had made much of her. But, when the celebrated pair had left and the little girl was asked how she liked cousin Gertrude and her friend, the child answered that she "liked the man part, but why did the lady have a mustache."

They had intended to cut down on all but the inescapable social engagements during their Baltimore visit, owing partly to Julian's illness and also to their own fatigue. During that week, as well, Alice planned to put in order the manuscript for the six lectures Gertrude had written at Bilignin; Bennett Cerf had arranged to publish the lectures in the spring. Aside from a lecture at the Baltimore Museum, they had scheduled no activities. Their Baltimore visit was to be the occasion for an unfortunate snub to Etta Cone. Having heard of Julian's illness, Etta had written to Gertrude offering the hospitality of her apartment at the Marlborough for any meetings that Gertrude might like to arange or that Etta could arrange for her. Etta suggested that Gertrude might like to meet George Boas of Johns Hopkins, as well as others interested in Gertrude's writing.

Gertrude had declined, pleading the pressure of events:

My dear Etta,

Thanks so much for your invitation, but I am not accepting any invitations. There is so much more happening than in our wildest dreams—I am

simply seeing no one except a few very dear friends. As I am lecturing in
Baltimore I will undoubtedly meet Dr. Boas and that will give me a great
deal of pleasure, but you can understand that with lecturing, broadcasting,
cinema newsreels and newspaper people and my editors, I must in between
go very easy.

Etta, who already had tickets for Gertrude's Baltimore lecture, evidently took Gertrude's decision to see "no one except a few very dear
friends" as a calculated slight. During Christmas week she made an unexpected visit to her relatives in Greensboro, North Carolina, leaving
her tickets for her young niece. Gertrude's snub may have been unin-
tentional; she seems to have thought Etta would not be in Baltimore
when they arrived, for she had added: "I am awfully sorry if you will
not be in Baltimore when we get there but sometime we will meet. Always lots of love." But, if the mistake with Etta was inadvertent, there
were occasions when Gertrude declined to meet old friends. At one of
the Columbia lectures Alice had been seated next to Mabel Weeks.
When Mabel asked Alice when she was going to see Gertrude, Alice
answered, frankly, that she did not know. For whatever reason—perhaps
because of the coolness that had developed between them over the
years—Gertrude did not plan to see Mabel.
    She did visit one old friend in sad circumstances, Scott Fitzgerald,
who was living in Baltimore. Zelda, who had been confined to a sanatorium after repeated bouts of mental illness, was home for the holidays. It was a sad occasion, taking place on December 24, in the living
room of the Fitzgeralds' Park Avenue apartment, in front of a gaily
decorated tree. Gertrude and Alice were driven there by Julian's stepdaughter, Ellen, and accompanied by young Julian. Fitzgerald was well
on his way to being drunk when they arrived, his once handsome features showing the traces of dissipation. Gertrude, experienced in talking
soberly to drunken friends, ignored his condition, and they chatted
pleasantly of old times. Zelda, rather apprehensively, brought out several
paintings that she had done at the sanatorium. She was surprised when
Gertrude expressed a genuine admiration for them, and promptly asked
Gertrude to select two. Their young daughter, Scottie, was brought in
to meet the guests. Gertrude apologized for not having brought a gift,
saying that she hadn't expected to see her. Gertrude got out a pen and
inscribed a little message on a hazel nut for her.
    When Gertrude and Alice left, later in the afternoon, Fitzgerald
walked out with them to the car. As he helped Gertrude in, he blurted
out, "Thank you. Having you come to the house was like—it was as if
Jesus Christ had stopped in!" Gertrude, who had become a little hard
of hearing in her later years, did not catch his remark. But Ellen,
seated behind the wheel, remembered it for years. Fitzgerald wrote Gertrude gratefully, a few days after their meeting:

Dearest Gertrude Stein:

It was a disappointment to think that you would not be here for another meeting. I was somewhat stupid—got with the Christmas spirit, but I enjoyed the one idea that you *did* develop and, like everything else you say, it will sing in my ears long after everything else about that afternoon is dust and ashes. You were the same fine fire to everyone who sat upon your hearth—for it was your hearth, because you carry home with you wherever you are—a home before which we have always warmed ourselves.

It meant so much to Zelda, giving her a tangible sense of her own existence, for you to have liked two of her pictures enough to want to own them. For the other people there, the impression was perhaps more vague, but everyone felt their Christmas eve was well spent in the company of your handsome face and wise mind—and sentences "that never leak."

Fitzgerald's letter was a burst of sentiment, commemorating a last meeting of old friends.

On December 30, Gertrude and Alice were invited to tea at the White House. It was an odd event, for Gertrude's occasional public references to the man in the White House were less than enthusiastic. When newsmen had queried her, asking if she intended to visit the White House, Gertrude had simply answered that she hadn't been asked. Now the invitation had come.

According to Alice, they were met by Mrs. Roosevelt, who told them that her husband, unfortunately, was indisposed and could not meet with them. In Gertrude's version, Eleanor told them that the President was busy with his annual message to Congress. The fact seemed to be confirmed by the activity—the men passing, coming "from somewhere going to somewhere"—while she and Alice sat, in a long hallway, sipping tea with the President's wife. Presidential adviser Louis Howe stopped for a moment but declined an offer of tea. Mrs. Roosevelt said, yes, they were "all writing the message to Congress." It was a form of writing that evidently piqued Gertrude's interest. "They were all writing it," she observed, "and each one and any one was changing it."

III

Like experienced politicians on a major political campaign, Gertrude and Alice criss-crossed the country, quadrant by quadrant. During and after their stay in Chicago, they had traveled—by plane, as often as possible—to Wisconsin, Minnesota, Michigan, Ohio, and Indiana. Gertrude lectured to university and college audiences and cultural groups,

visited friends, took in the local sights. After a flight in a three-seater
plane from Madison to Saint Paul, she wrote the Kiddie:

Just we two and the pilot, and over the snow hills and then the snow prairie
it was unbelievably beautiful, and the symmetry of the roads and farms and
turns, make something that fills me with a lot, and the shadows of the trees
on the wooded hills, well the more I see the more I do see what I like, I
cannot tell you how much we like it, last night my eyes were all full of it.

Near Minneapolis, they were entertained at the baronial estate of
Mrs. Walter Douglas, of Quaker Oats wealth. Mrs. Douglas, a survivor
of the *Titanic* disaster, in which her husband perished, was the friend
of Van Vechten's youth and the original model, so Gertrude and Alice
believed, of Van Vechten's *The Tattooed Countess*. At luncheon the
table was set with great clusters of hothouse grapes; the rooms were
filled with orchids, among them the first "Tiepolo blue" orchids Alice
had ever seen. Outside, the snow was falling gently. They were served
a sumptuous and subtle Lobster Archiduc, laced with brandy, port, and
whiskey, for which Alice acquired the recipe.

To Gertrude's regret, they missed Iowa. Both Van Vechten and William Cook had been born there, and according to Gertrude's theory,
there was a connection between geography and character: "After all,
anybody is as their land and air is." Cook and Van Vechten, according
to this theory, had some very special qualities: "You are brilliant and
subtle if you come from Iowa and really strange and you live as you
live and you are always very well taken care of if you come from Iowa."
But on the beautiful, clear evening that they flew from Saint Paul to
Chicago, where they were to catch a special plane to Iowa City, the
pilot, unexpectedly, landed in Milwaukee. There had been engine trouble before take-off, and they had had to transfer to a second plane.
When they set down in Milwaukee, Alice, fearing they were to be delayed by further engine trouble, cornered the copilot and reprimanded
him strenuously for taking on passengers that he obviously couldn't
deliver. She was told that no plane could land in Chicago because of
weather conditions. "Why not," Alice asked, "it's a lovely night."
"Maybe so," the copilot answered, "but lady, wouldn't you rather be
in Milwaukee than in your coffin." There was a fierce blizzard in Chicago, as they learned when they arrived there on the train they were
forced to take. Gertrude's lecture at Iowa City had to be canceled.

They went, next, to Detroit, putting up at a hotel. Gertrude was
afflicted with product loyalty and wanted to see the home of the Ford
car. But during her after-dinner walk, that evening, she was frightened
by a loudspeaker blaring out the news that a gunman was on the loose.
She promptly returned to the hotel. Alice called Joseph Brewer, then

the president of Olivet College, who had offered his services, if they should be in his area. Several years before, as a publisher, he had brought out Gertrude's *Useful Knowledge*. Brewer said he could come for them the next day. The following morning there were several cars waiting for them outside their hotel. What appeared to be the entire faculty of Olivet had come to escort them to Lansing. They stayed for a day or two and then were driven to Ann Arbor, where Gertrude was to lecture. It was on the drive to Ann Arbor that Gertrude discovered—and was delighted by—the Burma-Shave signs, with their rhymed "poems" spaced out along the highway.

At Columbus, Ohio, Gertrude visited the local museum and was surprised to find a room dedicated to the works of the Cubists, including several "really good" Picasso and Juan Gris paintings. She had not encountered modern works of that quality in any American museum thus far. She was told that they had been left to the museum by a wealthy local benefactor who had begun collecting at the age of seventy. Everywhere Gertrude went in America, she was "talked to" about American painting. She confessed that she had seen little that really impressed her: "The painting was like any learnt painting, it was good painting enough not awfully good painting as painting but good painting enough." But from "the standpoint of the Louvre," it was just not interesting. To the dismay of her inquirers, she maintained that "There was no painting like that in America there just was not, there was architecture there was writing but there was no painting."

From Columbus, she wrote the Kiddie about her appetite for the American landscape: "We have been so many places and we pretty well have liked them all . . . now we want to see a lot more of them until we have seen them all. I have been enormously interested in how different one state is from another, and why, and I don't know, I am tremendously moved by the simple facts and differences here and everywhere." In Toledo, she was asked how she wanted to be entertained, and she said she preferred not to be entertained but to be driven around the local countryside. On one of these trips they passed the estate of the manufacturer of Champion spark plugs. It was another of her American loyalties. Throughout World War I, with the French mechanics who overhauled her Ford, Gertrude had always insisted on Champion spark plugs. Asked if she would now like to visit the manufacturer, Gertrude gave a hearty, "Oh, yes." The manufacturer's wife was at home and received her graciously. Gertrude told her the saga of her experiences with her husband's product. Not long after her impromptu visit, she received a tiny steel watch charm in the shape of a spark plug. She kept it in her jewel box. She would have preferred, however, a silver one; but those had been discontinued because of the Depression.

After the Christmas holidays and their trip to Washington, Gertrude and Alice paid an extended visit to Springfield, Massachusetts, and the Kiddie and his wife—Rogers had recently married Mildred Weston. Gertrude had a comparatively strenuous schedule of lectures in the New England region, and they used their Springfield hotel as the base of operations. She also wanted to see the Connecticut River valley region. Although Rogers did not have a car, obliging neighbors provided all the necessary transportation. She and Alice were charmed by the picture-postcard scenery, the white-steepled churches settled in the snowy landscape. They visited Deerfield, saw the battered door in the old John Williams house, hacked by tomahawks in the Deerfield Massacre; at Longmeadow a friend of Rogers took them on a sleigh ride though the snow-laden woods. One evening Gertrude was escorted through the offices of the *Springfield Union*, Rogers's newspaper, to watch the morning edition go to press. In restaurants and bookstores, she was regularly sought after for autographs and enjoyed it immensely. One aspect of New England puzzled her, however; she encountered more drunks there than anywhere else in the country. She ascribed it to the puritanical fear of drink she had sensed in the novels of William Dean Howells and Louisa May Alcott. She began to realize that the "mysterious thing they used to talk about a taste for liquor did indeed matter." It was in Springfield, she conceded, that she became "more intimate with everything American."

Her lectures in New England brought Gertrude a new view of American education. She gave a special lecture, "How Writing Is Written," a discussion of the creative process, at the Choate School in Wallingford, Connecticut. She found the boys, aged twelve to sixteen, extremely attentive during the lecture and in the discussion period afterward. And she was impressed with the "extraordinary good writing" in the school's literary magazine. Yet the experience left her with a feeling of uneasiness. She wondered aloud to the Choate teachers, "if the boys can ever come to be themselves because you are all so reasonable and so sweet to them that inevitably they are convinced too soon. Is not that the trouble with American education that if they are to be convinced at all they are convinced too soon is it not the trouble with any republican education." At Amherst her lecture on "Poetry and Grammar," with its dismissal of most forms of punctuation as merely unnecessary conveniences, went down well with the students. As they filed out after the lecture, Rogers overheard one of the students saying, "She knows what she's doing."

Her experiences at men's and women's colleges gave her food for thought. At Wesleyan, following the lecture, she became deeply involved in a lengthy discussion about success and "why American men think that success is everything when they know that eighty percent of them are not going to succeed more than to just keep going." At Mount

Holyoke, which she considered the "best of the women's colleges in New England," she gave her lecture on "Plays" and found the audience surprisingly *au courant*. "Afterwards," she noted, "it seemed rather strange to me that the two colleges which were really made to make missionaries were more interesting than those that had been made to make culture and the other professions. It made me wonder a lot about what it is to be American."

At the end of her New England sojourn, she and Alice took a train to New York. "The train went along," she wrote Rogers, "but that is about all that it did, but gradually it got here." She was now making recordings, so she informed Rogers. The recording sessions had been held in the old Aeolian Hall, and she had recited segments from *The Making of Americans* and her word portraits of Picasso, Matisse, and Sherwood Anderson. Like everything else in her American tour, it was "rather wonderful."

Early in February, Gertrude and Alice started off on the first leg of their southern campaign. They were accompanied by Carl Van Vechten. They stopped at Charlottesville, where Gertrude lectured at the University of Virginia. They were met by a reception committee of students who brought a great cluster of balloons instead of the customary bouquet of flowers. Gertrude found the young men singularly attentive and attractive. Both she and Alice were impressed by the campus. Alice informed the Kiddie, "We quite lost our hearts to it."

At Richmond, Van Vechten had arranged for a reception by his novelist friend Ellen Glasgow. Miss Glasgow, a confirmed southern lady in the old tradition, was not an admirer of Gertrude Stein—or, at least, of Gertrude Stein's literary reputation. But, owing to her social standing in the community, she had agreed to entertain the "visiting royalty." "Usually I avoid modern fads and people who lecture," she had written Van Vechten, "but I have nothing against Miss Stein except her 'influence.' My private opinion is that the people she has influenced (especially Hemingway) couldn't have been much worse if she had left them alone." Other than her old friend James Branch Cabell, there were—so she told Van Vechten—"no literary people" in Richmond. But she would do her best.

The dinner, held in her Victorian home on West Street, went well. Despite their differences in outlook, Gertrude and Miss Glasgow had gotten on well together and they were to meet again in New York. Cabell, in an inquisitive and sly mood drew Van Vechten aside for an explanation of Gertrude's term the "continuous present." And, seated next to Alice at the dinner table, he asked: "Is Gertrude Stein serious?"

"Desperately," Alice answered. The author of *Jurgen* paused. "That puts a different light on it," he said. "For you," Alice said briskly, "not for me."

In the capital of the Confederacy, Gertrude gave her lecture on "Pictures" to the local women's club and visited the home of Edgar Allan Poe. She was struck by the still-thriving cult of Robert E. Lee, whom she could not take seriously as a hero since he had knowingly led his people to certain defeat. Richmond, so Alice wrote the Kiddie, "was amusing, the Confederacy and Mr. Lee are as present and familiar as a newsreel, but G. revenged herself by insisting upon being shown the site of Libbey prison."

From Richmond the pair proceeded on alone. Gertrude lectured at William and Mary, where she was mildly critical of the Rockefeller-funded restoration of colonial Williamsburg: "You put new where the old was and old where the new was and that makes restoration." They were driven to Sweet Briar, where the girls were "very good-looking." "Naturally," Gertrude observed, "the Northern girls came South but once there they might as well have come from there, it was charming." As they moved southward, they seemed to be meeting the advancing spring. They stopped at Chapel Hill, which Gertrude had never heard of before. At their hotel they ate very well. But they were even more impressed, on their drive to South Carolina, when they stopped at a planter's hotel, Cheraw, on the route to Charleston. At Charleston, Alice was enchanted with the long avenues of camellias coming into bloom. She reported to the Kiddie that she would have adored Charleston "if G. had not caught a most frightful cold when we spent a day on a plantation and were rowed for hours upon a swamp turned lake with hanging gardens in a torrential downpour." For Gertrude, the swamp gardens were strangely memorable, like the sleepwalking marathoners in Chicago, like "illustrations of Dante" in America. In Charleston they met the Southern writer Du Bose Heyward, whom Gertrude thought as "gentle" a man as his Porgy. (They had already met the composer George Gershwin, who played for them at a party in New York hosted by Carl Van Vechten.) From Charleston they took a plane to Atlanta, proceeding by train to Birmingham. At Birmingham they managed to scout up their doughboy friend Duncan, whose exploits Gertrude had chronicled in *The Autobiography of Alice B. Toklas*. Alabama had been the last address they had had for Duncan, and someone had managed to track him down. Duncan was totally unaware of his celebrity. Much to Gertrude's surprise—for she had been sure Duncan would be an "energetic something"—Duncan was an unsuccessful decorator.

Their next stop was New Orleans, where Gertrude lectured at Tulane University. Sherwood Anderson, who was there at the time, arrived at their hotel toting a huge bag of sweet oranges. At the hotel Gertrude struck up an acquaintance with the photographer who regu-

larly covered Huey Long, in whose political career Gertrude developed
a peculiar interest. She never met the Louisiana politician, but through
following the American newspapers, she became convinced that Long
was a genuine American phenomenon.

She and Alice dined at the famous Antoine's and at a smaller restaurant at which Alice thought the food was better. It was there that
they had Oysters Rockefeller for the first time. Each morning Alice
walked down to the bustling market, "realising that I would have to live
in the dream of it for the rest of my life." She was even prepared to
admit that New Orleans was "more varied and amusing than S. Francisco (alas that it should be so)."

In New Orleans they met Marc Connelly, the author of *The Green
Pastures*, and an old acquaintance of the early years in Paris, a Miss
Henderson, whose family had lived in New Orleans for generations and
who took them to see the old homes of her friends. They drove out
with Sherwood Anderson to inspect the Mississippi. Anderson was "indignant" when Gertrude complained that it somehow did not seem as
impressive as she had imagined it from reading Mark Twain's *Life
Along the Mississippi*. Literature, apparently, had a way of making
things seem larger than life.

From New Orleans they took a plane to Saint Louis, planning to
spend a few days there before proceeding to Chicago, where Gertrude
was to give her special course. The plane stopped at Memphis. But they
no longer bothered to complain when their flights did not reach their
destination. They were becoming seasoned air travelers.

In Chicago, Gertrude was the center of a lively but brief controversy.
transition, having opened up its pages to several former members of
her Parisian circle, disgruntled with *The Autobiography of Alice B.
Toklas*, had published its "Testimony Against Gertrude Stein," in February, 1935. In it, Eugene and Maria Jolas, Matisse, André Salmon,
Braque, and Tristan Tzara took issue with her book, partly on factual
grounds and partly on what Salmon termed its "confusion," its "incomprehension of an epoch." Eugene Jolas scored the *Autobiography*'s
"hollow, tinsel bohemianism and egocentric deformations"; his wife
noted Gertrude's "final capitulation to a Barnumesque publicity."
Matisse, the most sober-minded of her detractors, stuck largely to correcting some factual errors; he had not, for example, come to Paris to
study "pharmacy" but the law; he had not bought his Cézanne with
his wife's dowry; an incident that Gertrude described as having taken
place in Clamart had actually taken place at the boulevard des In-
valides. He was particularly distressed by Gertrude's description of
Madame Matisse as having "a firm large loosely hung mouth like a

horse." He also maintained that it was Sally Stein who was the "really intelligently sensitive member of the family," claiming that it was she who had instigated the purchase of the *Woman with a Hat*—both debatable issues—and added an error of his own by claiming that Sally had come into possession of the picture when Leo sold his collection. What the Jolases appeared to be most incensed about was Gertrude's favoritism toward Elliot Paul in her discussions of their magazine, even though they had several times tried to disabuse her of the notion that Paul was the operative intelligence of *transition.* Maria Jolas charged that Gertrude's dissatisfaction with the magazine had come about when the Jolases began promoting Joyce and neglecting her.

Questioned by the reporters in Chicago on March 4, Gertrude called the charges "babyish" and "infantish." And she responded only to Eugene Jolas's derogatory remarks about the book. "How can he know what he's talking about?" she asked the reporters. "He wasn't even in Paris during the period covered in the book from 1903 to 1914. He didn't go to Paris until 1920." She seems to have conveniently overlooked the fact that the book covered the period after World War I, although it was true that Jolas's knowledge of the prewar years could have come only by hearsay. On the following day, when a reporter brought up Matisse's complaint about her description of Madame Matisse, Gertrude rather disingenuously claimed that it had been meant as a "compliment." "I'm crazy about horses," she told the reporter. "You know there are many beautiful horses." Her calmer thoughts about the affair were confided to Carl Van Vechten: "Apparently Paris is amusing itself greatly about it all it seems to have made them forget politics for a brief moment and my French publishers are naturally very pleased."

During their two-week stay in Chicago, Gertrude and Alice lived in Thornton Wilder's apartment on Drexel Avenue. Wilder had vacated it so that Gertrude would be near the university. It had two bedrooms, a parlor, a dining room—and a modern kitchen. After months of hotel living they could dine at home and even have guests in for dinner. Although the kitchen was no larger than "a dining room table," Alice remembered their two weeks in Wilder's apartment as her "ideal of happy housekeeping." It was still winter when they arrived in Chicago; from their flat they could see the snowy Midway.

It was in Wilder's apartment that Gertrude wrote the four lectures on "Narration" that she gave to her special classes at the university. In some respects, her Chicago lectures were a reiteration, but in more concise form, of the literary problems she had taken up in the lectures she had written at Bilignin. Gertrude explained her view that the English language, as a literary instrument, had been evolved to express the "daily island life" of the English people. But, having been transplanted to America, it was being pressured into new usages, to fit the life of a continent. That, she avowed, was one of the exciting things about

America and American literature. It presented a new and unheard of situation: "History repeats itself anything repeats itself but all this had never happened before." American literature was not concerned with the soothing reassurance of daily life and routine habits. In a mobile society like that of the United States, what was wanted was not the confirmation of a settled and placid routine, but the quickening sense of activity both in life and in the language. "Think about American writing," she told her audience, "from Emerson, Hawthorne, Walt Whitman, Mark Twain, Henry James, myself, Sherwood Anderson, Thornton Wilder and Dashiell Hammett and you will see what I mean, as well as in advertising and in road signs, you will see what I mean, words left alone more and more feel that they are moving and all of it is detached and is detaching anything from anything and in this detaching and in this moving it is being in its way creating its existing. This is then the real difference between English and American writing and this then can then lead to anything."

She attempted, once more, to make a serviceable distinction between poetry and prose. Poetry, she claimed, was a "calling upon" the name of a thing until it had an existence of its own; it was, in a sense, "a narrative of calling upon that name." Prose, she maintained, repeating her idea of the unemotional sentences culminating in a paragraph that was emotional, had its narrative function, too. It concerned itself with a "progressive telling of things that were progressively happening." That, at least, was what narrative had been in earlier literature. "But," Gertrude maintained, "now we have changed all that we really have. We really now do not really know that anything is progressively happening and as knowledge is what you know and as now we do not know that anything is progressively happening where are we then in narrative writing and what has this to do with poetry and with prose." It was an open-ended question, but in her own view, modern writing no longer had any need of relating a story progressively through the conventional beginning, middle, and end. In one of her earlier lectures, "Portraits and Repetition," she had made a rare acknowledgment of her contemporary rival, Joyce, as well as Proust: "A thing you all know is that in the three novels written in this generation that are the important things written in this generation, there is, in none of them a story. There is none in Proust in The Making of Americans or in Ulysses." Her Chicago lectures once more raised the issue of the storyless modern narrative and the more consequential question of whether, in a sense, the conventions of the past had become superfluous: "Perhaps narrative and poetry and prose have all come where they do not have to be considered as being there." With this question, she could do no more than engage her audience with her own speculative approach, concluding, "You will perhaps say no and yes perhaps yes."

Her conferences, held each afternoon, with thirty or more students, hand-picked by Thornton Wilder, were lively and sometimes boisterous. When Wilder attempted to calm the students down, Gertrude indulgently waved him off—she was enjoying herself. Three of the students were confirmed partisans of proletarian literature, a subject they reverted to again and again. Gertrude would tease them about it a good deal. One day they arrived in class with their heads shaved as a gesture of solidarity. Inevitably, Gertrude was asked about her famous repetitive line "Rose is a rose is a rose is a rose." Gertrude answered volubly. It was "doubly hard," she claimed, to be a poet in a late age: "Now you all have seen hundreds of poems about roses and you know in your bones that the rose is not there. All those songs that sopranos sing as encores about 'I have a garden; oh, what a garden!' Now I don't want to put too much emphasis on that line, because it's just one line in a longer poem. But I notice that you all know it; you make fun of it, but you know it. Now listen! I'm no fool. I know that in daily life we don't go around saying 'is a . . . is a . . . is a. . . .' Yes, I'm no fool; but I think that in that line the rose is red for the first time in English poetry for a hundred years."

Gertrude, in turn, was teased by the students, who asked her whether her experimental writing was an example of "automatic writing." That charge had been in the air since the publication of *The Autobiography of Alice B. Toklas.* The psychologist B. F. Skinner, then a junior fellow at Harvard, had written an article, "Has Gertrude Stein a Secret?" for the January, 1934, issue of the *Atlantic Monthly.* Skinner had recently come upon Gertrude's two early contributions to the Harvard *Psychological Review*—one of them written with Leon Solomons—dealing with the experiments in automatic writing she had conducted under William James. Skinner felt that the two articles were "significant," and went on to suggest that Gertrude's eccentric writing style, in *Tender Buttons* and other works, was simply a continuation of the practice she had begun with William James.

In a letter to the *Atlantic*'s editor, Ellery Sedgwick, Gertrude had lightly dismissed the charges. "Thanks so very much for your good wishes and for the Atlantic with the Skinner article about my writing," she told Sedgwick. "No it is not so automatic as he thinks. If there is anything secret it is the other way to. I think I achieve by [e]xtra consciousness, [e]xcess, but then what is the use of telling him that, he being a psychologist and I having been one. Besides when he is not too serious he is a pretty good one."

With her Chicago students she gave a detailed account of the experiments and went on to add that she did not think, then or now, that the writing in those experiments was really automatic writing: "I do not think any university student is likely certainly not under observation is likely to be able to do genuinely automatic writing, I do not think so,

that is under normal conditions, where there is no hypnotism or anything of that kind."

Their two-week stay in Chicago was an island of calm in the generally
hectic progress of Gertrude's American tour. Gertrude hired a Drive-
Yourself-Car—"I adore the words," she told a reporter—and when not
lecturing, she and Alice took drives in and around the city, each day
picking a new route. Gertrude's driving was problematic on certain
occasions. She was unfamiliar with the road signs. "No left U turns,
that took me some time so much so that I did one," she recalled. On
that occasion, a policeman had hailed her. "Where do you think you
are going?" he asked. Gertrude said she was turning. "I guess you are a
stranger," the policeman suggested. Gertrude admitted she was. "Well,
go on," he told her, "but you will most likely get killed before you leave
town."

The Drive-Yourself-Car provided her with a few minor adventures
that gave her some odd insights into American life. She had a series of
flat tires, one of them while on her way to lecture. A student elected to
call the garage and have it taken care of. The car was ready when her
lecture was over. She had another flat, one day, when she and Alice were
shopping in Chicago. Since they were going to have lunch, Gertrude
simply gave her key to the doorman and asked him to call the garage
for her. When lunch was over, she had not only a new set of tires but
also a new car. And, one morning, she had looked out the window and
found her car buried under a mound of snow. Alice telephoned the
garage. The garage man suggested that they have the janitor in their
building clean it off and, of course, it was done. "Everything in America," Gertrude concluded, "is just as easy as that." She was blind to the
fact that her celebrity made it a good deal easier.

IV

Having failed with the Mississippi, Sherwood Anderson tried with the
Rio Grande; it was Anderson's descriptions of the Rio Grande Valley
with its miles of flat landscape that had whetted Gertrude's appetite for
Texas. Unfortunately, when they visited Texas after Gertrude's final
engagement at Chicago, they never managed to see the Rio Grande.
Gertrude and Alice flew first to Dallas, where they were the guests of
Miss Ela Hockaday of the Hockaday School for Girls, a junior college.
"The girls at Miss Hockaday's school," Gertrude found, "were very in-

teresting, as we were staying there we got to know them. They did understand what I had written, and that was a pleasure to me." And, she
added benignly, "to them a very great pleasure." Alice, with her culinary
interests, was impressed with the Hockaday kitchen: "the most beautiful one I have ever seen, all old coppers on the stove and on the walls,
with a huge copper hood over the stove. Everything else was modern
white enamel." She and Gertrude were particularly taken with the corn
sticks served at the meals. Later, when they boarded the *Champlain* for
the return voyage to France, Alice found a gift of a corn iron waiting
for her in the stateroom. It was from the thoughtful Miss Hockaday.
Gertrude confessed that they "ate too well almost too well" at the
school and offered her culinary opinion that since the cook came from
Louisiana, "Louisiana cooking in Texas is almost the best." Alice, however, had a different opinion, by way of Miss Hockaday: "All good
Texas food was Virginian."

From Dallas they went on to Austin and then to Houston. It was en
route to Houston that Gertrude, who preferred to sit next to the driver,
struck up a lengthy conversation with the Negro chauffeur. From him
she learned certain aspects of the racial situation of which, she confessed, she had been unaware. "Except as before the law," the driver
told her, Negroes "had nothing at all to complain of." When Gertrude
asked him what he meant by that, the driver answered that Negroes, in
Texas, had a good chance to go in for a profession and earn an "ordinary way of living," but that "if by any chance he does something and
the white man is against him and it comes up into court why then of
course it is another thing then he does not get the same justice as a
white man."

At Houston, Gertrude was surprised at the number of women that
attended her lecture. One woman, eighty years old, had driven from
Galveston to hear her; she had been reading Gertrude's work for years.
"You see," the woman explained, "it is the middle-aged people that
have no feeling, they are not young enough and not old enough to have
any understanding." Gertrude was convinced that the pioneering spirit
was still alive in the West—at least as far as literature was concerned.

They made a stop-over flight to Oklahoma City—"its towers, that is
its skyscrapers coming right up out of the flat oil country was as exciting
as when going to Alsace just after the armistice we first saw the Strasbourg Cathedral"—and then returned to Fort Worth. There they attended a performance of *Porgy and Bess*. Taken back stage to meet the
actors as they were making up, she told them she had met the author
several weeks before and promised she would write him about the performance. Then, early the next morning, they flew to California—
"God's own country," according to Alice, but Gertrude came to dislike
it. Her visit to the haunts of her childhood seemed to stir up only the
gloomy memories of her adolescence, not the happy ones.

They landed at Los Angeles and were driven to Pasadena, where Gertrude was to lecture. At the airport they had been met by a representative from Warner Brothers' studios who invited them to lunch and a tour of the studios, but they declined. Later, they accepted an invitation from the Pathé News studios for a private screening of the newsreel that had been made of Gertrude when she arrived in America. She and Alice had never seen the newsreel, in which Gertrude read aloud the "Pigeons on the grass alas" segment from *Four Saints*, putting on her glasses beforehand and taking them off afterward. She found the experience unaccountably alarming; when she saw herself "moving around and talking I did not like it particularly the talking, it gave me a very funny feeling and I did not like that funny feeling."

After her lecture at Pasadena, William Saroyan came up to introduce himself. Immediately after Gertrude's arrival in New York, Saroyan had heard her over the radio and had sent her a "charming" telegram, followed by a lengthy letter welcoming her to her native land. His letter noted, in Stein fashion, "Some critics say I have to be careful and not notice the writing of Gertrude Stein but I think they are fooling themselves when they pretend any American writing that is American and is writing is not partly the consequence of the writing of Gertrude Stein." Gertrude "liked" the "crazy Armenian," as Saroyan referred to himself, "not very much but I liked him." She was disappointed when she learned that the title of his book *The Daring Young Man on the Flying Trapeze* was not his invention but had come from a popular song.

She and Alice were entertained at a swank dinner party at the Beverly Hills home of Mrs. Ehrman, another friend of Carl Van Vechten's. Mrs. Ehrman had invited several members of the film industry, among them Charlie Chaplin and his wife, Paulette Goddard, as well as the writer Anita Loos. At Gertrude's request, she had sought out Dashiell Hammett, whom Gertrude particularly wanted to meet. After considerable difficulty she had succeeded in locating the mystery writer and sent him a telegram that Hammett, at first, thought was an April Fool's Day joke. He came to the party with Lillian Hellman. Gertrude's impression of Chaplin, whose films she admired, was that he was a "gentle person like any Spanish gypsy bull-fighter he is very like my favorite one Gallo who could not kill a bull but he could make him move better than any one ever could." Alice, trained to take stock of wives, pronounced Paulette Goddard an *"enfant terrible."*

With Dashiell Hammett, Gertrude became involved in a lengthy discussion about heroes and heroines in nineteenth- and twentieth-century literature:

I said to Hammett there is something that is puzzling. In the nineteenth century the men when they were writing did invent all kinds and a great number of men. The women on the other hand never could invent women they always made the women be themselves seen splendidly or sadly or heroically or beautifully or despairingly or gently, and they never could make any other kind of woman. From Charlotte Brontë to George Eliot and many years later this was true. Now in the twentieth century it is the men who do it. The men all write about themselves, they are always themselves as strong or weak or mysterious or passionate or drunk or controlled but always themselves as the women used to do in the nineteenth century.

Hammett, so Gertrude recalled, said the answer was simple; men no longer had the confidence in themselves that they had had in the nineteenth century, so they had to make themselves "more beautiful more intriguing more everything and they cannot make any other man because they have to hold on to themselves." Hammett told her that he hoped to circumvent this problem; he was thinking about creating a father and son. It was, Gertrude thought, an interesting confirmation of her theory. After dinner Gertrude stunned a group of cinema moguls who crowded around her wanting to know how she had gotten such extraordinary publicity. They were nonplussed and disbelieving when she told them, "by having a small audience."

At Los Angeles, Gertrude hired another Drive-Yourself-Car to make the journey north to San Francisco. They wanted to visit the Yosemite Valley, but Gertrude was afraid the roads might be precipitous. They hired a young man to drive them through. They traveled through the San Joaquin valley on their own, through "acres of orchards and artichokes," Alice recalled. At Monterey, where they stopped for a few days, Gertrude met Harry Leon Wilson, the gentle author of *Merton of the Movies*, "the best book about twentieth century American youth that has yet been done." For some reason, as they approached the hill region before San Francisco and saw the great drifts of California poppies blooming in the sun, Gertrude began to feel uneasy.

At their hotel in San Francisco they had a view of the bay. Their social engagements there had been taken in hand by the writer Gertrude Atherton, yet another of Van Vechten's friends whom Gertrude had already met in Paris. Miss Atherton took the pair to dine in the best restaurants the city had to offer and accompanied Gertrude to the Dominican convent in San Rafael. She also arranged another of the lively society parties to which Gertrude and Alice were treated by Van Vechten's women friends. "Not one regret have we received!" Gertrude Atherton had written to Gertrude well in advance of their arrival. "They fairly sputter over the telephone when asked. Already we are up to seventy-five, and hope to stop there, for if there are too many few will get a chance to talk to you."

There was one unfortunate episode connected with their California stay. Mabel Dodge Luhan, in roundabout fashion, was hoping to restore the long-discontinued friendship with Gertrude. Miss Atherton had written about it to Gertrude: "The other day, a friend of Mabel Luhan (who is staying at Carmel, an artists' colony near Monterey) called me up and said that Mrs. Robinson Jeffers was very anxious to bring about a 'reconciliation' between you and the High Priestess of Taos. I suggested that Mrs. Jeffers write to you and find out whether you cared to meet Mrs. Luhan or not. If you did I'd ask her to the cocktail party. Now, please tell me frankly how you feel about it. If you don't want her she doesn't get asked; that is certain. I like Mrs. Luhan, but this is your party and I want no jarring note." Neither Gertrude nor Alice wanted to see the High Priestess of Taos.

Years later, in *What Is Remembered*, Alice recalled—with evident satisfaction—Mabel's second unsuccessful attempt at reconciliation. She and Gertrude had stopped for several days in Del Monte, just before driving on to San Francisco. On their first night there, they had a call from Mabel. Alice answered the phone:

> She said, Hello, when am I going to see Gertrude? and I answered, I don't think you are going to. What? said she. No, said I, she's going to rest. Robinson Jeffers wants to meet her, she said. Well, I said, he will have to do without.

It was evident that Alice's painful memory of her humiliation at the Villa Curonia, years before, when Gertrude had cast such a meaningful glance at Mabel Dodge across the luncheon table, and she had burst out of the room in a fit of jealous tears, had remained with her. She now had her satisfaction. And Gertrude added insult to injury, by giving an interview, on the following day, that was an official snub to the entire Carmel colony, Mabel included. She had no use for artists' colonies, Gertrude told a reporter: "I like ordinary people who don't bore me. Highbrows, you know, always do."

But Mabel Luhan, too, was to have her revenge. She had already committed to paper her acid sketch of Alice at the Villa Curonia, giving a vivid account of Alice's humiliation. It was published in the second volume of her memoirs, *European Experiences*, published later that year.

While in San Francisco, Gertrude had had a strange inhibition about visiting the scenes of her childhood in Oakland. Finally she came to terms with her emotions: "I asked to go with a reluctant feeling to see the Swett School where I went to school and Thirteenth Avenue and Twenty-Fifth Street where we lived." Thirteenth Avenue was much the same as when she left, the houses large and shabby, the lawns overgrown with grass and bushes. But the house she had called the old

Stratton Place was not there. "The big house and the big garden and the eucalyptus trees and the rose hedge naturally were not any longer existing." It gave her a troubled feeling: "What was the use of my having come from Oakland it was not natural to have come from there yes write about it if I like or anything if I like but not there, there is no there there." At the heart of her remembered adolescence, it seems, she had discovered a feeling of vacancy.

V

Gertrude was harvesting her American impressions, and she had ample opportunities for discussing them. At virtually every stop of her American tour she had been interviewed and her lectures reported upon for the local citizenry. Not long after her arrival, she wrote a brief account of her initial impressions of being back in her native land after a thirty-year absence. Random House had sold an article, "I came and here I am," to *Cosmopolitan* for the princely sum of $1,500, the largest fee Gertrude had yet received for a magazine article. It appeared in the February, 1935, issue of the magazine.

The *New York Herald Tribune*, which had given her more continuous coverage than any other American newspaper—largely by way of Joseph Alsop's reporting—engaged her for a series of six articles on American subjects. The first of these, "The Capital and Capitals of the United States of America," appeared under a box headline, carrying her name in large type, in the March 9 issue of the newspaper. The remaining articles in the series ran on consecutive Saturdays after that. The articles were long and discursive, often falling into restatements of the same ideas, but they were pleasantly conversational in style and they offered some unique approaches to American institutions. The question posed in her first article—and for which she had no conclusive answer—was why the capital of the United States and of the various states, with a few exceptions, were never situated in the largest and most important cities. In Europe, Gertrude noted, the opposite was the case: "The capitals of important countries are in the big important city of the important country." Her tentative and hopeful answer was that this strange condition in America was an indication of the basic distrust that Americans felt toward government. She theorized: "Yes Americans are suspicious. What is the matter with it is a natural thing to say, show me I'm from Missouri is a natural thing to say. Americans are very friendly and very suspicious, that is what Americans are and that is what always upsets the foreigner who deals with them, they are so friendly how can they be so suspicious and they are so suspicious how can they be so friendly but they just are and that certainly has something to do historically has something to do with their having tucked their capital, their capitals away."

In line with the same reasoning, she made a distinction between being an employee and being a hired man. The latter was free to exercise his choice, unlike the employee, who sold himself to a system. A staunch Republican and believer in free enterprise, Gertrude was suspicious of government intervention. "I have been afraid," she noted, "these last years, that is before the depression, that [Americans] were changing, that they were getting to be not like a hired man but like an employee." Mindless of the breadlines and of the modest security her own private income provided her with, she was inclined to see some good issuing from the Depression: "Now that the depression has come in a funny way they seem to be going back again, back to being a hired man and not an employed one, at least I hope so." If she had doubts on that score, they were entirely due to her distrust of Roosevelt's New Deal policies.

Her article on "American Education and Colleges" was a plea for more individualism in education. There was an "extraordinary amount" of thought being given to the subject of education in America, particularly in New England, and Gertrude wondered if it were a good thing. "I was at a very nice boys' school the other day," she stated, referring to her visit at the Choate School, "and I know that anybody later seeing any of those boys would know that they had been at that school and I did think and I do think that that is rather a pity. It is of course necessary that anything does something to you and a pleasant school run by very competent people can perhaps do too much to you." She approved of the mobility of American society, of the fact that young people could now go to schools in any region of their choice, but she disliked the hard-sell mentality, the importance of success, that a college education seemed to be instilling in the young. It had a limiting function on the mind: "Naturally if you want to sell things your mind must be empty of everything except the thing to be sold but if you want to buy and make things your mind must necessarily be full of a great many things in other words a mind that is full of many things chooses, but a mind that is full of only one thing has to go on selling that thing and not choosing anything."

Gertrude's article on "American Newspapers," the third in the series, was in the nature of a causerie on her experiences with the press. In the days of the "yellow press," of muckraking journalism, the reporter had to strive for a sense of immediacy, as if the news were "hot off the press." But this convention, she claimed, had become a stereotyped approach in the metropolitan papers. "Think of any news that is fit to print, it all did happen the day before and once it is the day before it might just as well be the week before or the month before or the year before if you really do know that it was not on that day the newspaper day that it happened but on the day before." In an odd, homespun way, and simply as an exercise of literary analysis, she touched on what would later become an acute problem with the advent of television.

Gertrude noted, too, a distinction between metropolitan papers and small-town and country newspapers, by which she meant papers that served communities of "twenty or thirty thousand inhabitants." There, "because everybody knows everybody knows about everybody every day, and as they all know all the streets in the town and all the people in the town any news is such real news that even if it happened yesterday it is as if it really did happen today." Always happy to find some example of provincialism in large cities—she made a point of watching people reading their newspapers—she pointed out the case of the birth of the "quintettes," as she quaintly referred to the Dionne quintuplets, and of their doctor's visit to New York: "That interested the reader of the metropolitan paper as if it had been the news of a small town paper."

On the subject of "American Crimes and How They Matter," she gave a brief account of her ride in the Chicago squad car with the two detectives. She maintained that there were "two kinds of crime" that held the imagination: "the crime hero and the crime mystery, all the other crimes everybody forgets as soon as they find out who did them." She had been astonished that people still remembered Lizzie Borden, but it confirmed her view of the crime hero and the unsolved crime. She mentioned several topical crimes—the Lindbergh kidnaping and the Bruno Hauptmann trial, and the unsolved Hall-Mills case, in which a New Jersey minister and his paramour were found murdered in an orchard. The last case, she felt, was typically American: "Every one had so much openness and honesty and directness and nobody told any body anything and there was no feeling that anybody was lying." "The whole case was so American," Gertrude continued, "the orchard was American the surrounding family was American the person who had the pig farm and had something to say but never said anything, it was all so American, the causes which were there which were almost a poem and at the same time were filled with evil meaning, and it was all so simple so evident so subtle and so open . . . that is a kind of crime that means something as an expression of the American character, yes if you know what I mean." Dillinger was for her the most typical expression of the American crime hero—"The Al Capone crime is a different thing, that is a European thing, it is an organization to have something done"—but Dillinger's father could say that his son had been a good boy. "And he was right, that makes of any American a crime hero that his father can say that he is a good boy that he has always been a good boy. If they could not say that of him he would not have been on the front page of the newspaper."

Her report on "American States and Cities and How They Differ from Each Other" was the least interesting of her journalistic exercises, little more than a recital of the itinerary of her American tour and her conviction that the people in one state differed markedly from the people in another, though they were all Americans. But her final essay, "American Food and American Houses," allowed her, in her easygoing and repetitive way, to touch upon the changes in American cuisine that had taken place in her absence. She found some significant differences; the heavy American breakfast had disappeared. "Nobody seems to need them or eat them, just what has taken their place, well that seems hard to say." In earlier years, she also noted, "there were very few soups and not really good ones. Now there are lots of kinds of soups and all very good ones." The only thing that had remained constant, Gertrude decided, was American pie: "That is really the only thing really left over. And there are really no new kinds of pie."

On the subject of American houses, Gertrude expressed her mild puzzlement at the openness of the American home. In France she followed the European custom of shuttering her windows. At Bilignin, to the regret of some of her guests, she usually kept the windows, facing out on the spacious view of the valley, shuttered through the day and certainly at night. But there it was a matter of practical necessity, for Gertrude had a fear of bats, hornets, wasps, and other flying creatures. As Alice recalled, Gertrude "had no violent feeling about them out of doors, but in the house she would call for aid."

American homes, she discovered, placed no premium on privacy. "I took a walk one evening in Springfield and I found it more and more astonishing, people were sitting in a room talking and the blinds were up, or eating and the blinds were up. I said to my Springfield friend but suppose somebody suddenly got angry about something as they would in France and they began to quarrel and stamp around and perhaps throw things about does not that ever happen. I do not think so said my Springfield friend and if it did they would before it did happen they would pull down the curtain." There was, Gertrude felt, something trustful about the American character that she found pleasing. She concluded her American series on a hopeful note:

I like to think of all these millions of houses each one by itself each one all open each one with the moist food made of good material and each one with the American family inside it really not really afraid of anything in spite of everything in the way of woods and weather and snow and sun and hurricanes and thunder and blizzards and anything.

There are a great many things I like to look at and I wonder very often if it is not the most natural thing in the world to be an American.

She could hardly know that she was witnessing the American scene at the end of an era.

Well before the final days of her tour, Gertrude received a flattering letter from Joseph Alsop. A more than cordial relationship had developed between her and the reporter, and Gertrude had even visited Alsop's mother in Springfield. "Your lectures have been a revelation to me in many ways," Alsop wrote her, "The chief revelation has been yourself. You may possibly have gathered from my reports, if you have troubled to read them, that I have conceived a real admiration for you and for your work." Alsop wanted to be certain of seeing her before she returned to France. "Could I, perhaps, call on you some time before you leave New York. I want awfully to get a story on your impressions of this country after the long interval of your absence, but if you do not care to be interviewed again I should like more than I can say merely to see you."

Alsop visited her and Alice in their suite at the Algonquin several days before the May 4 sailing date of the *Champlain*. He found Gertrude buoyed up by their hectic tour: "Her cheerful sanguine-complexioned face was ruddier, her sharp eye was brighter." Alice, it seemed, was a "little exhausted by quartering every part of America except the Northwest and Southeast corners," but Gertrude "looked even healthier than ever." There were gifts and souvenirs scattered about the room, a "pink sugar woman donated by Carl Van Vechten," a shell necklace, a pair of cornelian earrings. Pictures of New England snow scenes were hanging in the place of the Algonquin's etchings. Gertrude, Alsop reported in the April 30 issue of the *Herald Tribune*, had made a rediscovery of America that "seems to have delighted her far more than Columbus' pioneer work possibly could have him." She had found everything "perfection except for California and the atmosphere." Her reason for disliking California, she admitted, was probably because it "recalled a disagreeable time in her early life." The air she found "agreeable enough, but unsuited to painters." "We've seen everything," she told the reporter. "We've seen it from the air, and we've seen it from the ground and in all kinds of ways, and in every way we've found it completely fascinating." She had developed an "especial fondness for Texas, among other places." And she was still pondering about American education. Women's colleges, she claimed, "ran their product too much to type, while at the men's the students ran just a shade too much on the serious side perhaps." When she returned to France, she and Alice would go to their country house in Bilignin. She hoped to find some "pretext" to come back to America soon. But she did not want to come back unless she found something to do.

During their final week in America, Gertrude and Alice rested comfortably in their hotel, made last-minute visits to friends, were entertained, kept up with their correspondence. The *Herald Tribune*, Gertrude wrote the Kiddie, had been very satisfied with her articles. They had been "enormously liked by the readers they care for most." She had heard the "gramophone records" and that had gone off very well. They were doing some last-minute shopping, and "next Saturday we are sailing on the Champlain, just the boat we came on." There was a note of regret in her conclusion: "Here we are and most reluctant to say goodby to you and our native land."

When she arrived in Paris, on May 12, she was still newsworthy—her American tour was to make her a public figure for years to come. An Associated Press reporter asked her how she felt about her American visit. She talked about it in the words of a lover: "I am already homesick for America. I never knew it was so beautiful. I was like a bachelor who goes along fine for twenty-five years and then decides to get married. That is the way I feel—I mean about America."

CHAPTER FIFTEEN

Here We Are and Here We Stay

I

About politics, Gertrude was willing to concede, she was "most generally always wrong." Nevertheless, she had her opinions on the subject. A week after her return to Paris, in an interview with an American reporter, she gave vent to her opinions in a manner that seemed almost vehement, as if she were satisfying an urge that had been held in check throughout her American tour. "Political theories bore me," she told the reporter, "because political theories end in nothing. Soviet Russia will end in nothing and so will the Roosevelt administration end in nothing because it is not stimulating it will end in nothing."

Huey Long, Gertrude announced four months before Long was assassinated, "will not end in nothing. He is stimulating, he is not ephemeral and he will not end in nothing because he has a capacity for knowing what men are doing and that will not end in nothing because he has a sense of human beings and is not boring the way Harding, President Roosevelt and Al Smith have been boring." It did not matter whether Long ever became President. "Most important political men never become president. Daniel Webster never became president, therefore one of the troubles of America is that we think it important that important people should become president. Democracies are more conservative than monarchies."

Nor did Gertrude believe there would be another European war. She had come to this conclusion out of a peculiar faith in her literary theory of the "audience" and a recognition that the balance of political power had shifted in the decades since World War I: "Europe is like a dog and a child playing together and when they see somebody looking it spoils their game because when they see anybody looking, they cannot get the same solemnity and intensity. I mean it is more difficult to have a convincing war or be convinced because the West[ern] world is the audience. In the old days, Europe was its own audience but now farthest North and South America are the audience. Europe cannot talk about the balance of power because European decisions are no longer world decisions for there is an audience and an audience is most important both to artists and nations." At the conclusion of her interview, she informed the reporter that "American interests" were negotiating with her to report on next year's Republican and Democratic conventions. The project never materialized, but the prospect of Gertrude's reporting on the Great American political circus in "the style she has created" seems to have an element of the surreal about it.

Before leaving New York, Gertrude had tentatively raised the issue of her future books with Bennett Cerf, and Cerf, mindful of the phenomenal publicity her American tour had generated, had promised her that Random House would publish one book a year, whether in her difficult manner or in the more accessible style of *The Autobiography of Alice B. Toklas*. With that security in mind, Gertrude began work, during a long summer at Bilignin, on a book of geographical and literary meditations, drawn from her recent American experiences, which she titled *The Geographical History of America, or The Relation of Human Nature to the Human Mind*.

Her exposure—indeed, her overexposure—to American audiences had once more raised the still-troublesome issue of her identity as a writer and of the writer's relation to his audience. She had touched upon the subject in one of her American lectures, distinguishing between two types of writing, writing for "God" and writing for "mammon."

When I say god and mammon concerning the writer writing, I mean that any one can use words to say something. And in using these words to say what he has to say he may use those words directly or indirectly. If he uses these words indirectly he says what he intends to have heard by somebody who is to hear and in so doing inevitably he has to serve mammon. Mammon may be a success, mammon may be an effort he is to produce, mammon may be a pleasure he has from hearing what he himself has done, mammon may be his way of explaining, mammon may be a laziness that needs nothing but going on, in short mammon may be anything that is done indirectly. Now serving god for a writer who is writing is writing anything directly, it makes no difference what it is but it must be direct, the relation between the thing done and the doer must be direct.

In *The Geographical History of America* she further refined this distinction in terms of new categories, "Human Nature" and the "Human Mind." As she had pointed out in her discussion of painting, wanting a "resemblance" was a pleasant human weakness, a product of human nature, but it had no true purpose for the purer function of the painting itself. In her new definition, serving God as a writer was an expression of the Human Mind.

In meditating on the subject of identity, Gertrude was to have recourse once again to canine allusions. She brought out her favorite nursery jingle, "I am I because my little dog knows me." To this she added another leitmotiv: "What is the use of being a little boy if you are going to grow up to be a man." The latter phrase, it seems, had been prompted by her gloomy reflections when she revisited her childhood scenes in Oakland. With these two themes, maddeningly repeated and rephrased throughout *The Geographical History*, she attempted to arrive at something beyond identity. In the course of her ruminations on the subject, she threw off observations about politics, the Roosevelt Administration, propaganda, journalism—in all of which the problem of identity was inextricably fixed. Identity was bound to the state of an audience, to states of memory; it was, like autobiography, a means of reassurance, a pleasant human weakness, a product of Human Nature. What she wanted was a purer state, a state of the Human Mind, out of which the artist and the genius could create. If, in the course of *The Geographical History*, she did not arrive at a successful definition or description of that state, she nonetheless was convinced that she had arrived at it in her own writing. It was from that empyrean height of the Human Mind that she could proclaim: "Why is it that in this epoch the only real literary thinking has been done by a woman."

Aside from meditating on history and politics and writing, Gertrude found the summer at Bilignin an unusually busy one. A detachment of French Army reservists had been stationed in the Belley region for summer training, and twenty-five of them were billeted in her barn at Bilignin. Other than being drunk a good deal of the time and pestering the two dogs, the reservists, Gertrude felt, were not especially bothersome. One of the reservists had an accordian, and in the evenings there was often singing, which she found pleasant. About the drunkenness, she was philosophic: "After all they cannot discipline reservists they can only keep them walking and however much they walk they must stop sometime and naturally if they stop they must occupy the time and the only way to occupy the time is by drinking that is natural enough."

When the reservists left, they were visited by Sir Robert Abdy and his wife, Lady Diana, whom they had known in Paris for several years. "Bertie" Abdy, an English baronet, was, according to Gertrude, gentle and sweet, but decidedly "peculiar." He disliked all modern art and all Americans "with a violence" that Gertrude found disconcerting. She and Alice, however, were exceptions. During his visit, Abdy kept insisting that she must lecture again at Oxford and Cambridge during the following winter, and Gertrude agreed, leaving it to her English friend to make the arrangements. The Abdys' visit was followed by the arrival of Thornton Wilder and a friend, Bob Davis, both on their way to Vienna. Gertrude and Wilder took long walks "up and down the hills near Bilignin," discussing literature and the ideas she had just set forth in *The Geographical History*. She gave Wilder a copy of the manuscript when he left.

From Vienna, Wilder wrote her an enthusiastic letter:

What a book! I mean what a book! I've been living for a month with ever-increasing intensity on the conceptions of Human Nature and the Human Mind, and on the relations of Master-pieces to their apparent subject-matter. Those things, yes and identity, have become cell and marrow in me and now at last I have more about them. And it's all absorbing and fascinating and intoxicatingly gay, even when it's terribly in earnest.

He had a cautious afterthought: "Don't be mad at me if I say again there are stretches I don't understand. This time it doesn't seem important that I don't understand, because there's so much I do understand and love and laugh at and feed on." A week later, after a visit with the famous Dr. Freud—"Really a beautiful old man," Wilder commented to Gertrude—he wrote her again on the subject, saying that he had begun "a vast apparatus of pencilled glosses" on the margin of her manuscript. "That's the way I close in on it and really digest. And the more I see, the more I see." They were to discuss the book at length, later that fall, when Wilder stopped off at Paris for several days, before returning to the States. He came to the rue de Fleurus daily, saw the famous picture collection for the first time, and for Gertrude's benefit read off his "glosses" on *The Geographical History*. Gertrude wanted him to provide a running commentary on her philosophical ideas to be published with her text when Random House brought out her book the following year. Wilder agreed to work up his marginal notes for that purpose. She was frankly disappointed when he wrote only a lengthy introduction to the book—although it was a detailed and graceful essay on her ideas—rather than the expected series of commentaries.

The subject of her new book was worth a lengthy report in the Paris

Herald Tribune and was picked up in the December 2 issue of the New York edition of the paper. The book, Gertrude told the reporter, was based on her "personal observations of last summer's activities of three members of her household"—Alice, Pépé the Chihuahua, and Basket, her poodle, which, as the reporter observed, "like Miss Stein is both affable and woolly."

Gertrude reverted to politics, once more, as if she had not finished with the subject. It was while observing Basket and Pépé, that summer, that she came to the conclusion "that politics formed a curiously isolated example of a trade based entirely on human nature without the constructive aid of the human mind." "People," she went on, "have a peculiar attitude toward being governed, in that they allow themselves to be governed not by people who think but by people who never have thought in their lives." "Do you think men like Hitler and Mussolini ever think," she asked. "Not on your life. Human nature, not the human mind guides their actions, and the people, mind you, put up with it. And yet in every other kind of human relations the people demand the use of the human mind as well as human nature. Obviously nothing constructive can develop in government so long as the leaders are in a state of identity instead of entity."

The Geographical History, she told the reporter, was written "somewhat more clearly" than some of her previous writings. Asked about the difficulties of her style, Gertrude maintained: "I cannot afford to be clear because if I was I would risk destroying my own thought. Most people destroy their thought before they create it. That is why I often repeat a word again and again—because I am fighting to hold the thought."

The subject of Gertrude's recent inspiration, Basket—so the reporter noted—had been lying quietly at his mistress's feet. Now he broke out into a "prodigious yawn. Struck by a sudden impulse, he left his mistress' side, growled slightly and slipped through the door into the night."

II

Through Kahnweiler, Gertrude heard that Picasso had stopped painting and was now writing poetry. It made her feel odd: "When I first heard he was writing I had a funny feeling one does you know. Things belong to you and writing belonged to me." She asked the dealer what kind of poetry it was and Kahnweiler answered, "Why, just poetry, you know, poetry like everybody writes." Gertrude's response was a noncommittal, "Oh."

She also learned that Picasso had separated from Olga. Given French laws on divorce and the division of communal property, it may have been one more reason why Picasso had for the moment ceased painting. When Gertrude met him, not long after, she asked Picasso how he had ever made the decision to leave Olga. More importantly, how had he ever stuck to the decision, once he had made it? "Yes," Picasso told her, "you and I we have weak characters and no initiative and if I had died before I did it you never would have thought that I had a strong enough character to do this thing." Gertrude agreed, saying that before, when Picasso made some drastic change in his personal situation, someone else had had to initiate the action, and she wondered how it had happened this time. "I suppose," Picasso said mournfully, "when a thing is where there is no life left then you either die or go on living, well . . . that is what happened to me."

Picasso was quite evidently going through a difficult period in his personal life and that fact was confirmed for Gertrude when Max Jacob visited her. Max complained bitterly about Picasso's treatment of him. The painter had spoken to him as "you who were a poet." "Why should he bark at me," Jacob said. "I am a sad and happy little old man, why should he?" "Everything is troubling him," Gertrude told the poet. Max, whose fortunes were far different from Picasso's at that moment, said, "But he has everything." "Yes," Gertrude answered, "but everything is troubling him." When Picasso brought up the subject of his poetry, therefore, Gertrude decided to deal with it as calmly and dispassionately as possible. Picasso asked her to come to his apartment to hear him read his work. Thornton Wilder was in Paris then, and Gertrude agreed to bring him and Alice one evening.

Although Gertrude was enormously curious about Picasso's poetry, the evening turned out to be uncomfortable. They sat at the dining-room table, Gertrude on one side and Wilder on the other, while Picasso read out the poems in French and in Spanish. When Picasso looked up at her, Gertrude drew a long breath and said, "It is very interesting." At one point Picasso looked across to Wilder to ask, "Did you follow?" Wilder answered, "Yes, it is very interesting." When the reading was over, they all talked about the beauty of words written on a white page and about the qualities of various languages, chiefly Spanish and French. With that, they left. On the way home, Gertrude said she was afraid "the miracle" had not happened. "The poetry was not poetry, it was—well . . ."

"Like the school of Jean Cocteau," Wilder interjected.

"For heaven's sake do not tell him," Gertrude answered.

According to Gertrude, Picasso made several roundabout attempts to find out her opinion of his literary efforts. When he visited her a few days later, he broached the subject obliquely by asking what her American friend, Wilder, had thought about the reading. Gertrude told him that Wilder had found it interesting. "And you, Gertrude," Picasso said, "you do not say much of anything." "Well you see, Pablo," Gertrude offered cautiously, "the egotism of a painter is an entirely different egotism than the egotism of a writer." When Picasso asked her what she meant by that, she decided to read him her lecture on "Pictures." Picasso sat listening while she translated as she read. When she finished, Picasso's comment was a diffident "That is very interesting." Gertrude answered, "Well, go on writing." Picasso said that he intended to, he liked the literary life; he went to the cafés, he thought, he wrote. It was very likely he would not paint again.

While in her studio, Picasso had not looked at any of the recent paintings Gertrude had acquired, but he mused that Francis Rose had "not come to anything." Gertrude agreed, Rose seemed to have reached a point of stasis, she felt, but then "everybody was kind of stopping." She felt that Rose would go on. "And Picabia," Picasso said, "after all he is the worst painter of anyone." Gertrude asked him why he felt that. Picasso said, "because he cannot paint at all." "Well," Gertrude answered, "his writing does not interest me."

The next episode in their wary sparring match occurred when Picasso asked if he might bring Dali and his wife to the rue de Fleurus one evening. He was seeing a good deal of his fellow Spaniard at the time. But on the evening that had been arranged, Picasso did not come, and Gertrude suspected it was a ploy. She and Dali talked a great deal that evening, but as she noted, "Neither of us listened very much to one another." Then Dali brought out a poem he had written about Picasso. Gertrude, knowing that the message would get back to her friend, said she was "bored with the hopelessness of painters and poetry." Painters, she maintained, did not know what poetry was. When Dali countered that it was only through Picasso's poetry that he had come to understand Picasso's painting, Gertrude could only sigh, "Oh, dear."

The issue was finally joined, one day, when she visited the Rosenberg Gallery, where an exhibition of Braque's paintings was in the process of being hung. Rosenberg asked her into the back room. Picasso and Braque were there, he told her. Gertrude shook hands with both; Braque, it seemed to Gertrude, looked a little pale. After some desultory conversation, Picasso confessed that he had sent Dali to her knowing that she would discuss his poetry with Dali though she would not do so with him. Gertrude, growing irritable, said, "Sure, I did . . . because you see one discusses things with stupid people but not with sensible ones, you know that very well." Picasso, growing excited, reminded her of her remark that painters could not write poetry.

"Well they can't," Gertrude said bluntly. "Look at you."

Picasso, on the defensive, remarked: "My poetry is good. Breton says so."

"Breton admires anything to which he can sign his name," Gertrude objected. "And you know as well as I do that a hundred years hence, nobody will remember his name."

"Oh, well, they say he can write."

"Yes," Gertrude continued, "you do not take their word for whether somebody can paint. Don't be an ass."

At this point, Braque spoke up to say that painters could write; he had been writing all his life.

"Well," Gertrude said, reminding him of his recent literary appearance in *transition*, "I only saw one thing of yours that was written and that in a language that you cannot understand and I did not think much of it."

She returned to the attack on Picasso. She reminded him that he loathed Cocteau's drawings: "It does something to you, they are more offensive than drawings that are just bad drawings now that's the way it is with your poetry it is more offensive than just bad poetry I do not know why but it just is." She then closed in on what she evidently regarded as her most telling argument: "You never read a book in your life that was not written by a friend and then not then and you never had any feelings about any words, words annoy you more than they do anything else so how can you write you know better you yourself know better."

Finally, as Gertrude later described it, their argument reached a marvelous run-on climax:

Well he said getting truculent, you yourself always said I was an extraordinary person well then an extraordinary person can do anything, ah I said catching him by the lapels of his coat and shaking him, you are extraordinary within your limits but your limits are extraordinarily there and I said shaking him hard, you know it, you know it as well as I know it, it is all right you are doing this to get rid of everything that has been too much for you all right all right go on doing it but don't go on trying to make me tell you it is poetry and I shook him again, well he said supposing I do know it, what will I do, what will you do said I and I kissed him, you will go on until you are more cheerful or less dismal and then you will, yes he said, and then you will paint a very beautiful picture and then more of them, and I kissed him again, yes said he.

With a perfect awareness of her audience, Gertrude included her lively scene with Picasso—the lapel-clutching, body-shaking episode, ending with a climactic yes that might have echoed the climactic yes of Molly Bloom's soliloquy in Joyce's *Ulysses*—in the new autobiography that she began writing in March, 1936. In *The Making of Americans*, she had wanted to write "an ordered history of every one." Now in *Everybody's Autobiography*, as she called her new book, she attempted to write the all-inclusive autobiography. "Alice B. Toklas did hers and now anybody will do theirs," she announced at the outset. The golden names—Picasso, Chaplin, Dashiell Hammett, Thornton Wilder—were to be dropped with regularity. But the common, or uncommon man—the unnamed Chicago detectives, the sleepwalking marathoners, the anonymous Negro chauffeur who had driven her from Dallas to Houston, the rather peculiar Miss Hennessy, who, in her walks around Paris, carried a carved wooden umbrella that looked very attractive on sunny days but that made her look foolish when it rained—were also to be crowded into its pages. The book was to be the best-selling mixture as before; but where the style of her earlier autobiography had imitated the terse manner in which Alice Toklas might relate an incident, the style of *Everybody's Autobiography* followed her own conversational manner—discursive, chatty, warm, and often long-winded.

Although the events related were recent in memory—for most of the book dealt with the events surrounding her American tour and her return to Europe—she was to make similar mistakes in memory. She did not, for instance, witness the Yale-Dartmouth football game after the performance of *Four Saints* in Chicago, thereby recognizing that the football players "moved some and . . . did nothing," just as the saints had done in Frederick Ashton's choreography. She had attended the game as Alfred Harcourt's guest on the weekend before she made her first flight to Chicago. And where, in *The Autobiography of Alice B. Toklas*, she had been content to declare her own genius and her literary importance, in *Everybody's Autobiography*, she was to up the ante considerably: "Einstein was the creative philosophic mind of the century and I have been the creative literary mind of the century." The success of her American tour had been heady.

Although Random House, which published the book in December, 1937, was happy to have it after the comparatively poor receptions accorded *Portraits and Prayers, Lectures in America, The Geographical History of America*, Gertrude's new autobiography did not repeat the huge success of her earlier autobiographical venture. There was only one printing of 3,000 copies of *Everybody's Autobiography*. Critics who had heaped praise on *The Autobiography of Alice B. Toklas* were inclined to be more circumspect with Gertrude's second memoir. And in some cases, more than circumspect. The reviewer for the *New York Times* panned it outright: "Easy to read and easy to forget, it is now obvious that Miss Stein's chief asset in writing is her colossal egotism and her chief inability to create character. . . . Her mind is acute and lively, as intelligent a recording instrument as one could wish for, but it is extraordinarily limited"—her rejoinder to Picasso came back to haunt her—"and almost purely parasitical."

The last charge is an odd one, for despite its disjunctive manner and its self-glorification, the book has its pervasive charms and represents the authentic conversational style of Gertrude Stein. Gertrude was to see the book as something more than another venture into autobiography. She saw it, in fact, as an authentic "narrative" and included her own apologia in the course of writing the book. Describing her walk with Thornton Wilder in Paris, on the night before he left for America, she noted: "I had really written poetry and I had really written plays and I had really written thinking and I had really written sentences and paragraphs but I said I had not simply told anything and I wanted to do that thing must do it. I would simply say what was happening which is what is narration." She had, it appears, become somewhat defensive about the book in relation to the *Autobiography of Alice B. Toklas*: "The first autobiography was not that, it was a description and a creation of something that having happened was in a way happening not again but as it had been which is history which is newspaper which is illustration but is not a simple narrative of what is happening. . . . And now in this book I have done it if I have done it." Her earlier success, it appears, had been a success of "identity" rather than a success for the Human Mind. Her evaluation of *Everybody's Autobiography*, when she received her first copies—"I must say that I read it through from cover to cover and I was fascinated," she wrote to Rogers, "I think it is an [e]xtraordinarily fascinating book"—was not, however, seconded by her public.

Their lives, following the American tour, had settled back into their normal routine—summers at Bilignin, winters in Paris. But before a second world war erupted in Europe, Gertrude and Alice made two brief trips to England. The first took place in February, 1936, when she delivered her lecture "What Are Masterpieces," a final restatement of her ideas on identity and entity, at Oxford and Cambridge, and "An American and France," a preview of her later tribute, *Paris France*, which she delivered to the French Club at Oxford.

At Oxford, she and Alice had stayed with Lord Gerald Berners, a minor English composer, and it had been agreed that Gertrude would supply him with a scenario for a ballet. The result of this effort was the ballet *A Wedding Bouquet*, a condensed and revised version of her play *They Must. Be Wedded. to Their Wife*, originally written in 1931. It was first produced by the Sadlers Wells Company in London, on April 27, 1937, with Robert Helpmann and Margot Fonteyn dancing, and Ninette de Valois in charge of production. As they had on the earlier trip, Gertrude and Alice flew to London for the occasion, arriving a few days in advance of the performance so that they could see the ballet in rehearsal. There they met, for the first time, Frederick Ashton, who was choreographing the work as he had done for *Four Saints*. Gertrude suspected Ashton was a genius and pressed Alice for confirmation, but the confirmation was not forthcoming. Gertrude had been thrilled by the performance and particularly taken with the quality of the English dancers. She was especially pleased with the dancing of the little dog Pépé, which formed part of the dramatis personae: "It was exciting, it was the first time I had ever been present when anything of mine had been played for the first time and I was not nervous but it was exciting, it went so very well. English dancers when they dance dance with freshness and agility and they know what drama is." When the curtains came down, there were calls for the composer and the author. Gertrude joined Berners on stage. She stood before the footlights, bowing to the audience, while the waves of applause broke in front of her. Her description of that moment has the quality of a dream: "And we went out and on to the stage and there where I never had been with everything in front all dark and we bowing and all of them coming and going and bowing, and then again not only bowing but coming again and then as if it was everything, it was all over and we went back to sit down."

At the opening-night party she was suitably lionized: "We met everyone and I always do like to be a lion, I like it again and again, and it is a peaceful thing to be one succeeding."

III

There were rumors of war. Hitler marched into the Rhineland; the French were demoralized. Civil war broke out in Spain while Gertrude was working on *Everybody's Autobiography:* "All the time that I am writing the Spanish revolution obtrudes itself. Not because it is a revolution, but because I know it all so well all the places they are mentioning and the things there they are destroying." The fall of Austria and the demoralizing Munich Pact were to come. Gertrude was convinced there would be no war. Her reasons for thinking so were odd: "Europe is not big enough for a war any more, it really is not, for a war countries should be bigger." Michael and Sarah Stein had returned to the States; they were now living in California. Michael cabled her, advising her to send her art collection to America for safekeeping. Gertrude wrote her brother that there was "no use in being too forethoughtful." Still, she was taking certain precautions. On Carl Van Vechten's advice, Alice was making typewritten copies of all Gertrude's unpublished works, which were later to be deposited at Yale. And through Thornton Wilder, her original handwritten manuscripts for her published and unpublished writings were deposited at the Yale Library in 1939. But Gertrude was inclined to be stoical. She and Alice, after their American trip, might well have decided to settle down in the Connecticut River valley, which—so she read in the newspapers, in the spring of 1936—had been the scene of a disastrous flood. "Everybody knows," she decided, "if you are too careful you are so occupied in being careful that you are sure to stumble over something."

During the years before the war, they stayed longer each summer at Bilignin. For Alice they were strenuous days, crowded with activities. She got up with the dawn, to gather in the vegetables and the ripened fruit. She picked the tiny *fraises des bois* for Gertrude's breakfast. With her basket and clippers in hand, a wide straw hat on her head, she cut fresh bouquets—the nameless, sweet-scented roses, the pastel-colored mallows—for the rooms at Bilignin. Each day she consulted with the cook—at first a succession of Annamese houseboys, then the Widow Roux—on the day's menu. Later in the morning she would retire to the small ground-floor room where, under a bare electric light, with stacks of paperback detective stories piled on the floor, she sat at the old black typewriter transcribing Gertrude's manuscripts.

On the *Champlain*, returning to France, they had had their fortunes told by a traveling American, who predicted continued success for Gertrude and a new career for Alice. They had wondered what Alice's career might be. For a time she considered writing a cookbook and had begun to gather material for it. Georges Maratier had found cookbooks for her from the first and second Empires; a country neighbor had given her recipes that had been written out by her mother and her grandmother. But there never seemed to be the time to work on it seriously, and Alice confessed that she would have to do research at the Bibliothèque Nationale. Gertrude, blithely taking for granted the devotion Alice spent on her own comfort, was optimistic but not, it appears, overeager to press Alice's writing project: "She has not yet had time, naturally enough who can and of course this she would not let me do for her and with reason." So the prophesied career was allowed to lapse.

Gertrude's routine remained normal. She came down from her bedroom around midday. In the afternoons she and Alice drove in the countryside and did the marketing. Or Gertrude would take the dogs walking, stopping to talk with the neighbors, discussing politics and the weather, the local gossip. In season, she devoted her walks to finding mushrooms and hazelnuts: "You go over the same ground ten or a dozen times and each time you see nuts that you had not taken. The pleasure is in the eye seeing them." She kept up a regular correspondence with old friends and with the young writers she had met on her American tour—Lloyd Lewis, Wendell Wilcox, Samuel Steward, Donald Sutherland. She read their manuscripts, tried to promote their works with publishers, reviewed them on the rare occasions when they were published, wrote recommendations for them when they applied for grants, but warned them that her name held no magic in those conservative quarters.

At times she even deigned to help Alice with the gardening chores: "I took to gardening and it was a great pleasure I cut all the box hedges and we have a great many and I cleared the paths more or less well, the box hedges I did very well and then the weeds came up in the garden." She had once asked Alice what she saw when she closed her eyes, and Alice had replied, numbly, "Weeds." That, said Gertrude, was not the answer. But even in the garden, politics could intrude. The Kiddie, who each year sent seed corn for the Bilignin garden, placed a political restriction on it, knowing the reactionary tendencies of some of her rural neighbors. Gertrude did not take the restriction seriously: "The Kiddie who sends it to us says now we must not give it to any fascists but why not if the fascists like it, and we liked the fascists, so I said please send us unpolitical corn." In the evenings she dallied before retiring: "I never go to sleep when I got to bed I always fool around in the evening." She read detective stories or, if there were guests, marched into their bedrooms just as they had settled down for the night. Plumping her ample body down on some uncomfortably small chair, clapping her hands on her knees, she could continue on with some discussion that had begun earlier. Conversations, once started, were not easily concluded.

At some point in each day, when inspiration served, Gertrude wrote. At Bilignin it was often in the late morning, behind the shuttered windows of her bedroom, which overlooked the courtyard and the plane tree. There was to be something desultory about Gertrude's literary output following her American tour, a casting about from one mode to another. She wrote prefaces for exhibitions by Elie Lascaux (1936) and Francis Rose (1937); for the *Saturday Evening Post* she did a series of five articles on the subject of "Money," a series of aimless speculations, based partly on her contention that in America, President Roosevelt was trying to spend money out of existence: "When you earn it and spend it you do know the difference between three dollars and a million dollars, but when you say it and vote it, it all sounds the same." The magazine ran the series between June and October, 1936. Her articles did not sit well with her protégés: "The young ones said I was reactionary and they said how could I be who had always been so well ahead of every one." For the *Chicago Tribune* she wrote a review of *Oscar Wilde in America*, by Lloyd Lewis, one of her newer young admirers she had met in Chicago. (Still hoping to collaborate on a biography of Grant, Gertrude proposed the subject to Lewis. The young writer declined: "With my situation what it is and my plodding scheme of research what it cannot help but be, I see time as the great obstacle.") She wrote plays: *Listen to Me* (1936), on which she hoped Francis Picabia might collaborate as scenic designer; *Dr. Faustus Lights the Lights* (1938), her version of the Faust legend, written as the libretto for an opera proposed by Gerald Berners—but neither of the schemes materialized.

Her most successful book during this period was the extended personal essay that she devoted to her friend Picasso. Written originally in French—Alice corrected the grammar and spelling—it was published by the Librairie Floury in March, 1938, with the English edition issued by B. T. Batsford in October. The American edition, brought out by Scribner's the following year, was the cause of some dismay for Bennett Cerf. Having published several of Gertrude's unpopular volumes, he found himself eased out of a book that was certain to have popular appeal. Cerf had written to her to that effect in August, 1938:

I am probably more distressed about the Picasso situation than even you are. We have endeavored—and I think succeeded—in creating the impression that we were your exclusive publishers in America. Now, to have another firm bringing out so important a book as this one breaks down, in one stroke, the whole structure that we were building so carefully. In my opinion, Batsford should have been told, when he bought the English rights, that he could sell sheets to us and to nobody else in America. This would have precluded his sending a cable—as he did on June 24th—demanding an immediate decision on the offer that he made us. . . . All this could have been worked out to everybody's satisfaction if it had been clearly understood at the beginning that he had no *right* to deal with anybody else but ourselves on this book. Just how this other offer developed is a mystery to me.

Cerf seems to have lulled himself into a sense of false security and delayed too long on the Batsford offer. He felt the price Batsford was asking for unbound sheets was prohibitive. By way of consolation, Gertrude had offered him *Dr. Faustus*, but Cerf declined: "Without a question of a doubt your book in America for next year will be the Picasso, and we feel that anything else of yours during that time is bound to suffer by comparison." Cerf, apparently, did not blame Gertrude for the misunderstanding, but it was clear that he had been overlooked. "I want you to know that I realize quite well that this mixup is absolutely no fault of yours." He concluded rather magnanimously, "I propose that we all forget about it as quickly as we can. I hope that Scribner's will do a bang-up job for you and that the book will sell 100,000 copies!" Cerf's overcompensated figure was not realized, but Gertrude could report joyfully to the Kiddie on the English edition: "The first edition of Picasso is about sold out 7500 not so bad in 3 months."

Gertrude's *Picasso* was not a conventional biographical study, though she set out the facts of Picasso's life as she knew them. Nor was it a standard critical approach to his paintings, several of which, including a number from her own collection, were included as illustrations in the book. It was an intimate recollection, containing episodes and incidents that she had touched upon in her earlier writings—sometimes with better effect. The purpose of her Picasso study seemed to be her need to define the underlying creative urge in the twentieth-century movement in art and literature. "Spaniards," she maintained, "know that there is no agreement, neither the landscape with the houses, neither the round with the cube, neither the great number with the small number, it was natural that a Spaniard should express this in the painting of the twentieth century, the century where nothing is in agreement, neither the round with the cube, neither the landscape with the houses. . . . America and Spain have this thing in common, that is why Spain discovered America and America Spain, in fact it is for this reason that both of them have found their moment in the twentieth century." For "Spain" and "America," one is invited to read "Picasso" and "Gertrude Stein."

In her attempts to define the genius of Picasso, however, Gertrude arrived at one of the prettiest definitions of the creative effort: "Picasso only sees something else, another reality. Complications are always easy but another vision than that of all the world is very rare. That is why geniuses are rare, to complicate things in a new way that is easy, but to see the things in a new way that is really difficult, everything prevents one, habits, schools, daily life, reason, necessities of daily life, indolence, everything prevents one, in fact there are very few geniuses in the world."

During those remaining years before the war, the stream of summer visitors at Bilignin had continued unabated. In the late summer of 1936 Bennett Cerf had come, bringing with him an old friend, Jo Davidson. They had flown to Geneva, and Gertrude drove to Switzerland to pick them up. The conversation during the drive back—the four of them and Basket, sitting in the car—was, Davidson recalled, "rich and furious" and nonstop, so much so that the scenery began to look strangely familiar. When they passed through the same village for the third time, the villagers cheered. "I must say," Gertrude remembered, "Bennett was astonished to the extent that we could lose ourselves in such a small country as Switzerland." Thornton Wilder, on his summer jaunts to Europe, regularly stopped to see them, and there were visits from Picabia and his wife, and Lord Berners. The latter visit was a matter of some consternation. Berners had asked to have some of the American seed corn for his English garden, and by mistake the whole package had been sent to his gardener. "But he is not a fascist, no certainly not," Gertrude wrote to the Kiddies. "I do not know what he is politically but I do not think he does either so that is alright." She pleaded for just a bit more seed, even though it was already late in the season for planting.

One of the more memorable visits, during those years, was from the Kiddies themselves. When Gertrude and Alice learned that Rogers and his wife, Mildred, would be coming to Europe in August, 1937, they decided to make an occasion of it. They planned a "sentimental journey" to the spots they had driven the Kiddie when he was a doughboy. "Do you know what we are going to do," Gertrude wrote the couple. "We are going to drive ourselves to Avignon, Arles, St. Rémy, Les Baux and then sleep at Nîmes and go to Uzès and St. Gilles and Aiguesmortes and Vienne and back to Bilignin and all the way Mrs. Kiddie will listen to the remembering of all of us and the very best time will be had by all." The itinerary, which Alice worked out beforehand, proved somewhat elusive. As Rogers observed in his memoir, titled after one of Gertrude's talisman phrases, *When This You See Remember Me*, Gertrude was "a fascinating person up to the line where practical affairs intervened, and a problem beyond that." Although Alice might calculate the driving distances and fix upon the proper restaurants and inns along the way, Gertrude, once behind the wheel, was all too likely to take off on tempting detours.

Rogers's affectionate account of the three-day tour gives a lively picture of the perplexing domestic routine that Alice was faced with managing. On the evening before they started, while they were all sitting in the living room, Alice made a point of stressing the fact—several times, for Gertrude's benefit—that they must start "early" in order to reach Chateauneuf-du-Rhône in time for lunch. Gertrude, in a mood of injured reasonableness, intimated that she had never before held Alice up. Alice's reply was a firm, "I think we ought to start at nine." Nine, it was settled, was a sensible hour for Gertrude: "Start whenever you please. Start at nine and I'll be ready. Nine is all right." Alice, once more, repeated, "early."

At that last obstinate "early," Miss Stein got up from her desk, passed the fireplace and reached the door between salon and garden. She filled the broad opening. Back to us and hands buried in the pockets of her skirt, she tipped her short-clipped gray head up toward the bright stars. She tramped back to the fireplace, hesitated and stopped. Balancing from one foot to the other—in a film new then an angry elephant tugging at its chains swayed from side to side just as she did—and with the fingers of one hand caressing the scalp over her broad temple, she announced positively, once and for all.

"Only of course I won't get up until eight. I wouldn't get up until eight no matter where I was going I wouldn't get up until eight."

Alice, bending over her knitting, declared: "We must start as early as we can."

The next morning, at ten-thirty, Gertrude settled herself behind the wheel of her Ford, announcing: "Here I am, and where is everybody else?" Alice, who had been up since five-thirty, Rogers recalled, "took an entire minute to open her door, plant one foot and then the other on the running board, pull herself up to the floor of the car, step inside, turn, begin to sit, sit, reach for the door, grasp the handle, pull it, and then lean back." In the tug of war in their domestic arrangements, Alice was often reduced to such small victories.

They lunched not at Chateauneuf-du-Rhône that day but at Viviers, which Gertrude had never seen before and which she insisted they must visit. At Orange, where the Kiddies were encouraged to view the ancient Roman theater, Gertrude took on as cargo a large yellow melon, bought in the market place. She had a penchant for melons and had eyed them favorably at an earlier stop, but made no purchase. The melon at Orange was the first of several. Along the way, Gertrude proposed, they would stop and have the melon.

"There, that's the place we're hunting for," Gertrude exclaimed after they had been driving for a while. She turned the car into a stubbled field. "This looks to me like a dump," Alice ventured. "It will end soon," Gertrude said as the Ford jounced along a primitive road past heaps of rubbish. They finally discovered a secluded spot, some distance into the field, screened from the dump by low bushes and clumps of wild lavender.

That night they stopped at the Hôtel d'Europe at Avignon and toured the Palace of the Popes by moonlight. The next morning, they set out for Les Baux and Saint Rémy. They lunched at Arles, where Gertrude discovered more melons, bought two and, out of Alice's hearing, inveigled Rogers into buying a very large one, which she assured him should cost no more than six francs. The price was seven and a half. From there, they went on to Aigues-mortes and Nîmes. At Nîmes, Gertrude bought another melon.

They had dinner that evening at Pont-du-Gard, in a restaurant within sight of the Roman aqueduct. After another evening at Avignon, they made a second brief trip to Nîmes, where Gertrude, Alice, and the Kiddie were photographed in front of the much-changed Hôtel Luxembourg, where they had met twenty years before. At Uzès, where they planned to inspect the cathedral, surrounded on three sides by avenues of chestnut trees, they were confronted with a *"défense de circuler"* sign, forbidding vehicles. Gertrude nevertheless proposed to drive through. "I don't want you to do it," Alice insisted. Gertrude remained firm of purpose. "Then, I'll walk," Alice said, grasping the door handle. "No, no, no, no, don't be silly," Gertrude objected. "We're in the car, it's smooth, it's level, it's like a road, it might as well be a road, it is a road." The car lurched forward down the forbidden drive.

It was now time for a picnic lunch. They had bought a roasted chicken, bread, figs, and oranges, but it was necessary to stop for wine. Driving along the Rhône, Gertrude stopped below a nondescript village, located on a steep incline. Rogers proceeded up the hill to the local café. In the meantime, while they waited, a peasant and his womenfolk came out of a nearby house to pass the time of day. The peasant presented Gertrude with a bottle of wine and sold her several more melons. In a large field, beside an old stone wall and hedge, they finally had their lunch.

The drive, that afternoon, was long and wearisome. At Vienne that evening, they stopped at the Pyramide, one of the gastronomical glories of the region. The menu—pâté, *écrevisses*, chicken with truffles, salad, a *bombe*, and *petits fours*—was "memorable," according to Rogers. They did not arrive at Bilignin until close to midnight and only then because Gertrude had been dissaded, at the last minute, from making a detour to Crémieu, which for some inexplicable reason had struck her fancy. "You see," Alice had exclaimed, "Gertrude wants to go to Crémieu when it's way off our road!" The Kiddies, both exhausted from the trip, sat quietly, hoping for a practical end to the journey. "It was as if," Rogers acknowledged, "Miss Stein's practical sense had been removed from her person and deposited in the person of Miss Toklas. The ego was in the front seat, and the alter ego in the back."

After their return to the states, the Kiddies had word of a surprising move. Gertrude and Alice were leaving their Parisian apartment for new quarters at 5, rue de Christine, a narrow, nondescript street that Apollinaire had made famous in his poem "*Lundi, rue Christine*," and where, supposedly, the profligate Swedish Queen Christina had had her apartments. The move was necessitated by Gertrude's landlord, who had commandeered their pavilion for his son, who was to be married shortly. Gertrude and Alice had found their new quarters through a Parisian friend, Méraude Guevara, and although they were somewhat taken aback by the dull, short street between the rue Dauphine and rue des Grands Augustins, they were impressed with the apartment with its fine old wainscotting and parquet floors. Alice, however, at first planned to carpet the floors to cut down on the noise and for warmth during the always chilly Parisian winters that troubled her. But their friend Elmer Harden and his friend Captain Peter, thought this was a desecration. They offered to pay for the restoration of the floors.

Gertrude and Alice planned to move in around the first of the year. It was always difficult to find the proper workmen, but this time, Alice, who had always extolled American plumbers, was unexpectedly surprised. As Gertrude wrote the Kiddies: "But gracious it is hard getting it ready, the funny part of it, the only angel of the lot was the plumber prompt efficient and obliging, so Alice does not sigh for an American plumber any more." Gertrude, who never lacked for proper assistance, informed the Kiddie that "A nice English boy is offering to move my books, we accept all offers." Early in 1938 they had moved into their new apartment.

After all their years and sentimental associations with the rue de Fleurus, they tried to take the move philosophically and without undue sentiment. As Gertrude had written the Kiddie: "We were tired of the present which also was the past because no servant would stand the kitchen, there was no air in the house, the garage they had built next door had made it uncomfortable." The past, it seemed, had become unlivable.

There had been few sorrows during those years before the war. The only tragedy they had to face was the death of Gertrude's poodle, Basket, late in 1938. "Basket died and it did us all up and we are just now able to smile and tell you about it," she wrote the Kiddies after the event. But she was soon able to report that there was now a Basket II: "We went to Bordeaux to get him and he is a beauty and came straight from the kennel and was scared of everything including stairways. . . . Baby Basket has lovely eyes so we feel he is Basket's baby and we feel so much better."

IV

In the troubled summer of 1939, Clare Boothe Luce and her husband, Henry Luce, the publisher of *Life* and *Time*, stopped at Belley for a visit. Gertrude and Alice lunched with them at the Hôtel Pernollet, and on the following day the Luces visited at Bilignin. Mrs. Luce was in the process of making a petit point map of the United States, a project that intrigued Alice. It somehow made her feel that Mrs. Luce "was convinced her husband would become President." The Luces, having just returned from a trip to Poland, were alarmed about the prospects of war. Gertrude had tried to allay their fears with her usual arguments, but without success. Back in America, in mid-August, Mrs. Luce wrote her: "I'm sick afraid that you're wrong about the war. Everywhere, in Poland and in the Balkans they've got too many guns, and now nobody can think what to do with them but shoot them off. That's 'raisonable' too, isn't it?"

Later in the month, Gertrude was still stoutly maintaining in front of her guests—Francis Rose and Cecil Beaton—that there would be no war. She ignored the black headlines—*Situation Plus Grave*—in the newspapers the two Englishmen bought on trips to Aix and Annecy. Beaton had visited Bilignin on several occasions and had taken innumerable photographs of the famous pair enjoying the settled routine of country life: Alice in her cretonne smock, picking the flowers for the household bouquets; Gertrude and Alice, sitting on the parapet wall in the terraced garden; Gertrude, alone, seated at a desk in the ground-floor salon. His August visit had begun pleasantly: He confided to his diary that the house, built in the mid-seventeenth century, "when domestic architecture in France was good," was ideal. "Each room is as satisfying as the solution of a mathematical problem." Alice's housekeeping was formidable: "The cakes of soap in the bathroom are placed in rigid, sharp-edged precision." And the meals were the "best food" because Alice watched over her cook with "a rapier eye." But he found Gertrude's continued optimism about the political situation "alarming." The usually serene atmosphere of Bilignin, however, turned to near panic on the morning that the butcher phoned to tell Alice he could not supply her order; the army had requisitioned his supplies. Gertrude promptly told her guests that she could "no longer take the responsibility" for their remaining. They were expected to leave.

On his last evening at Bilignin, Beaton had felt oppressed by the atmosphere and decided to take a walk before dinner: "I'd been closeted in this small house, or in the small car overrun with dogs, all day." When darkness came, and with it the drenching rains of a mountain squall, and Beaton had not returned, the two women and Rose became frightened. A neighbor stopped to ask Gertrude if she had heard the latest war news. "War?" Gertrude answered. "Who cares about war? We've lost Cecil Beaton!" Her panic had been transferred to her missing guest. After driving about in country lanes and calling aloud for him for what seemed an interminable time, Gertrude finally caught sight of the photographer in the glare of the headlights. Lost for nearly two hours, Beaton was brought home for a hot bath and a delayed dinner.

Gertrude and Alice were still at Bilignin on September 1, when Hitler invaded Poland. The war that Gertrude believed would never come had arrived. On the day that France declared war on Germany, she was visiting with Madame Pierlot and the d'Aiguys. "They all were upset but hopeful, but I was terribly frightened," Gertrude recalled. "I had been so sure there was not going to be war and here it was, it was war, and I made quite a scene. I said, 'They shouldn't! They shouldn't!' and they were very sweet, and I apologized and said I was sorry but it was awful, and they comforted me—they, the French, who had so much at stake, and I had nothing at stake comparatively."

Like many, during the first months of the war, they were optimistic that it would not last long. They decided to remain at Bilignin until the situation was more settled. But first they planned to go to Paris to get their papers and winter clothing, and to arrange about the paintings and valuables in the rue Christine apartment. Gertrude managed to finagle a military pass that allowed them to visit Paris for thirty-six hours.

As soon as they reached the French capital, they sent a message to Kahnweiler. (He had, this time, taken the precaution of becoming a French citizen, but as a Jew he was soon obliged to go into hiding in the country.) The dealer arrived at the rue Christine apartment to find Alice struggling to get the Cézanne *Portrait of Hortense* out of its frame, with her foot planted firmly on the frame. Fearing she would damage the painting, he set to work on it. At first they had planned to lay the paintings on the floor to protect them in case of bombing, but they found there was not enough room. They left them hanging on the walls. Gertrude took only the Cézanne and Picasso's portrait of her back to Bilignin. Alice, rummaging hurriedly through their papers, was unable to locate their passports, but she did find Basket's pedigree— luckily, as it turned out, since it enabled them to secure rations for the dog during the Occupation. They could not remain long; after a brief visit with Kahnweiler, they left immediately for the country. They were not to return to Paris for five years.

In Bilignin, they immediately received a telephone call from the American consul at Lyon, who advised them to leave the country while it was still possible. They were undecided, but as a precaution they drove to Lyon to have their papers put in order. When they found the consulate crowded, they did not bother to wait. The Kiddie had been warning them to leave, well before war was declared. But during the early months of the "phony war," a period of menacing quiet, they were reluctant. "We are for the present staying here," Gertrude wrote Rogers. "We have done everything we can for everybody and they for us, we see Madame Pierlot often, she is bearing up pretty well as Rob does not go any more, he is past age. . . . We have had a radio installed, I never listened to one before, there is a deplorable amount of music going on in the world, if they would suppress most of it perhaps the world would be more peaceful."

They were spending their first winter in the country in years. Their brief trip to Paris had made it apparent that they would find life a good deal easier in the country. In Bilignin, at least, there was the vegetable garden, and food would be more readily available from the local farmers than from the Parisian butchers. The main problem would be fuel; the house at Bilignin could be heated only with open fires, and they had only a short supply of coal for the kitchen stove. But

Singing her favorite song, "On the Trail of the Lonesome Pine," at Bilignin, summer, 1937. (Photo by W. G. Rogers. Courtesy Yale Collection of American Literature.)

Gertrude and Alice with Picasso, Paulot, and unidentified guests at Bilignin, the 1930's. (Courtesy
Yale Collection of American Literature.)

On the terrace with Bernard Faÿ, mid-1930's. (Courtesy Yale Collection of American Literature.)

With Pépé, the Chihuahua, at Bilignin, mid-1930's. (Courtesy Yale Collection of American Literature.)

With the Kiddie in front of the Hôtel Luxembourg at Nîmes, during the "sentimental journey," summer, 1937. (Photo by Mildred Weston.)

Alice and Gertrude on their first airplane trip to Chicago, November 7, 1934. (Photo by Carl Van Vechten. Courtesy Yale Collection of American Literature.)

With Carl Van Vechten during the American lecture tour, 1934. (Courtesy Yale Collection of American Literature.)

With Fanny Butcher, "Bobsy" Goodspeed, and Claire Dux Swift (*seated*) in Chicago, 1934. (Courtesy Yale Collection of American Literature.)

Alice and Gertrude with American GIs
on the terrace of the Berghof, Hitler's
mountain retreat at Berchtesgaden, Germany, summer, 1945. (Courtesy Yale
Collection of American Literature.)

Thornton Wilder at Bilignin, summer,
1937. (Courtesy Yale Collection of American Literature.)

Henry and Clare Boothe Luce at Bilignin,
summer, 1939. (Courtesy Yale Collection
of American Literature.)

Alice with Basket II, after Gertrude's death. (Photo by Carl Van Vechten.)

Alice alone at the rue Christine. (Courtesy Yale Collection of American Literature.)

they were, at least, in forested mountain country, and they could obtain wood.

During the early months of the war, Gertrude worked on the book she had already contracted for with Batsford, *Paris France*. Once again, Scribner's was to issue the American edition—this time, with tragic appropriateness, in June, 1940, when France fell to the Germans. Although she had begun the book before the war, it was to become, under the pressure of events, an ardent tribute to the country she had adopted as her second home. "Paris, France is exciting and peaceful," she maintained in the opening statement of the book. In its earlier segments, Gertrude expounded on the odd French sense of privacy; her *bonne* Hélène had turned dumb when she had asked her what her husband's political party was. Although Hélène had always talked freely about the intimate details of her family life, she would not discuss her husband's politics. When Gertrude asked if it were a secret, Hélène had replied firmly, "No Mademoiselle it is not a secret but one does not tell it." Gertrude discussed, too, the sense of privilege the French attached to the creative professions. Garagemen and policemen, she maintained, treated artists and writers with respect: "Well that too is intelligent on the part of France and unsentimental, because after all the way everything is remembered is by the writers and painters of the period, nobody really lives who has not been well written about and in realising that the French show their usual sense of reality." But much of the early segment of the book, including the incident with Hélène and her discussion of her introduction to French plays and French painting during her San Francisco childhood, was a repetition of material she had already used in *The Autobiography of Alice B. Toklas* and in her American lectures.

The latter portions of the book are more strenuously conceived. The war seems to have brought rigor to her style, given her more pertinent material to discuss. As if by way of explaining her own reluctance to accept the possibility of war, she told the story of her neighbor, Monsieur Lambert, a forty-five-year-old farmer, "a tall, thin man, a gentle soul, a good farmer and a good soldier," who had been mobilized during the war scare of 1938, the year before:

I met him with his wife and oxen. And I said you are leaving to go, Monsieur Lambert. Yes, he said, and my wife is crying. Is there going to be a war, I said. No, he said, my wife is crying but there is not going to be a war. Why not, I said. Because, said he, it is not logical. You see I am forty-five years old, I fought the whole of the last war, my son is seventeen years old, he and I would fight this war. It is not logical, mademoiselle that I at forty-five who fought the war, with a son of seventeen, should believe in a general European war. It is not logical.

Playing the role of devil's advocate, Gertrude suggested that the Germans and Italians might not be so logical. "Mademoiselle," the farmer answered, "they talk differently but they believe the same." A year later, with war declared, Gertrude clung optimistically to Monsieur Lambert's argument: "Monsieur Lambert is right therefore logic is logic and perhaps after all it will not be a general European war, and not a real war."

Against the backdrop of France at war—the glimpse of the Parisians they had seen carrying gas masks when they made their brief trip to the capital, the woman in the Belley market, in tears because her twenty-year-old horse, Kiki Vincent, had been requisitioned by the army because she did not have proof of the horse's age, of the young monks in the Abbey of Hautecombe mobilized—Gertrude introduced certain observations of French character and French *moeurs*. She noted, for example, "the very curious relation of every french man to his mother." There was no break, she maintained, in a Frenchman's dependence upon his mother: "He is always a son because he is always dependent upon his mother for his strength his morality, his hope and his despair, his future and his past. A frenchman always goes completely to pieces when his mother dies, he is fortunate if another woman has come into his life who is a mother to him."

There were lighter moments in the book; discussions of French fashions, in hats, in dogs, and—stealing a march on Alice, who had put aside her cookbook—cuisine. Gertrude's brief history of French cooking from Catherine de Medici, who made Italian desserts fashionable, to Madame Bourgeois, whose restaurant at Priay she and Alice regularly dined at, seems to have been gotten up from the material Alice had so far collected. The book was, as Gertrude's friend Kate Buss, from faraway Medford, Massachusetts, described it, a "love letter" to France. Kate Buss, so she wrote Gertrude, had read the book "in sorrow, in enchantment, in anguish, as I read, remembered, realized." It was, she felt, "such a tribute to France as few persons will ever be able to equal. But with all the deep delight of reading your book is mingled the anxiety of what may be happening to you—you will tell me of yourselves when you can. Meanwhile, very much love."

Despite Gertrude's faith in logic, by spring the war had become a "real war." With the defeat of Poland and the take-over of the Scandinavian countries, Hitler had turned his armies to the west. Gertrude regarded Belgium's surrender, unreasonably, as "the treason of the Belgian king." Enemy planes began flying sorties overhead. A few bombs were dropped at Culoz, a principal rail center for the region, twelve kilometers from Bilignin. The war was coming closer. The mayor of Belley came to the village to tell two women that their sons had been killed: "It was sad; they were each one the only sons of widows who had lost their husbands in the last war. . . . They were both hard-working quiet fellows twenty-six years old, and had gone to school together and worked together and one of them had just changed his company so as to be near the other, and now one bomb at the front had killed them both." The village was in mourning. Prophetically, Gertrude had praised the French attitude toward death in *Paris France:* "It is so friendly so simply friendly and though inevitable not a sadness and though occurring not a shock." Now the war was making it a reality.

They settled into a watchful routine, listening for the communiqués, three times a day, cultivating the garden at Bilignin: "I found that cutting box hedges was almost as soothing as sawing wood. I walked a great deal and I cut box hedges. . . . And none of us talked about the war because there was nothing to say." In the evenings Gertrude walked back and forth in the terrace garden, making up stories for a children's book, *To Do: A Book of Alphabets and Birthdays.* It helped to take her mind off the war.

The Kiddies had been urging them, that spring, to come back to America—there were opportunities for Gertrude to lecture. Gertrude, who had half-heartedly entertained the notion of making another lecture tour, reported that she had heard from two lecture agents but there would be difficulties in returning to France. "For various reasons," she wrote Rogers, "we could not stay away, in the first place we would go broke and the second place we would not want to." In the meantime, Carl Van Vechten was promoting the idea that there were "enormous" motion-picture possibilities for *The Autobiography of Alice B. Toklas,* suggesting that they go to Hollywood.

There were moments of dread as the reality of the war was borne in on them. "I write to you quite often because I know you want to hear," Gertrude told the Kiddie. "We go along very peacefully and then sometimes about 10 o'clock in the evening I get scared about everything and then I complete[ly] upset Alice and she goes to bed scared and I walk in the garden and I come in and I work and I am all peaceful and luckily Alice can sleep and that is the worst moment, during the day we are busy and that is the way that is."

When, early in June, Italy entered the war, Gertrude felt panic: "I was scared, completely scared, and my stomach felt very weak, because —well here we were right in everybody's path; any enemy that wanted to go anywhere might easily come here. I was frightened; I woke up completely upset. And I said to Alice Toklas, 'Let's go away.'" They telephoned to the American consul in Lyon, who told them: "I'll fix up your passports. Do not hesitate—leave."

But, still, from day to day they hesitated, in a panic of indecision, trying to make up their minds where to go—whether to Bordeaux or to

Spain or Switzerland. They made arrangements to leave the dogs with the Widow Roux, since they would not be able to take them. Then, perversely, they would decide to have one more discussion with the prefect at Bourg of the consul at Lyon, where they were told, once more, to leave. It was on one of their trips back from Lyon—on which, ominously, the traffic was stalled by the military, placing antiaircraft guns and making preparations for blowing up the bridges—that they encountered French friends, Dr. Chaboux and his wife, who resolved their indecision. The doctor was renewing his fishing permit. They asked him what they should do:

"Well," said Doctor Chaboux, reflecting, "I can't guarantee you anything, but my advice is stay. I had friends," he said, "who in the last war stayed in their homes all through the German occupation, and they saved their homes and those who left lost theirs." . . . He went on, "Everybody knows you here; everybody likes you; we all would help you in every way. Why risk yourself among strangers?" "Thank you," we said, "that is all we need. We stay."

They returned to the house and unpacked their bags and the spare gasoline, announcing to Madame Roux, "Here we are and here we stay." Gertrude took a walk down the country road she had walked so many times. The scene was peaceful, green with summer—the war seemed far away. She met a neighbor and told him of their decision. He answered, "*Vous faites bien, mademoiselle.* We all said, 'Why should these ladies leave? In this quiet corner they are as safe as anywhere,' and we have cows and milk and chickens and flour and we can all live and we know you will help us out in any way you can and we will do the same for you. Here in this little corner we are *en famille*, and if you left, to go where?—*aller, où?*"

They did not change their minds, a few days later, when Paris fell to the Germans on June 14, nor three days after that when the aged Marshal Pétain announced on the radio that further resistance was useless. These were grim days, but they went to Lyon, so they informed the Kiddie, to have their passports "made beautiful and neutral at the American consulate."

The German presence was soon established in their area. Gertrude and Alice had their first glimpse of German soldiers, one day, while shopping in Belley. Two German tanks rumbled into the city square. Frightened, they got into their car and drove back to Bilignin, where they remained for several days. A neighbor, a policeman at Belley, brought them news. Finally the armistice was signed, and on a gloomy, rain-soaked day, it was posted in Bilignin. Gertrude stood in the rain, reading it with a neighbor's wife who said, philosophically, "Well I suppose we will go on working even if we are no longer masters in our own home."

She and Alice were relieved on the following day, when the electricity, which had been cut for several days, was restored. The terms of the armistice were broadcast: Their region was part of the new Vichy government and presumably not to be officially occupied. They resumed their trips to Belley, to buy provisions. Gertrude seemed encouraged by the behavior of the Germans, but they took precautions: "We always stayed, one of us, in the car because of the dogs and the car—even though the Germans were very polite and very correct. That is what everybody was saying, 'They are correct.'" But there were moments when a sense of despair could not be held back. On a visit to a bookstore in Aix-les-Bains, Gertrude had lapsed into English. Alice warned her not to speak English so loudly. Gertrude moaned, "Nothing counts any more."

Under the terms of the armistice, most of the German troops were, at first, withdrawn from their region. There was a feeling of unreal calm. Gertrude wrote an account of the first year of the war, a straightforward narrative of the events as they had lived through them in the little village of Bilignin. She sent it to the *Atlantic Monthly*, where it was published in November, under the title "The Winner Loses." In it she recorded her hopes on August 8, 1940: "Our light is lit and the shutters are open, and perhaps everybody will find out, as the French know so well, that the winner loses, and everybody will be, too, like the French, that is, tremendously occupied with the business of daily living, and that that will be enough."

V

"In the beginning, like camels," Alice recalled, "we lived on our past." In the summer of 1939, friends had sent them ten pounds of Chinese tea. With careful rationing, Alice was to make it serve not only for the household but also for guests, until the Liberation. With the fall of France, Alice had stocked up on dried fruits and chicory for coffee, sardines and spices, corn meal. When sugar was no more to be had, they substituted honey. When meat was scarce, they had crayfish, at first supplied to them by the local butcher, but they learned to fish for them themselves, in the ingenious peasant fashion, with an open umbrella and bait attached to the prongs. Through the summer and fall, the Bilignin gardens supplied much of their needs; Alice put up quantities of tomatoes and string beans for the winter. Some of their resources were turned to unusual uses. They had a young friend, Hubert de

R————, whom they suspected of being in the newly formed Resistance. He frequently bicycled over from Savoy to bring them news. Hubert had a sweet tooth, and on one of his visits Alice concocted a dessert she called raspberry flummery, made from her own raspberry preserves and gelatin, of which she had a large supply. Their guest had shown an unusual interest in the gelatin, complaining that his wife could find none in Savoy. When he left, Alice gave him twenty sheets of it. Later they learned that he had needed it for making false papers.

The leanest years were 1941 and 1942. It was nearly impossible to find meat or eggs or milk. Their meager bread rations were usually given to the dogs. Alice had a recurrent, poignant dream of a thick slice of ham floating on a silver platter. Through their neighbor, Madame Pierlot, they discovered the black market. One didn't trade in the black market with one's money, the *baronne* told them, one traded with one's personality. Gertrude's walks became foraging expeditions. During the hardest years, she noticed that everywhere on the roads one encountered people with baskets under their arms or sacks over their shoulders, out searching for hard-to-get items on the menu. Their Ford had become a casualty of the war; when gasoline was no longer available, it was converted to run on wood alcohol. Then, when restrictions on travel were imposed, it was necessary to walk. At times Gertrude would walk twelve kilometers a day, armed with a "basket and big prospects." When she returned with an egg or a modest quantity of white flour or even, at times, a bit of country butter, she was welcomed as a hero. What seemed minor necessities—soap, darning cotton—became major luxuries. In the early years of the war, when mail between unoccupied France and America was fairly dependable, her letters to the Kiddies included odd pleas: "There is one thing though and that Mildred can help Alice, and that is white darning thread, there is no more and could you put a few yards in every letter." For a time the Kiddies sprinkled Ivory Soap flakes in each letter. Gertrude reported back that one of their neighbors had exclaimed that their mail smelled of "the American continent."

In adversity, Gertrude and Alice proved resourceful. On their first wartime Thanksgiving—an old-fashioned American custom that Gertrude clung to—she wrote the Kiddie that they were to have turkey and "near mince meat" and Hubbard squash, "but alas no sweet potatoes or Kiddie Korn." It was during the war years, faced with restrictions and shortages, that Alice maintained she had really learned to "cook seriously."

When their clothing had reached the threadbare stage, she wrote the Kiddie that they had fortunately met a young *couturier*—it was Pierre Balmain—a refugee in Aix, who had made them each a suit of clothes. They were now "most chic and warm." They even managed a full-fledged luncheon party in honor of Alice's sixty-fourth birthday, on

April 30. They had learned that their friend Monsieur Berrard of the Hôtel Berrard in Artemare, where they had often dined before the war, was now serving clandestine meals to his old clientele. Gertrude telephoned him. They were thinking of paying a visit, Gertrude told Monsieur Berrard discreetly. Monsieur Berrard said that he would be delighted to see them. As an afterthought, he asked how many would there be. Gertrude told him twelve. The guests were obliged to get there by all manner of conveyances. Gertrude and Alice rode over with Dr. Chaboux and his wife—the doctor had a small gasoline allowance and visited patients along the route. Several friends came in a farm wagon drawn by an ancient nag the Germans had not bothered to requisition. One couple came in a brightly decorated circus cart drawn by a Shetland pony; they had recently purchased the rig from gypsies they had met on the road. Monsieur Berrard's menu—*aspic de foie gras, truites en chemises*, braised pigeons, baron of spring lamb served with vegetables *en barquette*, truffle salad, wild strawberry tart—would have done justice to the happiest of times. For a few hours it seemed possible to forget the war.

Daily life, in their "small corner" of France, proved to be a salvation. Gertrude took her daily walks, held long conversations with anyone she encountered, read a good deal, sawed wood for the fireplaces in the cold, damp house. "I am writing an extra letter, too," she wrote the Kiddie. "It is snowing all day, and I have cut wood all day and read War and Peace of Tolstoy's all day." She read and reread English classics—Dickens and Byron, Shakespeare's plays. The present, with its violence and emotionalism, seemed Shakespearean to her. For consolation she turned to books of prophecy. In the early phases of the war she faithfully read her "bible," Leonardo Blake's *The Last Year of the War—and After*, a book of astrological predictions. When that proved unreliable, she turned to the prophetic writings of the Curé d'Ars and the fifteenth-century Saint Odile. The latter had been specially translated into French for her from a Latin document in the library at Lyon by a young seminarian from Belley. It comforted her to read, just at the time the Germans were meeting disaster in Russia, that Saint Odile had predicted that the battle of the Holy Mountain—and Moscow, she had been told, had been called the Holy Mountain because of its many churches—would be the beginning of the end of the war. "It is natural to believe in superstitions and hand-reading and predictions," she had claimed in *Everybody's Autobiography*.

Alice kept house, gardened, darned and redarned the stockings and the linen, read and reread her cookbooks. Somehow, each Christmas, Gertrude managed to give her a new one. One Christmas, when no communication with Paris was possible, "The 1,479 pages of Montagne's and Salle's *The Great Book of the Kitchen*," Alice recalled, "passed across the line with more intelligence than is usually credited to inanimate objects. Though there was not one ingredient obtainable it was abundantly satisfying to pore over its pages, imagination being as lively as it is." For a time she and Gertrude had thought of making an English translation of *Food in the Country of Brillat-Savarin* by Lucien Tendret, a protégé of the famous Brillat-Savarin and a celebrated gourmet in his own right. Tendret had been a native of the region, and Gertrude was given a copy of the book by Tendret's grandson.

As Jews and, later, as enemy nationals, they were obviously in danger. There was always, as Alice conceded, "a possible danger one refused to face," and by some tacit understanding between them, she and Gertrude refused to face it. In the beginning, Gertrude seems to have placed her faith in the Vichy government and the "correctness" of the German army as she had witnessed it. For perfectly selfish reasons, she believed that "Pétain was right to stay in France and he was right to make the armistice and little by little I understood it. I always thought he was right to make the armistice, in the first place it was more comfortable for us who were here." If American friends wrote that there seemed little difference, to them, between occupied and unoccupied France, her answer was adamant: "We who lived in the unoccupied we knew there was a difference all right. One might not be very free in the unoccupied but we were pretty free and in the occupied they were not free, the difference between being pretty free and not free at all is considerable." There were days, however, when their faith in simply living from one day to the next wavered. After Pearl Harbor and America's entry into the war, Gertrude confessed to the Kiddies: "When I write now I wonder if you will get it. . . . Now we do not know how you are and where you are, and what you are doing and feeling, it is the first time since the debacle that you seem far away and we hope every day that a letter will come from you and then that they will keep coming. . . . We think of you all as you all thought of us, only we think of you doubly because after all us is us."

Gertrude's early faith in Pétain needed something more, by way of justification, than her own sense of security. She was later to come to the conclusion that Pétain's armistice "was an important element in the ultimate defeat of the Germans." She had been amazed that the Germans had granted the conditions they had under the armistice when they could so easily have taken over the whole country. No one seemed able to give her a satisfactory explanation for this "miracle" until she was given one by a French officer she had met. The officer's opinion was that the German Army had planned an "arduous and fairly long campaign in France and then an attack on England." The Germans were completely surprised by France's surrender, the officer maintained, and then hurriedly decided to move up their timetable: "England this year instead of next year as it was intended and so they could not lose any more time so when Pétain suggested the armistice they were delighted because now their hands were free to turn back to England, they knew Pétain was a man of his word so they were not worried about what was behind them." According to the officer, the Germans' mistake was that they were not materially prepared to undertake their hurried invasion campaign, and by the time they were, American lend-lease had strengthened the English and it was "too late too late." Whatever might have been in the minds of the German General Staff, the officer's explanation satisfied Gertrude. She felt there was some justice to the anecdote about Pétain that was circulating at the time. Asked who was winning the war, the Germans or the English, the old marshal had "pointed to his own breast and answered I."

Gertrude's faith in Pétain was partly based on her understanding that during World War I, the marshal had, by shrewd administration, aborted the mutiny of the French troops. But she later confessed to a rather confused attitude toward Pétain: "So many points of view about him, so very many, I had lots of them, I was almost French in having so many." Her need to justify Pétain's decision to surrender to the Germans appears to have encouraged her to undertake one of her strangest literary exercises. Sometime in 1942 she began to translate Pétain's volume of speeches, *Paroles aux Français, Messages et écrits, 1934–1941*, evidently hoping for publication in America. The manuscript volumes—two of them, covering some 180 pages of Pétain's text, with Alice's corrections of Gertrude's literal rendition—were turned over to the Yale Library after Gertrude's death. The manuscript includes her brief preface, in which she offers the opinion that the defeat at Pearl Harbor might make Pétain's action more understandable to Americans. That she did not complete the project may indicate that she regarded the exercise as futile and not likely to reach publication. Or it may indicate some change in her own political attitudes. As the Occupation progressed, she began to have a greater dislike for the Vichy bureaucracy and a distrust of petty officialdom. She found it difficult to understand why civil servants could not see the handwriting on the wall—the fact that the Germans could not win the war. She wondered why they held to the same routines. "And now," she remarked in 1943, "everybody knows except the public servants they are still believing what they are supposed to believe nobody else believes it, not even all their families." Under the constraints of the occupation, she suddenly became eloquent on the subject of freedom. People wanted "to be free, not to be managed, threatened, directed, restrained, obliged, fearful, administered, they want none of these things they all want to feel free." She had become weary of propaganda. She wondered if "Laval and the rest of them think they are right now in 1943."

Their most important protector during these years was Bernard Faÿ, who had been appointed director of the Bibliothèque Nationale by the

Vichy government. With his strong connections with Vichy officials—
each month Faÿ conferred with Marshal Pétain in Vichy, and often
visited with Gertrude and Alice after these meetings—Faÿ was in a
position to alert her to any probable dangers. In a lengthy defense of
his wartime actions, written long after the war, Faÿ mentioned his protection of Gertrude and Alice: "I obtained from Pétain that the Pré-
fet and the Sous-Préfet should help them, watch over them."

If their situation in Vichy France was precarious, Gertrude did not
live meekly in hiding. She took part in local activities. In the spring of
1942 she helped organize an exhibition of local painters in Belley. She
was photographed at the opening of the salon by one of the local papers, *Le Petit Dauphinois.* In another, the local weekly, the *Bugiste,*
she gave an interview in which she announced her progress in translating Pétain. The reporter wrote glowingly about the project, describing
it as "the means of making the most fragile truths understood by the
great people of her country and others, without shocking anyone. It
will be an event, this presentation of the France of today to America."

Nor was Gertrude inclined to hold back on her opinions. When she
encountered Frenchmen who seemed "not sure that they did not want
the Germans to win," she asked them why, "pretty violently and pretty
often." Finally a bank clerk enlightened her on the subject. The clerk
told her that a man might have "a great many different points of
view" on the subject—if he were a businessman, he might want the
English to win so that his business would be secure, which it might not
be if the Germans won. If he had a son who was a prisoner, he might
be afraid the war would last too long, if the English were to win, and
his son might be killed. It was, Gertrude was forced to acknowledge, a
time of complex emotions: "The middle classes were once more torn,
if the Russians win, would there be communism, if the Germans win
would there be misery and oppression, if the English win would they
lose all their colonies."

She had personal knowledge of the complexity of the situation. The
lease on their house had run out, and her landlord, a captain in the
French Army, had served notice that he wanted to take possession of
the house at Bilignin. Gertrude had instituted a lawsuit—certainly a
move that might well have created enmities and that could have been
dangerous for the two of them during the German occupation. They
lost their suit, but the authorities had allowed them an indefinite stay
of execution. Later, however, when their landlord had been demobi-
lized and was considered as having just cause for reclaiming the house,
since he intended to live in it, Gertrude had begun proceedings for a
second suit against him.

Fortunately, friends found them a house in Culoz—a more modern
house, with a park, but, to Alice's sorrow, no large garden plot. It was
located some distance from Culoz itself, and it was being rented with a

staff of two servants, Olympe and Clothilde—one an expert cook, the other "a very perfect chamber maid." She and Alice decided to take the house and informed the lawyer to stop the second lawsuit.

The day before they were to make their move, early in February, 1943, Gertrude walked to Belley to say good-by to friends and her lawyer. Her lawyer told her that he had a serious message from Maurice Sivain, who had been the Sous-Préfet at Belley but was now working in Vichy, where the lawyer had met him on the previous day. Sivain told him flatly: "Tell these ladies that they must leave at once for Switzerland, tomorrow if possible, otherwise they will be put in a concentration camp." Gertrude was stunned:

But I said we are just moving. I know he said. I felt very funny, quite completely funny. But how can we go, as the frontier is closed, I said. That he said could be arranged. I think that could be arranged. You mean pass by fraud I said, Yes he said, it could be arranged.

She and Alice sat through a gloomy supper that night. Finally Gertrude said, "No, I am not going we are not going, it is better to go regularly wherever we are sent than to go irregularly where nobody can help us if we are in trouble." "They are always trying to get us to leave France," she added, "but here we are and here we stay." That night Gertrude and Alice walked back, in the dark, to tell the lawyer their decision. On the next day, they moved to Culoz.

As she had with their move to the rue Christine, Gertrude tried to put a good face on the change: "After you have been living in an old house for so long a new house has pleasant things about it, windows that fit and light and air." The house was called Le Colombier, and it was situated in a secluded park of fir trees against a mountain. She thought it large and comfortable. One of her first acts was to buy a white goat, for milk. She named it Bizerte, after the recent Allied victory.

Alice was less reconciled to the change. She missed the gardens at Bilignin. The cook, Clothilde, she soon discovered, "was old, tired and pessimistic," and claimed she could not cook on the meager rations that their coupons allowed. "So it fell upon me to do most of the cooking while a great cook sat by indifferent, inert." Years afterward, she recalled that last morning in February when they left Bilignin, a "cold winter day, all too appropriate to our feelings and the state of the world." It was the day when the German troops that had been occupying the southern zone moved into Belley. As Alice stood on the terrace, looking over the frozen gardens, the trim box hedges, the tall column of boxwood, "A sudden moment of sunshine peopled the gardens with all the friends and others who had passed through them."

CHAPTER SIXTEEN

The Liberation of Gertrude Stein

I

Shortly before the move to Culoz, Gertrude had begun writing a book about her wartime experiences. Early in the war the Kiddie had suggested that she write on that subject, and Gertrude had responded, "Yes perhaps I will write how it all is, I like to make you cry and to make money, bless you both." The result had been not a book, but an article, "The Winner Loses." The Kiddie's hint may well have prompted her to write *Wars I Have Seen*, her account of life in wartime France. But she had a forceful example in her old friend Mildred Aldrich, who had remained in her farmhouse near the Marne throughout World War I, recording her day-to-day experiences, the events of the war as it swirled around her.

Except for its opening pages, *Wars I Have Seen* is Gertrude's daybook of events in rural France during the war that occurred thirty years later. It begins with an excursion into her personal past as a jumping-off point for the episodes of the present. Gertrude recounts briefly the wars she could remember—the Boer War, the Spanish-American War, the Russo-Japanese War, World War I—some of which were so remote that they "did not particularly concern" her. She mentions, too, the wars she had been told about by her parents, such as the American Civil War. Her mother's vivid description of the Union soldiers transferring from one station to another in Baltimore, for instance, made that war especially "real" for her. And in the opening passages of the book there is some attempt to come to grips with the always-mysterious forces—the family wars, as it were—of childhood and adolescence. In one of these passages she makes an odd admission: "Naturally my mother being Baltimore there was the South, and naturally there was the North. My father I never took on in war although he was north." In childhood, it appears, her emotions were split along geographical lines.

Once the book assumes the task of describing the immediate events of World War II, ticking off the months and days—"Just tonight, June 1943 . . ." "Today, the eleventh of September, 1943 . . ."—it becomes an amazingly shrewd, warm, and humane account of beleaguered France, of the minor acts of heroism and endurance of her French friends and neighbors. The scenario for this segment of the book stretches from the wintry, moonlit night in January, 1943, when she was walking Basket and encountered a young gendarme from the village who had been made a bodyguard to Marshal Pétain, to the last weeks before the liberation, when the young Maquis were blowing up German trains and making Robin Hood raids on wealthy farmers guilty of collaboration. In the book, Gertrude set down the moments of personal danger, such as the evening she and Alice were warned to leave for Switzerland or risk the concentration camp, and the months of August and September, 1943, when first a German major and his orderly were billeted at their house at Culoz, and then a contingent of Italians. Although she and Alice had avoided seeing any more of the Germans than they had to, keeping to their rooms, Gertrude was surprised to find them "very meek, just as meek as that." With the Italians, they were not so cautious: "They were rather attaching, foolish and could not keep away from the young servant, they went in one door and came out another and then they were still there, but otherwise they were sad, and they hated the Germans and they liked everybody else."

And there were the dangerous moments, just before the end of the war, when one neighbor was denouncing another. Her friend Monsieur Berrard was taken off to prison for dealing in the black market—someone had denounced him: "Poor Madame Berrard said it was so sad to see her husband going off between two policemen just as if he was a criminal and to know that some of their neighbors were pleased to see it." The prisons were so full at the time that the situation had its comic aspect. One man, sentenced to three months for stealing, had to wait two months at home before there was a vacancy in the jail. Collaborators or those suspected of collaboration were being sent small black coffins. It was a frightening, anxious period. At one point Gertrude was afraid her disaffected servant Olympe might denounce them. Olympe's mistress, their landlady, was insisting that her maid come back to work for her, and the servant plainly did not want to go. In her anger, might Olympe reveal their situation: "Could those to whom she was loyal could she stop being loyal to them."

Gertrude recorded the heroism of the young men, slipping off into the mountains to serve in the Maquis, and of their friends who aided them. Her account is full of growing admiration for the young hotspurs. But there are moments of woe. The narrative is interrupted: "The son of our dentist a boy of eighteen has just been taken because he was helping and will he be shot or not. Oh dear. We all cry." But young Victor, the dentist's son, is resilient. He escapes from prison in Italy and makes his way back home to rejoin the Maquis. "After all that," Gertrude reports, "he went to Lyon on business for his friends, and was caught by the Germans and now is in prison again and his mother is desperate." She meets another escaped prisoner, an Alsatian: "Now all he had to do was to avoid big cities not that he really did, they never do and I asked him how he managed to get out of his troubles and he answered by patience and address and I suppose that is the way to get away." She receives a letter from the baker's son, a prisoner in Germany, who tells her: "I always liked you and your country and I have not changed my mind, far from it." She comments: "Well he is free to say what he will but that is very difficult to stop, very very difficult, even in prison."

Gertrude had words of comfort for those who were made of less heroic mettle:

And now it is June 1943 and two of the young men who are twenty-one have come to say good-bye, they hope they are not going to die right away but all who are twenty-one have to go to Germany as hostages to be put in a pen, they say to work in factories but there is no work, and if they go into hiding well it would be all right if it were not for the winter but will it be over before the winter, they ask me to tell them but can any one tell them, do I know, well anyway I can say that they might amuse themselves by learning and reading German and they might amuse themselves by saying that they are going traveling as students, and say they, if we do not consider them as enemies will the Americans like it, will they, might it not displease them, but said I you can learn their language and read their literature and contemplate them as if you were travelers and still know them to be enemies. Why not. Well said they why not. Anyway they said you have cheered us, and I kissed them each one of them and wished them well, and one of them came back to shake hands again and I kissed him again and said be prudent and he said I will and they went away up the hill. Oh dear me one cannot sleep very well.

In the course of the book, she registered unexpected acts of kindness to herself and others. After America's entry into the war their funds were running low and prices were rising. Neither she nor Alice had mentioned it to their friends, but they were clearly beginning to worry. "One day," Gertrude wrote, "a young man his name is Paul Genin and we had come to know him because they had bought a house in the neighborhood, he was a silk manufacturer from Lyon and he was interested in literature one day he said to me are you having trouble about money. I said not yet I still have a supply but it is beginning to run pretty low and he said can I help you and I said what can you do, well he said write out a check in dollars and I will see what I can do." Genin later returned the check; after investigating the possibilities, he decided that the procedure was too risky. Instead he offered to be her banker for six months, providing her with what she needed each month. "I said what do you want me to give you in the way of a paper, oh nothing he said, I think it is better not, but said I if I died or anything you have no evidence of anything, oh he said let us risk it." At the end of the six months, she noted, "I sold a picture I had with me quite quietly to some one who came to see me and so I thanked Paul Genin and paid him back and he said if you ever need me just tell me." The picture was her favorite Cézanne. Pierre Balmain, who lunched with her not long after the sale, noticed that the painting was no longer in its place in the dining room and asked what had become of it. "We are eating the Cézanne," Gertrude told him without a trace of sentiment.

There was, too, the brusque kindness of a departmental clerk in dealing with a woman Gertrude knew, a Jew who had fled occupied Paris when the persecutions against the Jews there had begun. She had moved to Chambéry. In the last days of the war, when the Germans were occupying the southern zone, there was a directive that all Jews would have to register and have their identity cards and food cards stamped. The woman had gone to the prefecture: "And the official whom she saw looked at her severely Madame he said, have you any proof with you that you are a Jewess, why no she said, well he said if you have no actual proof that you are a Jewess, why do you come and bother me, why she said I beg your pardon, no he said I am not interested unless you can prove you are a Jewess, good day." Her own situation and Alice's had long before been taken care of by the officials at Culoz. Their names had been completely left out of any lists that had been required by the Germans.

Some moments in her book were to be as graphically described as anything she had ever written, even though they dealt with unimportant episodes, such as the walk she took one winter evening on her way back home from a visit with a neighbor:

It was late in the afternoon and there was a glow in the sky and I went up the mountain there is a very big steep one right in back a real mountain and they bring wood down from the top of it by a cable. I went higher and higher and the water was falling down the mountain side louder and louder and it was very nice and cold quite cold and getting darker. I like it getting darker and as I was going up higher and higher and it was Sunday and nobody was working as it was getting darker I began to meet groups of men coming down from the mountain and I said how do you do and they said how do you do. And then as it was really getting darker I turned around to come down again, and it was very dark and darker and it began to rain and snow and sleet, and I could not see but I could feel the crunch of the gravel under my feet and so I could stay on the path and all around me I heard others coming down too and there were in little groups about twenty-five men who passed me and they went quickly and I went slower and I was getting wetter and wetter and I wondered why there were so many men of a Sunday coming down the mountain.

They were, Gertrude supposed, the Maquis coming down the mountain "to have a good dinner" with their families and spend the night.

She even recorded, in *Wars I Have Seen*, her comic exasperation in trying to explain American military strategy—or, at least, her view of it—to Frenchmen who were impatient for the American landings. The French, she observed, liked "good fighting":

They are as I am always telling them hopelessly European about all this, they cannot get into the point of America, that fighting consists in putting the other man out of business, there is no use just in going forward or back and using yourself up, it is just the difference between old fashioned dancing and American dancing, in old fashioned dancing you were always sashaying forward and back waltz or polka or anything but in dancing as Americans invented it you stay put you do it all on one spot. Well that is the American idea dont have your armies running all over the place but stay on one spot, bombard and bombard until all the enemy's material is destroyed and then the war is over.

But, she confessed, she had little success with her argument. And at one point, she was obliged to concede: "Enough said that is not the way the French mind works."

II

Gertrude and Alice were as impatiently awaiting the American Army as were their French friends. "It is darkest before the dawn," she writes in late April, 1944, "at least we all hope so, we are all terribly worried these days, alerts and airplanes and everybody wondering if everybody in Paris and Lyon are starving and indeed it is not impossible because with all the transport cut what can happen to them." The spring had not been promising. Their goat, Bizerte, had died in childbirth; the buzzards had carried off three of their baby chickens. Since the war, hunting had been restricted and the buzzards had multiplied. They had noticed that there were more spring birds, more quail, than usual that year; neighbors thought that it was the fighting in Italy that may have driven them northward. It was also the season of the "red moon." "We first heard of this dreadful lune rouge or red moon," she writes, "from Mildred Aldrich who during the last war lived in the country and thought agriculturally and in this war we are living in the country and thinking agriculturally and alas to-day . . . everything has frozen and as Easter was late and that made the red moon come late it is now the middle of May alas all the grapes were forward and the potatoes well up and they are all as the French say, scorched."

What became frightening was that, with the tide of the war turning, the Germans had become unpredictable and, sometimes, vicious. At Culoz two young boys who tried to run away were shot, and an old man, a drunk, who was out after curfew. The Germans had left his body on the road all night. All the townspeople attended his funeral. The body of a young schoolteacher from Seyssel, where there were, reportedly, many reprisals because the area was thick with Maquis, had been found washed up on one of the islands in the Rhône, a bullet through her head. The mayor's wife, Madame Rey, told Gertrude of a recent incident with the Germans. Her husband was required to go with them whenever they had something to be done. One day, they drove up for the mayor in a car. As they were leaving, the German officer had turned to Madame Rey and—out of earshot of her husband—said, "Madame weep because we are taking your husband away." Madame Rey refused and steadfastly insisted, "No," when the officer claimed that her husband was really being taken away. She had to wait three anxious hours before her husband returned. "Sadism," Gertrude said. "Yes," Madame Rey answered, "to make themselves feel masters."

The "bombardments" began, and Lyon was struck. Gertrude sold her car to a neighbor, a Red Cross worker, whose car was demolished during the bombing of Lyon: "I was sad to see it go but nevertheless there will sometime be lots of others. . . . we are all waiting yes waiting." She held firm to her conviction that there would be no Allied landing until Rome was taken, and to her faith in Saint Odile, who prophesied that when Rome was taken it would be the beginning of the end. She was joyous when she could report, "To-night Rome is taken, and now that Saint Odile's prophecy is being fulfilled it is a pleasure and such a pleasure." Two days later Gertrude was exultant: "To-day is the landing and we heard Eisenhower tell us he was here they were here and just yesterday a man sold us ten packages of Camel cigarettes, glory be, and we are singing glory hallelujah, and feeling very nicely, and everybody has been telephoning to us congratulatory messages upon my birthday which it isn't but we know what they mean."

For months, they waited for what Gertrude called the "liberation of Gertrude Stein." The cook was already fattening up a rooster, weighing it every day, for the "first dinner party of the first American general who comes this way." Early in July they had had a scare when a somewhat belligerent German officer and a contingent of soldiers commandeered the house: "I called the servants and told them to attend to them, I thought with that kind of a German it was just as well to keep our American accents out of it, and then they were at it, the German said he wanted two rooms for officers and mattresses for six men and he did not want any answering back and he did not care how much he upset the ladies of the house, and the servants said very well sir." Gertrude and Alice locked up what valuables they could and took the dog and went upstairs to bed. The soldiers were gone in the morning, after having stolen a pair of slippers belonging to the servant and the peaches that Alice had put up. Gertrude could not find her umbrella: "It turned out that it was used by a poor devil of an Italian whom they kept outside all night in the rain to sit with the horses."

Later that month she had had a strange preliminary announcement. Walking along the road near her house, where Germans had been encamped the night before, she poked about in the refuse with her stick and found a printed wrapper: "Half pound weight Swifts yellow American farmers cheese, distributed by Bright and Company Chicago Ill. and underneath it it said, buy war bonds and stamps regularly and then it said a natural source of vitamins and riboflavin, now what that is naturally we do not know, it seems to have come on since we knew about what they needed to have in America, but where oh where did the German army get this cheese." The American product had arrived in advance of the American Army.

Then, one day, early in August, the Maquis took over the village of Culoz and proclaimed the Fourth Republic, even though there were still twenty-five German soldiers remaining meekly in the village. They were mostly railroad workers, and no one bothered to gather them in. Alice began making the typescript of *Wars I Have Seen*; it had remained safely in manuscript until then. Gertrude acknowledged that her handwriting was so bad that no German was likely to be able to read it. The excitement mounted each day. The Americans, they heard, were at Grenoble, only eighty kilometers away. Then there was the radio announcement that Paris was free and unharmed. "I cant tell you how excited we all are," Gertrude wrote in her ledger book that day, "and now if I can only see the Americans come to Culoz I think all this about war will be finished yes I do."

She did not have long to wait. On September 1 she was able to exclaim, "What a day, what a day of days." The day before, the watchmaker's son brought her word that the Americans were at Culoz. "Really I said yes he said well I said lead me to them." They were at the local hotel, the boy told her. "I saw the proprietor of the hotel and I said is it true there are Americans, yes he said come on, and I followed and there we were Alice Toklas panting behind and Basket very excited and we went into a room filled with maquis and the mayor of Belley and I said in a loud voice are there any Americans here and three men stood up and they were Americans God bless them and were we pleased." She listed their names: Lieutenant Walter E. Oleson, 120th Engineers, and privates Edward Landry and Walter Hartze, adding, "how we talked and how we patted each other in the good American way." She and Alice were taken for their first jeep ride. Then it seemed as if the entire American Army was pouring into Culoz; but it turned out to be a false alarm—the French Army arriving in American trucks. They did, however, discover two more Americans: "I went over and said are you Americans and they said sure, and by that time I was confident and I said I was Gertrude Stein and did they want to come back with us and spend the night. They said well yes they thought that the war could get along without them for a few hours so they came." The soldiers were Lieutenant Colonel William O. Perry of the 47th Infantry Division and his driver, Private John Schmaltz. They were royally dined, talked at, talked to, questioned about their places of birth, and told that they were going to sleep in beds where German officers had slept only six weeks before. The next morning, after breakfast and more talk, Lieutenant Colonel Perry and his chauffeur left.

As Gertrude and Alice were sitting down to lunch, tired and happy, the cook, Clothilde, came running upstairs from the kitchen, calling wildly, "Madame there are Americans at the door." It was a pair of war correspondents: Eric Sevareid, whom Gertrude had met in Paris before the war, and Frank Gervasi of *Collier's*. Sevareid had been searching for her—Bilignin was the last address he had—but fortunately he had met Lieutenant Colonel Perry as he was returning from his visit to Culoz. Sevareid, in his memoir, *Not So Wild a Dream*, recalled a "magnificent lunch" but mostly the talk. Gertrude had wanted to be filled in on people with whom she had lost touch. Sevareid gave her news of Thornton Wilder, who was in Army Intelligence, and of Francis Rose, whom he had seen recently in London and who, much to their surprise, had recently married. When the correspondent mentioned having seen

Hemingway's wife, Martha Gellhorn, Alice "sniffed and said: 'That makes his third wife. Tch, Tch, Tch.'"

Gertrude, Sevareid remembered, did most of the talking. He noted that Gertrude had "a faint tone of sorrow that Pétain had turned out so miserably, and she said it was when he let the Germans round up the young men for service in Germany that people really turned against the old man. Laval was unspeakable." She mentioned that the mayor of Culoz and their neighbors had kept their secret, and Sevareid reported: "When the Germans began rounding up enemy aliens the mayor simply forgot to tell them about the Stein household, because, he said to Gertrude, 'you are obviously too old for life in a concentration camp. You would not survive it, so why should I tell them.'" Despite their difficulties, Gertrude told the correspondent that the past five years had been "the happiest years of her life." She felt she had come "very close to the ordinary French people" and had learned more about them by sharing their tribulations during that time than she had in all the years she had lived in the country. Gertrude, Sevareid observed, seemed "just a trifle more bent, a trifle heavier in her walk" than he remembered her. Alice was "still soft, small and warmly murmurous, but also a little more bowed." Gertrude had launched into a new theory, that Hitler was "essentially a nineteenth century person" and his war had destroyed the nineteenth century finally and irrevocably. Sevareid interrupted to remind her of a conversation they had had before the war in which she had claimed that Hitler was not a threat because he was a "German Romanticist" who might want the illusion of power but would hardly stand the blood and fighting involved in getting it. Gertrude hesitated, for the slightest moment, then resumed her argument as if she had not heard.

Gervasi, who was flying back to the United States, offered to deliver the manuscript of *Wars I Have Seen* to Bennett Cerf and to mail Gertrude's letters to friends she had not heard from for years. Sevareid arranged for her to make a broadcast to America from Voiron, some forty miles away. They came to get her two days later. At the press camp, Gertrude and Alice created "something of a sensation." Gertrude, settling down behind the microphone, informed her countrymen in a clear, cultivated voice: "I can tell everybody that none of you know what this native land business is until you have been cut off from that same native land completely for years. This native land business gets you all right." She spoke of the excitement of her meetings with the American soldiers of the past few days and named each of them and the states they had come from. She mentioned the long, "heartbreaking" period of the occupation and ended on a reflective note, with a typical Steinian repetition: "I can tell you that liberty is the most important thing in the world more important than food or clothes, more important than anything on this mortal earth, I who spent four years with the French under the German yoke tell you so. I am so happy to be talking to America today so happy."

She had learned about politics in one of the most severe schools.

III

It was mid-December when Gertrude and Alice returned to Paris. Gertrude managed to hire a car, as well as a truck for their larger possessions. It was a cold, dark night, and it was raining by the time the packing was finished and she and Alice were ready to start on their journey. The trip took all night; the roads were uncertain, many of them were still not passable and they encountered several detours. Toward dawn they were stopped, at gunpoint, by two men and a woman. They were members of the Resistance, wanting to know who the two women were and where they were going. When one of the men leaned too heavily on the Picasso portrait that they were transporting to Paris, Alice spoke up sharply: "Take care, that is a painting by Picasso, don't disturb it." The man said, "We congratulate you, Madame," and waved them on.

At the rue Christine, they were relieved to find that the picture collection was intact. In November they had been forewarned by an American neighbor, Katherine Dudley, that the Germans had broken into the apartment a few weeks before the Allies had taken Paris. A young secretary, on the floor below, had heard them rummaging around overhead and went upstairs to discover four members of the Gestapo, gesticulating in front of Picasso's large pink nude, swearing, "Jewish filth, that cow," and threatening to slash and burn the paintings. She summoned the gendarmes, who managed to put them out. There were some items stolen, however. It was not until the morning after their arrival that Alice learned what was missing—a small petit-point footstool that she had worked from a design by Picasso, a pair of Louis XIV silver candlesticks, and the cast iron cornstick pans that had been a gift from Miss Hockaday. She also discovered a bundle of small pictures already tied up.

On the day of their return, Picasso hurried over to the apartment to greet them. They embraced one another heartily, then wept and rejoiced together that the "treasures" of their youth, the paintings and drawings, had not been harmed. Picasso had heard of the break-in and contacted Bernard Faÿ who assured him that the situation had been taken care of. Gertrude thought it a "miracle" and Picasso agreed. It was a miracle, he said, "thanks to Bernard Faÿ." Alice made coffee. Picasso admired a Henri IV table they had brought with them from the country and Alice offered it to him on the spot. "Take it now," she said. "We have no place for it here."

In the next few days, there were joyous reunions with Katherine Dudley and Sylvia Beach, and with Kahnweiler and his wife, who had been in hiding under false names in the department of Lot-et-Garonne. There was even an unexpected reconciliation with Hemingway who, serving as a war correspondent, had "liberated" Paris earlier and returned in December, after covering a mopping-up operation in the Schnee-Eifel region. Hemingway, writing about the meeting to W. G. Rogers later, remarked that it had been brief but that he and Gertrude had agreed that they still loved one another. In his letter, Hemingway paid Gertrude the ultimate masculine compliment, saying that he had always had an urge to fuck her. Gertrude, he maintained, was well aware of this; it established a healthy bond between them. He attributed their former break to the fact that he had taught Gertrude how to write dialogue and she had found it necessary to attack him because of it. That, and Alice's jealousy of any of Gertrude's real men-friends—that is, men who worked seriously at their masculine functions.

In Paris, Gertrude became an immediate celebrity. American GIs swarmed to meet her, greeted her on the streets with shouts of "Hi ya, Gertie," sought her out for autographs. Young Americans stationed in Europe wrote to her and flocked to the rue Christine when they arrived in Paris. She read their manuscripts and offered them encouragement and tea. Only once did she become angry, when a soldier, as a joke, gave her a John Donne poem among those he left to be read. He was never allowed back. Still believing that American soldiers never wrote home often enough—that had been her experience during World War I—she sometimes wrote to their parents for them. From the mother of Pfc. John Breon, a twenty-one-year-old soldier who had first written her from Germany, Gertrude received a warm and grateful letter. Mrs. Breon told her: "He has been one of your most ardent admirers, spending many happy hours with such of your writings as he possesses. To have you say he is 'completely the young boy,' after all he has experienced as a soldier, rejoices my heart."

Leon Gordon Miller, later a noted industrial designer, was one of the GIs who met Gertrude in Paris and saw her frequently during the eight months he was stationed there. Miller was, at the time, interested in pursuing a career in art, and Gertrude introduced him to the painters Jacques Villon and André Lhote. Frequently the two of them took walks around Paris. On one of these occasions, Miller accompanied Gertrude to the butcher shop. Everywhere in Paris, after the war, there were long lines waiting in front of the shops. Food was scarce and people had to wait hours to fill their meager ration allowances. Gertrude, with perfect aplomb, simply walked to the head of the line, expecting service. There were catcalls from the angry housewives. The butcher explained, *"Elle est écrivaine"*—and the catcalls grew louder. One irate woman turned and spat. Miller was so embarrassed he left the store. When Gertrude came out, she lashed into him, calling him a "chicken coward." In France, she insisted, writers and creative people were privileged because they had "less time to spare on routine."

Among the writers she met was Joseph Barry, whom she labeled "Jo the Loiterer." During his radical student days at Ann Arbor, Barry had once been arrested while marching on a picket line. Since there was no law against picketing, he had been charged with "loitering." Barry was instrumental in having Gertrude lecture at American Army bases and service clubs. Gertrude also met the Negro writer Richard Wright, whose *Black Boy* she had admired. She was on the reception committee that welcomed him to Paris after the war. Wright, who had earlier written her about the racial problem in the United States—"We have made for ourselves a very tragic thing in America and we are afraid of it"—was troubled about prejudice at home, and Gertrude encouraged him to live in France, which he did. Young writers whom she had met on her American tour turned up as GIs. Donald Sutherland, stationed at "Camp Oklahoma City" in France, where he was writing the history of his regiment, visited her in Paris. And she met new young poets whom she considered extremely promising. One of these was George John, who knocked at her door, anxiously clutching a sheaf of poems. In his nervousness, he dropped them, scattering the poems all over the floor. Gertrude was "wildly impressed" with his work. When John returned a week later, she promptly introduced him to Henry Rago, an editor of *Poetry*, who was visiting. John's poems subsequently appeared in an issue of the magazine.

Gertrude was once more in the limelight and enjoying it immensely. Katherine Cornell, whom Gertrude and Alice had met in New York, lunched with them and invited them to a performance of *The Barretts of Wimpole Street*, in which she was touring for the USO. Pierre Balmain had set himself up as an independent couturier, and Gertrude and Alice were the aged stars of his first Parisian showing, which they attended with Cecil Beaton. "For God's sake," Alice had warned Gertrude, "don't tell anybody that we're wearing Pierre's clothes. We look too much like gypsies." When a New Jersey horticulturalist wrote to Gertrude asking to name a new rose after her, she agreed, but with the condition that it be "yellow, large and fragrant." It was one of the minor pleasures of her renewed fame.

Wars I Have Seen, published by Random House in the spring of 1945, became one of her most successful books and was warmly praised by the reviewers. Bennett Cerf wrote her late in March about the book, sending her several press notices: "I am sure you know by this time that *Wars I Have Seen* has been accorded a perfectly wonderful press and that the sale is already over the 10,000 mark. This will undoubtedly be by far the most popular success you've ever had in America." The $2,000 she was to receive from *Collier's* for publication of portions of the book, Cerf told her, was being invested in U.S. War Bonds, as she had requested. Gertrude's play *In Savoy*—later titled *Yes Is for a Very Young Man*—was being sought after for production. She had begun writing it before her return to Paris. Its theme was the conflicting loyalties, the divisions of family life, that she had witnessed in her corner of France during the occupation. Originally it was scheduled for production by an army group at the American University of Biarritz, but Gertrude had suddenly withdrawn it when she learned details about the production that did not please her. It was then offered to a group of actors touring Europe with the USO production of *Kind Lady* and was eventually—after much revision—produced by them at the Pasadena Playhouse in March, 1946. Interestingly, Gertrude had written the actor Lamont Johnson, one of the men responsible for the production, that its central character, Constance, had been inspired by Clare Boothe Luce. In her program note for the Pasadena production, Gertrude stated: "When I was in France during the occupation, knowing intimately all the people around me, I was struck with the resemblance to the stories my mother used to tell me, the divided families, the bitterness, the quarrels and sometimes the denunciations, and yet the natural necessity of their all continuing to live their daily life together, because after all that was all the life they had, besides they were after all the same family or their neighbors, and in the country neighbors are neighbors."

The liberation, Gertrude realized, had not brought an end to bitterness. In the midst of her personal "liberation" she was made aware of the sadder fate of others. Her friend Bernard Faÿ was imprisoned for life as a result of his collaboration with the Vichy government. In her mothering way, Gertrude remained loyal, sending him food and candy and the new vitamin pills she had wondered about, which were sent to her by way of Pfc. Breon's mother. She felt that while Faÿ may have done some things that were "wrong," he had never denounced anyone. In the Stein archives at Yale University's library, there is a lengthy testimonial which Gertrude wrote in Faÿ's defense, stating that Faÿ had never loved the Germans or Germany, pointing out his services to her, an American citizen, during the years of the occupation, and testifying to his services to Franco-American relations by way of his books and lectures. Faÿ, she claimed, had never ceased "to work for France."

Gertrude and Alice wrote Faÿ regularly while he was in prison. Faÿ thanked them for the "messages that are worth millions." He described the doldrums of prison life: "You cannot know how much talking and discussing there is in jails and concentration camps. It's incredible. Writing is a lot more difficult, because the main trouble of being in jail is the impossibility of dismissing a caller who calls on you." The luxury of a day to oneself, Faÿ wrote Gertrude, "costs a lot of cigarettes —cigarettes are the only money here."

Other friends, too, were in danger. On his first visit to the rue de Christine, Leon Gordon Miller had been studying a Picabia painting when Gertrude came up behind him, saying: "He may go to jail, you know. Picabia is like a child, not fully responsible for his acts. He's accused of collaboration, you know." It was difficult to know what stand to take; one had to go on living in the same human family. She was well aware of the complexity of the situation, for at the time of her meetings with Miller the French newspapers were running stories of those who had perished during the years of the Nazi terror. One of them was Max Jacob, who had died in a concentration camp at Drancy. Miller recalled that she had spoken of the poet with "much praise, not only for his work but for the man as a great and warm human being."

In June, 1945, Gertrude and Alice were flown to Germany where they toured U.S. Army bases. They visited Salzburg and Frankfort, were photographed on the terrace of the Berghof, Hitler's mountain retreat at Berchtesgaden, inspected the hoard of art treasures that Hermann Goering had confiscated from the conquered countries of Europe. Gertrude's account of the trip, "Off We All Went to See Germany," was featured in the August 6 issue of *Life* magazine, which had sponsored the tour. In her meetings with the American GIs in Germany, Gertrude was frankly disturbed when American soldiers expressed a preference for their former enemies, rather than the independent French. "Of course you do," she told them, "they flatter you and they obey you." Still, she was thrilled by the trip, as she told Miller afterward, showing him photographs of herself standing in chow lines with the American GIs. At least three times she told him about the excitement of eating out of a mess kit.

In the epilogue to *Wars I Have Seen*, Gertrude had quoted the American soldiers as saying, somewhat sadly, "Write about us." In August she began a book about the GIs of Europe, *Brewsie and Willie*. It is chiefly a record of GI conversations, using the lingo that she had readily picked up to describe the American soldiers' fears, hopes, satisfactions, and dissatisfactions, as they were reflected in her two principal characters—the first a reflective, pondering philosopher, the group thinker, the latter a brusque and cynical American male. Gertrude was convinced that World War II had killed off the last vestiges of the nineteenth century. What faced America and the returning American soldiers was a new world. They were in danger from American industrialism, which could easily make automatons of them, and from the American Government, which encouraged them, so she thought, to let others do their thinking for them. Her book, in which Willie stood for another aspect of her ideas, was a plea for individualism, for the distinction between the hired man and the employee mentality that she had underscored in her tour of America.

In an article written for the *New York Times* shortly before her trip to Germany, Gertrude had touched on some of the problems she thought the young men who visited her were facing. She did not think that this wartime generation could be referred to as all the "sad young men," as they had after World War I, for the "excellent" reason that they were "sad young men already." "I was so touched the other day," she remarked, "there was a young fellow here and we were talking about America and war, and the future and the young American said after all what have we to oppose to the world and to defend ourselves with except innocence and a kind heart." She recalled another American, a Californian, who for the first time had been on assignment with a contingent of Negroes. After four days, the soldier told her, "Well, I was glad in this year '45 that I had not been born black." Using Richard Wright as an example, Gertrude—prophetically—touched on something that was to become a problem in the postwar world, the racial issue. She saw it from her own queer angle, however. Talking with a southern soldier, she maintained:

The trouble is, as long as the Negro was just a native race, the white man's burden point of view, it's all right, but now when one Negro can write as Richard Wright does writing as a Negro about Negroes, writes not as a Negro but as a man, well the minute that happens the relation between the white and the Negro is no longer a difference of races but a minority question and ends not in ownership but in persecution. That is the trouble, when people have no equality there can be differences but no persecution, when they begin to have equality, then it is no longer separation, there is persecution.

American soldiers, she claimed, were beginning "to know what the words imprisoned and persecution mean, when they see the millions in prison, imprisoned for years, persecuted for years, they begin to realize what minorities in a country are bound to lead to, to persecution and to a sense of imprisonment."

The world that the new generation of young men was facing, Gertrude felt, was a world without answers. It was a world in which her hard-headed Willie—who seemed, in the course of the book, to gradually represent her more practical ego—claims that nothing is funny any more, "not even the comics." At one point, Willie bawls out: "I just tell you, and though I don't sound like it I've got plenty of sense, there ain't any answer, there ain't going to be any answer, there never has been an answer, that's the answer."

That mood of uncertainty and yet of the knowledge that one had to carry on was also reflected in the new opera libretto that Gertrude began writing that fall, in a new collaboration with Virgil Thomson. Thomson, who had been commissioned by the Alice M. Ditson Fund of Columbia University, had wired Gertrude earlier about the proposal, and they had discussed it frequently when he was in Paris during October and November. Although she was not an ardent supporter of the women's rights movement, Gertrude had proposed writing an opera based loosely on the life of Susan B. Anthony, the nineteenth-century suffragette. She had begun doing research on the nineteenth century, borrowing books from the American Library in Paris and from as far afield as the New York Public Library, and by October had shown one or two scenes to Thomson. Although Alice felt that Gertrude had not intended the heroine of the opera to be analagous with herself, the companionship between Susan B. Anthony and Dr. Anna Howard Shaw—represented by a character designated simply as Anne in the opera—seems to be a pointed reference to her lifelong relationship with Alice. Moreover, aside from historical figures such as Daniel Webster, Thaddeus Stevens, and Lillian Russell, the dramatis personae also included a number of Gertrude's acquaintances—including Jo the Loiterer, Donald Gallup, a young librarian from Yale whom she had recently met, a painter, Jean Atlan, and Virgil Thomson.

Thomson wrote her in April: "The libretto is sensationally handsome and Susan B. is a fine role." He felt that it would be easier to dramatize than *Four Saints* but did have reservations: "The number of characters who talk to the audience about themselves, instead of addressing the other characters, is a little terrifying." The beautiful score that Thomson composed for the opera (not completed until after Gertrude's death) was, as he later described it: "an evocation of nineteenth century America, with its gospel hymns and cocky marches, its sentimental ballads, waltzes, darn-fool ditties and intoned sermons." He saw the opera as a kind of "memory-book" of Victorian "play-games and passions," a "souvenir of all those sounds and kinds of tunes that were once the music of rural America."

Gertrude's scenario was a good deal more narrative than that for *Four Saints*, and the libretto ends in a scene, somewhat reminiscent of *Don Giovanni*, with a "replica of the statue of Susan B. Anthony and her comrades in the suffrage fight" in the halls of Congress. The voice from behind the statue reflects on "my long life of effort and strife, dear life, life is strife." The brief musings of Gertrude's heroine—*The Mother of Us All*, as the opera was titled—were drawn largely from her own reflections at the end of her career, with the assistance of a quote from another emancipated woman, Claribel Cone, whose "Dear life, life is strife" Gertrude liked to recall and frequently repeated.

Gertrude had been feeling tired. In November, she had flown to Brussels to lecture to American GIs stationed there. During her stay, she suffered from an attack of intestinal trouble, one of the few things that remained a persistent worry to her. In *Everybody's Autobiography*, she had remarked: "Indigestion and high places they are frightening. One well one always hopes that that will not happen but high places well there is nothing to do about them." When she returned to Paris she consulted a doctor, who advised her to see a specialist because the illness "might become grave." Nonetheless, Gertrude did not bother.

When Julian Stein's stepdaughter, Ellen Bloom, visited Paris in November while awaiting assignment as a Red Cross hospital worker, Gertrude did not mention her health. She seemed as alive and as spirited as ever to Ellen, though perhaps a bit thinner. When Ellen invited her and Alice to lunch at Red Cross headquarters in the Edward VII Hotel, Gertrude readily accepted but with the condition that Ellen call for them, since she refused to take the Métro and taxis were not plentiful. Her visitor managed to borrow a Red Cross jeep and arrived promptly at one o'clock, the time that Gertrude had specified. But Ellen was dismayed when she found that Gertrude had Basket with her. She told her that the hotel had a large sign forbidding dogs in the dining room. "Nonsense, Ellen," Gertrude said, "He *always* goes with us everywhere. The French love dogs. You'll see." At the hotel, they were stopped at the dining room by a waitress who told Gertrude the dog was not allowed. Gertrude simply swept past her, saying, "Basket *always* comes with me." After lunch, Gertrude had seemed particularly healthy, sitting in the lounge, laughing heartily with a group of young people who had immediately formed a circle around the celebrity.

During her stay in Paris, before she was assigned to a hospital in England, Ellen Bloom saw Gertrude on several occasions. In their walks together with Basket, "Cousin Gertrude" had seemed as autocratic as ever in her opinions. "She didn't leave much room for contradiction," Ellen recalled. Ellen especially remembered Gertrude's remark when she once ventured onto the subject of Hemingway. "Anyone who marries three girls from St. Louis hasn't learned much," Gertrude told her.

Gertrude did not seem ill to Virgil Thomson, who saw her that November. She was happy, engrossed in their plans for the opera. Thomson noted that one of her other projects that fall was to go over her correspondence and papers, which she had agreed to leave to the

Yale library as a result of her talks with Donald Gallup. "No thought of death was with her, I am sure," Thomson recalled, "for she planned, come spring, to buy a car again." But he had occasion to remember Gertrude's physical condition in the following summer, when he returned to Paris and they were once more involved in discussions about the opera. Thomson gave a dinner party for Gertrude and Alice and a few friends. He was in a teasing mood that evening and began to tease Gertrude until Alice warned him, "Don't scold her. She may cry."

The traveling, the lecturing, the constant visits of GIs had begun to prove tiring for both Gertrude and Alice. But Gertrude was also becoming increasingly irritable. Her outburst over the Biarritz production of *Yes Is for a Very Young Man* had had a legitimate cause. When she learned that the group planned to present the play as a symbolic drama for a select audience, she erupted. "Precious Baby blew a fuse," Alice later wrote to Carl Van Vechten. "We stayed up till the next morning getting the people at Biarritz on the phone. She wished her play to be produced in an ordinary way, simply, realistically, before ordinary theatre goers. She considered it a play like any other—except perhaps for its quality—that the characters were portraits and of ordinary people, that there was nothing mystical or symbolical about them or their actions."

Her irritability also erupted with her friend Picasso. Gertrude had bought her new car in the spring, and one day, as they were driving down the rue des Grands Augustins, they encountered the painter. "Is this the car you have bought?" Picasso asked. "It's not the car you wanted me to buy?" Gertrude said quizzically. "Oh dear no," Picasso answered. Gertrude said sharply, "I don't like second hand cars and that's what you proposed." She looked at Picasso and demanded, "Why are you so cross?" The painter responded that he wasn't. "Oh yes you are," Gertrude said. Picasso asked Alice what was the matter. She could only answer that Gertrude didn't agree with him about the car. With that, Gertrude announced: "It's what I wanted and I've gotten it. So goodbye, Pablo." She drove off, leaving the painter at the curb. It was their last meeting together.

A young writer, James Lord, who had been introduced to Gertrude by way of Picasso, was given an example of the Stein temper—and in time found himself in the middle of a crossfire between the two famous personalities. Lord's first visit had not been promising. Gertrude, who was about to take her customary walk, began pumping him with questions. "Now tell me everything about yourself," she said. Lord confessed that there wasn't much to tell. She turned on him. "Now listen to me," Gertrude said. "If that's the kind of answer you're going to give me when I ask a question, then it's quite obvious you and I will never have anything to say to each other and you might as well run along right now." Lord promptly supplied the facts of his age—

twenty-two—and his birthplace, Englewood, New Jersey. Mollified, Gertrude told him that this was a "curious coincidence," she knew an interesting young photographer from Englewood whose father was a clergyman there.

Lord's acquaintanceship with Gertrude did not last long. In fact, he soon had a disastrous falling out with her. He had brought a painter friend, Chapoval—Picasso was friendly with the artist as well—for a look at the famous Stein art collection. Gertrude answered the door. Lord apologized for what might be an inopportune visit, then somewhat tactlessly added that he did not want to disturb Gertrude. All he wanted was for Chapoval to have an opportunity to see her paintings. Gertrude frowned. "This is no museum," she said, "You can't just come around here to gawk any time you feel like it. Besides it's not convenient." Lord interjected that Chapoval was a friend of Picasso. The answer was abrupt: "Then let him go and ask Picasso to see some Picassos."

The two men stood at the door in embarrassed silence. After a pause, Gertrude softened and told them that she was going out on an errand and they might walk with her if they liked. The walk was even more unfortunate, for Gertrude began talking about the GIs who were now returning to America. She admitted that their visits had become wearying, but still she was sorry to see them go. It was sad that they would "go home and take off their army uniforms and be done with the war and the army, because they would never again in their lives be so happy." Lord disagreed with her—and said so. Most of the men he knew "were sick of the war, sick of the army." Gertrude irritably repeated her argument that soldiers' wartime experiences "were ones they would look back on all their lives with pleasure and nostalgia because they had been carefree among other men and because men loved fighting." It didn't matter what Lord thought. No, she maintained, he was too young to understand: "What matters is that I'm right, and you'll think so in due time." To that, Lord bluntly responded that she was a stupid old woman who didn't understand anything. He turned and walked away.

He walked straight to Picasso's apartment on the rue des Grands Augustins, where he made what was, obviously, another inopportune visit. Picasso clearly wasn't pleased to have a visitor, but when Lord mentioned his argument with Gertrude, the painter let him in. Picasso, on hearing the details, let loose with a string of epithets. Gertrude, he insisted, was "a real Fascist. She always had a weakness for Franco. Imagine! For Pétain, too. You know she wrote speeches for Pétain. Can you imagine it? An American. A Jewess, what's more." The diatribe continued for some minutes. Then the abrupt outburst was over. It was, so Lord recalled, as if "everything I had just told him and everything he had just said to me, as well as I myself were all at once nonexistent." Picasso explained that he was busy and that Lord would have to leave.

Even among the best of friends, old enmities could suddenly rise to the surface.

In July, Gertrude and Alice left Paris for a rest in the country. Bernard Faÿ had offered them the use of his country house at Luceaux in the *département* of Sarthe. Gertrude did not feel like making the long drive—it was more than two hundred kilometers—but Joe Barry had offered to drive the car, planning to stay a day or two before taking the train back to Paris. While there, Barry took them for a drive in the surrounding region. At Azay-le-Rideau, where Gertrude and Alice had once considered buying a house, Gertrude began to feel ill. Nonetheless, they stopped to look at the property. The house had been sold; they were dismayed to find that the lovely park she and Alice had admired was no longer in existence. Gertrude's symptoms became alarming. They took a room at an inn in Azay and called a doctor. After examining Gertrude, he told Alice, "Your friend will have to be cared for by a specialist, and at once!" Frightened, Alice called Allan Stein, asking him to meet them at the train the next day. They spent a restless night and the following day boarded the train for Paris. Gertrude refused to have a nurse accompany her. During the seemingly endless ride she was unable to settle down. Instead, she paced back and forth in the compartment, looking out the window, drinking in the landscape —the solitary farms, the trim villages, the open fields, the brakes of woods as they slipped away behind them. At Paris, she was embarrassed to find an ambulance waiting to take her to the American Hospital at Neuilly. Once there, she nevertheless thanked Allan for his trouble. She seemed, at least, to be more comfortable. Examinations proved that she was dangerously ill, and the doctors recommended that she undergo surgery after she had regained her strength.

On July 23, as a precaution, Gertrude made her will. She empowered her executors to pay "all my just debts," bequeathed her Picasso portrait to the Metropolitan Museum in New York City and her manuscripts and papers to the Yale University library in New Haven. Her unpublished works were still on her mind: Her fourth provision asked that the executors pay to Carl Van Vechten "such sum of money as the said Carl Van Vechten shall, in his own absolute discretion, deem necessary for the publication of my unpublished manuscripts."

In staid legal language, the fifth provision left "the rest and residue of my Estate of whatever kind and wheresoever situated" to "my friend Alice B. Toklas, of 5 rue Christine, Paris, to her use for life, and, in so far as it may become necessary for her proper maintenance and support, I authorize my Executors to make payments to her from the principal of my Estate, and, for that purpose, to reduce to cash any paintings or other personal property belonging to my Estate."

The will also provided that upon Alice's death the residuary estate should go to her nephew Allan Stein, and upon his death "in equal shares to such children of Allan Daniel Stein as may survive him."

Both Alice and Allan were then named executors of the estate with the request that "no bond be required of them for the proper performance of their duties." As a "citizen of the United States of America legally domiciled in Baltimore Maryland, but residing at 5 rue Christine, Paris," Gertrude asked that her will be probated in the State of Maryland.

The delay the doctors had recommended was not helpful. Gertrude was feeling more pain. But the doctors no longer felt that surgery was advisable in view of her weakened condition. A young surgeon was called in, and Gertrude told him bluntly, "I order you to operate. I was not made to suffer." It was the choice she made.

The operation was scheduled for the afternoon of July 27. Alice waited anxiously beside Gertrude's bed—Gertrude was already under heavy sedation. She turned to Alice and murmured, "What is the answer?" Alice, unable to answer, remained silent. Gertrude said, "In that case, what is the question?" The afternoon, Alice remembered, was "troubled, confused and very uncertain." Then the orderlies arrived and Gertrude was wheeled down the long corridor.

In the course of the operation, what was suspected proved to be true; Gertrude had inoperable cancer. At about 5:30 in the evening, she lapsed into a coma. Doctors worked on her for an hour. At 6:30, she was pronounced dead.

Knowledge had been her province. During the long years of the German occupation, she had drawn a valuable lesson from life. "You have to learn to do everything," she observed, "even to die."

CHAPTER SEVENTEEN

Alice Alone

In death, Gertrude was accorded the same public attention she had received during her "liberation." There were lengthy obituaries and editorials in the major papers in America and in France. Most emphasized her commanding public personality, acknowledged her influence upon younger writers, and expressed doubts about the validity of her literary experiments.

Alice, during the numbing days after Gertrude's death, clung to the shell of their former life, living on at the rue Christine apartment, surrounded by the paintings of Picasso and Juan Gris, amid the memories of their lifetime together. There were visits from friends. Virgil Thomson had learned of Gertrude's death from the newspapers while waiting for a train in Venice. In Paris he went straight to the rue Christine, found Alice "lonely in the large high rooms, but self-contained." There were letters of condolence from close friends and from the acquaintances of years. Bernard Faÿ wrote her from prison: "I know how much you are suffering and I want you to feel my deep and affectionate sympathy." Gertrude, he went on, "has been one of the few authentic experiences of my life—there are so few real human men and women—so few people really alive amongst the living ones, and so few of them are continuously alive as Gertrude was." In time, Alice was to answer most of the letters, writing in her fine, spidery script. James Lord, who, despite his quarrel with Gertrude, had written to Alice, was surprised to receive a reply. Alice told him "I am staying on here alone" and asked that he visit her when he came to Paris again. Although it was not true of her later years, it seemed to a friend such as Joe Barry that, in the years immediately after Gertrude's death, Alice had fixed upon only those people she had known with Gertrude. They were like "friendships in aspic."

In Italy, Leo took note of his sister's death with a matter-of-factness that may have belied his true feelings. In a postscript to a letter to his cousin Howard Gans, Leo noted: "I just saw in Newsweek that Gertrude was dead of cancer. It surprised me, for she seemed of late to be exceedingly alive. I can't say it touches me. I had lost not only all regard, but all respect, for her."

He and Nina had lived through the war in Settignano and had been liberated by the American Army. But Leo's liberation had excited little news. He had been aware of Gertrude's renewal in the limelight. Writing to Maurice Sterne, in the summer of 1945, he had been feeling "tired and ineffectual" and had composed some nonsense rhymes about various people. He included one about Gertrude in his letter to Sterne:

Gertrude writes a lot of stuff,
Sometimes she gives herself a puff
She's not afraid the puff will smother,
For soon she gives herself another.

Leo was seventy-four—old, deaf, and fatally ill; he was to die of cancer a year later. The shadow of Gertrude's fame seemed to fall across him even in death. He had written his most important book, *Appreciation: Painting Prose and Poetry*, a book of personal reminiscences and critical analyses of art and literature, published in 1947. Writing to his cousin Fred Stein about the manuscript, he mentioned: "In treating of Matisse and Picasso, I might have put in more of the purely anecdotic if Gertrude had not had the first innings and told or mistold most of the more amusing ones." When his book was published in 1947, he was rankled by critics and reviewers who compared him with Gertrude and spoke of their "feud." He had no "feudish feelings" about Gertrude. He hoped that the "critics will see that I am not concerned in any way with Gertrude and will leave her out of where she has no place."

Several days before his death, on July 29, 1947—he lived two days beyond the anniversary of Gertrude's death—he wrote out some notes on the irksome question of his relation to his sister. So much attention had been paid to it in the reviews of *Appreciation*, he felt "something should be said to put this matter straight." There were profound differences, Leo insisted, between Gertrude's character and his own. His critical interests were "in science and art." Gertrude's interests had always been "entirely in character, in people's personalities. She was practically inaccessible to ideas and I was accessible to nothing else." Since childhood, their private lives were "entirely independent" of each other. They had come to a tacit agreement "not to interfere with each other." About their supposed quarrel, he disagreed. "We never quarreled except for a momentary spat. We simply differed and went our own ways." There was, Leo maintained, "no more quarrel or feud in my relations to Gertrude than in my relations to Picasso. In both cases I have impressions and opinions which are not necessarily in agreement with certain opinions widely prevalent. That is all." The troublesome "family romance" nagged him to the edge of the grave.

The burial of Gertrude Stein took place on October 22, 1946. Although she had been a nonpracticing Jew, "special ceremonies" were held at the American Cathedral Church of the Holy Trinity, where her body—for unexplained reasons—had remained for several months before burial arrangements were completed. She was buried in Père Lachaise Cemetery, the resting place of many of the great French dead. Alice, Allan Stein and his wife, and a few friends attended. In time, a simple gravestone, designed by Francis Rose, marked the grave. The double plot was simple and square, edged in stone with a low box hedge surrounding the spot, rather like one of the flower beds at Bilignin. The face of the stone carried Gertrude's name and the dates and cities of her birth and death. Ironically, since Gertrude had always teased French officials with the spelling of Allegheny, Pennsylvania, the name of her birthplace is misspelled and the date of her death is given incorrectly as July 29, the day of Leo's death.

The slow years passed. As she had during Gertrude's lifetime, Alice continued to serve Gertrude's literary reputation. She was always available to help with the explication of Gertrude's difficult texts, which the Yale University Press began publishing under the editorship of Carl Van Vechten. In 1947 Yale brought out *Four in America*, with an introduction by Thornton Wilder. In 1951 it began issuing the eight volumes of the "Yale Edition of the Unpublished Work of Gertrude Stein." The first, *Two: Gertrude Stein and Her Brother and Other Early Portraits*, carried an introduction by Janet Flanner, who had recourse to Alice's expertise in identifying the cryptic personal references. Other volumes were prefaced with texts by Virgil Thomson, Natalie Clifford Barney, D.-H. Kahnweiler, and Donald Sutherland—the former Princeton graduate who wrote the first full-length critical study of Ger-

trude's writing, *Gertrude Stein: A Biography of Her Work*, published
in 1951. Sutherland and his wife became close personal friends of
Alice's and saw her regularly when they came to Europe.

Alice was also consulted by Gertrude's biographers: Elizabeth
Sprigge, whose *Gertrude Stein: Her Life and Work*, was issued in 1957,
and John Malcolm Brinnin, the poet, whose more detailed *The Third
Rose: Gertrude Stein and Her World* appeared two years later. Brinnin's book had resulted from a graceful and charming poem, a "Little
Elegy for Gertrude Stein," written on the occasion of Gertrude's death
and subsequently printed in *Harper's*. Friends had clipped it out and
sent it to Alice. She wrote the poet, thanking him for the "tender understanding" of his little elegy, telling him that she took it out to reread at intervals during each day.

Over the years, she was visited and sustained by old friends. Janet
Flanner, *The New Yorker's* Paris correspondent, accompanied her to
exhibitions and social affairs in Paris. Virgil Thomson, shuttling between Paris and New York, saw her often. As time passed, so Alice
wrote a friend, "A great appreciation and partiality has grown within
me for him." She found Thomson "mellower" but "not a speck less
witty." Carl Van Vechten wrote her often and regularly sent friends to
look in on her in Paris and to transport gifts.

She made new friends, as well. One of these was James Lord, who
took up her invitation a year after Gertrude's death. Although he had
found Alice an uncomfortable person when Gertrude was alive, he
warmed to her personality considerably. On that first occasion, after
Gertrude's death, Lord and Alice had sat beneath the spot where the
Picasso portrait usually hung. Lord commented sadly on its absence—
the room didn't seem the same. Alice turned around to look at the
blank spot on the wall. She had wanted to keep it as long as possible,
she told him. But eventually she had had to give it up. She had heard
that it was now on exhibition in the entrance hall of the Metropolitan.
"Gertrude would be pleased. That's what she wanted. But it's not the
same. You're right. Without the portrait it's not the same here at all.
But nothing at all is the same, anyway."

Among the newer friends Alice made were Minna and Mell Daniel.
They had made a trip to Paris in the winter of 1952–53, and Carl Van
Vechten had asked them to bring a warm woolen shawl to Alice, who
increasingly suffered from the raw Parisian winters. Mrs. Daniel had been
the editor and publisher of the magazine *Modern Music*, a prestigious
review of musical affairs for which Virgil Thomson was a frequent contributor. Mr. Daniel was a painter and a businessman. They were
surprised when they visited Alice to find her so tiny and fragile a
woman.

An old-fashioned correspondent, Alice had written to thank the

Daniels after they returned to the States. Though she did not frequently attend musical affairs, she tempered her letter to Minna Daniel's interests, remarking on a recent concert at which she had heard Virgil Thomson's *Six Studies*. It had been extremely well played. Thomson, she thought, "does know the mechanics of the piano as few of his contemporaries do." The friendship with the Daniels ripened considerably, encouraged by later visits. Minna Daniel sent her a gift of woolen underwear. Alice, at first protesting Mrs. Daniel's extravagance and kindness, thanked her profusely for the "enchanting rose-colored woolies."

Alice's career as a writer, deferred during Gertrude's lifetime, now began. She became a celebrity as the author of two cookbooks and a memoir. The first, and most famous, *The Alice B. Toklas Cookbook*, published in 1954, ran to several editions and was later issued in paperback. It was an unusual example of the genre, combining reminiscences with recipes. Alice recalled her American tour with Gertrude, and the foods they had eaten, their life in the country, and the deprivations of the wartime kitchen at Bilignin and Culoz. The second, *Aromas and Flavors of Past and Present*, written in collaboration with Poppy Cannon, contained a number of her favorite recipes, but the style of the writing was gushy and breathless in the fashion of women's magazines. Her collaborator, in conspiratorial tones, substituted processed foods and convenience ingredients for Alice's time-consuming directions. Alice regarded it as a failure that it was best to forget.

Her memoir, *What Is Remembered*, entailed a number of difficulties. It was begun as a collaboration with Max White, one of the younger writers she and Gertrude had met in America. But one day, "after four months—six times a week" of meetings, so she informed the Daniels, White "suddenly and inexplicably tore up the notes and left town. The publishers were aghast and are now hunting a successor." The volume was finally published by Holt, Rinehart and Winston, in 1963, with the collaboration of the firm's editor, Robert Lescher. On many points Alice's memory had begun to fail her, and her recall of the facts had to be corroborated from other sources. She had begun working on the book in 1958, she told the Daniels, because "it was necessary to earn some money." Her own resources and the royalties from Gertrude's writings were meager.

Memories of happier times still served her. When the Daniels reported that they had acquired a house in Rockland County and were planning a garden, Alice thought of her own: "I wish I could have shown you our flower garden at Bilignin—the terrace in front of the house—facing what we called the Corot valley, with the timbered mountains opposite—had twenty-eight large box-rimmed flower beds in a formal late seventeenth century design. We planted everything in

them until the occupation." Then they had been converted to vegetables, and it was "hard and fatiguing work." But, she added, "Though
Hitler and the presence of the occupants was a menacing nightmare, I
was happier then than today."

And with sufficient preparation, she could still entertain friends for
lunch. When the Daniels mentioned that they planned to make a trip
to Paris in the spring of 1957, she wrote them, hoping that the Daniels
did not believe "the exaggerated reports of Paris that are circulating in
the U.S." "Nothing but fuel scarcity has changed," she reported.
"Of course prices have gone up, but luxuries—in the best French manner—are abundant." She told them: "You must save me a lunch—a
plain one—for my really good cooking days are over I fear—but there is
really good Indian food which I've lately been enjoying—sole—filet of
course—with a rare sauce which will puzzle you and then there are
fraises des bois—enfin what the market offers."

She was growing old and infirm. Her arthritis was a chronic and progressive problem made worse by the Parisian winters. At first she had
tried to alleviate the situation by visits to the warm sun in Spain or in
Grasse, in southern France, before facing the rigors of a Paris winter.
The illness progressed, however, and she began to use a cane. She was
obliged to take cures for her condition in Acqui Terma, near Milan. In
1958, aged eighty-one, she wrote the Daniels: "The baths are just as
effective as last year and nearly as dull and the weather can be called
more suitable for truffle than for humans." She had not lost her sharp-
ness. She was also pursuing her literary interests, rereading Henry
James, and keeping herself aware of newer writers, reading Faulkner's
The Town and Jean Doutourd's *The Taxis of the Marne*, "a sad disturbing book of France," she told the Daniels, "my war, but I am frequently
not in agreement with his appraisement of present tendencies." Roger
Shattuck's *The Banquet Years*, which dealt with her past, as well—with
the Rousseau Banquet, and figures such as Satie and Apollinaire—was a
special pleasure. She found Shattuck's book "thrilling"—especially the
sections on Satie and Alfred Jarry.

In 1957, after long consideration, Alice rejoined the Church. She had
been "baptised as a child," so she reported to the Daniels. The move,
she noted, "has brought me a peace and comfort." Some of her friends
were dismayed. Virgil Thomson, however, was inclined to believe that it
was the promise of the afterlife in which she would certainly meet Gertrude that had prompted Alice's decision—"Since Gertrude, she could
not doubt, was immortal."

In the summer of 1959 Alice wrote the Daniels from a "sixteenth century priory—modernized" at Seine-et-Oise:

I haven't the courage to ask you to pardon my long silence but your understanding when you hear the causes encourages me to give you a little of the many reasons. A long severe winter followed by a bad spring gave me an acute attack of arthritis and it was late March before I could get to Acqui for the baths as before they were beneficial and I went over to Marseilles for a great Picasso show and to many accompanying festivities. I got back to Paris in good shape. There I collapsed and with a dozen symptoms had an illness from which I am now recovering at this pleasant spot.

She concluded her "sad tale" with a Jamesian "Basta!"

Unable to face the Parisian winters, she was spending longer periods away from her rue Christine apartment. In 1960 she went to Rome, hoping to stay with the Blue Nuns there—Santayana had remained with them during the war and until his death—but when that did not prove possible, she was taken in by a convent of Canadian nuns. It was then that the problem arose that was to plague her last years. In 1954 the apartments in her building on the rue Christine were offered for sale to the tenants. Alice could not afford to buy hers, but she lived on at the apartment, confident that the long legal process involved in evicting a tenant—especially an aged one—would protect her. While she was in Rome, a new landlord started eviction proceedings, claiming that the apartment was not properly occupied. As a result of the eviction proceedings, the heirs of the Stein estate—Allan Stein had died in 1951, and his three children had become the new heirs—discovered that the paintings were left unprotected while Alice was away. Gertrude had never insured her increasingly valuable collection. She claimed that she would have had to sell one picture a year in order to pay the insurance. Alice did insure them—but at well below their value. The heirs also discovered that Alice, needing funds to publish Gertrude's unpublished writings, had sold a portfolio of Picasso drawings without consulting them and at what was regarded as a disadvantageous price. To protect their interests, the heirs and Allan's second wife—"the Armenian," as Alice sarcastically referred to her—had engaged a lawyer friend, and by court order the collection was sequestered. While Alice was away, the paintings and drawings were taken from the apartment and deposited in a vault in the Chase Manhattan Bank in Paris. Alice's position in the matter was further compromised by the fact that in September, 1946, both she and Allan had relinquished their rights as executors of the estate.

She continued to live on in the rue Christine apartment for several more years—the eviction process was still in the courts—but without the pictures. There were only the blank spots on the faded walls. James Lord, who had visited her during this period, remarked on the bareness of the walls. Alice, whose vision was becoming increasingly poor—in 1965, at age eighty-eight, she submitted to an operation on a cataract—was nonetheless resigned. She couldn't see the blank spots, she told

Lord, "But I can see the pictures in my memory. I remember each one and where it was. I don't need to see them now."

Although the heirs agreed to pay her a monthly stipend until the collection could be sold, the meager sums were slow in coming. She sold one of the items that had been overlooked—an early Cubist construction by Picasso—this time at an advantageous price. The Steins' lawyer protested that the sale would have to be rescinded—but since it had been sold to a powerful French family, the matter was dropped. Other overlooked items—a small drawing by Picabia, for example— Alice simply gave away to close friends, saying, "At least, the heirs won't get that one."

In 1964, Alice was forced to move from the rue Christine apartment. When the officer of the court came to read her the eviction notice, Alice was in bed, recuperating from a broken hip. "I was born in 1877," she told him. "If I leave this apartment, it will be to go to Père Lachaise." Friends found her a small apartment on the rue de la Convention. She was bedridden much of the time. The friends who looked after her—Janet Flanner, Doda Conrad, Virgil Thomson when he was in Paris—supervised the maid who bought the groceries and cooked for her. The apartment was sparely furnished with such items of furniture as could be gotten into the small rooms. The walls were barren of pictures. Although the collection of paintings that was intended to provide for her "proper maintenance and support" was to be sold for several millions after her death, in life—during her last few years—she did not have the funds to sustain her. Again, friends—among them Donald Sutherland—came to her aid, providing her with what they could, although there was no guarantee that the sums would be returned when the collection was sold.

Alice was not a docile invalid; she could be demanding. She expected the luxuries, "in the best French manner," that she had been accustomed to: fresh peaches in November, groceries from Fauchon's, the most expensive victualer in Paris. As a last resort, when funds were low, the maid was provided with a black and white Fauchon shopping bag and sent to shop at the market around the corner. Alice could no longer see well enough to read or write. Like many invalids, she felt imprisoned in her cell-like bedroom, with a maid as a keeper. James Lord visited her on a bleak November day in 1965. Alice had stared after the maid as she closed the bedroom door. Lord asked her how she was. "I'd be fine if it weren't for that dreadful woman," Alice told him, "If it weren't for her I'd be cured. I'd be sturdy and cheerful as I like to be. She knows how I hate to have her slam the door, so she does it every time. She makes life miserable in every little way she can, and I'm at her mercy." They talked of America, where Lord was then living. Alice thought it wise for him to live there. It was no longer possible to live abroad as she and Gertrude had done. "Gertrude never left home in the same way I did," Alice mused. "She was always at home through the language, but I was at home only through her."

Alice's last letter to the Daniels was dictated on January 16, 1967, but it was not postmarked until February 4, a day after Gertrude's birthday. She thanked the Daniels for their Christmas card and wondered if they were planning another visit to Paris. "I hope so," she said, "for I shall never get to the U.S.A. again." "Have you a pretty garden this year?" she asked, mindless of the season. "I shall never have a garden again. I think and dream of one." She sent her love and best wishes.

On March 7, she died in her apartment on the rue de la Convention. She would have been ninety on April 30. Her will, written in French, left small bequests to friends: a Victorian tea service to Carl Van Vechten, a Renaissance inkwell to Donald Gallup, an English piecrust table to "dearest Virgil Thomson." The royalties from her cookbooks were left to her priest.

The will also noted that she wished to be buried "in the same tomb as Gertrude Stein in the Père Lachaise Cemetery." Before her burial, she stated, the tomb "must be consecrated to the Holy Catholic Religion." Her instructions as to the inscription were specific: "The inscriptions with regard to name, birth date and date of death must be placed on the back of the stone for which I have already paid Lecreux Frères." Even in death, she did not intend to intrude upon Gertrude's eminence.

Afterword

I wanted to hear their voices: Picasso's high, whinnying laugh as Gertrude Stein recalled it; Matisse's halting, carefully deliberated pronouncements; the terse self-consciousness of Hemingway; Robert McAlmon's aggravated, boozy malice; the tidy precision of Alice Toklas's observations; and, above all, the surprising, cultivated, contralto voice of Gertrude Stein repeating phrases, sentences, and odd judgments that I have remembered and turned over in my mind for what must be, now, a quarter of a century.

I wanted to re-create the texture of a life, a writer's daily life, out of memoirs, recollections, and old letters that, if not always literature, still carried the fire of issues and ambitions that had not burned out completely. I wanted, if I could, to recapture something of the special relationship of two lives—a difficult relationship, no doubt, but a durable and productive one—through the nearly forty years that Gertrude Stein and Alice Toklas lived together. And I wanted to catch something of the summery quality of those ordinary days—sunny days, I imagined, with sudden mountain squalls and drenching rains in the late afternoon —which they spent together in their country house at Bilignin.

Writing about the past is like attempting to restore an old house: You can never bring it back to what it once was, but you can hope to make it livable again.

—JRM.

Acknowledgments

When I began this biography of Gertrude Stein and her "circle" I had no ambitions about writing a "definitive" life, and I have not attempted to do so. I was interested in her life, her life-style, and the ways in which both informed her writing. That, largely, is what has occupied me in writing the book. If I have managed to present an honest woman—which is what I've always felt Gertrude Stein to have been—instead of the legend, then one of the aims of this biography has been accomplished.

For literary reasons, I am indebted to Leo Stein's observation that history is "a mare's nest of illusory knowledge." It became one of the underground themes of the book. I am also indebted to Leon Edel, not only for his kindness in answering my queries about Gertrude Stein's aborted visit to Henry James but for his masterful biography of James as well. Published in five volumes, it is nevertheless one of the most economically written biographies I know. Important episodes in James's life, his complex social relations, his impressions of people, and their impressions of him are managed within the space of one or two pages of narrative. It will be obvious to many readers that Edel's biography has been a model for my own.

On the practical level, I am most of all indebted to Donald Gallup, Curator of the Collection of American Literature, The Beinecke Rare Book and Manuscript Library, Yale University. My indebtedness to his research and writings on the subject of Gertrude Stein are acknowledged in the Notes and Bibliography. I am especially grateful for his permission to quote, without restrictions, from the unpublished letters of Gertrude Stein in advance of his own publication.

I am also deeply grateful to the Estate and/or Heirs of Gertrude Stein and the Estate of Alice B. Toklas for permission to quote from various Stein texts and from unpublished materials by Gertrude Stein in the Stein archives at Yale, as well as permission to quote passages from a series of unpublished letters by Alice B. Toklas. Calman A. Levin, of Daniel C. Joseph, Attorney at Law, has been unfailingly kind.

I am indebted to two recent Stein scholars: Richard Bridgman, whose *Gertrude Stein in Pieces* is a valuable addition to the Stein literature, and Leon Katz, whose discovery of several early versions of later Stein texts and of the personal relationships on which Gertrude's early novel *Q.E.D.* is based are acknowledged in my text and in the Notes. For mildly paranoid reasons on my part, I have not consulted Katz's 1963 doctoral dissertation, "The First Making of *The Making of Americans*." He is at present preparing a critical edition of the notebooks that Gertrude Stein kept while writing *The Making of Americans*, as well as a detailed biographical study based on his researches in the early Stein texts.

In the course of my biography, I quoted frequently from published memoirs and letters. Because I was dealing with a number of very literate people, I felt it was better to quote them directly rather than put words in their mouths by means of the conventional method of paraphrase. Where the amount of quotation exceeds "fair use" allowances, I am grateful to the publishers cited on the copyright page. I want to thank Charles Scribner's Sons for permission to quote necessary passages from Ernest Hemingway's *A Moveable Feast* and from *The Letters of F. Scott Fitzgerald*, edited by Andrew Turnbull. I am no less grateful to the publishers of less-quoted sources, listed in the Notes and Bibliography. With the exception of minor descriptive phrases, the sources of direct quotations are given in the Notes.

I depended heavily upon biographies and autobiographies of people who figured prominently in the lives of Gertrude Stein and Alice B. Toklas, and these are cited in the Bibliography. But I would especially like to acknowledge here the work of Gay Wilson Allen, Carlos Baker, Alfred H. Barr, Jr., Bruce Kellner, Arthur Mizener, Roland Penrose, Barbara Pollack, Francis Steegmuller, and Virgil Thomson.

For interviews, letters, and assistance, I am indebted to Joseph Barry, the late Eugene Berman, Janet Flanner, D.-H. Kahnweiler, the late Stanton Macdonald-Wright, and Julian Stein, Jr. James Lord and Leon Gordon Miller offered me their unpublished memoirs and allowed me to quote freely from them. Lord's memoir is scheduled for publication in a forthcoming edition of the magazine *Prose*.

Several New York art dealers—Lee Ault, Gertrude Dennis, Abe Sachs, Robert Schoelkopf, Joan Washburn, and Virginia Zabriskie—have helped me with photographs or alerted me to out-of-the-way source materials.

For various favors in the writing, editing, and production of this book, I am indebted to Jennifer Dunning, Steven Frankel, Martin Friedman, Mary Hemingway, Ellen B. Hirschland, Michael Janeway, William Jovanovich, Hilton Kramer, Gilda Kuhlman, Robert Lescher, John McKendry, Rita Myers, Mme. Ernest Pernollet, Margaret Potter, and W. G. Rogers.

I particularly want to thank John Hochmann, of Praeger Publishers, for his encouragement and advice during a project that lengthened into several more years than I had anticipated.

I owe a special debt of gratitude to Minna and Mell Daniel, for offering me, out of the blue, their letters from Alice B. Toklas, as well as a well-remembered luncheon alfresco.

I am more than grateful to the American Council of Learned Societies for a grant-in-aid toward the completion of this book.

And, lastly, I want to thank Augie Capaccio for the pleasures of the road —a winding country road—that led to an afternoon at Bilignin.

Notes

Works by Gertrude Stein, Alice B. Toklas, and Leo Stein that are frequently cited in the Notes are referred to by initials or abbreviations. A list of the principal works by these authors, with a key to the abbreviations used, appears at the front of the Bibliography. I also employ in the Notes two other abbreviations: *unp*. YCAL refers to letters in the Collection of American Literature, The Beinecke Rare Book and Manuscript Library, Yale University, that, so far as I know, have not been previously published; for letters that have been published, the published sources are cited. MOMA refers to the Museum of Modern Art, New York.

Works by other authors that I have quoted from or consulted are cited in shortened form in the Notes. When more than one work by an author has been cited, the short title as well as the author's name has been given. When only a single work by an author has been cited, only the author's name has been given. All titles appear in full in the Bibliography (pages 507–14).

A note on the method of citation of sources:
Passages that I have quoted directly, which appear within quotation marks in the text, are cited in the Notes by their opening phrases in italics. When several passages from the same source are quoted in sequence in the text, I have given the opening phrase of the first passage and the closing phrase of the last, as follows: From [*opening phrase*] to [*closing phrase:*]. Where I have commented on my own text without referring to directly quoted sources, I have given in roman the key words from the text pertinent to the subject of my note. Numbers to the left of each column refer to the pages of my text from which passages have been cited.

BOOK I. 27, RUE DE FLEURUS

CHAPTER ONE. THE ATMOSPHERE OF PROPAGANDA

3 *De la part de qui:* SW, 11
5 *not because they were rich:* App, 194
8 *The place was charged:* ibid., 84
  It happened that some hungarian: SW, 12
12 *He could often be tender:* Olivier, 64

Reunion in the Country: This group portrait was shown in the Apollinaire exhibition at the Bibliothèque Nationale in Paris in 1969 (no. 133 in the catalogue), along with a pen and ink sketch,

Portrait of Gertrude Stein (no. 132), obviously a study for the painting.

13 *There should be ten thousand:* WIR, 26

HRH finds you are delightful: Gallup, *Flowers,* 48

14 *I have never in my life:* This episode is recounted in Sweet's *Miss Mary Cassatt,* 196. George Biddle, however, in his memoir, *An American Artist's Story,* 223, reprints a letter from Mary Cassatt, dated March 26, 1913, in which she asserts that she had never visited the Steins, that she was "too old a bird to be caught by chaff." Her description of the Steins and their Saturday evenings—although she mistakenly believed Gertrude was Leo's wife— is detailed enough to be a first-hand account.

I know that people have tried: Vollard, 136–37

Give me new faces: AFAM, 40

16 *was and remained:* Meyer, 82

Most of the visitors: ibid., 81

From was very attractive to about the writings of others: Sterne, 47–49

17 *It took you a hell: ibid.,* 53

CHAPTER TWO. RICH, RIGHT AMERICAN LIVING

18 *not so much of death:* WIHS, 14

feel funny: EA, 134

19 Gertrude's characterizations of Simon and Bertha: *ibid.,* 135–37

stocky, positive, dominant: JIS, 187

From *splendid kind of person* to *free inside them:* MOA, 48–49

20 Immigration records: These were shown to me by a member of the Stein family. Although Daniel Stein's age is given as eight years old, he would have been nine on September 27, 1841.

good foreign woman: The move to America is described in MOA, 36–41

very competent but gentle person: JIS, 188

21 *perfect baby:* WIHS, 3. In a letter to Mabel Dodge (Jan. [?] 1913, YCAL) Gertrude states: "I was born Feb. 3, 1874 at 7:55 A.M. There it is exactly." In *UK,* 8, she declares, more poetically: "Two bits worth of birthday. I was born at eight o'clock."

And there was music: WIHS, 5

22 *gloves dozens of gloves:* SW, 60

that any one ever said: WIHS, 6

The sun was always shining: MOA, 90

23 *rich right american living: ibid.,* 527

Mostly they were honest: ibid., 97

some who were not good: ibid., 95

If that does happen: WIHS, 4

you go everywhere: EA, 70

Prize essay: As an example of Gertrude's inaccuracies, Leo, in a pedantic vein, notes in JIS, 190, that Gertrude was "nearer ten than eight" when she wrote this essay. It was one of the extraordinary sunsets that followed the eruption of Krakatoa in the autumn of 1883. Gertrude, who had an easy way with dates and did not claim otherwise, had said she was "about eight."

24 *What is the use:* EA, 75

From *to make a dozen neuroses* to *a headache:* Leo's account of the neurotic episodes in his childhood is given in JIS, 198–200.

led in everything: EA, 76

He found a good many: ibid., 72

From *a few stray novels* to *nineteenth century authors:* SW, 62

25 *endlessly about books:* JIS, 185

Death of Amelia Stein: A letter from Michael Stein to his uncle Meyer Stein, dated Jan. 28, 1891, (YCAL) gives the date of his mother's birth as April 16, 1842, and her death as July 29, 1888.

she had a gentle little bounty: MOA, 163

After my mother died: EA, 138

hastily, doing: JIS, 185

26 *Naturally, my father:* EA, 139

Then one morning: ibid., 139. Michael Stein's letter to Meyer Stein, Jan. 28, 1891, gives the date of Daniel Stein's death as January 24, 1891—neither in the spring nor the fall.

attended by many prominent: Michael Stein to Myer Stein, Jan. 28, 1891

There were so many debts: EA, 143

Mike's handling of the deal: see Golson, in MOMA, *Four Americans*, 36

perhaps a hundred and fifty dollars: JIS, 204

27 *Then our life:* EA, 142
So many things: WIHS, 36
From *to lose her lonesomeness* to *cheerful life:* SW, 63

28 Gertrude's grades at Radcliffe and Johns Hopkins are given in the very useful appendices of Richard Bridgman's *Gertrude Stein in Pieces*, 357–59.
a very good boarding-house keeper: EA, 155
She seems to have known: Miller, 147
"Browning's Theism": Letters from Royce and Santayana. See Gallup, *Flowers*, 6–7
We said if we have: Sprigge, 28

29 *dark-skinned girl:* Miller, 140
Now the time had come: ibid., 142

30 *She had not noticed:* ibid., 154
though unpleasant: ibid., 155
Is life worth living?: ibid., 146

31 *an impressionist in psychology:* Allen, 325
too lively to make: ibid., 324
The only states of consciousness: William James, "The Stream of Consciousness," in his *Psychology*, 153
One cannot come back: LIA, 11

32 *above all for that:* Gallup, *Flowers*, 4
Next she finds herself: Miller, 121
"Normal Motor Automatism": *Psychological Review* 3, no. 5 (Sept., 1896): 492–512

33 "Cultivated Motor Automatism," *Psychological Review* 5, no. 3 (May, 1898): 295–306
interesting to read: SW, 65
been doing automatic writing: EA, 267
From *never had subconscious* to *must not be cut out:* SW, 66

34 *Everything must come into:* Haas, *A Primer*, 34
the first view of Fujiyama: App, 145
couldn't leave the slightest: Hapgood, 120
He was almost always: ibid., 120

35 From *a mare's nest* to *I long ago called for:* JIS, 192

36 *with its mysterious:* App, 146

From *I've reached a stage* to *passage Perilous:* Gallup, *Flowers*, 5
It is now June 2nd: ibid., 9

37 *I write to tell you:* ibid., 10
Now for psychology: SW, 66. Leo disputed Gertrude's contention that James had said mathematics would be required for philosophy. See JIS, 135.
She said no reflectively: EA, 145

38 *Tell Leo that:* YCAL, Dec. 8, 1896, quoted by Gordon in MOMA, *Four Americans*, 15
From *wanted a metaphysic to people I knew:* App, 147
as was right and proper: JIS, 216
lack of enthusiasm: Gallup, *Flowers*, 8

39 *What do you mean by:* ibid., 12
From *He also wishes to* *notwithstanding:* ibid., 14

40 From *purely mechanical work* to *Chinamen:* JIS, 148
From *He dragged in the dirtiest* to *grades were always poor:* Wilson, *Upstate*, 61–63

42 *Etta, one night:* SW, 104
I had soon realized: JIS, 194

43 From *I also foolishly* to *Americanism is just a bluff:* ibid., 3–6

44 *was an ear:* Luhan, *European Experiences*, 326
From *could not remember* to *theory of medicine:* SW, 68–69
The chandelier in my room: Sprigge, 39

45 *What is all this nonmedicated:* Gallup, *Flowers*, 22
Gertrude, Gertrude: SW, 69
an aristocrat and a snob: Wilson, *Upstate*, 63
You have no idea: SW, 69
Dr. Mall set her a problem: Wilson, *Upstate*, 63

46 "nucleus of Darkschewitsch": Barker's report of Gertrude's research is included in a lengthy note in Bridgman, 38.
I have just gone through: Gallup, *Flowers*, 24

47 *Her apparently seamless garment:* Saarinen, 180
From *among some fine oaks* to *happily ever after:* JIS, 10–13

48 *The time comes when nothing:* Fern, 99

49 *no intimate acquaintances:* App, 151

CHAPTER THREE. THE VULGARITY OF VIRTUE

50 *growing into an artist: App,* 151
51 *What are your plans:* unp. YCAL, LS to MW, Apr. 8, 1903
52 *one could actually own: App,* 150
Cézanne, *The Spring House:* Leo appears to have bought this painting in 1904.
53 Leo's experiments with abstraction: discussed in *App,* 185
My brother needed to be: EA, 75
Well anyway he was painting: ibid., 14
she said she could stay: JIS, 320
54 *I simply rejoiced: Fern,* 101
college bred American women: ibid., 54
From *The contradiction isn't in me* to *vulgarity of vice: ibid.,* 56–57
55 *I am afraid: ibid.,* 63
From *intensely kissed* to *almost a duty: ibid.,* 66–67
At last the tension snapped: ibid., 86
56 From *I know therefore* to *not leave me: ibid.,* 97–98
From *turgid and complex world* to *world's opinion: ibid.,* 101–3
57 *This completeness of: ibid.,* 104
Just how it came about: ibid., 107
Oh it's simply prostitution: ibid., 127
From *Oh you know well enough to a dead-lock: ibid.,* 133
58 Unpublished manuscript of *Q.E.D.:* Leo, *JIS,* 137, claims to have read this early manuscript and found the writing "impossible." It seems more probable that he read the more amateurishly written *Fernhurst* story (see my discussion, page 66) which dealt with a more conventional emotional triangle.
Why it's like a bit: Fern, 67
Things as They Are: published by the Banyan Press, in a limited edition in 1950. In this edition, references to Baltimore were deleted and Mabel Neathe's name was altered to Sophie Neathe to avoid possible identification of the subject.
59 *Have you seen Miss Lounsbery:* unp. YCAL, MW to GS, Dec. 21, 1900
in a passion: Bridgman, 40
60 *I had a perfect devil: JIS,* 9
I did look disapproving: unp. YCAL, ELE to GS, Aug. 10, 1903
How were your friends: unp. YCAL, ELE to GS, Sept. 3, 1903

I was called off: unp. YCAL, ELE to GS, Nov. 3, 1903
Mabel Haynes is at present: unp. YCAL, ELE to GS, Feb. 15, 1904
61 *I'd like to see you:* unp. YCAL, ELE to GS, Mar. 20, 1906
In plain English: unp. YCAL, ELE to GS, May 14, 1906
62 *Now, Gertie:* unp. YCAL, ELE to GS, June 21, 1906
was married yesterday: unp. YCAL, ELE to GS, Aug. 16, 1906
criminal waste: App, 194
63 *a distribution of blacks: JIS,* 17
From *If this proves to be a treatise* to *most ideal of the four: ibid.,* 15–16. Leo's letter is undated, but was obviously written after the purchase of the paintings by Renoir, Gauguin, Cézanne and Maurice Denis, late in 1904. A letter from Mabel Weeks to Leo, in the Stein archives (YCAL), dated Mar. 25, 1905, refers to Leo's letter. Letters from Emma Lootz Erving to Gertrude, dated Nov. 20, 1904 and Dec. 13, 1904, suggest that the paintings were acquired during this period.
64 *But while eating: App,* 195
We is doin business: undated, YCAL. A segment of this letter has been quoted by Gordon in MOMA, *Four Americans,* 16
65 *used to go home:* Russell, 194
66 *Fernhurst:* The recovery of this manuscript is the work of Leon Katz.
trained in elaborate chivalry: Fern, 10
In this life: ibid., 47
strange stories: ibid., 49
full of moral purpose: ibid., 25
67 *You are a comrade: ibid.,* 26
How these trivial incidents: ibid., 13–14
fateful twenty-ninth year: ibid., 29–30
68 *You are an ungrateful brute:* Pollack, 66
69 *I did forty-five years:* Aldrich, *Hilltop,* 29
It seems a little foolish: This and the following letters from Gertrude to Etta Cone, in the Cone archives at the Baltimore Museum of Art, are quoted in Pollack, 66–69.
70 *She was quite amused:* Pollack, 50–51. Etta Cone's diaries are in the

Cone archives at the Baltimore Museum of Art.

72 *most admirable fooling:* JIS, 14
And I slave and slave: TL, 21

73 *always full with mystery: ibid.,* 89
Melanctha Herbert almost always: ibid., 90

74 *many ways that lead: ibid.,* 95
Heh, Sis, look out: ibid., 102
When the darkness: ibid., 102
She told Melanctha: ibid., 106

75 *You see Miss Melanctha: ibid.,* 121

Oh I know all about: ibid., 122
You certainly are just: ibid., 123

76 *You ain't got no right: ibid.,* 172
Jeff knew now always: ibid., 187

77 *I am afraid that:* undated letter, YCAL. Lovett is Robert Morss Lovett, one of the group of American writers, including William Vaughn Moody, who graduated from Harvard in the 1890's.
Baltimore is famous: SW, 44

CHAPTER FOUR. A GOOD-LOOKING BOOTBLACK

79 *The walls were covered:* Pollack, 70. The manuscript for Claribel Cone's memoir is owned by Ellen B. Hirschland.

80 *My master, Gustave Moreau:* E. Tériade, *Art News Annual* 21 (1952): 43

81 *All the paintings of this school: ibid.,* 42
The Cézanne portrait: SW, 30
a white-clothed woman: ibid., 29
It was a tremendous effort: App, 158

82 *I was winking at you:* SW, 34
an astonishing virility: ibid., 31

83 *every day and every day: ibid.,* 33
an act of considerable courage: Barr, *Matisse,* 56

84 *For the moment:* App, 162
Matisse brought people: SW, 35
there is nothing within you: SW, 55

85 *The weather has been fine:* Gallup, *Flowers,* 58
He wanted it: SW, 36
The ape looked: App, 169

86 *a born liaison officer: ibid.,* 170
Good, good, excellent: SW, 38
More and more your style: Gallup, *Flowers,* 56
a very earnest, very noble: SW, 37

87 *Now you've spoiled:* App, 173

88 *From a good-looking bootblack* to *I don't care for it:* SW, 38–39
forced to make it ugly: GSoP, 14

89 *Picasso never had the pleasure: ibid.,* 44
Spain and America: SW, 14

90 *Mademoiselle Gertrude: ibid.,* 54

91 *Gertrude's first sitting for Picasso: ibid.,* 39

92 *He was indeed quite overcome: ibid.,* 40
From Poor little Picasso to *for it's*

no use to: YCAL, quoted in Pollack, 86

93 *I can't see you:* SW, 44
I was and I still am: GSoP, 14
He needed ideas: ibid., 5

94 *In the twenties:* When Gertrude and Alice moved to the rue Christine, in 1938, Janet Flanner made an inventory of the Stein art works. (See Flanner, *Paris Was Yesterday,* 187.) The two Braques were still in her collection then. They are discernible in the Man Ray photograph of the studio room at the rue de Fleurus (1923). A note on the photographs of the Stein atelier: At the time that the Museum of Modern Art's exhibition of the Stein art was being organized, Margaret Potter, the director of the exhibition, and the author spent an afternoon collating the widely scattered photographs of the studio. It became quite clear that Gertrude and Leo had the studio photographed with some regularity. The photos could be arranged into complete sequences of three or four, taken at intervals of a year or two, from about 1905 until after 1914, when Gertrude and Leo divided the collection and the studio was renovated.

95 *every inch a chief:* SW, 48
extraordinarily brilliant: ibid., 49
He never wrote penetratingly: Steegmuller, *Apollinaire,* 141

96 *It is for that reason: ibid.,* 232
Few of the friends: ibid., 179
Who are all these: Olivier, 142

97 *Nobody but Guillaume:* SW, 82

As for punctuation: Steegmuller, *Apollinaire*, 253
vague scandal sheet: Apollinaire, *Apollinaire on Art*, 479
He is exhibiting: ibid., 29
98 *grew big and empty:* SW, 82
We have not seen: YCAL, quoted in Luhan, *Movers and Shakers*, 29. Gertrude's garbled translation apparently refers to Apollinaire's article, "Art et Curiosité: Les Commencements du Cubisme," in the October 14, 1912 issue of *Le Temps.* The sentence reads: "Delaunay, de son côté, inventait dans le silence un art de la couleur pure." (See Apollinaire, *Chroniques d'Art*, 265.) In the same letter, Gertrude mentions that Apollinaire intended to write a "portrait" of her for *Le Mercure de France*, but a check of the microfilms in the New York Public Library for this period, 1912–13, did not reveal one.

Gertrude shockingly ignorant of her French contemporaries: Kahnweiler, conversation with Mellow, October 16, 1969. Kahnweiler, however, professed great admiration for Gertrude's understanding of English literature and maintained that he had learned a great deal from her about the English writers of the seventeenth and eighteenth centuries.
99 *Et moi non plus:* McBride, 18
And when he balanced: Apollinaire, *Selected Writings*, 165
100 *We had just hung:* SW, 13
Details of probable luncheon menu: ABTC, 182
101 *ruined his promise:* App, 158
From *Manet for the impecunious* to *there you were:* SW, 42–43
Gee, don't tell me: YCAL, quoted in Pollack, 96
102 *Yes I know Mademoiselle Gertrude:* SW, 13

CHAPTER FIVE. THE NECESSARY LUXURY COMPANY

103 From *I hope they'll treat* to *news from San Francisco:* Allen, 453–54
104 *Do get up:* WIR, 13
Be calm madam: SW, 4
105 *unblinking steadiness:* Joseph Barry to Mellow, Apr. 21, 1970
gently bred existence: SW, 3
106 *We had a good deal of mail:* Gallup, *Flowers*, 32
I have had a pretty hot time: ibid., 37
From *Who did you say* to *charming young girl:* WIR, 18
107 *In September, 1907:* The date of Alice B. Toklas's arrival in Paris is problematic. Gertrude's account in *The Autobiography of Alice B. Toklas* has it that Alice first came to the rue de Fleurus on a Saturday evening that coincided with the eve of the *vernissage* of the *Salon des Indépendants* in the spring of 1907. Alice's account in *What Is Remembered* is more circumstantial. She indicates that she left California for Europe in September, 1907, stopping off in New York, where she saw an after-

noon performance of Nazimova in Ibsen's *A Doll's House.* Her first Saturday evening with the Steins, she claims, was on the eve of the *vernissage* of the *Salon d'Automne.* (The dates for the *Salon des Indépendants* that year are March 20 to April 30; for the *Salon d'Automne*, October 1 to October 22. In neither case is the opening day a Sunday.) A check of the theatrical pages in the *New York Times* for March, 1907, indicates that during that month Nazimova was appearing regularly in *Hedda Gabler* but gave only one performance in *A Doll's House*, a matinee on March 28—too late for Alice to arrive in Paris for the opening of the *Indépendants.*

During the first three weeks of September, 1907, Nazimova appeared in *Comtesse Coquette*, a comedy. On Monday, September 23, she opened in Ibsen's *The Master Builder*—too late, it would seem, for Alice to make the eight-day crossing and spend several days in Paris before September 28, the Saturday preceding the opening of the *Salon d'Automne*. Possibly she may have seen a rehearsal or preview of *The Master Builder* and in later years confused it with Ibsen's more famous play. (It was the one and only performance of Ibsen she claimed she was ever to see.) The reviewer for the *New York Times* characterized Nazimova as "hoydenish" in the role of Hilda Wangel. Alice expressed dissatisfaction with Nazimova's Slavic temperament in the role of Nora. Perhaps they had seen the same play.

107 From *She was a golden brown presence* to *autumn herbaceous border*: WIR, 23–24

109 *marvelous, all-seeing*: ibid., 27
From *there was something painful* to *she will take lessons*: SW, 19

110 From *That is a brutality* to *to Pablo by mistake*: ibid., 22

111 Matisse and Negro sculpture: See Matisse's interview with André Warnod, quoted in Barr, *Picasso*, 258
very ancient, very narrow: SW, 54
African art which was naïve: GSoP, 35

112 *a composition that had neither*: ibid., 19. In this particular instance Gertrude was making a comparison between the composition of Cubism and the "composition" of World War I.
It is true certainly: ibid., 23

113 *Matisse and all the others*: ibid., 30
They say I can draw: ibid., 23
horrible mess: App, 175
Picasso's interior resources: ibid., 174
Why don't you like my painting?: ibid., 187

114 *He would stand before a Cézanne*: ibid., 176
You have no right to judge: ibid., 187
I was alone: GSoP, 23
decent family's progress: MOA, 34
Early sketch for *The Making of Americans*: Leon Katz, who discovered this first version of Gertrude's novel, gives 1903 as the most plausible date. See *Fernhurst*, xv.

115 *I am sure no American publisher*: *Fern*, 179. For information on the minor twists and turns in the publication of *The Making of Americans* I am indebted to Donald Gallup's "The Making of *The Making of Americans*," first published in *New Colophon* 3 (1950), and reprinted and updated in *Fernhurst*.

I am writing for myself: MOA, 289
Once an angry man: ibid., 3. Apollinaire makes use of a very similar image for the war of the generations in *The Cubist Painters*, originally published in 1913: "You cannot carry around on your back the corpse of your father. You leave him with the other dead." (page 10 of the 1949 edition.) Might he have seen the opening pages of Gertrude's manuscript, which she began showing to friends around 1910–11?

116 *It has always seemed*: Fern, 137
Gertrude dispensing with two members of the family: She repeats her own family history by noting in the novel that two children had died in infancy.

117 *His hair was grey now*: MOA, 49
This is very true then: ibid., 441

118 *She was in the street*: ibid., 388
I began to get enormously: LIA, 138
history of every kind: MOA, 479

119 Gertrude's charts and diagrams: A critical edition of the notebooks Gertrude kept while writing *The Making of Americans*, edited by Leon Katz, will be published soon.
There must now then be: MOA, 345
a mushy mass: ibid., 384
just sort of bobbled: ibid., 419
cannon-ball resting: ibid., 562
Dean Hannah Charles: ibid., 467
dependent independent resisting being: ibid., 546
She was a child: ibid., 496
Frank Hackart: ibid., 442

120 *Loving being, I am filled*: ibid., 604
the most man-like woman: Weininger, 50
devoted wholly to sexual matters: ibid., 88
The most appallingly decisive: ibid., 286

121 *As there is no real dignity*: ibid., 308
By the way: Gallup, *Flowers*, 45
Pablo & Matisse: GSoP, 97
Always I love it: MOA, 304
It is sometimes a very hard: ibid., 573

I can never have really: ibid., 538
122 *the three novels written:* LIA, 184
     one hand in the past: Haas, *A*
     Primer, 29
     Nobody enters into: Haas, *Uclan*
     Review, Spring 1963, p. 48
123 *only mislay it:* SW, 74
124 *beautiful beyond words:* WIR, 51
     handsome and distinguished: ibid.,
     48
125 *It will certainly make:* YCAL, GS to
     MW, undated
     From *In the essentials to great ex-*
     cellence of your work: Gallup,
     Flowers, 31–32
126 *But to report at last: ibid.*, 34
     I have been delayed: ibid., 38
127 *supposed it was the agent's:* unp.
     YCAL, GS to MD, May [17 or
     24?], 1913
     Your manuscripts are in: unp. YCAL,
     MW to GS, Apr. 21, 1907
     doesn't in the least: unp. YCAL,
     MW to GS, Apr. 23, 1908
     From *My proofreaders report* to
     people take it seriously: Gallup,
     Flowers, 42–43
128 *It was like living history:* WIR, 54
     old-maid mermaid: ibid., 44
129 From *She had been a very good*
     daughter to *who ever will be living.*
     G&P, 15–16
130 *She was born in California:* AFAM,
     223
     Bridgman and Katz on Lesbianism:
     See also Virgil Thomson's article,
     "A Very Difficult Author," *New*
     York Review of Books, Apr. 8,
     1971, pp. 3–8, for a pertinent dis-
     cussion of this aspect of Gertrude's
     life.
131 *a woman who isn't a woman:*
     Cahiers d'Art (1934), p. 28
     I always did thank God: Fern, 58
132 *Give known or pin ware:* P&P, 26
     She did some things: "Two Women"
     was first published in the *Con-*
     tact Collection of Contemporary
     Writers, 1925; reprinted in Pol-
     lack, 275–300.
133 *Tell about the others:* manuscript
     version, YCAL; quoted in Pollack,
     314
     that touching pair: Wilson, *Shores*
     of Light, 583. For information on
     Miss Mars and Miss Squire, I am
     indebted to Virginia Zabriskie of
     the Zabriskie Gallery in New York,
     who supplied me with an unpub-

lished memoir by Anne Gold-
thwaite.
     They were both gay there: G&P, 17
134 From *that the vagueness that began*
     to remoteness in her personal re-
     lationships: Wilson, *Shores of*
     Light, 581–86
     From *Sometimes men are kissing* to
     in being such a one: Two, 310–15
135 *They are not men:* SW, 42
136 *Come home to lunch:* JIS, 173. Hap-
     good, in *A Victorian*, 215–20, gives
     a lively account of this three-sided
     relationship but does not indicate
     anything sexual in its arrange-
     ments. He gives an unpleasant pic-
     ture of Edstrom as a man who
     was a braggart about his sexual
     prowess and who "wept copiously."
     The cause of the quarrel between
     them was an autobiography of Ed-
     strom on which Hapgood collab-
     orated. Edstrom found it too re-
     vealing and ran off to Paris with
     the manuscript where he allowed
     a friend to burn it. Edstrom's re-
     marks about the burning of the
     manuscript, quoted by Hapgood,
     suggest something like a sexual
     violation: "If I could as easily have
     burned up the sense of having
     been violated, turned inside out,
     how happy I would have been!
     But a conviction that I had been
     mentally ravished, that another
     will than my own had stretched
     its hands into the delicate ma-
     chinery of my brain and seem-
     ingly scraped the nerve fibers for
     stuff that should never have been
     brought to the level of conscious-
     ness, would not leave me."
        Hapgood's account of a mur-
     derous fight between Sterne and
     Edstrom—evidently the one referred
     to in Gertrude's portrait—is also
     revealing: "It would have meant
     nothing to either to have gouged
     out the eyes of the other, and any
     handy object in the cafe, heavy
     and blunt enough was used by
     both in the service of the gigantic
     cause in which they were fighting,
     which was a dispute about the
     nature of art. This didn't prevent
     them for a time from being con-
     stant companions; and, under the
     influence of the surrounding art
     and the good wine of Florence,

they lived in the ecstatic heaven of mutual admiration; for each to the other was the greatest spirit yet. Sterne, of course, worked from

under, for with him, it was only a momentary illusion."
I had to find out: LIA, 183

CHAPTER SIX. COUPLES

138 *one of the most truthful:* Florent Fels, *Propos d'artistes,* 1925; quoted in Shattuck, *Banquet Years,* 67

139 *One day I had gone: App,* 191
It was Guillaume Apollinaire: SW, 86. Alice Toklas's account of the Rousseau Banquet, though differing in minor details, is similar to Gertrude's. Fernande Olivier's account is given in *Picasso and His Friends,* 68–71; André Salmon's, in *Souvenirs sans fin,* vol. 2, 48–65.

140 *a little small colourless:* SW, 88

141 *Nous sommes réunis:* Vallier, 87

144 *It is evident:* Salmon, in "Testimony," 15
Alice's servants: *ABTC,* 180

145 *put in the afternoon:* unp. YCAL, SS to GS, Aug. 7, 1909

146 *It is only in the last:* Gallup, *Flowers,* 69
Sirs, Will you have: unp. YCAL, GS to Harper & Co., undated
I told you: SW, 67

147 *I have had a bad conscience:* Gallup, *Flowers,* 50
Acute enlargement of the heart: Allen, 491
I got a really painful shock: JIS, 42
One of the greatest philosophical minds: Allen, 494
Three Lives's disappointing sale: the Grafton Press to GS, Feb. 23, 1910 and Feb. 28, 1910, YCAL

148 *As character study:* Kansas City *Star,* Dec. 18, 1909. This and the following reviews are in Gertrude's notebook of clippings at Yale.
From *most satisfactory establishment* to *stopping with you:* Gallup, *Flowers,* 48

149 From *She said she did not have to her plans for the winter: P&P,* 105–7

151 *Come on, we are getting:* WIR, 60
Caroline dear, you must: ibid., 61. That this episode took place in 1910 is confirmed by a note from Mildred Aldrich to Gertrude, May

6, 1910, saying that she expected Alice and Miss. Helbing that afternoon for tea.
Alice's father spent an afternoon: unp. YCAL, SS to GS, Aug. 17, 1910
That September: There has been some confusion about the year in which Alice moved into the rue de Fleurus, although Alice stated that it was after the summer vacation of 1910 (*ABTC,* 181). Her recollection is confirmed by two notes from Mildred Aldrich, one dated Apr. 13, 1910, addressed to Alice at rue Notre Dame des Champs, and the other, a postcard, dated Sept. 22, 1910, addressed to Alice "Chez Mlle. Stein" at the rue de Fleurus.

152 *Leo met her in 1909:* Leo's letter to Mabel Weeks, dated Feb. 15, 1910 (*JIS,* 21), says that they had met the previous winter and that just before the summer of 1909, Nina had made a "most desperate effort at seduction."
but paint innumerable bad: JIS, 23
loved her for her love: ibid., 23
From *Yes, you are right to her modernistic Sultan: ibid.,* 25–28. Nina's memoir gives May, 1905, as the date when she first noticed and was attracted to Leo, but also notes that it was years before she came to know him.

153 *My dearest, I have just received, ibid.,* 29
From *I deeply hope to results would be fearful: ibid.,* 30–31
I received today: ibid., 37

154 *Matters with Nina: ibid.,* 36.
She sends her postal cards: ibid., 43
From *In truth to music of the future: ibid.,* 46–47

155 *One was quite certain: P&P,* 12
Brutal egotism of Matisse: Katz, in MOMA, *Four Americans,* 55

156 *The antique above all:* Barr, *Matisse,* 550

157 *I am quite sure that:* GSoP, 96
    Do one about Pablo: ibid., 103
    From One whom some were cer-
    tainly to *a very pretty thing:* P&P,
    117–18
158 *All ages are heroic:* GSoP, 14
159 *engaged in what we felt:* Braque, in
    "Testimony," 13
    You forget we were young then: SW,
    6
160 *Fernande is certainly not: ibid.,* 92
    From Well, I will stay to *caramel*
    and meringue: WIR, 68–69
161 Letter from Leo: unp. YCAL, May
    29, 1912. "According to the De-
    launay version," Leo wrote her,
    "Fernande went off with some
    young futuriste of 22, and then

Pablo went to the Pyrenees with
that little woman whom Fernande
was constantly with. At all events,
Pablo is no longer in Paris & he
has gone off with a lady."
    I love her very much: Kahnweiler,
    Confessions, 128
162 *Not so dots:* SW, 486
    From like a grocer's family to *that*
    resort of all geniuses: Gallup,
    Flowers, 59
163 *If you had only told us:* WIR, 75
    At last, I begin to see: Fern, 69
    One day she was sitting: ibid., 68
164 *This is the sun in:* G&P, 65
    Well, Pablo is doing: Rönnebeck, 3
    I became more and more excited:
    LIA, 191

CHAPTER SEVEN. MADE IN AMERICA

165 *very pretty eyes:* SW, 107
166 *Is she completely mired:* unp. YCAL,
    GS to CVV
    From There are things hammered to
    book to get born: Gallup, *Flowers,*
    52–53
167 *Your letter was a great comfort:*
    YCAL, quoted in Luhan, *Movers*
    and Shakers, 32. The chronological
    sequence of Gertrude's letters pub-
    lished in Luhan's memoirs is often
    erroneous. The dates of the Futur-
    ist exhibition mentioned in the let-
    ter were February 5 to February
    24, 1912.
    writing automatically: Luhan, *Euro-*
    pean Experiences, 328
168 *The days are wonderful:* SW, 465
    What they see in it: Gallup, *Flowers,*
    65
    From wide, white-hung bed to *hung*
    loosely on the walls: Luhan, *Euro-*
    pean Experiences, 332
169 *From A walk that is not* to *not all*
    of any visit: SW, 467–68
    From the most important public event
    to *I'll send you some copies:* Gal-
    lup, *Flowers,* 71–72
170 *From She has taken the English lan-*
    guage to *their gradual charm: Arts*
    and Decoration, March, 1913, pp.
    172–74
171 *G is for Gertrude Stein's:* Brinnin,
    184
    I called the canvas: Brown, 111
172 *You are just on the eve:* Gallup,
    Flowers, 74

From I am completely delighted to
    seems he meant it: YCAL, quoted
    in Luhan, *Movers and Shakers,* 33
    It's a good time: unp. YCAL, GS to
    MD, Jan. [?] 1913
    awfully good about my work: YCAL,
    quoted in Luhan, *Movers and*
    Shakers, 34
173 *It made a deeper: ibid.,* 31
    the table a complete scheme: ibid.,
    34
    the incorrigible old Sapphist: Hol-
    royd, vol. 2, 77
    From Owing to the stress of poverty
    to *Bully for us, we are doing fine:*
    YCAL, quoted in Luhan, *Movers*
    and Shakers, 31–36
174 *He said he wanted: ibid.,* 33
175 *The lawyer expects:* Gallup, in *Fern,*
    181
    From I am delighted about to *giving*
    them away: YCAL, quoted in
    Luhan, *Movers and Shakers,* 32–35
176 *No decidedly not:* unp. YCAL, GS
    to MD, undated
    My bringing out the volume: Gallup,
    Flowers, 96
    What is the current: SW, 412
177 *Dining is west: ibid.,* 437
    Aider, why aider: ibid., 421
    From what is the use to *there be-*
    hind the door: ibid., 441–43
    Giving it away: ibid., 445
178 *Nothing:* GSoP, 14
    I knew nouns must go: LIA, 242
    You feel it all: ibid., 236
    I struggled I struggled: ibid., 238

Now in the first place: Gallup, *Flowers,* 96

179 From *for some obscure reason* to *leading the bear:* Luhan, *European Experiences,* 333
like Leah, out of the Old Testament: ibid., 324
What makes you contented: ibid., 332
did everything to save Gertrude: ibid., 327

180 From *Gertrude, sitting opposite me* to *her influencing and her wish:* ibid., 332–33

181 *Somehow in a little:* Jaffe, 34

182 *Telling Whitley about it:* Dawson, 4
Demuth's visits to Gertrude: Dated and undated notes from Demuth to Gertrude when he was in Paris in 1921 and 1922 indicate that he had visited her.
From *Demuth always sent word to* or *Henry James:* SW, 110–11

183 *I went to a couple of galleries:* A typescript of a taped interview with Charles Sheeler, dated June 18, 1959 was supplied to me by the interviewer, Martin Friedman.
it was a pity that Arthur: SW, 95
From *above everything to be a painter* to *lighter than air qualities:* Stanton Macdonald-Wright to Mellow, June 10, 1971.

184 *If he is a young one: Two,* 338
One was quite certain: ibid., 337
He certainly did listen: ibid., 332
I do miss 27: Gallup, "Weaving of a Pattern," 258. This article includes several of Hartley's letters to Gertrude quoted here.

185 *Get that real roundness:* Rönnebeck, *Books Abroad,* October, 1944, p. 6

186 *I feel like a neophyte:* Gallup, "Weaving of a Pattern," 258
From *I am without prescribed culture* to *one of my conversations:* Gallup, *Flowers,* 84–85
The exchange which is fanciful: "IIIIIIIIII" is printed in G&P, 189–98.

187 *It seems to have another kind:* Gallup, "Weaving of a Pattern," 259
I am glad you are all: unp. YCAL, GS to MD, [Autumn, 1913?]
In his painting: Gallup, "Weaving of a Pattern," 259. The segment dealing with Matisse has not been published before.

188 *She tries to express:* Hapgood, 290

189 *You are much talked of:* Gallup, "Weaving of a Pattern," 259
There is a Gertrude Stein: Gallup, *Flowers,* 93–94
Do keep me posted: ibid., 94
a new symbolic-associative language: Agee, 108

190 *Picabia the painter is here:* Gallup, *Flowers,* 94
If you want to have clean ideas: Camfield, 13. Catalogue for the Picabia exhibition at the Solomon R. Guggenheim Museum, New York.
To make love is not modern: ibid., 35

191 *I like him. He has no genius:* unp. YCAL, GS to MD, [Nov. 1913?]

192 *I have always liked:* Gallup, "Weaving of a Pattern," 259
There is an interesting: ibid., 258
temperamental: Gallup, *Flowers,* 74

193 From *in proportion to* to *a long way off:* McBride, 17
From *I am disgusted* to *allowed to help:* Gallup, *Flowers,* 83
You do make fun: unp. YCAL, GS to HMcB, Dec. 1, 1913
So you don't want: unp. YCAL, GS to HMcB, Dec. 29, 1913
a congenital contempt: unp. YCAL, MA to GS, Feb. 8, 1918

194 *It's about Vollard:* unp. YCAL, GS to HMcB, Mar. 27, 1915
Rogue was certainly astute: New York *Sun,* May 21, 1915
From *Your cablegram arrived* to *frequently asked to do so:* Gallup, *Flowers,* 108

195 *Carl Van Vechten writes with:* Van Vechten, 115
I'm so damn bored: Kellner, 16

196 *He wants me to tell:* YCAL, quoted in Kellner, 71

197 *He was dressed in evening clothes:* SW, 113
A touching white shining sash: G&P, 200

198 *"Cubist of Letters Writes a New Book":* This article does not appear in the microfilmed edition of the *New York Times.* A clipping of it, however, exists among the Van Vechten papers in the New York Public Library. It is hand-dated Feb. 24, 1913.

199 *The English language:* Kellner, 81

CHAPTER EIGHT. WAR ZONES

200 *A lot of Hungarians:* unp. YCAL,
     LS to GS, Feb. 3, 1913
     From *You people in New York* to
     What I can't do is just to write:
     JIS, 48–50
201 From *philosophical conceptions came*
     to be to *settle somewhere in sun-*
     shine land: ibid., 51–55
204 *Another is a study:* YCAL, quoted in
     Luhan, *Movers and Shakers*, 32
     The sound there is in them: Two, 1
205 *He had freedom: ibid.*, 106
     From *He was not monstrous* to *He*
     was not derogatory. ibid., 126–27
     From *This had never happened* to
     destroyed me for him: EA, 76–77
206 *We have after much:* unp. YCAL,
     GS to MD, [Dec., 1913? or Jan.,
     1914?]
     We have been very busy: YCAL, GS
     to HMcB, Dec. 29, 1913, incor-
     rectly transcribed in Bridgman.
     We have changed our minds: unp.
     YCAL, GS to MD, May [?] 1914
     Your brother-in-law is still: AFAM,
     125. Although "Possessive Case"
     is dated 1915 in Haas and Gallup,
     A Catalogue of the Published and
     Unpublished Writings of Gertrude
     Stein (Yale), timely references—
     to carpenters, plumbers, "building
     a vestibule," etc.—suggest that
     most of it was written during the
     period of renovation at the rue de
     Fleurus and completed in England
     during Gertrude's trip there in July,
     1914.
     So far as I can make out: JIS, 50
     I told you, one time: unp. YCAL,
     LS to GS, undated
207 Alice was obliged to carry paintings:
     Lord, "Where The Pictures Were"
     From *Dear Gertrude, It's impossible*
     to *our respective oranges:* YCAL,
     [Jan., 1914?]. Different segments
     of this letter have been published
     in Gallup, *Flowers*, 91, and *JIS*,
     56. (In the latter it has been mis-
     leadingly edited.) In the Stein
     archives at Yale, I discovered a
     note in Leo's hand, addressed to
     "Miss Gertrude Stein, Esq.," writ-
     ten on a large piece of notepaper
     folded to make a packet for a large
     letter. I believe it is a covering
     note for Leo's long letter about
     the division of the collection. Leo's
     note reads: "This letter which is

necessarily of a certain volume was
written in a state of cheerful calm
and will not to the best of my in-
tent and belief trouble any digestion."
208 *You did not suppose, did you:* unp.
     YCAL, MW to GS, undated
209 *At this time in Heidelberg:* Hapgood,
     131
     lots of fun and did poems: unp.
     YCAL, GS to HMcB, May 7, 1914
210 *a tormented and not particularly:*
     SW, 132
     We are still in Paris: unp. YCAL,
     GS to MD, undated
     the latest gossip: Gallup, *Flowers*, 97
     would rather begin with that: SW,
     120
211 *particularly amusing: ibid.*, 120
     the gentlest and most simply: ibid.,
     123
     had a most benign: WIR, 83
     liked us more than ever: SW, 121
212 *Alas, I have just:* Gallup, *Flowers*, 98
     Sorry to say unable: unp. YCAL, HJ
     to ALC, July 28, 1914
     It was a gratifying: SW, 121
213 *Where is Louvain: ibid.*, 122
     Paris is saved. ibid., 124
     Tout va bien: WIR, 85
214 *turned toward Fate:* Aldrich, *Hilltop*,
     100
     For seven days: Gallup, *Flowers*, 103
     Hilltop a best seller in America: the
     rediscovery of Mildred Aldrich,
     who is now virtually unknown, has
     been one of the greater pleasures
     of researching this biography. Her
     four books on life in wartime
     France—listed in the Bibliography
     —give a vivid account of the period
     and a picture, as well, of an extraor-
     dinarily vital and interesting
     woman.
215 From *neglect of the study* to *auto-*
     mobiles with Emerson: SW, 126
     the tired but watchful eyes: ibid.,
     128
216 *scared to death: ibid.*, 129
     125 francs a month: See Cooper in
     MOMA, *Four Americans*, 67
217 *For the present:* Gallup, *Flowers*, 106
     Wait a minute: SW, 130
     Well I am glad: Gallup, *Flowers*, 109
218 *It was a strange winter: SW*, 131
219 *We have made a vow: A&B*, 105
     We responded as well as: SW, 137
220 *incurable passion: ibid.*, 136

The story of Belmonte is: G&P, 70
221 Alright I will be natural: UK, 12
Dearest, supposing you tell me: ibid.,
17
If you had read the word: ibid., 12
How well I remember: ibid., 12
I can't remember the detail: ibid., 9
222 When I was wishing: ibid., 14
And some day we will be rich: ibid.,
15
I said I was careful: G&P, 271
You mean that I make it: ibid., 269
We are going to have a picnic: ibid.,
274
223 Pussy how pretty: BTV, 78
Do you love me sweetest: AFAM, 97
For instance our loving: PL, 23
Kiss my lips: BTV, 80
Lift brown eggs: G&P, 128
Oh you blessed: ibid., 127
I have very bad headaches: AFAM,
105
A splendid instance: G&P, 124
What did I say: BTV, 82
224 I don't understand: G&P, 341
I will write in the daytime: PL, 25
Oh shut up: ibid., 48
Can you recollect: G&P, 260
The play that I am doing: unp.
YCAL, GS to HMcB, Sept. 18,
1915
225 They knew it before we did: SW, 138
forty-five beds: Gallup, Flowers, 109
My life is a hell: ibid., 110
226 My poor Eva is dead: YCAL, quoted
in Sprigge, 110
227 bringing Paquerette: SW, 140
very Chicago: ibid., 141
228 One person was as good: ibid., 144
who always behaved admirably: ibid.,
143
armed with a Michelin: WIR, 95
229 She was an expert carver: ABTC, 63
Well I am proud of you: unp.
YCAL, MA to GS, Apr. [?] 1917
230 Fasten it fat: G&P, 392
Soldiers like a fuss: ibid., 394

It is astonishing: ibid., 398
I do hope that you ran: unp. YCAL,
MA to GS, Oct. 12, 1917
231 From Oh, just a village to big as a
washtub: SW, 152–53
232 They pumped me: Rogers, 8
I asked our mechanic: Gallup,
Flowers, 121
233 the youngest, the sweetest: SW, 146
Leo . . . is psycho-analyzing: Gallup,
Flowers, 118. Interestingly, to be
published in the Saturday Evening
Post became one of Gertrude's am-
bitions, one that she achieved in
1936 with her series of articles on
"Money."
234 They looked extremely strange:
Braque, in "Testimony," 14
Then I did a thing: Gallup, Flowers,
125
235 Compose yourself: WIR, 101
From Well here is peace to belonged
to no country: SW, 154–55
236 spoke a fluent incorrect German:
WIR, 103
Take care: Pollack, 127
Sweeter than water: G&P, 415
237 She had given it to: WIR, 104
Terrible as it all: Aldrich, When
Johnny, 236. Mildred Aldrich attributes this remark to "an American friend" passing through on
her way back to Paris. It is clearly
Gertrude that she is referring to
here, but Gertrude claimed that
it was late May when they returned to Paris. Mildred's letter,
however, is dated March 15, 1919.
more beautiful, vital: ABTC, 78. In
her memoir, published nine years
later, however, Alice remembered
the return to Paris somewhat differently: "The following day, after
lunch, we returned to Paris. The
city, like us, was sadder than when
we left it." (WIR, 104.)

BOOK II. THE LITERARY LIFE

CHAPTER NINE. THE OLD DOOR, A NEW BELL

241 From a second-class hearse to nor
cigarette lighter: ABTC, 81
242 Two penetrating eyes: Bryher, 210
Years ago: Ford, 179–80
243 Guillaume would have been: SW, 50

The old crowd had disappeared: ibid.,
160
Scratch a Russian: EA, 21
No I will not: SW, 157
244 I have circumvented: JIS, 65

raining women: ibid., 76
From *That froze the genial* to *isn't in the trenches*: ibid., 71
245 *In a letter of Rachel's*: Gallup, *Flowers*, 119
that the antagonism: JIS, 77–78
246 *Who was that?*: WIR, 106. Although Alice dates this episode as having occurred shortly after the acquisition of Godiva, the poem, "How She Bowed to Her Brother," which supposedly resulted from the incident, is dated 1931 in the Haas and Gallup *Catalogue* (Yale).
You can tell that the war: unp. YCAL, GS to HMcB, Dec. 12, 1919
247 *The war was over*: SW, 159
still in the shadow: ibid., 157
248 *for the moment overwhelmed*: Gallup, *Flowers*, 148
a pleasant female clerk: EA, 23
You French have no Alps: Beach, 32
249 *Yes, Braque and James Joyce*: SW, 175
Stein-Joyce meeting: There has been a good deal of confusion about the date of this meeting. Ellmann, in his biography of Joyce, without specifying a date, gives it as taking place at a party hosted by Eugene Jolas. His information was apparently drawn from a 1954 interview with Alice B. Toklas. (Ellmann, 543 and note.) Alice, however, without specifying a date, says it took place at a tea at Jo Davidson's. (WIR, 132.) Sylvia Beach gives the same story but dates it as "toward the end of 1930." (Beach, 32.) W. G. Rogers says it took place "a few years" before Joyce's death and quotes a letter from Gertrude Stein, referring to "a historic moment the other day," which confirms that it was at a party given by Jo Davidson. (Rogers, 74.)
Jacques, of course: Lipchitz, 23
From *an excellent gossip* to *content with what I say to you*: SW, 168.

In 1938, Lipchitz also did another bust of Gertrude wearing a cap.
250 *One night I heard friends*: Steegmuller, *Cocteau*, 92. Steegmuller's notes for this incident go into the apparently insoluble problem of what manuscript Cocteau could have seen.
251 *writing to each other*: SW, 169
your old admirer and: unp. YCAL, JC to GS, July 29, 1921
Your Picasso is a beautiful: unp. YCAL, JC to GS, Feb. 20, 1922
My dear Cocteau, Thanks so much: unp. YCAL, GS to JC, [Summer?], 1922
Gertrude l'admirable: unp. YCAL, JC to GS, Jan. 14, 1926
252 *le silence n'existe*: unp. YCAL, JC to GS, undated
The book came: Gallup, *Flowers*, 285
hammering at the Century Magazine: ibid., 149
Gertrude Stein was another powerful: Steffens, *Autobiography*, 834. See Steffens, *Letters*, vol. 2, 904, for Gertrude Stein's comments: "I liked the crime waves and I liked Roosevelt and I liked me." A letter from Steffens to Allen and Laura Suggett dated July 10, 1922 (page 594), indicates meetings in Paris with Gertrude and with Janet Scudder.
253 From *a village explainer* to *picking wildflowers*: SW, 166–67
254 *dictator of art*: Sanche de Gramont, 30
shouted belligerently: Man Ray, 182
who had an individual rhythm: SW, 164
pretty, velvety voice: WIR, 111
an almost mathematical lucidity: Coates, 213
From *not the first minute* to *mad at you*: Janet Flanner, conversation with Mellow, Oct., 1969
255 *there were only two*: SW, 172
256 *If you go to Provence*: Paul, 63
The weather: WIR, 121
This long winter: SW, 173

CHAPTER TEN. ALL HONORABLE MEN

257 *It excited me*: Anderson, *Story Teller's Story*, 362
258 *He is so anxious*: Gallup, *Flowers*, 138

Sherwood's deference: Beach, 31
kitchen of words: Sherwood Anderson, *Notebooks*, 48–49
You sometimes write: Sherwood

Anderson, *Memoirs*, 279

259 *a new book of your things:* Gallup, *Flowers*, 137

as an aid to the general: ibid., 143

Rose is a rose: G&P, 187

I was afraid: Gallup, *Flowers*, 145

It gives words an oddly: G&P, 5

From *There is a city* to *half forgotten city: ibid.*, 7–8

260 *As for Stein:* Sherwood Anderson, *Letters*, 88

From *I am trying to make* to *American I found you:* Gallup, *Flowers*, 152

261 *Very fine is my valentine:* P&P, 152

I like it: Gallup, *Flowers*, 153

From *There are four men* to *anyone writing to-day:* GS, in *Ex Libris* 2, no. 6 (Mar., 1925): 177

You always manage: Gallup, *Flowers*, 179

262 From *very beautiful places* to *mal entouré:* Hemingway, in *Ex Libris* 2, no. 6 (Mar., 1925): 176

crackerjack review: Gallup, *Flowers*, 179

instinctively in touch: ibid., 143

extraordinarily good-looking: SW, 175

263 From *She had beautiful eyes* to *and loosened it:* Hemingway, *Moveable Feast*, 14

There were almost never: ibid., 20

There is a great deal of description: SW, 176

That's not the question: Hemingway, *Moveable Feast*, 15

264 From *more about them as people* to *over to her side: ibid.*, 17

strictly to general principles: SW, 177

265 From *You know nothing about* to *lead happy lives together:* Hemingway, *Moveable Feast*, 20

From *If you keep on doing* to *sent him on his way:* SW, 176

266 *I am getting very fond:* Baker, 117

We were all born: SW, 177

267 *a sort of half-way house:* Gallup, *Flowers*, 166

Hemingway did it all: SW, 179

Ford alleges: Gallup, *Flowers*, 159

268 *It is up to us:* Gallup, in *Fern*, 187

But isn't writing a hard job: Gallup, *Flowers*, 165

Hemingway learned a great deal: SW, 179

began magnificently: Hemingway, *Moveable Feast*, 17

Over twenty thousand copies: Mizener, *Saddest Story*, 335

It is evidently the old: Fern, 191

269 *a spot of cosy low-brow conversation:* Mizener, *Saddest Story*, 348

Up to there: WIR, 113

Young man, it is I: SW, 182

The business management: Gallup, *Flowers*, 165

270 *By the way: ibid.*, 166

great, beautiful, warm: Hemingway, *Moveable Feast*, 27

271 *If you brought up Joyce: ibid.*, 28

From *had a genius for using* to *nothing to do with sentences:* SW, 180

From *No I don't think* to *skin their noses:* Wilson, *Shores of Light*, 117

the only American writer but one: ibid., 119

272 *the only man writing criticism: ibid.*, 123

From *so terribly bad* to *part of her apparatus:* Hemingway, *Moveable Feast*, 28

I have known all along: Mizener, *Far Side*, 196

273 Unpublished foreword to *The Sun Also Rises:* I am indebted to Carlos Baker's biography of Hemingway for alerting me to this foreword and to Mrs. Mary Hemingway for permission to study it.

From *You are all a génération perdue* to *lot of rot sometimes:* Hemingway, *Moveable Feast*, 29–31

274 *a number of people who:* EA, 67

He said that every man: ibid., 52

cross-eyed and really very sweet: Imbs, 228

1000 parties and no work: Mizener, *Far Side*, 180

275 From *really created for* to *contemporaries are forgotten:* SW, 180–81

I half bait: Fitzgerald, *Letters*, 345

There used to be: WIR, 117

But I am confused: Fitzgerald, *Letters*, 169

The real people: ibid., 187

276 *My wife and I: ibid.*, 174

is the cruellest thing: SW, 181

From *writing like a man of thirty* to *book you asked for?:* WIR, 117

From *Miss Toklas, I am sure to that is my idea: ibid.*, 116

277 Hemingway's "flame": See Mizener, *Far Side*, 212, and Turnbull, *Scott Fitzgerald*, 189

From *naturally was afraid* to *a favourite pupil:* SW, 178–79

278 From *a kind of funeral oration* to *sports for himself:* Sherwood Anderson, *Memoirs*, 463–64

From *just like the flat-boat men* to *a weakness:* SW, 179
Cut off my braids: WIR, 138. See also SW, 204.
279 *Have you never seen:* Williams, *Autobiography*, 229
some mystical complicated: Elizabeth Anderson, 161
280 *I just wish: ibid.*, 189
My dear, you don't: ibid., 163

beautiful to look upon: SW, 302
How about a drink?: Sherwood Anderson, *Memoirs*, 465
not at all sore: Baker, 181
281 *Keep in mind:* Elizabeth Anderson, 170
Don't you come home: SW, 182
From *had never heard one person* to *to be stuffy or righteous:* Hemingway, *Moveable Feast*, 116–17

CHAPTER ELEVEN. ENTRANCES, EXITS

283 *Only three books during the decade:* One might add, here, the publication of her Cambridge-Oxford lecture, "Composition As Explanation," published in 1926, by Leonard and Virginia Woolf, under their Hogarth Press imprint.
period of unreliability: Gallup, *Flowers*, 177
284 *The Little Review will be in Paris:* unp. YCAL, JH to GS, May 24, 1923
285 *no one can feel arrogant:* Margaret Anderson, 188
Margaret carries me about: ibid., 187
From *window trimmings* to *any more obscene literature: ibid.*, 219–22
turned up one afternoon: SW, 182
286 From *Good prose, by the way* to *call significant singularity:* Margaret Anderson, 249–51
287 *clasping its handle:* Alice B. Toklas, "They Who Came to Paris to Write," *New York Times Book Review*, Aug. 6, 1950, p. 25
very latest thing: WIR, 115
Don't bother to finish: SW, 166
most humbly for the long delay: Gallup, *Flowers*, 172
288 *the work of Gertrude Stein:* SW, 167
Preachers' sons will: EA, 66
too pitiful: Baker, 206. Hemingway had married Pauline Pfeiffer in 1927.
289 *Hemingway's thinking himself:* Beach, 78
driving about Paris: Knoll, 200
amazing: a clarified: Gallup, *Flowers*, 162
McAlmon's first meeting with Gertrude: Despite his professed reluctance, McAlmon's letters to Gertrude in the Stein archives (YCAL)

indicate that he was on invitational terms at the rue de Fleurus as early as 1923.
almost shy: Knoll, 200
the best criticism of Gertrude Stein: ibid., 204
290 From *the elephant's sensibility* to *tremendous pulsation: ibid.*, 204–5
very mature and very good-looking: SW, 166
abundance, he could: ibid., 181
in the labyrinthine: Knoll, 204
From *bitterly* to *questioned her genius:* Bryher, 211
291 *psychic factors:* Williams, *Autobiography*, 291. Williams mistakenly dates his meeting with Gertrude as having taken place in 1926. But McAlmon, who accompanied him, was no longer on speaking terms with Gertrude by then. A *petit bleu* from McAlmon to Gertrude, tentatively dated May, 1924 (YCAL), says that Bryher, Williams, and Hilda Doolittle wanted to see her.
If they were mine: Williams, *Autobiography*, 254
No, oh no, no, no, no: Knoll, 206
292 *Why in fact:* Williams, *Selected Essays*, 113
293 *delicacy and completeness:* SW, 192
From *verbally very interesting* to *considerable beauty:* Edith Sitwell, 159
From *bitterly disappointed* to *many fresh admirers:* Gallup, *Flowers*, 184
294 From *Peace* to *matter with it:* SW, 192
Granted that there are: Gallup, *Flowers*, 186
From *talk as quickly* to *prima donna:* SW, 193

295 *as if she were sitting:* Osbert Sitwell, 273

From *deflated* to *vague nervousness in the eyes:* Acton, vol. 1, 160–63

296 From *was not a question to enough of glory and excitement:* SW, 194

297 *entirely in accordance with my epoch:* ibid., 459

From *No one is ahead to several generations behind themselves:* ibid., 453–54

298 From *before we were dead* to *by almost thirty years:* ibid., 460

C'est nous: ibid., 75

a fine old femme: Baker, 91

299 From *all at sea* to *is paintable:* Gallup, *Flowers,* 169

Really, Henry: unp. YCAL, GS to HMcB, July 19, 1925

300 *You would not let me go:* SW, 195

the soft murmur: Miller, 119

having concluded that music: LIA, 117

always with the pedal down: Thomson, 11

changed my life, ibid., 46

301 From *We'll be seeing each other* to *satisfied with its looks:* ibid., 89–90

My portrait trick: ibid., 123

302 *in letters, for instance:* ibid., 91

From *I like to be told* to *named gradually:* A&B, 214

303 From *I think it should* to *as far as it has gone:* Thomson, 91–92

304 From *In narrative prepare for saints* to *necessary to go again:* SW, 511

My country 'tis of thee: ibid., 515

305 From *half in doors* to *Saint Therese not interested:* ibid., 515–16

completely imagine his suffering: EA, 90

From *Repeat First Act* to *Not more than as often:* SW, 516–18

306 *exist and converse: New York Times,* Nov. 17, 1934

A landscape does not move: LIA, 129

tried to tell what each one is: ibid., 121

The landscape has its formation: ibid., 125

Your emotion concerning the play: ibid., 93

307 *Pear trees cherry blossoms pink:* SW, 521

in wed in dead: ibid., 537

How many acts: ibid., 538

to break, crack open, and solve: Thomson, 90

308 *every word of it:* ibid., 107

everybody, in fact, seemed buoyed: ibid., 104

309 *I'm suffering now:* Gallup, *Flowers,* 202

From *Gertrude Stein has not written to write better about my painting than yourself:* quoted by Cooper in MOMA, *Four Americans,* 68–69

310 *Juan Gris is a Spaniard:* P&P, 46

It seduces me: ibid., 48

Tell me why you stand: SW, 175

311 *passion for exactitude:* ibid., 174

I can't find room: Soby, 97

Poor Juan is very low: Gallup, *Flowers* 206

You have no right to mourn: SW, 175

the most moving thing: ibid., 175

From *Josette equable intelligent* to *to be measured:* P&P, 48–50

312 *The funeral of Juan Gris:* See Kahnweiler, *Juan Gris,* 62

Who are all these people: SW, 17

CHAPTER TWELVE. THE GOOD LIFE AT BILIGNIN

314 *The country was beautiful:* ABTC, 100

315 *We are on our way:* YCAL, GS to HMcB, Sept., 8, 1924. Bridgman, in his Chronology (*Gertrude Stein in Pieces,* p. 361), gives the year as 1923, but the postmark, readable with a magnifying glass, is clearly 1924.

much of what great French cooking: ABTC, 101

316 Reading the proofs was a tedious job:

In the manuscript of *The Autobiography of Alice B. Toklas,* Alice has written an emphatic "Never" in red pencil over the passage describing this episode.

Lots of people will think: Fern, 199

I'm sorry Boni's did not: unp. YCAL, RMcA to GS, Sept. 16, 1925

317 *What the dickens is the matter:* unp. YCAL, GS to RMcA, undated

There is a syndicate which: Fern, 205

You know perfectly well: ibid., 206
318 *What are you talking about: ibid.,*
208
Had you wished to give: ibid., 208
You do forget from one letter: ibid.,
209
319 *With sentences so regularly rhythmical: ibid.,* 211
Reviews in *The Irish Statesman* and
The Dial: ibid., 211
From *Contrary to your verbal statements* to *by the pulping proposition:* Gallup, *Flowers,* 189–90
320 *Will you without fail: Fern,* 204
321 *Painting now after its great moment:*
HTW, 13
From *any one who would listen to*
to *have been the creator of an
idea:* SW, 190
322 *And then my opera:* unp. YCAL, GS
to HMcB, Aug. [?] 1927
They go out of the door naturally:
SW, 188
323 *The boy needs some tea:* Imbs, 176
Bébé almost died: Gallup, *Flowers,*
205
One must always yield: Imbs, 162
We are peacefully and completely:
Thomson, 126
324 From *a mirroring of it* to *friends too
strong for me: ibid.,* 185
girls' high school stuff: Acton, vol. 1,
180
Curious and poor fellow: Gallup,
Flowers, 198
young and violent and ill: SW, 196
325 From *exhilarated with exasperation*
to *contemplate them with indifference: ibid.,* 187
I am unhappy just now: Gallup,
Flowers, 232
with tears in the eyes: ibid., 221
to the accompaniment of some: ibid.,
234
326 *just another YMCA secretary:* Imbs,
119
*You have the gift of true brilliancy:
ibid.,* 121
Don't, don't get mixed up: ibid., 203
to give the young generation: SW, 8
Helen is very pleased: A&B, 202
327 *Gertrude does not like silent men:*
Imbs, 128
After all, we do want: SW, 198
Transition died: ibid., 199
piled compliment upon compliment:
Imbs, 228
328 *I can't see why anyone: ibid.,* 235

From *the troubles of senility* to *low
in my mind:* Imbs, 239–40
329 *When I put it down:* Gallup,
Flowers, 214
I got up quite early: ibid., 215
330 *I will drive you up there:* WIR, 123
331 *Allez doucement:* SW, 189
From *It does seem very foolish* to
George went off and said nothing:
EA, 24
We would get two influential friends:
ABTC, 102
Alice Toklas' conscience troubled her:
EA, 25
333 From *In the morning she would read*
to *fullness as an overflowing:* Thom-
son, 169–70
334 *They talk a great deal:* EA, 68
Alice driving a cow: According to
Thomson, Alice maintained that it
was Gertrude who drove the cow.
(Thomson, 171.)
It takes a lot of time: EA, 70
From *I like moving around to mem-
ory and eternity: ibid.,* 116
*I am writing a lot, grammatically
speaking:* unp. YCAL, GS to
HMcB, Sept. 15, 1928
From *I am writing a lot about sentences* to *in retirement, perhaps:*
unp. YCAL, GS to HMcB, May
22, 1929
335 *Way-laid made it known:* HTW, 26
A rain makes transplanting: ibid., 15
What is a sentence for: ibid., 19
Hers and his the houses: ibid., 20
*What happened to Mabel Haynes:
ibid.,* 222
vastly interesting: Gallup, *Flowers,*
249
336 From *Because he knows all about
gardens* to *liked each other as
writers:* SW, 205
I often wondered whether: HTW,
244. As indicated, Gertrude took
up this idea at length in *Four in
America.* The book involved four
basic "conceits." She began "If
Ulysses S. Grant had been a religious leader who was to become a
saint what would he have done."
(FIA, 1.) She raised similar questions about the Wright brothers as
painters, Henry James as a general,
and George Washington as a
novelist. The idea about James is
not altogether far-fetched. James
was a superb tactician and strate-
gist as a writer of fiction. More-

over, he had an enduring fascination with Napoleon. As Leon Edel reported, James on his deathbed suffered delusions of being the French Emperor, and dictated "two letters from Napoleon Bonaparte to one of his married sisters." (Edel, *The Master*, 551.)

337 From *an institution* to *it was sublime:* ABTC, 297

338 And *one of the principal things:* Amory and Bradlee, 280
Pavlik's long face froze: Thomson, 182

339 *by inference that she found it:* ibid., 183
a sleepy vulture look: Imbs, 123
an impossible woman: Berman, conversation with Mellow, 1972

340 *My holiday with you:* Gallup, *Flowers,* 238
a sort of courteous revenge: Berman to Mellow, June 8, 1972 and Aug. 1, 1972
I do not care about anybody's painting: EA, 98
I did not care for the way: ibid., 57
From *the problem that a line* to *the creator and his followers:* SW, 174, 111

341 *Admirable Gertrude:* Gallup, *Flowers,* 243

342 From *for Gertrude Stein to improvise* to *very sweet love to you:* Thomson, 190–92

343 *Those whom I have questioned:* Gallup, *Flowers,* 244
From *The last act of the drama* to *It isn't what was asked for:* Thomson, 194

344 *This seems to be all right:* ibid., 194
Did you want something?: ibid., 196
Losing friends is a sad matter: Gallup, *Flowers,* 247

345 *Miss Gertrude Stein has asked me:* Imbs, 296

346 *putting all I can spare:* YCAL, quoted in Pollack, 160
My very dear Etta: quoted by Hirschland in MOMA, *Four Americans,* 84

347 *understanding sympathy:* Pollack, 198
When a Jew dies: Thomson, 378
My dear Miss Stein, Your poems: Gallup, *Flowers,* 129
Here there is no group: ibid., 130
unsympathetic with the present: ibid., 210

348 From *Lack of popular success* to *patriotism is fundamental, instinctive:* New York World, May 18, 1930

349 *And when she told Picasso:* WIR, 136
stick to the booksellers: SW, 200
What do you expect, Madame: WIR, 136

350 *You must get me out of a mess:* ibid., 136

CHAPTER THIRTEEN. THE LAST TOUCH OF BEING

351 *If there had not been:* EA, 9

352 *last touch of being:* MOA, 180
Except in daily life: EA, 106
Just think what a lot of money: SW, 207

353 From *Of course I shall be delighted* to *effect of your story on the general public:* Gallup, *Flowers,* 259–61

354 The book ran to four printings: Financial information was very kindly supplied by Mr. William Jovanovich, of Harcourt Brace Jovanovich, Inc., and by Mr. Michael Janeway, of the *Atlantic Monthly*.
for sentimental reasons: EA, 48
the most expensive coat: ibid., 40
There is no doubt about it: ibid., 47

355 *nothing but words of praise:* Gallup, *Flowers,* 266–67
a bit sorry and sad: Sherwood Anderson, *Letters,* 295
He would prefer, it seems: Gallup, *Flowers,* 266–67

356 *that woman:* EA, 14
From *maintained very well the tone* to *practically eliminate me:* JIS, 134
Menopausal phenomena: See Baker, 240 and notes.
Hemingway threatening to write his memoirs: His letter is paraphrased in Stock, 311.

357 *We did not yet use:* EA, 91
wisdom, its distinction: Wilson, *Shores of Light,* 579

not nearly so isolated: Troy, 134

From *sell one's personality* to *any of us will really go over:* EA, 50

358 *I had written and was writing nothing: ibid.,* 64

What happened to me was this: Amory and Bradlee, 280

359 The summer at Bilignin: The sequence of servants that summer differs somewhat, chronologically, as given in *Blood on the Dining-Room Floor* and later in *Everybody's Autobiography.* I have followed the earlier chronology.

She had everything the matter: EA, 56

360 *big good-looking woman: ibid.,* 79. It is not clear whether the names of Madame Caesar and Madame Steiner are actual or disguised.

361 *Then I went out to speak: ibid.,* 61–62

For that price: Thomson, 93

Anybody called Francis: EA, 57

362 *the four permanent friendships:* SW, 205

had nothing in particular: ibid., 196

stimulating and comforting: ibid., 203

read eagerly everything: Gallup, *Flowers,* 193

It came after a joke: Faÿ, Preface to his abridged version of *The Making of Americans* (Harcourt, Brace, 1934), ix

363 *wanted to read her books: ibid.,* xiii

As our food is made up: ibid., xi

Amongst all the English writers: ibid., xviii

The greatest and most beautiful: ibid., xi

Once in a while: EA, 53

From *a very large woman who was not moving* to *frightened of her and about her: ibid.,* 82–83

364 *How many houses and families:* BoDF, 27. There is something puerile and unsatisfactory about Gertrude Stein's novels after *The Making of Americans.* Books like *Lucy Church Amiably* and *Ida,* for example, seem rather "gotten up" —like children's books in mothers' dresses. Her remarks in Haas, *A Primer* (p. 22), might be taken as a confession of failure: "To my mind the novel form has not been a successful affair in the Twentieth Century. There has been nothing that you can honestly call a novel.

There has not been one in the Twentieth Century with the possible exception of Proust. That makes the novel scheme quite out of the question."

It was a funny thing that summer: EA, 51

365 From *would be happy to have* to *that very equality:* Thomson, 229

My dear Virgil, Have just received: ibid., 231

366 *And dear Gertrude, if you knew: ibid.,* 232

My dear Virgil, Yes yes yes: ibid., 233

Yes, of course, you are to: ibid., 234

367 *Negro singers have the most perfect:* New York *World Telegram,* Dec. 16, 1933

a more direct and unself-conscious: New York *Times,* Feb. 8, 1934

it begins to look: Houseman, 109

the movements would be sedate: Thomson, 230

368 *Everything about the opera: ibid.,* 241

To know to know: SW, 511

Pigeons on the grass alas: ibid., 533

369 *Four Saints, in our vivid:* Gallup, *Flowers,* 275

A spirit of inspired madness: New York *Times,* Feb. 8, 1934

there were so many references: Gallup, *Flowers,* 276

Toscanini was in the orchestra: ibid., 277

It's like Grand Opera: Houseman, 117

doubtful aid to Stein's prose: Williams, *Selected Essays,* 161

The most important event: Houseman, 117

370 *for positively you can have had:* Gallup, *Flowers,* 277–78

No music publisher wished: Thomson, 243

371 From *their inspiration comes from without* to *elected a second time:* New York *Times,* Jan. 3, 1934

From *a very real and efficient personality* to *difficult to read:* Warren, 9, 23

373 *the United States is a country:* transition, Fall, 1928, 97–98

374 *rather wild place:* Gallup, *Flowers,* 273

My dear Kiddie: Rogers, 40

375 *Mme. Pierlot was much pleased: ibid.,* 108

What did America think: ibid., 114

We always believe: EA, 159

squeezed insultingly into: Rogers, 115

376 From *There have been so many alarms* to *I guess it's pretty good:* ibid., 116

From *Bernard Faÿ is here* to *they*

are not too easy: ibid., 118–19

377 *There is not enough money:* New York Herald Tribune, Oct. 5, 1934

I don't at all approve: Gallup, Flowers, 285

378 *I was awfully scared:* Rogers, 119

CHAPTER FOURTEEN. REDISCOVERING AMERICA

380 From *speaking a language every one to the last child is always most loved:* Gertrude's shipboard remarks are taken from the published reports in both the *New York Times* and the *New York Herald Tribune*, October 25, 1934.

382 *the ubiquitous honeydew melon:* ABTC, 133

anything should be American: EA, 174

As if we didn't know it: WIR, 144

after the thirty years we went: EA, 175

Have we had a hectic time: Rogers, 129

383 *I lost everything, I was excited:* EA, 176

very pleasant but quite firm: New York Herald Tribune, Oct. 29, 1934

Well, this is it: unp. YCAL, ABT to WGR, Nov. 18, 1934. The schedule for Gertrude's lectures in New England in January which Alice gives here is strenuous: the 7th, Springfield; 9th, Amherst; 10th, Northampton; 11th, Pittsfield; 12th, Wallingford; 15th, Wesleyan; 16th, South Hadley; 18th, Hartford; 21st, Providence; 23rd, Springfield.

Hearing his voice was: EA, 169

Besides it was silly: ibid., 177

384 From *It is natural that I should tell* to *what an oil painting is:* LIA, 59–90

385 *no unanimity of opinion:* New York Times, Nov. 2, 1934

386 *variously pleased, mystified:* New York Herald Tribune, Nov. 2, 1934

You don't need any special preparation: New York American, Nov. 3, 1934

After all once you know: EA, 178

There are so many of them: ibid., 182

387 *And we are flying to Chicago:* Rogers, 130

The wandering line of Masson: EA, 191

looked very lovely: ibid., 194

Everything has been wonderful: Rogers, 130

388 From *all the Negro intellectuals* to *and so let us keep them:* EA, 199–200

From *said she wished she knew more French* to *she melted away:* ibid., 7–8

389 From *so different that it was* to *was not there for ten cents:* ibid., 187–88

390 *I never tired of seeing them:* ibid., 202, 201

It seemed as if Europe: ibid., 212

391 From *in English there have really been* to *Madame the police:* ibid., 206–7

Baby Face Nelson: George "Baby Face" Nelson was entrapped by Federal agents on November 27, 1934. His bullet-riddled body was found in an abandoned car near Barrington, Ill., on the following day.

mostly from somewhere in the South: EA, 208

392 *They were all young ones:* ibid., 209

Pretty soon we were all talking: ibid., 213

393 *On Christmas morning:* Details of the Christmas Day festivities from Julian Stein, Jr., conversation with Mellow, May 31, 1972.

The romantic thing about America: EA, 232

My dear Etta, Thanks so much: Pollack, 231

394 *Thank you. Having you come:* Bloom, 19

395 *Dearest Gertrude Stein: It was a disappointment:* Fitzgerald, Letters, 518

from somewhere going to somewhere:
EA, 234

396 *Just we two and the pilot:* Rogers,
133
After all, anybody is as their land:
Narr, 46
You are brilliant and subtle: EA,
224
Why not: ibid., 223

397 *The painting was like any learnt
painting: ibid.*, 228
We have been so many places:
Rogers, 133

398 *mysterious thing they:* EA, 237
if the boys can ever come: ibid., 241
*why American men think that suc-
cess: ibid.*, 239

399 *The train went along:* Rogers, 149
We quite lost our hearts to it: ibid.,
132
Usually I avoid modern fads: Van
Vechten, 103
Is Gertrude Stein serious?: WIR,
150

400 *was amusing, the Confederacy:*
Rogers, 132
You put new where the old was: EA,
250
*if G. had not caught a most fright-
ful cold:* Rogers, 132
illustrations of Dante: EA, 253

401 *realising that I would have to live:*
ABTC, 139
more varied and amusing: Rogers,
132
confusion: Salmon, in "Testimony,"
15
hollow, tinsel bohemianism: Eugene
Jolas, in *ibid.*, 2
final capitulation: Maria Jolas, in
ibid., 11
*From pharmacy to sensitive member
of the family:* Matisse, in *ibid.*, 3–
4

402 *How can he know what he's talking
about?: New York Evening Post,*
Mar. 4, 1935
*I'm crazy about horses: New York
Herald Tribune,* Mar. 5, 1935
Apparently Paris is amusing itself:
Sprigge, 198
a dining room table: ABTC, 140

403 *History repeats itself:* Narr, 7
Think about American writing: ibid.,
10
calling upon: ibid., 26
progressive telling of things: ibid., 17
A thing you all know: LIA, 184
*Perhaps narrative and poetry and
prose:* Narr, 29

404 *Now you have all seen hundreds:*
FIA, vi
Thanks so very much for your good:
A transcript of this letter was sup-
plied by Mr. B. F. Skinner.
I do not think any university student:
EA, 267 .

405 *From No left U turns to is just as
easy as that: ibid.*, 262–63
*The girls at Miss Hockaday's school:
ibid.*, 272

406 *the most beautiful one I have:*
ABTC, 140
ate too well almost too well: EA, 272
all good Texas food was Virginian:
ABTC, 140
Except as before the law: EA, 274
*You see it is the middle-aged people:
ibid.*, 276
God's own country: ABTC, 140

407 *moving around and talking:* EA, 280
Some critics say I have to be careful:
Gallup, *Flowers*, 291
gentle person like any Spanish gypsy:
EA, 282
I said to Hammett: ibid., 5

408 *by having a small audience: ibid.*,
284
acres of orchards and artichokes:
ABTC, 141
*From Not one regret to want no jar-
ring note:* Gallup, *Flowers*, 296

409 *She, said, Hello:* WIR, 153
*I like ordinary people: New York
Herald Tribune,* Apr. 7, 1935
I asked to go: EA, 291

410 *What was the use of my having:
ibid.*, 289
*From The capitals of important
countries to at least I hope so:
New York Herald Tribune,* Mar. 9,
1935, 11

411 *From extraordinary amount to not
choosing anything: ibid.*, Mar. 16,
1935, 15
*From Think of any news that to
news of a small town paper: ibid.*,
Mar. 23, 1935, 15

412 *From two kinds of crime to on the
front page of the newspaper: ibid.*,
Mar. 30, 1935, 13

413 *From Nobody seems to need them to
natural thing in the world to be
an American: ibid.*, Apr. 13, 1935,
13

414 *Your lectures have been a revelation:*
Gallup, *Flowers*, 298
*From Her cheerful sanguine-com-
plexioned face to on the serious
side perhaps: New York Herald*

Tribune, Apr. 30, 1935
enormously liked by the readers:
Rogers, 150

415 I am already homesick for America:
New York Herald Tribune, May,
13, 1935

CHAPTER FIFTEEN. HERE WE ARE AND HERE WE STAY

416 most generally always wrong: EA, 40
From Political theories bore me to
the style she has created: New
York Herald Tribune, May 19,
1935
417 When I say god and mammon: LIA,
23–24
418 What is the use of being: GHoA, 25
Why is it that in this epoch: ibid.,
182
After all they cannot discipline: EA,
299
419 up and down the hills near Bilignin:
ibid., 301
What a book: Gallup, Flowers, 305
Really a beautiful old man: ibid.,
307
420 From personal observations of last
summer's to slipped through the
door into the night: New York
Herald Tribune, Dec. 2, 1935
When I first heard: EA, 15
French laws on divorce: Picasso's biographer Roland Penrose notes
that the painter had contemplated
divorce but his Spanish nationality made the process very complicated. (Picasso, 250.)
421 Yes, you and I we have weak: EA,
14
you who were a poet: ibid., 18
From It is very interesting to his
writing does not interest me: ibid.,
17–19. Gertrude may have had
cause for worrying about Picasso's
poetry. Penrose gives a specimen
of it ("give wrench twist and kill
I make my way set alight,"
Picasso, 252) and notes that the
painter had dispensed with the
usual forms of punctuation as unnecessary and had written a "word-
portrait" of his friend Sabartès.
422 Neither of us listened very much:
EA, 30–31
From Sure I did . . . because to
him again, yes said he: ibid., 36–37
423 an ordered history of every one:
MOA, 284
Alice B. Toklas did hers: EA, 3
424 Einstein was the creative: ibid., 21
Easy to read and easy to forget: New

York Times, Dec. 5, 1937
425 I had really written poetry: EA, 302
I must say that I read it: Rogers, 234
426 From It was exciting to to be one
succeeding: EA, 317–18
All the time that I am writing: ibid.,
88
no use in being too forethoughtful:
ibid., 11
427 She has not yet had time: ibid., 296
You go over the same ground: ibid.,
131
428 I took to gardening: ibid., 309
When you earn it and spend it: Gertrude Stein: Writings and Lectures,
333
The young ones said I was reactionary: EA. 310
With my situation what it is: Gallup, Flowers, 322
429 I am probably more distressed: ibid.,
330
The first edition of Picasso: Rogers,
228
430 Spaniards know that there is no:
GSoP, 36
Picasso only sees something else:
ibid., 65
rich and furious: Davidson, 312
I must say Bennett was astonished:
EA, 309
But he is not a fascist: Rogers, 91
431 Do you know what: ibid., 153
a fascinating person: ibid., 157
From I think we ought to start at
nine to and then lean back: ibid.,
156–58
432 There, that's the place: ibid., 166
I don't want you to do it: ibid., 174
433 You see Gertrude wants to go: ibid.,
179
But gracious it is hard: ibid., 83
434 We were tired of the present: Bridgman, 364
Basket died: Rogers, 97
was convinced her husband: WIR,
161
I'm sick afraid that you're wrong:
Gallup, Flowers, 341
435 when domestic architecture: Beaton,
377

I'd been closeted in this small house:
    ibid., 379
War? Who cares about war?: ibid.,
    381
They all were upset but hopeful:
    SW, 543
436 *We are for the present staying here:*
    Rogers, 188
437 *Paris, France is exciting and peaceful:* PF, 1
Well that too is intelligent: ibid., 21
*From a tall, thin man to not a real
    war: ibid.,* 42–43
438 *the very curious relation: ibid.,* 27
in sorrow, in enchantment: Gallup,
    Flowers, 352
the treason of the Belgian king: SW,
    547
439 *It was sad; they were each: ibid.,* 549
It is so friendly: PF, 13
I found that cutting box hedges:
    SW, 549
*From For various reasons to that is
    the way that is:* Rogers, 190–91
I was scared, completely scared: SW,
    549
440 *From "Well," said Dr. Chaboux to
    —aller, où?: ibid.,* 551
made beautiful and neutral: Rogers,
    193
441 *Well I suppose we will go on:* SW,
    556
We always stayed, one of us: ibid.,
    557
Nothing counts any more: WIR, 162
Our light is lit: SW, 563
In the beginning, like camels: ABTC,
    215
442 *There is one thing though:* Rogers,
    194

most chic and warm: ibid., 195
443 *I am writing an extra letter:* Rogers,
    194
The 1,479 pages: ABTC, 227
444 *a possible danger one refused to face:*
    ibid., 227
Pétain was right to stay in France:
    WIHS, 87
When I write now I wonder: Rogers,
    198
*From was an important element to
    pointed to his own breast and answered I:* WIHS, 87–88
445 *So many points of view: ibid.,* 82.
    Gertrude's reactions to the Vichy
    Government and her report on the
    mixed motivations of the people
    she met seem to confirm, at
    ground level, the overview given in
    a recent book, Robert O. Paxton's
    *Vichy France: Old Guard and
    New Order, 1940–1944.*
And now everybody knows except:
    WIHS, 53
to be free, not to be managed: ibid.,
    75
Laval and the rest of them: ibid., 37
446 *I obtained from Pétain:* Bridgman,
    316
the means of making: Rogers, 213
not sure that they did not want:
    WIHS, 81
*The middle classes were once more
    torn: ibid.,* 82
447 *From Tell these ladies to but here
    we are and here we stay: ibid.,* 50
After you have been living: ibid., 49
So it fell upon me: ABTC, 223
cold winter day, all too appropriate:
    ibid., 297

CHAPTER SIXTEEN. THE LIBERATION OF GERTRUDE STEIN

448 *Yes perhaps I will write:* Rogers, 227
449 *Naturally my mother being Baltimore:* WIHS, 8
very meek, just as meek as that:
    ibid., 59
They were rather attaching, foolish:
    ibid., 70
Poor Madame Berrard: ibid., 37
450 *Could those to whom she was loyal:*
    ibid., 41
The son of our dentist: ibid., 40
After all that he went to Lyon: ibid.,
    120
Now all he had to do: ibid., 121
I always liked you and your country:
    ibid., 54

And now it is June 1943: ibid., 35
451 *One day a young man his name is
    Paul Genin: ibid.,* 112
We are eating the Cézanne: Balmain, 90
And the official whom she saw:
    WIHS, 243. Gertrude seems to
    have settled in a region which afforded some protection against the
    Nazi deportations of the Jews, not
    through the Vichy Government,
    but through the Italians occupying
    the French Alpine territories. Paxton notes: "When deportations
    from the costal zone increased in
    early 1943, the Italian occupation

authorities obstructed them east of the Rhône, warning the French government that while it could do what it wanted with French Jews, foreign Jews in the Italian-occupied zone were exclusively a matter for the Italian authorities. In March the Italian authorities stepped in to prevent the French prefects of Valence, Chambéry, and Annecy from arresting foreign Jews there. In June 1943 Italian police prefect Lospinosa blocked the French arrest of 7,000 foreign Jews at Mégève." (*Vichy France*, 182–83.)

452 *It was late in the afternoon*: WIHS, 98

They are as I am always telling them: ibid., 93

Enough said that is not the way: ibid., 80

It is darkest before the dawn: ibid., 175

453 *We first heard of this dreadful lune rouge*: ibid., 184

Madame weep because we are taking: ibid., 193

From *I was sad to see it go* to *it is a pleasure and such a pleasure*: ibid., 192

454 *To-day is the landing*: ibid., 194

I called the servants: ibid., 211

Half pound weight Swifts yellow: ibid., 218

455 *I cant tell you how excited*: ibid., 237

From *What a day, what a day of days* to *a few hours so they came*: ibid., 244–45

Madame there are Americans: WIR, 166

From *magnificent lunch* to *to be talking to America today so happy*: Sevareid, 457–62

457 *Take care, that is a painting*: WIR, 167

thanks to Bernard Faÿ: unp. deposition in defense of Bernard Faÿ, YCAL. See note, page 460.

458 *Take it now*: WIR, 168

Hemingway's letter to W. G. Rogers: The letter, dated July 29, 1948, is a touching document in its way. Hemingway generously acknowledges having learned from both Gertrude and Ezra Pound; but his assertion that Gertrude had learned dialogue from him is somewhat amiss. She had developed a feeling for the conversational idiom as early as *Three Lives*, and it is the

bits and snatches of dialogue in her Majorcan poems and plays, around 1915–16, that provide the real strength of her work in that period.

He has been one of your most ardent: Gallup, *Flowers*, 382

459 *Elle est écrivaine*: Leon Gordon Miller, unpublished memoir

We have made for ourselves: Gallup, *Flowers*, 379

For God's sake: WIR, 171

yellow, large and fragrant: ibid., 109

I am sure you know by this time: Gallup, *Flowers*, 376

460 *When I was in France during the occupation*: LO& P, xv

to work for France: unp. YCAL. This deposition, written in French and addressed to Maître Chresteil, Avocat à la Cour, is dated March 14, 1946. In it Gertrude testifies to Faÿ's lifelong services, by way of his books and lectures, to Franco-American culture, and states that Faÿ "n'a jamais aimé ni les Allemands ni l'Allemagne." A note in Alice's hand states that foreigners could only give written testimony, not oral testimony, in the French court.

messages that are worth millions: Gallup, *Flowers*, 388

461 *He may go to jail*: Leon Gordon Miller, unpublished memoir

Of course you do: *Life*, Aug. 6, 1945, p. 58

462 From *sad young men* to *a sense of imprisonment*: "The New Hope in Our 'Sad Young Men' ", *New York Times Magazine*, June 3, 1945, p. 5

I just tell you, and though: B&W, 30

463 *The libretto is sensationally handsome*: Gallup, *Flowers*, 397

an evocation of nineteenth century America: *New York Times*, Apr. 15, 1956

my long life of effort and strife: LO& P, 87

464 *Indigestion and high places*: EA, 190

might become grave: WIR, 171

Nonsense, Ellen: Bloom, 15

She didn't leave: ibid., 22

465 *No thought of death was with her*: Thomson, 366

Don't scold her: ibid., 373

Precious Baby blew a fuse: LO& P, xv

From *Is this the car* to *So goodbye, Pablo:* WIR, 171–72

From *Now tell me everything* to *as I myself were all at once non-exis-tent:* Lord, "Where The Pictures Were"

467 *Your friend will have to be cared for:* WIR, 172
468 *I order you to operate:* Thomson, 377
What is the answer?: WIR, 173
You have to learn to do: WIHS, 126

CHAPTER SEVENTEEN. ALICE ALONE

469 *lonely in the large high rooms:* Thomson, 377
I know how much you are suffering: Gallup, *Flowers,* 402
470 *friendships in aspic:* Joe Barry, conversation with Mellow, October, 1969.
I just saw in Newsweek: JIS, 276
Gertrude writes a lot of stuff: ibid., 251
In treating of Matisse and Picasso: ibid., 269
critics will see that I: ibid., 292
From something should be said to *That is all: ibid.,* 298
472 *A great appreciation and partiality:* unp. ABT to Minna Daniel, Feb. 5, 1953
Gertrude would be pleased: Lord, "Where the Pictures Were"
473 *does know the mechanics:* ABT to MD, Feb. 5, 1953
after four months—six times a week: unp. ABT to MD, Aug. 15, 1958
it was necessary to earn: unp. ABT to MD, Apr. 18, 1958
I wish I could have shown you: unp. ABT to MD, July 24, 1957
474 *the exaggerated reports of Paris:* unp. ABT to MD, Jan. 8, 1957
You must save me a lunch—a plain one: unp. ABT to MD, Mar. 13, 1957. Alice's recipe for sole "with a rare sauce" which she sent to Minna Daniel in a later letter is as follows:
2 lbs fish (sole)   1 tsp. tumeric
½ pint yoghurt   Salt

1 cup powdered almonds
5 tbls. butter
1 inch stick cinnamon
1 pint heavy cream
¾ tsp. black pepper
3 onions
1 cup light cream

Wash and soak fish 1 hour in water. I use filet of sole or trout. Melt 2½ tbls butter and fry onions. (Diced with cinnamon.) When lightly browned place the fish on them. Sprinkle with tumeric, salt, pepper and light cream and 2½ tbls. butter. Shake the casserole or skillet until the fish is almost done. Mix almonds, yoghurt and heavy cream. Pour over fish. Cover and simmer for ½ hour over lowest flame. If too dry, add small quantity heavy cream.
The baths are just as effective: unp. ABT to MD, Oct. 9, 1958
a sad disturbing book of France: unp. ABT to MD, June 3, 1957
baptised as a child: unp. ABT to MD, Apr. 18, 1958
Since Gertrude: Thomson, 378
475 *I haven't the courage:* unp. ABT to MD, July 13, 1959
Sale of Picasso drawings: See SoA, 401
476 *But I can see the pictures:* Lord, "Where The Pictures Were"
I was born in 1877: Barry, 8
I'd be fine if: Lord, "Where The Pictures Were"
477 *Have you a pretty garden this year?:* unp. ABT to MD, Jan. 16, 1967

𝒷ibliography

Abbreviations listed here are used in citations in the Notes.
See page 481 for explanation.

PRINCIPAL WORKS OF GERTRUDE STEIN

A&B   *Alphabets and Birthdays.* Introduction by Donald Gallup. New Haven: Yale University Press, 1957.

AFAM   *As Fine as Melanctha.* Foreword by Natalie Clifford Barney. New Haven: Yale University Press, 1954.

BTV   *Bee Time Vine and Other Pieces.* Preface and notes by Virgil Thomson. New Haven: Yale University Press, 1953.
Before the Flowers of Friendship Faded Friendship Faded. Paris: Plain Edition, 1931.

BoDF   *Blood on the Dining-Room Floor.* Foreword by Donald Gallup. Pawlet, Vt.: Banyon Press, 1948.

B&W   *Brewsie and Willie.* New York: Random House, 1946.
Composition as Explanation. London: Hogarth Press, 1926.

EA   *Everybody's Autobiography.* New York: Random House, 1937.

Fern   *Fernhurst, Q.E.D., and Other Early Writings by Gertrude Stein.* Edited with introduction by Leon Katz. Appendix by Donald Gallup. New York: Liveright, 1971.

FIA   *Four in America.* Introduction by Thornton Wilder. New Haven: Yale University Press, 1947.

GHoA   *The Geographical History of America or The Relation of Human Nature to the Human Mind.* Introduction by Thornton Wilder. New York: Random House, 1936.

G&P   *Geography and Plays.* Boston: Four Seas, 1922.
Gertrude Stein: Writings and Lectures 1909–1945. Edited by Patricia Meyerowitz. Baltimore: Penguin, 1971.

GSoP   *Gertrude Stein on Picasso.* Edited by Edward Burns. Afterword by Leon Katz and Edward Burns. New York: Liveright, 1970. Includes *Picasso* (1938).

HTW   *How to Write.* Paris: Plain Edition, 1931.
Ida. New York: Random House, 1941.

LO&P   *Last Operas and Plays.* Edited with introduction by Carl Van Vechten. New York: Rinehart, 1949.

LIA   *Lectures in America.* New York: Random House, 1935.
Lucy Church Amiably. New York: Something Else Press, 1969.

MOA   *The Making of Americans.* New York: Something Else Press, 1966.
             Matisse Picasso and Gertrude Stein with Two Shorter Stories. Paris: Plain Edition, 1933.
             Mrs. Reynolds and Five Earlier Novelettes. Foreword by Lloyd Frankenberg. New Haven: Yale University Press, 1952.
Narr   *Narration: Four Lectures by Gertrude Stein.* Introduction by Thornton Wilder. Chicago: University of Chicago Press, 1935.
             A Novel of Thank You. Introduction by Carl Van Vechten. New Haven: Yale University Press, 1958.
PL   *Painted Lace and Other Pieces.* Introduction by Daniel-Henry Kahnweiler. New Haven: Yale University Press, 1955.
PF   *Paris France.* London: Batsford, 1940.
P&P   *Portraits and Prayers.* New York: Random House, 1934.
SW   *Selected Writings of Gertrude Stein.* Edited by Carl Van Vechten. New York: Random House, 1946. Includes *The Autobiography of Alice B. Toklas, Tender Buttons, Four Saints in Three Acts,* and "The Winner Loses."
             Stanzas in Meditation and Other Poems. Preface by Donald Sutherland. New Haven: Yale University Press, 1956.
             Things as They Are. Pawlet, Vt.: Banyan Press, 1950.
TL   *Three Lives.* Norfolk, Conn.: New Directions, 1933.
Two   *Two: Gertrude Stein and Her Brother and Other Early Portraits.* Foreword by Janet Flanner. New Haven: Yale University Press, 1951.
UK   *Useful Knowledge.* London: Bodley Head, 1929.
WIHS   *Wars I Have Seen.* New York: Random House, 1945.
WAM   *What Are Masterpieces.* Foreword by Robert Bartlett Haas. Los Angeles: Conference Press, 1940.
             The Yale Edition of the Unpublished Writings of Gertrude Stein. New Haven: Yale University Press, 1951–58. Includes *Alphabets and Birthdays* (1957), *As Fine as Melanctha* (1954), *Bee Time Vine and Other Pieces* (1953), *Mrs. Reynolds and Five Earlier Novelettes* (1952), *A Novel of Thank You* (1958), *Painted Lace and Other Pieces* (1955), *Stanzas in Meditation and Other Poems* (1956), and *Two: Gertrude Stein and Her Brother and Other Early Portraits* (1951).

PRINCIPAL WRITINGS OF LEO STEIN

             The ABC of Aesthetics. New York: Boni & Liveright, 1927.
App   *Appreciation: Painting, Poetry and Prose.* New York: Crown Publishers, 1947.
JIS   *Journey into the Self: Being the Letters, Papers and Journals of Leo Stein.* Edited by Edmund Fuller. New York: Crown Publishers, 1950.

PRINCIPAL WRITINGS OF ALICE B. TOKLAS

ABTC   *The Alice B. Toklas Cookbook.* New York: Anchor Books, by arrangement with Harper & Bros., 1960.

      Aromas and Flavors of Past and Present. With introduction and comments by Poppy Cannon. New York: Harper & Bros., 1958.

SoA   *Staying on Alone: Letters of Alice B. Toklas.* Edited by Edward Burns. With an introduction by Gilbert Harrison. New York: Liveright, 1973.

WIR   *What Is Remembered.* New York: Holt, Rinehart & Winston 1963.

OTHER BOOKS AND ARTICLES CONSULTED OR CITED IN THE TEXT

ACTON, HAROLD. *Memoirs of an Aesthete.* London: Methuen, 1948.

ADHEMAR, JEAN, LISE DUBIEF, and GÉRARD WILLEMETZ (eds.). *Apollinaire.* Paris: Bibliothèque Nationale, 1969.

AGEE, WILLIAM. "New York Dada, 1910–1930." *Art News Annual: The Avant-Garde* 34 (1968):104–13.

ALDRICH, MILDRED. *A Hilltop on the Marne.* Boston: Houghton Mifflin, 1915.

———. *On the Edge of the War Zone.* Boston: Small, Maynard, 1917.

———. *The Peak of the Load.* Boston: Small, Maynard, 1918.

———. *When Johnny Comes Marching Home.* Boston: Small, Maynard, 1919.

ALLEN, GAY WILSON. *William James.* New York: Viking Press, 1967.

AMORY, CLEVELAND, and FREDERIC BRADLEE (eds.). *Vanity Fair: A Cavalcade of the 1920s and 1930s.* New York: Viking Press, 1960.

ANDERSON, ELIZABETH, and GERALD R. KELLY. *Miss Elizabeth.* Boston: Little, Brown, 1969.

ANDERSON, MARGARET. *My Thirty Years' War.* New York: Covici, Friede, 1930.

ANDERSON, SHERWOOD. *The Letters of Sherwood Anderson.* Edited by Howard Mumford Jones and Walter B. Rideout. Boston: Little, Brown, 1953.

———. *Sherwood Anderson's Memoirs: A Critical Edition.* Edited by Ray Lewis White. Chapel Hill: University of North Carolina Press, 1969.

———. *Sherwood Anderson's Notebooks.* New York: Boni & Liveright, 1926.

———. *A Story Teller's Story.* New York: B. W. Huebsch, 1924.

APOLLINAIRE, GUILLAUME. *Apollinaire on Art.* Edited by Leroy C. Breunig. New York: Viking Press, 1972 (Published in France as *Chroniques d'art.* Textes réunis avec préface et notes, par L. C. Breunig. Paris: Gallimard, 1960).

———. *The Cubist Painters: Aesthetic Meditations.* New York: Wittenborn, Schultz, 1949.

———. *The Selected Writings of Guillaume Apollinaire.* Translated with critical introduction by Roger Shattuck. New York: New Directions, 1971.

BAKER, CARLOS. *Ernest Hemingway: A Life Story.* New York: Charles Scribner's Sons, 1969.

BALMAIN, PIERRE. *My Years and Seasons.* New York: Doubleday, 1965.

BARR, ALFRED H., JR. *Matisse: His Art and His Public.* New York: Museum of Modern Art, 1951. Reprint: New York: Arno Press, 1966.

———. *Picasso: Fifty Years of His Art.* New York: Museum of Modern Art, 1946.

BARRY, JOSEPH. "Alice B. Toklas." *Village Voice,* March 16, 1967, p. 8.

BEACH, SYLVIA. *Shakespeare and Company.* New York: Harcourt, Brace, 1959.

BEATON, CECIL. *The Wandering Years: Diaries, 1922–1939.* Boston: Little, Brown, 1961.

BELL, CLIVE. *Old Friends.* New York: Harcourt, Brace, 1956.

BIDDLE, GEORGE. *An American Artist's Story.* Boston: Little, Brown, 1939.

BLOOM, ELLEN F. "Three Steins." *Texas Quarterly,* Summer, 1970, pp. 15–22.

BOWEN, STELLA. *Drawn from Life.* London: Collins, 1941.

BREESKIN, ADELYN D. H. *Lyman Sayen.* Catalogue for an exhibition at the National Collection of Fine Arts, Washington, D.C., September 25 to November 1, 1970.

BRIDGMAN, RICHARD. *Gertrude Stein in Pieces.* New York: Oxford University Press, 1970.

BRINNIN, JOHN MALCOLM. *The Third Rose: Gertrude Stein and Her World.* Boston: Little, Brown, 1959.

BROMFIELD, LOUIS. *Pleasant Valley.* New York: Harper & Bros., 1945.

BROWN, MILTON W. *The Story of the Armory Show.* Greenwich, Conn.: Joseph H. Hirshhorn Foundation, 1963.

BRYHER, WINIFRED. *The Heart to Artemis.* New York: Harcourt, Brace, 1962.

CABANNE, PIERRE. *Dialogues with Marcel Duchamp.* New York: Viking Press, 1971.

CALLAGHAN, MORLEY. *That Summer in Paris.* New York: Coward-McCann, 1963.

CAMFIELD, WILLIAM A. *Francis Picabia.* New York: Solomon R. Guggenheim Museum, 1970.

CHAMBERLAIN, SAMUEL. *Bouquet de France.* New York: Gourmet Society, 1957.

COATES, ROBERT M. *The View from Here.* New York: Harcourt, Brace, 1960.

COBURN, ALVIN LANGDON. *Alvin Langdon Coburn, Photographer: An Autobiography.* Edited by Helmut and Alison Gernsheim. New York: Praeger, 1966.

COCTEAU, JEAN. *My Contemporaries.* Edited with introduction by Margaret Crosland. Philadelphia: Chilton, 1968.

———. *Professional Secrets: An Autobiography of Jean Cocteau.* Edited by Robert Phelps. New York: Farrar, Straus & Giroux, 1970.

DAVIDSON, JO. *Between Sittings: An Informal Autobiography.* New York: Dial Press, 1951.

DAWSON, MANIERRE. *Manierre Dawson: Paintings, 1909–1913.* Catalogue for an exhibition at the Ringling Museum of Art, Sarasota, Florida, November 6 to November 26, 1967.

ELLMANN, RICHARD. *James Joyce.* New York: Oxford University Press, 1959.

———. *Ulysses on the Liffey.* New York: Oxford University Press, 1972.

FARNHAM, EMILY. *Charles Demuth: Behind a Laughing Mask.* Norman: University of Oklahoma Press, 1971.

FENTON, CHARLES A. *The Apprenticeship of Ernest Hemingway.* New York: Viking Press, 1968.

FITZGERALD, F. SCOTT. *The Crack Up.* Edited by Edmund Wilson. New York: New Directions, 1956.

———. *The Letters of F. Scott Fitzgerald.* Edited by Andrew Turnbull. New York: Charles Scribner's Sons, 1963.

FLANNER, JANET [GENÊT]. "Letter from Paris." *New Yorker,* March 25, 1967, pp. 172–78.

———. *Paris Journals: 1944–1965.* New York: Atheneum, 1965.

———. *Paris Was Yesterday, 1925–1939.* Edited by Irving Drutman. New York: Viking Press, 1972.

FORD, FORD MADOX. *It Was the Nightingale.* Philadelphia: J.B. Lippincott, 1933.

GALLUP, DONALD. "The Making of *The Making of Americans.*" *New Colophon* 3 (1950):54–74. Reprinted in *Fernhurst, Q.E.D., and Other Early Writings by Gertrude Stein.*

———. "The Weaving of a Pattern: Marsden Hartley and Gertrude Stein." *Magazine of Art* 41 (November, 1948):256–61.

——— (ed.). *The Flowers of Friendship: Letters Written to Gertrude Stein.* New York: Alfred A. Knopf, 1953.

GILOT, FRANÇOISE, and CARLTON LAKE. *Life with Picasso.* New York: McGraw-Hill, 1964.

GLASSCO, JOHN. *Memoirs of Montparnasse.* New York: Oxford University Press, 1970.

GOLDRING, DOUGLAS. *Trained for Genius: The Life and Writings of Ford Madox Ford.* New York: E.P. Dutton, 1949.

GRAMONT, ELIZABETH DE. *Souvenirs du monde.* Paris: Bernard Grasset, 1966.

GRAMONT, SANCHE DE. "Remember Dada: Man Ray at 80." *New York Times Magazine,* September 6, 1970, p. 30.

HAAS, ROBERT BARTLETT. "Gertrude Stein Talking: A Transatlantic Interview." *Uclan Review* 8 (Summer, 1962):3–11; 9 (Spring, 1963):40–48; 10 (Winter, 1964):44–48.

——— (ed.). *A Primer for the Gradual Understanding of Gertrude Stein.* Los Angeles: Black Sparrow Press, 1971.

HAAS, ROBERT BARTLETT, and DONALD CLIFFORD GALLUP (eds.). *A Catalogue of the Published and Unpublished Writings of Gertrude Stein.* New Haven: Yale University Library, 1941.

HAPGOOD, HUTCHINS. *A Victorian in the Modern World.* New York: Harcourt, Brace, 1939.

HARRISON, GILBERT A. (ed.). *Gertrude Stein's America.* Washington, D.C.: (Luce) McKay, 1965.

HEMINGWAY, ERNEST. *By-Line: Ernest Hemingway.* Edited by William White. New York: Charles Scribner's Sons, 1967.

———. *A Moveable Feast.* Bantam, by arrangement with Charles Scribner's Sons, 1969.

HOLROYD, MICHAEL. *Lytton Strachey.* 2 vols. New York: Holt, Rinehart & Winston, 1968.

HOUSEMAN, JOHN. *Run-through: A Memoir.* New York: Simon & Schuster, 1972.

IMBS, BRAVIG. *Confessions of Another Young Man.* New York: Henkle-Yewdale, 1936.

JAFFE, IRMA B. *Joseph Stella.* Cambridge, Mass.: Harvard University Press, 1970.

JAMES, WILLIAM. *Psychology.* New York: Henry Holt, 1913.

JOOST, NICHOLAS. *Ernest Hemingway and the Little Magazine: The Paris Years.* Barre, Mass.: Barre, 1968.

JOSEPHSON, MATTHEW. *Life Among the Surrealists.* New York: Holt, Rinehart & Winston, 1962.

KAHNWEILER, DANIEL-HENRY. *Confessions esthétiques.* Paris: Gallimard, 1963.

———. *Juan Gris: His Life and Work.* Translated by Douglas Cooper. New York: Harry N. Abrams, 1969.

KAHNWEILER, DANIEL-HENRY, and FRANCIS CRÉMIEUX. *My Galleries and Painters.* Translated by Helen Weaver. New York: Viking Press, 1971.

KAZIN, ALFRED. *Contemporaries.* Boston: Little, Brown, 1962.
KELLNER, BRUCE. *Carl Van Vechten and the Irreverent Decades.* Norman: University of Oklahoma Press, 1968.
KIRSTEIN, LINCOLN. *The Sculpture of Elie Nadelman.* New York: Museum of Modern Art, 1948.
KNOLL, ROBERT E. (ed.). *McAlmon and the Lost Generation.* Lincoln: University of Nebraska Press, 1962.
KOCH, VIVIENNE. *William Carlos Williams.* Norfolk, Conn.: New Directions, 1950.
LIPCHITZ, JACQUES, and H. H. ARNASON. *My Life in Sculpture.* New York: Viking Press, 1972.
LOEB, HAROLD. *The Way It Was.* New York: Criterion, 1959.
LORD, JAMES. "Where the Pictures Were." Unpublished memoir.
LUDWIG, RICHARD M. (ed.). *Letters of Ford Madox Ford.* Princeton, N.J.: Princeton University Press, 1965.
LUHAN, MABEL DODGE. *Intimate Memories.* 4 vols. New York: Harcourt, Brace. Vol. 2: *European Experiences* (1935). Vol. 3: *Movers and Shakers* (1936).
McBRIDE, HENRY. "Pictures for a Picture of Gertrude." *Art News* 49, no. 10 (February, 1951):16–18.
MAN RAY. *Self Portrait.* Boston: Little, Brown, 1963.
MEYER, AGNES E. *Out of These Roots.* Boston: Little, Brown, 1953.
MILLER, LEON GORDON. "The Willies and Miss Gertrude." Unpublished memoir.
MILLER, ROSALIND. *Gertrude Stein: Form and Intelligibility.* New York: Exposition Press, 1949.
MIZENER, ARTHUR. *The Far Side of Paradise.* Boston: Houghton Mifflin, 1949.
———. *The Saddest Story: A Biography of Ford Madox Ford.* New York: World Publishing, 1971.
Museum of Modern Art. *Four Americans in Paris.* Introduction by Margaret Potter. Essays by Douglas Cooper, Lucile M. Golson, Irene Gordon, Ellen B. Hirschland, and Leon Katz. New York: Museum of Modern Art, 1970.
OLIVIER, FERNANDE. *Picasso and His Friends.* Translated by Jane Miller. New York: Appleton-Century, 1965.
PACH, WALTER. *Queer Thing, Painting.* New York: Harper & Bros., 1938.
PAUL, ELLIOT. *Understanding the French.* New York: Random House, 1955.
PAXTON, ROBERT O. *Vichy France: Old Guard and New Order, 1940–1944.* New York: Alfred A. Knopf, 1972.
PENROSE, ROLAND. *Picasso: His Life and Work.* New York: Schocken, 1966.
POLLACK, BARBARA. *The Collectors: Dr. Claribel and Miss Etta Cone.* New York: Bobbs-Merrill, 1962.
PORTER, KATHERINE ANNE. *The Collected Essays and Occasional Writings of Katherine Anne Porter.* New York: Delacorte Press, 1970.
PUTNAM, SAMUEL. *Paris Was Our Mistress.* New York: Viking Press, 1947.
REID, B. L. *Art by Subtraction: A Dissenting Opinion of Gertrude Stein.* Norman: University of Oklahoma Press, 1958.
———. *The Man from New York: John Quinn and His Friends.* New York: Oxford University Press, 1968.
RICH, DANIEL CATTON. "The Conscience of a Critic: Henry McBride, 1867–1962." *Arts Magazine* 37, no. 2 (November, 1962):48–52.
ROGERS, W. G. *When This You See Remember Me: Gertrude Stein in Person.* New York: Rinehart, 1948.

Rönnebeck, Arnold. "Gertrude Was Always Giggling." *Books Abroad* 18, no. 4 (October, 1944):2–7.
Rose, Sir Francis. *Saying Life.* London: Cassell, 1961.
Russell, Bertrand. *The Autobiography of Bertrand Russell: 1872–1914.* Boston: Little, Brown, 1967.
Saarinen, Aline B. *The Proud Possessors.* New York: Vintage, 1968.
Sabartès, Jaime. *Picasso: Documents iconographiques.* Genève: Pierre Cailler, 1954.
Salmon, André. *Souvenirs sans fin.* Vol. 2. Paris: Gallimard, 1956.
Schneider, Pierre. *Henri Matisse.* Catalogue for the Matisse Centenary Exhibition at the Grand Palais, Paris, April–September, 1970.
Scudder, Janet. *Modeling My Life.* New York: Harcourt, Brace, 1925.
Sevareid, Eric. *Not So Wild a Dream.* New York: Alfred A. Knopf, 1946.
Shattuck, Roger. *The Banquet Years.* New York: Vintage, 1968.
Sitwell, Edith. *Take Care Of: The Autobiography of Edith Sitwell.* New York: Atheneum, 1965.
Sitwell, Osbert. *Laughter in the Next Room.* Boston: Little, Brown, 1948.
Smith, Logan Pearsall. *Unforgotten Years.* Boston: Little, Brown, 1939.
Soby, James Thrall. *Juan Gris.* New York: Museum of Modern Art, 1958.
Sprigge, Elizabeth. *Gertrude Stein: Her Life and Work.* New York: Harper & Bros., 1957.
Steegmuller, Francis. *Apollinaire: Poet Among the Painters.* New York: Farrar, Straus, 1963.
———. *Cocteau: A Biography.* Boston: Little, Brown, 1970.
Steffens, Lincoln. *The Autobiography of Lincoln Steffens.* New York: Harcourt, Brace, 1931.
———. *The Letters of Lincoln Steffens.* Edited by Ella Winter and Granville Hicks. Harcourt, Brace, 1938.
Stephens, Robert O. *Hemingway's Nonfiction: The Public Voice.* Chapel Hill: University of North Carolina Press, 1968.
Sterne, Maurice. *Shadow and Light.* New York: Harcourt, Brace, 1965.
Stewart, Allegra. *Gertrude Stein and the Present.* Cambridge, Mass.: Harvard University Press, 1967.
Stock, Noel. *The Life of Ezra Pound.* New York: Pantheon, 1970.
Sutherland, Donald. *Gertrude Stein: A Biography of Her Work.* New Haven: Yale University Press, 1951.
Sweet, Frederick A. *Miss Mary Cassatt.* Norman: University of Oklahoma Press, 1966.
Tériade, E. "Matisse Speaks." *Art News Annual* 21 (1952):40–71.
"Testimony Against Gertrude Stein." Supplement to *transition*, February, 1935.
Thomson, Virgil. *Virgil Thomson.* New York: Alfred A. Knopf, 1966.
Tomkins, Calvin. *Living Well Is the Best Revenge.* New York: New American Library, 1972.
Troy, William. *William Troy: Selected Essays.* Edited by Stanley Edgar Hyman. New Brunswick, N.J.: Rutgers University Press, 1967.
Turnbull, Andrew. *Scott Fitzgerald.* New York: Charles Scribner's Sons, 1962.
Vallentin, Antonina. *Picasso.* New York: Doubleday, 1963.
Vallier, Dora. *Henri Rousseau.* New York: Harry N. Abrams, 1962.
Van Vechten, Carl. "Some 'Literary Ladies' I Have Known." *Yale University Library Gazette* 26, no. 3 (January, 1952):97–116.
Vollard, Ambroise. *Recollections of a Picture Dealer.* Boston: Little, Brown, 1936.

WAKEFIELD, ELEANOR. "Stormy Petrel of Modernism Is Patriotic." *New York World*, May 18, 1930.

WARREN, LANSING. "Gertrude Stein Views Life and Politics." *New York Times Magazine*, May 6, 1934, p. 9.

WEININGER, OTTO. *Sex and Character*. New York: G.P. Putnam's Sons, 1906.

WILLIAMS, WILLIAM CARLOS. *The Autobiography of William Carlos Williams*. New York: Random House, 1951.

———. *Selected Essays*. New York: New Directions, 1954.

———. *The Selected Letters of William Carlos Williams*. Edited by John C. Thirwall. New York: McDowel, Obolensky, 1957.

WILSON, EDMUND. *Axel's Castle*. New York: Charles Scribner's Sons, 1959.

———. *The Shores of Light*. New York: Farrar, Straus & Young, 1952.

———. *Upstate: Records and Recollections of Northern New York*. New York: Farrar, Straus & Giroux, 1971.

Index

Index